75
READINGS
PLUS

75
READINGS
PLUS

FIFTH EDITION

Santi V. Buscemi
Middlesex County College

Charlotte Smith
Adirondack Community College

Boston   Burr Ridge, IL   Dubuque, IA   Madison, WI
New York   San Francisco   St. Louis
Bangkok   Bogotá   Caracas   Lisbon   London   Madrid   Mexico City
Milan   New Delhi   Seoul   Singapore   Sydney   Taipei   Toronto

McGraw-Hill Higher Education

A Division of The **McGraw-Hill** *Companies*

75 READINGS PLUS

This book is printed on acid-free paper.

3 4 5 6 7 8 9 0 FGR/FGR   0 9 8 7 6 5 4 3 2 1 0

ISBN 0-07-229265-2

Editorial director: *Philip A. Butcher*
Senior sponsoring editor: *Lisa Moore*
Editorial assistant*: Emily Sparano*
Director of marketing: *Margaret Metz*
Project editor: *Paula M. Krauza*
Production supervisor: *Rose Hepburn*
Designer: *Kiera Cunningham*
Supplement coordinator: *Craig S. Leonard*
Compositor: *Carlisle Communications, Ltd.*
Typeface: *10/12 Times Roman*
Printer: *Quebecor Printing Book Group/Fairfield*

Library of Congress Cataloging-in-Publication Data
75 readings plus / Santi V. Buscemi, Charlotte Smith. — 5th ed.
    p. cm.
  Includes index.
  ISBN 0-07-229265-2
  1. College readers. 2. English language—Rhetoric Problems,
exercises, etc. I. Buscemi, Santi V. II. Smith, Charlotte.
III. Title: Seventy-five readings plus.
PE1417.A14 2000
 808'.0427—dc21   99-23204

http://www.mhhe.com

ABOUT THE AUTHORS

Santi Buscemi teaches reading and writing and chairs the English Department at Middlesex County College in Edison, New Jersey.

Charlotte Smith teaches English composition and technical writing at Adirondack Community College in Queensbury, New York.

CONTENTS

CHAPTER 3

Process Analysis 98

CHAPTER 4

Definition 139

CHAPTER 5

Division and Classification 174

CHAPTER 6

Comparison and Contrast 218

CHAPTER 7

Illustration   255

CHAPTER 8

Cause and Effect   306

CHAPTER 9

Analogy   349

CHAPTER 10

Argument and Persuasion   386

THEMATIC CONTENTS

Portraits

Growing Up, Growing Old

Power and Politics

Problems, Solutions, and Consequences

Culture and Identity

The Media and the Arts

Science and Technology

Health and Medicine

Use and Abuse of Language

TO THE INSTRUCTOR

75 Readings Plus is an expanded version of *75 Readings,* the popular and inexpensive collection of essays for freshman composition first published in 1987 and now in its seventh edition. Tables of contents for the two texts are identical, but the presentation of instructional materials differs.

Questions for discussion, suggestions for writing, and other instructional apparatus for *75 Readings* are presented in a manual from which teachers may copy materials for students as needed. In *75 Readings Plus,* on the other hand, instructional materials appear in the text. Accompanying each selection are an author biography, a set of discussion questions on content and strategy, and at least two suggestions for sustained writing. In addition, to help instructors exploit the connection between reading, writing, and critical thinking, *75 Readings Plus* again offers a set of prompts for short writing inspired by each essay selection. These prompts can also be used as journal assignments or as warm-up exercises for projects such as those described in Suggestions for Sustained Writing. In some cases, they can even be expanded into assignments for complete essays.

The table of contents of the fifth edition of *75 Readings Plus* contains nine new essays. "Traveling South" by James Weldon Johnson, first published in 1912, and Naton Leslie's fascinating and multilayered "Don't Get Comfortable" have been added to Chapter 1: Narration. Chapter 5: Division and Classification now contains Donald Hall's classic "Four Kinds of Reading," and Chapter 7: Illustration features "Fecundity," a challenging and thought-provoking piece by Annie Dillard, America's premier essayist.

Chapter 10 has undergone the most extensive revision. Essays in this chapter are now categorized under Argument and Persuasion, with five new selections having been added. They include Mike Wallace's "The Press Needs a National Monitor" (with a response by Don Hewitt); Debra Dickerson's "Who Shot Johnny?"; Richard Rodriguez's "Bilingual Education: Outdated and Unrealistic"; Ann N. Martin's "Food Pets Die For"; and The Nature of Wellness's "Next Time You Are Sick, You'd Better Go to the Vet . . .," one of the few selections with group authorship ever to have appeared in this text.

Special thanks are due to the following colleagues who made suggestions for the fifth edition:

Tammy DiBenedetto from Riverside Community College
Terry Telfer from Monroe County Community College

Nancy Schneider from University of Maine at Augusta
Joe Safdie from lake Washington Technical College
Fred Misurella from East Stroudsberg University
Sonja Lynch from Southside Virginia Community College

We are grateful for the comments and suggestions of all of our colleagues who have used *75 Readings* and *75 Readings Plus* over the last 10 years. We welcome their ongoing contributions as we continue to improve these texts and make them even more responsive to the needs of our students. We would also like to thank our friends at McGraw-Hill, who encouraged us and helped us continue these projects.

Santi Buscemi
Charlotte Smith

1

Narration

One of the things that defines us as human is the universal desire and ability to create narrative. "Tell me a story," the child implores; and we willingly oblige by reciting an old favorite passed down through the generations or by making up one of our own.

We are naturally curious creatures, wanting to know what happened, when, and to whom—even if none of it is true. Perhaps that is why we feel compelled to create mythologies on one hand and to report the news or write history on the other.

Some narratives contain long evocative descriptions of setting. Others present fascinating characters whose predicaments rivet our attention or whose lives mirror our own. Still others seem more like plays, heavy with dialogue by which writers allow their characters to reveal themselves. Whatever combination of techniques authors use, all stories—from the briefest anecdotes to the longest novels—have a plot. They recount events in a more-or-less chronological order. They reveal what happened, and, in most cases, allow readers or listeners to draw their own conclusions about the significance of those events.

This is perhaps the chief difference between what you will read in Chapter One and the essays in other parts of this text. While some types of writing are aimed at explaining or persuading, narration dramatizes important human concerns by presenting events that, when taken together, create a world the author wants the reader to share.

Moving from beginning to end by order of time, narration generally relies on a more natural pattern of organization than other types of writing, but it is no less sophisticated or powerful a tool for explaining complex ideas or for changing readers' opinions than, say, analogy, classification, or formal argument. All story tellers, no matter how entertaining their tales, have something to say about human beings and the world they inhabit. If you have already read selections from the chapters that follow, you know that writers often couple narration with other techniques to develop ideas and support opinions that otherwise might have remained

1

abstract, unclear, or unconvincing. A good story may reveal more about a person or a place, than physical description, and it can sometimes help readers understand an important problem or issue beyond our most valiant attempts to explain it "logically."

The point is that writers of narrative writers are not compelled to underscore the connection between the events in a story and the point it makes. Readers can find their own "theses."

Many of the essays you will read in this chapter are autobiographical: Maya Angelou, Langston Hughes, Virginia Bell Dabney, and James Weldon Johnson show how they confronted difficult situations and, in the process, gained significant insight into themselves, their families, and the human personality. Although very different in content and purpose, Naton Leslie's "Don't Get Comfortable" provides similar insight into the human character, not to mention into a few real characters! The writing of essays like theirs often results from a profound compulsion to find meaning in what once seemed devoid of it, a process that may define the act of narration itself.

The selections by George Orwell, and Maxine Hong Kingston might be placed in another category. They point beyond themselves to social and political issues that are universal and perennial.

However the pieces in this chapter seem to be related—and you will surely find connections of your own to talk about—remember that each has been included because it has a poignant story to tell. Read each selection carefully, and learn what you can about the techniques of narration. Here's hoping that at least a few will inspire you to narrate a personal vision of the world that will enrich both you and your readers.

A Hanging

George Orwell

George Orwell is the pseudonym of Eric Blair (1903–1950). Born in India, where his father served in the British colonial government, Orwell was educated at Eton. As a young man, he served as a British policeman in Burma, the setting for this selection. Later, he was wounded while fighting for the loyalists in the Spanish Civil War, about which he wrote in Homage to Catalonia. *Orwell despised the "Big Brother" mentalities of both the fascists and the communists, who backed opposing sides in that war. However, he also condemned the crass bureaucracy of the democratic governments of his time. In short, Orwell became an enemy of politics and politicians in general. He is remembered for* Animal Farm (1946) *and* 1984 (1949), *classics of political satire, and for his many essays.*

It was in Burma, a sodden morning of the rains. A sickly light, like yellow tinfoil, 1 was slanting over the high walls into the jail yard. We were waiting outside the condemned cells, a row of sheds fronted with double bars, like small animal cages. Each cell measured about ten feet by ten and was quite bare within except for a plank bed and a pot of drinking water. In some of them brown silent men were squatting at the inner bars, with their blankets draped round them. These were the condemned men, due to be hanged within the next week or two.

One prisoner had been brought out of his cell. He was a Hindu, a puny wisp 2 of a man, with a shaven head and vague liquid eyes. He had a thick, sprouting moustache, absurdly too big for his body, rather like the moustache of a comic man in the films. Six tall Indian warders were guarding him and getting him ready for the gallows. Two of them stood by with rifles and fixed bayonets, while the others handcuffed him, passed a chain through his handcuffs and fixed it to their belts, and lashed his arms tight to his sides. They crowded very close about him, with their hands always on him in a careful, caressing grip, as though all the while feeling him to make sure he was there. It was like men handling a fish which is still alive and may jump back into the water. But he stood quite unresisting, yielding his arms limply to the ropes, as though he hardly noticed what was happening.

Eight o'clock struck and a bugle call, desolately thin in the wet air, floated 3 from the distant barracks. The superintendent of the jail, who was standing apart from the rest of us, moodily prodding the gravel with his stick, raised his head at the sound. He was an army doctor, with a grey toothbrush moustache and a gruff voice. "For God's sake hurry up, Francis," he said irritably. "The man ought to have been dead by this time. Aren't you ready yet?"

Francis, the head jailer, a fat Dravidian in a white drill suit and gold specta- 4 cles, waved his black hand. "Yes sir, yes sir," he bubbled. "All iss satisfactorily prepared. The hangman iss waiting. We shall proceed."

"Well, quick march, then. The prisoners can't get their breakfast till this 5 job's over."

We set out for the gallows. Two warders marched on either side of the pris- 6 oner, with their rifles at the slope; two others marched close against him, gripping

3

him by arm and shoulder, as though at once pushing and supporting him. The rest of us, magistrates and the like, followed behind. Suddenly, when we had gone ten yards, the procession stopped short without any order or warning. A dreadful thing had happened—a dog, come goodness knows whence, had appeared in the yard. It came bounding among us with a loud volley of barks, and leapt round us wagging its whole body, wild with glee at finding so many human beings together. It was a large woolly dog, half Airedale, half pariah. For a moment it pranced round us, and then, before anyone could stop it, it had made a dash for the prisoner, and jumping up tried to lick his face. Everyone stood aghast, too taken aback even to grab at the dog.

"Who let that bloody brute in here?" said the superintendent angrily. "Catch it, someone!"   7

A warder, detached from the escort, charged clumsily after the dog, but it danced and gambolled just out of his reach, taking everything as part of the game. A young Eurasian jailer picked up a handful of gravel and tried to stone the dog away, but it dodged the stones and came after us again. Its yaps echoed from the jail walls. The prisoner, in the grasp of the two warders, looked on incuriously, as though this was another formality of the hanging. It was several minutes before someone managed to catch the dog. Then we put my handkerchief through its collar and moved off once more, with the dog still straining and whimpering.   8

It was about forty yards to the gallows. I watched the bare brown back of the prisoner marching in front of me. He walked clumsily with his bound arms, but quite steadily, with that bobbing gait of the Indian who never straightens his knees. At each step his muscles slid neatly into place, the lock of hair on his scalp danced up and down, his feet printed themselves on the wet gravel. And once, in spite of the men who gripped him by each shoulder, he stepped slightly aside to avoid a puddle on the path.   9

It is curious, but till that moment I had never realised what it means to destroy a healthy, conscious man. When I saw the prisoner step aside to avoid the puddle, I saw the mystery, the unspeakable wrongness, of cutting a life short when it is in full tide. This man was not dying, he was alive just as we were alive. All the organs of his body were working—bowels digesting food, skin renewing itself, nails growing, tissues forming—all toiling away in solemn foolery. His nails would still be growing when he stood on the drop, when he was falling through the air with a tenth of a second to live. His eyes saw the yellow gravel and the grey walls, and his brain still remembered, foresaw, reasoned—reasoned even about puddles. He and we were a party of men walking together, seeing, hearing, feeling, understanding the same world; and in two minutes, with a sudden snap, one of us would be gone—one mind less, one world less.   10

The gallows stood in a small yard, separate from the main grounds of the prison, and overgrown with tall prickly weeds. It was a brick erection like three sides of a shed, with planking on top, and above that two beams and a crossbar with the rope dangling. The hangman, a grey-haired convict in the white uniform of the prison, was waiting beside his machine. He greeted us with a servile crouch   11 as we entered. At a word from Francis the two warders, gripping the prisoner more closely than ever, half led, half pushed him to the gallows and helped him clumsily up the ladder. Then the hangman climbed up and fixed the rope round the prisoner's neck.

We stood waiting, five yards away. The warders had formed in a rough cir- 12 cle round the gallows. And then, when the noose was fixed, the prisoner began crying out on his god. It was a high, reiterated cry of "Ram! Ram! Ram! Ram!", not urgent and fearful like a prayer or a cry for help, but steady, rhythmical, almost like the tolling of a bell. The dog answered the sound with a whine. The hangman, still standing on the gallows, produced a small cotton bag like a flour bag and drew it down over the prisoner's face. But the sound, muffled by the cloth, still persisted, over and over again: "Ram! Ram! Ram! Ram! Ram!"

The hangman climbed down and stood ready, holding the lever. Minutes 13 seemed to pass. The steady, muffled crying from the prisoner went on and on, "Ram! Ram! Ram!" never faltering for an instant. The superintendent, his head on his chest, was slowly poking the ground with his stick; perhaps he was counting the cries, allowing the prisoner a fixed number—fifty, perhaps, or a hundred. Everyone had changed colour. The Indians had gone grey like bad coffee, and one or two of the bayonets were wavering. We looked at the lashed, hooded man on the drop, and listened to his cries—each cry another second of life; the same thought was in all our minds: oh, kill him quickly, get it over, stop that abominable noise!

Suddenly the superintendent made up his mind. Throwing up his head he 14 made a swift motion with his stick. "Chalo!" he shouted almost fiercely.

There was a clanking noise, and then dead silence. The prisoner had van- 15 ished, and the rope was twisting on itself. I let go of the dog, and it galloped immediately to the back of the gallows; but when it got there it stopped short, barked, and then retreated into a corner of the yard, where it stood among the weeds, looking timorously out at us. We went round the gallows to inspect the prisoner's body. He was dangling with his toes pointed straight downwards, very slowly revolving, as dead as a stone.

The superintendent reached out with his stick and poked the bare body; it 16 oscillated slightly. "*He's* all right," said the superintendent. He backed out from under the gallows, and blew out a deep breath. The moody look had gone out of his face quite suddenly. He glanced at his wrist-watch. "Eight minutes past eight. Well, that's all for this morning, thank God."

The warders unfixed bayonets and marched away. The dog, sobered and 17 conscious of having misbehaved itself, slipped after them. We walked out of the gallows yard, past the condemned cells with their waiting prisoners, into the big central yard of the prison. The convicts, under the command of warders armed with lathis, were already receiving their breakfast. They squatted in long rows, each man holding a tin pannikin, while two warders with buckets marched round ladling out rice; it seemed quite a homely, jolly scene, after the hanging. An enormous relief had come upon us now that the job was done. One felt an impulse to sing, to break into a run, to snigger. All at once everyone began chattering gaily.

The Eurasian boy walking beside me nodded towards the way we had come, 18 with a knowing smile: "Do you know, sir, our friend (he meant the dead man), when he heard his appeal had been dismissed, he pissed on the floor of his cell. From fright. Kindly take one of my cigarettes, sir. Do you not admire my new silver case, sir? From the boxwallah, two rupees eight annas. Classy European style."

Several people laughed—at what, nobody seemed certain.   19

Francis was walking by the superintendent, talking garrulously: "Well, sir, 20 all has passed off with the utmost satisfactoriness. It wass all finished—flick! like that. It iss not always so—oah, no! I have known cases where the doctor wass obliged to go beneath the gallows and pull the prisoner's legs to ensure decease. Most disagreeable!"

"Wriggling about, eh? That's bad," said the superintendent.   21

"Ach, sir, it iss worse when they become refractory! One man, I recall, clung 22 to the bars of hiss cage when we went to take him out. You will scarcely credit, sir, that it took six warders to dislodge him, three pulling at each leg. We reasoned with him. 'My dear fellow,' we said, 'think of all the pain and trouble you are causing to us!' But no, he would not listen! Ach, he wass very troublesome!"

I found that I was laughing quite loudly. Everyone was laughing. Even the su- 23 perintendent grinned in a tolerant way. "You'd better all come out and have a drink," he said quite genially. "I've got a bottle of whisky in the car. We could do with it."

We went through the big double gates of the prison, into the road. "Pulling 24 at his legs!" exclaimed a Burmese magistrate suddenly, and burst into a loud chuckling. We all began laughing again. At that moment Francis's anecdote seemed extraordinarily funny. We all had a drink together, native and European alike, quite amicably. The dead man was a hundred yards away.

1931

QUESTIONS FOR DISCUSSION

Content

a. Does this narrative essay have a "message," or do you think Orwell deliberately avoided one?
b. Orwell avoids saying anything directly about the English presence in Burma— he neither explains the presence nor states his opinion explicitly. Nevertheless, his opinion is voiced. What is his attitude toward his country's presence in Burma?
c. How would you characterize Orwell's description of the Burmese in this piece? Of the Hindu prisoners? How do these descriptions relate to his attitude toward the British?
d. What details of the hanging does Orwell treat as significant? What are his reasons for including these details? What effect do they have on you?

Strategy and Style

e. In which paragraphs does Orwell use descriptive details most effectively? What other paragraphs do you find effective? Why?

f. Orwell is careful to tell us the dimensions of the prisoners' cells, the time, the number of people, the distance to the gallows, the distance between the officials and the prisoner, etc. Why are these numerical references important?

g. "A Hanging" is a mature writer's recollection of an earlier time in his life. Does Orwell present himself sympathetically, or does he describe himself with a satiric edge? Point to details that support your answer.

h. How does the use of dialogue affect the tone of the essay? In what way would your reaction have been different if Orwell had not used dialogue?

SUGGESTIONS FOR SHORT WRITING

a. Write a letter to Orwell, telling him what you do not understand about his essay. As best you can, tell him why you do not understand it.

b. Ask a question (or questions) about this essay, and then try to answer the question(s) by piecing together phrases drawn from the essay itself. Then write your own answer, or write a response to Orwell's "answer."

SUGGESTIONS FOR SUSTAINED WRITING

a. In paragraph 10, Orwell writes of an epiphany of sorts: "It is curious, but till that moment I had never realised what it means to destroy a healthy, conscious man. When I saw the prisoner step aside to avoid the puddle, I saw the mystery, the unspeakable wrongness, of cutting a life short. . . ." Tell the story of a time when something happened during an ordinary day that suddenly and profoundly changed your thinking. What details of the day do you remember? Make those details seem as significant to your readers as they are to you.

b. Orwell communicates his feelings about capital punishment and other issues in this essay. Use narration to present an issue about which you feel strongly. Present your opinion(s) implicitly by drawing on Orwell's narrative techniques: the use of dialogue, the detailed descriptions of characters, the chronological sequence of events, and the inclusion of humor, to name a few. In short, imbed your opinion within the framework of a story.

c. Orwell learned much about himself from this wrenching experience. Narrate a traumatic experience in your life that revealed something important about yourself.

Salvation

Langston Hughes

Among the chief figures of the Harlem Renaissance in the 1920s, Langston Hughes (1902–1967) is one of the best known poets and playwrights in America. A native of Mississippi, Hughes also wrote numerous essays that detail life in the South during the early part of this century. His novels and his autobiography, I Wonder as I Wander, *are still read widely. In this selection, he captures the trauma and disillusionment he experienced during a childhood incident.*

I was saved from sin when I was going on thirteen. But not really saved. It happened 1
like this. There was a big revival at my Auntie Reed's church. Every night for weeks
there had been much preaching, singing, praying, and shouting, and some very hardened sinners had been brought to Christ, and the membership of the church had
grown by leaps and bounds. Then just before the revival ended, they held a special
meeting for children, "to bring the young lambs to the fold." My aunt spoke of it for
days ahead. That night I was escorted to the front row and placed on the mourners'
bench with all the other young sinners, who had not yet been brought to Jesus.

My aunt told me that when you were saved you saw a light, and something 2
happened to you inside! And Jesus came into your life! And God was with you
from then on! She said you could see and hear and feel Jesus in your soul. I believed her. I had heard a great many old people say the same thing and it seemed
to me they ought to know. So I sat there calmly in the hot, crowded church, waiting for Jesus to come to me.

The preacher preached a wonderful rhythmical sermon, all moans and 3
shouts and lonely cries and dire pictures of hell, and then he sang a song about the
ninety and nine safe in the fold, but one little lamb was left out in the cold. Then
he said: "Won't you come? Won't you come to Jesus? Young lambs, won't you
come?" And he held out his arms to all us young sinners there on the mourners'
bench. And the little girls cried. And some of them jumped up and went to Jesus
right away. But most of us just sat there.

A great many old people came and knelt around us and prayed, old women 4
with jet-black faces and braided hair, old men with work-gnarled hands. And the
church sang a song about the lower lights are burning, some poor sinners to be
saved. And the whole building rocked with prayer and song.

Still I kept waiting to *see* Jesus.   5

Finally all the young people had gone to the altar and were saved, but one 6
boy and me. He was a rounder's son named Westley. Westley and I were surrounded by sisters and deacons praying. It was very hot in the church, and getting
late now. Finally Westley said to me in a whisper: "God damn! I'm tired o' sitting
here. Let's get up and be saved." So he got up and was saved.

Then I was left all alone on the mourners' bench. My aunt came and knelt at 7
my knees and cried, while prayers and songs swirled all around me in the little
church. The whole congregation prayed for me alone, in a mighty wail of moans
and voices. And I kept waiting serenely for Jesus, waiting, waiting—but he didn't

come. I wanted to see him, but nothing happened to me. Nothing! I wanted something to happen to me, but nothing happened.

I heard the songs and the minister saying: "Why don't you come? My dear 8
child, why don't you come to Jesus? Jesus is waiting for you. He wants you. Why
don't you come? Sister Reed, what is this child's name?"

"Langston," my aunt sobbed.   9

"Langston, why don't you come? Why don't you come and be saved? Oh, 10
Lamb of God! Why don't you come?"

Now it was really getting late. I began to be ashamed of myself, holding every- 11
thing up so long. I began to wonder what God thought about Westley, who certainly
hadn't seen Jesus either, but who was now sitting proudly on the platform, swinging
his knickerbockered legs and grinning down at me, surrounded by deacons and old
women on their knees praying. God had not struck Westley dead for taking his name
in vain or for lying in the temple. So I decided that maybe to save further trouble, I'd
better lie, too, and say that Jesus had come, and get up and be saved.

So I got up.   12

Suddenly the whole room broke into a sea of shouting, as they saw me rise. 13
Waves of rejoicing swept the place. Women leaped in the air. My aunt threw her
arms around me. The minister took me by the hand and led me to the platform.

When things quieted down, in a hushed silence, punctuated by a few ecstatic 14
"Amens," all the new young lambs were blessed in the name of God. Then joyous
singing filled the room.

That night, for the last time in my life but one—for I was a big boy twelve 15
years old—I cried. I cried, in bed alone, and couldn't stop. I buried my head under the quilts, but my aunt heard me. She woke up and told my uncle I was crying
because the Holy Ghost had come into my life, and because I had seen Jesus. But
I was really crying because I couldn't bear to tell her that I had lied, that I had deceived everybody in the church, that I hadn't seen Jesus, and that now I didn't believe there was a Jesus any more, since he didn't come to help me.

1940

QUESTIONS FOR DISCUSSION

Content

a. What is Hughes's purpose in recalling this event?
b. The author's portrayal of the revival meeting is extremely realistic. What
   rhetorical techniques make it so?
c. What exactly is a religious revival?
d. What Biblical metaphor is Hughes alluding to when he tells the reader that this
   was to be a special meeting "to bring the young lambs to the fold"?
e. Why does Hughes spend time talking about Westley? How is young Langston
   different from this boy?

f. What does the author's waiting so long before going up to be "saved" tell you
    about him?

g. Explain why Langston cries so much after coming home. Is there only one reason
    behind his tears? What does the last paragraph tell you about the young Langston?

Strategy and Style

h. The telling of this story is enhanced by the author's description of the church
    and the members of the congregation. In which paragraphs is Hughes's facility
    with description most evident?

i. What examples of metaphoric language do you find in this essay? How do such
    figures of speech help Hughes accomplish his purpose?

j. Hughes often makes use of a childlike perspective to relate the incident at his
    aunt's church. What details help him create that perspective? Does he use
    words like those a child might use?

k. What is Hughes's attitude or tone when recalling this incident?

SUGGESTIONS FOR SHORT WRITING

a. Write about one of your religious experiences, comparing or contrasting it to
    that of Hughes.

b. Write an advertisement for Salvation (the concept or the essay).

SUGGESTIONS FOR SUSTAINED WRITING

a. Describe a religious ceremony that has or used to have significance for you. As
    clearly and convincingly as you can, describe the emotional or spiritual bene-
    fits you derive or derived from that ceremony. Address your essay to someone
    who you know is skeptical about the value of religious or social ceremonies and
    observances.

b. At one time or another, we have all been pressured into doing things we did
    not want to do. Recount such an incident from your experience; make sure to
    describe your feelings both during and after it occurred. If appropriate, narrate
    the incident in a letter addressed to the individual or individuals who did the
    pressuring.

c. This brief recollection allows us only a peek into the author's personality. But
    the details are so vibrant that we are tempted to imagine what Langston Hughes
    was like as a child. Write about an incident from your own childhood that il-
    lustrates something about your personality or about the personality of a close
    friend or relative.

d. Recount a childhood incident that disillusioned you about a belief, an event, or a
    person. Describe what caused this disillusionment and explain how you coped
    with it. Please, no essays about the day you found out there was no Santa Claus!

Grandmother's Victory

Maya Angelou

Born Marguerita Johnson in 1928, Maya Angelou spent most of her childhood in Stamps, Arkansas, where her family owned the general store that is the setting for this selection. After a difficult youth, Angelou became a dancer, actress, and writer. She has performed all over the world, most notably in the U.S. State Department–sponsored production of Porgy and Bess, *in the television miniseries "Roots," and in a production of Jean Genet's* The Blacks. *She has also taught dance in Rome and Tel Aviv. Active in the civil rights movement, Angelou was appointed northern director for the Southern Christian Leadership Conference by Martin Luther King, Jr., in the 1960s. In 1970, she published the first volume of her autobiography,* I Know Why the Caged Bird Sings, *of which this selection is the fifth chapter. Three other volumes followed. Angelou has also written several books of poetry, including* And Still I Rise *(1978) and* I Shall Not Be Moved *(1990). Recent works include three autobiographies:* The Heart of a Woman *(1981),* Shaker, Why Don't You Sing? *(1983), and* All God's Children Need Traveling Shoes *(1986).*

"Thou shall not be dirty" and "Thou shall not be impudent" were the two commandments of Grandmother Henderson upon which hung our total salvation. 1

Each night in the bitterest winter we were forced to wash faces, arms, necks, legs, and feet before going to bed. She used to add, with a smirk that unprofane people can't control when venturing into profanity, "and wash as far as possible, then wash possible." 2

We would go to the well and wash in the ice-cold, clear water, grease our legs with the equally cold stiff Vaseline, then tiptoe into the house. We wiped the dust from our toes and settled down for schoolwork, cornbread, clabbered milk, prayers, and bed, always in that order. Momma was famous for pulling the quilts off after we had fallen asleep to examine our feet. If they weren't clean enough for her, she took the switch (she kept one behind the bedroom door for emergencies) and woke up the offender with a few aptly placed burning reminders. 3

The area around the well at night was dark and slick, and boys told about how snakes love water, so that anyone who had to draw water at night and then stand there alone and wash knew that moccasins and rattlers, puff adders, and boa constrictors were winding their way to the well and would arrive just as the person washing got soap in her eyes. But Momma convinced us that not only was cleanliness next to Godliness, dirtiness was the inventor of misery. 4

The impudent child was detested by God and a shame to its parents and could bring destruction to its house and line. All adults had to be addressed as Mister, Missus, Miss, Auntie, Cousin, Unk, Uncle, Buhbah, Sister, Brother, and a thousand other appellations indicating familial relationship and the lowliness of the addressor. 5

Everyone I knew respected these customary laws, except for the powhitetrash children. 6

Some families of powhitetrash lived on Momma's farm land behind the school. Sometimes a gaggle of them came to the Store, filling the whole room, 7 chasing out the air, and even changing the well-known scents. The children crawled over the shelves and into the potato and onion bins, twanging all the time in their sharp voices like cigar-box guitars. They took liberties in my Store that I would never dare. Since Momma told us that the less you say to white-folks (or even powhitetrash) the better, Bailey and I would stand, solemn, quiet, in the displaced air. But if one of the playful apparitions got close to us, I pinched it. Partly out of angry frustration and partly because I didn't believe in its flesh reality.

They called my uncle by his first name and ordered him around the Store.   8
He, to my crying shame, obeyed them in his limping dip-straight-dip fashion.

My grandmother, too, followed their orders, except that she didn't seem to   9
be servile because she anticipated their needs.

"Here's sugar, Miz Potter, and here's baking powder. You didn't buy soda   10
last month, you'll probably be needing some."

Momma always directed her statements to the adults, but sometimes, Oh   11
painful sometimes, the grimy, snotty-nosed girls would answer her.

"Naw, Annie . . ."—to Momma? Who owned the land they lived on? Who   12
forgot more than they would ever learn? If there was any justice in the world, God should strike them dumb at once!—"Just give us some extra sody crackers, and some more mackerel."

At least they never looked in her face, or I never caught them doing so. No-   13
body with a smidgen of training, not even the worst roustabout, would look right in a grown person's face. It meant the person was trying to take the words out before they were formed. The dirty little children didn't do that, but they threw their orders around the Store like lashes from a cat-o'-nine-tails.

When I was around ten years old, those scruffy children caused me the most   14
painful and confusing experience I had ever had with my grandmother.

One summer morning, after I had swept the dirt yard of leaves, spearmint-   15
gum wrappers and Vienna-sausage labels, I raked the yellow-red dirt, and made half-moons carefully, so that the design stood out clearly and mask-like. I put the rake behind the Store and came through the back of the house to find Grandmother on the front porch in her big, wide white apron. The apron was so stiff by virtue of the starch that it could have stood alone. Momma was admiring the yard, so I joined her. It truly looked like a flat redhead that had been raked with a big-toothed comb. Momma didn't say anything but I knew she liked it. She looked over to-ward the school principal's house and to the right at Mr. McElroy's. She was hop-ing one of those community pillars would see the design before the day's business wiped it out. Then she looked upward to the school. My head had swung with hers, so at just about the same time we saw a troop of powhitetrash kids marching over the hill and down by the side of the school.

I looked to Momma for direction. She did an excellent job of sagging from   16
her waist down, but from the waist up she seemed to be pulling for the top of the oak tree across the road. Then she began to moan a hymn. Maybe not to moan, but the tune was so slow and the meter so strange that she could have been moaning.

She didn't look at me again. When the children reached halfway down the hill, halfway to the Store, she said without turning, "Sister, go on inside."

I wanted to beg her, "Momma, don't wait for them. Come on inside with me. 17 If they come in the Store, you go to the bedroom and let me wait on them. They only frighten me if you're around. Alone I know how to handle them." But of course I couldn't say anything, so I went in and stood behind the screen door.

Before the girls got to the porch I heard their laughter crackling and popping 18 like pine logs in a cooking stove. I suppose my lifelong paranoia was born in those cold, molasses-slow minutes. They came finally to stand on the ground in front of Momma. At first they pretended seriousness. Then one of them wrapped her right arm in the crook of her left, pushed out her mouth and started to hum. I realized that she was aping my grandmother. Another said, "Naw, Helen, you ain't standing like her. This here's it." Then she lifted her chest, folded her arms and mocked that strange carriage that was Annie Henderson. Another laughed, "Naw, you can't do it. Your mouth ain't pooched out enough. It's like this."

I thought about the rifle behind the door, but I knew I'd never be able to hold 19 it straight, and the .410, our sawed-off shotgun, which stayed loaded and was fired every New Year's night, was locked in the trunk and Uncle Willie had the key on his chain. Through the fly-specked screen door, I could see that the arms of Momma's apron jiggled from the vibrations of her humming. But her knees seemed to have locked as if they would never bend again.

She sang on. No louder than before, but no softer either. No slower or faster. 20

The dirt of the girls' cotton dresses continued on their legs, feet, arms, and 21 faces to make them all of a piece. Their greasy uncolored hair hung down, un-combed, with a grim finality. I knelt to see them better, to remember them for all time. The tears that had slipped down my dress left unsurprising dark spots, and made the front yard blurry and even more unreal. The world had taken a deep breath and was having doubts about continuing to revolve.

The girls had tired of mocking Momma and turned to other means of agita- 22 tion. One crossed her eyes, stuck her thumbs in both sides of her mouth and said, "Look here, Annie." Grandmother hummed on and the apron strings trembled. I wanted to throw a handful of black pepper in their faces, to throw lye on them, to scream that they were dirty, scummy peckerwoods, but I knew I was as clearly im-prisoned behind the scene as the actors outside were confined to their roles.

One of the smaller girls did a kind of puppet dance while her fellow clowns 23 laughed at her. But the tall one, who was almost a woman, said something very qui-etly, which I couldn't hear. They all moved backward from the porch, still watching Momma. For an awful second I thought they were going to throw a rock at Momma, who seemed (except for the apron strings) to have turned into stone herself. But the big girl turned her back, bent down and put her hands flat on the ground—she didn't pick up anything. She simply shifted her weight and did a hand stand.

Her dirty bare feet and long legs went straight for the sky. Her dress fell 24 down around her shoulders, and she had on no drawers. The slick pubic hair made a brown triangle where her legs came together. She hung in the vacuum of that lifeless morning for only a few seconds, then wavered and tumbled. The other girls clapped her on the back and slapped their hands.

Momma changed her song to "Bread of Heaven, bread of Heaven, feed me 25 till I want no more."

I found that I was praying too. How long could Momma hold out? What new 26 indignity would they think of to subject her to? Would I be able to stay out of it? What would Momma really like me to do?

Then they were moving out of the yard, on their way to town. They bobbed 27 their heads and shook their slack behinds and turned, one at a time:

"Bye, Annie." 28

"Bye, Annie." 29

"Bye, Annie." 30

Momma never turned her head or unfolded her arms, but she stopped 31 singing and said, "'Bye, Miz Helen, 'bye, Miz Ruth, 'bye, Miz Eloise."

I burst. A firecracker July-the-Fourth burst. How could Momma call them 32 Miz? The mean nasty things. Why couldn't she have come inside the sweet, cool store when we saw them breasting the hill? What did she prove? And then if they were dirty, mean, and impudent, why did Momma have to call them Miz?

She stood another whole song through and then opened the screen door to 33 look down on me crying in rage. She looked until I looked up. Her face was a brown moon that shone on me. She was beautiful. Something had happened out there, which I couldn't completely understand, but I could see that she was happy. Then she bent down and touched me as mothers of the church "lay hands on the sick and afflicted" and I quieted.

"Go wash your face, Sister." And she went behind the candy counter and 34 hummed, "Glory, glory, hallelujah, when I lay my burden down."

I threw the well water on my face and used the weekday handkerchief to 35 blow my nose. Whatever the contest had been out front, I knew Momma had won.

I took the rake back to the front yard. The smudged footprints were easy to 36 erase. I worked for a long time on my new design and laid the rake behind the wash pot. When I came back in the Store, I took Momma's hand and we both walked outside to look at the pattern.

It was a large heart with lots of hearts growing smaller inside, and piercing 37 from the outside rim to the smallest heart was an arrow. Momma said, "Sister, that's right pretty." Then she turned back to the Store and resumed, "Glory, glory, hallelujah, when I lay my burden down."

1970

QUESTIONS FOR DISCUSSION

Content

a. Is this simply a story about bad-mannered children and racism? Or is Angelou's intent more complex?

b. Why does the speaker bother to tell us that she made careful patterns when she raked the yard? Why did Momma admire these designs?

c. Angelou describes a number of outdated social observances such as never looking "right in a grown person's face." What other examples can you find in this selection? Why does she make it a point to include them in this recollection of her childhood?

d. Grandmother Henderson addresses each of the white girls as "Miz." Does her doing so have anything to do with her strange victory over these brats?

e. What details does Angelou use to create this obviously unflattering picture of "powhitetrash children"?

f. What does Angelou mean when she describes her uncle's limping in "dip-straight-dip fashion"?

Strategy and Style

g. In light of what she says early in the narrative, is it important for her to quote all three of the girls as they leave the store (paragraphs 28 through 30)? In general, what effect does Angelou's extensive use of dialogue create?

h. This selection begins with two rather odd commandments, which both startle and amuse the reader. Why are they important to the rest of the essay?

i. Angelou's use of metaphor is brilliant. In paragraph 18, she tells us that her "paranoia was born in those cold, molasses-slow minutes." What other examples of figurative language can you find?

j. How would you describe the speaker's tone at the beginning of this essay? When, exactly, does this tone change?

SUGGESTIONS FOR SHORT WRITING

a. What is victory to Angelou's grandmother?

b. Write your own definition of *victory*. What does it mean to you personally?

SUGGESTIONS FOR SUSTAINED WRITING

a. What kind of person is Grandmother Henderson? Based upon the details Angelou provides, jot down a few notes that might help explain her character to other readers. Then, relying on your own experiences, narrate an incident from the life of a close family relative. Through the use of description, dialogue, and action, make sure to include the kind of details that will provide the reader with a fairly vivid picture of the person you are recalling. Address your essay to someone who has never met this person and/or knows very little about him or her.

b. Grandmother Henderson's triumph may well have resided in the fact that she had done a far better job of raising children than many of her "powhitetrash" neighbors. Analyze Angelou's essay in order to explain this and other sources of "Momma's" victory.

c. The term *powhitetrash* has many connotations, several of which are apparent in this narrative. Choose a label often used in conversation to describe a type of person or group of persons. Using events from your life as illustrations, explain the kind of person(s) the label describes. Examples might include a hero/heroine, a creep, a spoiled brat, a winner/loser, an egghead, a yuppie, a jock, a nerd, a giver/taker, a witch.

No Name Woman

Maxine Hong Kingston

Born in 1940 to recently arrived immigrants from China, Maxine Hong Kingston grew up having to negotiate between two very different cultures. Her gender in a culture that valued males over females created further difficulties. These two issues are the main themes that inform much of Hong Kingston's work, most notably The Woman Warrior: Memoirs of a Girlhood among Ghosts *(1975), a collection of autobiographical narrative essays through which she seeks to understand her female ancestors and the ways they helped to form her own identity. "No Name Woman" is from this collection. The most well known of her other books are* China Men *(1980), a collection of character sketches from real and legendary sources; and* Tripmaster Monkey: His Fake Book *(1989), a novel. She has received over twenty awards, fellowships, and honorary degrees, including a National Book Critics Circle Award for* The Woman Warrior, *an American Book Award for* China Men, *and a PEN West Award in Fiction for* Tripmaster Monkey.

1   "You must not tell anyone," my mother said, "what I am about to tell you. In China your father had a sister who killed herself. She jumped into the family well. We say that your father has all brothers because it is as if she had never been born.

2   "In 1924 just a few days after our village celebrated seventeen hurry-up weddings—to make sure that every young man who went 'out on the road' would responsibly come home—your father and his brothers and your grandfather and his brothers and your aunt's new husband sailed for America, the Gold Mountain. It was your grandfather's last trip. Those lucky enough to get contracts waved goodbye from the decks. They fed and guarded the stowaways and helped them off in Cuba, New York, Bali, Hawaii. 'We'll meet in California next year,' they said. All of them sent money home.

3   "I remember looking at your aunt one day when she and I were dressing; I had not noticed before that she had such a protruding melon of a stomach. But I did not think, 'She's pregnant,' until she began to look like other pregnant women, her shirt pulling and the white tops of her black pants showing. She could not have been pregnant, you see, because her husband had been gone for years. No one said anything. We did not discuss it. In early summer she was ready to have the child, long after the time when it could have been possible.

4   "The village had also been counting. On the night the baby was to be born the villagers raided our house. Some were crying. Like a great saw, teeth strung with lights, files of people walked zigzag across our land, tearing the rice. Their lanterns doubled in the disturbed black water, which drained away through the broken bunds. As the villagers closed in, we could see that some of them, probably men and women we knew well, wore white masks. The people with long hair hung it over their faces. Women with short hair made it stand up on end. Some had tied white bands around their foreheads, arms, and legs.

5   "At first they threw mud and rocks at the house. Then they threw eggs and began slaughtering our stock. We could hear the animals scream their deaths—the

17

roosters, the pigs, a last great roar from the ox. Familiar wild heads flared in our night windows; the villagers encircled us. Some of the faces stopped to peer at us, their eyes rushing like searchlights. The hands flattened against the panes, framed heads, and left red prints.

"The villagers broke in the front and the back doors at the same time, even 6 though we had not locked the doors against them. Their knives dripped with the blood of our animals. They smeared blood on the doors and walls. One woman swung a chicken, whose throat she had slit, splattering blood in red arcs about her. We stood together in the middle of our house, in the family hall with the pictures and tables of the ancestors around us, and looked straight ahead.

"At that time the house had only two wings. When the men came back, we 7 would build two more to enclose our courtyard and a third one to begin a second courtyard. The villagers pushed through both wings, even your grandparents' rooms, to find your aunt's, which was also mine until the men returned. From this room a new wing for one of the younger families would grow. They ripped up her clothes and shoes and broke her combs, grinding them underfoot. They tore her work from the loom. They scattered the cooking fire and rolled the new weaving in it. We could hear them in the kitchen breaking our bowls and banging the pots. They overturned the great waist-high earthenware jugs; duck eggs, pickled fruits, vegetables burst out and mixed in acrid torrents. The old woman from the next field swept a broom through the air and loosed the spirits-of-the-broom over our heads. 'Pig.' 'Ghost.' 'Pig,' they sobbed and scolded while they ruined our house.

"When they left, they took sugar and oranges to bless themselves. They cut 8 pieces from the dead animals. Some of them took bowls that were not broken and clothes that were not torn. Afterward we swept up the rice and sewed it back up into sacks. But the smells from the spilled preserves lasted. Your aunt gave birth in the pigsty that night. The next morning when I went for the water, I found her and the baby plugging up the family well.

"Don't let your father know that I told you. He denies her. Now that you 9 have started to menstruate, what happened to her could happen to you. Don't humiliate us. You wouldn't like to be forgotten as if you had never been born. The villagers are watchful."

Whenever she had to warn us about life, my mother told stories that ran like 10 this one, a story to grow up on. She tested our strength to establish realities. Those in the emigrant generations who could not reassert brute survival died young and far from home. Those of us in the first American generations have had to figure out how the invisible world the emigrants built around our childhoods fits in solid America.

The emigrants confused the gods by diverting their curses, misleading them 11 with crooked streets and false names. They must try to confuse their offspring as well, who, I suppose, threaten them in similar ways—always trying to get things straight, always trying to name the unspeakable. The Chinese I know hide their names; sojourners take new names when their lives change and guard their real names with silence.

Chinese-Americans, when you try to understand what things in you are Chi-   12
nese, how do you separate what is peculiar to childhood, to poverty, insanities, one
family, your mother who marked your growing with stories, from what is Chinese?
What is Chinese tradition and what is the movies?

If I want to learn what clothes my aunt wore, whether flashy or ordinary, I   13
would have to begin, "Remember Father's drowned-in-the-well sister?" I cannot
ask that. My mother has told me once and for all the useful parts. She will add
nothing unless powered by Necessity, a riverbank that guides her life. She plants
vegetable gardens rather than lawns; she carries the odd-shaped tomatoes home
from the fields and eats food left for the gods.

Whenever we did frivolous things, we used up energy; we flew high kites.   14
We children came up off the ground over the melting cones our parents brought
home from work and the American movie on New Year's Day—*Oh, You Beautiful Doll* with Betty Grable one year, and *She Wore a Yellow Ribbon* with John
Wayne another year. After the one carnival ride each, we paid in guilt; our tired father counted his change on the dark walk home.

Adultery is extravagance. Could people who hatch their own chicks and eat   15
the embryos and the heads for delicacies and boil the feet in vinegar for party food,
leaving only the gravel, eating even the gizzard lining—could such people engender a prodigal aunt? To be a woman, to have a daughter in starvation time was a
waste enough. My aunt could not have been the lone romantic who gave up everything for sex. Women in the old China did not choose. Some man had commanded
her to lie with him and be his secret evil. I wonder whether he masked himself
when he joined the raid on her family.

Perhaps she had encountered him in the fields or on the mountain where the   16
daughters-in-law collected fuel. Or perhaps he first noticed her in the marketplace.
He was not a stranger because the village housed no strangers. She had to have
dealings with him other than sex. Perhaps he worked an adjoining field, or he sold
her the cloth for the dress she sewed and wore. His demand must have surprised,
then terrified her. She obeyed him; she always did as she was told.

When the family found a young man in the next village to be her husband,   17
she had stood tractably beside the best rooster, his proxy, and promised before they
met that she would be his forever. She was lucky that he was her age and she would
be the first wife, an advantage secure now. The night she first saw him, he had sex
with her. Then he left for America. She had almost forgotten what he looked like.
When she tried to envision him, she only saw the black and white face in the group
photograph the men had had taken before leaving.

The other man was not, after all, much different from her husband. They   18
both gave orders: she followed. "If you tell your family, I'll beat you. I'll kill you.
Be here again next week." No one talked sex, ever. And she might have separated
the rapes from the rest of living if only she did not have to buy her oil from him
or gather wood in the same forest. I want her fear to have lasted just as long as rape
lasted so that the fear could have been contained. No drawn-out fear. But women
at sex hazarded birth and hence lifetimes. The fear did not stop but permeated

everywhere. She told the man, "I think I'm pregnant." He organized the raid against her.

On nights when my mother and father talked about their life back home, 19 sometimes they mentioned an "outcast table" whose business they still seemed to be settling, their voices tight. In a commensal tradition, where food is precious, the powerful older people made wrongdoers eat alone. Instead of letting them start separate new lives like the Japanese, who could become samurais and geishas, the Chinese family, faces averted but eyes glowering sideways, hung on to the offenders and fed them leftovers. My aunt must have lived in the same house as my parents and eaten at an outcast table. My mother spoke about the raid as if she had seen it, when she and my aunt, a daughter-in-law to a different household, should not have been living together at all. Daughters-in-law lived with their husbands' parents, not their own; a synonym for marriage in Chinese is "taking a daughter-in-law." Her husband's parents could have sold her, mortgaged her, stoned her. But they had sent her back to her own mother and father, a mysterious act hinting at disgraces not told me. Perhaps they had thrown her out to deflect the avengers.

She was the only daughter; her four brothers went with her father, husband, 20 and uncles "out on the road" and for some years became western men. When the goods were divided among the family, three of the brothers took land, and the youngest, my father, chose an education. After my grandparents gave their daughter away to her husband's family, they had dispensed all the adventure and all the property. They expected her alone to keep the traditional ways, which her brothers, now among the barbarians, could fumble without detection. The heavy, deep-rooted women were to maintain the past against the flood, safe for returning. But the rare urge west had fixed upon our family, and so my aunt crossed boundaries not delineated in space.

The work of preservation demands that the feelings playing about in one's 21 guts not be turned into action. Just watch their passing like cherry blossoms. But perhaps my aunt, my forerunner, caught in a slow life, let dreams grow and fade and after some months or years went toward what persisted. Fear at the enormities of the forbidden kept her desires delicate, wire and bone. She looked at a man because she liked the way the hair was tucked behind his ears, or she liked the question-mark line of a long torso curving at the shoulder and straight at the hip. For warm eyes or a soft voice or a slow walk—that's all—a few hairs, a line, a brightness, a sound, a pace, she gave up family. She offered us up for a charm that vanished with tiredness, a pigtail that didn't toss when the wind died. Why, the wrong lighting could erase the dearest thing about him.

It could very well have been, however, that my aunt did not take subtle en- 22 joyment of her friend, but, a wild woman, kept rollicking company. Imagining her free with sex doesn't fit, though. I don't know any women like that, or men either. Unless I see her life branching into mine, she gives me no ancestral help.

To sustain her being in love, she often worked at herself in the mirror, guess- 23 ing at the colors and shapes that would interest him, changing them frequently in order to hit on the right combination. She wanted him to look back.

On a farm near the sea, a woman who tended her appearance reaped a rep- 24
utation for eccentricity. All the married women blunt-cut their hair in flaps about
their ears or pulled it back in tight buns. No nonsense. Neither style blew easily
into heart-catching tangles. And at their weddings they displayed themselves in
their long hair for the last time. "It brushed the backs of my knees," my mother
tells me. "It was braided, and even so, it brushed the backs of my knees."

At the mirror my aunt combed individuality into her bob. A bun could have 25
been contrived to escape into black streamers blowing in the wind or in quiet wisps
about her face, but only the older women in our picture album wear buns. She
brushed her hair back from her forehead, tucking the flaps behind her ears. She
looped a piece of thread, knotted into a circle between her index fingers and
thumbs, and ran the double strand across her forehead. When she closed her fingers as if she were making a pair of shadow geese bite, the string twisted together
catching the little hairs. Then she pulled the thread away from her skin, ripping the
hairs out neatly, her eyes watering from the needles of pain. Opening her fingers,
she cleaned the thread, then rolled it along her hairline and the tops of her eye-
brows. My mother did the same to me and my sisters and herself. I used to believe
that the expression "caught by the short hairs" meant a captive held with a depila-
tory string. It especially hurt at the temples, but my mother said we were lucky we
didn't have to have our feet bound when we were seven. Sisters used to sit on their
beds and cry together, she said, as their mothers or their slaves removed the band-
ages for a few minutes each night and let the blood gush back into their veins. I
hope that the man my aunt loved appreciated a smooth brow, that he wasn't just a
tits-and-ass man.

Once my aunt found a freckle on her chin, at a spot that the almanac said 26
predestined her for unhappiness. She dug it out with a hot needle and washed the
wound with peroxide.

More attention to her looks than these pullings of hairs and pickings at spots 27
would have caused gossip among the villagers. They owned work clothes and
good clothes, and they wore good clothes for feasting the new seasons. But since
a woman combing her hair hexes beginnings, my aunt rarely found an occasion to
look her best. Women looked like great sea snails—the corded wood, babies, and
laundry they carried were the whorls on their backs. The Chinese did not admire
a bent back; goddesses and warriors stood straight. Still there must have been a
marvelous freeing of beauty when a worker laid down her burden and stretched
and arched.

Such commonplace loveliness, however, was not enough for my aunt. She 28
dreamed of a lover for the fifteen days of New Year's, the time for families to exchange visits, money, and food. She plied her secret comb. And sure enough she
cursed the year, the family, the village, and herself.

Even as her hair lured her imminent lover, many other men looked at her. 29
Uncles, cousins, nephews, brothers would have looked, too, had they been home
between journeys. Perhaps they had already been restraining their curiosity, and
they left, fearful that their glances, like a field of nesting birds, might be startled

and caught. Poverty hurt, and that was their first reason for leaving. But another, final reason for leaving the crowded house was the never-said.

She may have been unusually beloved, the precious only daughter, spoiled 30 and mirror gazing because of the affection the family lavished on her. When her husband left, they welcomed the chance to take her back from the in-laws; she could live like the little daughter for just a while longer. There are stories that my grandfather was different from other people, "crazy ever since the little Jap bayoneted him in the head." He used to put his naked penis on the dinner table, laughing. And one day he brought home a baby girl, wrapped up inside his brown western-style greatcoat. He had traded one of his sons, probably my father, the youngest, for her. My grandmother made him trade back. When he finally got a daughter of his own, he doted on her. They must have all loved her, except perhaps my father, the only brother who never went back to China, having once been traded for a girl.

Brothers and sisters, newly men and women, had to efface their sexual color 31 and present plain miens. Disturbing hair and eyes, a smile like no other, threatened the ideal of five generations living under one roof. To focus blurs, people shouted face to face and yelled from room to room. The immigrants I know have loud voices, unmodulated to American tones even after years away from the village where they called their friendships out across the fields. I have not been able to stop my mother's screams in public libraries or over telephones. Walking erect (knees straight, toes pointed forward, not pigeon-toed, which is Chinese-feminine) and speaking in an inaudible voice, I have tried to turn myself American-feminine. Chinese communication was loud, public. Only sick people had to whisper. But at the dinner table, where the family members came nearest one another, no one could talk, not the outcasts nor any eaters. Every word that falls from the mouth is a coin lost. Silently they gave and accepted food with both hands. A preoccupied child who took his bowl with one hand got a sideways glare. A complete moment of total attention is due everyone alike. Children and lovers have no singularity here, but my aunt used a secret voice, a separate attentiveness.

She kept the man's name to herself throughout her labor and dying; she did 32 not accuse him that he be punished with her. To save her inseminator's name she gave silent birth.

He may have been somebody in her own household, but intercourse with a 33 man outside the family would have been no less abhorrent. All the village were kinsmen, and the titles shouted in loud country voices never let kinship be forgotten. Any man within visiting distance would have been neutralized as a lover—"brother," "younger brother," "older brother"—one hundred and fifteen relationship titles. Parents researched birth charts probably not so much to assure good fortune as to circumvent incest in a population that has but one hundred surnames. Everybody has eight million relatives. How useless then sexual mannerisms, how dangerous.

As if it came from an atavism deeper than fear, I used to add "brother" silently 34 to boys' names. It hexed the boys, who would or would not ask me to dance, and made them less scary and as familiar and deserving of benevolence as girls.

But, of course, I hexed myself also—no dates. I should have stood up, both 35
arms waving, and shouted out across libraries, "Hey, you! Love me back." I had no
idea, though, how to make attraction selective, how to control its direction and magnitude. If I made myself American-pretty so that the five or six Chinese boys in the
class fell in love with me, everyone else—the Caucasian, Negro, and Japanese
boys—would too. Sisterliness, dignified and honorable, made much more sense.

Attraction eludes control so stubbornly that whole societies designed to or- 36
ganize relationships among people cannot keep order, not even when they bind
people to one another from childhood and raise them together. Among the very
poor and the wealthy, brothers married their adopted sisters, like doves. Our family allowed some romance, paying adult brides' prices and providing dowries so
that their sons and daughters could marry strangers. Marriage promises to turn
strangers into friendly relatives—a nation of siblings.

In the village structure, spirits shimmered among the live creatures, bal- 37
anced and held in equilibrium by time and land. But one human being flaring up
into violence could open up a black hole, a maelstrom that pulled in the sky. The
frightened villagers, who depended on one another to maintain the real, went to
my aunt to show her a personal, physical representation of the break she had made
in the "roundness." Misallying couples snapped off the future, which was to be
embodied in true offspring. The villagers punished her for acting as if she could
have a private life, secret and apart from them.

If my aunt had betrayed the family at a time of large grain yields and peace, 38
when many boys were born, and wings were being built on many houses, perhaps she
might have escaped such severe punishment. But the men—hungry, greedy, tired of
planting in dry soil—had been forced to leave the village in order to send food-money
home. There were ghost plagues, bandit plagues, wars with the Japanese, floods. My
Chinese brother and sister had died of an unknown sickness. Adultery, perhaps only
a mistake during good times, became a crime when the village needed food.

The round moon cakes and round doorways, the round tables of graduated 39
sizes that fit one roundness inside another, round windows and rice bowls—these
talismans had lost their power to warn this family of the law: A family must be
whole, faithfully keeping the descent line by having sons to feed the old and the
dead, who in turn look after the family. The villagers came to show my aunt and
her lover-in-hiding a broken house. The villagers were speeding up the circling of
events because she was too shortsighted to see that her infidelity had already
harmed the village, that waves of consequences would return unpredictably, sometimes in disguise, as now, to hurt her. This roundness had to be made coin-sized so
that she would see its circumference: Punish her at the birth of her baby. Awaken
her to the inexorable. People who refused fatalism because they could invent small
resources insisted on culpability. Deny accidents and wrest fault from the stars.

After the villagers left, their lanterns now scattering in various directions to- 40
ward home, the family broke their silence and cursed her. "Aiaa, we're going to
die. Death is coming. Death is coming. Look what you've done. You've killed us.
Ghost! Dead ghost! Ghost! You've never been born." She ran out into the fields,

far enough from the house so that she could no longer hear their voices, and pressed herself against the earth, her own land no more. When she felt the birth coming, she thought that she had been hurt. Her body seized together. "They've hurt me too much," she thought. "This is gall, and it will kill me." With forehead and knees against the earth, her body convulsed and then relaxed. She turned on her back, lay on the ground. The black well of sky and stars went out and out and out forever; her body and her complexity seemed to disappear. She was one of the stars, a bright dot in blackness, without home, without a companion, in eternal cold and silence. An agoraphobia rose in her, speeding higher and higher, bigger and bigger; she would not be able to contain it; there would be no end to fear.

Flayed, unprotected against space, she felt pain return, focusing her body. **41** This pain chilled her—a cold, steady kind of surface pain. Inside, spasmodically, the other pain, the pain of the child, heated her. For hours she lay on the ground, alternately body and space. Sometimes a vision of normal comfort obliterated reality: She saw the family in the evening gambling at the dinner table, the young people massaging their elders' backs. She saw them congratulating one another, high joy on the mornings the rice shoots came up. When these pictures burst, the stars drew yet further apart. Black space opened.

She got to her feet to fight better and remembered that old-fashioned women **42** gave birth in their pigsties to fool the jealous, pain-dealing gods, who do not snatch piglets. Before the next spasms could stop her, she ran to the pigsty, each step a rushing out into emptiness. She climbed over the fence and knelt in the dirt. It was good to have a fence enclosing her, a tribal person alone.

Laboring, this woman who had carried her child as a foreign growth that **43** sickened her every day, expelled it at last. She reached down to touch the hot, wet, moving mass, surely smaller than anything human, and could feel that it was human after all—fingers, toes, nails, nose. She pulled it up on to her belly, and it lay curled there, butt in the air, feet precisely tucked one under the other. She opened her loose shirt and buttoned the child inside. After resting, it squirmed and thrashed and she pushed it up to her breast. It turned its head this way and that until it found her nipple. There, it made little snuffling noises. She clenched her teeth at its preciousness, lovely as a young calf, a piglet, a little dog.

She may have gone to the pigsty as a last act of responsibility: she would **44** protect this child as she had protected its father. It would look after her soul, leaving supplies on her grave. But how would this tiny child without family find her grave when there would be no marker for her anywhere, neither in the earth nor the family hall? No one would give her a family hall name. She had taken the child with her into the wastes. At its birth the two of them had felt the same raw pain of separation, a wound that only the family pressing tight could close. A child with no descent line would not soften her life but only trail after her, ghostlike, begging her to give it purpose. At dawn the villagers on their way to the fields would stand around the fence and look.

Full of milk, the little ghost slept. When it awoke, she hardened her breasts   45
against the milk that crying loosens. Toward morning she picked up the baby and
walked to the well.

Carrying the baby to the well shows loving. Otherwise abandon it. Turn its   46
face into the mud. Mothers who love their children take them along. It was probably a girl; there is some hope of forgiveness for boys.

"Don't tell anyone you had an aunt. Your father does not want to hear her   47
name. She has never been born." I have believed that sex was unspeakable and
words so strong and fathers so frail that "aunt" would do my father mysterious
harm. I have thought that my family, having settled among immigrants who had
also been their neighbors in the ancestral land, needed to clean their name, and a
wrong word would incite the kinspeople even here. But there is more to this silence: They want me to participate in her punishment. And I have.

In the twenty years since I heard this story I have not asked for details nor   48
said my aunt's name; I do not know it. People who can comfort the dead can also
chase after them to hurt them further—a reverse ancestor worship. The real punishment was not the raid swiftly inflicted by the villagers, but the family's deliberately forgetting her. Her betrayal so maddened them, they saw to it that she
would suffer forever, even after death. Always hungry, always needing, she
would have to beg food from other ghosts, snatch and steal it from those whose
living descendants give them gifts. She would have to fight the ghosts massed at
crossroads for the buns a few thoughtful citizens leave to decoy her away from
village and home so that the ancestral spirits could feast unharassed. At peace,
they could act like gods, not ghosts, their descent lines providing them with paper suits and dresses, spirit money, paper houses, paper automobiles, chicken,
meat, and rice into eternity—essences delivered up in smoke and flames, steam
and incense rising from each rice bowl. In an attempt to make the Chinese care
for people outside the family, Chairman Mao encourages us now to give our paper replicas to the spirits of outstanding soldiers and workers, no matter whose
ancestors they may be. My aunt remains forever hungry. Goods are not distributed evenly among the dead.

My aunt haunts me—her ghost drawn to me because now, after fifty years   49
of neglect, I alone devote pages of paper to her, though not origamied into
houses and clothes. I do not think she always means me well. I am telling on
her, and she was a spite suicide, drowning herself in the drinking water. The
Chinese are always very frightened of the drowned one, whose weeping ghost,
wet hair hanging and skin bloated, waits silently by the water to pull down a
substitute.

1975

QUESTIONS FOR DISCUSSION

Content

a. Is Hong Kingston's family ashamed of No Name Woman because she committed suicide or because she became pregnant by a man who was not her husband? Is the distinction important?

b. Why doesn't the author ever learn her aunt's name?

c. In what way does the story of No Name Woman cast light on Kingston's claim that her mother is guided "by Necessity" (paragraph 13)?

d. Why does Hong Kingston refer to her aunt as "prodigal" (paragraph 15)? What meanings does she associate with this term?

e. Does she see an affinity between herself and her aunt not shared by other members of the family? In what ways is this a defense of No Name Woman? Of all Chinese women? Of all women?

f. "The villagers punished [No Name Woman] for acting as if she could have a private life, secret and apart from them" (paragraph 37). How does this statement shed light upon the culture Hong Kingston is describing?

g. What motives does she ascribe to No Name Woman? To the man who raped her? To the villagers? To her family?

Strategy and Style

h. The author uses her mother's voice to relate the story of the villagers' attack. Would she have done better to tell this story from her own point of view?

i. Why does she address Chinese-Americans directly in paragraph 12? Is she writing to a limited audience?

j. What does she mean when, at the end of paragraph 20, she says, "the rare urge west had fixed upon our family, and so my aunt crossed boundaries not delineated in space"?

k. Why does she spend so much time describing the setting of her story?

l. Comment upon the author's use of verbs in the passage that recalls the attack of the townspeople. What effect does her choice of verbs create?

m. Among other things, "No Name Woman" is an indictment of sexism, intolerance, and violence against women. Is Hong Kingston's tone appropriate? Should she have made her criticism fiercer and more apparent? Should she have focused on this issue alone?

n. How would you describe the function of the writer in this selection? Is she simply a reporter, or does she have other functions? What might they be?

o. The author says she has participated in her aunt's punishment. What does she mean? Why might she have written this essay?

SUGGESTIONS FOR SHORT WRITING

a. Spend a few minutes explaining how people of the town in which you grew up might react to learning that one of their neighbors had become pregnant while her husband was away. Would attention focus on the woman, on her husband, or on the "other" man? Would the woman be condemned by some people no matter what the circumstances?

b. Review or reread "No Name Woman." As you do this, record your reactions to the sexism, violence, and intolerance in the culture Kingston is describing. Can you find examples of such phenomena in your own environment?

c. Sketch out a few details that might serve as the outline to a story about a traumatic event in the history of your family. Choose an event that you experienced firsthand or that you learned about from a parent or other relative.

SUGGESTIONS FOR SUSTAINED WRITING

a. You can probably recall an interesting story about an ancestor or a living relative. Write this story down just as you heard it. Then, rewrite the story from at least two other perspectives: from the ancestor's or relative's perspective, from the perspective of another person involved in the story, and/or from the perspective you might use if you were to pass on the story to your children. How does the story change from one point of view to another? What elements are based on fact in each? What elements are based on speculation? Which version, in your opinion, is the most "truthful"?

b. Hong Kingston tells her versions of what might have happened to her aunt in order to lend substance to her memory of this woman and implicitly to explain the cruelty toward women that can be imbedded in a culture. Collect several personal memories that might illustrate some unfairness or injustice to you (as representative of a larger group) or to a subgroup within your culture. Then turn these memories into a coherent narrative essay. Though you need not make your work as detailed or complex as Hong Kingston's, try to interweave these memories closely so as to create a clear and coherent discussion of the injustice you wish to illustrate.

Traveling South*

James Weldon Johnson

"Traveling South" (editors' title) is a chapter from The Autobiography of an Ex-Colored Man, *a purported account of the early life of James Weldon Johnson (1871–1938). First published anonymously in 1912, the book's discussion of racial issues—especially of miscegenation—is both startling and convincing. Although it was a work of fiction, Johnson's* Autobiography *was based upon many of his own travels and experiences as a young man. A poet, diplomat, and anthologist of African-American literature, Johnson was one of the founders of the National Association for the Advancement of Colored People (NAACP).* The Autobiography of an Ex-Colored Man *was republished in 1927 under the author's name. "Traveling South" begins as the narrator journeys from New England to Atlanta, where he plans to enroll in a university.*

The farther I got below Washington the more disappointed I became in the ap- 1
pearance of the country. I peered through the car windows, looking in vain for the luxuriant semi-tropical scenery which I had pictured in my mind. I did not find the grass so green, nor the woods so beautiful, nor the flowers so plentiful, as they were in Connecticut. Instead, the red earth partly covered by tough, scrawny grass, the muddy straggling roads, the cottages of unpainted pine boards, and the clay daubed huts imparted a "burnt up" impression. Occasionally we ran through a little white and green village that was like an oasis in a desert.

When I reached Atlanta my steadily increasing disappointment was not less- 2
ened. I found it a big, dull, red town. This dull red color of that part of the South I was then seeing had much, I think, to do with the extreme depression of my spirits— no public squares, no fountains, dingy street-cars, and, with the exception of three or four principal thoroughfares, unpaved streets. It was raining when I arrived and some of these unpaved streets were absolutely impassable. Wheels sank to the hubs in red mire, and I actually stood for an hour and watched four or five men work to save a mule, which stepped into a deep sink, from drowning, or, rather, suffocating in the mud. The Atlanta of today is a new city.

On the train I had talked with one of the Pullman car porters, a bright young 3
fellow who was himself a student, and I told him that I was going to Atlanta to attend school. I had also asked him to tell me where I might stop for a day or two until the University opened. He said I might go with him to the place where he stopped during his "layovers" in Atlanta. I gladly accepted his offer, and went with him along one of those muddy streets until we came to a rather rickety looking frame house, which we entered. The proprietor of the house was a big, fat, greasy looking brown-skinned man. When I asked him if he could give me accommodation he wanted to know how long I would stay. I told him perhaps two days, not more than three. In reply he said, "Oh, dat's all right den," at the same time leading the way up a pair of creaky stairs. I followed him and the porter to a room, the

*Editors' title.

28

door of which the proprietor opened while continuing, it seemed, his remark, "Oh, dat's all right den," by adding, "You kin sleep in dat cot in de corner der. Fifty cents please." The porter interrupted by saying, "You needn't collect from him now, he's got a trunk." This seemed to satisfy the man, and he went down leaving me and my porter friend in the room. I glanced around the apartment and saw that it contained a double bed and two cots, two wash-stands, three chairs, and a time-worn bureau with a looking glass that would have made Adonis appear hideous. I looked at the cot in which I was to sleep and suspected, not without good reasons, that I should not be the first to use the sheets and pillowcase since they had last come from the wash. When I thought of the clean, tidy, comfortable surroundings in which I had been reared, a wave of homesickness swept over me that made me feel faint. Had it not been for the presence of my companion, and that I knew this much of his history—that he was not yet quite twenty, just three years older than myself, and that he had been fighting his own way in the world, earning his own living and providing for his own education since he was fourteen—I should not have been able to stop the tears that were welling up in my eyes.

I asked him why it was that the proprietor of the house seemed unwilling to **4** accommodate me for more than a couple of days. He informed me that the man ran a lodging house especially for Pullman porters, and as their stays in town were not longer than one or two nights it would interfere with his arrangements to have anyone stay longer. He went on to say, "You see this room is fixed up to accommodate four men at a time. Well, by keeping a sort of table of trips, in and out, of the men, and working them like checkers, he can accommodate fifteen or sixteen in each week, and generally avoid having an empty bed. You happen to catch a bed that would have been empty for a couple of nights." I asked him where he was going to sleep. He answered, "I sleep in that other cot tonight; tomorrow night I go out." He went on the tell me that the man who kept the house did not serve meals, and that if I was hungry we would go out and get something to eat.

We went into the street, and in passing the railroad station I hired a wagon **5** to take my trunk to my lodging place. We passed along until, finally, we turned into a street that stretched away, up and down hill, for a mile or two; and here I caught my first sight of colored people in large numbers. I had seen little squads around the railroad stations on my way south; but here I saw a street crowded with them. They filled the shops and thronged the sidewalks and lined the curb. I asked my companion if all the colored people in Atlanta lived in this street. He said they did not, and assured me that the ones I saw were of the lower class. I felt relieved, in spite of the size of the lower class. The unkempt appearance, the shambling, slouching gait and loud talk and laughter of these people aroused in me a feeling of almost repulsion. Only one thing about them awoke a feeling of interest; that was their dialect. I had read some Negro dialect and had heard snatches of it on my journey down from Washington; but here I heard it in all of its fullness and freedom. I was particularly struck by the way in which it was punctuated by such exclamatory phrases as "Lawd a mussy!" "G'wan man!" "Bless ma soul!" "Look heah chile!" These people talked and laughed without restraint. In fact, they talked straight from their lungs, and laughed from the pits of their stomachs. And this hearty laughter was often justified by the droll humor of some remark. I paused long enough to hear one man say to another, "W'at's de mattah wid you an' yo' fr'en' Sam?" And the other came back like a flash, "Ma fr'en? He ma fr'en? Man! I'd go to his funeral jes de same as I'd go to a minstrel show." I have since learned that this ability to laugh heartily is, in part, the salvation of the American Negro; it does much to keep him from going the way of the Indian.

The business places of the street along which we were passing consisted 6 chiefly of low bars, cheap dry-goods and notion stores, barber shops, and fish and bread restaurants. We, at length, turned down a pair of stairs that led to a basement, and I found myself in an eating-house somewhat better than those I had seen in passing; but that did not mean much for its excellence. The place was smoky, the tables were covered with oil-cloth, the floor covered with sawdust, and from the kitchen came a rancid odor of fish fried over several times, which almost nauseated me. I asked my companion if this were the place where we were to eat. He informed me that it was the best place in town where a colored man could get a meal. I then wanted to know why somebody didn't open a place where respectable colored people who had money could be accommodated. He answered, "It wouldn't pay; all the respectable colored people eat at home, and the few who travel generally have friends in the towns to which they go, who entertain them." He added, "Of course, you could go in any place in the city; they wouldn't know you from white."

I sat down with the porter at one of the tables, but was not hungry enough to 7 eat with any relish what was put before me. The food was not badly cooked; but the iron knives and forks needed to be scrubbed, the plates and dishes and glasses needed to be washed and well dried. I minced over what I took on my plate while my companion ate. When we finished we paid the waiter twenty cents each and went out. We walked around until the lights of the city were lit. Then the porter said that he must get to bed and have some rest, as he had not had six hours' sleep since he left Jersey City. I went back to our lodging-house with him.

When I awoke in the morning there were, besides my newfound friend, two 8 other men in the room, asleep in the double bed. I got up and dressed myself very quietly, so as not to awake anyone. I then drew from under the pillow my precious roll of greenbacks, took out a ten dollar bill, and very softly unlocking my trunk, put the remainder, about three hundred dollars, in the inside pocket of a coat near the bottom; glad of the opportunity to put it unobserved in a place of safety. When I had carefully locked my trunk, I tiptoed toward the door with the intention of going out to look for a decent restaurant where I might get something fit to eat. As I was easing the door open, my porter friend said with a yawn, "Hello! You're going out?" I answered him, "Yes." "Oh!" he yawned again, "I guess I've had enough sleep; wait a minute, I'll go with you." For the instant his friendship bored and embarrassed me. I had visions of another meal in the greasy restaurant of the day before. He must have divined my thoughts; for he went on to say, "I know a woman across town who takes a few boarders; I think we can go over there and get a good breakfast." With a feeling of mingled fears and doubts regarding what the breakfast might be, I waited until he had dressed himself.

When I saw the neat appearance of the cottage we entered my fears van- 9
ished, and when I saw the woman who kept it my doubts followed the same course. Scrupulously clean, in a spotless white apron and colored head handkerchief, her round face beaming with motherly kindness, she was picturesquely beautiful. She impressed me as one broad expanse of happiness and good nature. In a few minutes she was addressing me as "chile" and "honey." She made me feel as though I should like to lay my head on her capacious bosom and go to sleep.

And the breakfast, simple as it was, I could not have had at any restaurant in Atlanta at any price. There was fried chicken, as it is fried only in the South, homily boiled to the consistency where it could be eaten with a fork, and biscuits so light and flaky that a fellow with any appetite at all would have no difficulty in disposing of eight or ten. When I had finished I felt that I had experienced the realization of, at least, one of my dreams of Southern life.

During the meal we found out from our hostess, who had two boys in school, 10
that Atlanta University opened on that very day. I had somehow mixed my dates. My friend the porter suggested that I go out to the university at once and offered to walk over and show me the way. We had to walk because, although the university was not more than twenty minutes distance from the center of the city, there were no street-cars running in that direction. My first sight of the school grounds made me feel that I was not far from home; here the red hills had been terraced and covered with green grass; clean gravel walks, well shaded, led up to the buildings; indeed, it was a bit of New England transplanted. At the gate my companion said he would bid me goodby, because it was likely that he would not see me again before his car went out. He told me that he would make two more trips to Atlanta, and that he would come out and see me; that after his second trip he would leave the Pullman service for the winter and return to school in Nashville. We shook hands, I thanked him for all his kindness, and we said goodby.

I walked up to a group of students and made some inquiries. They directed 11
me to the president's office in the main building. The president gave me a cordial welcome; it was more than cordial; he talked to me, not as the official head of a college, but as though he were adopting me into what was his large family, to personally look after my general welfare as well as my education. He seemed especially pleased with the fact that I had come to them all the way from the North. He told me that I could have come to the school as soon as I had reached the city, and that I had better move my trunk out at once. I gladly promised him that I would do so. He then called a boy and directed him to take me to the matron, and to show me around afterwards. I found the matron even more motherly than the president was fatherly. She had me to register, which was in effect to sign a pledge to abstain from the use of intoxicating beverages, tobacco, and profane language, while I was a student in the school. This act caused me no sacrifice; as, up to that time, I was free from either habit. The boy who was with me then showed me about the grounds. I was especially interested in the industrial building.

The sounding of a bell, he told me, was the signal for the students to gather 12
in the general assembly hall, and he asked me if I would go. Of course I would.
There were between three and four hundred students and perhaps all of the teachers gathered in the room. I noticed that several of the latter were colored. The president gave a talk addressed principally to new comers; but I scarcely heard what he
said, I was so much occupied in looking at those around me. They were of all types
and colors, the more intelligent types predominating. The colors ranged from jet
black to pure white, with light hair and eyes. Among the girls especially there were
many so fair that it was difficult to believe that they had Negro blood in them. And,
too, I could not help but notice that many of the girls, particularly those of the delicate brown shades, with black eyes and wavy dark hair, were decidedly pretty.
Among the boys, many of the blackest were fine specimens of young manhood, tall,
straight, and muscular, with magnificent heads, these were the kind of boys who
developed into the patriarchal "uncles" of the old slave régime.

When I left the University it was with the determination to get my trunk, and 13
move out to the school before night. I walked back across the city with a light step
and a light heart. I felt perfectly satisfied with life for the first time since my
mother's death. In passing the railroad station I hired a wagon and rode with the
driver as far as my stopping place. I settled with my landlord and went upstairs to
put away several articles I had left out. As soon as I opened my trunk a dart of suspicion shot through my heart; the arrangement of things did not look familiar. I began to dig down excitedly to the bottom till I reached the coat in which I had concealed my treasure. My money was gone! Every single bill of it. I knew it was
useless to do so, but I searched through every other coat, every pair of trousers,
every vest, and even into each pair of socks. When I had finished my fruitless
search I sat down dazed and heartsick. I called the landlord up, and informed him
of my loss; he comforted me by saying that I ought to have better sense than to
keep money in a trunk, and that he was not responsible for his lodgers' personal
effects. His cooling words brought me enough to my senses to cause me to look
and see if anything else was missing. Several small articles were gone, among
them a black and gray necktie of odd design upon which my heart was set; almost
as much as the loss of the money, I felt the loss of my tie.

After thinking for awhile as best I could, I wisely decided to go at once back 14
to the university and lay my troubles before the president. I rushed breathlessly back
to the school. As I neared the grounds the thought came across me, would not my
story sound fishy? Would it not place me in the position of an impostor or beggar?
What right had I to worry these busy people with the results of my carelessness? If
the money could not be recovered, and I doubted that it could, what good would it
do to tell them about it? The shame and embarrassment which the whole situation
gave me caused me to stop at the gate. I paused, undecided, for a moment; then
turned and slowly retraced my steps, and so changed the whole course of my life.

If the reader has never been in a strange city without money or friends, it is 15
useless to try to describe what my feelings were; he could not understand. If he has
been, it is equally useless, for he understands more than words could convey.

When I reached my lodgings I found in the room one of the porters who had slept there the night before. When he heard what misfortune had befallen me he offered many words of sympathy and advice. He asked me how much money I had left, I told him that I had ten or twelve dollars left in my pocket. He said, "That won't last you very long here, and you will hardly be able to find anything to do in Atlanta. I'll tell you what you do, go down to Jacksonville and you won't have any trouble to get a job in one of the big hotels down there, or in St. Augustine." I thanked him, but intimated my doubts of being able to get to Jacksonville on the money I had. He reassured me be saying, "Oh, that's all right. You express your trunk on through, and I'll take you down in my closet." I thanked him again, not knowing then, what it was to travel in a Pullman porter's closet. He put me under a deeper debt of gratitude by lending me fifteen dollars, which he said I could pay back after I had secured work. His generosity brought tears to my eyes, and I concluded that, after all, there were some kind hearts in the world.

I now forgot my troubles in the hurry and excitement of getting my trunk 16 off in time to catch the train, which went out at seven o'clock. I even forgot that I hadn't eaten anything since morning. We got a wagon—the porter went with me—and took my trunk to the express office. My new friend then told me to come to the station at about a quarter of seven, and walk straight to the car where I should see him standing, and not to lose my nerve. I found my rôle not so difficult to play as I thought it would be, because the train did not leave from the central station, but from a smaller one, where there were no gates and guards to pass. I followed directions, and the porter took me on his car, and locked me in his closet. In a few minutes the train pulled out for Jacksonville.

I may live to be a hundred years old, but I shall never forget the agonies I 17 suffered that night. I spent twelve hours doubled up in the porter's basket for soiled linen, not being able to straighten up on account of the shelves for clean linen just over my head. The air was hot and suffocating and the smell of damp towels and used linen was sickening. At each lurch of the car over the none too smooth track, I was bumped and bruised against the narrow walls of my narrow compartment. I became acutely conscious of the fact that I had not eaten for hours. Then nausea took possession of me, and at one time I had grave doubts about reaching my destination alive. If I had the trip to make again, I should prefer to walk.

1912

QUESTIONS FOR DISCUSSION

Content

a. How old is the narrator of this story?
b. What does Johnson mean when he says that laughter is "the salvation of the American Negro; it does much to keep him from going the way of the Indian" (paragraph 5)?

c. Johnson writes about a time when racial segregation was prominent in the South. What evidence of segregation do you see in this selection?

d. Johnson contrasts the narrator's reaction to the people and places in paragraphs 3, 4, 5, 6, and 7 with those in paragraphs 9, 10, and 11. What does this contrast tell us about the narrator's character, upbringing, and lifestyle?

e. The narrator feels "shame and embarrassment" over having lost his money. What might be the cause of that embarrassment?

f. Why does the narrator decide not to seek help from the university after discovering that he has been robbed? What does his reaction to this incident tell us about the way he views the world? What does it tell us about his character in general?

g. Explain how "Traveling South" might be interpreted as the story of a young person's initiation into adulthood. In your answer, make sure to consider what happens to the narrator on his way to Jacksonville.

h. Does this essay have a thesis? If so, what is it?

Strategy and Style

i. Why does Johnson use dialect to recreate the language of the proprietor of the boarding house and the people on the street? Wouldn't his story have been easier to read had he put their words into standard English?

j. What function does description play in this narrative? Where is it most prominent?

k. Why, in paragraph 3, does the narrator bother to tell us about the life of the young porter who befriends him?

l. Analyze the vocabulary used in paragraph 5. How would you describe the narrator's tone (his attitude toward his subject) in this part of the essay?

m. Where, in paragraph 13 does the author use irony? What effect does this device have on distinguishing the narrator from the author?

SUGGESTIONS FOR SHORT WRITING

a. Speculate on who might have stolen the narrator's money and necktie.

b. Compare and contrast the character of the narrator in this story with that of Sister in Angelou's "Grandmother's Victory," which also appears in this chapter.

SUGGESTIONS FOR SUSTAINED WRITING

a. Recall an incident in which you had to face a serious setback, difficulty, or reversal such as the one confronting the narrator of "Traveling South." Explain how you faced that setback. Then, as a way to give focus and purpose to your essay, explain what your reaction revealed about your character and personality at the time.

b. Write a letter to the narrator of "Traveling South" as a hypothetical attempt to persuade him to return to Atlanta and the university. Begin your assignment by rereading the essay and making notes in the margins so as to help you gather details that will make your writing convincing. As you draft your letter, refer to the text by paraphrasing and including direct quotations. In addition, anticipate and answer the objections the narrator might use to respond to your arguments. Make sure to respond to these objections convincingly.

The Day the Fire Came

Virginia Bell Dabney

Virginia Bell Dabney (b. 1919) lives in central Virginia, near the farm on which she was raised. "The Day the Fire Came" is a childhood memoir that first appeared in Harper's Magazine *in 1990. It is part of a full-length book,* Once There Was a Farm . . . : A Country Childhood Remembered. *From 1952 to 1983, Dabney worked as a writer and director of publications for the American Lung Association of Virginia in Richmond. During the 1960s, she wrote a novel for young people, which was accepted and then rejected by a large publishing house whose editors feared its positive portrayal of African Americans might alienate some readers. For Dabney, authors develop their skills "through good reading" and "by writing the best one can, every day." This is especially good advice for college writers.*

The last rain in these mountains this summer was about July 11. It is now the 1
twenty-first day of August and it has not rained for one month and ten hot days. All of us who live here think some computer glitch has been made in weather deliveries and we are getting Arizona weather by mistake. Days that usually have a high of eighty degrees now reach into the parching nineties. Thunderheads rise in the west, look us over, and then go somewhere else to rain. Grass crackles underfoot, the birds quit singing after the sun is up. Many have packed it up and left; the indigo buntings are gone and the wood thrush has taken his flute to damper places.

I sit limply on the porch with a cold drink; the dog lies at my feet eyeing my 2
glass. Finally I give him an ice cube and he crunches it, licking up the tiny ice puddles. I give him another and he wants it, but not now, so he takes it over to a dusty bush and buries it. It is the first drink the bush has had in forty-two days.

A wind comes up in the afternoon, leaving the dogwoods limp and the 3
poplars yellowing prematurely. There is a smell in the air that I remember from another time; it is of green leaves hot and burned in the sun. I keep watching the horizon and sniffing for any faint whiff of fire starting in the woods, made wary for all time by what happened when I was eleven.

On a Sunday in April 1930, my mother was pacing from the yard to our up- 4
stairs hallway window and then down again. She was watching a column of smoke rising beyond our woods to the west. I caught her nervousness and watched also, but without her added awareness that there had been very little rainfall during the winter and early spring. There were new leaves on the trees, but on the forest floor the old leaves were as dry and separate as cornflakes.

I heard Mother report to my sister Allison that the smoke seemed to be moving 5
our way. Allison was in bed, feverish and coughing. She wanted to get up and help us, but my mother said, "Only if necessary," and started gathering possessions we could take with us if the fire came nearer. Allison was coughing more, the smoke was bothering her. Mother was dumping drawer contents into a box. I lugged down books I wanted to save and Mother told me, "There's no room in the car for those, Vallie."

Our neighbor Carl Stevens drove into the yard and my mother met him on 6 the porch. There was a tense conversation. "Mrs. Bell, you and the girls better get out right quick. That fire is picking up fast. You all better come over to our house. It's got so much plowed land around it I think it will be safe."

"Allison is sick in bed," Mother told him. "You can take the girls and I can 7 come behind you."

But she had hardly finished when I burst into tears. I grabbed her arm and 8 said, "I won't go unless you go too!" I was sure she would be caught in the fire if we left first. Carl looked at my stricken face and said, "I'll just take Allison." He went into the bedroom with my mother, picked Allison up in her blankets, and carried her out to his car.

The wind picked up, smoke was blueing the air around us, and the smell of 9 burning leaves stung our noses. My mother pulled her Model T near the porch and put a box with our silver, her photographs, and her handmade linens into the tiny trunk space. She had already put our suitcases on the running board. Now she hastily gathered up some new WearEver pots and pans packed in salesmen's suitcases and flung them on the bare sand of the tennis court. Burning ash was flying over us. "Get in," Mother yelled at me, and I did so only because she had her foot on the running board itself. She backed the car out, and as we fled through smoke growing thicker every minute, she leaned out of the window and called Mac, the dog. He came running. "Lean out and call him," she told me, and I did. He ran easily not far behind us; he had never followed the car before but understood this was a crisis.

I thought but didn't ask about the cows in the pasture and the chickens in the 10 chicken houses. There were new chicks under the brooder, and I told myself that the brooder house was off by itself and maybe . . .

At Carl's house my mother parked the car near their drive. We all ran toward 11 the open field on the north side of the Stevenses' big house to watch the fire. I could see our house standing calmly among its oak trees. Behind it to the north the fire seemed to be going away, though the smoke was so thick it was hard to tell. We could see great rolling balls of fire in the treetops and I thought I could feel the heat on my face.

"If the wind just doesn't change . . . ," my mother said.   12

We stood there until I couldn't stand the tension and began to cry, but Mother 13 said, "Hush, that only makes things worse," and I stopped, wanting to watch and at the same time afraid to see what would happen. The whole woods beyond our house, our orchard in its grassy clearing, were in flames. There was a crackling sound as branches broke and fell from trees like burning logs in a fireplace, showering sparks. Over our heads birds were flying from the fire. Our house stood peacefully silhouetted against the orange-and-black swirl of smoke and flame.

Suddenly I heard my mother say tightly. "The wind's shifted," and we 14 watched as a great ball of fire, tumbling and rolling on the wind, came toward our house. It caught first in the highest oak-tree branches, and they flared like torches. My mother turned away and said. "That's it." I stared long enough to see burning branches drop on our roof and the entire scene obliterated by smoke that had tongues of flames roaring through it.

My mother and I walked back to the Stevenses' back porch and sat on the steps, she silent and her face white. After a while Carl came over and said, "It's 15 not coming here. Your fields just burned over and it stopped at the road."

"The house gone?" she said, looking up.   16

"It's gone," he said. "All those trees dropped fire on it."   17

I can remember almost nothing else about the rest of that day. My mother 18 could not go back to our place because some of the old trees were still burning and the ground was still hot.

We had supper at the Stevenses' big table, and afterward Miss Lou, Carl's 19 wife, took me upstairs to a tiny room under sloping eaves and showed me a bed with a feather mattress. When I sank into it its billows rose around me. It was warm and cozy and I snuggled in deeply.

I was still asleep at faint daylight when Mother, unable to rest, went to the 20 kitchen and found Carl, Miss Lou, and Carl's mother fixing breakfast. They gave her coffee and a hot biscuit and then Carl went with her to look at the smoking ruins of our farm.

The barn was gone, the machine shed vanished, the woodshed and its at- 21 tached room, where my mother kept her equipment for developing photographs, were ash heaps. One of the chicken houses was a mass of hot melted asphalt roofing over incinerated birds and twisted metal feeders. Another still stood, the new one set off by itself and built for the largest new brood of chickens, which were now gone with the brooder house.

My mother and Carl walked down the pasture hill, seeking the cows they be- 22 lieved might have escaped. At the bottom, up to their knees in the stream, the devastated woods behind them, both of them stood, their udders distended with milk. Carl went back to his house to get milk buckets.

Neither Allison nor I was allowed to go back to view the ruins. We stood 23 with Miss Lou looking across the fields at the black skeletons of trees around the dark pile of rubble that had been our house. We stared numbly, trying to sort out what had happened.

My mother was walking from one pile of rubble to another, feeling, she said 24 later, in a daze, when our neighbors the Woodfords drove up in their wagon. Their own house and buildings were safe but they had lost some good forest. Mrs. Woodford put her arm around Mother and said, "We've been praying for you and the girls. Now we want you all to come stay with us until things are straightened out. We'll be so glad to have you, you know."

Her earnest goodness touched my mother, but it was not her way to turn to 25 others. "I'm not sure yet what I have to do," she said, "but it's wonderfully kind of you to offer." She laid a hand briefly on Mrs. Woodford's arm. "I just have to work things out."

Mother and Mrs. Woodford moved from ruin to ruin, picking up pieces of 26
things, trying to identify them. One was a darkened dish with a garland of roses;
looking at it in her neighbor's hand, Mother said, "Those were my best dessert
bowls." She carried it around with her as they walked.

Before the day was half over, people from miles around were coming to find 27
out what had happened to the Bells, to ask if they could help, and to wander about
the stricken farmyard. Tom Walker came on foot and asked my mother what she
was going to do now. "Ye ain't wantin' to stay here, are ye?"

"I don't have any other home, Mr. Walker."   28

He spat with no change of expression. "I tole my wife that's what ye'd say. 29
Ye ain't no quitter, I tole her."

The Painters also urged my Mother to move in with them until she could de- 30
cide what to do, but she thanked them with the same words she'd said to others.
She did not say that she had already decided what to do; she was probably not
ready to put it into words. When the others had gone, she asked Carl to come with
her to look at the chicken house that had been untouched by fire. It still smelled of
recently poured cement and new wood. As she opened the door she said, "You see
this little room we set off for feed? I think I can stay in here while a place is fixed
up for all of us."

"It's right small . . . ," Carl said doubtfully.   31

"But look, I could put a cot over there, and some kind of stove here. And a 32
table and chair. That's all I need right now."

He shook his head. "You know you can stay with us. You'd be comfortable 33
and real close by."

"But Carl, I need to be here. I'll have the dog, you know."   34

That, of course, is how it was. I was sent to stay with my other sister, Daphne, 35
so I could finish out the school year. Allison, still running a fever, was put to bed at
the home of a friend who was a nurse. As she had already decided, Mother moved
into the feed room of the chicken house, from which she directed and helped with the
cleanup of all that was left of our house, barn, and sheds. She kept finding remnants
of her life that she turned over and over: a solidified aluminum puddle on the tennis
court where the pots and pans she'd tried to save had melted; the handles to her bread
mixer and meat grinder, the wooden parts burned off, the machines twisted and useless; fragments of rose glass from the shattered hanging lamp in the living room.

Before they were hauled away, she touched the warped brass bedsteads, 36
the broken shards of pitchers and basins, and the cracked, streaked pieces of
my father's plate collection that had once shone from a plate rail in our new
dining room.

Mother did not allow herself to sigh over these things for long; there was too 37
much to do. One of the first things she did was to walk through deep ash in the ruined woods to see what was left. The young silver-green white pines were gone, and
the hollies, once so thick, were unrecognizable. But the trunks of the large blackened
oaks and maples still stood, two or three large barren branches left pointing upward.

Walking behind my mother with an ax, our hired man, Solomon, cut a notch here and there in the charred bark; underneath there was solid, unburned wood.

"There's a lot of timber here good for building if we can get it out," my **38** mother told Solomon. "Enough for all of us," she said thoughtfully. In her mind, a plan was already taking shape that would distract her from despair and keep her from always watching the skies and listening for rain.

1990

QUESTIONS FOR DISCUSSION

Content

a. What is the author's purpose? Is it simply to explain how a fire destroyed her home?
b. The story is set in 1930, the beginning of the Great Depression. What can you infer about the Bells' standard of living from details about their home and farm?
c. What does the author reveal about herself as a child? As an adult?
d. Analyze the essay's first three paragraphs. What is Dabney trying to accomplish in this introduction?
e. "Ye ain't no quitter," Mr. Walker says of Mrs. Bell. What other evidence can you find that the speaker's mother was an extraordinary person?
f. What does the essay's conclusion tell us about Mrs. Bell? In what way does the conclusion relate to the essay's introduction?

Strategy and Style

g. Overall, this essay appeals to the visual, but the author includes details that appeal to other senses as well. Find such details and explain how they help move the story along.
h. Discuss examples of Dabney's use of figurative language. To what end(s) does she use such language?
i. Dabney's style is relatively simple and straightforward. Is it appropriate to this narrative?
j. The author makes excellent use of dialogue. Given the essay's purpose, should she have included more of it?

SUGGESTIONS FOR SHORT WRITING

a. In paragraph 3, Dabney writes that she has been "made wary for all time by what happened when [she] was eleven." Have you had such an experience? Try to recall this incident and record details about it through freewriting, listing, or some other information-gathering technique you have learned in class. Accumulate as many specific details—narrative and descriptive—as you can.

b. If you were given an opportunity to interview Dabney about the incident in this essay or about her motivation for writing, what would you ask? Write a set of questions—at least five—that you might use in such an interview.

SUGGESTIONS FOR SUSTAINED WRITING

a. If you responded to the first suggestion for short writing, reread your notes. Then, expand them into a full-length essay in which you recall an incident that has made you "wary for all time."

b. Using Dabney's work as inspiration, write a narrative essay that recalls a terrifying incident involving the loss of property or life. If possible, rely on personal experience or observation as your primary source of information. In addition, however, speak with other participants or observers to gather details and insights that will enrich your story.

c. Write a character analysis of Mrs. Bell. Use evidence from "The Day the Fire Came" to explain the kind of person you think she was. Then, compare—draw similarities between—Mrs. Bell and someone you know well. Use direct quotations as well as incidents from your subject's life to elucidate his or her character and to show what character traits he or she shares with Mrs. Bell.

Don't Get Comfortable

Naton Leslie

Naton Leslie (b. 1956) teaches at Siena College in Loudonville, New York. He has published essays and poetry in the North American Review, *the* Ohio Review, *and the* Kansas Quarterly, *among other periodicals in the United States. "Don't Get Comfortable" is from his collection entitled* Places Cursed by John Brown and Other Essays on History.

This story is about a railroad detective named Charley Best. Best worked in the 1920s on the narrow-gauge lines between Pittsburgh and the lumber and mining hill towns of northwestern Pennsylvania. My father tells this story and said his father told it to him, having known Best or known others who knew him. Or maybe my grandfather rode those rails to work in the camps; I know he worked for the railroad, lighting kerosene lamps on the bridge over the Allegheny River and during winter breaking ice from cables that hoisted lanterns high above the girders.

My father tells that story too, how when he was five years old his father would take him out at night when he made his rounds on the bridge over the Allegheny in Mahoning, Pennsylvania. His father would climb over the side, hanging on to the slick catwalk while he broke cables free after an ice storm. The night would be filled with frigid gusts, and the wind was particularly strong that high above the river. On the swaying iron bridge my grandfather ordered my father to "take a holt" of the side railing. He was never frightened during these trips because his father was so strong, sure-footed, and careful. It must have been like watching an athlete, my grandfather climbing catlike over the rail, hitting the ice-bound cables with steady blows from the ball-peen. He was a compact man, and every movement, every swing of the hammer, seemed to come from the center of his body.

This was 1934, and my grandfather was lucky to have this bit of a job, this small paycheck, in the mountains of Pennsylvania where no farm made it, where the mines had begun to play out. So, though the job was dangerous and hard, he did it, and because I remember my grandfather as a meticulous man, I'm sure he did it well. Why he took my father along is less clear, though my grandmother may have asked him to get him out of her hair for a while, not realizing the danger, or perhaps my grandfather assumed his son would have to do the job someday. He'd been taught how to plant, to shoe horses, to make medicines, and to build outbuildings by his own father on the homestead farm. Perhaps my grandfather was teaching his son about the railroad.

Once, as my father tells it, a train crossed the bridge while they were on it. It was a bitterly cold, moonless night, and the lanterns seemed to light only the barest arc of the old iron bridge. My grandfather was hanging from a side rail, breaking ice and edging a cable through the pulley, when the headlamp of the train broke the darkness. He hollered to my father to hop over the side of the bridge and hold on, to "get a purchase and don't let go no matter what." Then, as the train caused the bridge to quake and sway, my father felt his father's arm around him

42

and his own weight release from his arms as his father held them both by one arm, sixty feet above the icy Allegheny. "Imagine," my father says when he tells the story," a five-year-old boy and I wasn't even scared," though I wonder if he says that in tribute to his naive courage or in acknowledgment of trusting his father so utterly that fear never occurred to him.

I don't know where my grandfather heard of Charley Best. The area was 5 sparsely populated; it had been homesteaded in the mid-nineteenth century and remained wholly wilderness until the first oil well in the nation, the Drake Well, was drilled in Titusville. Those who worked in the lumber and mining camps, and later in oil fields and railroad yards, were all like Charley Best and my grandfather, raised on hardscrabble farms in the Allegheny Mountains, farms now part of the Allegheny National Forest, a mixed old-growth-second-growth wilderness replacing their hard-won clearings and plantings. They were coarse, often violent people for whom fighting was merely another kind of work. For Charley Best, his work became violence. Best had a fierce reputation, and my father, who used to see him at Walker's store in Mahoning, said he looked the part. The railroad detective bought cigars at Walker's, and even there he carried a sidearm, what my father thought was an enormous Colt. He was a big man, and my father also remembers his wide hat, the high leather boots with the pant cuffs tucked inside, and the huge chain stretched across his chest, Prince Albert style, upon which hung a nickel-plated railroad watch my father thought was as big as an alarm clock. Mostly, though, he remembers that handgun and a handlebar mustache Best had cultivated to curl around his wide face. My father poses as Best as he tells the story, striding the catwalks and tops of railcars, wind whipping his mustache back like flames. But it's the same picture he paints of his grandfather, Doc, one of the original homesteaders in Forest County. We have a photograph of him, published in a volume of local history, his reportedly immense size diminished by a team of oxen behind him, that same mustache flaring like horns.

My father heard a story about Doc at the funeral of one of his uncles, and in 6 it his mustache and oxen are part of the scenery. Doc Leslie had taken cattle into Brookville, Pennsylvania, to sell. Later, while he was having a drink at the Sigel Hotel, one of the men from town said, "Aren't you scared traveling all the way back to Blue Jay Ridge with that much money on you, Doc?"

My father doesn't say what Doc said back—some grunt or mumble through 7 his mustache—but later, on Blood Road in his oxcart, Doc was jumped by three men wearing bandannas, like the outlaws they had read about in dime novels.

It was only a joke. These were friends of Doc's, out only to put a scare in 8 him, but when one of them said "Stick 'em up," Doc replied, "Stick 'em up, hell. There'll be feet up and shit flying," as he leaped from the cart, scattering the men with his bullwhip. When my father tells it, he pantomimes rolling up one sleeve to signify the fight, his eyes fierce and fixed. The story is frozen at that point: Doc poised for action, the flight of the men inevitable.

Part of Charley Best's story is arrested as well. Best patrolled the tops of 9 railcars as they sped across the hills toward the coal fields. My father said those who hopped trains rode Charley's line only twice: the first time you were warned, and if you took Detective Best's warning with humility, you got where you wanted to go. But Best remembered, and the second time he caught you riding free, you were off.

"Off?" I once asked, interrupting my father for once as he told the story. His [10] irritation was clear.

"Yeah, *off,*" he said, his arms poised in the act of grabbing someone by the [11] scruff of the neck and back of the trousers. I remembered a postcard drawn by Wobbly leader Joe Hill, a comic portrait of himself being booted from a train, and had less admiration for Best and more sympathy for the hoboes who just wanted a ride and ended up flying.

I could see them soaring, sprawling like skydivers over the empty air of the [12] railroad cut, over the sixty-foot drop from the bridge in Mahoning. I've always been hesitant about heights—not actually frightened, only concerned and reluctant about climbing, a controllable vertigo. Not that I have suffered many spectacular falls. Once I fell off, or more accurately, ran off, the top of an extension ladder when a wasp landed on my nose. I simply turned around, stepped off the top of the ladder, and began to run, heading straight down to a gravel parking lot of the car dealership where I was working. I was pretty skinned up, landing on my forearms to protect my face from the gravel, and my coworker, a young biker named Rocky, said, "Man, did you crash 'n' burn!" Perhaps I got this timidity from my mother, who also shied from heights. I remember my father, mother, older sister, and myself climbing a fire tower in the Allegheny Mountains. My mother and I made it about halfway up when the open sides and the lack of a railing sent me back down. My father and sister made it to the top, and I watched from the ground as they laughed and climbed impossibly higher.

My sister trusted my wild and unpredictable father and would follow him, [13] while my trust in him had limits. Probably he had learned not to fear heights from his father on that railroad bridge; he even took a job as a tree-topper for a lumber company and later as a lineman for the power company. When he was sixteen he got a job as a ground hand, or "ground squirrel," as they called the young boys who dragged limbs by the butt to the burn pile. He grew to love the work, part of the postwar rural electrification program, and when not piling brush he watched the men high in trees worrying off limbs with bow saws.

Finally he got his own climbing gear: long hooks like bayonets that strapped [14] to his high-topped boots and a wide leather belt to wrap around tree trunks. He got so good he'd climb a tree, and eventually a utility pole, with only his hooks and hands on the trunk, using the belt only when he reached the top. He said he loved heights; on top of a tree on a mountain he said he could see all of Forest County, see deer move in herds and bears trailing cubs on the ridge miles away. Working for the power company, my father climbed poles on wide rights of way cut across the mountains, high power lines carrying thousands of volts from transformer substations to light lamps in a farmhouse on remote Blue Jay Ridge.

But he fell. Twice. The first time, he says, they were putting up new lines on 15
poles in residential Brookville. Poles were originally treated with creosote to prevent decay, a dark, oil-based coating that smelled vaguely of kerosene and urine,
now outlawed in favor of a pressure treatment with brine. These were old poles,
put up at the turn of the century during the first wave of utility construction, and
that morning my father climbed the first one. He says he had just hooked on his
belt and was looking up at the late autumn sky, a mix of clouds and high blue. He
thought, "Those clouds sure are moving fast," and then he realized it was he who
was moving, not the clouds, as the pole was falling, breaking off at the rotten base.
He tells how he managed to take off his belt and scamper to the other side, riding
the pole to the ground as it bent, then snapped.

The other time he fell was more dangerous, and more miraculous. He was 16
at the top of a forty-five-foot pole, and according to the newspaper article from the
Oil City Derrick his belt snapped and he pitched backward. My father says that after he felt the belt give he reached for the crossarm. His fingertips barely reached
the class insulators on his right, but he was unable to grasp them or the wooden
beam, and he fell. He flipped backward twice in the air, landed on his feet,
bounced, and fell on his side. He stood up, apparently unhurt, but when he tried to
unbuckle his tool harness he found the fingers on his left hand would not work; he
had broken his wrist in two places. Later he would develop severe back problems
and would suffer years of pain, caused I'm sure by that jarring fall, though he
never seemed to connect the two.

He doesn't tell either of those stories often. You don't tell stories that could 17
have ended so finally. I heard him once admit to waking up in the middle of the night,
years later, a dream of fingertips grazing the crossarm tearing him into sweaty wake-
fulness. And these stories are among the few illustrating a point or a moral. My father would sometimes say, after telling one of these stories, that there's only one
thing you need to know to do "high work": "Don't get comfortable." What he means
goes beyond the commonplace "Keep your wits about you." It's the lesson I forgot
when I ran off the top of that ladder—whenever doing anything high up, do it with
the knowledge of where you are. I use this advice whenever I work on ladders or
roofs—whenever I am moving about and stop thinking about being up high, I force
myself to remember, I stop and say aloud, "Don't get comfortable."

Charley Best would not have told his own story either. Perhaps that's why oth- 18
ers told the story for him. My father claims he grew mean and that his father did not
like Best, not because he threw men off trains but because he shot a twelve-year-old
boy in the back for stealing coal from the railyard at night. The boy, a homeless child
the railroad workers called Hard Rock Pete, hung around the railyards, and the
gandy dancers and switch operators often shared their lunches with him, casually
adopting him. My grandfather said he was shy and weak, and they all assumed he
slept in abandoned works shacks or boxcars in the yard. Best, my grandfather
claimed, saw the boy at night, stooping over and pulling lumps of coal into a shirt
hooped to make a sack. Best claimed at the investigation that he couldn't tell it was

Hard Rock Pete—the boy was tall and wore bulky clothes that late fall evening, hiding his frail frame. When he stood up and lit a cigarette, Best saw him, and when the detective's menacing voiced called out, the boy ran. That's when Charley Best shot him with the big Colt.

But that's not the story of Charley Best my father often tells; that's another 19 story, or actually part of the longer version of the story, because it shows how mean Best got afterward, how what happened changed him. I remember once my father was telling the story at my grandmother Harnish's house, a gathering of men in his mother-in-law's parlor listening, among them Sam, her second husband, who in the last year had been forced to sit on the couch with an oxygen tank beside him, alternately reaching for the hose and mask to give him the oxygen black lung denied him and bending over, panting with effort, to spit tobacco juice into a plastic bucket.

My father began telling the story sitting down, but was standing by the time 20 he began describing Best, the Harnish men listening closely though they had heard the story before, while I sat watching the story being retold as I leaned forward in the straight-backed chair moved into the room and parked near the television. I had recently turned thirteen and was splitting my time between the room where adult men sat, talking slowly, and the cousins outside exploring the forty-acre farm I had already mapped over the years of visits. Sam's son Warren had finally finished a long-winded story that made my father edgy and restless, and how he had managed to get to the story of Charley Best I'm not sure, but the story was well under way.

Best had been assigned jurisdiction, lacking any other police, over several min- 21 ing camps in northwestern Pennsylvania, and was sent to arrest a miner in Chickasaw, near the New York border, who was accused of stealing. My father added that he probably only had stolen coal from the railyard, as everyone did in the 1930s. Warren interrupted briefly to tell how he and his brothers stole coal from the Clarion yards, but my father skillfully steered the conversation back to Best.

"Chickasaw was a rough mining camp, just up the river from Mahoning, and 22 Charley Best was sent there, where there was no other law, to arrest that miner," he began again, and everyone leaned comfortably back into the story, glad Warren had been stopped. He explained how Best arrived in town, Colt revolver displayed prominently, cigar under his ample mustache, and how he walked over to the tavern, a slapped-up, long and low shed affair, where he assumed he would find the thief. The men inside sat on rough stools, and the ceiling of plank was held up with twelve-inch rough-cut beams. "One of them eyes Best, and Best figured that was him and that he'd have to slug it out with the miner to take him." My father's eyes grew narrow and menacing.

I'd heard this story many times and knew the men in the room had heard it 23 too; they were sitting through the telling as though it were a ritual, a stage in their conversation they always reached, and passed. But then an unexpected reaction from Sam drew their attention from my father, who was perched on his knees at the end of the story. Sam did not speak much in those last years because speech was breath, and each breath was bought with larger portions of his strength. Yet there in the room filled with his sons and the husbands of his daughters, he pushed out a hurried "Yes," and quickly drawing on the oxygen as the heads of the men turned to him, added, "I drove those miners to Chickasaw every day in an old buckboard—they were usually drunk. A rough, wild bunch," he said, spitting a brown stream and reaching for the hose again. "Yes, that's how it happened."

My father never worked in the mines, so was spared the black lung from 24 which Sam and so many others suffered, but he often spoke of the mines as though he had worked there, as he had lived among the miners, played with their children, fought with their sons, and eventually drunk and laughed with them after work on the power lines. In his father's day the miners began forming unions, and these hardened men formed even harder coal-black clumps of strikers. One of them, Piercy MacIntyre, was an organizer and therefore was even rougher than most. The bosses in Chickasaw claimed he had been sent in from the outside, an agitator, but some of the men said he came from around Blue Jay Ridge, from a hill farm so far back "the owls carried knapsacks."

My father had met Piercy MacIntyre, but he knew his son Jackie better. The 25 miners said Piercy had been a boxer in France during World War I, and whether true or not, he did teach his son Jackie how to box. He'd take the boy, eight or nine years old, down to Walker's store, and men would clear a makeshift ring in the corner, moving stock to form a rough square. Walker would then hold the bets as Jackie's opponent, usually an older boy of twelve or so, was announced. My father claims Jackie beat all comers, and my father, younger by two or three years, always rooted for him as fervently as he did for Joe Louis when his father would struggle to pick up Louis's fights through the static on KDKA radio. He tells how Louis knocked out Max Schmeling, the Nazi superman, so quickly that once they got the station in, all they heard was the count to ten.

Twenty-five years later, after my father had moved one hundred miles away to 26 work in the mills of Ohio, he ran into Jackie MacIntyre at Republic Steel. He spoke to him, and though Jackie, now John, didn't remember him as one of his youngest fans among the dozens or more who had watched him fight as a kid, my father said they talked briefly of people they knew, even about Charley Best. My father said he was puzzled to see how the guys in the mill picked on him, and MacIntyre didn't seem to care. My father thought, "You guys don't know who you're dealing with."

Although my father had moved to the edge of the industrial Midwest, the 27 mountains and forests remained home to him, and we went back every weekend to visit. And he hunted in Pennsylvania, not along the industrial riverbanks of Ohio. My father liked only two sports, boxing and hunting, and he tried to teach me both. I never caught on to boxing, partly because my father couldn't coach me while we sparred without beginning to fight in earnest, burying me in a flurry of open-palmed combinations and jabs. I liked the fluidity of the movements, the backpedaling, the duck-and-jab; however, I was not destined to be a boxer. I have a glass jaw, a nerve positioned in my face that makes a knockout a matter of one punch. My father found this fatal flaw one day while we sparred in the living room. One quick jab to my left jaw and I felt nothing—I saw pinpoints of light and awoke to my father shaking his head and saying, "The kid's got a glass jaw." As a boxer I was finished.

But hunting was another matter. Early on, my father declared I was a natu-   28
ral good shot, that I had a "good eye" that made up, I suppose, for my bad jaw. I
cold pick off pennies at twenty-five yards with a .22 caliber rifle, and after I got a
shotgun, a 16-gauge, my father spent one long afternoon throwing clay pigeons,
which I shot out of the air. He threw more than seventy, and I missed two. I enjoyed target shooting not only because I was good at it but because I did it without thinking. I simply knew when I was on target and then pulled the trigger. I
guess it was instinct or something reflexive.

Yet, by age eighteen, I had pretty much lost interest in hunting. Animals   29
made poor targets; they were hard to find, but when found, too big and easy. For
a target shooter, walking all day for one shot at an easy target was not much of a
thrill. I still went hunting with my father when in my teens, but I had no real enthusiasm for the sport, as he did. I tried to find it; I remember not eating one day,
thinking that it would make me a keener hunter, but it only made me a hungry one.
What I liked was the evening, getting comfortable down at Archie's camp, near his
stone fireplace, listening to hunting stories.

The last time I went hunting with my father I was eighteen. I hadn't been   30
deer hunting that last fall because the season fell during final exam week at college, and it was with some relief that I realized this would happen every year.
However, I went hunting for turkey that spring. I think I liked turkey hunting most
because the hunt occurred in midautumn and midspring, the two most beautiful
times of the year to be in the forest. You also could go deeper into the woods because, unlike a deer, once a turkey was shot it was not hard to pull it out of the
woods. Dragging a hundred pounds of deer carcass over several miles of rough
terrain quickly dampened the thrill of the hunt.

It was a cold April in the mountains that year; patches of snow still clung to   31
rocks and roots in the forest, and springs remained frozen, even in the bright sun-
shine. My father led the way through the woods we hunted north of Brookville,
stepping around the icy stones and fallen limbs with sure-footed grace and speed.
Every hour or so we would stop and cradle our shotguns, and my father would
bring out the wooden turkey call, a cedar box with a top that wagged loosely when
shaken, chalk between box and lid giving off a decent gobble.

The turkey call was a new addition to our hunting gear. My father had never   32
gone in for gimmicks as a hunter, although he thought my aunt Clair's trick of rubbing apple cores on her boots to attract deer might account for her yearly success.
However, in the over twenty-five years he had been hunting, he had never bagged
a wild turkey. He was well known among the locals for regularly bringing out a
deer. He'd have a deer within the first couple of hours of the opening day of the season and could be found down at Archie's camp or at the Sigel Hotel by early afternoon, telling how the deer, never a trophy buck but respectable, would have risen
from his bed twenty-five yards from my father's stand at first light. But turkeys had
always eluded him, so he bought the call and had been practicing for months, brief
chirps and throaty gobbles rising from our basement ever since September.

That day we had walked farther into the woods than usual, so far that we 33
found ourselves on Windfall Ridge, or so it was called on my father's topo map.
The ridge was steep and treeless, and the North Fork Creek ran noisily below. My
father had noticed a stand of beech, and knowing turkey like beechnuts, we had
stopped to look for signs. Sure enough, my father found a large patch where turkey
had been scratching the winter-decayed leaves, a large flock probably discovered
and broken up by other hunters earlier in the morning. The turkeys would still be
in the area, scattered over Windfall, calling out to regroup. We stood and listened,
but all I heard was the icy North Fork and a high wind in the trees.

So my father decided to try calling them in, making first a few hesitant 34
chirps, then a long and short gobble that he'd heard was the turkey equivalent of
"I'm over here."

And a turkey answered. The bird sounded like it was on the edge of the 35
ridge, about fifty yards in front of us, but neither of us could see it. We walked cau-
tiously toward the sound, my heart pounding for my father, hoping he'd at long
last get a shot at the turkey. As we reached the ridge we split, my father wander-
ing to the right of a tall pine growing in the fragile earth of the rim of the ridge, I
to the left. The turkey flew out of the tree in a great bluster of wings. It flew left
and was clearly my shot.

I snapped up my shotgun and found him quickly, flying high but in range. 36
Then I thought about it. I wished the bird had flown right, to give my father the
shot, wished it was not flying over the icy-filmed North Fork into which I would
surely have to wade, waist high, to retrieve the bird. And I knew I did not want to
kill the turkey; I had no need of it.

So I shot behind it, the bird's wings flapping comically faster after the sound 37
echoed over the ridge. The turkey flew higher, out of range of another shot from
me or my father, not landing until it reached the next ridge. I turned to look at my
father, who said, "How'd you miss him?"

"Jerked the trigger, I think," I said, still looking over at the ridge where the 38
bird had disappeared. "Or choked; I don't know," I added.

"Hell, a good shot like you must have hit him," he said. "Maybe he went 39
down with a few shot in him."

"Nah, he was too high up, out of range," I answered, not wanting to have to 40
wade the creek anyway and hike the next ridge looking for the bird.

But we did cross the creek, over the back of a windfallen tree, and after 41
searching for the bird for a while decided we had had our shot for the day and gave
up. It was midafternoon, and it was a long way back, and I, having slipped into the
North Fork on the return crossing, wearily tramped behind my father, one boot
sloshing with creek water.

By the time we arrived at the Sigel Hotel my father was convinced I had hit 42
the gobbler but that, as he said, "death is invisible, while life can be seen." A slain
animal is still, and the natural camouflage is perfect. He believed we didn't find a
dead turkey because it blended in with the rocks and undergrowth.

At the Sigel Hotel we sat at the long bar, adding our hunting outfits of red   43
wool caps and canvas game vests to those of other hunters gathered there. My father began telling the story of our hunt to the man at his right elbow, and eventually to two or three down the counter. "The boy here got a shot, and I know he hit
him—you should have seen the feathers fly! This kid is a great wingshot," he continued, telling of my slaughter of clay pigeons.

The other men answered his story with others, and through that, through the   44
progress of stories to the next, he began telling the story of Charley Best. "He
walked into this bar, a smoky place with a low ceiling supported by big, twelve-
inch rough-cut post," he said, his hands surrounding one in the air, "rough like
everything else in those camps."

Best looked around the smoky room, and when he spotted the man eyeing   45
him he said, "You'd better finish that drink, because you're coming with me.
You're under arrest."

The man sat with his stool tipped backward against a post, and when Best   46
approached he said, "Well, I guess you're going to have to pull that big revolver,
because I'm not going anywhere." Best was standing over him, and my father was
on his feet in the Sigel Hotel, doing his best to look down at me as Best must have
glared at the miner.

Then my father said, "The guy suddenly pulls a knife, cuts Best across the   47
gut, and slips behind the thick post." My father's knees buckle.

Best was not used to working in the camps, so he was out of his element and   48
forgot to watch himself. He was too comfortable, my father would say, and should
have reminded himself that Chickasaw was a rough mining camp and that the man
he sought could be armed and was drunk, that he was not simply approaching a
frightened hobo on top of a rushing train. At this point my father's voice became
a little squeezed, imitating the pain of the knife wound, but he continued, "He cut
Best clear across the stomach, and his guts bulged and began to spill. With his left
arm Best reached down and pulled his own guts back in, and with the right drew
his gun and shot the miner." My father was fully on his knees now, his arm and
hand holding in intestines, his other arm raising a Colt revolver.

"He hit him in the mouth. Killed him deader than hell."   49

This is where the story of Charley Best generally ends, though sometimes   50
my father tells how they took him by train to a hospital in Brookville, how he got
mean after that. But with my father on his knees, clutching his stomach in agony,
this is when Charley Best appeared, or should have. He could have been a little
fellow, age having shrunken him, a glass of clay-colored liquor in front of him at
the bar, his mustache trimmed to a salt-and-pepper line under his nose. He'd sit
near the opposite end of the counter, listening to but not telling his own story.

Best wouldn't wear hunting clothes. He'd stand up and, pulling out his flan-   51
nel shirttails, say, "That's just the way it happened." Then he'd raise his shirt
quickly, and we'd see the brutish pucker circling his waist. When Best sat back
down he would drain the liquor in front of him, no one noticing that his left arm

rested across his lap and against his body, holding the organs in, still trying to get comfortable with the wound.

1996

QUESTIONS FOR DISCUSSION

Content

a. In paragraph 3, the author tells us that in 1934 his grandfather was lucky to have a job. What circumstances or period is he referring to?
b. What does Charley Best's story have in common with other stories in this essay?
c. In what way was Charley Best similar to the author's grandfather and great-grandfather and their contemporaries? Begin your answer with reference to paragraph 5.
d. The narrator tells us a great deal about his father, grandfather, and great-grandfather. Explain what he also reveals about his own character.
e. Discuss the relationship that the narrator had with his father.
f. The thesis of this essay is expressed concisely in its three-word title. Citing details from the text, expand on that statement by explaining Leslie's point and purpose in this essay.

Strategy and Style

g. Why does the author tell about his and his father's falling from heights? How do these stories help the reader understand Charley Best? How do they help develop the essay's thesis?
h. The introduction and conclusion of this essay seem to reflect some uncertainty. Explain how and why the author expresses that uncertainty.
i. "Don't Get Comfortable" uses an introduction different from those found in other selections of this type. The essay begins by mentioning Charley Best, then quickly moves to stories about the author's father and grandfather before returning to Best in paragraph 5. What is it about the first four paragraphs that holds our attention?
j. Unlike other narratives in this chapter, "Don't Get Comfortable" does not follow a conventional plot line (events proceeding from beginning to end without interruption). The story of Charley Best is interrupted several times with other interesting tales, which apparently have nothing to do with it. Take a few minutes to outline the plot of this story; then, explain why the author has inserted these tales.
k. Where does the author use humor? What function does it serve in this essay?

l. In what way is the structure of this essay (not its contents) reflective of its title and thesis?

m. What does the author's tone reveal about the audience for this essay?

SUGGESTIONS FOR SHORT WRITING

a. Read David Quammen's "Alias Benowitz Shoe Repair" in Chapter 2. Compare the plot structure of Naton Leslie's "Don't Get Comfortable" with what Quammen uses. Then, discuss whether the authors of these pieces are aiming at similar purposes.

b. Read Sam Pickering's "Faith of the Father" in Chapter 4. In what ways is this essay similar to and different from "Don't Get Comfortable"?

SUGGESTIONS FOR SUSTAINED WRITING

a. Using your own experiences and/or the experiences of people you know well, write an essay that develops the same thesis as Leslie's "Don't Get Comfortable." You might choose a number of short tales or anecdotes to illustrate your thesis, or you might tell one longer story in full. Either way, make sure that all of the details that you include relate directly to your thesis. Finally, state the thesis in an introduction that, like Leslie's, captures and holds the reader's attention.

b. Narrate an exciting or frightening experience like one of the ones Leslie tells in his essay. This story need not be taken from personal experience; incidents from the history of your family or your community might work just as well. However you choose to approach this assignment, make your story exciting and colorful. Try using the kind of language and detail Leslie uses to recreate the incident in which his father and grandfather nearly fell off a railroad bridge or the one in which Charlie Best was knifed by a miner.

c. Read your responses to the Suggestions for Short Writing. Extend one of them into a fully developed essay.

2

Description

Description makes for diversity. The people, places, and things described in the eight selections that follow vary as widely as the distinctive styles and perspectives of their authors. Nonetheless, each essay is a portrait sketched in details that are at once concrete, specific, and vivid.

Good description is never hurried; it is crafted with carefully chosen details that *show* the reader something. Take "Where the World Began," for example. Not content to tell us that watching the hometown fire company answer an alarm was "exciting, colorful, and noisy," Margaret Laurence savors the moment and helps us do the same:

> . . . the wooden tower's bronze bell would clonk and toll like a
> thousand speeded funerals in a time of plague, and in a few minutes
> the team of giant black horses would cannon forth, pulling the fire
> wagons like some scarlet chariot of the Goths, while the firemen
> clung with one hand, adjusting their helmets as they went.

Appealing to the senses—in this case sight and sound—is fundamental to the process of describing. Some writers rely almost solely upon vision and hearing as sources of descriptive detail, but the authors in this chapter teach us that we can use the other senses as well—taste, smell, and touch—to guide readers through our private worlds. Indeed, Simeti's "Easter in Sicily" invites us to a banquet for all the senses. As a result, we come away with a genuine taste of the place.

The above excerpt from "Where the World Began" also shows that writers of description exploit techniques often associated with narration, especially the use of verbs that are informative and evocative. More important, Laurence's use of figurative language—her comparison of the alarm to the sounds of bells at a "thousand speeded funerals," for example—reminds us that invoking facts and images from the knowledge we share with readers is a good way to show them something new. Flashes of brilliance appear throughout the chapter. Virginia Woolf's reference to the "narrow and intricate corridors" of her brain, for example, and James Baldwin's reminder that the residents of the ghetto "must struggle stolidly, incessantly, to keep [a] sense [of honor] alive in themselves in spite of the insults, the indifference, and the cruelty they are certain to encounter in their working day" testify to the power and clarity with which they invest their writing.

While relying heavily on physical description, none of the essays collected here is a purely sensate record of its subject. More often than not, describing is a means to an end. It is hard to read a narrative, for example, without stumbling over details that reveal setting and character. Even writers of scientific prose use information that appeals to the senses as a way to discuss the lives of plants and animals or to explore the workings of machines and processes.

Whether they are describing people, places, or things, the authors in this chapter use description to reveal the character or capture the essence of their subjects, though their purpose may not be immediately apparent. Consider Doris Lessing, who transcends physical appearance to expose the psychology of her father by allowing him to speak to us directly and by recalling his memories, his dreams, and his failures. Fascinating anecdotes and dialogue also enrich Laurence's portrait of home, allowing us to understand the place that nurtured the author and helped form her character. And Mary Taylor Simeti's vivid evocation of Easter festivals in Sicily reveals her ability to manipulate narrative and descriptive details brilliantly as she explores the unique character of her adopted homeland.

Like other writers in this chapter, Joan Didion and N. Scott Momaday remind us that discussing the people who inhabit a place is a way to reveal its soul. David Quammen, on the other hand, reveals the Rockies' natural beauty by describing the passion and energy of a man who is determined to save it. Finally, in recalling the death of a moth Virginia Woolf engages a seemingly banal subject not simply to describe an exterior reality but to tell us about herself, the real subject of her essay. Of course, something of this can also be said of Momaday and Laurence.

As always, you are invited to make your own comparisons and to draw conclusions as you see fit. What makes the selections in this chapter so enjoyable is that each reveals the strong and distinctive voice of its author. Enjoy the artists behind the subjects they describe. They will teach you that your personal commitment to a subject—the "wonder" with which it fills you, Woolf might say—is worth sharing with others.

Where the World Began

Margaret Laurence

Born in Manitoba, Margaret (Wemyss) Laurence (1926–1987) was one of Canada's foremost novelists, essayists, and writers of short fiction and of children's books. She based much of her work on her travels in Africa and on her life in the small Canadian prairie town in which she was born. The former yielded A Tree for Poverty *(1954), a translation of Somali poems and stories she gathered during two years in the harsh Haud desert;* This Side Jordan *(1960), a novel;* The Tomorrow Tamer and Other Stories *(1963); and* The Prophet's Camel Bell *(1963), a travel memoir. Neepawa, the hometown that she renamed Manawaba in her fiction, figures in* The Stone Angel *(1964);* A Jest of God *(1966), republished as* Rachel, Rachel; Fire Dwellers *(1969); and* A Bird in the House *(1970). It is on the Manawaba books that Laurence's fame chiefly rests. However, she is also noted for her essays, a collection of which she published as* Heart of a Stranger *(1976). In a* Book Forum, *John Caldwell cited "the search for the lost Eden, for Jerusalem the Golden, for the promised land of one's own freedom" as an important ingredient in her work. For Laurence, that little prairie town "Where the World Began" might very well have contained the "promised land."*

A strange place it was, that place where the world began. A place of incredible happenings, splendors, and revelations, despairs like multitudinous pits of isolated hells. A place of shadow-spookiness, inhabited by the unknowable dead. A place of jubilation and of mourning, horrible and beautiful. 1

It was, in fact, a small prairie town. 2

Because that settlement and that land were my first and for many years my only real knowledge of this planet, in some profound way they remain my world, my way of viewing. My eyes were formed there. Towns like ours, set in a sea of land, have been described thousands of times as dull, bleak, flat, uninteresting. I have had it said to me that the railway trip across Canada is spectacular, except for the prairies, when it would be desirable to go to sleep for several days, until the ordeal is over. I am always unable to argue this point effectively. All I can say is— well, you really have to live there to know that country. The town of my childhood could be called bizarre, agonizingly repressive or cruel at times, and the land in which it grew could be called harsh in the violence of its seasonal changes. But never merely flat or uninteresting. Never dull. 3

In winter, we used to hitch rides on the back of the milk sleigh, our moccasins squeaking and slithering on the hard rutted snow of the roads, our hands in ice-bubbled mitts hanging onto the box edge of the sleigh for dear life, while Bert grinned at us through his great frosted mustache and shouted the horse into speed, daring us to stay put. Those mornings, rising, there would be the perpetual fascination of the frost feathers on windows, the ferns and flowers and eerie faces traced there during the night by unseen artists of the wind. Evenings, coming back from skating, the sky would be black but not dark, for you could see a cold glitter of stars from one side of the earth's rim to the other. And then the 4

55

sometime astonishment when you saw the Northern Lights flaring across the sky, like the scrawled signature of God. After a blizzard, when the snowplow hadn't yet got through, school would be closed for the day, the assumption being that the town's young could not possibly flounder through five feet of snow in the pursuit of education. We would then gaily don snowshoes and flounder for miles out into the white dazzling deserts, in pursuit of a different kind of knowing. If you came back too close to night, through the woods at the foot of the town hill, the thin black branches of poplar and chokecherry now meringued with frost, sometimes you heard coyotes. Or maybe the banshee wolf-voices were really only inside your head.

Summers were scorching, and when no rain came and the wheat became   5
bleached and dried before it headed, the faces of farmers and townsfolk would not smile much, and you took for granted, because it never seemed to have been any different, the frequent knocking at the back door and the young men standing there, mumbling or thrusting defiantly their requests for a drink of water and a sandwich if you could spare it. They were riding the freights, and you never knew where they had come from, or where they might end up, if anywhere. The Drought and Depression were like evil deities which had been there always. You understood and did not understand.

Yet the outside world had its continuing marvels. The poplar bluffs and the   6
small river were filled and surrounded with a zillion different grasses, stones, and weed flowers. The meadowlark sang undaunted from the twanging telephone wires along the gravel highway. Once we found an old flat-bottomed scow, and launched her, poling along the shallow brown waters, mending her with wodges of hastily chewed Spearmint, grounding her among the tangles of yellow marsh marigolds that grew succulently along the banks of the shrunken river, while the sun made our skins smell dusty-warm.

My best friend lived in an apartment above some stores on Main Street (its   7
real name was Mountain Avenue, goodness knows why), an elegant apartment with royal-blue velvet curtains. The back roof, scarcely sloping at all, was corrugated tin, of a furnace-like warmth on a July afternoon, and we would sit there drinking lemonade and looking across the back lane at the Fire Hall. Sometimes our vigil would be rewarded. Oh joy! Somebody's house burning down! We had an almost-perfect callousness in some ways. Then the wooden tower's bronze bell would clonk and toll like a thousand speeded funerals in a time of plague, and in a few minutes the team of giant black horses would cannon forth, pulling the fire wagon like some scarlet chariot of the Goths, while the firemen clung with one hand, adjusting their helmets as they went.

The oddities of the place were endless. An elderly lady used to serve, as her   8
afternoon tea offering to other ladies, soda biscuits spread with peanut butter and topped with a whole marshmallow. Some considered this slightly eccentric, when compared with chopped egg sandwiches, and admittedly talked about her behind her back, but no one ever refused these delicacies or indicated to her that they thought she had slipped a cog. Another lady dyed her hair a bright and cherry orange, by strangers often mistaken at twenty paces for a feather hat. My own beloved stepmother wore a silver fox neckpiece, a whole pelt, *with the embalmed*

(?) head still on. My Ontario Irish grandfather said, "sparrow grass," a more interesting term than asparagus. The town dump was known as "the nuisance grounds," a phrase fraught with weird connotations, as though the effluvia of our lives was beneath contempt but at the same time was subtly threatening to the determined and sometimes hysterical propriety of our ways.

Some oddities were, as idiom had it, "funny ha ha"; others were "funny peculiar." Some were not so very funny at all. An old man lived, deranged, in a shack in the valley. Perhaps he wasn't even all that old, but to us he seemed a wild Methuselah figure, shambling among the underbrush and the tall couchgrass, muttering indecipherable curses or blessings, a prophet who had forgotten his prophecies. Everyone in town knew him, but no one knew him. He lived among us as though only occasionally and momentarily visible. The kids called him Andy Gump, and feared him. Some sought to prove their bravery by tormenting him. They were the medieval bear baiters, and he the lumbering bewildered bear, half blind, only rarely turning to snarl. Everything is to be found in a town like mine. Belsen, writ small but with the same ink. 9

All of us cast stones in one shape or another. In grade school, among the vulnerable and violet girls we were, the feared and despised were those few older girls from what was charmingly termed "the wrong side of the tracks." Tough in talk and tougher in muscle, they were said to be whores already. And may have been, that being about the only profession readily available to them. 10

The dead lived in that place, too. Not only the grandparents who had, in local parlance, "passed on" and who gloomed, bearded or bonneted, from the sepia photographs in old albums, but also the uncles, forever eighteen or nineteen, whose names were carved on the granite family stones in the cemetery, but whose bones lay in France. My own young mother lay in that graveyard, beside other dead of our kin, and when I was ten, my father, too, only forty, left the living town for the dead dwelling on the hill. 11

When I was eighteen, I couldn't wait to get out of that town, away from the prairies. I did not know then that I would carry the land and town all my life within my skull, that they would form the mainspring and source of the writing I was to do, wherever and however far away I might live. 12

This was my territory in the time of my youth, and in a sense my life since then has been an attempt to look at it, to come to terms with it. Stultifying to the mind it certainly could be, and sometimes was, but not to the imagination. It was many things, but it was never dull. 13

The same, I now see, could be said for Canada in general. Why on earth did generations of Canadians pretend to believe this country dull? We knew perfectly well it wasn't. Yet for so long we did not proclaim what we knew. If our upsurge of so-called nationalism seems odd or irrelevant to outsiders, and even to some of our own people (*what's all the fuss about?*), they might try to understand that for many years we valued ourselves insufficiently, living as we did under the huge shadows of those two dominating figures, Uncle Sam and Britannia. We have only just begun to value ourselves, our land, our abilities. We have only just begun to recognize our legends and to give shape to our myths. 14

There are, God knows, enough aspects to deplore about this country. When 15
I see the killing of our lakes and rivers with industrial wastes, I feel rage and despair. When I see our industries and natural resources increasingly taken over by
America, I feel an overwhelming discouragement, especially as I cannot simply
say "damn Yankees." It should never be forgotten that it is we ourselves who have
sold such a large amount of our birthright for a mess of plastic Progress. When I
saw the War Measures Act being invoked in 1970, I lost forever the vestigial remains of the naïve wish-belief that repression could not happen here, or would not.
And yet, of course, I had known all along in the deepest and often hidden caves of
the heart that anything can happen anywhere, for the seeds of both man's freedom
and his captivity are found everywhere, even in the microcosm of a prairie town.
But in raging against our injustices, our stupidities, I do so *as family,* as I did, and
still do in writing, about those aspects of my town which I hated and which are always in some ways aspects of myself.

The land still draws me more than other lands. I have lived in Africa and in 16
England, but splendid as both can be, they do not have the power to move me in
the same way as, for example, that part of southern Ontario where I spent four
months last summer in a cedar cabin beside a river. "Scratch a Canadian, and you
find a phony pioneer," I used to say to myself in warning. But all the same it is
true, I think, that we are not yet totally alienated from physical earth, and let us
only pray we do not become so. I once thought that my lifelong fear and mistrust
of cities made me a kind of old-fashioned freak; now I see it differently.

The cabin has a long window across its front western wall, and sitting at 17
the oak table there in the mornings, I used to look out at the river and at the tall
trees beyond, green-gold in the early light. The river was bronze; the sun caught
it strangely, reflecting upon its surface the near-shore sand ripples underneath.
Suddenly, the crescenting of a fish, gone before the eye could clearly give image to it. The old man next door said these leaping fish were carp. Himself, he
preferred muskie, for he was a real fisherman and the muskie gave him a fight.
The wind most often blew from the south, and the river flowed toward the
south, so when the water was windriffled, and the current was strong, the river
seemed to be flowing both ways. I liked this, and interpreted it as an omen, a
natural symbol.

A few years ago, when I was back in Winnipeg, I gave a talk at my old col- 18
lege. It was open to the public, and afterward a very old man came up to me and
asked me if my maiden name had been Wemyss. I said yes, thinking he might have
known my father or my grandfather. But no. "When I was a young lad," he said,
"I once worked for your great-grandfather, Robert Wemyss, when he had the sheep
ranch at Raeburn." I think that was a moment when I realized all over again something of great importance to me. My long-ago families came from Scotland and
Ireland, but in a sense that no longer mattered so much. My true roots were here.

I am not very patriotic, in the usual meaning of that word. I cannot say "My 19
country right or wrong" in any political, social, or literary context. But one thing
is inalterable, for better or worse, for life.

This is where my world began. A world which includes the ancestors—both 20
my own and other people's ancestors who become mine. A world which formed
me, and continues to do so, even while I found it in some of its aspects, and continue to do so. A world which gave me my own lifework to do, because it was here
that I learned the sight of my own particular eyes.

1976

QUESTIONS FOR DISCUSSION

Content

a. Do you find Laurence's title intriguing? What exactly does she mean by it?
Think about various Biblical allusions that John Caldwell, in the biography,
makes in his remarks about Laurence.

b. The author's purpose goes beyond simply describing a prairie town. What is that
purpose, and how does her use of descriptive details help her accomplish it?

c. How would you describe the audience to whom Laurence is writing?

d. What important distinction does Laurence draw in paragraph 3? Why is this
distinction important? In what other parts of the essay does she allude to it?

e. In what way does her recollection of the "almost-perfect callousness" (paragraph 7) she possessed as a girl help develop the thesis? Why does she devote
two entire paragraphs to "the oddities of the place" (paragraphs 8 and 9)?

f. What are the "Drought and Depression" mentioned in paragraph 5? In what
ways does the author's mention of these "evil deities" help her recapture her
childhood?

g. Who were "the young men . . . thrusting defiantly their requests for a drink of
water and a sandwich" (paragraph 5)? What do they add to Laurence's description of her home?

h. In which of the world wars did the "uncles . . . whose bones lay in France" die
(paragraph 11)? What are some of the context clues that help us determine the
answer?

i. What is the one insidious notion about both Canada and her birthplace that Laurence wishes to dispel?

j. What does she mean by "plastic Progress" (paragraph 15)?

k. Paragraphs 16 and 17 explain Laurence's belief that she and other Canadians
are "not yet totally alienated from physical earth. . . ." Why is it important for
her to tell us this? What is the "omen" she describes in paragraph 17?

Strategy and Style

l. To a great degree this selection is really two essays. Where does one end and
the other begin? In what way is the little town in which Laurence grew up a
"microcosm" of the whole of Canada?

m. Like all good descriptive pieces, this selection uses details "to show" rather than "to tell." Nowhere is that statement more applicable than in paragraph 4. Explain why this paragraph is so effective in helping Laurence counter the charge that her prairie town was "dull."

n. Comment upon the author's choice of verbs in paragraph 4. In what other paragraphs of the essay is her language nearly as vivid and exciting?

o. Laurence's use of metaphors, similes, and other kinds of figurative language is superb. In paragraph 7, she compares a fire truck to "some scarlet chariot of the Goths." In paragraph 11, she uses an oxymoron (a rhetorical figure that contains contradictory elements) to tell us that the "dead lived in that place, too." What other examples of figurative language do you find?

p. Near the end of the essay, Laurence becomes almost rhapsodic in explaining how growing up as a Canadian influenced her writing. In what way does her chance meeting with one of her great-grandfather's farm workers help her create an appropriate conclusion for this essay?

q. What is the author's attitude toward herself, both as the adult who wrote this essay and as the child who is one of its subjects?

SUGGESTIONS FOR SHORT WRITING

a. Choose a passage (a sentence or a paragraph) and relate that passage to your own life.

b. Describe one of the "oddities of the place" (paragraph 8) of your hometown.

SUGGESTIONS FOR SUSTAINED WRITING

a. Describe your hometown or community. In what ways has it helped shape you as an individual and helped determine what you want out of life?

b. In what ways is your hometown a "microcosm" of your country? As Laurence has done, compare both positive and negative aspects.

c. Describe the small town (or big city, for that matter) in which you were raised in such a way as to prove that living there was anything but dull.

d. Everyone's community has its oddities. Describe some of the people, places, laws, rituals, etc., of your hometown that you find odd.

The Metropolitan Cathedral in San Salvador

Joan Didion

*Born in Sacramento, California, Didion (b. 1934) served as associate feature editor
for* Vogue, *as a regular columnist for* The Saturday Evening Post, *and as a
contributing editor to the* National Review. *Her essays are subtle portraits of the
American experience. Her major works include novels:* Play It As It Lays *(1971),* A
Book of Common Prayer *(1977), and* Democracy *(1984); collections of essays:*
Slouching Toward Bethlehem *(1968) and* The White Album *(1979); and nonfiction:*
Salvador *(1983) and* Miami *(1987). She is also coauthor of several screenplays,
including* The Panic in Needle Park *(1971),* A Star Is Born *(1976), and* True
Confessions *(1981). This excerpt is from* Salvador, *a book about her experiences in El
Salvador.*

During the week before I flew down to El Salvador a Salvadoran woman who 1
works for my husband and me in Los Angeles gave me repeated instructions
about what we must and must not do. We must not go out at night. We must stay
off the street whenever possible. We must never ride in buses or taxis, never leave
the capital, never imagine that our passports would protect us. We must not even
consider the hotel a safe place: people were killed in hotels. She spoke with considerable vehemence, because two of her brothers had been killed in Salvador in
August of 1981, in their beds. The throats of both brothers had been slashed. Her
father had been cut but stayed alive. Her mother had been beaten. Twelve of her
other relatives, aunts and uncles and cousins, had been taken from their houses
one night the same August, and their bodies had been found some time later, in a
ditch. I assured her that we would remember, we would be careful, we would in
fact be so careful that we would probably (trying for a light touch) spend all our
time in church.

  She became still more agitated, and I realized that I had spoken as a 2
norteamericana: Churches had not been to this woman the neutral ground they
had been to me. I must remember: Archbishop Romero killed saying mass in
the chapel of the Divine Providence Hospital in San Salvador. I must remember: More than thirty people killed at Archbishop Romero's funeral in the Metropolitan Cathedral in San Salvador. I must remember: More than twenty people killed before that on the steps of the Metropolitan Cathedral. CBS had
filmed it. It had been on television, the bodies jerking, those still alive crawling over the dead as they tried to get out of range. I must understand: The
Church was dangerous.

  I told her that I understood, that I knew all that, and I did, abstractly, 3
but the specific meaning of the Church she knew eluded me until I was actually there, at the Metropolitan Cathedral in San Salvador, one afternoon
when rain sluiced down its corrugated plastic windows and puddled around
the supports of the Sony and Philips billboards near the steps. The effect of
the Metropolitan Cathedral is immediate, and entirely literary. This is the

cathedral that the late Archbishop Oscar Arnulfo Romero refused to finish, on the premise that the work of the Church took precedence over its display, and the high walls of raw concrete bristle with structural rods, rusting now, staining the concrete, sticking out at wrenched and violent angles. The wiring is exposed. Fluorescent tubes hang askew. The great high altar is backed by warped plyboard. The cross on the altar is of bare incandescent bulbs, but the bulbs, that afternoon, were unlit: there was in fact no light at all on the main altar, no light on the cross, no light on the globe of the world that showed the northern American continent in gray and the southern in white; no light on the dove above the globe, *Salvador del Mundo.* In this vast brutalist space that was the cathedral, the unlit altar seemed to offer a single ineluctable message: At this time and in this place the light of the world could be construed as out, off, extinguished.

In many ways the Metropolitan Cathedral is an authentic piece of politi- 4 cal art, a statement for El Salvador as *Guernica* was for Spain. It is quite devoid of sentimental relief. There are no decorative or architectural references to familiar parables, in fact no stories at all, not even the Stations of the Cross. On the afternoon I was there the flowers laid on the altar were dead. There were no traces of normal parish activity. The doors were open to the barricaded main steps, and down the steps there was a spill of red paint, lest anyone forget the blood shed there. Here and there on the cheap linoleum inside the cathedral there was what seemed to be actual blood, dried in spots, the kind of spots dropped by a slow hemorrhage, or by a woman who does not know or does not care that she is menstruating.

There were several women in the cathedral during the hour or so I spent 5 there, a young woman with a baby, an older woman in house slippers, a few others, all in black. One of the women walked the aisles as if by compulsion, up and down, across and back, crooning loudly as she walked. Another knelt without moving at the tomb of Archbishop Romero in the right transept. "Loor a Monsenor Romero," the crude needlepoint tapestry by the tomb read, "Praise to Monsignor Romero from the Mothers of the Imprisoned, the Disappeared, and the Murdered," the *Comité de Madres y Familiares de Presos, Desaparecidos, y Asesinados Politicos de El Salvador.*

The tomb itself was covered with offerings and petitions, notes decorated 6 with motifs cut from greeting cards and cartoons. I recall one with figures cut from a Bugs Bunny strip, and another with a pencil drawing of a baby in a crib. The baby in this drawing seemed to be receiving medication or fluid or blood intravenously, through the IV line shown on its wrist. I studied the notes for a while and then went back and looked again at the unlit altar, and at the red paint on the main steps, from which it was possible to see the guardsmen on the balcony of the National Palace hunching back to avoid the rain. Many Salvadorans are offended by the Metropolitan Cathedral, which is as it should be, because the place remains perhaps the only unambiguous political statement in El Salvador, a metaphorical bomb in the ultimate power station.

1983

QUESTIONS FOR DISCUSSION

Content

a. Is Didion simply describing the Metropolitan Cathedral, or is she using her description as a metaphor for something else? If so, what is the metaphor?
b. Why does she describe the interior of the cathedral in such detail?
c. What senses does Didion appeal to in this description?
d. What does she tell us about the people who worship at the cathedral? How do references to people enrich her description of this place?
e. The author says that the churches in El Salvador are not "neutral ground" (paragraph 2). What does she mean? Does Didion give us an indication about why the Church is involved in Salvadoran politics?
f. What is the "specific meaning of the Church" (paragraph 3) that Didion says eluded her until she came to El Salvador?

Strategy and Style

g. Why does Didion begin by recalling the advice of the Salvadoran woman who works for her?
h. Is your overall reaction to the cathedral generally positive or negative? What details in the essay account for your reaction?
i. Is Didion justified in saying in paragraph 6 that "many Salvadorans are offended by the Metropolitan Cathedral, which is as it should be . . ."? Why would Salvadorans be offended by the cathedral?
j. Is she justified in saying that it is the "only unambiguous political statement in El Salvador . . ."? What is this statement saying?
k. How objective is Didion? Is she praising, criticizing, or trying to be neutral?
l. How would you describe her tone, and what elements in this essay reveal that tone?

SUGGESTIONS FOR SHORT WRITING

a. Try describing a place that is very familiar to you as if you had never seen it before. You might want to find a place in which you can sit, observe, and write unnoticed. First, sit for a while and try to see the place as a stranger would; then, write your description of it.

b. Try rewriting paragraph 4, excising all political language. What do you end up
    with? What words did you consider to be political?

SUGGESTIONS FOR SUSTAINED WRITING

a. Think of a building that you believe symbolizes a political or social situation.
    What physical details of this building mirror aspects of the situation? Write a
    description of the building in which you make the connection clear.
b. Describe the government of the United States, of another country, of your state,
    or of your hometown through the use of an extended metaphor developed
    through description. Like Didion, use carefully chosen descriptive details to
    show how a building or a place mirrors major aspects of that government.
c. Recall a time when you were an outsider—for example, when you traveled to a
    foreign country or moved to a new community. What were your thoughts about
    and reactions to this new place? Do you think your outsider status allowed you
    to see the situation more clearly than the "natives" did? Try describing this sit-
    uation so that these "natives" might see their culture in a new way.

Fifth Avenue, Uptown

James Baldwin

*James Baldwin (1924–1987) was born in Harlem. In 1927 his mother married David
Baldwin, a minister who had moved to New York from New Orleans and who preached in
a storefront church. With both of his parents working, James became the caretaker of his
eight siblings and balanced his time between tending to them and going to school. His
teachers at DeWitt Clinton High School encouraged his literary talent, and he began
writing poems, stories, plays, and essays while editing the school's literary magazines. At
14 he had a religious awakening and began preaching, becoming increasingly popular
while his stepfather's congregation decreased. But his religious calling was short-lived,
and Baldwin, becoming disillusioned with Christianity, stopped preaching after three
years. In 1942, he moved to New Jersey but returned to New York a year later when his
father was dying. After his father's death, he moved to Greenwich Village to focus on his
literary career; after five difficult years he published his first work in 1947, book reviews
for the* Nation *and the* New Leader. *In 1948 he received a fellowship and left the United
States to live in France. There he wrote his most famous works,* Go Tell It on the
Mountain *(1953), a novel about a boy's religious awakenings;* Giovanni's Room *(1956),
a novel about a young homosexual man living in Paris; and* Notes of a Native Son
*(1955), a nonfiction work about racism in American society. In 1957 he returned to the
United States and became active in the Civil Rights Movement, publishing* Another
Country *(1962) and* The Fire Next Time *(1963). His other works include novels,
nonfiction, essays, and plays. Disillusioned by the assassinations of Martin Luther King,
Jr., and Malcolm X, he returned to France, where he lived the rest of his life.*

There is a housing project standing now where the house in which we grew up 1
once stood, and one of those stunted city trees is snarling where our doorway used
to be. This is on the rehabilitated side of the avenue. The other side of the avenue—
for progress takes time—has not been rehabilitated yet and it looks exactly as it
looked in the days when we sat with our noses pressed against the windowpane,
longing to be allowed to go "across the street." The grocery store which gave us
credit is still there, and there can be no doubt that it is still giving credit. The people in the project certainly need it—far more, indeed, than they ever needed the
project. The last time I passed by, the Jewish proprietor was still standing among
his shelves, looking sadder and heavier but scarcely any older. Farther down the
block stands the shoe-repair store in which our shoes were repaired until reparation became impossible and in which, then, we bought all our "new" ones. The
Negro proprietor is still in the window, head down, working at the leather.

These two, I imagine, could tell a long tale if they would (perhaps they 2
would be glad to if they could), having watched so many, for so long, struggling
in the fishhooks, the barbed wire, of this avenue.

The avenue is elsewhere the renowned and elegant Fifth. The area I am de- 3
scribing, which, in today's gang parlance, would be called "the turf," is bounded
by Lenox Avenue on the west, the Harlem River on the east, 135th Street on the
north, and 130th Street on the south. We never lived beyond these boundaries; this

65

is where we grew up. Walking along 145th Street—for example—familiar as it is, and similar, does not have the same impact because I do not know any of the people on the block. But when I turn east on 131st Street and Lenox Avenue, there is first a soda-pop joint, then a shoeshine "parlor," then a grocery store, then a dry cleaners', then the houses. All along the street there are people who watched me grow up, people who grew up with me, people I watched grow up along with my brothers and sisters; and, sometimes in my arms, sometimes underfoot, sometimes at my shoulder—or on it—their children, a riot, a forest of children, who include my nieces and nephews.

When we reach the end of this long block, we find ourselves on wide, filthy,   4
hostile Fifth Avenue, facing that project which hangs over the avenue like a monument to the folly, and the cowardice, of good intentions. All along the block, for anyone who knows it, are immense human gaps, like craters. These gaps are not created merely by those who have moved away, inevitably into some other ghetto; or by those who have risen, almost always into a greater capacity for self-loathing and self-delusion; or yet by those who, by whatever means—World War II, the Korean war, a policeman's gun or billy, a gang war, a brawl, madness, an overdose of heroin, or, simply, unnatural exhaustion—are dead. I am talking about those who are left, and I am talking principally about the young. What are they doing? Well, some, a minority, are fanatical churchgoers, members of the more extreme of the Holy Roller sects. Many, many more are "moslems," by affiliation or sympathy, that is to say that they are united by nothing more—and nothing less—than a hatred of the white world and all its works. They are present, for example, at every Buy Black street-corner meeting—meetings in which the speaker urges his hearers to cease trading with white men and establish a separate economy. Neither the speaker nor his hearers can possibly do this, of course, since Negroes do not own General Motors or RCA or the A & P, nor, indeed, do they own more than a wholly insufficient fraction of anything else in Harlem (those who *do* own anything are more interested in their profits than in their fellows). But these meetings nevertheless keep alive in the participators a certain pride of bitterness without which, however futile this bitterness may be, they could scarcely remain alive at all. Many have given up. They stay home and watch the TV screen, living on the earnings of their parents, cousins, brothers, or uncles, and only leave the house to go to the movies or to the nearest bar. "How're you making it?" one may ask, running into them along the block, or in the bar. "Oh, I'm TV-ing it"; with the saddest, sweetest, most shamefaced of smiles, and from a great distance. This distance one is compelled to respect; anyone who has traveled so far will not easily be dragged again into the world. There are further retreats, of course, than the TV screen or the bar. There are those who are simply sitting on their stoops, "stoned," animated for a moment only, and hideously, by the approach of someone who may lend them the money for a "fix." Or by the approach of someone from whom they can purchase it, one of the shrewd ones, on the way to prison or just coming out.

And the others, who have avoided all of these deaths, get up in the morning 5 and go downtown to meet "the man." They work in the white man's world all day and come home in the evening to this fetid block. They struggle to instill in their children some private sense of honor or dignity which will help the child to survive. This means, of course, that they must struggle, stolidly, incessantly, to keep this sense alive in themselves, in spite of the insults, the indifference, and the cruelty they are certain to encounter in their working day. They patiently browbeat the landlord into fixing the heat, the plaster, the plumbing; this demands prodigious patience; nor is patience usually enough. In trying to make their hovels habitable, they are perpetually throwing good money after bad. Such frustration, so long endured, is driving many strong, admirable men and women whose only crime is color to the very gates of paranoia.

One remembers them from another time—playing handball in the play- 6 ground, going to church, wondering if they were going to be promoted at school. One remembers them going off to war—gladly, to escape this block. One remembers their return. Perhaps one remembers their wedding day. And one sees where the girl is now—vainly looking for salvation from some other embittered, trussed, and struggling boy—and sees the all-but-abandoned children in the streets.

1948

QUESTIONS FOR DISCUSSION

Content

a. What is the image of Harlem that Baldwin creates in your mind? How does that image mesh with or conflict with other images you may have of Harlem?
b. What do the metaphors "fishhooks" and "barbed wire" in paragraph 2 mean? What other metaphors would make the same point?
c. How does Baldwin feel about Harlem? Where in the essay is this feeling revealed?
d. What are the main landmarks along the way? What does Baldwin see as significant about each one?
e. Why have many of the people in Harlem "given up"?
f. Why does Baldwin choose Fifth Avenue as the street to describe?

Strategy and Style

g. Besides the fishhooks and barbed wire metaphors in paragraph 2, what other metaphors does Baldwin use, and why?
h. This essay is from a book written in the 1950s. What do you find in the sentence style or word choice that recalls that time?
i. This is an excerpt from a longer work. From what this essay leads you to expect, what does Baldwin most likely describe immediately before and after the piece? What about this piece sets up those expectations?

j. How does Baldwin sequence this essay? In what order does he take us along this street in Harlem?
k. Baldwin uses a literary tone—calm, dispassionate, evenly paced. What sentences and words in particular create this tone?

SUGGESTIONS FOR SHORT WRITING

a. Rewrite a paragraph or short passage to create a different tone, such as one of excitement, anger, romance, or nostalgia. Note the words you remove from Baldwin and the ones you use instead.
b. Make a list and describe briefly the most important places in the neighborhood in which you grew up.

SUGGESTIONS FOR SUSTAINED WRITING

a. Write an extended description of one of the streets or roads in the neighborhood or rural area in which you grew up. Take the reader along the street or road, pointing out the important landmarks along the way and explaining why these landmarks create a particular identity for the area.
b. Research Baldwin's life. (The brief biographical headnote provided here does not begin to describe Baldwin's interesting life.) Write a biographical essay, focusing on the aspect of his life you find most significant.

The Death of the Moth

Virginia Woolf

The daughter of the British essayist and scholar Leslie Stephen, Virginia Woolf (1882–1941) was at the center of the Bloomsbury Group, a circle that included Lytton Strachey and John Maynard Keynes as well as several other important intellectuals, poets, and artists. With her husband, Leonard, Woolf founded the Hogarth Press and published the work of brilliant young writers such as T. S. Eliot and E. M. Forster. Her fiction is important because of her experimentation with the stream-of-consciousness technique and her ability to expose the psychology of her characters in a way that is at once subtle and vivid. Among her most memorable novels are Mrs. Dalloway *(1925),* To the Lighthouse *(1927),* Orlando *(1928), and* The Waves *(1931). Her nonfiction works include* A Room of One's Own *(1929) and* The Death of the Moth *(1942).*

Moths that fly by day are not properly to be called moths; they do not excite that pleasant sense of dark autumn nights and ivy-blossom which the commonest yellow-underwing asleep in the shadow of the curtain never fails to rouse in us. They are hybrid creatures, neither gay like butterflies nor sombre like their own species. Nevertheless the present specimen, with his narrow hay-coloured wings, fringed with a tassel of the same colour, seemed to be content with life. It was a pleasant morning, mid-September, mild, benignant, yet with a keener breath than that of the summer months. The plough was already scoring the field opposite the window, and where the share had been, the earth was pressed flat and gleamed with moisture. Such vigour came rolling in from the fields and the down beyond that it was difficult to keep the eyes strictly turned upon the book. The rooks too were keeping one of their annual festivities; soaring round the tree tops until it looked as if a vast net with thousands of black knots in it had been cast up into the air; which, after a few moments sank slowly down upon the trees until every twig seemed to have a knot at the end of it. Then, suddenly, the net would be thrown into the air again in a wider circle this time, with the utmost clamour and vociferation, as though to be thrown into the air and settle slowly down upon the tree tops were a tremendously exciting experience.

The same energy which inspired the rooks, the ploughmen, the horses, and even, it seemed, the lean bare-backed downs, sent the moth fluttering from side to side of his square of the windowpane. One could not help watching him. One was, indeed, conscious of a queer feeling of pity for him. The possibilities of pleasure seemed that morning so enormous and so various that to have only a moth's part in life, and a day moth's at that, appeared a hard fate, and his zest in enjoying his meagre opportunities to the full, pathetic. He flew vigorously to one corner of his compartment, and, after waiting there a second, flew across to the other. What remained for him but to fly to a third corner and then to a fourth? That was all he could do, in spite of the size of the downs, the width of the sky, the far-off smoke of houses, and the romantic voice, now and then, of a steamer out at sea. What he could do he did. Watching him, it seemed as if a fibre, very thin but pure, of the enormous energy of the world had been thrust into his frail and diminutive body.

69

As often as he crossed the pane, I could fancy that a thread of vital light became visible. He was little or nothing but life.

Yet, because he was so small, and so simple a form of the energy that was 3 rolling in at the open window and driving its way through so many narrow and intricate corridors in my own brain and in those of other human beings, there was something marvellous as well as pathetic about him. It was as if someone had taken a tiny bead of pure life and decking it as lightly as possible with down and feathers, had set it dancing and zig-zagging to show us the true nature of life. Thus displayed one could not get over the strangeness of it. One is apt to forget all about life, seeing it humped and bossed and garnished and cumbered so that it has to move with the greatest circumspection and dignity. Again, the thought of all that life might have been had he been born in any other shape caused one to view his simple activities with a kind of pity.

After a time, tired by his dancing apparently, he settled on the window ledge in 4 the sun, and, the queer spectacle being at an end, I forgot about him. Then, looking up, my eye was caught by him. He was trying to resume his dancing, but seemed either so stiff or so awkward that he could only flutter to the bottom of the window-pane; and when he tried to fly across it he failed. Being intent on other matters I watched these futile attempts for a time without thinking, unconsciously waiting for him to resume his flight, as one waits for a machine, that has stopped momentarily, to start again without considering the reason of its failure. After perhaps a seventh attempt he slipped from the wooden ledge and fell, fluttering his wings, on to his back on the window sill. The helplessness of his attitude roused me. It flashed upon me that he was in difficulties; he could no longer raise himself; his legs struggled vainly. But, as I stretched out a pencil, meaning to help him to right himself, it came over me that the failure and awkwardness were the approach of death. I laid the pencil down again.

The legs agitated themselves once more. I looked as if for the enemy against 5 which he struggled. I looked out of doors. What had happened there? Presumably it was midday, and work in the fields had stopped. Stillness and quiet had replaced the previous animation. The birds had taken themselves off to feed in the brooks. The horses stood still. Yet the power was there all the same, massed outside, indifferent, impersonal, not attending to anything in particular. Somehow it was opposed to the little hay-coloured moth. It was useless to try to do anything. One could only watch the extraordinary efforts made by those tiny legs against an oncoming doom which could, had it chosen, have submerged an entire city, not merely a city, but masses of human beings; nothing, I knew, had any chance against death. Nevertheless after a pause of exhaustion the legs fluttered again. It was superb this last protest, and so frantic that he succeeded at last in righting himself. One's sympathies, of course, were all on the side of life. Also, when there was nobody to care or to know, this gigantic effort on the part of an insignificant little moth, against a power of such magnitude, to retain what no one else valued or desired to keep, moved one strangely. Again, somehow, one saw life, a pure bead. I lifted the pencil again, useless though I knew it to be. But even as I did so, the unmistakable tokens of death showed themselves. The body relaxed, and instantly grew stiff. The struggle was over. The insignificant little creature now knew death. As I looked at the dead moth, this minute wayside triumph of so great a force over so mean an antagonist filled me with wonder. Just as life had been strange a few minutes before, so death was now as strange. The moth having righted himself now lay most decently and uncomplainingly composed. O yes, he seemed to say, death is stronger than I am.

1942

QUESTIONS FOR DISCUSSION

Content

a. Woolf's essay is obviously a serious discussion of the inevitability of death. Why does she rely on the death of so inconsequential a creature to convey her impressions? Why did she not describe the death of a human being instead?

b. To what is Woolf referring in paragraph 2 when she says, "The same energy which inspired the rooks, the ploughmen, the horses . . . sent the moth fluttering . . ."?

c. In the same paragraph, Woolf indicates that the moth was "little or nothing but life." Yet, by paragraph 5, the insect has died. Did the same power that gave him life strike him down?

d. What connection does Woolf draw between the moth and the world of living things outside her window? Why is it appropriate that the moth die at midday?

Strategy and Style

e. Throughout the first three paragraphs, Woolf refers to herself in the third person ("one"). In paragraphs 4 and 5, however, she uses the more familiar first-person pronoun ("I"). Does this change indicate a change in tone?

f. What other differences do you notice between the first three paragraphs and the last two in regard to both content and rhetorical strategy?

g. At the end of paragraph 1, Woolf uses an extended metaphor. What other interesting uses of figurative language can you identify?

SUGGESTIONS FOR SHORT WRITING

a. Choose a window or some equally limited area at home and describe the "world" of that area.

b. Study Woolf's opening paragraph, looking at the way she structures each sentence, the way she uses punctuation, the subject matter of each sentence. Then, with some animal other than a moth, write an opening paragraph of your own in Woolf's style.

SUGGESTIONS FOR SUSTAINED WRITING

a. Woolf's perspective on the death of the moth is, for the most part, subjective. As such, it is a perfect example of the extent to which our personal vision of the world can color our perceptions of natural objects and events. Spend some time observing the night sky, a field of corn in autumn, a newborn calf, the backyard outside your bedroom window, a potted geranium, or some other natural subject. Write two short essays about it. In the first, be objective. Describe things accurately and scientifically. Use factual details only, and make reference to exact sizes, shapes, and colors. In the second, flex the muscles of your imagination by writing a subjective description. Let your emotions color your perceptions. If possible, use metaphors and other figures of speech to convey your personal impressions of the subject.

b. Woolf proves that even a creature as insignificant as a moth is an appropriate subject for an essay that explores significant human questions. Go out and watch the activity in an anthill for ten or fifteen minutes, observe what a bird must go through to keep her chicks alive, or recall the birth of a puppy or kitten. What lessons can the natural world teach us about how to live our lives?

The Way to Rainy Mountain

N. Scott Momaday

Half Kiowan and part Cherokee, N. Scott Momaday (b. 1934) was born in Lawton, Oklahoma, and grew up on Navajo, Apache, and Pueblo reservations in northern New Mexico. A distinguished writer and professor of English at the University of Arizona, Momaday is also an accomplished painter, photographer, and tribal dancer. His prose, poetry, illustrations, and photographs celebrate the culture of Native Americans and their reverence for the land. Momaday is best known for The Way to Rainy Mountain *(1969), a book that grew from an autobiographical essay, "The Journey of Tai-me," published two years earlier. But his works are many and varied. In 1968, he won the Pulitzer Prize for* House Made of Dawn, *a novel. He has written two volumes of poetry:* Angle of Geese and Other Poems *(1973) and* The Gourd Dancer *(1976). A second autobiographical work,* The Names: A Memoir, *appeared in 1977. In 1982, he coauthored a pictorial history entitled* American Indian Photographic Images 1868–1931.

A single knoll rises out of the plain in Oklahoma, north and west of the Wichita 1 Range. For my people, the Kiowas, it is an old landmark, and they gave it the name Rainy Mountain. The hardest weather in the world is there. Winter brings blizzards, hot tornadic winds arise in the spring, and in summer the prairie is an anvil's edge. The grass turns brittle and brown, and it cracks beneath your feet. There are green belts along the rivers and creeks, linear groves of hickory and pecan, willow and witch hazel. At a distance in July or August the steaming foliage seems almost to writhe in fire. Great green-and-yellow grasshoppers are everywhere in the tall grass, popping up like corn to sting the flesh, and tortoises crawl about on the red earth, going nowhere in the plenty of time. Loneliness is an aspect of the land. All things in the plain are isolate; there is no confusion of objects in the eye, but *one* hill or *one* tree or *one* man. To look upon that landscape in the early morning, with the sun at your back, is to lose the sense of proportion. Your imagination comes to life, and this, you think, is where Creation was begun.

I returned to Rainy Mountain in July. My grandmother had died in the 2 spring, and I wanted to be at her grave. She had lived to be very old and at last infirm. Her only living daughter was with her when she died, and I was told that in death her face was that of a child.

I like to think of her as a child. When she was born, the Kiowas were living 3 that last great moment of their history. For more than a hundred years they had controlled the open range from the Smoky Hill River to the Red, from the headwaters of the Canadian to the fork of the Arkansas and Cimarron. In alliance with the Comanches, they had ruled the whole of the southern Plains. War was their sacred business, and they were among the finest horsemen the world has ever known. But warfare for the Kiowas was preeminently a matter of disposition rather than of survival, and they never understood the grim, unrelenting advance of the U.S. Cavalry. When at last, divided and ill-provisioned, they were driven onto the Staked Plains in the cold rains of autumn, they fell into panic. In Palo Duro Canyon they abandoned their

73

crucial stores to pillage and had nothing then but their lives. In order to save themselves, they surrendered to the soldiers at Fort Sill and were imprisoned in the old stone corral that now stands as a military museum. My grandmother was spared the humiliation of those high gray walls by eight or ten years, but she must have known from birth the affliction of defeat, the dark brooding of old warriors.

Her name was Aho, and she belonged to the last culture to evolve in North   4
America. Her forebears came down from the high country in western Montana nearly three centuries ago. They were a mountain people, a mysterious tribe of hunters whose language has never been positively classified in any major group. In the late seventeenth century they began a long migration to the south and east. It was a long journey toward the dawn, and it led to a golden age. Along the way the Kiowas were befriended by the Crows, who gave them the culture and religion of the Plains. They acquired horses, and their ancient nomadic spirit was suddenly free of the ground. They acquired Tai-me, the sacred Sun Dance doll, from that moment the object and symbol of their worship, and so shared in the divinity of the sun. Not least, they acquired the sense of destiny, therefore courage and pride. When they entered upon the southern Plains, they had been transformed. No longer were they slaves to the simple necessity of survival; they were a lordly and dangerous society of fighters and thieves, hunters and priests of the sun. According to their origin myth, they entered the world through a hollow log. From one point of view, their migration was the fruit of an old prophecy, for indeed they emerged from a sunless world.

Although my grandmother lived out her long life in the shadow of Rainy   5
Mountain, the immense landscape of the continental interior lay like memory in her blood. She could tell of the Crows, whom she had never seen, and of the Black Hills, where she had never been. I wanted to see in reality what she had seen more perfectly in the mind's eye, and traveled fifteen hundred miles to begin my pilgrimage.

Yellowstone, it seemed to me, was the top of the world, a region of deep   6
lakes and dark timber, canyons and waterfalls. But, beautiful as it is, one might have the sense of confinement there. The skyline in all directions is close at hand, the high wall of the woods and deep cleavages of shade. There is a perfect freedom in the mountains, but it belongs to the eagle and the elk, the badger and the bear. The Kiowas reckoned their stature by the distance they could see, and they were bent and blind in the wilderness.

Descending eastward, the highland meadows are a stairway to the plain. In   7
July the inland slope of the Rockies is luxuriant with flax and buckwheat, stonecrop and larkspur. The earth unfolds and the limit of the land recedes. Clusters of trees and animals grazing far in the distance cause the vision to reach away and wonder to build upon the mind. The sun follows a longer course in the day, and the sky is immense beyond all comparison. The great billowing clouds that sail upon it are shadows that move upon the grain like water, dividing light. Farther down, in the land of the Crows and Blackfeet, the plain is yellow. Sweet clover takes hold of the hills and bends upon itself to cover and seal the soil. There the Kiowas paused on their way; they had come to the place where they must

change their lives. The sun is at home on the plains. Precisely there does it have the certain character of a god. When the Kiowas came to the land of the Crows, they could see the dark lees of the hills at dawn across the Bighorn River, the profusion of light on the grain shelves, the oldest deity ranging after the solstices. Not yet would they veer southward to the caldron of the land that lay below; they must wean their blood from the northern winter and hold the mountains a while longer in their view. They bore Tai-me in procession to the east.

A dark mist lay over the Black Hills, and the land was like iron. At the top 8 of a ridge I caught sight of Devil's Tower upthrust against the gray sky as if in the birth of time the core of the earth had broken through its crust and the motion of the world was begun. There are things in nature that engender an awful quiet in the heart of man; Devil's Tower is one of them. Two centuries ago, because they could not do otherwise, the Kiowas made a legend at the base of the rock. My grandmother said:

> Eight children were there at play, seven sisters and their brother.
> Suddenly the boy was struck dumb; he trembled and began to run
> upon his hands and feet. His fingers became claws, and his body was
> covered with fur. Directly there was a bear where the boy had been.
> The sisters were terrified; they ran, and the bear after them. They
> came to the stump of a great tree, and the tree spoke to them. It bade
> them climb upon it, and as they did so, it began to rise into the air.
> The bear came to kill them, but they were just beyond its reach. It
> reared against the tree and scored the bark all around with its claws.
> The seven sisters were borne into the sky, and they became the stars
> of the Big Dipper.

From that moment, and so long as the legend lives, the Kiowas have kinsmen in the night sky. Whatever they were in the mountains, they could be no more. However tenuous their well-being, however much they had suffered and would suffer again, they had found a way out of the wilderness.

My grandmother had a reverence for the sun, a holy regard that now is all but 9 gone out of mankind. There was a wariness in her, and an ancient awe. She was a Christian in her later years, but she had come a long way about, and she never forgot her birthright. As a child she had been to the Sun Dances; she had taken part in those annual rites, and by them she had learned the restoration of her people in the presence of Tai-me. She was about seven when the last Kiowa Sun Dance was held in 1887 on the Washita River above Rainy Mountain Creek. The buffalo were gone. In order to consummate the ancient sacrifice—to impale the head of a buffalo bull upon the medicine tree—a delegation of old men journeyed into Texas, there to beg and barter for an animal from the Goodnight herd. She was ten when the Kiowas came together for the last time as a living Sun Dance culture. They could find no buffalo; they had to hang an old hide from the sacred tree. Before the dance could begin, a company of soldiers rode out from Fort Sill under orders to disperse the tribe. Forbidden without cause the essential act of their faith, having seen the wild herds slaughtered and left to rot upon the ground, the Kiowas backed away forever from the medicine tree. That was July 20, 1890, at the great bend of the Washita. My grandmother was there. Without bitterness, and for as long as she lived, she bore a vision of deicide.

Now that I can have her only in memory, I see my grandmother in the several postures that were peculiar to her: standing at the wood stove on a winter morning and turning meat in a great iron skillet; sitting at the south window, bent above her beadwork, and afterwards, when her vision had failed, looking down for a long time into the fold of her hands; going out upon a cane, very slowly as she did when the weight of age came upon her; praying. I remember her most often at prayer. She made long, rambling prayers out of suffering and hope, having seen many things. I was never sure that I had the right to hear, so exclusive were they of all mere custom and company. The last time I saw her she prayed standing by the side of her bed at night, naked to the waist, the light of a kerosene lamp moving upon her dark skin. Her long, black hair, always drawn and braided in the day, lay upon her shoulders and against her breasts like a shawl. I do not speak Kiowa, and I never understood her prayers, but there was something inherently sad in the sound, some merest hesitation upon the syllables of sorrow. She began in a high and descending pitch, exhausting her breath to silence; then again and again—and always the same intensity of effort, of something that is, and is not, like urgency in the human voice. Transported so in the dancing light among the shadows of her room, she seemed beyond the reach of time. But that was illusion; I think I knew then that I should not see her again.

1969

QUESTIONS FOR DISCUSSION

Content

a. Is this essay the description of a place, of a person, or of both? What other purpose does Momaday have in writing this piece?

b. In what way does describing what he saw on his 1,500-mile journey help Momaday tell us about his grandmother?

c. Who is Tai-me, and what function does he serve in this essay?

d. What is the "deicide" that Momaday talks about near the end of this essay? How does the event help him explain the consciousness of his grandmother? What does it tell us about the Kiowas?

e. What is Momaday's point in telling us that his grandmother was born when "the Kiowas were living that last great moment of their history" (paragraph 3)?

f. The earth, for Momaday, is a redemptive force. What signs of this belief do you find in "The Way to Rainy Mountain"?

Strategy and Style

g. In what way does the Kiowa myth about the eight children help us understand the author's grandmother and her culture?

h. Momaday uses concrete details to describe the landscape he sees. What devices does he use to describe his grandmother?

i. Why is it important for the reader to learn about developments in Kiowan history?

j. Comment upon the author's use of figurative language. Where, for example, does he use similes and metaphors? What is the effect of such language?

k. Momaday's prose often has a rhythmic beauty. In paragraph 5, for example, he says that his grandmother "could tell of the Crows, whom she had never seen, and of the Black Hills, where she had never been." What other examples of parallelism and balance do you find in this selection?

l. Good description relies heavily on the use of concrete and specific nouns. Find a paragraph or two that illustrate Momaday's reliance on both common and proper names to make his writing believable.

SUGGESTIONS FOR SHORT WRITING

a. This essay begins with a startling snapshot of Rainy Mountain. Focus on a natural object or scene, and use your five senses to re-create it in a paragraph or two.

b. As you know, Momaday seems fond of mentioning the names of things he sees on his travels: plants, rivers, geologic formations, people, etc. Briefly recall a memorable trip you took recently by listing the interesting things you saw. You need not describe each object, place, etc., but you should give it a name.

c. Near the end of this selection, the author tells us about the sound of his grandmother's voice. Other parts of the essay appeal to our sense of touch. Describe a person or place you know well by using details that appeal to any of the five senses but sight.

SUGGESTIONS FOR SUSTAINED WRITING

a. Go through your family albums and select a series of photographs that "tell the story" of one member of your family or one of your ancestors. If you can, take the photos out and arrange them in their "storytelling" sequence. Then, write the story they tell, adding your own memories about your subject as you do so. Momaday does something similar in his book *The Way to Rainy Mountain;* you might want to find a copy in your library and use it as a source for ideas.

b. Momaday emphasizes the connection between his grandmother and the land. Write a story about a family member or someone else you know well, and explain that person's connection to the land, to some aspect of nature, or to a particular place. Show your readers how that connection is an unbroken bond that helped create the person's identity and that maintains his or her culture and sense of tradition.

Alias Benowitz Shoe Repair

David Quammen

David Quammen (b. 1948) has taken degrees at Oxford and Yale universities and has been a Rhodes scholar and Guggenheim fellow. At age 22, he published his first novel, To Walk the Line *(1970), which was based upon his work in a Chicago ghetto. Other fiction by Quammen includes* Stories of Fathers and Sons *(1987) and two political thrillers:* The Zolta Configuration *(1983) and* The Soul of Victor Tronko *(1987). Though not a scientist, Quammen writes "Natural Acts," a regular column on science, nature, and the environment for* Outside *magazine. Collected in* Natural Acts: A Sidelong View of Science and Nature *(1985) and in* The Flight of the Iguana: A Sidelong View of Science and Nature *(1988), these essays ask probing, often humorous questions about the natural world and the way we see it. "Alias Benowitz Shoe Repair," one such column, first appeared in 1985.*

1 I first heard about George Ochenski from a friend of mine who happens to be president of the Montana River-Snorkelers Association. We were in a fancy restaurant, as I recall, and there was wine involved. Ochenski had come to my friend's attention in the course of his (the friend's) presidential duties, which are in strict point of fact nonexistent. I should explain that the MRSA presidency is a purely honorary title, self-bestowed actually, because the MRSA is a mythical organization. This is all quite different, please note, from labeling the organization itself nonexistent. Certainly the Montana River-Snorkelers Association does exist (mainly over wine and beer at various bars and restaurants, occasionally also around a campfire); it just isn't *real*. An actual mythical entity, then, the MRSA, of roughly the same ontological status as the NCAA national championship in football, or the domino theory of international relations. You should look into this fellow Ochenski, my friend told me. He can be reached care of Benowitz Shoe Repair, in a tiny town called Southern Cross, up in the Flint Mountains above Anaconda. Have some more cabernet, I said. But sure enough it turned out to be true. Benowitz Shoe Repair is another mythical entity, existent in its own way but not real. George Ochenski is both mythical and real. Are you with me so far?

2 George Ochenski must certainly be the preeminent river-snorkeler in the Rocky Mountains. He has talent, commitment, infectious enthusiasm, broad experience, state-of-the-art equipment, and a measure of lunatic daring. He has precious little competition. Most important, he has self-abnegating dedication to a larger purpose.

3 Sometimes you have to snorkel a river, Ochenski believes, in order to save it.

4 So dedicated is George Ochenski, and so scornful of risk, that—if necessary to make a point—he is willing even to snorkel the Clark Fork River downstream from the Anaconda smelter.

5 Now a river-snorkeler (in case this isn't self-evident) is someone who swims downstream in a river with his face under water, enjoying the ride, watching the scenery, breathing through his little tube. A lazy, hypnotic pastime best practiced on pellucid trout streams in midsummer. A few of us have been toying at it for years.

78

But George Ochenski does not toy. He jimmies himself into a full wet suit, 6
adds fins and a hood and neoprene gloves and a fanny pack holding three cans of
beer, pulls a pair of skateboarding knee pads into place, defogs his mask, and
jumps into rivers. Gentle rivers and raging whitewater monsters. Last year, for instance, he did thirty-eight miles of the Salmon in Idaho without benefit of a boat.
Also last year, he leapt into the Quake Lake trench—an earthquake-contorted
stretch of the Madison River famous for biting kayaks in half—and nearly died.
On that run his mask was ripped off six times while he tumbled head over teaket-
tle through a garden of sharp boulders; the trench, George admits today, was a mis-
calculation. In Montana this kind of behavior does not pass unnoticed. By word,
and more discreetly by the looks on their faces, people frequently tell him: *Son,
you must be out of your everlovin' skull.* But they said that to Orville Wright, and
they were wrong. Then again, they said it to Evel Knievel, and they were right.
George Ochenski figures somewhere in between.

He has an enduring though ambivalent attraction to what he himself classi- 7
fies "death sports." Huge squinting grin from George as he acknowledges this am-
bivalence. Mountaineering. Iceclimbing. Scuba. Never a major injury, never a bad
accident—unless you count the time he fell 600 feet down a steep rock slope in
the Alaska Range and did a self-arrest on his nose. Back in those years he traveled
exotically for serious climbing, with generous sponsorship from the equipment
people, and took part in the first successful ascent of the west face of Alaska's Mt.
Hayes. Scaled some breathtaking frozen waterfalls. Around the same time, a consummate autodidact, he turned himself into an expert cobbler, because he wasn't
satisfied with the professional repair work on his climbing boots; before long he
was doing work for his friends too, and they had rechristened him, whimsically
and metonymically, "Benowitz Shoe Repair." Today he mostly stays close to the
little wood-heated cabin at Southern Cross, in the front room of which stands a
bass fiddle. The fiddle is a logical switch from tuba, which he played for thirteen
years. Benowitz is a man of many skills.

Several years ago, in response to pressure both internal and external, he gave 8
up the glorious climbing, thanked the sponsors, and settled down to being useful
politically. He had come to feel that he owed something back to the mountains and
rivers; meanwhile there happened to be a certain crisis brewing near home. He
now makes his living as an editorial assistant to an author of textbooks on environmental science. The cabin is filled ceiling-high with an eclectic library. On one
wall is a quote from Congressman Ron Dellums: "Democracy is not about being
a damn spectator against the backdrop of tapdancing politicians swinging in the
winds of expediency." By disposition, George is certainly no spectator. Some people, particularly of the opposition, might still take him on first impression for a
wild-haired, good-timing, reckless flake. They would be grievously mistaken.
George Ochenski has an excellent brain, he has chutzpah, he has focus.

And in a small trailer up the hill behind his own cabin, where the ash from 9
his cook stove can't fuddle its circuits, he has an Apple II computer, its floppy
discs full of damning information concerning the Anaconda Minerals Company.

On September 29, 1980, the Anaconda Company announced that it was clos- 10
ing its copper-smelting operations at the town of Anaconda. This came as a severe
shock to the 1,000 smelter workers suddenly unemployed, and marked the end of
a century of awesome environmental pillage. For one hundred years the Company
had cut down forests, poisoned streams, smelted copper, piled up vast mounds of
slag, and filled the air of the country with a sulfurous smog, in exchange for the
regular paychecks dispensed. Now the economics of copper had shifted. Goodbye,
thanks for everything. "The Company thought they could just lock the doors and
walk away," says George Ochenski.

He and a few other Anaconda folk, some of them former smelter workers, 11
think otherwise. They are after the Company like a fierce dog after a bear. They
have formed an enraged-citizens' organization, pressured the governor, pressured
the senators, pressured the EPA. They want more than goodbyes. They want recla-
mation. They want accountability. At very least they want precise information
about the nature and magnitude of the poisonous mess left behind.

With sulfur dioxide no longer pouring from the smelter stack, the chief con- 12
cern now is over toxic metals: lead, cadmium, mercury, zinc, copper itself, and especially arsenic. One hundred years of copper-smelting have left various concentrations of some or all of these in the waters, in the plants, in the soil, in the animals
of the county. George Ochenski and his compatriots want to know: *How much?*
How much was dumped in the ponds, how much was buried, how much is still
blowing free off the smelter site? How much is already in our lungs and our bones?
How much is ingested with each brown trout from the Clark Fork River, if a person should be so lucky as to catch one of the surviving fish, and so foolhardy as
to eat it?

How much lead? How much cadmium? How much arsenic? The Anaconda 13
Company, no doubt, devoutly wishes that these questions would go away.

Sometimes you have to snorkel a river in order to save it. Guided by this dic- 14
tum, George Ochenski loaded his gear into the back of my car. It was late in the
season, Labor Day weekend, with the air already growing cool. We paused briefly,
where the gravel lane down from Southern Cross joined the larger road, to check
the Benowitz Shoe Repair mailbox. Then George led me off on a pair of brief but
illuminating tours.

We went to the Big Hole River, across the Continental Divide from Ana- 15
conda and clear of the war zone over heavy metals. The Big Hole is still a pellucid trout stream. We jimmied ourselves into wet suits, added fins and hoods and
neoprene gloves; I pulled George's one extra skateboarding pad into position over
my favorite knee. Masks were defogged, snorkels adjusted, and we jumped in.

The view was beautiful. Trout and whitefish looked me in the eye, aghast, 16
and skittered away. Sculpins darted discreetly for cover. I observed the differences
in underwater behavior among three different species of stonefly. I gazed at the
funnel webs of *Arctopsyche* caddisfly larvae, down between rocks in the fast water, that I had read about often but never before seen. I found a mayfly nymph
equipped with an elephantine pair of tusks. We passed through a few modest sets

of rapids, where the current abruptly accelerated and the boulders came at me like blitzing linebackers who must be straight-armed away. After two hours of cruising we were nearly hypothermic, but the experience had been delightful.

Our second tour was to the Clark Fork River, downstream from the settling 17 ponds into which the Anaconda Company has voided its years of industrial offal. "We're off to snorkel the Clark Fork," George told a friend as we pulled out of town. The friend looked puzzled. Huge squinting grin from George. "Then we'll come back and glow in the dark."

We snorkeled a long section of the Clark Fork. Here the water was turbid, 18 visibility was poor. The rocks of the stream bed were largely cemented together with silt, leaving no habitat for stoneflies or *Arctopsyche*. I didn't see a single fish. I didn't see a single insect. Some people claim that the Clark Fork today is actually much improved over its sorry condition two decades ago, before the Company adopted certain technical measures to mitigate the toxicity of its releases. Maybe those people are right. But I remain skeptical. The river I was swimming through, with my eyes open and my nose very close to the bottom, was definitely no basis for passing out congratulations.

This dramatic lack of vitality proves nothing, of course, about what causal 19 role the smelter wastes, and the erosion from denuded hillsides around Anaconda, may or may not still be playing. It simply correlates. Consider it, if you wish to, purest coincidence. It is not, however, mythical. It is real.

Later Benowitz and I were careful to shower ourselves down with clean wa- 20 ter. "River-snorkeling," he told me, and he should know, "is not supposed to be a death sport."

1985

QUESTIONS FOR DISCUSSION

Content

a. This is as much a description of a person as it is of a place. What does the environment in which "Benowitz" has chosen to live tell us about him?
b. What is "chutzpah"? How does Quammen prove that Benowitz has this quality and that he "has focus" (paragraph 8)?
c. Behavior reveals personality. What does the author tell us about "Benowitz's" behavior and lifestyle that provides clues to his personality?
d. Why does Quammen entitle this piece "Alias . . . "? Why didn't he just call it "George Ochenski"?

Strategy and Style

e. Description can be put to many purposes. What has Quammen set out to do in this essay?

f. Why does he spend so much time explaining the difference between "mythical" and "real"? Is the distinction important to his purpose?

g. Why does he mention Orville Wright and Evel Knievel (paragraph 6) when trying to describe "Benowitz"?

h. Is this essay aimed solely at scientific readers? What can we assume about the educational background, interests, and values of Quammen's intended audience?

i. What examples of figurative language can you find in this essay? Is figurative language appropriate to "scientific" writing? Why or why not?

j. Find examples of irony. How do they affect the tone of this essay? Is this tone appropriate to scientific writing?

k. Though Quammen is not a scientist, his writing is convincing. How does the author establish his expertise?

SUGGESTIONS FOR SHORT WRITING

a. Write briefly about someone you know who has "chutzpah" or "focus." Try to record the kinds of details that you might later use in a clear and convincing character sketch of this individual.

b. You need not snorkel the Clark Fork River to find evidence of pollution. Take a stroll in any natural setting near your campus that has been damaged by pollution of one sort or another. With notebook or journal in hand, use your powers of observation to record specific details about what you see, hear, smell, or taste. Try to reveal the extent to which this environment has been affected.

SUGGESTIONS FOR SUSTAINED WRITING

a. Write a character sketch about a person you admire greatly and whom you met recently. Or, write about a person in your community who is well known and whose ways of getting things done are considered a bit eccentric. You can use the method Quammen chose by narrating your own experiences with the person, or you can experiment with other methods, such as using third-person point of view or relying on fragmented descriptions rather than narration. Whatever method you choose, make the sketch both informative and entertaining.

b. Write an essay about an environmental problem that focuses on a particular person involved in either solving or creating the problem. If the former, explain how that person has worked to find a solution; if she or he has had a lot of difficulty, show your readers the struggle and get them to sympathize with the person or even to join in that struggle. If the latter, show your readers why you think the person has caused the problem, and explain what they can do to help solve it.

My Father

Doris Lessing

Doris Lessing (b. 1919) was born in Persia, the daughter of English parents who had moved there hoping to make a good living in banking. When that venture did not turn out as her father had hoped, the family moved to Rhodesia where they settled as farmers. In 1949, Doris Lessing moved to London, where her first novel, The Grass Is Singing *(1950), won her instant fame. Soon after, she won the Somerset Maugham Award for Five* Short Novels *(1954).* The Golden Notebook *(1962), a complex autobiographical novel that weaves an exploration of the psychology of women with Lessing's views of social history, is her best-known work. An experimenter with form and subject, she covers a wide range of themes and motifs in her novels. In* Briefing for a Descent into Hell *(1971) and* Memoirs of a Survivor *(1974), for example, she deals with psychological disturbances, engages in dreamlike fantasy, and portrays a pessimistic view of history. In 1979, she began a series of "space fiction" novel beginning with the novel* Shikasta. *Recent nonfiction includes* Prisons We Choose to Live Inside *(1986) and* The Wind Blows Away Our Worlds *(1987).*

1 We use our parents like recurring dreams, to be entered into when needed; they are always there for love or for hate; but it occurs to me that I was not always there for my father. I've written about him before, but novels, stories, don't have to be "true." Writing this article is difficult because it has to be "true." I knew him when his best years were over.

2 There are photographs of him. The largest is of an officer in the 1914–18 war. A new uniform—buttoned, badged, strapped, tabbed—confines a handsome, dark young man who holds himself stiffly to confront what he certainly thought of as his duty. His eyes are steady, serious, and responsible, and show no signs of what he became later. A photograph at sixteen is of a dark, introspective youth with the same intent eyes. But it is his mouth you notice—a heavily-jutting upper lip contradicts the rest of a regular face. His moustache was to hide it: "Had to do something—a damned fleshy mouth. Always made me uncomfortable, that mouth of mine."

3 Earlier a baby (eyes already alert) appears in a lace waterfall that cascades from the pillowy bosom of a fat, plain woman to her feet. It is the face of a head cook. "Lord, but my mother was a practical female—almost as bad as you!" as he used to say, or throw at my mother in moments of exasperation. Beside her stands, or droops, arms dangling, his father, the source of the dark, arresting eyes, but otherwise masked by a long beard.

4 The birth certificate says: Born 3rd August, 1886, Walton Villa, Creffield Road, S. Mary at the Wall, R.S.D. Name, Alfred Cook. Name and surname of Father: Alfred Cook Tayler. Name and maiden name of Mother: Caroline May Batley. Rank or Profession: Bank Clerk. Colchester, Essex.

5 They were very poor. Clothes and boots were a problem. They "made their own amusements." Books were mostly the Bible and *The Pilgrim's Progress.* Every Saturday night they bathed in a hipbath in front of the kitchen fire. No servants.

83

Church three times on Sundays. "Lord, when I think of those Sundays! I dreaded them all week, like a nightmare coming at you full tilt and no escape." But he rabbited with ferrets along the lanes and fields, bird-nested, stole fruit, picked nuts and mushrooms, paid visits to the blacksmith and the mill and rode a farmer's carthorse.

They ate economically, but when he got diabetes in his forties and subsisted 6 on lean meat and lettuce leaves, he remembered suet puddings, treacle puddings, raisin and currant puddings, steak and kidney puddings, bread and butter puddings, "batter cooked in the gravy with the meat," potato cake, plum cake, butter cake, porridge with treacle, fruit tarts and pies, brawn, pig's trotters and pig's cheek and homesmoked ham and sausages. And "lashings of fresh butter and cream and eggs." He wondered if this diet had produced the diabetes, but said it was worth it.

There was an elder brother described by my father as: "Too damned clever 7 by half. One of those quick, clever brains. Now I've always had a slow brain, but I get there in the end, damn it!"

The brothers went to a local school and the elder did well, but my father was 8 beaten for being slow. They both became bank clerks in, I think, the Westminster Bank, and one must have found it congenial, for he became a manager, the "rich brother," who had cars and even a yacht. But my father did not like it, though he was conscientious. For instance, he changed his writing, letter by letter, because a senior criticised it. I never saw his unregenerate hand, but the one he created was elegant, spiky, careful. Did this mean he created a new personality for himself, hiding one he did not like, as he hid his "damned fleshy mouth"? I don't know.

Nor do I know when he left home to live in Luton, or why. He found family 9 life too narrow? A safe guess—he found everything too narrow. His mother was too down-to-earth? He had to get away from his clever elder brother?

Being a young man in Luton was the best part of his life. It ended in 1914, 10 so he had a decade of happiness. His reminiscences of it were all of pleasure, the delight of physical movement, of dancing in particular. All his girls were "a beautiful dancer, light as a feather." He played billiards and ping-pong (both for his country); he swam, boated, played cricket and football, went to picnics and horse races, sang at musical evenings. One family of a mother and two daughters treated him "like a son only better. I didn't know whether I was in love with the mother or the daughters, but oh I did love going there; we had such good times." He was engaged to one daughter, then, for a time, to the other. An engagement was broken off because she was rude to a waiter. "I could not marry a woman who allowed herself to insult someone who was defenseless." He used to say to my wryly smiling mother: "Just as well I didn't marry either of *them;* they would never have stuck it out the way you have, old girl."

Just before he died he told me he had dreamed he was standing in a kitchen 11 on a very high mountain holding X in his arms. "Ah, yes, that's what I've missed in my life. Now don't you let yourself be cheated out of life by the old dears. They take all the colour out of everything if you let them."

But in that decade—"I'd walk 10, 15 miles to a dance two or three times a 12 week and think nothing of it. Then I'd dance every dance and walk home again over the fields. Sometimes it was moonlight, but I liked the snow best all crisp and fresh. I loved walking back and getting into my digs just as the sun was rising. My little dog was so happy to see me, and I'd feed her, and make myself porridge and tea, then I'd wash and shave and go off to work."

The boy who was beaten at school, who went too much to church, who car- 13 ried the fear of poverty all his life, but who nevertheless was filled with the memories of country pleasures; the young bank clerk who worked such long hours for so little money, but who danced, sang, played, flirted—this naturally vigorous, sensuous being was killed in 1914, 1915, 1916. I think the best of my father died in that war, that his spirit was crippled by it. The people I've met, particularly the women, who knew him young, speak of his high spirits, his energy, his enjoyment of life. Also of his kindness, his compassion and—a word that keeps recurring— his wisdom. "Even when he was just a boy he understood things that you'd think even an old man would find it easy to condemn." I do not think these people would have easily recognised the ill, irritable, abstracted, hypochondriac man I knew.

He "joined up" as an ordinary soldier out of a characteristically quirky scru- 14 ple: it wasn't right to enjoy officers' privileges when the Tommies had such a bad time. But he could not stick the communal latrines, the obligatory drinking, the collective visits to brothels, the jokes about girls. So next time he was offered a commission he took it.

His childhood and young man's memories, kept fluid, were added to, grew, as 15 living memories do. But his war memories were congealed in stories that he told again and again, with the same words and gestures, in stereotyped phrases. They were anonymous, general, as if they had come out of a communal war memoir. He met a German in no-man's-land, but both slowly lowered their rifles and smiled and walked away. The Tommies were the salt of the earth, the British fighting men the best in the world. He had never known such comradeship. A certain brutal officer was shot in a sortie by his men, but the other officers, recognising rough justice, said nothing. He had known men intimately who saw the Angels at Mons. He wished he could force all the generals on both sides into the trenches for just one day, to see what the common soldiers endured—*that* would have ended the war at once.

There was an undercurrent of memories, dreams, and emotions much 16 deeper, more personal. This dark region in him, fate-ruled, where nothing was true but horror, was expressed inarticulately, in brief, bitter exclamations or phrases of rage, incredulity, betrayal. The men who went to fight in that war believed it when they said it was to end war. My father believed it. And he was never able to reconcile his belief in his country with his anger at the cynicism of its leaders. And the anger, the sense of betrayal, strengthened as he grew old and ill.

But in 1914 he was naïve, the German atrocities in Belgium inflamed him, 17 and he enlisted out of idealism, although he knew he would have a hard time. He knew because a fortuneteller told him. (He could be described as uncritically superstitious or as psychically gifted.) He would be in great danger twice, yet not die—he was being protected by a famous soldier who was his ancestor. "And sure enough, later I heard from the Little Aunties that the church records showed we were descended the backstairs way from the Duke of Wellington, or was it Marl-borough? Damn it, I forget. But one of them would be beside me all through the war, she said." (He was romantic, not only about this solicitous ghost, but also about being a descendant of the Huguenots, on the strength of the "e" in Tayler; and about "the wild blood" in his veins from a great uncle who, sent unjustly to prison for smuggling, came out of a ten-year sentence and earned it, very effi-ciently, along the coasts of Cornwall until he died.)

The luckiest thing that ever happened to my father, he said, was getting his leg shattered by shrapnel ten days before Passchendaele. His whole company was killed. He knew he was going to be wounded because of the fortuneteller, who had said he would know. "I did not understand what she meant, but both times in the trenches, first when my appendix burst and I nearly died, and then just before Pass-chendaele, I felt for some days as if a thick, black velvet pall was settled over me. I can't tell you what it was like. Oh, it was awful, and the second time it was so bad I wrote to the old people and told them I was going to be killed." 18

His leg was cut off at mid-thigh, he was shell-shocked, he was very ill for many months, with a prolonged depression afterwards. "You should always re-member that sometimes people are all seething underneath. You don't know what terrible things people have to fight against. You should look at a person's eyes, that's how you tell. . . . When I was like that, after I lost my leg, I went to a nice doctor man and said I was going mad, but he said, don't worry, everyone locks up things like that. You don't know—horrible, horrible, awful things. I was afraid of myself, of what I used to dream. I wasn't myself at all." 19

In the Royal Free Hospital was my mother, Sister McVeagh. He married his nurse which, as they both said often enough (though in different tones of voice), was just as well. That was 1919. He could not face being a bank clerk in England, he said, not after the trenches. Besides, England was too narrow and conventional. Besides, the civilians did not know what the soldiers had suffered, they didn't want to know, and now it wasn't done even to remember "The Great Unmentionable." He went off to the Imperial Bank of Persia, in which country I was born. 20

The house was beautiful, with great stone-floored high-ceilinged rooms whose windows showed ranges of snow-streaked mountains. The gardens were full of roses, jasmine, pomegranates, walnuts. Kermanshah he spoke of with lik-ing, but soon they went to Teheran, populous with "Embassy people," and my gre-garious mother created a lively social life about which he was irritable even in rec-ollection. 21

Irritableness—that note was first struck here, about Persia. He did not like, he said, "the graft and the corruption." But here it is time to try and describe some-thing difficult—how a man's good qualities can also be his bad ones, or if not bad, a danger to him. 22

My father was honourable—he always knew exactly what that word meant. He had integrity. His "one does not do that sort of thing," his "no, it is *not* right," sounded throughout my childhood and were final for all of us. I am sure it was true he wanted to leave Persia because of "the corruption." But it was also because he 23 was already unconsciously longing for something freer, because as a bank official he could not let go into the dream-logged personality that was waiting for him. And later in Rhodesia, too, what was best in him was also what prevented him from shaking away the shadows: it was always in the name of honesty or decency that he refused to take this step or that out of the slow decay of the family's fortunes.

In 1925 there was leave from Persia. That year in London there was an Em- 24
pire Exhibition, and on the Southern Rhodesian stand some very fine maize cobs and a poster saying that fortunes could be made on maize at 25/ -a bag. So on an impulse, turning his back forever on England, washing his hands of the corruption of the East, my father collected all his capital, £800, I think, while my mother packed curtains from Liberty's, clothes from Harrods, visiting cards, a piano, Persian rugs, a governess and two small children.

Soon, there was my father in a cigar-shaped house of thatch and mud on the 25
top of a kopje that overlooked in all directions a great system of mountains, rivers, valleys, while overhead the sky arched from horizon to empty horizon. This was a couple of hundred miles south from the Zambesi, a hundred or so west from Mozambique, in the district of Banket, so called because certain of its reefs were of the same formation as those called *banket* on the Rand. Lomagundi—gold country, tobacco country, maize country—wild, almost empty. (The Africans had been turned off it into reserves.) Our neighbours were four, five, seven miles off. In front of the house . . . no neighbours, nothing; no farms, just wild bush with two rivers but no fences to the mountains seven miles away. And beyond these mountains and bush again to the Portuguese border, over which "our boys" used to escape when wanted by the police for pass or other offences.

And then? There was bad luck. For instance, the price of maize dropped 26
from 25/ - to 9/ -a bag. The seasons were bad, prices bad, crops failed. This was the sort of thing that made it impossible for him ever to "get off the farm," which, he agreed with my mother, was what he most wanted to do.

It was an absurd country, he said. A man could "own" a farm for years that 27
was totally mortgaged to the Government and run from the Land Bank, meanwhile employing half-a-hundred Africans at 12/-a month and none of them knew how to do a day's work. Why, two farm labourers from Europe could do in a day what twenty of these ignorant black savages would take a week to do. (Yet he was proud that he had a name as a just employer, that he gave "a square deal.") Things got worse. A fortuneteller had told him that her heart ached when she saw the misery ahead for my father: this was the misery.

But it was my mother who suffered. After a period of neurotic illness, which 28
was a protest against her situation, she became brave and resourceful. But she never saw that her husband was not living in a real world, that he had made a captive of her common sense. We were always about to "get off the farm." A miracle would do it—a sweepstake, a goldmine, a legacy. And then? What a question! We would go to England where life would be normal with people coming in for musical evenings and nice supper parties at the Trocadero after a show. Poor woman, for the twenty years we were on the farm, she waited for when life would begin

for her and for her children, for she never understood that what was a calamity for her was for them a blessing.

Meanwhile my father sank towards his death (at 61). Everything changed in 29 him. He had been a dandy and fastidious, now he hated to change out of shabby khaki. He had been sociable, now he was misanthropic. His body's disorders— soon diabetes and all kinds of stomach ailments—dominated him. He was brave about his wooden leg, and even went down mine shafts and climbed trees with it, but he walked clumsily and it irked him badly. He greyed fast, and slept more in the day, but would be awake half the night pondering about. . . .

It could be gold divining. For ten years he experimented on private theories 30 to do with the attractions and repulsions of metals. His whole soul went into it but his theories were wrong or he was *unlucky*—after all, if he had found a mine he would have had to leave the farm. It could be the relation between the minerals of the earth and of the moon; his decision to make infusions of all the plants on the farm and drink them himself in the interests of science; the criminal folly of the British Government in not realizing that the Germans and the Russians were con- spiring as Anti-Christ to . . . the inevitability of war because no one would listen to Churchill, but it would be all right because God (by then he was a British Is- raelite) had destined Britain to rule the world; a prophecy said 10 million dead would surround Jerusalem—how would the corpses be cleared away?; people who wished to abolish flogging should be flogged; the natives understood nothing but a good beating; hanging must not be abolished because the Old Testament said "an eye for an eye and a tooth for a tooth. . . ."

Yet, as this side of him darkened, so that it seemed all his thoughts were of 31 violence, illness, war, still no one dared to make an unkind comment in his pres- ence or to gossip. Criticism of people, particularly of women, made him more and more uncomfortable till at last he burst out with: "It's all very well, but no one has the right to say that about another person."

In Africa, when the sun goes down, the stars spring up, all of them in their 32 expected places, glittering and moving. In the rainy season, the sky flashed and thundered. In the dry season, the great dark hollow of night was lit by veld fires: the mountains burned through September and October in chains of red fire. Every night my father took out his chair to watch the sky and the mountains, smoking, silent, a thin shabby fly-away figure under the stars. "Makes you think—there are so many worlds up there, wouldn't really matter if we did blow ourselves up— plenty more where we came from."

The Second World War, so long foreseen by him, was a bad time. His son 33 was in the Navy and in danger, and his daughter a sorrow to him. He became very ill. More and more often it was necessary to drive him into Salisbury with him in a coma, or in danger of one, on the back seat. My mother moved him into a pretty little suburban house in town near the hospitals, where he took to his bed and a couple of years later died. For the most part he was unconscious under drugs. When awake he talked obsessively (a tongue licking a nagging sore place) about "the old war." Or he remembered his youth. "I've been dreaming—Lord, to see those horses come lickety-split down the course with their necks stretched out and the sun on their coats and everyone shouting. . . . I've been dreaming how I walked along the river in the mist as the sun was rising. . . . Lord, lord, lord, what a time that was, what good times we all had then, before the old war."

1956

QUESTIONS FOR DISCUSSION

Content

a. What was Lessing's motivation for writing this article? Does she ever reveal her motives?

b. What role does physical description play in this brilliant psychological portrait? To what extent does Lessing combine description with techniques normally associated with narration?

c. Does the overall image Lessing builds of her father satisfy you? Is the behavior of her father accounted for in her description of specific, perhaps isolated, events?

d. What image does Lessing build of her father by contrasting his youth with his old age? By contrasting remembrances of the past with the present?

e. Does Lessing ever reveal who or what is the main cause of her father's deterioration? What do you think is the main cause?

f. How does World War I change Lessing's father? Why were the changes significant? What are Lessing's feelings about them?

g. Besides showing that her father relied on reminiscences to justify current situations, Lessing shows that he dreamt of future successes as a way to justify current hardships (paragraphs 26 through 28). What do reminiscing and dreaming reveal about the author's father? What do they reveal about the author?

Strategy and Style

h. In the first paragraph, Lessing says that this essay "has to be 'true.' " Why does she tell us this, and how does her insistence that the essay be true affect its content and tone?

i. Why does Lessing put quotation marks around "true"? How do you define this word? How closely does this essay conform to your definition? Must an essay be factual in order to be true?

j. Lessing uses details of her father's youth to counterbalance those about his old age, yet she must rely on his own reminiscences for information about his youth. In what ways might these reminiscences affect the essay's truthfulness?

k. Lessing distinguishes between types of memories: reminiscences (paragraph 10), living memories (paragraph 15), congealed war stories (paragraph 15), undercurrent of personal memories (paragraph 16), hallucinatory dreaming (paragraph 33). Why does she make these distinctions?

l. How objective is Lessing in recalling her father? Are there any phrases or passages that reveal positive or negative feelings about him?

SUGGESTIONS FOR SHORT WRITING

a. Annotate this essay, writing down, as well as you can remember, what you were thinking as you read. Write your comments in the margins or jot them down in your notebook.

b. Then, choose one of your annotations and write a short explanation to yourself about why you wrote that annotation.

SUGGESTIONS FOR SUSTAINED WRITING

a. Write a history of your father or mother in which you rely on photographs and reminiscences to build a "truthful" image of him or her. Keep in mind your motivation for doing this history.

b. What might a history of yourself, written by your parents, be like? How objective and/or truthful would it be? Write a history of yourself from either parent's point of view.

c. Read other essays in this anthology that use memory and personal reminiscence as a framework (for example, "No Name Woman," "Salvation," "Grandmother's Victory"). Write a reflective essay on the significance of memory as a means to create meaning and order out of past events.

Easter in Sicily*

Mary Taylor Simeti

*Born and raised in New York City, Mary Taylor Simeti (b. 1941) celebrated her
graduation from Radcliffe College in 1962 with a trip to Sicily. There she worked as a
volunteer at a center for community development started by Danilo Dolci, the social
reformer whose writings on social, cultural, and economic life in Sicily had caught
Simeti's attention while in college. After completing graduate work, she returned to Sicily,
married a young agronomist ("Tonino"), and settled there. "Easter in Sicily" first
appeared in* On Persephone's Island: A Sicilian Journal *(1986). Set against the story of
Persephone, the Greek vegetation myth about the changing of the seasons, Simeti's
journal is both a meditation and an evocative exploration of Sicilian folklore, history,
religion, and natural environment. It explains why Simeti decided to settle on this "island
of dazzling sun and bright colors." Among her other works are* Pomp and Sustenance:
Twenty-Five Centuries of Sicilian Food (1991) and A Taste of Ancient Rome *(1992).*

Beyond the vague intention of ending up at Prizzi to see the devils dance on Easter   1
afternoon, we have no set itinerary for the rest of the day and decide to drive east along
the southern coast, turning or stopping at whim. And whim soon declares itself: only
a short distance from Castelvetrano there are road signs indicating the turnoff for Selinunte, and it seems sinful not to make a stop when we have all the time in the world.

Selinunte is to me the least accessible of the Greek sites I have seen in Sicily.   2
The bare bones of a city sacked by man and toppled by earthquake lie in careless heaps
on low cliffs overlooking the sea, building blocks abandoned by some infant Titan
who has centuries since outgrown them. They are illegible in their very size, with the
tourists clambering over the enormous fluted drums of fallen columns like tiny, multicolored ants. Today it is very crowded; parking is difficult and the air rings with a
many-tongued babble and with the nagging claxons of the tourist buses gathering their
various broods. We mingle with the crowds, wander through the eastern temples, and
stroll along the road that leads down into the river valley and up to the acropolis on
the opposite cliff until the heat and the confusion persuade us to turn back.

Selinunte was a revelation the first time I came, exactly twenty years ago yes-   3
terday. Apart from Tonino and me there were no more than a dozen people here,
and even these disappeared, swallowed up by the vast sweep of sea and plain and
the immoderate proportions of the ruins. We sat for hours on some stones and stared
out across sea and centuries, the sea of flowers in the foreground no less brilliant
than the Mediterranean that sparkled in the distance. The *selinon,* the wild celery
that gave the ancient city its name, was submerged by the red of the sulla, the yellow of mayflowers and mustard, the blue of bugloss and borage, bobbing and trembling under the insistent and noisy prodding of thousands of bees. It was my first
immersion in the Sicilian spring, in its colors and its perfumes and its heat, a bap-
tism that caught and held me convert. Today the flowers are still as beautiful, the

*Editors' title.

sun perhaps even hotter, but the crowd and the confusion drown out the bees, and
the ruins are silent, unable despite their size to cope with this Lilliputian invasion.

We continue eastward and then turn north on the road for Caltabellotta, which 4
winds up over the ridge of low mountains that separates the southern coastal plain
east of Selinunte from the rolling hills of the interior. These mountains are quite barren, with patches of vineyard or wheat exploiting the rare flat spaces, an occasional
olive or almond tree clinging to the steep and rocky slopes, and, as closer inspection reveals, a sparse carpeting of the crouching, grasping plants of arid soil and
high altitudes: Purple squill, delicate white clusters of star-of-Bethlehem, the single tiny yellow-and-brown orchids of the lutea family, and the many-flowered
stalks of the *orchis italica,* bristling with minute pink tentacles.

The village of Caltabellotta lies at the summit of the highest mountain in this 5
southern ridge, topped only by two great spurs of rock that thrust up behind it like
giant tusks. The streets are narrow and zigzag steeply up the hillside; a policeman
directing all five cars' worth of traffic instructs us to park the car and continue on
foot if we want to see the procession. Of course we do, so we quickly park and follow the main street up to a point where it splits, one fork leading farther up a very
steep slope, the other curving down to the right into a tiny piazza. The "procession"
is here—townspeople and bandsmen, their instruments tucked forgotten under their
elbows, have gathered in a circle to cheer and applaud a dancing saint, a life-size
plaster statue of the Archangel Michael, the town's patron. Michael, dressed in the
armor of a Roman legionary, is leaning against a column that has been completely
wrapped in purple phlox, with a young laurel tree tied next to it so that the purple
flowers glow against the dark leaves. As in Tràpani and Castelvetrano, the flower-
decked platform that bears the statue is mounted on two poles—in this case very
long, thick wooden beams that of themselves must weigh an enormous amount—
and requires some thirty hefty young men to carry it. But "carry" is not the right
word: they rock and jostle and bounce the statue in the most extraordinary manner,
accompanied and encouraged by a crescendo of cheering and clapping from the
crowd that presses in around them. Sweat pouring off their faces, the young men
push and pull still harder on their poles, and the Archangel rocks and sways and
reels in a frenzied dance, until his porters can bear it no longer, the movement sub-
sides into a faint bobbing, and the statue itself seems to pant as the men fight to
catch their breath, still holding all the weight on their shoulders.

Bottles of water and beer are passed around, the band recovers its role and 6
starts to play again, and considerable maneuvering is necessary to effect the passage of the statue around the curve and into the main street, where it pauses at the
foot of the rise, gathering strength. Meanwhile another statue arrives, a little
winged cherub about two feet high, with platform, poles, and porters in proportion: a handful of boys about twelve years old bounce the baby statue about in
great excitement, egged on by an amused crowd.

The music dies out, and, at a sign from one of the porters, the drummer 7
sounds a roll. On the final snap of the drumsticks the men charge up the street, running and stumbling with their heavy burden up a slope so steep that the statue
seems almost horizontal. The cheers of the onlookers assist them over the top and

around the corner, quickly followed by the angel, who bobs gaily and effortlessly up the rise in the wake of his big brother.

We too turn and climb. We have lost the statues, but echoes of their progress 8 parallel to ours reach us at the street corners. A final hike up a street so sheer that the sidewalk is a flight of stairs brings us out onto the Piano della Matrice, the open square of the mother church, unexpectedly spectacular. In front of us a wide checkerboard of cobble and grass slopes gently up to the steps of the Matrice, built by Count Roger after he took Caltabellotta from the Saracens in 1090. The weathered gray stone of the Norman church blends into the sharp-toothed rock that rises abruptly behind it. On the left-hand side of the square stands the chapel of San Michele, its Gothic portal garlanded in laurel branches, and next to it a gate and a stairway carved into the live rock lead off toward the second, bigger pinnacle, ringed by the trees of the town park where the ruins of the Norman castle lie.

Commotion rising from below tells us that Saint Michael is about to make his 9 final assault on the mountain. The last steep rise is rendered more problematical by telephone wires and shop signs, and considerable measuring accompanied by animated discussion is necessary before a strategy can be agreed upon. At last somebody climbs out on a balcony and unties a laundry line, final directions are shouted out, and the group braces itself. Up they come, the initial momentum waning as they scramble up the cobbled street, their boots slipping and straining to find a grip on the polished stones. A final push and they burst into the square, where they bring up sharply, the statue swaying back and forth, evidently in some confusion as to where to go next.

One of the townsmen who has followed the progress of the statue explains 10 to us that the municipal *pro loco* committee has decided that Caltabellotta should cash in on the "Easter in Sicily" tourist boom and has organized a new procession for the afternoon, a version of the Castelvetrano Aurora, but the details have not been thought out all that well, and no one knows whether Michael should spend his lunch hour in the Matrice or in the chapel of San Michele, where the garlands declare a readiness to receive him sooner or later.

After a few false starts and some rather languishing discussion, Michael is car- 11 ried up the steps and into the dark interior of the Matrice. We start to follow it, but a priest, heretofore absent from the scene, closes the door firmly in our faces. Lunchtime. The Matrice is closed, the chapel is closed, the gate to the castle is closed. The best we can do is climb up some stone steps that lead around behind the Matrice, to discover that the rock is sheltering a miniature Alpine meadow, shaded by pine trees whose sun-warmed resin fills the air and dotted with tiny daisies, the kind whose white petals have had their tips dipped in red. I remember the flowers from a French children's book I had when I was little, and it is surprising yet suitable to find their smiling faces here in the shadow of the Norman walls. The view from the meadow is spectacular: We can look north toward the mountains of Palermo across the whole of Sicily, the hills and valleys flattened from this height into a gentle pool of green, flecked with the white foam of the blossoming fruit trees.

The priest had something, however. Our stomachs call us to more prosaic 12 questions. We discover that Caltabellotta offers a choice of two restaurants, one in the town itself and one just outside, around the back of the peak that rises above the castle ruins. Walking down toward the car we pass the first, which is occupied by a baptismal party and has no free tables. A winding road takes us out of town, past vegetable plots and tiny vineyards, to a huge baroque monastery, this too flanked by a cliff and by a charming restaurant with a trellised terrace. The proprietor is polite and extremely apologetic: A wedding reception is in progress, and there isn't a free chair in the place. Tonino, undaunted or perhaps desperate, asks if they couldn't fix us a little antipasto to go. After a brief wait the obliging host produces three foil-covered plates, a bottle of mineral water, and a round kilo loaf of fragrant, crusty bread. We drive back along the road a little way to a curve that offers space to park and some rocks to sit on. Our plates turn out to hold spicy olives, some slices of *prosciutto crudo* and of a peppery local salame, and two kinds of pecorino cheese, one fresh and mild, the other aged and sharper. With a bag of oranges from the car, the sun warm on our backs, the mountains rolling down at our feet to the southern coast and the sea beyond, where the heat haze clouds the horizon and hides Africa from view, we have as fine an Easter dinner as I have ever eaten.

The drive north to Prizzi, a rapid descent switchbacking down the north side 13 of the mountain to the green valleys we had seen from above, takes us along luxuriant riverbeds, over hills of green wheat, past isolated pear and apple trees in bloom. The hedgerows are overflowing with flowers, unable to contain such a riot of color, such an exuberance of form and texture. It is difficult to believe that in the space of a few months the velvet softness of the wheat fields, shifting from emerald to chartreuse with the wind, will give way to bristling, colorless stubble; these are the hills that the Lampedusa family cross in the Visconti film of *The Leopard,* in blinding light and smothering dust, their carriages creaking to the shrill song of the locusts.

But the extravagant hand of spring is less and less successful in concealing 14 the poverty of the agriculture the farther north we go. Our destination, the village of Prizzi, is quite high, slapped down on a hill of rock soil and stunted vegetation with none of the cozy shifting and filling with which most Sicilian towns have accommodated themselves to the bones of that island. The outskirts of the town are ringed with the usual half-finished houses, fruit of the emigrants' remittances, but once past them the streets are small and close and we are hard put to find a parking space and then to fight our way through the crowds that are thronging toward the center of town, the ranks of the Prizzitani being very much swollen by both foreign and Sicilian tourists. Tonino greets several of his students from the university, then most unexpectedly a hand claps down on my shoulder. It is Nicolò, a man who served on the school board with me. He is a native of Prizzi, a linesman for the telephone company, and after a period of technical schooling in Milan now lives in Palermo, where, fortified by his northern experience, he has become very active in the local section of the Communist party, in the neighborhood council, the trade union, and the school board. He proved a most unusual and valuable addition to the school board, able and willing to work on two levels in a way that is rare among Sicilians, ready to debate the ideological or educational implications of a policy decision and at the same time to fix a light plug or repair a busted slide projector himself rather than trusting to the lengthy meanderings of the school bureaucracy. But today he is here in Prizzi to be with his family and to see the devils dance.

We are lucky to run into him. We have arrived too late for the distribution of 15
the *cannateddi,* Prizzi's special Easter cakes, but Nicolò carries us off to the Cir-
colo della Caccia, the Hunters' Club, which the Chamber of Commerce has been
using as its headquarters for the occasion, and there he sets various cousins scur-
rying around to unearth some last undistributed *cannateddi* for us, oval cakes of
biscuit dough braided about an egg.

Cannateddi in hand, we follow Nicolò out again and push our way along the 16
main street, which dips sharply down, then rises again in the distance. Nicolò
guides us to the lowest point in the street, where he tells us to stay put, this being
a grandstand seat for watching the triumph of Good over Evil. The street is filled
with people, strolling, talking, and shouting across from one crowded balcony to
another. Here at the bottom we can look up in either direction at a sea of faces. A
small and hornèd vortex is descending upon us from the eastern end: the devils are
coming, accompanied by the clanking of their chains and the squealing and shouting of a swarm of little boys. There are three masked figures, two devils escorting
Death. Death is dressed in yellow, a big, loose-fitting yellow jump suit and a yellow mask of soldered tin covering his whole head in the shape of a skull, in which
have been cut eyeholes, a black dent for the nose, and a mouth grinning around a
few long and crooked teeth. Under his arm is a crossbow with which he menaces
the crowd. The devils have rust-colored jump suits, ample enough to accommodate a variety of figures over the years, and their masks are large, flat tin ovals,
painted brown, with curved horns, long noses, and tongues sticking out from leer-
ing mouths. The backs of their heads and shoulders are covered by heavy, long-
haired goat pelts, black for one, white for the other, a touch of the genuine that is
somehow much more menacing than the masks themselves. The multicolored
stripes of Adidas sneakers show underneath the baggy trouser legs.

Comfortable shoes are a must for the devils, whose loping, lolloping dance be- 17
trays considerable weariness. Well it may, says Nicolò: they have been dancing ever
since the hour of the Crucifixion on Friday, chasing about the town making mischief
and teasing all they encounter. Nicolò was a devil one year and assures us that the costumes are unbearably hot and heavy, especially on a sunny day like today—the only
thing that keeps you going is the wine. Anyone whom Death manages to hit with his
crossbow is obliged to stand the devils a round at the nearest tavern, and if Death is a
good shot, they all have quite a bit under their jump suits by the end of the day.

There is movement up at either end of the street, and for the second time to- 18
day we are shoved back against the buildings by white-gloved policemen. The
street is long and I can barely make out the Madonna to the east, Christ to the west,
and just hear the loudest notes of the band. Down the hill come the forces of Good,
two angels in armor, with cardboard wings, red capes, ropes of beads and gilt chains
across their breasts, swords in hand, and strange flat-topped helmets that Francesco
is quick to notice have been cut out from Alemagna panettone boxes. The devils at
first have the best of these bizarre apparitions; a brief skirmish leads to a hasty retreat, and then a counterattack. Back and forth they run and clash and feint as the
statues continue their slow but steady descent. The battlefield shrinks as the statues
draw nearer, the dance and the swordwork grow more and more frenzied as the dev-

ils find themselves hemmed in between the advancing figures, until a last and desperate leap marks the meeting between the risen Christ and the rejoicing Madonna, and Death and the devils fall to earth, vanquished and immobile.

This scene will be repeated four more times this evening, the last time in the dark in the big piazza in front of the Matrice, at the top of the hill. Nicolò urges us to stay, but it is a long way back to Bosco and it is already half past five, so we say good-bye. Drunk with all that we have seen, my cheeks burning from the sun and wind, and my eyes watering, I can hardly take in the landscape we drive through, nor do I notice where we are when Tonino turns his attention from the road to give me a reproachful glance.   19

"When I was a boy, I spent all my time *avoiding* processions!"   20

1986

QUESTIONS FOR DISCUSSION

Content

a. Simeti finds examples of both Gothic and Norman architectural styles in Caltabellota. Use an encyclopedia or unabridged dictionary to learn more about these styles. You might also want to consult an encyclopedia to learn a little about the history and geography of Sicily.

b. Is Simeti describing religious rituals, or is her focus on the people and places that give those rituals their special characters? Can you think of another reason she might have written this essay?

c. Why aren't Simeti and her husband, Tonino, upset about not being able to follow the statue of St. Michael into the Matrice? What does this tell you about the writer and her attitude about what she is witnessing?

d. At the essay's conclusion, we learn that the author and her husband are "Drunk with all that [they] have seen." What is Simeti driving at? If you could write a thesis statement for this essay, what would it be?

Strategy and Style

e. This essay is about the most important feast in the Christian calendar. Why, then, does the author begin with a visit to the ruins of Selinunte, a pre-Christian Greek settlement?

f. Paragraphs 4 and 5 reveal Simeti's ability to focus closely on a subject and describe it in fine detail. Where else in the essay is her ability to do this evident?

g. "Easter in Sicily" is heavy with narrative detail, yet its primary purpose is to describe, not to narrate. What defines this essay as descriptive?

h. This is a three-part essay, organized around places Simeti visits: Selinunte, Caltabellota, and Prizzi. Nonetheless, it remains unified and flows smoothly. What do the three parts of this essay have in common? What is the "glue" that holds them together?

i. What in Simeti's style tells us that this essay is aimed at readers who may not know much about Sicilian culture?
j. How would you define Simeti's tone—her attitude toward her subject? In what way is it appropriate to an essay that describes religious rituals?
k. What is the author's attitude toward the people who take part in the processions she observes?
l. This essay incorporates details from all of the senses. Identify places in the text that appeal to each of the five senses.

SUGGESTIONS FOR SHORT WRITING

a. Using a list, an outline, or freewriting, write down what you consider the most important features or aspects of a religious or civic ceremony with which you are very familiar or in which you have participated.
b. This essay displays Simeti's ability to paint lavish word pictures. Take paragraphs 12 and 18, for example. Write a paragraph that focuses on a street scene or landscape. Describe your subject by filling your paragraph with visual details (color, size, shape, etc.) about the people, animals, vegetation, and objects you see. However, try to use information from the other senses as well.

SUGGESTIONS FOR SUSTAINED WRITING

a. Write a letter to a friend or classmate who is planning a first visit to a city or area that you have been to and remember well. Make your letter a kind of travel guide that will describe buildings, monuments, shops, markets, museums, historic homes, natural phenomena, or other points of interest. Like Simeti, also prepare your reader for the people and attractions he or she might encounter. Whether the place you write about is in your own country or in another country, focus on a limited area. For example, writing about three or four neighborhoods in San Francisco is preferable to recalling your two-week trip to northern California.
b. Simeti uses description to explain ritual, specifically how she and others celebrated a religious holiday. Take your lead from "Easter in Sicily" by describing the rituals associated with a holiday, religious or not, that you know well. Focus on the visual, but whenever possible, rely on your other senses for information. For example, Simeti uses both visual and auditory details in paragraph 16. In paragraph 12, she appeals to several senses. If you responded to the first of the Suggestions for Short Writing above, you may have already gathered material to use in your essay.

3

Process Analysis

Often thought of as a way to develop scientific papers, process analysis can be used with a variety of topics and in combination with many of the other methods of development illustrated in this text. It is the type of writing used to convey instructions—how to change a tire, write a research paper, take someone's temperature, cook a carp, or paint a fresco! Process analysis can also explain how something happens or happened—the birth of a planet, the way you convinced your boss to give you a raise, or even the workings of a rodeo.

Like narratives, essays on such topics generally follow chronological order, with each step in the process likened to events in a well-developed plot. Much is made of transitional words and phrases to keep the reader on the right track. "First," Euell Gibbons tells us, "instead of merely scaling the fish [my brother] skinned them." And like any good storyteller, the writer of process analysis usually begins at the beginning and follows through to the end, sometimes listing steps by number but always providing sufficient detail to help the reader picture the activity accurately and concretely.

Sometimes writers of process analysis infuse their work with vivid, if not unnerving, description like the kind we find in Jessica Mitford's "Behind the Formaldehyde Curtain." More often than not, however, process papers also explain the relationship of causes and effects, as in Alexander Petrunkevitch's "The Spider and the Wasp."

Nonetheless, the purpose of process analysis is instructive in the most practical sense: Narration and description may show *what* happens, causal analysis may explain *why* it happens, but process analysis always focuses on *how* it happens. The most important aspect of any process essay, therefore, is clarity. Readers will not follow unless your explanations are complete, your language is familiar, and your organization is simple. Take your lead from Richard Marius, who lists important advice and information about writing in easy-to-follow steps. And

98

whenever you give instructions, pay your readers the courtesy of preparing them for the task by mentioning required tools, materials, and expectations, as does Adam Goodheart in "How to Paint a Fresco."

Of course, explaining a process does not give you license to produce prose that is dull. Gretel Ehrlich's "The Rules of the Game: Rodeo," a spirited explanation of what happens at an Oklahoma rodeo, keeps us riveted to the page while offering advice on, of all things, "starting out fresh in a marriage." Sue Hubbell's "Honey Harvest" offers comic relief while explaining a process that is potentially painful and dangerous.

Like selections in other parts of this text, those that appear here represent a variety of subjects, approaches, and styles. But there is a common denominator. As you might expect, the selections that follow are models of clarity, but their authors never seem cold and detached, even when explaining what might first seem recondite or abstract. The committed, sometimes impassioned, voice of the writer always comes through. That is probably why we read these sometimes "technical" pieces with alacrity. Each selection has something important to teach us, but the lesson has relatively little to do with the process its author describes. What we learn here is a need to respect the reader, to understand our attitude toward the subject, and to believe that what we have to say is important.

The Spider and the Wasp

Alexander Petrunkevitch

Alexander Petrunkevitch (1875–1964) arrived in the United States around the turn of the century after having studied in Russia, his native country, and in Germany. A world-famous zoologist, Petrunkevitch taught at several American universities including Harvard and Yale. As an expert on spiders, he published what is now a standard reference in the field: Index Catalogue of Spiders of North, Central and South America. *Like James Rettie and Claudia Glenn Dowling, Petrunkevitch writes scientific prose that, while accurate and well documented, is colorful, exciting, and accessible to readers with little scientific training. "The Spider and the Wasp" first appeared in* Scientific American *in 1952.*

To hold its own in the struggle for existence, every species of animal must have a 1 regular source of food, and if it happens to live on other animals, its survival may be very delicately balanced. The hunter cannot exist without the hunted; if the latter should perish from the earth, the former would, too. When the hunted also prey on some of the hunters, the matter may become complicated.

This is nowhere better illustrated than in the insect world. Think of the com- 2 plexity of a situation such as the following: There is a certain wasp, *Pimpla inquisitor,* whose larvae feed on the larvae of the tussock moth. *Pimpla* larvae in turn serve as food for the larvae of a second wasp, and the latter in their turn nourish still a third wasp. What subtle balance between fertility and mortality must exist in the case of each of these four species to prevent the extinction of all of them! An excess of mortality over fertility in a single member of the group would ultimately wipe out all four.

This is not a unique case. The two great orders of insects, Hymenoptera and 3 Diptera, are full of such examples of interrelationship. And the spiders (which are not insects but members of a separate order of arthropods) also are killers and victims of insects.

In the feeding and safeguarding of their progeny the insects and spiders ex- 4 hibit some interesting analogies to reasoning and some crass examples of blind instinct. The case I propose to describe here is that of the tarantula spiders and their arch-enemy, the digger wasps of the genus Pepsis. It is a classic example of what looks like intelligence pitted against instinct—a strange situation in which the victim, though fully able to defend itself, submits unwittingly to its destruction.

A fertilized female tarantula lays from 200 to 400 eggs at a time; thus it is 5 possible for a single tarantula to produce several thousand young. She takes no care of them beyond weaving a cocoon of silk to enclose the eggs. After they hatch, the young walk away, find convenient places in which to dig their burrows and spend the rest of their lives in solitude. Tarantulas feed mostly on insects and millipedes. Once their appetite is appeased, they digest the food for several days before eating again. Their sight is poor, being limited to sensing a change in the intensity of light and to the perception of moving objects. They apparently have little or no sense of hearing, for a hungry tarantula will pay no attention to a loudly chirping cricket placed in its cage unless the insect happens to touch one of its legs.

But all spiders, and especially hairy ones, have an extremely delicate sense 6 of touch. Laboratory experiments prove that tarantulas can distinguish three types of touch: pressure against the body wall, stroking of the body hair, and riffling of certain very fine hairs on the legs called trichobothria. Pressure against the body, by a finger or the end of a pencil, causes the tarantula to move off slowly for a short distance. The touch excites no defensive response unless the approach is from above where the spider can see the motion, in which case it rises on its hind legs, lifts its front legs, opens its fangs and holds this threatening posture as long as the object continues to move. When the motion stops, the spider drops back to the ground, remains quiet for a few seconds and then moves slowly away.

The entire body of a tarantula, especially its legs, is thickly clothed with hair. 7 Some of it is short and woolly, some long and stiff. Touching this body hair produces one of two distinct reactions. When the spider is hungry, it responds with an immediate and swift attack. At the touch of a cricket's antennae the tarantula seizes the insect so swiftly that a motion picture taken at the rate of 64 frames per second shows only the result and not the process of capture. But when the spider is not hungry, the stimulation of its hairs merely causes it to shake the touched limb. An insect can walk under its hairy belly unharmed.

The trichobothria, very fine hairs growing from disklike membranes on the 8 legs, were once thought to be the spider's hearing organs, but we now know that they have nothing to do with sound. They are sensitive only to air movement. A light breeze makes them vibrate slowly without disturbing the common hair. When one blows gently on the trichobothria, the tarantula reacts with a quick jerk of its four front legs. If the front and hind legs are stimulated at the same time, the spider makes a sudden jump. This reaction is quite independent of the state of its appetite.

These three tactile responses—to pressure on the body wall, to moving of 9 the common hair and to flexing of the trichobothria—are so different from one another that there is no possibility of confusing them. They serve the tarantula adequately for most of its needs and enable it to avoid most annoyances and dangers. But they fail the spider completely when it meets its deadly enemy, the digger wasp Pepsis.

These solitary wasps are beautiful and formidable creatures. Most species 10 are either a deep shiny blue all over, or deep blue with rusty wings. The largest have a wing span of about four inches. They live on nectar. When excited, they give off a pungent odor—a warning that they are ready to attack. The sting is much worse than that of a bee or common wasp, and the pain and swelling last longer. In the adult stage the wasp lives only a few months. The female produces but a few eggs, one at a time at intervals of two or three days. For each egg the mother must provide one adult tarantula, alive but paralyzed. The tarantula must be of the correct species to nourish the larva. The mother wasp attaches the egg to the paralyzed spider's abdomen. Upon hatching from the egg, the larva is many hundreds of times smaller than its living but helpless victim. It eats no other food and drinks no water. By the time it has finished its single gargantuan meal and becomes ready for wasphood, nothing remains of the tarantula but its indigestible chitinous skeleton.

The mother wasp goes tarantula-hunting when the egg in her ovary is almost 11 ready to be laid. Flying low over the ground late on a sunny afternoon, the wasp looks for its victim or for the mouth of a tarantula burrow, a round hole edged by a bit of silk. The sex of the spider makes no difference, but the mother is highly discriminating as to species. Each species of Pepsis requires a certain species of tarantula, and the wasp will not attack the wrong species. In a cage with a tarantula which is not its normal prey the wasp avoids the spider, and is usually killed by it in the night.

Yet when a wasp finds the correct species, it is the other way about. To iden- 12 tify the species the wasp apparently must explore the spider with her antennae. The tarantula shows an amazing tolerance to this exploration. The wasp crawls under it and walks over it without evoking any hostile response. The molestation is so great and so persistent that the tarantula often rises on all eight legs, as if it were on stilts. It may stand this way for several minutes. Meanwhile the wasp, having satisfied itself that the victim is of the right species, moves off a few inches to dig the spider's grave. Working vigorously with legs and jaws, it excavates a hole 8 to 10 inches deep with a diameter slightly larger than the spider's girth. Now and again the wasp pops out of the hole to make sure that the spider is still there.

When the grave is finished, the wasp returns to the tarantula to complete 13 her ghastly enterprise. First she feels it all over once more with her antennae. Then her behavior becomes more aggressive. She bends her abdomen, protruding her sting, and searches for the soft membrane at the point where the spider's leg joins its body—the only spot where she can penetrate the horny skeleton. From time to time, as the exasperated spider slowly shifts ground, the wasp turns on her back and slides along with the aid of her wings, trying to get under the tarantula for a shot at the vital spot. During all this maneuvering, which can last for several minutes, the tarantula makes no move to save itself. Finally the wasp corners it against some obstruction and grasps one of its legs in her powerful jaws. Now at last the harassed spider tries a desperate but vain defense. The two contestants roll over and over on the ground. It is a terrifying sight and the outcome is always the same. The wasp finally manages to thrust her sting into the soft spot and holds it there for a few seconds while she pumps in the poison. Almost immediately the tarantula falls paralyzed on its back. Its legs stop twitching; its heart stops beating, yet it is not dead, as is shown by the fact that if taken from the wasp it can be restored to some sensitivity by being kept in a moist chamber for several months.

After paralyzing the tarantula, the wasp cleans herself by dragging her body 14 along the ground and rubbing her feet, sucks the drop of blood oozing from the wound in the spider's abdomen, then grabs a leg of the flabby, helpless animal in her jaws and drags it down to the bottom of the grave. She stays there for many minutes, sometimes for several hours, and what she does all that time in the dark we do not know. Eventually she lays her egg and attaches it to the side of the spider's abdomen with a sticky secretion. Then she emerges, fills the grave with soil carried bit by bit in her jaws, and finally tramples the ground all around to hide any trace of the grave from prowlers. Then she flies away, leaving her descendant safely started in life.

In all this the behavior of the wasp evidently is qualitatively different from   15
that of the spider. The wasp acts like an intelligent animal. This is not to say that instinct plays no part or that she reasons as man does. But her actions are to the point; they are not automatic and can be modified to fit the situation. We do not know for certain how she identifies the tarantula—probably it is by some olfactory or chemo-tactile sense—but she does it purposefully and does not blindly tackle a wrong species.

On the other hand, the tarantula's behavior shows only confusion. Evidently   16
the wasp's pawing gives it no pleasure, for it tries to move away. That the wasp is not simulating sexual stimulation is certain, because male and female tarantulas react in the same way to its advances. That the spider is not anesthetized by some odorless secretion is easily shown by blowing lightly at the tarantula and making it jump suddenly. What, then, makes the tarantula behave as stupidly as it does?

No clear, simple answer is available. Possibly the stimulation by the wasp's   17
antennae is masked by a heavier pressure on the spider's body, so that it reacts as when prodded by a pencil. But the explanation may be much more complex. Initiative in attack is not in the nature of tarantulas; most species fight only when cornered so that escape is impossible. Their inherited patterns of behavior apparently prompt them to avoid problems rather than attack them. For example, spiders always weave their webs in three dimensions, and when a spider finds that there is insufficient space to attach certain threads in the third dimension, it leaves the place and seeks another, instead of finishing the web in a single plane. This urge to escape seems to arise under all circumstances, in all phases of life and to take the place of reasoning. For a spider to change the pattern of its web is as impossible as for an inexperienced man to build a bridge across a chasm obstructing his way.

In a way the instinctive urge to escape is not only easier but often more ef-   18
ficient than reasoning. The tarantula does exactly what is most efficient in all cases except in an encounter with a ruthless and determined attacker dependent for the existence of her own species on killing as many tarantulas as she can lay eggs. Perhaps in this case the spider follows its usual pattern of trying to escape, instead of seizing and killing the wasp, because it is not aware of its danger. In any case, the survival of the tarantula species as a whole is protected by the fact that the spider is much more fertile than the wasp.

1952

QUESTIONS FOR DISCUSSION

Content

a. In paragraph 1, Petrunkevitch claims that, for some species, "survival may be very delicately balanced." How does this statement relate to the rest of the essay?

b. How does the word "complicated" (paragraph 1) prepare the reader for what is to follow?

c. Based on your reading of this essay, in what way(s) is process analysis similar to narration?

d. Petrunkevitch makes it a point to describe a number of significant differences between the spider and the wasp. Identify a few of these. Why are they significant?

e. As you probably inferred from the two questions before this one, a variety of techniques, including narration and contrast, can be used to explain a process. What function does description play in this essay?

f. What, according to Petrunkevitch, may account for the tarantula's unwitting acceptance of its own destruction?

Strategy and Style

g. Outline Petrunkevitch's major points in an attempt to trace the organization of the essay.

h. Given the fact that this selection was first published in *Scientific American,* it is probably safe to assume that Petrunkevitch was writing for a highly educated reader but one who may not have had formal training in zoology. Comment upon his use of technical language. Why does the author stop to define unfamiliar words?

i. Petrunkevitch's tone is typically scientific—detached and objective—through most of this selection. At times, however, his language seems highly emotional and charged with excitement. Analyze his choice of words in these instances. What are the connotations of words such as *desperate* and *ghostly?* What images does Petrunkevitch evoke with phrases such as "she pumps in the poison" (paragraph 13)?

SUGGESTIONS FOR SHORT WRITING

a. Summarize, the battle between the spider and the wasp in one short paragraph.

b. Closely observe a pet, if you have one, or an animal in a park or zoo for fifteen or twenty minutes, and describe its behavior.

SUGGESTIONS FOR SUSTAINED WRITING

a. Write an explanation (process analysis) about the way in which an animal undertakes a task necessary to its survival or the survival of its species. Topics to choose from might include how a beaver constructs a dam, how ants build colonies, how deer forage for food, or how birds care for their young. In addition to observing animals firsthand, you might also want to research this topic in your college library.

b. In many ways, "The Spider and the Wasp" is a study in contrasts. Choose two animals or types of animals that, while apparently similar, exhibit distinctive differences in "personality" or behavior. For instance, compare two house pets, two kinds of saltwater fish you have caught, a hawk and a crow, or two common insects.

c. As the author points out, nature can be cruel and terrifying. Write a description of a natural process that you find frightening, painful, or unpleasant. Be as specific as you can in conveying an objective picture of the process but, like Petrunkevitch, do not hesitate to allow your emotions to influence your writing.

How to Cook a Carp

Euell Gibbons

Euell Gibbons (1911–1975) was born and raised in Clarkesville, Texas, but left home when he was 15. He worked in Texas and New Mexico as a harvest hand, a cowboy, a carpenter, and a trapper before joining the army in 1934. After his discharge in 1936, he moved to Washington where he continued working odd jobs. He joined the Communist party but resigned when the Soviet Union attacked Finland in 1939. During World War II, he worked for the U.S. Navy as a civilian boat builder. After the war, he moved to Hawaii and turned beachcomber, living in a thatched hut for two years and subsisting entirely on wild food. He entered the University of Hawaii as a freshman at the age of 36. Shortly thereafter, he began a career of teaching, writing, and lecturing about wild foods. His books on foraging for wild foods combine detailed how-to instructions and recipes with delightfully entertaining narrative. Among his best-known works are Stalking the Wild Asparagus *(1962), from which "How to Cook a Carp" is taken;* Stalking the Blue-Eyed Scallop *(1964);* Stalking the Healthful Herbs *(1966); and* Euell Gibbons's Beachcomber's Handbook *(1967).*

When I was a lad of about eighteen, my brother and I were working on a cattle ranch in New Mexico that bordered on the Rio Grande. Most Americans think of the Rio Grande as a warm southern stream, but it rises among the high mountains of Colorado, and in the spring it is fed by melting snows. At this time of the year, the water that rushed by the ranch was turbulent, icy-cold and so silt-laden as to be semisolid. "A little too thick to drink, and a little too thin to plow" was a common description of the waters of the Rio Grande.

A few species of fish inhabited this muddy water. Unfortunately, the most common was great eight- to ten-pound carp, a fish that is considered very poor eating in this country, although the Germans and Asiatics have domesticated this fish, and have developed some varieties that are highly esteemed for the table.

On the ranch where we worked, there was a drainage ditch that ran through the lower pasture and emptied its clear waters into the muddy Rio Grande. The carp swimming up the river would strike this clear warmer water and decide they preferred it to the cold mud they had been inhabiting. One spring day, a cowhand who had been riding that way reported that Clear Ditch was becoming crowded with huge carp.

On Sunday we decided to go fishing. Four of us armed ourselves with pitch-forks, saddled our horses and set out. Near the mouth of the ditch, the water was running about two feet deep and twelve to sixteen feet wide. There is a saying in that part of the country that you can't get a cowboy to do anything unless it can be done from the back of a horse, so we forced our mounts into the ditch and started wading them upstream, four abreast, herding the carp before us.

By the time we had ridden a mile upstream, the water was less than a foot deep and so crystal clear that we could see our herd of several hundred carp still fleeing from the splashing, wading horses. As the water continued to shallow, our fish began to get panicky. A few of the boldest ones attempted to dart back past us and were impaled on pitchforks. We could see that the whole herd was getting rest-

106

less and was about to stampede back downstream, so we piled off our horses into the shallow water to meet the charge. The water boiled about us as the huge fish swirled past us and we speared madly in every direction with our pitchforks, throwing each fish we managed to hit over the ditch bank. This was real fishing— cowhand style. The last of the fish herd was by us in a few minutes and it was all over, but we had caught a tremendous quantity of fish.

Back at the ranch house, after we had displayed our trophies, we began won- 6 dering what we were going to do with so many fish. This started a series of typical cowboy tall tales on "how to cook a carp." The best of these yarns was told by a griz- zled old *vaquero,* who claimed he had made his great discovery when he ran out of food while camping on a tributary of the Rio Grande. He said that he had found the finest way to cook a carp was to plaster the whole fish with a thick coating of fresh cow manure and bury it in the hot ashes of a campfire. In an hour or two, he said, the casing of cow manure had become black and very hard. He then related how he had removed the fish from the fire, broken the hard shell with the butt of his Winchester and peeled it off. He said that as the manure came off the scales and skin adhered to it, leaving the baked fish, white and clean. He then ended by saying, "Of course, the carp still wasn't fit to eat, but the manure in which it was cooked tasted pretty good."

There were also some serious suggestions and experiments. The chief ob- 7 jection to the carp is that its flesh is full of many forked bones. One man said that he had enjoyed carp sliced very thin and fried so crisp that one could eat it, bones and all. He demonstrated, and you really could eat it without the bones bothering you, but it was still far from being an epicurean dish. One cowboy described the flavor as "a perfect blend of Rio Grande mud and rancid hog lard."

Another man said that he had eaten carp that had been cooked in a pressure 8 cooker until the bones softened and became indistinguishable from the flesh. A pressure cooker is almost a necessity at that altitude, so we had one at the ranch house. We tried this method, and the result was barely edible. It tasted like the poorest possible grade of canned salmon flavored with a bit of mud. It was, how- ever, highly appreciated by the dogs and cats on the ranch, and solved the prob- lem of what to do with the bulk of the fish we had caught.

It was my brother who finally devised a method of cooking carp that not only 9 made it fit for human consumption, but actually delicious. First, instead of merely scaling the fish, he skinned them. Then, taking a large pinch, where the meat was thickest, he worked his fingers and thumb into the flesh until he struck the median bones, then he worked his thumb and fingers together and tore off a handful of meat. Using this tearing method, he could get two or three goodsized chunks of flesh from each side of the fish. He then heated a pot of bland vegetable shortening, rubbed the pieces of fish with salt and dropped them into the hot fat. He used no flour, meal, crumbs or seasoning other than salt. They cooked to a golden brown in a few min- utes, and everyone pronounced them "mighty fine eating." The muddy flavor seemed to have been eliminated by removing the skin and the large bones. The forked bones were still there, but they had not been multiplied by cutting across them, and one only had to remove several bones still intact with the fork from each piece of fish.

For the remainder of that spring, every few days one or another of the cow- 10
boys would take a pitchfork and ride over to Clear Ditch and spear a mess of carp.
On these evenings, my brother replaced the regular *cocinero* and we enjoyed some
delicious fried carp.

The flavor of carp varies with the water from which it is caught. Many years 11
after the above incidents I attended a fish fry at my brother's house. The main
course was all of his own catching, and consisted of bass, catfish and carp, all from
Elephant Butte Lake farther down the Rio Grande. All the fish were prepared exactly alike, except that the carp was pulled apart as described above, while the bass
and catfish, being all twelve inches or less in length, were merely cleaned and fried
whole. None of his guests knew one fish from another, yet all of them preferred
the carp to the other kinds. These experiences have convinced me that the carp is
really a fine food fish when properly prepared.

Carp can, of course, be caught in many ways besides spearing them with 12
pitchforks from the back of a horse. In my adopted home state, Pennsylvania, they
are classed as "trash fish" and one is allowed to take them almost any way. They
will sometimes bite on worms, but they are vegetarians by preference and are more
easily taken on dough balls. Some states allow the use of gill nets, and other states,
because they would like to reduce the population of this unpopular fish, will issue
special permits for the use of nets to catch carp.

A good forager will take advantage of the lax regulations on carp fishing 13
while they last. When all fishermen realize that the carp is really a good food fish
when prepared in the right way, maybe this outsized denizen of our rivers and
lakes will no longer be considered a pest and will take his rightful place among
our valued food and game fishes

1962

QUESTIONS FOR DISCUSSION

Content

a. What do you think is Gibbons's goal in writing this essay? How successful is
   he in reaching this goal?
b. How would you describe Gibbons's ideal reader? If you were that reader, what
   use would this essay be to you?
c. Is there an argument implied in this essay? If so, how would you phrase the argument? What would the counterargument be?
d. Carp is common throughout North America. Besides the obvious reason that
   the essay is based on personal experience, why would Gibbons set his narrative in the ranch country along the Rio Grande and not some other locale? How
   would the essay be different if it were set in, for example, Gibbons's "adopted
   home state, Pennsylvania"?

Strategy and Style

e. Though Gibbons titles his essay "How to Cook a Carp," he does not actually describe the process until paragraph 9. What does he do first, and what are his reasons for providing this long introduction?

f. Gibbons was an expert on foraging for and cooking wild plants and game, and this essay appears in one of his popular books about foraging. Why, then, does he describe so many failed attempts at cooking carp? Do these accounts add to or detract from his authority as an expert?

g. How do anecdotes such as the account of catching carp with pitchforks or the tale of the "old *vaquero*" (paragraphs 5 and 6) affect the essay? What purpose do they serve other than entertaining the reader?

h. What metaphors does Gibbons use to describe carp and the process of catching them? What effect do these metaphors have on the essay? On you?

SUGGESTIONS FOR SHORT WRITING

a. Have some fun and write a recipe for an inedible, or seemingly inedible, product. Include directions on how to capture or collect it, how to prepare it, and how to serve it.

b. Write an anecdote of a time when you tried an unusual food.

SUGGESTIONS FOR SUSTAINED WRITING

a. Write a narrative essay that explains how you accomplished a common but important task. Limit your essay to a simple process that can be explained fully in three or four typewritten pages. For example, explain how you learned to hang wallpaper, cook a Thanksgiving turkey, load software into a home computer, do laundry, set up an aquarium, change the oil in a car, or plant a vegetable patch. Put your comments in the form of a letter to a friend or classmate who has asked for instructions about a process you know well. Assume that your reader knows little about the process.

b. Recall (or create) a personal experience in which you learned by trial and error how to do something well. Write a descriptive account of this series of processes.

c. Write an essay in which you convince your readers to change their minds about some process they now consider uninteresting, difficult, or unimportant. Make them see that washing the dog, studying for final exams, or going on a special diet, for instance, might be fun, easy, or beneficial if they only understood the process as well as you do. Include an account of the process.

d. Conduct interviews and collect anecdotes and tall tales that relate to a process. Include them in an essay in which you explain, record, or satirize the process.

Behind the Formaldehyde Curtain

Jessica Mitford

Born in Great Britain to parents who were members of the nobility, Jessica Mitford (b. 1917) immigrated to the United States in 1939. In 1960, she published the first volume of her autobiography, Daughters and Rebels, *in which she described what it is like to grow up in an aristocratic English household and to receive one's education at home. The title of this book was to prove prophetic, for much of Mitford's later work is social criticism. For instance,* The American Way of Death *(1963), from which this selection is taken, is an indictment of morticians and their profession as well as of American funeral customs in general. In* Kind and Unusual Punishment: The Prison Business *(1973), Mitford exposes the scandal of the U.S. corrections system. In 1977, Mitford published the second part of her autobiography,* A Fine Old Madness. *Since then, she has published* Faces of Philip: A Memoir of Philip Toynbee *(1984) and* Grace Had an English Heart: The Story of Grace Darling *(1988).*

The drama begins to unfold with the arrival of the corpse at the mortuary.   1

Alas, poor Yorick! How surprised he would be to see how his counterpart of   2 today is whisked off to a funeral parlor and is in short order sprayed, sliced, pierced, pickled, trussed, trimmed, creamed, waxed, painted, rouged and neatly dressed—transformed from a common corpse into a Beautiful Memory Picture. This process is known in the trade as embalming and restorative art, and is so universally employed in the United States and Canada that the funeral director does it routinely, without consulting corpse or kin. He regards as eccentric those few who are hardy enough to suggest that it might be dispensed with. Yet no law requires embalming, no religious doctrine commends it, nor is it dictated by considerations of health, sanitation, or even of personal daintiness. In no part of the world but in Northern America is it widely used. The purpose of embalming is to make the corpse presentable for viewing in a suitably costly container; and here too the funeral director routinely, without first consulting the family, prepares the body for public display.

Is all this legal? The processes to which a dead body may be subjected are   3 after all to some extent circumscribed by law. In most states, for instance, the signature of next of kin must be obtained before an autopsy may be performed, before the deceased may be cremated, before the body may be turned over to a medical school for research purposes; or such provision must be made in the decedent's will. In the case of embalming, no such permission is required nor is it ever sought. A textbook, *The Principles and Practices of Embalming,* comments on this: "There is some question regarding the legality of much that is done within the preparation room." The author points out that it would be most unusual for a responsible member of a bereaved family to instruct the mortician, in so many words, to *"embalm"* the body of a deceased relative. The very term "embalming" is so seldom used that the mortician must rely upon custom in the matter. The author concludes that unless the family specifies otherwise, the act of entrusting the body to the care of a funeral establishment carries with it an implied permission to go ahead and embalm.

Embalming is indeed a most extraordinary procedure, and one must wonder 4 at the docility of Americans who each year pay hundreds of millions of dollars for its perpetuation, blissfully ignorant of what it is all about, what is done, how it is done. Not one in ten thousand has any idea of what actually takes place. Books on the subject are extremely hard to come by. They are not to be found in most libraries or bookshops.

In an era when huge television audiences watch surgical operations in the 5 comfort of their living rooms, when, thanks to the animated cartoon, the geography of the digestive system has become familiar territory even to the nursery school set, in a land where the satisfaction of curiosity about almost all matters is a national pastime, the secrecy surrounding embalming can, surely, hardly be attributed to the inherent gruesomeness of the subject. Custom in this regard has within this century suffered a complete reversal. In the early days of American embalming, when it was performed in the home of the deceased, it was almost mandatory for some relative to stay by the embalmer's side and witness the procedure. Today, family members who might wish to be in attendance would certainly be dissuaded by the funeral director. All others, except apprentices, are excluded by law from the preparation room.

A close look at what does actually take place may explain in large measure 6 the undertaker's intractable reticence concerning a procedure that has become his major *raison d'être*. It is possible he fears that public information about embalming might lead patrons to wonder if they really want this service? If the funeral men are loath to discuss the subject outside the trade, the reader may, understandably, be equally loath to go on reading at this point. For those who have the stomach for it, let us part the formaldehyde curtain. . . .

The body is first laid out in the undertaker's morgue—or rather, Mr. Jones 7 is reposing in the preparation room—to be readied to bid the world farewell.

The preparation room in any of the better funeral establishments has the 8 tiled and sterile look of a surgery, and indeed the embalmer-restorative artist who does his chores there is beginning to adopt the term "dermasurgeon" (appropriately corrupted by some mortician-writers as "demi-surgeon") to describe his calling. His equipment, consisting of scalpels, scissors, augers, forceps, clamps, needles, pumps, tubes, bowls, and basins, is crudely imitative of the surgeon's, as is his technique, acquired in a nine- or twelve-month post-highschool course in an embalming school. He is supplied by an advanced chemical industry with a bewildering array of fluids, sprays, pastes, oils, powders, creams, to fix or soften tissue, shrink or distend it as needed, dry it here, restore the moisture there. There are cosmetics, waxes and paints to fill and cover features, even plaster of Paris to replace entire limbs. There are ingenious aids to prop and stabilize the cadaver: A Vari-Pose Head Rest, the Edwards Arm and Hand Positioner, the Repose Block (to support the shoulders during the embalming), and the Throop Foot Positioner, which resembles an old-fashioned stock.

Mr. John H. Eckels, president of the Eckels College of Mortuary Science, 9 thus describes the first part of the embalming procedure: "In the hands of a skilled practitioner, this work may be done in a comparatively short time and without mutilating the body other than by slight incision—so slight that it scarcely would cause serious inconvenience if made upon a living person. It is necessary to remove the blood, and doing this not only helps in the disinfecting, but removes the principal cause of disfigurements due to discoloration."

Another textbook discusses the all-important time element: "The earlier this 10 is done, the better, for every hour that elapses between death and embalming will add to the problems and complications encountered. . . ." Just how soon should one get going on the embalming? The author tells us, "On the basis of such scanty information made available to this profession through its rudimentary and haphazard system of technical research, we must conclude that the best results are to be obtained if the subject is embalmed before life is completely extinct—that is, before cellular death has occurred. In the average case, this would mean within an hour after somatic death." For those who feel that there is something a little rudimentary, not to say haphazard, about this advice, a comforting thought is offered by another writer. Speaking of fears entertained in early days of premature burial, he points out, "One of the effects of embalming by chemical injection, however, has been to dispel fears of live burial." How true; once the blood is removed, chances of live burial are indeed remote.

To return to Mr. Jones, the blood is drained out through the veins and re- 11 placed by embalming fluid pumped in through the arteries. As noted in *The Principles and Practices of Embalming,* "every operator has a favorite injection and drainage point—a fact which becomes a handicap only if he fails or refuses to forsake his favorites when conditions demand it." Typical favorites are the carotid artery, femoral artery, jugular vein, subclavian vein. There are various choices of embalming fluid. If Flextone is used, it will produce a "mild, flexible rigidity. The skin retains a velvety softness, the tissues are rubbery and pliable. Ideal for women and children." It may be blended with B. and G. Products Company's Lyf-Lyk tint, which is guaranteed to reproduce "nature's own skin texture . . . the velvety appearance of living tissue." Suntone comes in three separate tints: Suntan; Special Cosmetic Tint, a pink shade "especially indicated for female subjects"; and Regular Cosmetic Tint, moderately pink.

About three to six gallons of a dyed and perfumed solution of formaldehyde, 12 glycerin, borax, phenol, alcohol and water is soon circulating through Mr. Jones, whose mouth has been sewn together with a "needle directed upward between the upper lip and gum and brought out through the left nostril," with the corners raised slightly "for a more pleasant expression." If he should be bucktoothed, his teeth are cleaned with Bon Ami and coated with colorless nail polish. His eyes, meanwhile, are closed with flesh-tinted eye caps and eye cement.

The next step is to have at Mr. Jones with a thing called a trocar. This is a 13 long, hollow needle attached to a tube. It is jabbed into the abdomen, poked around the entrails and chest cavity, the contents of which are pumped out and replaced with "cavity fluid." This done, and the hole in the abdomen sewn up, Mr. Jones's face is heavily creamed (to protect the skin from burns which may be caused by leakage of the chemicals), and he is covered with a sheet and left unmolested for a while. But not for long—there is more, much more, in store for him. He has been embalmed, but not yet restored, and the best time to start the restorative work is eight to ten hours after embalming, when the tissues have become firm and dry.

The object of all this attention to the corpse, it must be remembered, is to 14 make it presentable for viewing in an attitude of healthy repose. "Our customs require the presentation of our dead in the semblance of normality . . . unmarred by the ravages of illness, disease or mutilation," says Mr. J. Sheridan Mayer in his *Restorative Art.* This is rather a large order since few people die in the full bloom of health, unravaged by illness and unmarked by some disfigurement. The funeral industry is equal to the challenge: "In some cases the gruesome appearance of a mutilated or disease-ridden subject may be quite discouraging. The task of restoration may seem impossible and shake the confidence of the embalmer. This is the time for intestinal fortitude and determination. Once the formative work is begun and affected tissues are cleaned or removed, all doubts of success vanish. It is surprising and gratifying to discover the results which may be obtained."

The embalmer, having allowed an appropriate interval to elapse, returns to 15 the attack, but now he brings into play the skill and equipment of sculptor and cosmetician. Is a hand missing? Casting one in plaster of Paris is a simple matter. "For replacement purposes, only a cast of the back of the hand is necessary; this is within the ability of the average operator and is quite adequate." If a lip or two, a nose or an ear should be missing, the embalmer has at hand a variety of restorative waxes with which to model replacements. Pores and skin texture are simulated by stippling with a little brush, and over this cosmetics are laid on. Head off? Decapitation cases are rather routinely handled. Ragged edges are trimmed, and head joined to torso with a series of splints, wires and sutures. It is a good idea to have a little something at the neck—a scarf or a high collar—when time for viewing comes. Swollen mouth? Cut out tissue as needed from inside the lips. If too much is removed, the surface contour can easily be restored by padding with cotton. Swollen necks and cheeks are reduced by removing tissue through vertical incisions made down each side of the neck. "When the deceased is casketed, the pillow will hide the suture incisions . . . as an extra precaution against leakage, the suture may be painted with liquid sealer."

The opposite condition is more likely to present itself—that of emaciation. 16 His hypodermic syringe now loaded with massage cream, the embalmer seeks out and fills the hollowed and sunken areas by injection. In this procedure the backs of the hands and fingers and the under-chin area should not be neglected.

Positioning the lips is a problem that recurrently challenges the ingenuity of 17 the embalmer. Closed too tightly, they tend to give a stern, even disapproving expression. Ideally, embalmers feel, the lips should give the impression of being ever so slightly parted, the upper lip protruding slightly for a more youthful appearance. This takes some engineering, however, as the lips tend to drift apart. Lip drift can sometimes be remedied by pushing one or two straight pins through the inner margin of the lower lip and then inserting them between the two front upper teeth. If Mr. Jones happens to have no teeth, the pins can just as easily be anchored in his Armstrong Face Former and Denture Replacer. Another method to maintain lip closure is to dislocate the lower jaw, which is then held in its new position by a wire run through holes which have been drilled through the upper and lower jaws at the midline. As the French are fond of saying, *il faut souffrir pour être belle.*

If Mr. Jones has died of jaundice, the embalming fluid will very likely turn   18 him green. Does this deter the embalmer? Not if he has intestinal fortitude. Masking pastes and cosmetics are heavily laid on, burial garments and casket interiors are color-correlated with particular care, and Jones is displayed beneath rose-colored lights. Friends will say "How *well* he looks." Death by carbon monoxide, on the other hand, can be rather a good thing from the embalmer's viewpoint: "One advantage is the fact that this type of discoloration is an exaggerated form of a natural pink coloration." This is nice because the healthy glow is already present and needs but little attention.

The patching and filling completed, Mr. Jones is now shaved, washed and   19 dressed. Cream-based cosmetic, available in pink, flesh, suntan, brunette and blond, is applied to his hands and face, his hair is shampooed and combed (and, in the case of Mrs. Jones, set), his hands manicured. For the horny-handed son of toil special care must be taken; cream should be applied to remove ingrained grime, and the nails cleaned. "If he were not in the habit of having them manicured in life, trimming and shaping is advised for better appearance—never questioned by kin."

Jones is now ready for casketing (this is the present participle of the verb "to   20 casket"). In this operation his right shoulder should be depressed slightly "to turn the body a bit to the right and soften the appearance of lying flat on the back." Positioning the hands is a matter of importance, and special rubber positioning blocks may be used. The hands should be cupped slightly for a more life like, relaxed appearance. Proper placement of the body requires a delicate sense of balance. It should lie as high as possible in the casket, yet not so high that the lid, when lowered, will hit the nose. On the other hand, we are cautioned, placing the body too low "creates the impression that the body is in a box."

Jones is next wheeled into the appointed slumber room where a few last   21 touches may be added—his favorite pipe placed in his hand or, if he was a great reader, a book propped into position. (In the case of little Master Jones a Teddy bear may be clutched.) Here he will hold open house for a few days, visiting hours 10 AM to 9 PM.

All now being in readiness, the funeral director calls a staff conference to   22 make sure that each assistant knows his precise duties. Mr. Wilber Kriege writes: "This makes your staff feel that they are a part of the team, with a definite assignment that must be properly carried out if the whole plan is to succeed. You never heard of a football coach who failed to talk to his entire team before they go on the field. They have drilled on the plays they are to execute for hours and days, and yet the successful coach knows the importance of making even the bench-warming third-string substitute feel that he is important if the game is to be won." The winning of *this* game is predicated upon glass-smooth handling of the logistics. The funeral director has notified the pallbearers whose names were furnished by the family, has arranged for the presence of clergyman, organist, and soloist, has provided transportation for everybody, has organized and listed the flowers sent by friends. In *Psychology of Funeral Service* Mr. Edward A. Martin points out: "He may not always do as much as the family thinks he is doing, but it is his helpful guidance that they appreciate in knowing they are proceeding as they should. . . . The important thing is how well his services can be used to make the family believe they are giving unlimited expression to their own sentiment."

The religious service may be held in a church or in the chapel of the funeral   23
home; the funeral director vastly prefers the latter arrangement, for not only is it more convenient for him but it affords him the opportunity to show off his beautiful facilities to the gathered mourners. After the clergyman has had his say, the mourners queue up to file past the casket for a last look at the deceased. The family is *never* asked whether they want an open-casket ceremony; in the absence of their instruction to the contrary, this is taken for granted. Consequently well over 90 percent of all American funerals feature the open casket—a custom unknown in other parts of the world. Foreigners are astonished by it. An English woman living in San Francisco described her reaction in a letter to the writer:

> I myself have attended only one funeral here—that of an elderly
> fellow worker of mine. After the service I could not understand why
> everyone was walking towards the coffin (sorry, I mean casket), but
> thought I had better follow the crowd. It shook me rigid to get there
> and find the casket open and poor old Oscar lying there in his brown
> tweed suit, wearing a suntan makeup and just the wrong shade of
> lipstick. If I had not been extremely fond of the old boy, I have a
> horrible feeling that I might have giggled. Then and there I decided
> that I could never face another American funeral—even dead.

The casket (which has been resting throughout the service on a Classic   24
Beauty Ultra Metal Casket Bier) is now transferred by a hydraulically operated device called Porto-Lift to a balloon-tired, Glide Easy casket carriage which will wheel it to yet another conveyance, the Cadillac Funeral Coach. This may be lavender, cream, light green—anything but black. Interiors, of course, are color-correlated, "for the man who cannot stop short of perfection."

At graveside, the casket is lowered into the earth. This office, once the pre-   25
rogative of friends of the deceased, is now performed by a patented mechanical lowering device. A "Lifetime Green" artificial grass mat is at the ready to conceal the sere earth, and overhead, to conceal the sky, is a portable Steril Chapel Tent ("resists the intense heat and humidity of summer and the terrific storms of winter . . . available in Silver Grey, Rose or Evergreen"). Now is the time for the ritual scattering of earth over the coffin, as the solemn words "earth to earth, ashes to ashes, dust to dust" are pronounced by the officiating cleric. This can today be accomplished "with

a mere flick of the wrist with the Gordon Leak-Proof Earth Dispenser. No grasping of a handful of dirt, no soiled fingers. Simple, dignified, beautiful, reverent! The modern way!" The Gordon Earth Dispenser (at $5) is of nickel-plated brass construction. It is not only "attractive to the eye and long wearing"; it is also "one of the 'tools' for building better public relations" if presented as "an appropriate noncommercial gift" to the clergyman. It is shaped something like a saltshaker.

Untouched by human hand, the coffin and the earth are now united.   26

It is in the function of directing the participants through this maze of gad-   27 getry that the funeral director has assigned to himself his relatively new role of "grief therapist." He has relieved the family of every detail, he has revamped the corpse to look like a living doll, he has arranged for it to nap for a few days in a slumber room, he has put on a well-oiled performance in which the concept of *death* has played no part whatsoever—unless it was inconsiderately mentioned by the clergyman who conducted the religious service. He has done everything in his power to make the funeral a real pleasure for everybody concerned. He and his team have given their all to score an upset victory over death.

1963

QUESTIONS FOR DISCUSSION

Content

a. What is Mitford's purpose? Do you agree that "public information about embalming might lead patrons to wonder if they really want this service" (paragraph 6)?

b. In what ways does this selection resemble a narrative? What aspects are arranged in chronological order? How does Mitford indicate the passage of time?

c. According to Mitford, why is it odd that embalming remains so secretive a business? What can we infer about the reasons for the persistence of embalming as a widespread practice only in this part of the world?

d. Do you know of any important differences between funeral practices in North America and those in other parts of the world? Why does Mitford bother to mention such differences at the start of this essay?

e. The beginning of paragraph 2 alludes to Shakespeare's *Hamlet*. Who was Yorick, and why has Mitford chosen to include him in her introduction?

f. Why does the author make it a point to mention the brand names of the supplies and equipment used by undertakers?

Strategy and Style

g. Mitford's use of detail seems to be accurate and thorough. Is it too thorough? Could she have achieved her purpose without being so detailed?

h. Mitford relies heavily on the use of quoted material from embalming textbooks to develop her indictment of morticians. Explain how these citations help her achieve her purpose.

i. In paragraph 6, before parting "the formaldehyde curtain," Mitford warns us about what is to follow. Why?

j. What other interesting metaphors does Mitford use? Do they help "enliven" her prose?

k. What is ironic about her calling the embalming procedure the mortician's *raison d'être*? Identify other examples of irony in this selection.

l. Look up the roots of the term *dermasurgeon* in a good dictionary. What do their meanings suggest? Now look up *demi*. What does the corruption *demi-surgeon* (paragraph 8) tell you about Mitford's view of undertakers? What does Mitford mean by "grief therapist" (paragraph 27)? Why does she say that funeral directors have "assigned" themselves this role?

m. How would you describe Mitford's tone? Analyze at least one paragraph closely (paragraph 13, 14, or 15 would be a good choice). How does her use of language make her attitude about the subject clear?

n. When does irony turn to sarcasm? Reread paragraph 25. What makes Mitford's treatment of graveside ceremonies so caustic?

SUGGESTIONS FOR SHORT WRITING

a. Write a response entirely made up of exclamatory statements.

b. Address a response to Mitford. Tell her what you think of her essay, and why.

SUGGESTIONS FOR SUSTAINED WRITING

a. Do you agree with Mitford's assessment of the undertaker's profession? If not, write an essay in which you refute her by explaining the important role current funeral customs and practices play. Address your essay to Mitford directly, perhaps in the form of a letter.

b. Funeral customs differ from country to country and from culture to culture. Have you ever witnessed or read about funeral rites that are distinctive from those one might consider typically American? If so, write an essay in which you explain how such rites are carried out.

c. Do you believe funeral customs should be changed? What aspect of the way in which people deal with the dead do you object to most? Write an essay in which you explain the basis for your objection and suggest alternatives to current practices.

d. Mitford focuses on only one method of laying the dead to rest; actually there are many alternatives. One is cremation; another is burial at sea. Explain the process involved in any funeral practice other than the one she discusses.

Writing Drafts

Richard Marius

A native of Tennessee, Richard Marius (b. 1933) took his bachelor's degree in journalism at the University of Tennessee and his master's and doctorate in history at Yale University. He also holds a B.D. from Southern Baptist Theological Seminary. Marius is the author of several historical studies and has received wide acclaim for his full-length biographies of Martin Luther and Thomas More. He has also written three novels, including The Coming of Rain *(1969) and* Bound for the Promised Land *(1976). Now director of the Expository Writing Program at Harvard University, Marius has published several books on writing including* The McGraw-Hill College Handbook, *which he coauthored with Harvey Wiener, and* A Short Guide to Writing About History *(1987).* "Writing Drafts" *first appeared in* The Writer's Companion *(1985), his splendid guide for both novice and experienced writers.*

Finally the moment comes when you sit down to begin your first draft. It is always 1 a good idea at the start to list the points you want to cover. A list is not as elaborate as a formal outline. In writing your first list, don't bother to set items down in the order of importance. List your main points and trust your mind to organize them. You will probably make one list, study it, make another, study it, and perhaps make another. You can organize each list more completely than the last. This preliminary process may save you hours of starting and stopping.

Write with your list outline in front of you. Once you begin to write, commit 2 yourself to the task at hand. Do not get up until you have written for an hour. Write your thoughts quickly. Let one sentence give you an idea to develop in the next. Organization, grammar, spelling, and even clarity of sentences are not nearly as important as getting the first draft together. No matter how desperate you feel, keep going.

Always keep your mind open to new ideas that pop into your head as you 3 write. Let your list outline help you, but don't become a slave to it. Writers often start an essay with one topic in mind only to discover that another pushes the first one aside as they work. Ideas you had not even thought of before you began to write may pile onto your paper, and five or six pages into your first draft you may realize that you are going to write about something you did not imagine when you started.

If such a revelation comes, be grateful and accept it. But don't immediately 4 tear up or erase your draft and start all over again. Make yourself keep on writing, developing these new ideas as they come. If you suddenly start all over again, you may break the train of thought that has given you the new topic. Let your thoughts follow your new thesis, sailing on that tack until the wind changes.

When you have said everything you can say in this draft, print it out if you are 5 working on a computer. Get up from your desk and go sit in a chair somewhere else to read it without correcting anything. Then put it aside, preferably overnight. If possible, read your rough draft just before you go to sleep. Many psychological tests have shown that our minds organize and create while we sleep if we pack them full before bedtime. Study a draft just before sleep, and you may discover new ideas in the morning.

Be willing to make radical changes in your second draft. If your thesis 6 changed while you were writing your first draft, you will base your second draft on this new subject. Even if your thesis has not changed, you may need to shift paragraphs around, eliminate paragraphs, or add new ones. Inexperienced writers often suppose that revising a paper means changing only a word or two or adding a sentence or two. This kind of editing is part of the writing process, but it is not the most important part. The most important part of rewriting is a willingness to turn the paper upside down, to shake out of it those ideas that interest you most, to set them in a form where they will interest the reader, too.

I mentioned earlier that some writers cut up their first drafts with a pair of 7 scissors. They toss some paragraphs into the trash; others they paste up with rubber cement in the order that seems most logical and coherent. Afterward they type the whole thing through again, smoothing out the transitions, adding new material, getting new ideas as they work. The translation of the first draft into the second nearly always involves radical cutting and shifting around. Now and then you may firmly fix the order of your thoughts in your first draft, but I find that the order of my essays is seldom established until the second draft.

With the advent of computers the shifting around of parts of the essays has 8 become easy. We can cut and paste electronically with a few strokes of the keyboard. We can also make back-up copies of our earlier drafts so we can go back to them if we wish. But as I said earlier, computers do not remove from us the necessity to think hard about revising.

Always be firm enough with yourself to cut out thoughts or stories that have 9 nothing to do with your thesis, even if they are interesting. Cutting is the supreme test of a writer. You may create a smashing paragraph or sentence only to discover later that it does not help you make your point. You may develop six or seven examples to illustrate a point and discover you need only one.

Now and then you may digress a little. If you digress too often or too far, read- 10 ers will not follow you unless your facts, your thoughts, and your style are so compelling that they are somehow driven to follow you. Not many writers can pull such digressions off, and most editors will cut out the digressions even when they are interesting. In our hurried and harried time, most readers get impatient with the rambling scenic route. They want to take the most direct way to their destination. To appeal to most of them, you must cut things that do not apply to your main argument.

In your third draft, you can sharpen sentences, add information here and there, 11 cut some things, and attend to other details to heighten the force of your writing. In the third draft, writing becomes a lot of fun (for most of us). By then you have usually decided what you want to say. You can now play a bit, finding just the right word, choosing just the right sentence form, compressing here, expanding there.

I find it helpful to put a printed draft down beside my keyboard and type the 12 whole thing through again as a final draft, letting all the words run through my mind and fingers one more time rather than merely deleting and inserting on the computer screen. I wrote four drafts of the first edition of this book; I have preserved the final draft of that edition on computer diskettes. But I am writing this draft by propping the first edition up here beside me and typing it all over again. By comparing the first draft and the second draft, one can see how many changes I have made, most of them unforeseen until I sat down here to work.

I have outlined here my own writing process. It works for me. You must find 13 the process that works for you. It may be different from mine. A friend tells me that his writing process consists of writing a sentence, agonizing over it, walking around the room, thinking, sitting down, and writing the next sentence. He does not revise very much. I think it unnecessarily painful to bleed out prose that way, but he bleeds out enough to write what he needs to write. Several of my friends tell me they cannot compose at a typewriter; they must first write with a pencil on a yellow pad. These are the people most likely to cut up their drafts with scissors and paste them together in a different form. They also tend to be older. Most young writers are learning to compose at a keyboard, and they cannot imagine another way to write. Neither can I—though on occasion yet I go back to my pencil for pages at a time.

The main thing is to keep at it. B. F. Skinner has pointed out that if you write 14 only fifty words a night, you will produce a good-sized book every two or three years. That's not a bad record for any writer. William Faulkner outlined the plot of his Nobel Prize–winning novel *A Fable* on a wall inside his house near Oxford, Mississippi. You can see it there to this day. Once he got the outline on the wall, he sat down with his typewriter and wrote, following the outline to the end. If writing an outline on a kitchen wall does the trick for you, do it. You can always repaint the wall if you must.

Think of writing as a process making its way toward a product—sometimes 15 painfully. Don't imagine you must know everything you are going to say before you begin. Don't demean yourself and insult your readers by letting your first draft be your final draft. Don't imagine that writing is easy or that you can do it without spending time on it. And don't let anything stand in your way of doing it. Let your house get messy. Leave your magazines unread and your mail unanswered. Put off getting up for a drink of water or a cup of tea. (Never mix alcohol with your writing; true, lots of writers have become alcoholics, but it has not helped their writing.) Don't make a telephone call. Don't straighten up your desk. Sit down and write. And write, and write, and write.

1988

QUESTIONS FOR DISCUSSION

Content

a. Marius advises using a list outline, but he cautions us not to follow it slavishly. Why not?

b. "Cutting is the supreme test of a writer," the author tells us in paragraph 9. What does he mean?

c. How is rewriting different from simple editing?

d. In what way is writing the second draft different from writing the first? In what way is writing the third draft different from writing the second?

e. How does Marius's suggested process compare with the way you usually write a paper? Which of his suggestions have you tried with success? Which without success? Which suggestions might you try for your next paper?

f. Are there any suggestions in "Writing Drafts" that you disagree with? What is the basis of your disagreement?

Strategy and Style

g. The author's personal voice can be heard clearly and distinctly throughout this selection. Is this subjective approach appropriate to writing that instructs?

h. If the writing process Marius follows may not work for you, why does he explain that process in careful detail?

i. Marius draws on several metaphors to help him describe the drafting process. One is the sailing metaphor at the end of paragraph 4: "Let your thoughts follow your new thesis, sailing on that tack until the wind changes." What connection does he want us to see between writing and sailing? What other metaphors can you find in the essay?

j. How does including personal experience, as in paragraph 13, help the author achieve his purposes? Why does he make reference to the experiences of well-known writers such as B. F. Skinner and William Faulkner?

k. Marius writes directly to you, the student. What was your reaction to this technique when you first read the essay? Why did he choose this technique?

SUGGESTIONS FOR SHORT WRITING

a. Quickly, and without looking back at Marius's essay, list the steps he suggests in writing drafts. Check what you have written against Marius's essay.

b. What piece of advice in "Writing Drafts" did you find most helpful? In what way do you think it will help you improve your writing?

SUGGESTIONS FOR SUSTAINED WRITING

a. Outline your own writing process. You may want to use as an example the last academic paper you wrote. Then, roughly following Marius's essay as a model, describe your *ideal* process for writing papers. As you complete this assignment, keep in mind techniques and practices you might try out with your *next* academic paper.

b. Write an essay similar to Marius's in which you set forth a set of sequenced suggestions for doing something other than writing drafts for an academic paper. The task you explain could be another kind of writing—poetry or short stories, for instance—or it might be any activity that people often find intimidating. Either way, make the activity seem both unintimidating and fruitfully challenging.

The Rules of the Game: Rodeo

Gretel Ehrlich

Gretel Ehrlich (b. 1946) studied at Bennington College, UCLA Film School, and the New School for Social Research. She went to Wyoming to make a film documentary, but she stayed on and now lives there with her husband on a remote ranch, dividing her time between ranch work and writing. "I often write—notepad balanced on saddlehorn— gathering cattle," she says, "and when I'm in my writing room, . . . I often get up mid- sentence to fix a panel of fence or change an irrigation dam, or put a stray horse away. . . . Our ranch, and the entire ecosystem in which it lies, is my laboratory." For Ehrlich, this combination is essential to her writing, which is characterized by closely observed detail and moving images, a blending of the ordinary and wondrous. A versatile writer, she has published poetry, To Touch the Water *(1981); short stories,* Wyoming Stories *(1986) and* Drinking Dry Clouds *(1991); a novel,* Heart Mountain *(1988); and essays,* The Solace of Open Spaces *(1986), from which "The Rules of the Game" is taken. Other essays by Ehrlich have appeared in the* New York Times, *the* Atlantic, Harper's, Sierra, *and* Antaeus.

1 Instead of honeymooning in Paris, Patagonia, or the Sahara as we had planned, my new husband and I drove through a series of blizzards to Oklahoma City. Each De- cember the National Finals Rodeo is held in a modern, multistoried colosseum next to buildings that house banks and petroleum companies in a state whose flat- ness resembles a swimming pool filled not with water but with oil.

2 The National Finals is the "World Series of Professional Rodeo," where not only the best cowboys but also the most athletic horses and bucking stock com- pete. All year, rodeo cowboys have been vying for the honor to ride here. They've been to Houston, Las Vegas, Pendleton, Tucson, Cheyenne, San Francisco, Cal- gary; to as many as eighty rodeos in one season, sometimes making two or three on a day like the Fourth of July, and when the results are tallied up (in money won, not points) the top fifteen riders in each event are invited to Oklahoma City.

3 We climbed to our peanut gallery seats just as Miss Rodeo America, a lanky brunette swaddled in a lavender pantsuit, gloves, and cowboy hat, loped across the arena. There was a hush in the audience; all the hats swimming down in front of us, like buoys, steadied and turned toward the chutes. "Out of chute number three, Pat Linger, a young cowboy from Miles City, Montana, making his first appear- ance here on a little horse named Dillinger." And as fast as these words sailed across the colosseum, the first bareback horse bumped into the lights.

4 There's a traditional order to the four timed and three rough stock events that make up a rodeo program. Bareback riders are first, then steer wrestlers, team rop- ers, saddle bronc riders, barrel racers, and finally, the bull riders.

5 After Pat Linger came Steve Dunham, J. C. Trujillo, Mickey Young, and the defending champ, Bruce Ford on a horse named Denver. Bareback riders do just that: they ride a horse with no saddle, no halter, no rein, clutching only a handhold riveted into a girth that goes around the horse's belly. A bareback rider's loose style suggests a drunken, comic bout of lovemaking: he lies back on the horse and, with

each jump and jolt, flops delightfully, like a libidinous Raggedy Andy, toes turned out, knees flexed, legs spread and pumping, back arched, the back of his hat bumping the horse's rump as if nodding, "Yes, let's do 'er again." My husband, who rode saddle broncs in amateur rodeos, explains it differently: "It's like riding a runaway bicycle down a steep hill and lying on your back; you can't see where you're going or what's going to happen next."   6

Now the steer wrestlers shoot out of the box on their own well-trained horses: There is a hazer on the right to keep the steer running straight, the wrestler on the left, and the steer between them. When the wrestler is neck and neck with the animal, he slides sideways out of his saddle as if he's been stabbed in the ribs and reaches for the horns. He's airborne for a second; then his heels swing into the dirt, and with his arms around the horns, he skids to a stop twisting the steer's head to one side so the animal loses his balance and falls to the ground. It's a fast-paced game of catch with a thousand-pound ball of horned flesh.   7

The team ropers are next. Most of them hail from the hilly, oak-strewn valleys of California where dally roping originated.* Ropers are the graceful technicians, performing their pas de deux (plus steer) with a precision that begins to resemble a larger clarity—an erudition. Header and heeler come out of the box at the same time, steer between them, but the header acts first: He ropes the horns of the steer, dallies up, turns off, and tries to position the steer for the heeler who's been tagging behind this duo, loop clasped in his armpit as if it were a hen. Then the heeler sets his generous, unsweeping loop free and double-hocks the steer. It's a complicated act which takes about six seconds. Concomitant with this speed and skill is a feminine grace: they don't clutch their stiff loop or throw it at the steer like a bag of dirty laundry the way I do, but hold it gently, delicately, as if it were a hoop of silk. One or two cranks and both arm and loop vault forward, one becoming an appendage of the other, as if the tendons and pulse that travel through the wrist had lengthened and spun forward like fishing line until the loop sails down on the twin horns, then up under the hocks like a repeated embrace that tightens at the end before it releases.   8

The classic event at rodeo is saddle bronc riding. The young men look as serious as academicians: They perch spryly on their high-kicking mounts, their legs flicking forward and back, "charging the point" "going back to the cantle" in a rapid, staccato rhythm. When the horse is at the high point of his buck and the cowboy is stretched out, legs spurring above the horse's shoulder, rein-holding arm straight as a board in front, and free hand lifted behind, horse and man look like a propeller. Even their dismounts can look aeronautical: Springing off the back of the horse, they land on their feet with a flourish—hat still on—as if they had been ejected mechanically from a burning plane long before the crash.   9

Barrel racing is the one women's event. Where the men are tender in their movements, as elegant as if Balanchine had been their coach, the women are prodigies of Wayne Gretzky, all speed, bully, and grit. When they charge into the

---

*The word dally is a corruption of the Spanish *da la vuelta,* meaning to take a turn, as with a rope around the saddle horn.

arena, their hats fly off; they ride brazenly, elbows, knees, feet fluttering, and by the time they've careened around the second of three barrels, the whip they've had clenched between their teeth is passed to a hand, and on the home stretch they urge the horse to the finish line.   10

Calf ropers are the whiz kids of rodeo: They're expert on the horse and on the ground, and their horses are as quick-witted. The cowboy emerges from the box with a loop in his hand, a piggin' string in his mouth, coils and reins in the other, and a network of slack line strewn so thickly over horse and rider, they look as if they'd run through a tangle of kudzu before arriving in the arena. After roping the calf and jerking the slack in the rope, he jumps off the horse, sprints down the length of nylon, which the horse keeps taut, throws the calf down, and ties three legs together with the piggin' string. It's said of Roy Cooper, the defending calf-roping champion, that "even with pins and metal plates in his arm, he's known for the fastest groundwork in the business; when he springs down his rope to flank the calf, the resulting action is pure rodeo poetry." The six or seven separate movements he makes are so fluid they look like one continual unfolding.   11

Bull riding is last, and of all the events it's the only one truly dangerous. Bulls are difficult to ride: They're broadbacked, loose-skinned, and powerful. They don't jump balletically the way a horse does; they jerk and spin, and if you fall off, they'll try to gore you with a horn, kick, or trample you. Bull riders are built like the animals they ride: Low to the ground and hefty. They're the tough men on the rodeo circuit, and the flirts. Two of the current champs are city men: Charlie Samson is a small, shy black from Watts, and Bobby Del Vecchio, a brash Italian from the Bronx who always throws the audience a kiss after a ride with a Catskill-like showmanship not usually seen here. What a bull rider lacks in technical virtuosity—you won't see the fast spurring action of a saddle bronc rider in this event—he makes up for in personal flamboyance, and because it's a deadlier game they're playing, you can see the belligerence rise up their necks and settle into their faces as the bull starts his first spin. Besides the bull and the cowboy, there are three other men in the ring—the rodeo clowns—who aren't there to make children laugh but to divert the bull from some of his deadlier tricks, and, when the rider bucks off, jump between the two—like secret service men—to save the cowboy's life.   12

Rodeo, like baseball, is an American sport and has been around almost as long. While Henry Chadwick was writing his first book of rules for the fledgling ball clubs in 1858, ranch hands were paying $25 a dare to a kid who would ride five outlaw horses from the rough string in a makeshift arena of wagons and carts. The first commercial rodeo in Wyoming was held in Lander in 1895, just nineteen years after the National League was formed. Baseball was just as popular as bucking and roping contests in the West, but no one in Cooperstown, New York, was riding broncs. And that's been part of the problem. After 124 years, rodeo is still misunderstood. Unlike baseball, it's a regional sport (although they do have rodeos in New Jersey, Florida, and other eastern states); it's derived from and stands for the western way of life and the western spirit. It doesn't have the universal appeal of a sport contrived solely for the competition and winning; there is no ball bandied about between opposing players.

Rodeo is the wild child of ranch work and embodies some of what ranching 13
is all about. Horsemanship—not gunslinging—was the pride of western men, and
the chivalrous ethics they formulated, known as the western code, became the
ground rules for every human game. Two great partnerships are celebrated in this
Oklahoma arena: The indispensable one between man and animal that any rancher
or cowboy takes on, enduring the joys and punishments of the alliance; and the
one between man and man, cowboy and cowboy.

Though rodeo is an individualist's sport, it has everything to do with team- 14
work. The cowboy who "covers" his bronc (stays on the full eight seconds) has
become a team with that animal. The cowboys' competitive feelings amongst each
other are so mixed with western tact as to appear ambivalent. When Bruce Ford,
the bareback rider, won a go-round he said, "The hardest part of winning this year
was taking it away from one of my best friends, Mickey Young, after he'd worked
so hard all year." Stan Williamson, who'd just won the steer wrestling, said, "I just
drew a better steer. I didn't want Butch to get a bad one. I just got lucky, I guess."

Ranchers, when working together, can be just as diplomatic. They'll apolo- 15
gize if they cut in front of someone while cutting out a calf, and their thanks to
each other at the end of the day has a formal sound. Like those westerners who still
help each other out during branding and roundup, rodeo cowboys help each other
in the chutes. A bull rider will steady the saddle bronc rider's horse, help measure
out the rein or set the saddle, and a bareback rider might help the bull rider set his
rigging and pull his rope. Ropers lend each other horses, as do barrel racers and
steer wrestlers. This isn't a show they put on; they offer their help with the utmost
goodwill and good-naturedness. Once, when a bucking horse fell over backward
in the chute with my husband, his friend H.A., who rode bulls, jumped into the
chute and pulled him out safely.

Another part of the "westernness" rodeo represents is the drifting cowboys 16
do. They're on the road much of their lives the way turn-of-the-century cowboys
were on the trail, but these cowboys travel in style if they can—driving pink Lin-
colns and new pickups with a dozen fresh shirts hanging behind the driver, and the
radio on.

Some ranchers look down on the sport of rodeo; they don't want these 17
"drugstore cowboys" getting all the attention and glory. Besides, rodeo seems
to have less and less to do with real ranch work. Who ever heard of gathering
cows on a bareback horse with no bridle, or climbing on a herd bull? Ranchers are
generalists—they have to know how to do many things—from juggling the futures
market to overhauling a tractor or curing viral scours (diarrhea) in calves—while
rodeo athletes are specialists. Deep down, they probably feel envious of each
other: The rancher for the praise and big money; the rodeo cowboy for the stay-at-
home life among animals to which their sport only alludes.

People with no ranching background have even more difficulty with the 18
sport. Every ride goes so fast, it's hard to see just what happened, and perhaps because of the Hollywood mythologizing of the West which distorted rather than dis-
tilled western rituals, rodeo is often considered corny, anachronistic, and cruel to

animals. Quite the opposite is true. Rodeo cowboys are as sophisticated athletically as Bjorn Borg or Fernando Valenzuela. That's why they don't need to be from a ranch anymore, or to have grown up riding horses. And to undo another myth, rodeo is not cruel to animals. Compared to the arduous life of any "using horse" on a cattle or dude ranch, a bucking horse leads the life of Riley. His actual work load for an entire year, i.e., the amount of time he spends in the arena, totals approximately 4.6 minutes, and nothing done to him in the arena or out could in any way be called cruel. These animals aren't bludgeoned into bucking; they love to buck. They're bred to behave this way, they're athletes whose ability has been nurtured and encouraged. Like the cowboys who compete at the National Finals, the best bulls and horses from all the bucking strings in the country are nominated to appear in Oklahoma, winning money along with their riders to pay their own way.

     The National Finals run ten nights. Every contestant rides every night, so it is easy to follow their progress and setbacks. One evening we abandoned our rooftop seats and sat behind the chutes to watch the saddle broncs ride. Behind the chutes two cowboys are rubbing rosin—part of their staying power—behind the saddle swells and on their Easter-egg-colored chaps which are pink, blue, and light green with white fringe. Up above, standing on the chute rungs, the stock contractors direct horse traffic: "Velvet Drums" in chute #3, "Angel Sings" in #5, "Rusty" in #1. Rick Smith, Monty Henson, Bobby Berger, Brad Gjermudson, Mel Coleman, and friends climb the chutes. From where I'm sitting, it looks like a field hospital with five separate operating theaters, the cowboys, like surgeons, bent over their patients with sweaty brows and looks of concern. Horses are being haltered; cowboys are measuring out the long, braided reins, saddles are set: One cowboy pulls up on the swells again and again, repositioning his hornless saddle until it sits just right. When the chute boss nods to him and says, "Pull 'em up, boys," the ground crew tightens front and back cinches on the first horse to go, but very slowly so he won't panic in the chute as the cowboy eases himself down over the saddle, not sitting on it, just hovering there. "Okay, you're on." The chute boss nods to him again. Now he sits on the saddle, taking the rein in one hand, holding the top of the chute with the other. He flips the loose bottoms of his chaps over his shins, puts a foot in each stirrup, takes a breath, and nods. The chute gate swings open releasing a flood—not of water, but of flesh, groans, legs kicking. The horse lunges up and out in the first big jump like a wave breaking whose crest the cowboy rides, "marking out the horse," spurs well above the bronc's shoulders. In that first second under the lights, he finds what will be the rhythm of the ride. Once again he "charges the point," his legs pumping forward, then so far back his heels touch behind the cantle. For a moment he looks as though he were kneeling on air, then he's stretched out again, his whole body taut but released, free hand waving in back of his head like a palm frond, rein-holding hand thrust forward: *"En garde!"* he seems to be saying, but he's airborne; he looks like a wing that has sprouted suddenly from the horse's broad back. Eight seconds. The whistle blows. He's covered the horse. Now two gentlemen dressed in white chaps and satin shirts

19

gallop beside the bucking horse. The cowboy hands the rein to one and grabs the waist of the other—the flank strap on the bronc has been undone, so all three horses move at a run—and the pickup man from whom the cowboy is now dangling slows almost to a stop, letting him slide to his feet on the ground.

Rick Smith from Wyoming rides, looking pale and nervous in his white 20 shirt. He's bucked off and so are the brash Monty "Hawkeye" Henson, and Butch Knowles, and Bud Pauley, but with such grace and aplomb, there is no shame. Bobby Berger, an Oklahoma cowboy, wins the go-round with a score of 83.

By the end of the evening we're tired, but in no way as exhausted as these 21 young men who have ridden night after night. "I've never been so sore and had so much fun in my life," one first-time bull rider exclaims breathlessly. When the performance is over we walk across the street to the chic lobby of a hotel chock full of cowboys. Wives hurry through the crowd with freshly ironed shirts for tomorrow's ride, ropers carry their rope bags with them into the coffee shop, which is now filled with contestants, eating mild midnight suppers of scrambled eggs, their numbers hanging crookedly on their backs, their faces powdered with dust, and looking at this late hour prematurely old.

We drive back to the motel, where, the first night, they'd "never heard of us" 22 even though we'd had reservations for a month. "Hey, it's our honeymoon," I told the night clerk and showed him the white ribbons my mother had tied around our duffel bag. He looked embarrassed, then surrendered another latecomer's room.

The rodeo finals in Oklahoma may be a better place to honeymoon than 23 Paris. All week, we've observed some important rules of the game. A good rodeo, like a good marriage, or a musical instrument when played to the pitch of perfection, becomes more than what it started out to be. It is effort transformed into effortlessness; a balance becomes grace, the way love goes deep into friendship.

In the rough stock events such as the one we watched tonight, there is no vic- 24 tory over the horse or bull. The point of the match is not conquest but communion: The rhythm of two beings becoming one. Rodeo is not a sport of opposition; there is no scrimmage line here. No one bears malice—neither the animals, the stock contractors, nor the contestants; no one wants to get hurt. In this match of equal talents, it is only acceptance, surrender, respect, and spiritedness that make for the midair union of cowboy and horse. Not a bad thought when starting out fresh in a marriage.

1985

QUESTIONS FOR DISCUSSION

Content

a. What two great partnerships are celebrated in the rodeo arena?
b. Ehrlich uses two similes for bareback riding in paragraph 5. What is the main difference between the two? Why are they both apt similes?

c. Why is rodeo a particularly American sport? What is the "western code" mentioned in paragraph 13?

d. What myths about the rodeo does the author attempt to dispel? Are her arguments convincing?

e. The events she describes in paragraphs 5 through 11 happen in a matter of seconds, but they are slowed down by her describing each step of the process. Is she successful at re-creating these brief events? Why or why not?

f. In the same paragraphs, Ehrlich describes only the parts of the events that actually get judged. For example, she leaves out what happens immediately after the steer wrestlers throw the steers to the ground. What does stopping these events in midaction add to her essay?

g. In paragraph 10, what did the unidentified speaker mean when he called Roy Cooper's skill "rodeo poetry"?

h. Why is rodeo a misunderstood sport (paragraph 12)? In what way do people misunderstand it?

i. What is the distinction Ehrlich makes between rodeo athletes and ranchers? How does this distinction help her explain rodeo?

j. What do rodeo and marriages have in common, in Ehrlich's opinion? Why does a trip to the National Rodeo Finals make a particularly good honeymoon for Ehrlich and her husband?

Strategy and Style

k. Why does Ehrlich include the names of so many actual rodeo cowboys?

l. What does the author mean by saying that a precision is a "larger clarity" (paragraph 7)? Of what is it a larger clarity of?

m. Process writers often rely on analogies. Where in this essay do analogies appear, and in what way do they help Ehrlich achieve her purpose?

n. Do you find the essay's introduction appropriate to a process paper? Why or why not?

SUGGESTIONS FOR SHORT WRITING

a. Ehrlich's love for the rodeo and its people is clear. Do about ten minutes of freewriting about a sport, game, or other activity you "love," such as baseball, soccer, tennis, chess, reading, acting, going to the movies, cooking, or repairing old cars. After you complete this assignment, write a sentence that explains the one thing you love most about this activity.

b. Dispel some myths about a game, activity, or job you know well. For example, explain one or two reasons that ballet is definitely not for weaklings, that football players can be sensitive, or that women can make good police officers.

SUGGESTIONS FOR SUSTAINED WRITING

a. Explain a fast-moving, complicated sport or activity. Attempt to make your description evocative enough to re-create the event *in action* in your reader's mind.

b. Explain another quintessential American sport or communal activity. Make sure you tell your readers what makes the sport "American." If you know of a related foreign sport or activity, compare and contrast it with your topic in order to point out its American elements.

c. Explain a sport or communal activity popular in a country other than the United States or Canada.

d. For a longer, researched paper, write a history and description of the sport or activity you chose for *b* or *c* above.

Honey Harvest*

Sue Hubbell

Born in 1935 in Kalamazoo, Michigan, Hubbell attended Swarthmore College and the University of Michigan before getting a bachelor's degree from the University of Southern California in 1956 and a master's degree from Drexel Institute in 1963. She worked as a bookstore manager in New Jersey and as a school librarian in New Jersey and Rhode Island before boldly changing careers in 1973 to become a commercial beekeeper in the Ozark Mountains. In 1985 she added writing to beekeeping when she began writing A Country Year: Living the Questions *(1986), a collection of essays on life and nature. Since then she has published two books about insects,* A Book of Bees: . . . and How to Keep Them *(1988) and* Broadsides from the Other Orders: A Book of Bugs *(1993), which prompted a book reviewer to call her "one of the two or three best writers-about-bugs now living." She has also published collections of her essays,* On This Hilltop *(1991) and* Far Flung Hubbell *(1995), and contributes regularly to magazines such as the* New Yorker, Smithsonian, Time, *and* Newsweek. *She currently splits her time between her 18 million bees in Missouri and her husband in Washington, D.C. "Honey Harvest" (editor's title) is taken from* A Country Year.

I keep twenty hives of bees here in my home beeyard, but most of my hives are 1 scattered in outyards across the Ozarks, where I can find the thickest stands of wild blackberries and other good things for bees. I always have a waiting list of farmers who would like the bees on their land, for the clover in their pastures is more abundant when the bees are there to pollinate it.

One of the farmers, a third-generation Ozarker and a dairyman with a lively 2 interest in bees, came over today for a look at what my neighbors call my honey factory. My honey house contains a shiny array of stainless-steel tanks with clear plastic tubing connecting them, a power uncapper for slicing open honey comb, an extractor for spinning honey out of the comb, and a lot of machinery and equipment that whirs, thumps, hums, and looks very special. The dairyman, shrewd in mountain ways, looked it all over carefully and then observed, "Well . . . ll . . . ll, wouldn't say for sure now, but it looks like a still to me."

There have been droughty years and cold wet ones when flowers refused to 3 bloom and I would have been better off with a still back up here on my mountain top, but the weather this past year was perfect from a bee's standpoint, and this August I ran 33,000 pounds of honey through my factory. This was nearly twice the normal crop, and everything was overloaded, starting with me. Neither I nor my equipment is set up to handle this sort of harvest, even with extra help.

I always need to hire someone, a strong young man who is not afraid of be- 4 ing stung, to help me harvest the honey from the hives.

The honey I take is the surplus that the bees will not need for the winter; they 5 store it above their hives in wooden boxes called supers. To take it from them, I

*Editors' title.

stand behind each hive with a gasoline-powered machine called a bee-blower and blow the bees out of the supers with a jet of air. Meanwhile, the strong young man carries the supers, which weigh about sixty pounds each, and stacks them on pallets in the truck. There may be thirty to fifty supers in every outyard, and we have only about half an hour to get them off the hives, stacked and covered before the bees get really cross about what we are doing. The season to take the honey in this part of the country is summer's end, when the temperature is often above ninety-five degrees. The nature of the work and the temper of the bees require that we wear protective clothing while doing the job: a full set of coveralls, a zippered bee veil and leather gloves. Even a very strong young man works up a considerable sweat wrapped in a bee suit in hot weather hustling sixty-pound supers—being harassed by angry bees at the same time.

This year my helper has been Ky, my nephew, who wanted to learn some- 6 thing about bees and beekeeping. He is a sweet, gentle, cooperative giant of a young man who, because of a series of physical problems, lacks confidence in his own ability to get on in the world.

As soon as he arrived, I set about to desensitize him to bee stings. The first 7 day, I put a piece of ice on his arm to numb it; then, holding the bee carefully by her head, I placed her abdomen on the numbed spot and let her sting him there. A bee's stinger is barbed and stays in the flesh, pulling loose from her body as she struggles to free herself. Lacking her stinger, the bee will live only a short time. The bulbous poison sac at the top of the stinger continues to pulsate after the bee has left, its muscles pumping the venom and forcing the barbed stinger deeper into the flesh.

I wanted Ky to have only a partial dose of venom that first day, so after a 8 minute I scraped the stinger out with my fingernail and watched his reaction closely. A few people—about one percent of the population—are seriously sensitive to bee venom. Each sting they receive can cause a more severe reaction than the one before, reactions ranging from hives, difficulty in breathing and accelerated heartbeat, to choking, anaphylactic shock, and death. Ky had been stung a few times in his life and didn't think he was seriously allergic, but I wanted to make sure.

The spot where the stinger went in grew red and began to swell. This was a nor- 9 mal reaction, and so was the itchiness that Ky felt the next day. That time I let a bee sting him again, repeating the procedure, but leaving the stinger in his arm a full ten minutes, until the venom sac was emptied. Again the spot was red, swollen and itchy, but had disappeared the next day. Thereafter Ky decided that he didn't need the ice cube any more, and began holding the bee himself to administer his own stings. I kept him at one sting a day until he had no redness or swelling from the full sting, and then had him increase to two stings daily. Again the greater amount of venom caused redness and swelling, but soon his body could tolerate them without an allergic reaction. I gradually had him build up to ten full stings a day with no reaction.

To encourage Ky, I had told him that what he was doing might help protect 10 him from the arthritis that runs in our family. Beekeepers generally believe that getting stung by bees is a healthy thing, and that bee venom alleviates the symptoms of arthritis. When I first began keeping bees, I supposed this to be just another one of the old wives' tales that make beekeeping such an entertaining occupation, but after my hands were stung the pain in my fingers disappeared and I too became a believer. Ky was polite, amused and skeptical of what I told him, but he welcomed my taking a few companionable stings on my knuckles along with him.

In desensitizing Ky to bee venom, I had simply been interested in building 11 up his tolerance to stings so that he could be an effective helper when we took the honey from the hives, for I knew that he would be stung frequently. But I discovered that there had been a secondary effect on Ky that was more important: He was enormously pleased with himself for having passed through what he evidently regarded as a rite of initiation. He was proud and delighted in telling other people about the whole process. He was now one tough guy.

I hoped he was prepared well enough for our first day of work. I have had 12 enough strong young men work for me to know what would happen the first day: He would be stung royally.

Some beekeepers insist that bees know their keeper—that they won't sting 13 that person, but *will* sting a stranger. This is nonsense, for summertime bees live only six weeks and I often open a particular hive less frequently than that, so I am usually a stranger to my bees; yet I am seldom stung. Others say that bees can sense fear or nervousness. I don't know if this is true or not, but I do know that bees' eyes are constructed in such a way that they can detect discontinuities and movement very well and stationary objects less well. This means that a person near their hives who moves with rapid, jerky motions attracts their attention and will more often be blamed by the bees when their hives are being meddled with than will the person whose motions are calm and easy. It has been my experience that the strong young man I hire for the honey harvest is always stung unmercifully for the first few days while he is new to the process and a bit tense. Then he learns to become easier with the bees and settles down to his job. As he gains confidence and assurance, the bees calm down too, and by the end of the harvest he usually is only stung a few times a day.

I knew that Ky very much wanted to do a good job with me that initial day 14 working in the outyards. I had explained the procedures we would follow in taking the honey from the hives, but of course they were new to him and he was anxious. The bees from the first hive I opened flung themselves on him. Most of the stingers could not penetrate his bee suit, but in the act of stinging a bee leaves a chemical trace that marks the person stung as an enemy, a chemical sign other bees can read easily. This sign was read by the bees in each new hive I opened, and soon Ky's bee suit began to look like a pincushion, bristling with stingers. In addition, the temperature was starting to climb and Ky was sweating. Honey oozing from combs broken between the supers was running down the front of his bee suit when he carried them to the truck. Honey and sweat made the suit cling to him, so that the stingers of angry bees could penetrate the suit and he could feel the prick of each one as it entered his skin. Hundreds of bees were assaulting him and finally drove him out of the beeyard, chasing him several hundred yards before they gave up the attack. There was little I could do to help him but try to complete the job quickly, so I took the supers off the next few hives myself, carried them to the truck and loaded them. Bravely, Ky returned to finish the last few hives. We tied down the load and drove away. His face was red with exertion when he unzipped his bee veil. He didn't have much to say as we drove to the next yard, but sat beside me gulping down ice water from the thermos bottle.

At the second yard the bees didn't bother Ky as we set up the equipment. I 15 hoped that much of the chemical marker the bees had left on him had evaporated, but as soon as I began to open the hives they were after him again. Soon a cloud of angry bees enveloped him, accompanying him to the truck and back. Because of the terrain, the truck had to be parked at an odd angle and Ky had to bend from the hips as he loaded it, stretching the fabric of the bee suit taut across the entire length of his back and rear, allowing the bees to sting through it easily. We couldn't talk over the noise of the beeblower's engine, but I was worried about how he was taking hundreds more stings. I was removing the bees from the supers as quickly as I could, but the yard was a good one and there were a lot of supers there.

In about an hour's time Ky carried and stacked what we later weighed in as a 16 load of 2500 pounds. The temperature must have been nearly a hundred degrees. After he had stacked the last super, I drove the truck away from the hives and we tied down the load. Ky's long hair was plastered to his face and I couldn't see the expression on it, but I knew he had been pushed to his limits and I was concerned about him. He tried to brush some of the stingers out of the seat of his bee suit before he sat down next to me in the truck in an uncommonly gingerly way. Unzipping his bee veil, he tossed it aside, pushed the hair back from his sweaty face, reached for the thermos bottle, gave me a sunny and triumphant grin and said, "If I ever get arthritis of the ass, I'll know all that stuff you've been telling me is a lot of baloney."

1983

QUESTIONS FOR DISCUSSION

Content

a. What about beekeeping does Hubbell find particularly appealing?
b. What are supers and what is their place in the process of collecting honey?
c. What is the process for being desensitized to bee venom, and how does it work?
d. How does harvesting honey benefit Hubbell's nephew, Ky?
e. What are some of the theories explaining why bees sting some people who work with them more than others?

Strategy and Style

f. What is the ideal audience for this essay? Who would most enjoy reading it? What in the essay indicates this audience?

g. Why does Hubbell describe the process of being stung by a bee in such detail (paragraph 7)? What purpose does this detailed and rather gruesome description serve?

h. How does this essay compare to one or two of the other selections in this chapter, in terms of style and organization? What do each of the writers do particularly well in describing processes?

i. In paragraphs 14, 15, and 16 Hubbell describes getting the honey from two outyards. What descriptive words and phrases are especially effective?

j. Where does Hubbell use humor? How does humor help the story?

SUGGESTIONS FOR SHORT WRITING

a. List the steps in collecting honey.

b. Describe a "rite of initiation" (paragraph 11) of your own.

SUGGESTIONS FOR SUSTAINED WRITING

a. Describe the process of one of your hobbies or sports. Avoid writing this as a dull straightforward description; instead, write the process in story form, using lively examples and dialogue. If the hobby or sport is familiar to most readers, such as stamp collecting or basketball, find something about it that is new and surprising. If the hobby or sport is unfamiliar to your readers, such as palm reading or ice climbing, be sure to explain it as well as to tell a story about it.

b. Research a hobby, sport, or career that you might like to have. Describe how the hobby is done, the sport is played, or the career pursued.

How to Paint a Fresco

Adam Goodheart

An associate editor of Civilization, *the magazine of the Library of Congress, Adam Goodheart (b. 1970) writes a column called "Lost Arts," which contains essays on how to master arts that have passed into history. Among these interesting process essays are "How to Bleed a Patient," "How to Elect a Holy Roman Emperor," "How to Fight a Duel," "How to Hunt a Woolly Mammoth," "How to Mummify a Pharaoh," and "How to Paint a Fresco," which appeared in 1995. Goodheart, who was born in Philadelphia, attended Harvard University and has studied history and archaeology in Italy. His favorite Renaissance frescoes are those on the life of Pope Pius II by Pintoricchio. They can be found in Sienna's cathedral library.*

Although it must be painted in a very short time, a fresco will last a very long time— 1 that is its great advantage. Many of the masterpieces of the golden age of fresco (from the 14th through the 18th centuries) are as brilliant now as when they were first painted. If you want to fresco a cathedral or palazzo today, you may have a few problems—papal and ducal commissions are scarcer than they once were, and the great Renaissance masters are no longer accepting applications for apprenticeships. Fortunately, a few of their trade secrets have come down to us through the ages.

EQUIPMENT

Lime 2
Sand
Water
A trowel
Paper
A needle
A small bag of charcoal dust
The bristles of a white hog
The hair of bears, sables and martens
The quills of vultures, geese, hens and doves
Ocher, burnt grapevines, lapis lazuli
Egg yolks
Goat's milk

    1. Preparing the wall. Cennino Cennini, a Tuscan master, advised pupils in 3 1437 to "begin by decking yourselves with this attire: Enthusiasm, Reverence, Obedience, and Constancy." You'd do better to deck yourself with some old clothes, though, since the first stage of the process is quite messy. Soak the wall thoroughly and coat it with coarse plaster, two parts sand to one part lime, leaving the surface uneven. (Andrea Pozzo, a 17th-century expert, recommended hiring a

135

professional mason to do this, since "the lime makes a foul odor, which is injurious to the head.")

2. Tracing your design. You should already have extensive drawings for   4
your fresco—these will be much sought by scholars and collectors in centuries to come. Make a full-size sketch, on sturdy paper, of a section of the fresco that you can paint in a day. Then go over the drawing with a needle, pricking holes along every line. Lay a coat of fine plaster on a section of the wall corresponding to the location, size, and shape of the sketch, and press the sketch against the plaster. Fill a loosely woven bag with charcoal dust and strike it lightly all over the surface of the paper. Now peel the sketch off. Your design will be outlined in black dots on the wet plaster, giving you a guide for the day's work.

3. Painting. Time is of the essence: You must paint the plaster while it is   5
wet, so that the pigments bind chemically with the lime. That gives you about six hours, although some painters had tricks to prolong drying. (Piero della Francesca packed the plaster with wet rags; problem was, this left indentations that are still visible after 500 years.) Use top-quality brushes. One 17th-century Flemish master recommended those made of "fish hair" (he probably meant seal fur), but most painters made brushes from bear, marten, or sable hairs inserted in hollow quills. Cennini suggested the bristles of a white hog for the coarser work. As for paints, every artist had his own favorite recipes, but all agreed that mineral pigments such as ocher or ground stone mixed with water were best. Avoid white lead. One 14th-century Umbrian used it to paint a nursing infant; the lime turned the white black and the milky babe into a "devilish changeling." A few pigments, such as dark blue azurite (often used for the Virgin Mary's mantle), must be mixed with egg yolk or goat's milk and added after the fresco is dry. Such colors will prove less durable.

Money is a consideration in choosing materials. When Michelangelo fres-   6
coed the Sistine ceiling, expenses came out of his fee, so he used cheap blue smalt for the sky. Twenty years later, when he did the *Last Judgment,* Michelangelo used semiprecious lapis lazuli for blue, since the pope was paying for the paint. (He made up for it by using burnt grapevines for black.)

4. Casualties of style. Realism, while a worthy goal, has its perils. Spinello   7
Aretino, a 14th-century Tuscan, is said to have painted a fresco that depicted Lucifer with such hideous accuracy that the Evil One himself came to the artist in a dream and demanded an explanation. Spinello went half-mad with fear and died shortly thereafter. On the other hand, a Florentine woodcut from 1500 depicts a painter who has portrayed the Virgin so skillfully that when he falls off the scaffold, she reaches out of the fresco and saves him.

WARNING

Frescoing ceilings can be rough on your back. While working on the Sistine   8
Chapel, Michelangelo wrote a poem complaining: "I've already grown a goiter at

this drudgery . . . With my beard toward heaven . . . I am bent like a bow." Don't be discouraged, though. Bad posture is a small price to pay for immortality.

1995

QUESTIONS FOR DISCUSSION

Content

a. What are some of the problems painters of frescoes faced?
b. Why, according to Goodheart, would an artist want to attempt fresco?
c. Why is time essential when painting a fresco?
d. What does the quotation from Cennini (paragraph 3) tell us about the art of fresco? What use, other than explanation, does Goodheart make of it?
e. Where is Tuscany? Where and what is the Sistine Chapel?

Style and Strategy

f. What is the effect of Goodheart's listing the equipment needed in a separate paragraph? Why didn't he simply mention tools and supplies in the course of explaining the process?
g. Explain the organizational logic behind this essay.
h. The author includes several examples (illustrations) in this essay. Where do they appear, and what is their function?
i. Where does Goodheart use comparison and contrast? To what end?
j. What kind of audience does this essay address? Explain your answer with reference to both style and content.
k. Identify important transitional devices—common to narrative and process analysis—in Goodheart's essay. Then, discuss other ways in which this essay resembles a narrative.

SUGGESTIONS FOR SHORT WRITING

a. Freewrite for ten minutes about a task you know a great deal about. For example, consider what it takes to write a college research paper, to paint the exterior of an old house, to set a large table for a holiday party, or to plan a wedding. Then, read your freewriting and list three or four of the major steps involved in the process. You might be able to use these steps as a rough outline for a full-length paper. Use the four steps in "How to Paint a Fresco" as your blueprint.
b. Notice that "How to Paint a Fresco" contains a warning at the end. From what you have learned about the art of fresco, what might you add to this warning?

SUGGESTIONS FOR SUSTAINED WRITING

a. Follow the outline you made above (in response to item *a* of Short Writing) and write a full-length process paper that explains how to complete a task with which you are familiar. Use the details you gathered during freewriting to get you started.

b. In your college library, research a "lost art" that interests you. Take notes from at least three sources. Then, write a process paper on this activity. For example, as Goodheart has, you might explain how to fight a duel or hunt a woolly mammoth. Then again, you can explain how to complete a cave painting, build a drawbridge, shoot a crossbow, weave a tapestry, smoke meat, make medicines from herbs, or build a Roman aqueduct. Make sure to give your sources credit by including internal citations as appropriate and a works-cited or references page.

4

Definition

Generally speaking, definitions fall into three broad categories: lexical, stipulative, and extended. The dictionary is of course the best place to begin familiarizing yourself with new concepts, but lexical definitions tend to be abstract, for they sometimes explain terms without reference to particular contexts. And stipulative definitions, while practical, are by their very nature limited to special purposes. Say you were writing a paper on the advantages and disadvantages of being a part-time student. You might *stipulate* that, for the purposes of your essay, "a part-timer is someone enrolled for less than 2 credits." Thus, while both lexical and stipulative definitions have their uses, extended definitions are the type used most often to explain complex topics like those discussed in this chapter.

The many practical uses to which extended definition can be applied make it a powerful tool for exposition. In the hands of writers like Claudia Glenn Dowling and Susan Sontag, it becomes a systematic way to grapple with social, moral, or even scientific questions. It can correct common, sometimes dangerous, misconceptions, as in Gloria Steinem's "Erotica and Pornography" or Jo Goodwin Parker's "What Is Poverty?" It can be used to expose abuses of language, as in the essay by John Leo, or to satirize "Good Souls" as Dorothy Parker has shown. And it can even explain something as delicate as a one's relationship to his or her faith, as in Sam Pickering's amusing "Faith of the Father."

Like process essays, extended definitions are developed by using a number of methods. Among the most common are analogy and comparison/contrast. Sontag discusses two notions of beauty in Catholic and Protestant countries, and Pickering contrasts a religion of "soft feeling" to one of "sharp thought."

As a matter of fact, many techniques can be used to develop extended definitions. The examples and anecdotes (brief, illustrative stories) Jo Goodwin Parker uses to define poverty are powerful and incisive tools for correcting social myopia. Illustration and anecdote, though used for a different purpose, also appear in Dorothy Parker's "Good Souls."

139

    Approaches to the process of defining, then, are as varied as the authors who use them. Sontag launches her discussion of beauty by tracing its etymology from the Greeks to the present. Leo analyzes the current uses of important words to show how badly those in positions of influence and power abuse the language. Sontag and Steinem rely on lexical and etymological information to introduce or clarify specific points in a larger context.

    You can learn a great deal more about techniques for writing extended definitions by considering the Questions for Discussion and by addressing the Suggestions for Short Writing and for Sustained Writing that follow each selection in this chapter. Another good way to learn the skills of definition is to read each of the essays in this chapter twice. On your first pass, simply make sure you understand each selection thoroughly and accurately. The second time around, ask yourself how you might define the term being explained, whether you agree with the author's perception, or if you can add information to make the definition even more credible. The method described above might require more time than you had planned to spend on this chapter, but it is the kind of mental exercise that will strengthen your analytical muscles and help you use definition as a powerful tool whenever you need to explain complex ideas.

Beauty

Susan Sontag

Susan Sontag (b. 1933) took her BA at the University of Chicago and her M.A. at Radcliffe College. She also studied at Oxford University. She is an accomplished novelist, film director, and writer of screenplays. Through her essays, which have been published in magazines and journals across the country, Sontag has established a reputation as a critic of modern culture. She will probably be best remembered, however, for her contribution to the theory of aesthetics. In her best-known work, Against Interpretation *(1966), Sontag enunciates a theory of art based upon a reliance on the senses and not the intellect. Her place of authority in the contemporary world of art criticism was confirmed when, in 1976, she published* On Photography. *Her novels include* The Benefactor *(1964) and* Death Kit *(1967). Sontag's nonfiction—*Trip to Hanoi *(1969),* Styles of Radical Will *(1969),* Vudu Urbano *(1985), and* AIDS and Its Metaphors *(1989)—demonstrate her ability to address current social and political realities with the same incisiveness that she approaches questions of art. In "Beauty," which she first published in* Vogue *in 1975, Sontag provides us with a feminist interpretation of the uses and misuses of that word throughout history.*

For the Greeks, beauty was a virtue: A kind of excellence. Persons then were as- 1
sumed to be what we now have to call—lamely, enviously—*whole* persons. If it
did occur to the Greeks to distinguish between a person's "inside" and "outside,"
they still expected that inner beauty would be matched by beauty of the other
kind. The well-born young Athenians who gathered around Socrates found it
quite paradoxical that their hero was so intelligent, so brave, so honorable, so se-
ductive—and so ugly. One of Socrates' main pedagogical acts was to be ugly—
and teach those innocent, no doubt splendid-looking disciples of his how full of
paradoxes life really was.

They may have resisted Socrates' lesson. We do not. Several thousand years 2
later, we are more wary of the enchantments of beauty. We not only split off—with
the greatest facility—the "inside" (character, intellect) from the "outside" (looks);
but we are actually surprised when someone who is beautiful is also intelligent,
talented, good.

It was principally the influence of Christianity that deprived beauty of the 3
central place it had in classical ideals of human excellence. By limiting excellence
(*virtus* in Latin) to *moral* virtue only, Christianity set beauty adrift—as an alienated, arbitrary, superficial enchantment. And beauty has continued to lose prestige.
For close to two centuries it has become a convention to attribute beauty to only
one of the two sexes: The sex which, however Fair, is always Second. Associating
beauty with women has put beauty even further on the defensive, morally.

A beautiful woman, we say in English. But a handsome man. "Handsome" is 4
the masculine equivalent of—and refusal of—a compliment which has accumulated
certain demeaning overtones, by being reserved for women only. That one can call
a man "beautiful" in French and in Italian suggests that Catholic countries—unlike
those countries shaped by the Protestant version of Christianity—still retain some

141

vestiges of the pagan admiration for beauty. But the difference, if one exists, is of degree only. In every modern country that is Christian or post-Christian, women *are* the beautiful sex—to the detriment of the notion of beauty as well as of women.

To be called beautiful is thought to name something essential to 5 women's character and concerns. (In contrast to men—whose essence is to be strong, or effective, or competent.) It does not take someone in the throes of advanced feminist awareness to perceive that the way women are taught to be involved with beauty encourages narcissism, reinforces dependence and immaturity. Everybody (women and men) knows that. For it is "everybody," a whole society, that has identified being feminine with caring about how one *looks.* (In contrast to being masculine—which is identified with caring about what one *is* and *does* and only secondarily, if at all, about how one looks.) Given these stereotypes, it is no wonder that beauty enjoys, at best, a rather mixed reputation.

It is not, of course, the desire to be beautiful that is wrong but the obligation 6 to be—or to try. What is accepted by most women as a flattering idealization of their sex is a way of making women feel inferior to what they actually are—or normally grow to be. For the ideal of beauty is administered as a form of self-oppression. Women are taught to see their bodies in *parts,* and to evaluate each part separately. Breasts, feet, hips, waistline, neck, eyes, nose, complexion, hair, and so on—each in turn is submitted to an anxious, fretful, often despairing scrutiny. Even if some pass muster, some will always be found wanting. Nothing less than perfection will do.

In men, good looks is a whole, something taken in at a glance. It does not 7 need to be confirmed by giving measurements of different regions of the body, nobody encourages a man to dissect his appearance, feature by feature. As for perfection, that is considered trivial—almost unmanly. Indeed, in the ideally good-looking man a small imperfection or blemish is considered positively desirable. According to one movie critic (a woman) who is a declared Robert Redford fan, it is having that cluster of skin-colored moles on one cheek that saves Redford from being merely a "pretty face." Think of the depreciation of women—as well as of beauty—that is implied in that judgment.

"The privileges of beauty are immense," said Cocteau. To be sure, beauty is 8 a form of power. And deservedly so. What is lamentable is that it is the only form of power that most women are encouraged to seek. This power is always conceived in relation to men; it is not the power to do but the power to attract. It is a power that negates itself. For this power is not one that can be chosen freely—at least, not by women—or renounced without social censure.

To preen, for a woman, can never be just a pleasure. It is also a duty. It is her 9 work. If a woman does real work—and even if she has clambered up to a leading position in politics, law, medicine, business, or whatever—she is always under pressure to confess that she still works at being attractive. But in so far as she is keeping up as one of the Fair Sex, she brings under suspicion her very capacity to be objective, professional, authoritative, thoughtful. Damned if they do—women are. And damned if they don't.

One could hardly ask for more important evidence of the dangers of consid- 10
ering persons as split between what is "inside" and what is "outside" than that interminable half-comic half-tragic tale, the oppression of women. How easy it is to
start off by defining women as caretakers of their surfaces, and then to disparage
them (or find them adorable) for being "superficial." It is a crude trap, and it has
worked for too long. But to get out of the trap requires that women get some critical
distance from that excellence and privilege which is beauty, enough distance to see
how much beauty itself has been abridged in order to prop up the mythology of the
"feminine." There should be a way of saving beauty *from* women—and *for* them.

1975

QUESTIONS FOR DISCUSSION

Content

a. What is Sontag's thesis?

b. Sontag makes it a point to explain the differences between the connotations
of the word *handsome* and those of *beautiful*. How does this contrast help her
develop her thesis? In what other ways does she use contrast as a method of
development?

c. Is Sontag's message aimed at a predominantly female audience? At a predominantly male audience? At a mixed audience?

d. Consult appropriate sources in the reference section of your college library.
Who are Socrates and Cocteau? Why does Sontag mention them (paragraphs
1 and 8 respectively)?

e. What was it that caused beauty to "lose prestige" (paragraph 3)? How does our
conception of beauty differ from the one the Greeks had?

f. What is Sontag referring to when she talks about countries that are "post-
Christian" (paragraph 4)?

g. If beauty is "a form of power" (paragraph 8), what about it is "lamentable"?

h. What does Sontag mean when she claims that women are "Damned if they
do. . . . And damned if they don't" (paragraph 9)?

Strategy and Style

i. Sontag launches the essay by spending considerable time discussing notions of
beauty through history. Is such a long introduction justified? Why or why not?

j. Does the essay's conclusion echo its introduction? Explain.

k. In some instances, Sontag seems to be addressing the reader directly. Find a
few such instances, and explain their effect on you.

l. Analyze the author's style. What is the effect of her insistence on varying sentence length and structure?

m. Overall, how would you describe Sontag's tone?

SUGGESTIONS FOR SHORT WRITING

a. Rewrite Sontag's essay as song lyrics. An easy way to do this is to use the melody of a well-known song for the structure of your lyrics. Try to remain true to what you believe to be Sontag's meaning.
b. Write a short definition of *ugliness*. Is it the antithesis of beauty, or do beauty and ugliness share some of the same characteristics?

SUGGESTIONS FOR SUSTAINED WRITING

a. In paragraph 5, the author claims that "the way women are taught to be involved with beauty encourages narcissism, reinforces dependence and immaturity." Think about some relevant television or magazine advertisements for beauty products. Is Sontag correct? Write an analytical essay in which you explain how such ads define *beauty*.
b. Is there such a thing as "inner beauty" as distinguished from one's physical appearance? Establish your own definition of *inner beauty*, but make sure to illustrate it with concrete details about a person or persons you know quite well.
c. Sontag seems to have concentrated on the negative effects of our preoccupation with physical beauty. Are there any positive effects? Write an essay from the other side of the issue.

What Is Poverty?

Jo Goodwin Parker

The author has requested that no biographical information be provided.

You ask me what is poverty? Listen to me. Here I am, dirty, smelly, and with no 1
"proper" underwear on and with the stench of my rotting teeth near you. I will tell
you. Listen to me. Listen without pity. I cannot use your pity. Listen with understanding. Put yourself in my dirty, worn out, ill-fitting shoes, and hear me.

Poverty is getting up every morning from a dirt- and illness-stained mat- 2
tress. The sheets have long since been used for diapers. Poverty is living in a smell
that never leaves. This is a smell of urine, sour milk, and spoiling food sometimes
joined with the strong smell of long-cooked onions. Onions are cheap. If you have
smelled this smell, you did not know how it came. It is the smell of the outdoor
privy. It is the smell of young children who cannot walk the long dark way in the
night. It is the smell of the mattresses where years of "accidents" have happened.
It is the smell of the milk which has gone sour because the refrigerator long has
not worked, and it costs money to get it fixed. It is the smell of rotting garbage. I
could bury it, but where is the shovel? Shovels cost money.

Poverty is being tired. I have always been tired. They told me at the hospi- 3
tal when the last baby came that I had chronic anemia caused from poor diet, a bad
case of worms, and that I needed a corrective operation. I listened politely—the
poor are always polite. The poor always listen. They don't say that there is no
money for iron pills, or better food, or worm medicine. The idea of an operation
is frightening and costs so much that, if I had dared, I would have laughed. Who
takes care of my children? Recovery from an operation takes a long time. I have
three children. When I left them with "Granny" the last time I had a job, I came
home to find the baby covered with fly specks, and a diaper that had not been
changed since I left. When the dried diaper came off, bits of my baby's flesh came
with it. My other child was playing with a sharp bit of broken glass, and my oldest was playing alone at the edge of a lake. I made twenty-two dollars a week, and
a good nursery school costs twenty dollars a week for three children. I quit my job.

Poverty is dirt. You can say in your clean clothes coming from your clean 4
house, "Anybody can be clean." Let me explain about housekeeping with no
money. For breakfast I give my children grits with no oleo or cornbread without
eggs and oleo. This does not use up many dishes. What dishes there are, I wash in
cold water and with no soap. Even the cheapest soap has to be saved for the baby's
diapers. Look at my hands, so cracked and red. Once I saved for two months to
buy a jar of Vaseline for my hands and the baby's diaper rash. When I had saved

enough, I went to buy it and the price had gone up two cents. The baby and I suffered on. I have to decide every day if I can bear to put my cracked sore hands into
the cold water and strong soap. But you ask, why not hot water? Fuel costs money.
If you have a wood fire it costs money. If you burn electricity, it costs money. Hot
water is a luxury. I do not have luxuries. I know you will be surprised when I tell
you how young I am. I look so much older. My back has been bent over the wash
tubs every day for so long, I cannot remember when I ever did anything else. Every
night I wash every stitch my school age child has on and just hope her clothes will
be dry by morning.

Poverty is staying up all night on cold nights to watch the fire knowing one   5
spark on the newspaper covering the walls means your sleeping child dies in
flames. In summer, poverty is watching gnats and flies devour your baby's tears
when he cries. The screens are torn and you pay so little rent you know they will
never be fixed. Poverty means insects in your food, in your nose, in your eyes, and
crawling over you when you sleep. Poverty is hoping it never rains because diapers won't dry when it rains and soon you are using newspapers. Poverty is seeing your children forever with runny noses. Paper handkerchiefs cost money and
all your rags you need for other things. Even more costly are antihistamines.
Poverty is cooking without food and cleaning without soap.

Poverty is asking for help. Have you ever had to ask for help, knowing your   6
children will suffer unless you get it? Think about asking for a loan from a relative, if this is the only way you can imagine asking for help. I will tell you how it
feels. You find out where the office is that you are supposed to visit. You circle that
block four or five times. Thinking of your children, you go in. Everyone is very
busy. Finally, someone comes out and you tell her that you need help. That never
is the person you need to see. You go see another person, and after spilling the
whole shame of your poverty all over the desk between you, you find that this
isn't the right office after all—you must repeat the whole process, and it never is
any easier at the next place.

You have asked for help, and after all it has a cost. You are again told to wait.   7
You are told why, but you don't really hear because of the red cloud of shame and
the rising cloud of despair.

Poverty is remembering. It is remembering quitting school in junior high   8
because "nice" children had been so cruel about my clothes and my smell. The attendance officer came. My mother told him I was pregnant. I wasn't, but she
thought that I could get a job and help out. I had jobs off and on, but never long
enough to learn anything. Mostly I remember being married. I was so young then.
I am still young. For a time, we had all the things you have. There was a little house
in another town, with hot water and everything. Then my husband lost his job.
There was unemployment insurance for a while and what few jobs I could get.
Soon, all our nice things were repossessed and we moved back here. I was pregnant then. This house didn't look so bad when we first moved in. Every week it
gets worse. Nothing is ever fixed. We now had no money. There were a few odd
jobs for my husband, but everything went for food then, as it does now. I don't

know how we lived through three years and three babies, but we did. I'll tell you something, after the last baby I destroyed my marriage. It had been a good one, but could you keep on bringing children in this dirt? Did you ever think how much it costs for any kind of birth control? I knew my husband was leaving the day he left, but there were no goodbys between us. I hope he has been able to climb out of this mess somewhere. He never could hope with us to drag him down.

That's when I asked for help. When I got it, you know how much it was? It 9 was, and is, seventy-eight dollars a month for the four of us; that is all I ever can get. Now you know why there is no soap, no needles and thread, no hot water, no aspirin, no worm medicine, no hand cream, no shampoo. None of these things for-ever and ever and ever. So that you can see clearly, I pay twenty dollars a month rent, and most of the rest goes for food. For grits and cornmeal, and rice and milk and beans. I try my best to use only the minimum electricity. If I use more, there is that much less for food.

Poverty is looking into a black future. Your children won't play with my 10 boys. They will turn to other boys who steal to get what they want. I can already see them behind the bars of their prison instead of behind the bars of my poverty. Or they will turn to the freedom of alcohol or drugs, and find themselves enslaved. And my daughter? At best, there is for her a life like mine.

But you say to me, there are schools. Yes, there are schools. My children 11 have no extra books, no magazines, no extra pencils, or crayons, or paper and most important of all, they do not have health. They have worms, they have infections, they have pink-eye all summer. They do not sleep well on the floor, or with me in my one bed. They do not suffer from hunger, my seventy-eight dollars keeps us alive, but they do suffer from malnutrition. Oh yes, I do remember what I was taught about health in school. It doesn't do much good. In some places there is a surplus commodities program. Not here. The county said it cost too much. There is a school lunch program. But I have two children who will already be damaged by the time they get to school.

But, you say to me, there are health clinics. Yes, there are health clinics and 12 they are in the towns. I live out here eight miles from town. I can walk that far (even if it is sixteen miles both ways), but can my little children? My neighbor will take me when he goes; but he expects to get paid, *one way or another.* I bet you know my neighbor. He is that large man who spends his time at the gas station, the barbershop, and the corner store complaining about the government spending money on the immoral mothers of illegitimate children.

Poverty is an acid that drips on pride until all pride is worn away. Poverty is 13 a chisel that chips on honor until honor is worn away. Some of you say that you would do *something* in my situation, and maybe you would, for the first week or the first month, but for year after year after year?

Even the poor can dream. A dream of a time when there is money. Money 14 for the right kinds of food, for worm medicine, for iron pills, for toothbrushes, for hand cream, for a hammer and nails and a bit of screening, for a shovel, for a bit of paint, for some sheeting, for needles and thread. Money to pay *in money* for a trip to town. And, oh, money for hot water and money for soap. A dream of when asking for help does not eat away the last bit of pride. When the office you visit is as nice as the offices of other governmental agencies, when there are enough workers to help you quickly, when workers do not quit in defeat and despair. When you have to tell your story to only one person, and that person can send you for other help and you don't have to prove your poverty over and over and over again.

I have come out of my despair to tell you this. Remember I did not come   15
from another place or another time. Others like me are all around you. Look at us with an angry heart, anger that will help you help me. Anger that will let you tell of me. The poor are always silent. Can you be silent too?

1971

QUESTIONS FOR DISCUSSION

Content

a. How would you define the author's purpose? Besides paragraph 15, in what parts of the essay is that purpose most apparent?

b. Why does the speaker address her audience directly, especially in paragraphs 4 and 10? How would you describe that audience?

c. What is the speaker's attitude toward her estranged husband? Do you find it curious? What does it tell you about her? What does it tell you about Parker's purpose?

d. In paragraph 8, the speaker seems to describe a cycle of poverty into which the poor are born and in which they remain. Explain. In what other sections of the essay does she allude to this cycle?

e. How does she account for her inability to keep her family clean? Why is it futile for her to seek a job?

f. What is the distinction between "hunger" and "malnutrition" that she makes in paragraph 11? Why does she deny the usefulness of school lunch programs?

g. The speaker relates incidents in which she has had to endure both public and private humiliation in order to obtain help for her family. What is the source of such humiliation? How does Parker's inclusion of these incidents help her define *poverty*?

Strategy and Style

h. Often, the speaker makes sure to anticipate and to discuss opposing arguments. What is the effect of her doing so? How does this practice help illuminate her character?

i. Parker has organized the essay by having her speaker enunciate a series of characteristics that define *poverty*. What is the effect of her beginning several paragraphs with "Poverty is . . . "?

j. Comment upon the author's use of illustrations. To what physical senses does she appeal most often? What use does she make of metaphor?

k. Parker has created a "persona" or speaker who tells her story by using the first-person pronoun ("I"). How would you describe this "persona"?

l. What is the purpose of paragraph 15 besides concluding the essay? How would you describe the speaker's tone in this paragraph? Does it differ from the tone she uses in other parts of the essay?

SUGGESTIONS FOR SHORT WRITING

a. Write a dictionary definition of *poverty* without using a dictionary. Then look the word up and compare your definition with the dictionary's. How specific were you or the dictionary able to get?

b. Now write a definition by using examples drawn from life. In your opinion, which of the definitions is clearer?

SUGGESTIONS FOR SUSTAINED WRITING

a. Parker has done an excellent job of defining an abstract term by using concrete illustrations. Think about one abstract term that describes a human reality with which you are thoroughly familiar: power, personal ambition, grief, hunger, physical pain, pride, for example. Explain what that term means to you. Use your own personal experiences as illustrations.

b. The speaker tells us about material poverty. Are there other kinds of poverty that are less frequently talked about—intellectual, spiritual, or moral poverty, for instance? Try to define one of these less commonly discussed types of poverty by using concrete details and illustrations as Parker does in this selection.

c. Does Parker believe that many of her readers harbor unfair and unrealistic assumptions about the poor? If so, what are these assumptions? Do you agree that they are unfair and unrealistic? Use what you know about poverty and the poor to write an essay that addresses such assumptions.

Faith of the Father

Sam Pickering

A graduate of the University of the South, Cambridge University, and Princeton University, Sam Pickering (b. 1941) has taught at Dartmouth College and is now a full professor at the University of Connecticut, where he teaches courses in nature writing and children's literature. He has written numerous scholarly books and articles on eighteenth- and nineteenth-century English literature and children's literature. A prolific writer, he regularly publishes familiar and critical essays in College English, *the* Kenyon Review, National Review, *the* Virginia Quarterly Review, Sewanee Review, *and other prestigious journals. Pickering was the recipient of Fulbright Lectureships in both Lebanon and Syria. He has published several essay collections including* The Right Distance, A Continuing Education, *and* May Days. *In some ways, "Faith of the Father" contrasts markedly with other essays in this chapter, for it is, as Pickering might say, "more concerned with people than ideas." More important, it reveals unmistakably, Pickering's sharp insight into the human character and his ability to extract wondrous things from lives that to lesser writers might seem ordinary. "Faith of the Father" first appeared in* The Southwest Review.

On weekdays Campbell's store was the center of life in the little Virginia town in   1
which I spent summers and Christmas vacations. The post office was in a corner of
the store, and the train station was across the road. In the morning men gathered on
Campbell's porch and drank coffee while they waited for the train to Richmond.
Late in the afternoon, families appeared. While waiting for their husbands, women
bought groceries, mailed letters, and visited with one another. Children ate cups of
ice cream and played in the woods behind the store. Sometimes a work train was
on the siding, and the engineer filled his cab with children and took them for short
trips down the track. On weekends life shifted from the store to St. Paul's Church.
Built in a grove of pine trees in the nineteenth century, St. Paul's was a small, white
clapboard building. A Sunday School wing added to the church in the 1920s jutted
out into the graveyard. Beyond the graveyard was a field in which picnics were held
and on the Fourth of July, the yearly Donkey Softball Game was played.

St. Paul's was familial and comfortable. Only a hundred people attended   2
regularly, and everyone knew everyone else and his business. What was private
became public after the service as people gathered outside and talked for half an
hour before going home to lunch. Behind the altar inside the church was a stained
glass window showing Christ's ascension to heaven. A red carpet ran down the
middle aisle, and worn, gold cushions covered the pews. On the walls were
plaques in memory of parishioners killed in foreign wars or who had made large
donations to the building fund. In summer the minister put fans out on the pews.
Donated by a local undertaker, the fans were shaped like spades. On them, besides the undertaker's name and telephone number, were pictures of Christ performing miracles: Walking on water, healing the lame, and raising Lazarus from
the dead.

150

Holidays and funerals were special at St. Paul's. Funerals were occasions for ³
reminiscing and telling stories. When an irascible old lady died and her daughter
had "Gone to Jesus" inscribed on her tombstone, her son-in-law was heard to say
"poor Jesus"—or so the tale went at the funeral. Christmas Eve was always cold
and snow usually fell. Inside the church at midnight, though, all was cheery and
warm as the congregation sang the great Christmas hymns: "O Come, All Ye
Faithful," "The First Noel," "O Little Town of Bethlehem," and "Hark! The Herald Angels Sing." The last hymn was "Silent Night." The service did not follow
the prayer book; inspired by Christmas and eggnog, the congregation came to
sing, not to pray. Bourbon was in the air, and when the altar boy lit the candles, it
seemed a miracle that the first spark didn't send us all to heaven in a blue flame.

Easter was almost more joyous than Christmas. Men stuck greenery into ⁴
their lapels and women blossomed in bright bonnets, some ordering hats not simply from Richmond but from Baltimore and Philadelphia. On a farm outside town
lived Miss Emma and Miss Ida Catlin. Miss Emma was the practical sister, running the farm and bringing order wherever she went. Unlike Miss Emma, Miss Ida
was shy. She read poetry and raised guinea fowl and at parties sat silently in a corner. Only on Easter was she outgoing; then like a day lily she bloomed tri-
umphantly. No one else's Easter bonnet ever matched hers, and the congregation
eagerly awaited her entrance which she always made just before the first hymn.

One year Miss Ida found a catalogue from a New York store which adver- ⁵
tised hats and their accessories. For ten to twenty-five cents ladies could buy artificial flowers to stick into their bonnets. Miss Ida bought a counter full, and that
Easter her head resembled a summer garden in bloom. Daffodils, zinnias, and
black-eyed Susans hung yellow and red around the brim of her hat while in the
middle stood a magnificent pink peony.

In all his glory Solomon could not have matched Miss Ida's bonnet. The ⁶
congregation could not take its eyes off it; even the minister had trouble concentrating on his sermon. After the last hymn, everyone hurried out of the church, eager to get a better look at Miss Ida's hat. As she came out, the altar boy began ring-
ing the bell. Alas, the noise frightened pigeons who had recently begun to nest and
they shot out of the steeple. The congregation scattered, but the flowers on Miss
Ida's hat hung over her eyes, and she did not see the pigeons until it was too late
and the peony had been ruined.

Miss Ida acted like nothing had happened. She greeted everyone and asked ⁷
about their healths and the healths of absent members of families. People tried not
to look at her hat but were not very successful. For two Sundays Miss Ida's "accident" was the main subject of after-church conversation; then it was forgotten for
almost a year. But, as Easter approached again, people remembered the hat. They
wondered what Miss Ida would wear to church. Some people speculated that since
she was a shy, poetic person, she wouldn't come. Even the minister had doubts. To
reassure Miss Ida, he and his sons borrowed ladders two weeks before Easter, and
climbing to the top of the steeple, chased the pigeons away and sealed off their
nesting place with chicken wire.

Easter Sunday seemed to confirm the fears of those who doubted Miss Ida   8
would appear. The choir assembled in the rear of the church without her. Half-
heartedly the congregation sang the processional hymn, "Hail Thee, Festival
Day." Miss Ida's absence had taken something bright from our lives, and as we sat
down after singing, Easter seemed sadly ordinary.

We were people of little faith. Just as the minister reached the altar and turned   9
to face us, there was a stir at the back of the church. Silently the minister raised his
right hand and pointed toward the door. Miss Ida had arrived. She was wearing the
same hat she wore the year before; only the peony was missing. In its place was a wonderful sunflower; from one side hung a black and yellow garden spider building a web
while fluttering above was a mourning cloak, black wings, dotted with blue and a yellow border running around the edges. Our hearts leaped up, and at the end of the service people in Richmond must have heard us singing "Christ the Lord Is Risen Today."

St. Paul's was the church of my childhood, that storied time when I thought lit-   10
tle about religion but knew that Jesus loved me, yes, because the Bible told me so. In
the Morning Prayer of life I mixed faith and fairy tale, thinking God a kindly giant,
holding in his hands, as the song put it, the corners of the earth and the strength of the
hills. Thirty years have passed since I last saw St. Paul's, and I have come down from
the cool upland pastures and the safe fold of childhood to the hot lowlands. Instead of
being neatly tucked away in a huge hand, the world now seems to bound erratically,
smooth and slippery, forever beyond the grasp of even the most magical deity. Would
that it were not so, and my imagination could find a way through his gates, as the prayer
says, with thanksgiving. Often I wonder what happened to the "faith of our fathers."
Why if it endured dungeon, fire, and sword in others, did it weaken so within me?

For me religion is a matter of story and community, a congregation rising to-   11
gether to look at an Easter Bonnet, unconsciously seeing it as an emblem of hope
and vitality, indeed of the Resurrection itself. For me religion ought to be more concerned with people than ideas, creating soft feeling rather than sharp thought. Often I associate religion with small, backwater towns in which tale binds folk one to
another. Here in a university in which people are separated by idea rather than
linked by story, religion doesn't have a natural place. In the absence of community,
ceremony becomes important. Changeable and always controversial, subject to dispassionate analysis, ceremony doesn't tie people together like accounts of pigeons
and peonies and thus doesn't promote good feeling and finally love for this world
and hope for the next. Often when I am discouraged, I turn for sustenance, not to
formal faith with articled ceremony but to memory, a chalice winey with story.

Not long ago I thought about Beagon Hackett, a Baptist minister in   12
Carthage, Tennessee. Born in Bagdad in Jackson County, Beagon answered the
call early in life. Before he was sixteen, he had preached in all the little towns in
Jackson County: Antioch, Nameless, McCoinsville, Liberty, and Gum Springs.
Although popular in country churches, Beagon's specialty was the all-day revival,
picnic, and baptizing, usually held back in the woods near places like Seven
Knobs, Booger Hill, Backbone Ridge, Chigger Hollow, and Twelve Corners.
Beagon made such a name that the big Baptist church in Carthage selected him as
minister. Once in Carthage, Beagon tempered his faith to suit the mood of the

county seat. Only once a year did he hold a meeting out of doors. For his first four or five years in Carthage, he led a revival near Dripping Rock Bluff across Hell Bend on the Caney Fork River, the spot being selected for name not location.

The narrows of the river were swift and deep, and crossing Hell Bend was dan-   13
gerous, a danger Beagon celebrated, first reminding the faithful that Jesus was a fisher of men and then buoying their spirits up on a raft of watery Christian song: "Shall We Gather at the River," "The Rock That Is Higher Than I," and "Sweet By and By." Beagon's meetings across the Caney Fork were a success with people traveling from as far as Macon and Trousdale counties to be baptized. But then one spring Gummert Capron or Doodlebug Healy, depending on whose memory is accurate, became frightened in mid-river and tipping over a rowboat changed "Throw Out the Life-Line" from word to deed. If Homer Nye had not grabbed Clara Jakeways by the hair, the dark waters, as the hymn puts it, would have swept her to eternity's shore. As it turned out Clara's salvation turned into romance, and three months later she and Nye were married, much to the disappointment of Silas Jakeways who owned a sawmill and the Eagle Iron Works and who disapproved of Nye, until that time an itinerant bricklayer. Clara, Silas was reported to have said, would "have been better off if love hadn't lifted her from the deep to become the wife of a no-account." Whatever the case, however, Beagon never led another revival across Hell Bend; instead he stayed dry on the Carthage side of the Caney Fork, once a year holding a temperate affair, more Sunday outing than revival, on Myers Bottom.

After Beagon had been in Carthage for twenty years, he grew heavy and dig-   14
nified. No longer would he preside at river baptizings. In his church he erected, as Silas Jakeways said "a marble birdbath," a baptismal font, copied from one he saw in an Episcopal Church at Monteagle. In Carthage, though, pretension was always liable to be tipped over, if not by simple-minded folk like Gummert Capron or Doodlebug Healy, then by daily life. Addicted to drink, Horace Armitage, the disreputable brother of Benbow Armitage, occasionally cut hair at King's Barber Shop. One morning after a long night of carousing at Enos Mayfield's in South Carthage, Horace was a bit shaky, and while shaving Beagon cut him slightly on the chin. "That's what comes of taking too much to drink," said Beagon, holding a towel to his chin. "Yes, sir, Reverend," Horace replied, "Alcohol does make the skin tender."

1985

QUESTIONS FOR DISCUSSION

Content

a. Explain the allusion at the beginning of paragraph 6. (Look up Solomon in a dictionary, an encyclopedia, or the Old Testament if you have to.) To what end does Pickering make this allusion?

b. How does the question at the end of paragraph 10 relate to the author's purpose?

c. What does Pickering mean when he writes that "religion ought to be more concerned with people than ideas, creating soft feeling rather than sharp thought" (paragraph 11)? How might this idea serve as his thesis?

d. What is his purpose in mentioning that, on Christmas Eve at St. Paul's, "Bourbon was in the air" (paragraph 3)?

e. Why is the congregation so elated at the return of Miss Ida and her hat (paragraph 9)? In what ways is the story of Miss Ida related to the Easter theme and to the essay's thesis?

f. How the author's faith—his vision of God and the world—has changed in the thirty years since he attended St. Paul's?

g. Why does Pickering believe that "religion doesn't have a natural place" in a university (paragraph 11)?

h. "In Carthage," we are told, "pretension was always liable to be tipped over" (paragraph 14). How is this point illustrated?

i. How might Pickering defend the notion that humor can be used to define something as serious as religious faith?

Strategy and Style

j. What details about St. Paul's in the first paragraph make that paragraph an appropriate introduction?

k. Find examples of irony in this piece.

l. The essay might have ended with paragraph 11. Why, then, does the author tell the story of Beagon Hackett?

m. Pickering mentions the titles of several Christian hymns. What does that accomplish other than helping to create atmosphere and establish the setting?

n. This selection is in three parts. What is the function of each? Is this organization appropriate?

o. Pickering's thesis appears in paragraph 11. Would the essay have been more effective had paragraph 11 come at the essay's very beginning or at its very end?

SUGGESTIONS FOR SHORT WRITING

a. We each worship in a different way. If you believe in a supreme being or in some spiritual power that controls the universe, write a paragraph of between 50 and 100 words that explains how you worship, recognize, or communicate with that being or power.

b. "Faith of the Father" makes use of humorous anecdotes to illustrate the human quality in even the most serious and spiritual of ceremonies. In a short paragraph or two, recall a humorous event that occurred during a ritual or holiday celebration, religious or not, which you attended. Include elements that will bring out the human qualities in even the most solemn observance.

c. Do you agree with Pickering that religion should create "soft feeling"? Freewrite for about 10 minutes on the function or role that religion—however you define it—plays in your life.

d. In paragraph 10, Pickering tells us that his childhood vision of religion was a mixture of "faith and fairy tale." What was your childhood faith like? Use freewriting, listing, or any other prewriting technique to gather details that might help you recall how you saw religion when you were a child.

SUGGESTIONS FOR SUSTAINED WRITING

a. If you responded to either or both of the last two Suggestions for Short Writing (items *c* and *d*), use the information you collected to get started on a well-developed essay that compares and contrasts your childhood vision of religion with the way you see religion today.

b. In many ways, Pickering's essay addresses the same questions and topics as Simeti's "Easter in Sicily" (Chapter 2). Read or reread Simeti's essay. Then, write a well-developed essay that compares and contrasts Simeti's description of Easter rituals with what is described in "Faith of the Father." Start by asking yourself if Simeti would accept Pickering's definition of religion. Then, discuss ways in which the rituals these authors discuss—although from very different cultures—are similar.

c. Easter is the most important of Christian holidays. Discuss a ritual or ceremony used in the celebration of a holiday important to your faith. Develop your essay with details that are specific and vivid. Use description, narration, and dialogue if appropriate. Make sure you explain what important tenet(s) of your faith are exemplified in the ceremony you have chosen to discuss.

Erotica and Pornography

Gloria Steinem

Born in Toledo, Ohio, Gloria Steinem (b. 1934) took her BA at Smith College, then studied at the University of Delhi and the University of Calcutta in India. Early in her career, she was a television news writer for NBC's "That Was the Week That Was." She went on to write for a number of America's most important magazines including Vogue, Life, Cosmopolitan, *and* Glamour, *and she served as an editorial consultant to* Seventeen *and* Show. *One of the founders and leaders of the contemporary American feminist movement, Steinem went undercover for* Show *magazine in 1963 to write "I Was a Playboy Bunny," an article that brought her journalistic acclaim. However, she is best known for her work as cofounder of and contributing editor to* New York *magazine and* Ms. *magazine. Today, she is among the most influential women in American public life, and her work has brought her numerous awards and honors, including the United Nations Ceres Medal and the Front Page Award. Among her full-length works are* Outrageous Acts *and* Everyday Rebellions *(1983),* Marilyn: Norma Jean *(1986),* A Revolution from Within *(1993), and* Moving Beyond Words *(1994). "Erotica and Pornography" was first published in 1978 in* Ms.

Human beings are the only animals that experience the same sex drive at times 1 when we can—and cannot—conceive.

Just as we developed uniquely human capacities for language, planning, 2 memory, and invention along our evolutionary path, we also developed sexuality as a form of expression, a way of communicating that is separable from our need for sex as a way of perpetuating ourselves. For humans alone, sexuality can be and often is primarily a way of bonding, of giving and receiving pleasure, bridging differentness, discovering sameness, and communicating emotion.

We developed this and other human gifts through our ability to change our 3 environment, adapt physically, and in the long run, to affect our own evolution. But as an emotional result of this spiraling path away from other animals, we seem to alternate between periods of exploring our unique abilities to change new boundaries and feelings of loneliness in the unknown that we ourselves have created; a fear that sometimes sends us back to the comfort of the animal world by encouraging us to exaggerate our sameness.

The separation of "play" from "work," for instance, is a problem only in the 4 human world. So is the difference between art and nature, or an intellectual accomplishment and a physical one. As a result, we celebrate play, art, and invention as leaps into the unknown; but any imbalance can send us back to nostalgia for our primate past and the conviction that the basics of work, nature, and physical labor are somehow more worthwhile or even moral.

In the same way, we have explored our sexuality as separable from concep- 5 tion: A pleasurable, empathetic bridge to strangers of the same species. We have even invented contraception—a skill that has probably existed in some form since our ancestors figured out the process of birth—in order to extend this uniquely hu-

156

man difference. Yet we also have times of atavistic suspicion that sex is not complete—or even legal or intended-by-god—if it cannot end in conception.

No wonder the concepts of "erotica" and "pornography" can be so crucially 6 different, and yet so confused. Both assume that sexuality can be separated from conception, and therefore can be used to carry a personal message. That's a major reason why, even in our current culture, both may be called equally "shocking" or legally "obscene," a word whose Latin derivative means "dirty, containing filth." This gross condemnation of all sexuality that isn't harnessed to childbirth and marriage has been increased by the current backlash against women's progress. Out of fear that the whole patriarchal structure might be upset if women really had the autonomous power to decide our reproductive futures (that is, if we controlled the most basic means of production), right-wing groups are not only denouncing pro-choice abortion literature as "pornographic," but are trying to stop the sending of all contraceptive information through the mails by invoking obscenity laws. In fact, Phyllis Schlafly recently denounced the entire Women's Movement as "obscene."

Not surprisingly, this religious, visceral backlash has a secular, intellectual 7 counterpart that relies heavily on applying the "natural" behavior of the animal world to humans. That is questionable in itself, but these Lionel Tigerish studies make their political purpose even more clear in the particular animals they select and the habits they choose to emphasize. The message is that females should accept their "destiny" of being sexually dependent and devote themselves to bearing and rearing their young.

Defending against such reaction in turn leads to another temptation: To 8 merely reverse the terms, and declare that *all* nonprocreative sex is good. In fact, however, this human activity can be as constructive or destructive, moral or immoral, as any other. Sex as communication can send messages as different as life and death; even the origins of "erotica" and "pornography" reflect that fact. After all, "erotica" is rooted in *eros* or passionate love, and thus in the idea of positive choice, free will, the yearning for a particular person. (Interestingly, the definition of erotica leaves open the question of gender.) "Pornography" begins with a root meaning "prostitution" or "female captives," thus letting us know that the subject is not mutual love, or love at all, but domination and violence against women. (Though, of course, homosexual pornography may imitate this violence by putting a man in the "feminine" role of victim.) It ends with a root meaning "writing about" or "description of" which puts still more distance between subject and object, and replaces a spontaneous yearning for closeness with objectification and a voyeur.

The difference is clear in the words. It becomes even more so by example. 9

Look at any photo or film of people making love; really making love. The 10 images may be diverse, but there is usually a sensuality and touch and warmth, an acceptance of bodies and nerve endings. There is always a spontaneous sense of people who are there because they *want* to be, out of shared pleasure.

Now look at any depiction of sex in which there is clear force, or an un- 11 equal power that spells coercion. It may be very blatant, with weapons or torture or bondage, wounds and bruises, some clear humiliation, or an adult's sexual power being used over a child. It may be much more subtle: A physical attitude of conqueror and victim, the use of race or class difference to imply the same thing, perhaps a very unequal nudity, with one person exposed and vulnerable while the other is clothed. In either case, there is no sense of equal choice or equal power.

The first is erotic: A mutually pleasurable, sexual expression between peo- 12 ple who have enough power to be there by positive choice. It may or may not strike the sense-memory in the viewer, or be creative enough to make the unknown seem real; but it doesn't require us to identify with a conqueror or a victim. It is truly sensuous, and may give us a contagion of pleasure.

The second is pornographic: Its message is violence, dominance, and con- 13 quest. It is sex being used to reinforce some inequality, or to create one, or to tell us the lie that pain and humiliation (ours or someone else's) are really the same as pleasure. If we are to feel anything, we must identify with conqueror or victim. That means we can only experience pleasure through the adoption of some degree of sadism or masochism. It also means that we may feel diminished by the role of conqueror, or enraged, humiliated, and vengeful by sharing identity with the victim.

Perhaps one could simply say that erotica is about sexuality, but pornogra- 14 phy is about power and sex-as-weapon—in the same way we have come to understand that rape is about violence, and not really about sexuality at all.

Yes, it's true that there are women who have been forced by violent families 15 and dominating men to confuse love with pain; so much so that they have become masochists. (A fact that in no way excuses those who administer such pain.) But the truth is that, for most women—and for men with enough humanity to imagine themselves into the predicament of women—true pornography could serve as aversion therapy for sex.

Of course, there will always be personal differences about what is and is not 16 erotic, and there may be cultural differences for a long time to come. Many women feel that sex makes them vulnerable and therefore may continue to need more sense of personal connection and safety before allowing any erotic feelings. We now find competence and expertise erotic in men, but that may pass as we develop those qualities in ourselves. Men, on the other hand, may continue to feel less vulnerable, and therefore more open to such potential danger as sex with strangers. As some men replace the need for submission from childlike women with the pleasure of cooperation from equals, they may find a partner's competence to be erotic, too.

Such group changes plus individual differences will continue to be reflected in 17 sexual love between people of the same gender, as well as between women and men. The point is not to dictate sameness, but to discover ourselves and each other through sexuality that is an exploring, pleasurable, empathetic part of our lives; a human sexuality that is unchained both from unwanted pregnancies and from violence.

But that is a hope, not a reality. At the moment, fear of change is increas- 18 ing both the indiscriminate repression of all nonprocreative sex in the religious and "conservative" male world, and the pornographic vengeance against women's sexuality in the secular world of "liberal" and "radical" men. It's almost futuristic to debate what is and is not truly erotic, when many women are again being forced into compulsory motherhood, and the number of pornographic murders, tortures, and woman-hating images are on the increase in both popular culture and real life.

It's a familiar division: wife or whore, "good" woman who is constantly 19 vulnerable to pregnancy or "bad" woman who is unprotected from violence. *Both* roles would be upset if we were to control our own sexuality. And that's exactly what we must do.

In spite of all our atavistic suspicions and training for the "natural" role of 20 motherhood, we took up the complicated battle for reproductive freedom. Our bodies had borne the health burden of endless births and poor abortions, and we had a greater motive for separating sexuality and conception.

Now we have to take up the equally complex burden of explaining that all 21 nonprocreative sex is *not* alike. We have a motive: Our right to a uniquely human sexuality, and sometimes even to survival. As it is, our bodies have too rarely been enough our own to develop erotica in our own lives, much less in art and literature. And our bodies have too often been the objects of pornography and the womanhating, violent practice that it preaches. Consider also our spirits that break a little each time we see ourselves in chains or full labial display for the conquering male viewer, bruised or on our knees, screaming a real or pretended pain to delight the sadist, pretending to enjoy what we don't enjoy, to be blind to the images of our sisters that really haunt us—humiliated often enough ourselves by the truly obscene idea that sex and the domination of women must be combined.

Sexuality *is* human, free, separate—and so are we.   22

But until we untangle the lethal confusion of sex with violence, there will be 23 more pornography and less erotica. There will be little murders in our beds—and very little love.

1978

QUESTIONS FOR DISCUSSION

Content

a. What is the distinction between *erotica* and *pornography*?
b. What place does the notion of choice have in that distinction?
c. Why is Steinem's separating the notions of sexuality and conception important to this essay?
d. This selection was published in 1978. What does Steinem mean by "the current backlash against women's progress" (paragraph 6)?

e. Strong opinions are voiced in paragraphs 6 and 7. To what extent do you agree or disagree with them?

f. What, according to Steinem, is the danger in declaring "that *all* nonprocreative sex is good" (paragraph 8)?

g. In paragraph 13, we read that only by adopting "some degree of sadism or masochism" can we derive pleasure from pornography. Why is this notion central to Steinem's distinction between *erotica* and *pornography*?

h. What changes does Steinem predict in the attitudes of women and men toward sex? To what extent do you believe those changes have been realized since the publication of this essay?

i. Summarize Steinem's arguments in paragraphs 18 and 19. Then, explain to what extent you agree or disagree.

j. How do you interpret the phrase "little murders" (paragraph 23)?

Strategy and Style

k. Steinem sometimes uses etymology, the study of word origins. In what way does her explaining the origins of *erotica* and *pornography* help her differentiate them (paragraph 8)?

l. As you know, this essay first appeared in Ms., a magazine whose readership consists largely of women. What in the essay's content also reveals that Steinem is addressing women?

m. Based on the language used in this piece, what else can you say about Steinem's audience?

n. Analyze the vocabulary in paragraphs 6 and 7. Regardless of the opinions stated, how would you characterize Steinem's tone in those paragraphs?

o. What use does the author make of illustration in this definition essay?

p. How does she use contrast and analysis?

q. Where do you find an example of descriptive writing?

r. In what way is Steinem's conclusion (paragraphs 21–23) a call to action?

SUGGESTIONS FOR SHORT WRITING

a. Paraphrase paragraphs 3 through 5. Then explain the function of these paragraphs in Steinem's essay. How do they relate to or help further her thesis?

b. Steinem's essay hinges on the distinction between two terms that are often confused. It is successful because the author is able to make that distinction clear. Choose two other terms that are often confused. Then list or explain differences between them. Here are topics like those you might choose to distinguish: sensuous/sensual, ideology/philosophy, art/craft, love/infatuation, discipline/denial, intelligence/cleverness, democracy/republicanism, knowledge/wisdom, leadership/intimidation, faith/orthodoxy, criticism/disapproval, naïveté/gullibility, stupidity/ignorance, tragic/disastrous.

SUGGESTIONS FOR SUSTAINED WRITING

a. If you responded to the second of the Suggestions for Short Writing above, use the details you have gathered in an essay that draws a distinction between two often confused concepts. Your goal will be to define each concept clearly and to allow your readers to distinguish one from the other easily. You may want to illustrate each concept by making reference to people or events that you have read about or learned about through personal experience.

b. Pretend that this is 1978 and that you have just read "Erotica and Pornography" in *Ms.* magazine. Write a letter to the editor of this periodical in which you defend or attack Steinem's thesis. Begin by identifying key points in her definition of *pornography.* Then, support or deny each of those points with facts and opinions of your own.

Good Souls

Dorothy Parker

Dorothy Parker (1893–1967) began her career shortly after graduating from high school by writing essays, sketches, and poetry for Vogue *and* Vanity Fair. *Later, she published in* The New Yorker *and, on occasion, in the* Saturday Evening Post. *Parker was one of the "charter members" of the Algonquin Round Table, an informal literary club that included humorist Robert Benchley and Harold Ross, the founder of* The New Yorker. *Versatile as well as witty, Parker published books of poetry, collections of essays, and stories, and wrote many plays and screenplays, including* A Star Is Born, *which she coauthored with her husband, Alan Campbell. "Big Blonde," for which she won the O. Henry Award in 1929, is her best-known short story. Parker also helped found the Screen Writers Guild in 1934 and the Anti-Nazi League in 1936. But her life was not all happiness and success. She was often troubled and twice attempted suicide. Her outspoken Marxist politics landed her before the House Un-American Activities Committee in 1952. Yet she always survived, perhaps supported by humor, the possession of which she felt to be essential to living. Her suggestions for an epitaph reveal an ability to chuckle even over her own demise: "Excuse my dust" and "If you can read this, you've come too close." "Good Souls" is an early piece by this brilliant American wit; it appeared in* Vanity Fair *in 1919.*

1   All about us, living in our very families, it may be, there exists a race of curious creatures. Outwardly, they possess no marked peculiarities; in fact, at a hasty glance, they may be readily mistaken for regular human beings. They are built after the popular design; they have the usual number of features, arranged in the conventional manner; they offer no variations on the general run of things in their habits of dressing, eating, and carrying on their business.

2   Yet, between them and the rest of the civilized world, there stretches an impassable barrier. Though they live in the very thick of the human race, they are forever isolated from it. They are fated to go through life, congenital pariahs. They live out their little lives, mingling with the world, yet never a part of it.

3   They are, in short, Good Souls.

4   And the piteous thing about them is that they are wholly unconscious of their condition. A Good Soul thinks he is just like anyone else. Nothing could convince him otherwise. It is heartrending to see him, going cheerfully about, even whistling or humming as he goes, all unconscious of his terrible plight. The utmost he can receive from the world is an attitude of good-humored patience, a perfunctory word of approbation, a praising with faint damns, so to speak—yet he firmly believes that everything is all right with him.

5   There is no accounting for Good Souls.

6   They spring up anywhere. They will suddenly appear in families which, for generations, have had no slightest stigma attached to them. Possibly they are throwbacks. There is scarcely a family without at least one Good Soul somewhere in it at the present moment—maybe in the form of an elderly aunt, an unmarried sister, an unsuccessful brother, an indigent cousin. No household is complete without one.

162

The Good Soul begins early; he will show signs of his condition in extreme 7 youth. Go now to the nearest window, and look out on the little children playing so happily below. Any group of youngsters that you may happen to see will do perfectly. Do you observe the child whom all the other little dears make "it" in their merry games? Do you follow the child from whom the other little ones snatch the cherished candy, to consume it before his streaming eyes? Can you get a good look at the child whose precious toys are borrowed for indefinite periods by the other playful youngsters, and are returned to him in fragments? Do you see the child upon whom all the other kiddies play their complete repertory of childhood's winsome pranks—throwing bags of water on him, running away and hiding from him, shouting his name in quaint rhymes, chalking coarse legends on his unsuspecting back?

Mark that child well. He is going to be a Good Soul when he grows up.   8

Thus does the doomed child go through early youth and adolescence. So does 9 he progress towards the fulfillment of his destiny. And then, some day, when he is under discussion, someone will say of him, "Well, he means well, anyway." That settles it. For him, that is the end. Those words have branded him with the indelible mark of his pariahdom. He has come into his majority; he is a full-fledged Good Soul.

The activities of the adult of the species are familiar to us all. When you are 10 ill, who is it that hastens to your bedside bearing molds of blanc-mange, which, from infancy, you have hated with unspeakable loathing? As usual, you are way ahead of me, gentle reader—it is indeed the Good Soul. It is the Good Souls who efficiently smooth out your pillow when you have just worked it into the comfortable shape, who creak about the room on noisy tiptoe, who tenderly lay on your fevered brow damp cloths which drip ceaselessly down your neck. It is they who ask, every other minute, if there isn't something that they can do for you. It is they who, at great personal sacrifice, spend long hours sitting beside your bed, reading aloud the continued stories in the *Woman's Home Companion,* or chatting cozily on the increase in the city's death rate.

In health, as in illness, they are always right there, ready to befriend you. No 11 sooner do you sit down, than they exclaim that they can see you aren't comfortable in that chair, and insist on your changing places with them. It is the Good Souls who just *know* that you don't like your tea that way, and who bear it masterfully away from you to alter it with cream and sugar until it is a complete stranger to you. At the table, it is they who always feel that their grapefruit is better than yours and who have to be restrained almost forcibly from exchanging with you. In a restaurant the waiter invariably makes a mistake and brings them something which they did not order—and which they refuse to have changed, choking it down with a wistful smile. It is they who cause traffic blocks, by standing in subway entrances arguing altruistically as to who is to pay the fare.

At the theater, should they be members of a box-party, it is the Good Souls 12 who insist on occupying the rear chairs; if the seats are in the orchestra, they worry audibly, all through the performance, about their being able to see better than you, until finally in desperation you grant their plea and change seats with them. If, by so doing, they can bring a little discomfort on themselves—sit in a draught, say, or behind a pillar—then their happiness is complete. To feel the genial glow of martyrdom—that is all they ask of life. . . .

The lives of Good Souls are crowded with Occasions, each with its own rit- 13 ual which must be solemnly followed. On Mother's Day, Good Souls conscientiously wear carnations; on St. Patrick's Day, they faithfully don boutonnieres of shamrocks; on Columbus Day, they carefully pin on miniature Italian flags. Every feast must be celebrated by the sending out of cards—Valentine's Day, Arbor Day, Groundhog Day, and all the other important festivals, each is duly observed. They have a perfect genius for discovering appropriate cards of greeting for the event. It must take hours of research.

If it's too long a time between holidays, then the Good Soul will send little 14 cards or little mementoes, just by way of surprises. He is strong on surprises, anyway. It delights him to drop in unexpectedly on his friends. Who has not known the joy of those evenings when some Good Soul just runs in, as a surprise? It is particularly effective when a chosen company of other guests happens to be present—enough for two tables of bridge, say. This means that the Good Soul must sit wistfully by, patiently watching the progress of the rubber, or else must cut in at intervals, volubly voicing his desolation at causing so much inconvenience, and apologizing constantly during the evening.

His conversation, admirable though it is, never receives its just due of at- 15 tention and appreciation. He is one of those who believe and frequently quote the exemplary precept that there is good in everybody; hanging in his bedchamber is the whimsically phrased, yet vital, statement, done in burned leather— "There is so much good in the worst of us and so much bad in the best of us that it hardly behooves any of us to talk about the rest of us." This, too, he archly quotes on appropriate occasions. Two or three may be gathered together, intimately discussing some mutual acquaintance. It is just getting really absorbing, when comes the Good Soul, to utter his dutiful, "We mustn't judge harshly—after all, we must always remember that many times our own actions may be misconstrued." Somehow, after several of these little reminders, there seems to be a general waning of interest; the little gathering breaks up, inventing quaint excuses to get away and discuss the thing more fully, adding a few really good details, some place where the Good Soul will not follow. While the Good Soul pitifully ignorant of their evil purpose glows with the warmth of conscious virtue, and settles himself to read the Contributors' Club, in the *Atlantic Monthly,* with a sense of duty well done. . . .

Good Souls are no mean humorists. They have a time-honored formula of 16 fun-making, which must be faithfully followed. Certain words or phrases must be whimsically distorted every time they are used. "Over the river," they dutifully say, whenever they take their leave. "Don't you cast any asparagus on me," they warn, archly; and they never fail to speak of "three times in concussion." According to their ritual, these screaming phrases must be repeated several times, for the most telling effect, and are invariably followed by hearty laughter from the speaker, to whom they seem eternally new.

Perhaps the most congenial role of the Good Soul is that of advice-giver. He 17 loves to take people aside and have serious little personal talks, all for their own good. He thinks it only right to point out faults or bad habits which are, perhaps unconsciously, growing on them. He goes home and laboriously writes long, intricate letters, invariably beginning, "Although you may feel that this is no affair of mine, I think that you really ought to know," and so on, indefinitely. In his desire to help, he reminds one irresistibly of Marcelline, who used to try so pathetically and so fruitlessly to be of some assistance in arranging the circus arena, and who brought such misfortunes on his own innocent person thereby.

The Good Souls will, doubtless, gain their reward in Heaven; on this earth, 18 certainly, theirs is what is technically known as a rough deal. The most hideous outrages are perpetrated on them. "Oh, he won't mind," people say. "He's a Good Soul." And then they proceed to heap the rankest impositions upon him. When Good Souls give a party, people who have accepted weeks in advance call up at the last second and refuse, without the shadow of an excuse save that of a subsequent engagement. Other people are invited to all sorts of entertaining affairs; the Good Soul, unasked, waves them a cheery good-bye and hopes wistfully that they will have a good time. His is the uncomfortable seat in the motor car; he is the one to ride backwards in the train; he is the one who is always chosen to solicit subscriptions and make up deficits. People borrow his money, steal his servants, lose his golf balls, use him as a sort of errand boy, leave him flat whenever something more attractive offers—and carry it all off with their cheerful slogan, "Oh, he won't mind—he's a Good Soul."

And that's just it—Good Souls never do mind. After each fresh atrocity they 19 are more cheerful, forgiving and virtuous, if possible, than they were before. There is simply no keeping them down—back they come, with their little gifts, and their little words of advice, and their little endeavors to be of service, always anxious for more.

Yes, there can be no doubt about it—their reward will come to them in the 20 next world.

Would that they were even now enjoying it!   21

1919

QUESTIONS FOR DISCUSSION

Content

a. Parker takes a well-worn phrase and treats it as worthy of a thorough definition. How would her definition of *Good Souls* sound if it were to be defined seriously in a standard dictionary?

b. The many touches of humor and sarcasm aside, do you feel that Parker is attempting to be serious or humorous? What specific details do you find to support either answer?

c. What is Parker's opinion of Good Souls? Does she sympathize with them at all? How do you know?

d. Do Good Souls as Parker defines them, really exist? If so, suppose that one of them happened to read this essay. What would his or her reaction be? To what extent would he or she agree or disagree with Parker?

e. This essay was written more than seventy years ago. Is Parker's definition of *Good Souls* still relevant? In what way?

Strategy and Style

f. How does the author's use of imagined situations and conversations affect the essay? In what way would the essay have been different had Parker named real people and recalled real conversations?

g. Find examples of irony in this essay.

h. Sometimes, Parker uses language that is affected (archaic, sentimental, or overblown—even for 1919!): for example, "little dears" and "merry games" in paragraph 7; "gentle reader" and "fevered brow" in paragraph 10; and "rankest impositions" in paragraph 18. What were her reasons for using these words? How do they affect the tone of the essay?

i. What purpose do the one-sentence paragraphs near the beginning of the essay serve?

j. Why does Parker include the last sentence? Does this sentence clarify the essay's purpose? Does it alter the essay's tone?

SUGGESTIONS FOR SHORT WRITING

a. Write a brief description of any Good Souls of your acquaintance.

b. Drawing from your own experience, write a different introduction for "Good Souls." Use dialogue or an anecdote instead of Parker's more or less straight-forward description.

SUGGESTIONS FOR SUSTAINED WRITING

a. In the first paragraph, Parker distinguishes between Good Souls and "regular human beings." Write an essay in which you define and describe these "regular human beings." Could "Regular Human Beings" be the title of your essay? One way to organize and develop your essay is to compare "regular human beings" with Good Souls.

b. Do you know any Good Souls? Write a sequel or extension to Parker's essay in which you show that this person or these persons fit Parker's definition.

c. Write an essay in which you define a cliché or a well-worn descriptive phrase as Parker did with Good Souls. For example: Bleeding Hearts, Hardened Criminals, Femme Fatales, Mr. (or Ms.) Right, Gentle Readers, True Loves.

Fire in the Sky

Claudia Glenn Dowling

Two years after taking a degree in Chinese at Vassar College, Dowling began working for People *magazine, where she became a senior writer and editor of the movie column. She then became a staff writer for* Life, *covering a variety of subjects from the Gulf War to space exploration to treatments for breast cancer. Her thirteen years with* Life *have been exciting, taking her around the world and giving her the opportunity to race a Porsche through Mexico, visit with the Cofan Indians in the Amazon, and tour Kyrgyzstan with Al Gore. She even climbed part of the way up Mt. Everest with a British Special Forces team and got her passport taken away in China. Dowling is a fellow of the world-famous explorer's club and a winner of several awards for excellence in journalism. She is also the author of Warner Books' photo version of* The Bridges of Madison County. *"Fire in the Sky" was first published in* Life *in 1994.*

Nights are long and bitter in the polar winters, but the compensations can be spec- 1
tacular: The skies blaze in a display of energy called the aurora borealis in the Arctic, aurora australis in the Antarctic. Ancient tribes who saw the lights believed
they were caused by the bonfires of spirits; today we know that awe-inspiring
physical forces create the heavenly arrays. And we're about to know more: A
hardy breed of scientists—who don't mind odd hours or sub-zero temperatures—
are investigating the powerful magnetic storms hidden within the aurora's glory.
A few years ago some of these researchers put up a sign outside their University
of Alaska lab near the tiny village of Poker Flats. It said it all: "Center for the Study
of Something which, on the face of it, might seem trivial, but on closer examination takes on Global Significance."

Auroras are born on the sun, where thermonuclear storms tear apart hydro- 2
gen atoms, blasting protons and electrons toward earth at up to 1,000 miles per
second. As this solar wind approaches earth's magnetic field, particles are drawn
to the poles like iron filings to the ends of a bar magnet. When the particles collide with gases in the earth's atmosphere, they create electrical discharges that
glow purple, green, red and white. The effect is similar to the collision of electrons
and gases inside a color television tube.

The beauty of an auroral storm hides its violence—the release of millions of 3
amperes of electricity, 20 times that found in a bolt of lightning. Surges within auroras, called substorms, tap energy trapped by the earth's magnetic field on the
side of the planet away from the sun. One physicist poetically calls this energy
pool earth's "electromagnetic soul."

A series of such storms knocked out power in all of Quebec as well as sev- 4
eral U.S. states in 1989. Earlier this year surges damaged two communications
satellites. NASA researchers theorize that the substorms, which produce nitrogen
oxides, may also damage the ozone layer above the poles. No one knows what effect the electrical charge may have on human beings, although Japanese travel

167

agencies book tours to the Arctic specifically for couples who believe that their chances of conceiving a child are better under the aurora.

Lately, interest in mapping and predicting substorms has led to increased 5 government spending. (That may be why, not long ago, the sign at Poker Flats was changed to read: "This facility is uniquely dedicated to studies of the aurora borealis and other atmospheric research studies for the paying customer such as the National Aeronautics and Space Administration, the United States Air Force. . . .") Last month NASA launched a satellite—dubbed Wind—to monitor the solar wind as it howls toward earth. Another, called Polar, the size of a school bus, is planned to orbit closer to the planet, photographing auroras with sensitive cameras. Next year Russia will launch two similar probes. And in November a consortium of European nations will open a radar installation in Spitsbergen, Norway, with high-powered dishes that will collect information about the velocity, density and temperature of solar particles. A European satellite that is designed to circle the Arctic will collect similar data from above.

Still, a nonscientific observer need only be in the right place at the right time 6 to study this natural wonder. A jargon-filled recorded message from the National Oceanic and Atmospheric Administration in Boulder, Colo. (303-497-3235), tells aficionados when conditions are favorable for a good show. Although the aurora can be seen year-round—the atmosphere is always being bombarded by the solar wind—and is sometimes visible as far away as the equator, it occurs most often in the extreme north and south and is easiest to see on a clear, dark winter night. Photographer Norbert Rosing's favorite site is Churchill, Manitoba, where winter skies are cloudless 80 percent of the time. There, every February and March, he waits in the cold, warming his film with his car heater so it won't crack. "When you see the northern lights," he says, "you're in love."

1994

QUESTIONS FOR DISCUSSION

Content

a. How would you define the term *aurora?*
b. What are some of the effects scientists have attributed to auroral substorms?
c. What advice does Dowling give amateur astronomers who want to see the northern lights?
d. Besides definition, for what other purposes was this essay intended?

Strategy and Style

e. Analyze Dowling's introduction. What about that first paragraph makes the reader want to continue?

f. Besides the fact that this essay was first published in *Life* magazine, how can we tell that Dowling is addressing a general audience?
g. This essay makes excellent use of figurative language to explain natural phenomena. Identify at least two examples of such language.

SUGGESTIONS FOR SHORT WRITING

a. Dowling mentions both ancient and contemporary human reactions to the aurora. Do some library research on a natural phenomenon—such as an earthquake, a lightning storm, or a solar eclipse—and report on the folklore associated with it. Discuss one or two ways in which people have accounted for, explained, or reacted to this phenomenon.
b. Summarize the ideas in paragraph 3.
c. Dowling has conveyed the excitement and fascination that many professional and amateur stargazers experience when viewing the aurora. Think about a natural phenomenon that arouses your interest. Freewrite for about ten minutes to describe that phenomenon.

SUGGESTIONS FOR SUSTAINED WRITING

a. If you responded to item *a* in Suggestions for Short Writing, continue researching your topic and turn your short writing and other notes into a full-length essay that explains how people in the past accounted for, explained, or reacted to a particular natural phenomenon.
b. If you responded to item *c* in Suggestions for Short Writing, use your freewriting as the basis of a fully developed discussion of a natural occurrence that interests you. To gather even more information, try interviewing a professor who has knowledge of your subject, or continue doing library research on it.

Stop Murdering the Language

John Leo

John Leo writes "On Society," a weekly column for US News & World Report, *which also appears in 150 U.S. newspapers. Before joining* US News & World Report, *Leo wrote for* Time *magazine and for the* New York Times. *He has also been an associate editor at* Commonweal; *a writer for* Society *magazine; a columnist for the* Village Voice; *the editor of* The Catholic Messenger, *a weekly paper in Davenport, Iowa; and a deputy administrator for the City of New York's Environmental Protection Administration. He currently serves as an editorial advisor to the* Columbia Journalism Review. *Leo's* US News & World Report *columns have been collected in* Two Steps Ahead of the Thought Police *(1994); he has also published a humorous collection entitled* How the Russians Invented Baseball and Other Essays of Enlightenment *(1989). "Stop Murdering the Language" appeared in* US News & World Report *in 1993.*

If you doubt that word games are becoming crucial to our social and political 1
struggles, listen to Derek Humphry. A leading figure in the euthanasia movement, Humphry says his side lost at the polls in Washington State last fall largely because it lost the battle over language. The pro-euthanasia campaigners talked broadly about "aid in dying." But the media and public, Humphry says, "used the real words with relish"—suicide and euthanasia—and Initiative 119 went down.

In passing, Humphry pointed out the vagueness of "aid in dying." It can mean, 2
he says, "anything from a physician's lethal injection all the way to holding hands with a dying patient and saying, 'I love you.'" Anyone who stretches a phrase to cover both killing and moral support is a serious player in the language games.

This is, in fact, a big trend in the fast-growing field of language manipula- 3
tion. Specific terms give way to ever broader and gassier ones. "Blind" or "legally blind" was replaced by "visually impaired," which includes everyone who wears glasses. "Child abuse" now seems to cover almost anything a parent or a parental figure can do wrong. "Substance abusers" (formerly addicts and winos) now include any person who overuses or misuses anything at all. William Lutz, editor of the *Quarterly Review of Doublespeak,* says, "The whole world is composed of substance. . . . This doesn't promote clarity of discussion."

More often word stretching occurs for frankly polemic reasons. "Family has 4
been stretched to make nonfamilies eligible for various family benefits. Now the word is seriously used to refer to group renters, childless couples and even single people living alone. To circumvent zoning restrictions, two groups of recovering alcoholics in Cherry Hill, N.J., insisted they were families. A spokesman said, "Residents consider themselves a family, and no other family in the country has to announce itself or explain itself." As in "Alice in Wonderland," the word means what the speaker wants it to mean.

Another popular form of stretching is to associate some low-level complaint 5
with a higher-level one involving violence, thus presumably startling everyone

into paying attention. A *Washington Post* columnist complained recently about "intellectual genocide" in D.C. public schools, meaning that students aren't taught well and aren't learning basic skills. Betty Friedan regularly complains about the media's "symbolic annihilation of women" (she means there still aren't enough news stories by and about women). A Manhattan man, dying of AIDS, said his death should be seen as "a form of political assassination" (he means Bush should have spent more on AIDS).

These stretching exercises are often more than publicity-grabbing hyper- 6
bole. Sometimes they are conscious attempts to ratchet up a minor offense into a major one. Ogling a woman, once considered harmless, or merely rude, is considered sexual harassment now and is often mentioned in the same breath as rape. Notice how the University of Minnesota's definition of sexual harassment blurs all lines between a glance, lack of sensitivity, serious harassment and rape: "Sexual harassment can be as blatant as rape or as subtle as a look. Harassment . . . often consists of callous insensitivity to the experience of women."

The verbal work of folding the entire category of harassment into the cate- 7
gory of rape goes on all the time. "Sexual harassment is a subtle rape," a psychologist named John Gottman told the *New York Times*. "Sexual harassment is a subset of rape with overtones of blackmail and extortion," columnist Carole Agus told her readers in *New York Newsday*.

Looser definitions keep blurring categories. The term "domestic violence," 8
for instance, once referred to physical assault in the home. Now it includes psychological abuse. Lenore Walker, a specialist in the field, defines wife battering to include bullying and manipulation ("making women do things they otherwise wouldn't . . . by eroding their self-esteem"). This mimics what happened when some definitions of date rape were expanded to include "psychological coercion," presumably including wheedling and pleading for sex.

A similar blurring occurs in the hate crime field. Often it's not very clear 9
whether we are talking about violence or nonviolence, crimes or noncriminal bias incidents, serious social offenses or minor and ambiguous run-ins. The National Institute Against Prejudice and Violence in Baltimore keeps feeding the media statistics on campus "ethnoviolence," but it defines violence to include slurs, graffiti and perceptions of slights (e.g., "I went to talk to someone who was black, and his friend stared at me the whole time as though she didn't want me there"). The effect of this tactic is to increase alarm about what's happening on campus and to raise doubts about the aims and methods of the statistics keepers.

The constant use of violent language for nonviolent incidents reflects the 10
current tensions among races and between sexes. But it probably also helps magnify those tensions by linking minor incidents to major assaults and putting everyone on full-time alert for offense. It's one price we're paying for these polemic word games.

1993

QUESTIONS FOR DISCUSSION

Content

a. What is Leo's thesis?
b. In what way does the statement by William Lutz support that thesis?
c. Definition can be used for a variety of purposes. To what end has Leo used it in this essay?
d. What, according to Leo, are some of the more common reasons that writers and speakers consciously manipulate language?

Strategy and Style

e. Does the reference to Derek Humphry in paragraphs 1 and 2 make for an appropriate introduction?
f. Where in this essay does Leo use illustration? Where does he use contrast?
g. The author's choice of words provides clues to his tone. How would you describe Leo's attitude toward his subject?
h. Why does Leo use so many direct quotations in this essay? Could he have paraphrased instead?
i. What is the effect of his referring to "Alice in Wonderland" in paragraph 4?
j. Where in this essay does Leo make an appeal to authority to support his thesis?

SUGGESTIONS FOR SHORT WRITING

a. Do you agree with Leo that "family" has been stretched to include groups that are not really families? Or do you believe that group renters, single people, and groups of recovering alcoholics, for example, might also be considered families? Freewrite for about 15 minutes to gather details about your personal definition of the term.
b. As Leo says, very specific terms often "give way to broader and gassier ones." Make a short list of such terms and their "gassier" alternatives.
c. Reread paragraphs 8 and 9. Respond to either of the two issues in these paragraphs by explaining why you agree or disagree with Leo's position.

SUGGESTIONS FOR SUSTAINED WRITING

a. Reread the University of Minnesota's definition of sexual harassment quoted in this essay. Is this close to your definition of the term? Would you advocate adopting such a policy at your school? Explain why or why not. If you are against adopting this kind of policy, use your essay as an opportunity to write your own definition of sexual harassment and to make a statement of policy that you would like adopted at your institution.

b. Though Leo makes several significant criticisms about the way in which some contemporary writers and speakers abuse language, one might argue that certain common terms can mean very different things to different people. Write an essay in which you compare your definition of an abstract term—such as *family, education, culture, wealth,* or *kindness*—with the definitions of this term held by two or three of your friends, classmates, or family members. Brainstorm with or interview these people to gather details for your essay. Make sure to take careful notes, and include direct quotations whenever possible.

5

Division and Classification

Division and classification are attempts to explain the nature and connections between bits of information that may, at first, seem unrelated and confusing. Writers often find it useful to identify like qualities or characteristics among various facts, ideas, people, or things so as to create related categories or classes by which the material can be divided logically and discussed systematically.

If you are a people watcher, you know that public places—a bus station, a sports stadium, or even a college library—offer a variety of subjects. Let's say that two days before a math midterm, you resolve to study hard in the library. As you walk into the main reading room, you hear the giggles of young lovers seated in a corner. A few yards beyond, you spot one of the college's maintenance workers who is spending her lunch hour noisily turning the pages of a large newspaper. To your right, you begin to eavesdrop on a few students discussing a fraternity party, and you realize that their chatter is annoying a woman trying to take notes for a term paper. In a less-crowded part of the room, two of your friends kill time by browsing through a few magazines they found lying about. After a while, you decide that the reading room offers too many distractions, so you find a corner in the basement where you can hide. It is no coincidence that other members of your math class had the same idea, so you sit down quietly and begin studying.

The decision to join your classmates and not stay in the reading room resulted from dividing the group of people you found at the library into three smaller categories: fun-seekers, browsers, and serious students! Your analysis may have been quick and informal, but it was effective. What's more, it revealed something important about the nature and function of classification: You began by observing similarities among various individuals; you created categories based on those similarities and placed each individual you observed into one of them; and you made a decision—to study in one place and not another—based upon what your classification revealed.

174

Classification is a versatile tool. It can be used to explain stages in human development as in Gail Sheehy's "Predictable Crises of Adulthood," to discuss current thinking about morality as in Meg Greenfield's "Why Nothing Is 'Wrong' Anymore," or to define one's ethnic, cultural, and sexual identity as in Kesaya E. Noda's "Growing Up Asian in America." As Donald Hall shows in "Four Kinds of Reading," it can help us analyze and understand the processes and motivations behind the way we read, think, and comprehend. As a matter of fact, Kesaya E. Noda and Susan Allen Toth show that classification makes an effective tool for self-analysis and for shedding light on aspects of our personalities and our lives that might parallel those of our readers.

The success of a classification paper depends upon how logically an author divides the material and how thoroughly and concretely he or she develops each category. Among the most effective methods to develop such an essay is illustration. Examples like those in Judith Viorst's "The Truth about Lying" are often essential to the writer's purpose. Without them, an essay might remain a list of ill-defined labels and abstractions. But good writers use a variety of techniques to keep readers interested. The essays by Ludlum and Toth, though different in style and approach, all contain anecdotes (narration) to support important points; Greenfield and Sheehy make excellent use of definition; Noda relies on definition, contrast, and anecdote; and Ludlum contrasts what we know and what we once believed in order to define *climythology* and to explain its causes and effects.

As you read the selections that follow, remember that almost any conglomeration of seemingly unrelated information can be classified to reveal patterns of meaning readers will find valuable and interesting. The perspectives from which you view a subject and the choices you make to impose order on the material should be determined only by your purpose. Read the Suggestions for Short Writing and for Sustained Writing after each selection. They describe activities that will help you use classification to accomplish a well-defined purpose. But even if you approach a writing assignment without a clear notion of purpose—something not uncommon even among experienced writers—you may still want to use classification in the early stages of your project to review the raw information you have collected, to group facts, ideas, and insights logically, and, ultimately, to improve your understanding both of the material and of your purpose.

Cinematypes

Susan Allen Toth

Born in Ames, Iowa, in 1940, Susan Allen Toth earned a PhD. at the University of Minnesota in 1969. She also holds a BA from Smith College (1961) and an MA from the University of California at Berkeley (1963). Since 1969, she has been on the faculty of Macalester College in St. Paul, Minnesota, where she teaches courses in the British and American novel, contemporary American literature, and creative writing. Toth's first book, Blooming: A Small-Town Girlhood *(1981), was named by the* New York Times *as one of the "notable books of the year."* Ivy Days: Making My Way Out East *was published in 1984, followed by* How to Prepare for Your High-School Reunion: And Other Mid-Life Musings *in 1988. Toth's stories, essays, and reviews have appeared in the* New York Times Book Review, Harper's, Ms., *and other publications. She has also written scholarly essays on late-nineteenth-century American local-color literature. She is currently working on a fictional memoir about her grandmother. "Cinematypes" first appeared in* Harper's *in May 1980.*

Aaron takes me only to art films. That's what I call them, anyway: strange movies   1
with vague poetic images I don't always understand, long dreamy movies about a
distant Technicolor past, even longer black-and-white movies about the general
meaninglessness of life. We do not go unless at least one reputable critic has found
the cinematography superb. We went to *The Devil's Eye*, and Aaron turned to me
in the middle and said, "My God, this is *funny*." I do not think he was pleased.

When Aaron and I go to the movies, we drive our cars separately and meet   2
by the box office. Inside the theater he sits tentatively in his seat, ready to move if
he can't see well, poised to leave if the film is disappointing. He leans away from
me, careful not to touch the bare flesh of his arm against the bare flesh of mine.
Sometimes he leans so far I am afraid he may be touching the woman on his other
side. If the movie is very good, he leans forward, too, peering between the heads
of the couple in front of us. The light from the screen bounces off his glasses; he
gleams with intensity, sitting there on the edge of his seat, watching the screen.
Once I tapped him on the arm so I could whisper a comment in his ear. He jumped.

After *Belle de Jour* Aaron said he wanted to ask me if he could stay overnight.   3
"But I can't," he shook his head mournfully before I had a chance to answer, "be-
cause I know I never sleep well in strange beds." Then he apologized for asking.
"It's just that after a film like that," he said, "I feel the need to assert myself."

Pete takes me only to movies that he thinks have redeeming social value. He   4
doesn't call them "films." They tend to be about poverty, war, injustice, political
corruption, struggling unions in the 1930s, and the military-industrial complex.
Pete doesn't like propaganda movies, though, and he doesn't like to be too depressed, either. We stayed away from *The Sorrow and the Pity;* it would be, he
said, just too much. Besides, he assured me, things are never that hopeless. So
most of the movies we see are made in Hollywood. Because they are always top-
ical, these movies offer what Pete calls "food for thought." When we saw *Coming*

176

Home, Pete's jaw set so firmly with the first half-hour that I knew we would end up at Poppin' Fresh Pies afterward.

When Pete and I go to the movies, we take turns driving so no one owes any- 5 one else anything. We leave the car far from the theater so we don't have to pay for a parking space. If it's raining or snowing, Pete offers to let me off at the door, but I can tell he'll feel better if I go with him while he finds a spot, so we share the walk too. Inside the theater Pete will hold my hand when I get scared if I ask him. He puts my hand firmly on his knee and covers it completely with his own hand. His knee never twitches. After a while, when the scary part is past, he loosens his hand slightly and I know that is a signal to take mine away. He sits companionably close, letting his jacket just touch my sweater, but he does not infringe. He thinks I ought to know he is there if I need him.

One night, after *The China Syndrome,* I asked Pete if he wouldn't like to stay 6 for a second drink, even though it was past midnight. He thought a while about that, considering my offer from all possible angles, but finally he said no. Relationships today, he said, have a tendency to move too quickly.

Sam likes movies that are entertaining. By that he means movies that Will 7 Jones in the *Minneapolis Tribune* loved and either *Time* or *Newsweek* rather liked; also movies that do not have sappy love stories, are not musicals, do not have subtitles, and will not force him to think. He does not go to movies to think. He liked *California Suite* and *The Seduction of Joe Tynan,* though the plots, he said, could have been zippier. He saw it all coming too far in advance, and that took the fun out. He doesn't like to know what is going to happen. "I just want my brain to be tickled," he says. It is very hard for me to pick out movies for Sam.

When Sam takes me to the movies, he pays for everything. He thinks that's 8 what a man ought to do. But I buy my own popcorn, because he doesn't approve of it; the grease might smear his flannel slacks. Inside the theater, Sam makes himself comfortable. He takes off his jacket, puts one arm around me, and all during the movie he plays with my hand, stroking my palm, beating a small tattoo on my wrist. Although he watches the movie intently, his body operates on instinct. Once I inclined my head and kissed him lightly just behind his ear. He beat a faster tattoo on my wrist, quick and musical, but he didn't look away from the screen.

When Sam takes me home from the movies, he stands outside my door and 9 kisses me long and hard. He would like to come in, he says regretfully, but his steady girlfriend in Duluth wouldn't like it. When the *Tribune* gives a movie four stars, he has to save it to see with her. Otherwise her feelings might be hurt.

I go to some movies by myself. On rainy Sunday afternoons I often sneak 10 into a revival house or a college auditorium for old Technicolor musicals, *Kiss Me Kate, Seven Brides for Seven Brothers, Calamity Jane,* even, once, *The Sound of Music.* Wearing saggy jeans so I can prop my feet on the seat in front, I sit toward the rear where no one can see me. I eat large handfuls of popcorn with double butter. Once the movie starts, I feel completely at home. Howard Keel and I are old friends; I grin back at him on the screen. I know the sound tracks by heart. Sometimes when I get really carried away I hum along with Kathryn Grayson, remembering how I once thought I would fill out a formal like that. I am rather glad now I never did. Skirts whirl, feet tap, acrobatic young men perform impossible feats, and then the camera dissolves into a dream sequence I know I can comfortably follow. It is not, thank God, Bergman.

If I can't find an old musical, I settle for Hepburn and Tracy, vintage Grant 11 or Gable, on adventurous days Claudette Colbert or James Stewart. Before I buy my ticket I make sure it will all end happily. If necessary, I ask the girl at the box office. I have never seen *Stella Dallas* or *Intermezzo*. Over the years I have developed other peccadilloes: I will, for example, see anything that is redeemed by Thelma Ritter. At the end of *Daddy Long Legs* I wait happily for the scene when Fred Clark, no longer angry, at last pours Thelma a convivial drink. They smile at each other, I smile at them, I feel they are smiling at me. In the movies I go to by myself, the men and women always like each other.

1980

QUESTIONS FOR DISCUSSION

Content

a. What does the last sentence in the essay reveal about Toth's experiences with movies and men? How does it reveal Toth's thesis? What is that thesis?
b. Why is it necessary to classify the activity of movie going? What benefits are gained from classifying this subject?
c. For whom is Toth writing? What might be their reasons for reading this essay?
d. Into what categories does Toth divide movies and men? Why does she choose these categories?
e. How does she distinguish between *film* and *movie*? Do her definitions of these terms match yours? What words does Toth use to reveal her opinion of them?
f. Into which category do you place yourself and your own boyfriend, girlfriend, or spouse? Do you find that you agree or disagree with Toth's opinions of movies and men?
g. Has Toth left any categories out? Has she overgeneralized with the categories she has chosen? If so, what might be her reasons for doing so?

Strategy and Style

h. Each category is structured in the same way: name of boyfriend, type of movie, titles of representative movies, mode of transportation to the movie, behavior during the movie, etc. How do the components of one category relate to those of the others? What effect does this rigid structure have on the essay as a whole?
i. Why does Toth focus her description on her friends in the first three categories, leaving herself out until the fourth category?

j. The author does not use a standard introduction or conclusion. How effective is the essay without a standard beginning and ending? Does the abruptness increase or decrease the essay's effectiveness?

k. Why does Toth title her essay "Cinematypes"? Do you think these types refer to cinemas, movies, or moviegoers? What is the benefit of having an ambiguous title?

l. Describe Toth's tone. Is she being serious or humorous? What words, phrases, or sentences reveal her tone?

SUGGESTIONS FOR SHORT WRITING

a. Write the story of one of your own experiences with a date at a movie. Which cinematype did he or she resemble most closely?

b. Write personals ads for Toth, any of her cinematypes, and/or yourself, seeking to find the perfect movie date. You might find examples of such ads in the classified section of your newspaper.

SUGGESTIONS FOR SUSTAINED WRITING

a. Write an essay classifying a popular activity. Be sure that your reasons for classifying are clear to you and to your readers. Take into account the types of people and the types of behavior associated with each category.

b. Write an essay in which you extend Toth's classification, discussing cinematypes that she did not include.

c. Write "Cinematypes" from a man's point of view. What aspects will remain the same? Which will differ?

Climythology

David Ludlum

An expert on weather history, David Ludlum wrote "Climythology" for Weatherwise, *a magazine he founded in 1946.*

History is full of myths, and so is climatology. Every generation of historians gives 1 rise to a revisionist school that reinterprets the past in light of new material and facts. Sometimes the revisions join the body of history; other times they are revised by the next generation. Overall, the process leads to a richer and more truthful history.

The settlement of America produced a series of myths about the climate of 2 different regions of our country. Even before the first British settlements in North America, Europeans held certain concepts concerning the supposed climate of the New World, and those concepts greatly influenced their efforts to establish colonies from Newfoundland to the Carolinas.

Once the seaboard was occupied, new myths arose about the lands west of 3 the Allegheny Mountains. Other unfounded beliefs appeared to influence the oc-cupation of the Mississippi Valley and Great Plains until, in the last decade of the nineteenth century, the land office in Washington officially declared the frontier closed, though much territory remained unsettled. Most of this, however, was thought to be wasteland unsuitable for cultivation. This belief would be dispelled in the next century by the introduction of scientific methods of agriculture and the construction of huge irrigation projects.

THE EQUAL-LATITUDE MYTH

The intellectual content of climatology had made little progress from the time of 4 Ptolemy, the Greek astronomer and geographer of the second century A.D., to the year 1601, which marked the beginning of the century of colonization of North America by the English and the French. The concept of *clima,* or parallel bands around the world which shared comparable temperatures and hence weather con-ditions, was the generally accepted view of global arrangements. So much so, in fact, that the word clima was used by English writers interchangeably with "lati-tude." This gave rise to what I shall call the equal-latitude myth.

The planners and backers of the new colonies held to the classical view of 5 the distribution of global temperatures and thus were greatly surprised and cha-grined when their environmental expectations were not met by the realities of the New World. The French were perplexed by the harsh winter conditions they met in Nova Scotia and the St. Lawrence Valley because both lay at the same latitudes as northern and central France. The British ultimately gave up constant efforts to settle Newfoundland in the early years of the seventeenth century because of the severe winters, despite the fact that it lay at the same latitude as southernmost Eng-land, where winters were usually moderate in temperature.

180

The history of all the British colonies from Maine to the Carolinas ran much **6** the same. The commercial backers of each colony expressed surprise and dismay that these settlements, though at the latitudes of France and Spain, could not produce the exotic agricultural products of those countries.

Believing Virginia to have a Mediterranean climate, the proprietors tried silk **7** culture until the realities of the winter killed all hopes of producing such a tropical product.

Almost a century passed before the backers of the colonies realized that the **8** American climate differed from the European at the same latitudes. By the beginning of the eighteenth century, a more realistic viewpoint prevailed about the climate of the New World. Facts replaced the equal-latitude myth.

THE CLIMATE CHANGE MYTH

During the first two centuries of settlement of the American seaboard, a popular **9** misconception arose about the observed climate. Where were the record snows of yesteryear? Why did we not have the harsh winters so often mentioned by grandfather and great-grandfather? Many homespun philosophers pondered these questions and suggested answers. Though no actual facts were brought forth, most colonists believed that conditions had grown milder and that the seasons had changed, with spring coming later and autumn lasting longer.

These ideas were expressed in an article by Dr. Hugh Williamson of North **10** Carolina in the first issue of the *Transactions of the American Philosophical Society* in 1771: "An attempt to account for the change observed in the Middle Colonies in North America."

Williamson's thesis was that the cutting down of the forests for farms and **11** settlements had produced a warming of the soil for two reasons. First, the felling of the trees allowed easterly winds to penetrate more deeply into the country, bringing temperate marine influences inland. Second, the bare soil received and stored more solar heat than did forested lands, and snow melted more quickly when exposed to direct sunlight.

In addition, some colonials suggested that the rise of urban communities **12** with heated buildings and smokepots was leading to a milder climate, as they claimed had occurred in Europe. These ideas were the first of many about climate change that were to arise and claim a body of believers among Americans.

THE OHIO COUNTRY MYTH

After almost 200 years of English settlement along the Atlantic seaboard, the vast **13** interior of the North American continent remained a *terra incognita* as far as an exact knowledge of its geography and climate was concerned. The French had sent voyageurs, couriers de bois and missionaries deep into the interior, but their first-hand knowledge of the conditions encountered did not reach the seaboard-bound British. Though the barrier of the Appalachian Mountains was breached during the war years that marked the closing decades of the eighteenth century, few scientific men went westward to observe and report on the physical and atmospheric geography of the interior.

A vigorous controversy as to the nature of the climate of the Ohio Country 14 beyond the Allegheny Mountains arose as the century drew to a close and continued to spark lively arguments well into the next century. The controversy became known as the Ohio Country myth.

Between October 1795 and June 1796, Constantin Francois de Chaseboeuf, 15 Comte de Volney, traveled from Washington, D.C., to Vincennes on the Wabash River in Indiana. He was familiar with Jefferson's view, expressed in his *Notes on the State of Virginia,* that the annual temperature west of the mountains was several degrees warmer than at the same latitude east of the mountains along the Atlantic seaboard. Jefferson based his opinion on the different types of plants thriving on opposite sides of the mountains. Volney's seeming confirmation of Jefferson's opinion received wide dissemination in the *View of the Climate and Soil of the United States,* published in London and Paris in 1804.

The first refutation of the ideas promulgated by Volney came from Dr. Daniel 16 Drake in *Notices Concerning Cincinnati,* published in 1810, which produced actual comparative temperature readings. Others soon took up their scientific cudgels. In an address before the Albany Institute in 1823, Dr. Lewis Beck took each of Volney's statements and demolished them with facts from more recent material.

William Darby, in his *View of the United States: Historical, Geographical* 17 *and Statistical* (1828), referred to Volney's "by no means innoxious vulgar error." As late as 1842, Dr. Samuel Forry, in the first climatological survey to employ meteorological observations, felt constrained to criticize Volney's opinions as being "barren of precise data."

In 1857, Lorin Blodget put the Ohio Country myth to final rest in his compre- 18 hensive *Climatology of the United States:* "The early distinction between the Atlantic States and the Mississippi has been quite dropped, as the progress of observation has shown them to be essentially the same, or to differ only in unimportant particulars."

THE GREAT AMERICAN DESERT MYTH

"When I was a schoolboy my map of the United States showed between the Mis- 19 souri River and the Rocky Mountains a long, broad white blotch, upon which was printed in small capitals 'THE GREAT AMERICAN DESERT—UNEXPLORED.'" So wrote Colonel Richard Irving Dodge in 1877 when commencing his revealing survey, *The Great Plains of the Great West.* He concluded: "What was then 'unexplored' is now almost thoroughly known. What was regarded as a desert supports, in some portions, thriving populations. The blotch of thirty years ago is now known as 'The Plains.'"

Sergeant John Ordway, who had accompanied Lewis and Clark in 1804, had 20
stated ". . . this country may with propriety be called the Deserts of North America." Captain Zebulon Pike in exploring the headwaters of the Arkansas River had
declared that ". . . these vast plains of the western hemisphere may become in time
as celebrated as the sandy deserts of Africa." And Major Stephen H. Long had
written, ". . . the Great Desert at the Base of the Rocky Mountains . . . is almost
wholly unfit for cultivation, and of course uninhabitable. . . ."

When Lorin Blodget published his comprehensive *Climatology of the* 21
United States in 1857, he marked a zone running east of the 100° W meridian on
his precipitation chart "the eastern limit of the dry plains," and labeled the area of
western Kansas and Nebraska "the Desert Plains."

Following the Civil War, a counterattack was launched on the pessimistic 22
opinion about the future of the plains. The pressure for new lands to settle caused
a change of view regarding the farming possibilities of the plains west of the Missouri River. Optimistic projections were penned by enthusiastic travelers, booster-
type editors and eager business promoters. Their hopes were bolstered by several
years of above-normal rainfall in the late 1860s and early 1870s. The concept that
"Rain Follows the Plough" was broadcast in chamber-of-commerce style by agricultural improvement societies and business enterprises. This was the "Garden
Myth"—that planting trees and crops on the dry plains would result in increased
rainfall in a self-perpetuating manner. The climate pendulum, however, underwent
several swings from adequate to inadequate rainfall until a nadir was reached in the
late 1880s and early 1890s, resulting in disaster for the many cattle ranchers and the
abandonment of farming in much of western Kansas and western Nebraska.

The occupation of the central plains by farmers, the western plains by cat- 23
tlemen, the mountains by miners, and the Pacific Northwest by lumbermen
brought more adequate knowledge of the actual climates of these regions. The filling in of the nation's climatological charts was completed about 1890, when the
availability of free land ended and the frontier was considered closed.

THE SOUTHERN CALIFORNIA HEALTH MYTH

During the first 30 years of American settlement Southern California remained a 24
frontier country with ranching and agriculture dominating the economy. The last
two decades of the century, however, brought a change. Promoters and develop-
ers exploited the region's prime natural attraction, a beneficent climate, to make it
the health frontier of the United States. Its favorable features were widely promoted in a tidal wave of publicity, and hordes of Easterners responded by migrat-
ing to the promised land in search of restored health. Thanks to man's ingenuity,
the barren outlands had suddenly become habitable and even attractive.

During the decades from 1850 to 1880, native Angelenos might have been 25
forgiven for doubting their climate would turn out to be the most promising feature
of the region. Damaging floods occurred in 1862 and 1868, devastating droughts

came in 1862–64 and 1876–77, and a long spell of recurrent cold weather in the late 1870s and early 1880s set many still-standing date records for coldness. In addition, a destructive earthquake struck in 1857 and every year there were "tremblos."

Despite the lack of knowledge of the effect of California's climate on dis-   26
ease, publicity for the region's salubrity soon poured forth. A pamphlet entitled *Southern California: The Italy of America* claimed for the area the "only perfect climate in the world and the grandest scenery under the sun." *The Los Angeles Star* in 1872 carried an article, "Land of Glorious Sunsets," which was considered by historian Oscar O. Winther (in 1946) as "the opening trumpet blast of a climate promotion campaign that has not ended."

Concerted efforts to attract visitors and settlers became an increasingly ac-   27
tive industry in the 1880s. The local Chamber of Commerce was careful to point out that not all parts of California enjoyed the salubrious climate claimed for the southern region. The results soon became apparent. A great boom in real estate and business developed in the mid-1880s, similar to those previously experienced in other sections of the western frontier country.

In the 1890s, climate continued to be the principal pitch of promotion agen-   28
cies. In 1892, the Southern California Information Bureau asserted: ". . . we sell the climate at so much an acre and throw in the land." To a complaint that the region had nothing to sell except climate, one enthusiast declared: "That's right, and we sell it, too—$10 for an acre of land, $490 an acre for the climate."

The health angle and longevity prospects were emphasized in the promo-   29
tional publications of the 1890s. Dr. Peter C. Remondino stated the extreme claim for the region in his book, *The Mediterranean Shores of America: Southern California:* "from my personal observations, I can say that at least an extra ten years' lease on life is gained by a removal to this coast from the Eastern States; not ten years to be added with its extra weight of age and infirmity, but ten years more with additional benefit of feeling ten years younger during the time."

They came at first by the thousands, and finally by the millions; today more   30
than 15 million people live in Southern California where a century ago there were only 32,000.

Ironically, the concentration of population with attendant urban sprawl and   31
congested freeways affected the climate in a way none of its promoters of the late 1800s foresaw. The effusions of millions of combustion engines, trapped in the area's natural basins by the almost daily inversions in the lower atmosphere, have created smog conditions detrimental to health.

ALASKAN CLIMYTHOLOGY

The bill for $7,200,000 to pay for Alaska "loosed a storm in the House of Repre-   32
sentatives. I shall not attempt to say whether it was a hurricane or tornado, but it was accompanied by a lot of wind, by a great flood—a flood of oratory and some verbal thunder," declared Senator Ernest Gruening at a meeting of the American

Meteorological Society at the University of Alaska on June 27, 1962. The former Russian colony was portrayed as "a frozen waste with a savage climate, where little or nothing could grow, and where few could or would live."

Typical of the statements of these pioneer climythologists was that of Benjamin F. Loan of St. Louis, who declared: 33

". . . the acquisition of this inhospitable and barren waste will never add a dollar to the wealth of our country or furnish any homes to our people. It is utterly worthless. . . . To suppose that anyone would leave the United States . . . to seek a home . . . in the regions of perpetual snow is simply to suppose such a person insane." 34

Another climatic pessimist, Representative Orange Ferris of Glens Falls, New York, asserted that Alaska "is a barren and unproductive region covered with ice and snow" and "will never be populated by an enterprising people." 35

A representative from New York, Dennis McCarthy of Syracuse, cited "reports that every foot of the soil of Alaska is frozen from five to six feet in depth" and ventured that his colleagues would soon hear that Greenland was on the market. 36

And the minority report of the House Committee on Foreign Relations, in a scathing denunciation, declared Alaska "had no capacity as an agricultural country . . . no value as a mineral country . . . its timber generally of poor quality and growing upon inaccessible mountains . . . its fur trade . . . of insignificant value, and, will speedily come to an end . . . the fisheries of doubtful value . . . in a climate unfit for the habitation of civilized men." 37

Today, Alaska supports a population of more than one half million people and an annual economy worth more than $9 billion. 38

1987

QUESTIONS FOR DISCUSSION

Content

a. What is Ludlum's purpose? What do you gain from reading about the history of climate myths?
b. Ludlum has coined a new term with *climythology.* How does he define this word?
c. Look up the definition of the word *myth.* How does a myth differ from a legend, a history, a folktale? Look up *climate* and *weather.* How do the two differ?
d. How does Ludlum's discussion of the European's misconceptions about the climate of North America help explain the colonization of North America? What did European settlers do in order to adapt to the climate?
e. What is a "homespun philosopher" (paragraph 9)? Are the writers whom Ludlum quotes in this and other paragraphs examples of homespun philosophers? If not, in what ways do the writers quoted differ from them?
f. Ludlum writes that explorers used words such as *desert* to describe the Great Plains. What effect would the use of such words have on the formation of climate myths?

g. What effect did marketing and advertising have on the formation and maintenance of the "Southern California Health Myth"?

h. Do any myths about climate still exist? Do you recall hearing any from your parents or grandparents? Are there any you believe to be true?

i. Has Ludlum left out any myths? How would climate and weather help to explain other historical events and developments?

Strategy and Style

j. Why does Ludlum provide headings for each of the climate myths? How does dividing his essay in this way affect the essay as a whole? How do you account for the sequence in which the myths appear?

k. Ludlum begins his article with a three-paragraph introduction, yet ends the article abruptly. What might be his reasons for doing this?

l. In the sentence "Others soon took up their scientific cudgels" (paragraph 16), why does Ludlum use the word *cudgel*? What does this reveal about the nature of belief in the climate myths?

m. What is it about the way Ludlum develops this essay that makes it so convincing?

n. Describe the tone and language in this essay by comparing them with what you have read in another essay in this chapter. Are they different from the tone and word choice in this other essay? Why and in what way?

SUGGESTIONS FOR SHORT WRITING

a. Write a climate myth of your own. The myth can be regional or global in scope; for example, there has been a lot of talk lately about global warming–are there any myths attached to this issue?

b. Choose one of the climate myths that Ludlum presents and write it as a narrated myth, as if you were telling or hearing it as a story with mythological characters and action.

SUGGESTIONS FOR SUSTAINED WRITING

a. What other misconceptions do people have about climate or weather (for example, that lightning never strikes the same place twice, or that the winters of one's childhood were much worse than recent winters)? Write a sequel or continuation of Ludlum's essay in which you expose these misconceptions.

b. What other bodies of modern mythology can you think of? For example, think about the misconceptions people have about particular ethnic groups, sexes, religions, diseases, professions, cities, states, or parts of the world. Write an essay in which you catalog and explain a set of beliefs.

c. Write a myth of your own that explains the origin or existence of something. Upon what existing beliefs or knowledge will you base your myth?

Predictable Crises of Adulthood

Gail Sheehy

Born in New York City and educated at the University of Vermont and Columbia University, Gail Sheehy (b. 1937) has been a contributing editor for New York Magazine *and has written for* Paris Match, *the* London Sunday Telegraph, *the* New York Times Magazine, Cosmopolitan, *and* Glamour. *Sheehy's first sustained work was* Lovesounds *(1970), a novel, which has been followed by several pieces of nonfiction, including* Hustling: Prostitution in Our Wide Open Society *(1973);* Character: America's Search for Leadership *(1988); and* Gorbachev: The Man Who Changed the World *(1990). In 1986, Sheehy published* Spirit of Survival, *the story of a Cambodian girl she found and later adopted as a result of a journalistic assignment on refugee children in Southeast Asia.* Passages *(1976), from which "Predictable Crises of Adulthood" is taken, discusses several natural crises through which everyone must pass and which, if understood and handled properly, can lay the foundation for a stable and fulfilling life.*

We are not unlike a particularly hardy crustacean. The lobster grows by developing and shedding a series of hard, protective shells. Each time it expands from within, the confining shell must be sloughed off. It is left exposed and vulnerable until, in time, a new covering grows to replace the old. 1

With each passage from one stage of human growth to the next we, too, must shed a protective structure. We are left exposed and vulnerable—but also yeasty and embryonic again, capable of stretching in ways we hadn't known before. These sheddings may take several years or more. Coming out of each passage, though, we enter a longer and more stable period in which we can expect relative tranquility and a sense of equilibrium regained. . . . 2

As we shall see, each person engages the steps of development in his or her own characteristic *step-style.* Some people never complete the whole sequence. And none of us "solves" with one step—by jumping out of the parental home into a job or marriage, for example—the problems in separating from the caregivers of childhood. Nor do we "achieve" autonomy once and for all by converting our dreams into concrete goals, even when we attain those goals. The central issues or tasks of one period are never fully completed, tied up, and cast aside. But when they lose their primacy and the current life structure has served its purpose, we are ready to move on to the next period. 3

Can one catch up? What might look to others like listlessness, contrariness, a maddening refusal to face up to an obvious task may be a person's own unique detour that will bring him out later on the other side. Developmental gains won can later be lost—and rewon. It's plausible, though it can't be proven, that the mastery of one set of tasks fortifies us for the next period and the next set of challenges. But it's important not to think too mechanistically. Machines work by units. The bureaucracy (supposedly) works step by step. Human beings, thank God, have an individual inner dynamic that can never be precisely coded. 4

Although I have indicated the ages when Americans are likely to go through each stage, and the differences between men and women where they are striking, 5

187

do not take the ages too seriously. The stages are the thing, and most particularly the sequence.

Here is the briefest outline of the developmental ladder.   **6**

PULLING UP ROOTS

Before 18, the motto is loud and clear: "I have to get away from my parents." But **7** the words are seldom connected to action. Generally still safely part of our families, even if away at school, we feel our autonomy to be subject to erosion from moment to moment.

After 18, we begin Pulling Up Roots in earnest. College, military service, **8** and short-term travels are all customary vehicles our society provides for the first round trips between family and a base of one's own. In the attempt to separate our view of the world from our family's view, despite vigorous protestations to the contrary—"I know exactly what I want!"—we cast about for any beliefs we can call our own. And in the process of testing those beliefs we are often drawn to fads, preferably those most mysterious and inaccessible to our parents.

Whatever tentative memberships we try out in the world, the fear haunts us **9** that we are really kids who cannot take care of ourselves. We cover that fear with acts of defiance and mimicked confidence. For allies to replace our parents, we turn to our contemporaries. They become conspirators. So long as their perspective meshes with our own, they are able to substitute for the sanctuary of the family. But that doesn't last very long. And the instant they diverge from the shaky ideals of "our group," they are seen as betrayers. Rebounds to the family are common between the ages of 18 and 22.

The tasks of this passage are to locate ourselves in a peer group role, a sex role, **10** an anticipated occupation, an ideology or world view. As a result, we gather the impetus to leave home physically and the identity to *begin* leaving home emotionally.

Even as one part of us seeks to be an individual, another part longs to restore **11** the safety and comfort of merging with another. Thus one of the most popular myths of this passage is: We can piggyback our development by attaching to a Stronger One. But people who marry during this time often prolong financial and emotional ties to the family and relatives that impede them from becoming self-sufficient.

A stormy passage through the Pulling Up Roots years will probably facili- **12** tate the normal progression of the adult life cycle. If one doesn't have an identity crisis at this point, it will erupt during a later transition, when the penalties may be harder to bear.

THE TRYING TWENTIES

The Trying Twenties confront us with the question of how to take hold in the adult **13** world. Our focus shifts from the interior turmoils of late adolescence—"Who am I?" "What is truth?"—and we become almost totally preoccupied with working out the externals. "How do I put my aspirations into effect?" "What is the best way to start?" "Where do I go?" "Who can help me?" "How did *you* do it?"

In this period, which is longer and more stable compared with the passage 14 that leads to it, the tasks are as enormous as they are exhilarating: To shape a Dream, that vision of ourselves which will generate energy, aliveness, and hope. To prepare for a lifework. To find a mentor if possible. And to form the capacity for intimacy without losing in the process whatever consistency of self we have thus far mustered. The first test structure must be erected around the life we choose to try.

Doing what we "should" is the most pervasive theme of the twenties. The 15 "shoulds" are largely defined by family models, the press of the culture, or the prejudices of our peers. If the prevailing cultural instructions are that one should get married and settle down behind one's own door, a nuclear family is born. If instead the peers insist that one should do one's own thing, the 25-year-old is likely to harness himself onto a Harley-Davidson and burn up Route 66 in the commitment to have no commitments.

One of the terrifying aspects of the twenties is the inner conviction that the 16 choices we make are irrevocable. It is largely a false fear. Change is quite possible, and some alteration of our original choices is probably inevitable.

Two impulses, as always, are at work. One is to build a firm, safe structure 17 for the future by making strong commitments, to "be set." Yet people who slip into a ready-made form without much self-examination are likely to find themselves *locked* in.

The other urge is to explore and experiment, keeping any structure tentative 18 and therefore easily reversible. Taken to the extreme, these are people who skip from one trial job and one limited personal encounter to another, spending their twenties in the *transient* state.

Although the choices of our twenties are not irrevocable, they do set in mo- 19 tion a Life Pattern. Some of us follow the lock-in pattern, others the transient pattern, the wunderkind pattern, the caregiver pattern, and there are a number of others. Such patterns strongly influence the particular questions raised for each person during each passage. . . .

Buoyed by powerful illusions and belief in the power of the will, we com- 20 monly insist in our twenties that what we have chosen to do is the one true course in life. Our backs go up at the merest hint that we are like our parents, that two decades of parental training might be reflected in our current actions and attitudes.

"Not me," is the motto, "I'm different."   21

CATCH-30

Impatient with devoting ourselves to the "shoulds," a new vitality springs from within 22 as we approach 30. Men and women alike speak of feeling too narrow and restricted. They blame all sorts of things, but what the restrictions boil down to are the outgrowth of career and personal choices of the twenties. They may have been choices perfectly suited to that stage. But now the fit feels different. Some inner aspect that was left out is striving to be taken into account. Important new choices must be made, and commitments altered or deepened. The work involves great change, turmoil, and often crisis—a simultaneous feeling of rock bottom and the urge to bust out.

One common response is the tearing up of the life we spent most of our 23
twenties putting together. It may mean striking out on a secondary road toward a new vision or converting a dream of "running for president" into a more realistic goal. The single person feels a push to find a partner. The woman who was previously content at home with children chafes to venture into the world. The childless couple reconsiders children. And almost everyone who is married, especially those married for seven years, feels a discontent.

If the discontent doesn't lead to a divorce, it will, or should, call for a seri- 24
ous review of the marriage and of each partner's aspirations in their Catch-30 condition. The gist of that condition was expressed by a 29-year-old associate with a Wall Street law firm:

"I'm considering leaving the firm. I've been there four years now; I'm getting 25
good feedback, but I have no clients of my own. I feel weak. If I wait much longer, it will be too late, too close to that fateful time of decision on whether or not to become a partner. I'm success-oriented. But the concept of being 55 years old and stuck in a monotonous job drives me wild. It drives me crazy now, just a little bit. I'd say that 85 percent of the time I thoroughly enjoy my work. But when I get a screwball case, I come away from court saying, 'What am I doing here?' It's a *visceral* reaction that I'm wasting my time. I'm trying to find some way to make a social contribution or a slot in city government. I keep saying, 'There's something more.' "

Besides the push to broaden himself professionally, there is a wish to expand 26
his personal life. He wants two or three more children. "The concept of a home has become very meaningful to me, a place to get away from troubles and relax. I love my son in a way I could not have anticipated. I never could live alone."

Consumed with the work of making his own critical lifesteering decisions, 27
he demonstrates the essential shift at this age: An absolute requirement to be more self-concerned. The self has new value now that his competency has been proved.

His wife is struggling with her own age-30 priorities. She wants to go to law 28
school, but he wants more children. If she is going to stay home, she wants him to make more time for the family instead of taking on even wider professional commitments. His view of the bind, of what he would most like from his wife, is this:

"I'd like not to be bothered. It sounds cruel, but I'd like not to have to worry 29
about what she's going to do next week. Which is why I've told her several times that I think she should do something. Go back to school and get a degree in social work or geography or whatever. Hopefully that would fulfill her, and then I wouldn't have to worry about her line of problems. I want her to be decisive about herself."

The trouble with his advice to his wife is that it comes out of concern with *his* 30
convenience, rather than with *her* development. She quickly picks up on this lack of goodwill: He is trying to dispose of her. At the same time, he refuses her the same latitude to be "selfish" in making an independent decision to broaden her horizons. Both perceive a lack of mutuality. And that is what Catch-30 is all about for the couple.

ROOTING AND EXTENDING

Life becomes less provisional, more rational and orderly in the early thirties. We 31
begin to settle down in the full sense. Most of us begin putting down roots and
sending out new shoots. People buy houses and become very earnest about climbing career ladders. Men in particular concern themselves with "making it." Satisfaction with marriage generally goes downhill in the thirties (for those who have
remained together) compared with the highly valued, vision-supporting marriage
of the twenties. This coincides with the couple's reduced social life outside the
family and the inturned focus on raising their children.

THE DEADLINE DECADE

In the middle of the thirties we come upon a crossroads. We have reached the 32
halfway mark. Yet even as we are reaching our prime, we begin to see there is a
place where it finishes. Time starts to squeeze.

The loss of youth, the faltering of physical powers we have always taken for 33
granted, the fading purpose of stereotyped roles by which we have thus far identified ourselves, the spiritual dilemma of having no absolute answers—any or all
of these shocks can give this passage the character of crisis. Such thoughts usher
in a decade between 35 and 45 that can be called the Deadline Decade. It is a time
of both danger and opportunity. All of us have the chance to rework the narrow
identity by which we defined ourselves in the first half of life. And those of us who
make the most of the opportunity will have a full-out authenticity crisis.

To come through this authenticity crisis, we must reexamine our purposes 34
and reevaluate how to spend our resources from now on. "Why am I doing all this?
What do I really believe in?" No matter what we have been doing, there will be
parts of ourselves that have been suppressed and now need to find expression.
"Bad" feelings will demand acknowledgment along with the good.

It is frightening to step off onto the treacherous footbridge leading to the sec- 35
ond half of life. We can't take everything with us on this journey through uncertainty. Along the way, we discover that we are alone. We no longer have to ask permission because we are the providers of our own safety. We must learn to give
ourselves permission. We stumble upon feminine or masculine aspects of our na-
tures that up to this time have usually been masked. There is grieving to be done
because an old self is dying. By taking in our suppressed and even our unwanted
parts, we prepare at the gut level for the reintegration of an identity that is ours and
ours alone—not some artificial form put together to please the culture or our
mates. It is a dark passage at the beginning. But by disassembling ourselves, we
can glimpse the light and gather our parts into a renewal.

Women sense this inner crossroads earlier than men do. The time pinch of- 36
ten prompts a woman to stop and take an all-points survey at age 35. Whatever options she has already played out, she feels a "my last chance" urgency to review

those options she has set aside and those that aging and biology will close off in the now *foreseeable* future. For all her qualms and confusion about where to start looking for a new future, she usually enjoys an exhilaration of release. Assertiveness begins rising. There are so many firsts ahead.

Men, too, feel the time push in the mid-thirties. Most men respond by pressing down harder on the career accelerator. It's "my last chance" to pull away from the pack. It is no longer enough to be the loyal junior executive, the promising young novelist, the lawyer who does a little *pro bono* work on the side. He wants now to become part of top management, to be recognized as an established writer, or an active politician with his own legislative program. With some chagrin, he discovers that he has been too anxious to please and too vulnerable to criticism. He wants to put together his own ship. 37

During this period of intense concentration on external advancement, it is common for men to be unaware of the more difficult, gut issues that are propelling them forward. The survey that was neglected at 35 becomes a crucible at 40. Whatever rung of achievement he has reached, the man of 40 usually feels stale, restless, burdened, and unappreciated. He worries about his health. He wonders, "Is this all there is?" He may make a series of departures from well-established life-long base lines, including marriage. More and more men are seeking second careers in midlife. Some become self-destructive. And many men in their forties experience a major shift of emphasis away from pouring all their energies into their own advancement. A more tender, feeling side comes into play. They become interested in developing an ethical self. 38

RENEWAL OR RESIGNATION

Somewhere in the mid-forties, equilibrium is regained. A new stability is achieved, which may be more or less satisfying. 39

If one has refused to budge through the midlife transition, the sense of staleness will calcify into resignation. One by one, the safety and supports will be withdrawn from the person who is standing still. Parents will become children; children will become strangers; a mate will grow away or go away; the career will become just a job—and each of these events will be felt as an abandonment. The crisis will probably emerge again around 50. And although its wallop will be greater, the jolt may be just what is needed to prod the resigned middle-ager toward seeking revitalization. 40

On the other hand . . . 41

If we have confronted ourselves in the middle passage and found a renewal of purpose around which we are eager to build a more authentic life structure, these may well be the best years. Personal happiness takes a sharp turn upward for partners who can now accept the fact: "I cannot expect *anyone* to fully understand me." Parents can be forgiven for the burdens of our childhood. Children can be let go without leaving us in collapsed silence. At 50, there is a new warmth and mellowing. Friends be- 42 come more important than ever, but so does privacy. Since it is so often proclaimed by people past midlife, the motto of this stage might be "No more bullshit."

1976

QUESTIONS FOR DISCUSSION

Content

a. The author explains that each of us has our own "stepstyle." What does she mean?

b. Do any people you know—your parents for example—fit neatly into Sheehy's ladder? Explain.

c. What qualifications does the author include in her introductory paragraphs to allow her to generalize?

d. Why should we not think "too mechanistically" (paragraph 4) when it comes to understanding how people move through life stages?

e. Why are "rebounds to the family" (paragraph 9) common between the ages of 18 and 21?

f. What, according to Sheehy, is the common response to approaching age 30?

g. How is establishing identity during the Deadline Decade different from establishing it during earlier years? What does Sheehy mean by "disassembling ourselves" (paragraph 35)?

h. In what way might reaching age 50 bring renewal? In what way might it bring resignation?

Strategy and Style

i. Is the analogy in the introduction appropriate? Does it help prepare us for what is to follow?

j. Sheehy's approach is, for the most part, objective, even detached. At times, however, she does express her personal reaction to the material. Find places in which the author's personal voice can be heard.

k. Why are explanations of the steps on the developmental ladder written in fairly generalized terms? Would it have been possible to be more specific? What are some of the strategies Sheehy uses to make these explanations seem specific?

SUGGESTIONS FOR SHORT WRITING

a. Sheehy begins this passage with an analogy linking humans to lobsters. What other animals could you use in an analogy to describe human development? Make a list of two or three, and explain the analogy you see.

b. Briefly explain to what extent your chosen "course in life" is different from that of your parents or of other members of your family.

SUGGESTIONS FOR SUSTAINED WRITING

a. Where are you on Sheehy's developmental ladder? Write a narrative essay, using specific examples from your life, to discuss how your life fits Sheehy's categories, or how it does not fit. This essay can be extended to include other members of your family.

b. Do you know someone who has gone through the "middle passage" Sheehy discusses in paragraphs 39–42? Briefly tell the story of this passage, and explain whether this individual experienced a "renewal" or a "resignation."

c. For a researched essay, find other theories of adult development. Categorize each of them by applying age groups as Sheehy has done. Then, compare and contrast the theories, speculating on which most accurately describes adult development. Use your own experiences and your observations of your family and friends to form criteria for judging the theories.

Why Nothing Is "Wrong" Anymore

Meg Greenfield

Meg Greenfield (b. 1930) studied in Rome and as a Fulbright scholar at Cambridge University in England before she returned in 1957 to the United States to work for The Reporter, *first as a writer and later as an editor. When The* Reporter *ceased publication in 1968, she took a job with* The Washington Post *as an editorial writer. In 1978 she won a Pulitzer for editorial writing. She is now* The Washington Post's *editorial page editor and also writes a regular column for* Newsweek, *in which "Why Nothing Is 'Wrong' Anymore" appeared on July 28, 1986.*

There has been an awful lot of talk about sin, crime, and plain old antisocial be- 1 havior this summer—drugs and pornography at home, terror and brutality abroad. Maybe it's just the heat; or maybe these categories of conduct (sin, crime, etc.) are really on the rise. What strikes me is our curiously deficient, not to say defective, way of talking about them. We don't seem to have a word anymore for "wrong" in the moral sense, as in, for example, "theft is wrong."

Let me quickly qualify. There is surely no shortage of people condemning 2 other people on such grounds, especially their political opponents or characters they just don't care for. Name-calling is still very much in vogue. But where the concept of wrong is really important—as a guide to one's own behavior or that of one's own side in some dispute—it is missing; and this is as true of those on the religious right who are going around pronouncing great masses of us sinners as it is of their principal antagonists, those on the secular left who can forgive or "understand" just about anything so long as it has not been perpetrated by a right-winger.

There is a fairly awesome literature that attempts to explain how we have 3 changed as a people with the advent of psychiatry, the weakening of religious institutions and so forth, but you don't need to address these matters to take note of a simple fact. As a guide and a standard to live by, you don't hear so much about "right and wrong" these days. The very notion is considered politically, not to say personally, embarrassing, since it has such a repressive, Neanderthal ring to it. So we have developed a broad range of alternatives to "right and wrong." I'll name a few.

Right and stupid: This is the one you use when your candidate gets caught 4 stealing, or, for that matter, when anyone on your side does something reprehensible. "It was really so dumb of him"—head must shake here—"I just can't understand it." Bad is dumb, breathtakingly dumb and therefore unfathomable; so, conveniently enough, the effort to fathom it might just as well be called off. This one had a big play during Watergate and has had mini-revivals ever since whenever congressmen and senators investigating administration crimes turn out to be guilty of something similar themselves.

Right and not necessarily unconstitutional: I don't know at quite what 5 point along the way we came to this one, the avoidance of admitting that something is wrong by pointing out that it is not specifically or even

195

inferentially prohibited by the Constitution or, for that matter, mentioned by name in the criminal code or the Ten Commandments. The various parties that prevail in civil-liberty and civil-rights disputes before the Supreme Court have gotten quite good at making this spurious connection: it is legally permissible, therefore it is morally acceptable, possibly even good. But both as individuals and as a society we do things every day that we know to be wrong even though they may not fall within the class of legally punishable acts or tickets to eternal damnation.

Right and sick: Crime or lesser wrongdoing defined as physical and/or psy-   6
chological disorder—this one has been around for ages now and as long ago as 1957 was made the butt of a great joke in the "Gee Officer Krupke!" song in "West Side Story." Still, I think no one could have foreseen the degree to which an originally reasonable and humane assumption (that some of what once was regarded as wrongdoing is committed by people acting out of ailment rather than moral choice) would be seized upon and exploited to exonerate every kind of misfeasance. This route is a particular favorite of caught-out officeholders who, when there is at last no other recourse, hold a press conference, announce that they are "sick" in some wise and throw themselves and their generally stunned families on our mercy. At which point it becomes gross to pick on them; instead we are exhorted to admire them for their "courage."

Right and only to be expected: You could call this the tit-for-tat school; it   7
is related to the argument that holds moral wrongdoing to be evidence of sickness, but it is much more pervasive and insidious these days. In fact it is probably the most popular dodge, being used to justify, or at least avoid owning up to, every kind of lapse: The other guy, or sometimes just plain circumstance, "asked for it." For instance, I think most of us could agree that setting fire to live people, no matter what their political offense, is— dare I say it?—wrong. Yet if it is done by those for whom we have sympathy in a conflict, there is a tendency to extenuate or disbelieve it, receiving it less as evidence of wrongdoing on our side than as evidence of the severity of the provocation or as enemy-supplied disinformation. Thus the hesitation of many in the antiapartheid movement to confront the brutality of so-called "necklacing," and thus the immediate leap of Sen. Jesse Helms to the defense of the Chilean government after the horrifying incineration of protesters there.

Right and complex: This one hardly takes a moment to describe; you know   8
it well. "Complex" is the new "controversial," a word used as "controversial" was for so long to flag trouble of some unspecified, dismaying sort that the speaker doesn't want to have to step up to. "Well, you know, it's very complex. . . ." I still can't get this one out of my own vocabulary.

In addition to these various sophistries, we also have created a rash of 9 "ethics committees" in our government, of course, whose function seems to be to dither around writing rules that allow people who have clearly done wrong—and should have known it and probably did—to get away because the rules don't cover their offense (see Right and not necessarily unconstitutional). But we don't need any more committees or artful dodges for that matter. As I listen to the moral arguments swirling about us this summer I become ever more persuaded that our real problem is this: the "still, small voice" of conscience has become far too small—and utterly still.

1986

QUESTIONS FOR DISCUSSION

Content

a. Summarize Greenfield's argument. Do you agree or disagree with it?
b. What is her purpose? Is it simply to explain a series of excuses people use to justify their irresponsibility?
c. What is the significance of her indicting both the "religious right" and the "secular left" (paragraph 2)? Is there evidence elsewhere in this essay that Greenfield's approach is balanced?
d. We don't hear so much about "right and wrong" anymore as "a guide and a standard to live by," claims Greenfield in paragraph 3. Why not? What purpose does the word *wrong* now serve?
e. Look up "sophistries" (paragraph 9). How are the categories Greenfield creates examples of sophistry?

Strategy and Style

f. How do the subheads lend clarity to this essay? Do they also help strengthen Greenfield's argument? Why or why not?
g. How would you describe Greenfield's intended audience?
h. What is the author's attitude toward her subject? Is her tone appropriate to an essay on contemporary moral attitudes?
i. Given Greenfield's purpose, is classification an appropriate method to organize her material? What other methods could she have used?
j. What use does she make of illustration?
k. Greenfield occasionally uses high-level vocabulary—"exonerate every kind of misfeasance," for example (paragraph 6). However, these words can usually be defined from their context. Using context clues, define *exonerate* and *misfeasance*; then, check your definitions in the dictionary. How would you define other unfamiliar words?

SUGGESTIONS FOR SHORT WRITING

a. Brainstorm with classmates to find other categories that might continue Green-field's list. Title each category in your list "right and _____."

b. Identify and briefly discuss one or two acts you have observed, read about, or done yourself that might be classified as "right and stupid" or "right and sick" or that might fit one of Greenfield's other categories.

c. Discuss another term people avoid using because it seems unpleasant, embar-rassing, or threatening. Begin by listing two or three popular alternatives. Then explain differences in meaning between the term you are discussing and its "more acceptable" synonyms. Some terms you might discuss are *selfish, ego-tistical, materialistic, promiscuous, irresponsible, greedy, ostentatious, self-centered, rude,* or *fanatical.*

SUGGESTIONS FOR SUSTAINED WRITING

a. Write a rebuttal to Greenfield's column. Point out to your readers why you think the author is being overly pessimistic about the current state of things. Make sure you take into account each of her points.

b. If you basically agree with Greenfield, apply her list, and any other categories you can add to it, to current events and/or to current political candidates. Find specific examples to illustrate each of her categories.

Four Kinds of Reading

Donald Hall

A prolific writer of prose and poetry, Donald Hall was born in New Haven, Connecticut, in 1928. He studied at Harvard, Stanford, and Oxford universities, and he has taught at both Stanford University and the University of Michigan. From 1953–1961, he was poetry editor for the Paris Review, *a prestigious literary journal. He has twice won National Book Awards, in 1968 and 1992. Hall's books of poetry include* Exiles and Marriages *(1955),* A Roof of Tiger Lilies *(1963),* The One Day *(1988), and* The Museum of Clear Ideas *(1993). Among his essay collections are* To Keep Moving *(1980),* Fathers Playing Catch with Sons: Essays on Sport *(1985), and* Here at Eagle Pond *(1989). Hall has also written biography, short fiction, and drama, as well as several volumes of children's literature. "Four Kinds of Reading" was first published in* The New York Times *in 1969.*

Everywhere one meets the idea that reading is an activity desirable in itself. It is 1
understandable that publishers and librarians—and even writers—should promote
this assumption, but it is strange that the idea should have general currency. People surround the idea of reading with piety, and do not take into account the purpose of reading or the value of what is being read. Teachers and parents praise the
child who reads, and praise themselves, whether the text be *The Reader's Digest*
or *Moby Dick.* The advent of TV has increased the false values ascribed to reading, since TV provides a vulgar alternative. But this piety is silly; and most reading is no more cultural nor intellectual nor imaginative than shooting pool or
watching *What's My Line.*

It is worth asking how the act of reading became something to value in it- 2
self, as opposed for instance to the act of conversation or the act of taking a walk.
Mass literacy is a recent phenomenon, and I suggest that the aura which decorates
reading is a relic of the importance of reading to our great-great-grandparents.
Literacy used to be a mark of social distinction, separating a small portion of humanity from the rest. The farm laborer who was ambitious for his children did not
daydream that they would become schoolteachers or doctors; he daydreamed that
they would learn to read, and that a world would therefore open up to them in
which they did not have to labor in the fields fourteen hours a day for six days a
week in order to buy salt and cotton. On the next rank of society, ample time for
reading meant that the reader was free from the necessity to spend most of his
waking hours making a living. This sort of attitude shades into the contemporary
man's boast of his wife's cultural activities. When he says that his wife is interested in books and music and pictures, he is not only enclosing the arts in a female world, he is saying that he is rich enough to provide her with the leisure to
do nothing. Reading is an inactivity, and therefore a badge of social class. Of
course, these reasons for the piety attached to reading are never acknowledged.
They show themselves in the shape of our attitudes toward books; reading gives
off an air of gentility.

199

It seems to me possible to name four kinds of reading, each with a charac- 3
teristic manner and purpose. The first is reading for information—reading to learn
about a trade, or politics, or how to accomplish something. We read a newspaper
this way, or most textbooks, or directions on how to assemble a bicycle. With most
of this material, the reader can learn to scan the page quickly, coming up with what
he needs and ignoring what is irrelevant to him, like the rhythm of the sentence,
or the play of metaphor. Courses in speed reading can help us read for this purpose, training the eye to jump quickly across the page. If we read the *New York
Times* with the attention we should give a novel or a poem, we will have time for
nothing else, and our mind will be cluttered with clichés and dead metaphor. Quick
eye-reading is a necessity to anyone who wants to keep up with what's happening,
or learn much of what has happened in the past. The amount of reflection, which
interrupts and slows down the reading, depends on the material.

But it is not the same activity as reading literature. There ought to be another 4
word. If we read a work of literature properly, we read slowly, and we *hear* all the
words. If our lips do not actually move, it's only laziness. The muscles in our
throat move, and come together when we see the word "squeeze." We hear the
sounds so accurately that if a syllable is missing in a line of poetry we hear the
lack, though we may not know what we are lacking. In prose we accept the
rhythms, and hear the adjacent sounds. We also register a track of feeling through
the metaphors and associations of words. Careless writing prevents this sort of attention, and becomes offensive. But the great writers reward it. Only by the full
exercise of our powers to receive language can we absorb their intelligence and
their imagination. This kind of reading goes through the ear—though the eye takes
in the print, and decodes it into sound—to the throat and the understanding, and it
can never be quick. It is slow and sensual, a deep pleasure that begins with touch
and ends with the sort of comprehension that we associate with dream.

Too many intellectuals read in order to reduce images to abstractions. One 5
reads philosophy slowly, as if it were literature, but much time must be spent with
the eyes turned away from the page, reflecting on the text. To read literature this
way is to turn it into something it is not—to concepts clothed in character, or philosophy sugar-coated. I think that most literary intellectuals read this way, including brighter professors of English, with the result that they miss literature completely, and concern themselves with a minor discipline called the history of ideas.
I remember a course in Chaucer at my university in which the final exam required
the identification of a hundred or more fragments of Chaucer, none as long as a
line. If you like poetry, and read Chaucer through a couple of times slowly, you
found yourself knowing them all. If you were a literary intellectual, well-informed
about the great chain of being, chances are you had a difficult time. To read literature is to be intimately involved with the words on the page, and never to think
of them as the embodiments of ideas which can be expressed in other terms. On
the other hand, intellectual writing—closer to mathematics on a continuum that
has at its opposite pole lyric poetry—requires intellectual reading, which is slow
because it is reflective and because the reader must pause to evaluate concepts.

But most of the reading which is praised for itself is neither literary nor in- 6
tellectual. It is narcotic. Novels, stories, and biographies—historical sagas,
monthly regurgitations of book clubs, four- and five-thousand word daydreams of
the magazines—these are the opium of the suburbs. The drug is not harmful except to the addict himself, and is no more injurious to him than Johnny Carson or
a bridge club, but it is nothing to be proud of. This reading is the automated daydream, the mild trip of the housewife and the tired businessman, interested not in
experience and feeling but in turning off the possibilities of experience and feeling. Great literature, if we read it well, opens us up to the world, and makes us
more sensitive to it, as if we acquired eyes that could see through walls and ears
that could hear the smallest sounds. But by narcotic reading, one can reduce great
literature to the level of *The Valley of the Dolls*. One can read *Anna Karenina* pas-
sively and inattentively, and float down the river of lethargy as if one were reading a confession magazine: "I Spurned My Husband for a Count."

I think that everyone reads for narcosis occasionally, and perhaps most con- 7
sistently in late adolescence, when great readers are born. I remember reading to
shut the world out, away at a school where I did not want to be; I invented a word
for my disease: "Bibliolepsy," on the analogy of narcolepsy. But after a while the
books became a window on the world, and not a screen against it. This change
doesn't always happen. I think that late adolescent narcotic reading accounts for
some of the badness of English departments. As a college student, the boy loves
reading and majors in English because he would be reading anyway. Deciding on
a career, he takes up English teaching for the same reason. Then in graduate school
he is trained to be a scholar, which is painful and irrelevant, and finds he must
write papers and publish them to be a Professor—and at about this time he no
longer requires reading for narcosis, and he is left with nothing but a Ph.D. and the
prospect of fifty years of teaching literature; and he does not even like literature.

Narcotic reading survives the impact of television, because this type of read- 8
ing has even less reality than melodrama; that is, the reader is in control: Once the
characters reach into the reader's feelings, he is able to stop reading, or glance away,
or superimpose his own daydream. The trouble with television is that it embodies
its own daydream. Literature is often valued precisely because of its distance from
the tangible. Some readers prefer looking into the text of a play to seeing it performed. Reading a play, it is possible to stage it oneself by an imaginative act; but
it is also possible to remove it from real people. Here is Virginia Woolf, who was
lavish in her praise of the act of reading, talking about reading a play rather than seeing it: "Certainly there is a good deal to be said for reading *Twelfth Night* in the book
if the book can be read in a garden, with no sound but the thud of an apple falling
to the earth, or of the wind ruffling the branches of the trees." She sets her own stage;
the play is called *Virginia Woolf Reads Twelfth Night in a Garden*. Piety moves into
narcissism, and the high metaphors of Shakespeare's lines dwindle into the flowers
of an English garden; actors in ruffles wither, while the wind ruffles branches.

1968

QUESTIONS FOR DISCUSSION

Content

a. What are the four types of reading discussed in this selection?
b. What assumption does Hall tell us about in paragraph 1? To what end does he do this?
c. Explain "the aura which decorates reading," mentioned in paragraph 2.
d. What, according to Hall, accounts for the "piety" that we attach to reading?
e. What does Hall imply about the role of a reader in appreciating literature?
f. To what end does Hall recommend taking courses in speed reading (paragraph 3)?
g. In what ways are reading for information and reading literature dissimilar?
h. What distinction does the author make between literature and the history of ideas in paragraph 5?
i. What fault does Hall find in television?
j. Write one sentence of your own that might serve as this essay's thesis.

Strategy and Style

k. Is Hall's two-paragraph introduction appropriate to this essay? In what way?
l. What methods of development, other than classification, are used in this essay?
m. How does Hall support his argument that the fourth type of reading is "nothing to be proud of" (paragraph 6)?
n. Explain the order in which Hall chose to address the four types of reading. For example, why does he begin with informational reading and end with narcotic reading?
o. Describe the intended audience for this essay.
p. Hall's tone is formal, and his style is somewhat elevated. Could he have approached his subject using a lighter tone and more familiar language?

SUGGESTIONS FOR SHORT WRITING

a. "The trouble with television is that it embodies its own daydream," Hall claims in paragraph 8. What does he mean? Cite examples from your own television viewing that would support or oppose this notion.
b. Write a paragraph explaining Hall's belief that books should be "a window on the world, and not a screen against it" (paragraph 7). Do you agree with this statement? Why or why not? Under what circumstances, if any, might you find it appropriate to use reading as a screen?
c. Make an outline of the four types of reading Hall discusses. Then, list the titles of books, magazines, and other materials you have read under the appropriate category. What does your list tell you about your reading habits? Should you change them?

SUGGESTIONS FOR SUSTAINED WRITING

a. Write an essay that discusses at least four different reasons for pursuing a particular goal, activity, or pastime. For example, write about the different reasons for which you go to the movies, explain why people choose a particular college major, or discuss four different reasons that people have babies.

b. Interview a few friends and classmates on the subject of study habits. Then, write a paper in which you explain three or four good methods you might recommend to someone who is trying to become a successful student. If you want, include a discussion of study methods that you would not recommend in the last section of your paper.

c. Read what you wrote in response to items *a* or *b* in the Suggestions for Short Writing above. Expand that material into a full essay.

Growing Up Asian in America

Kesaya E. Noda

Born in a Japanese community in California, Kesaya E. Noda (b. 1950) was raised in New England. She studied Japanese after graduating from high school and lived in Japan for a year and a half. Noda is the author of Yamato Colony *(1981), a history of the California community where her grandparents settled after immigrating to America. She earned a Master of Divinity degree from Harvard University in 1987. "Growing Up Asian in America" first appeared in a collection of essays entitled* Making Waves *(1989), which was published by Asian Women United in California.*

Sometimes when I was growing up, my identity seemed to hurtle toward me and paste 1
itself right to my face. I felt that way, encountering the stereotypes of my race perpetuated by non-Japanese people (primarily white) who may or may not have had contact with other Japanese in America. "You don't like cheese, do you?" someone would ask. "I know your people don't like cheese." Sometimes questions came making allusions to history. That was another aspect of the identity. Events that had happened quite apart from the me who stood silent in that moment connected my face with an incomprehensible past. "Your parents were in California? Were they in those camps during the war?" And sometimes there were phrases or nicknames: "Lotus Blossom." I was sometimes addressed or referred to as racially Japanese, sometimes as Japanese-American, and sometimes as an Asian woman. Confusions and distortions abounded.

How is one to know and define oneself? From the inside—within a context 2
that is self-defined, from a grounding in community and a connection with culture and history that are comfortably accepted? Or from the outside—within terms of messages received from the media and people who are often ignorant? Even as an adult I can still see two sides of my face and past. I can see from the inside out, in freedom. And I can see from the outside in, driven by the old voices of childhood and lost in anger and fear.

I AM RACIALLY JAPANESE

A voice from my childhood says: "You are other. You are less than. You are unalter- 3
ably alien." This voice has its own history. We have indeed been seen as other and alien since the early years of our arrival in the United States. The very first immigrants were welcomed and sought as laborers to replace the dwindling numbers of Chinese, whose influx had been cut off by the Chinese Exclusion Act of 1882. The Japanese fell natural heir to the same anti-Asian prejudice that had arisen against the Chinese. As soon as they began striking for better wages, they were no longer welcomed.

I can see myself today as a person historically defined by law and custom as 4
being forever alien. Being neither "free white," nor "African," our people in California were deemed "aliens, ineligible for citizenship," no matter how long they intended to stay here. Aliens ineligible for citizenship were prohibited from owning,

204

buying, or leasing land. They did not and could not belong here. The voice in me remembers that I am always a *Japanese*-American in the eyes of many. A third-generation German-American is an American. A third-generation Japanese-American is a Japanese-American. Being Japanese means being a danger to the country during the war and knowing how to use chopsticks. I wear this history on my face.

I move to the other side. I see a different light and claim a different context. 5 My race is a line that stretches across ocean and time to link me to the shrine where my grandmother was raised. Two high, white banners lift in the wind at the top of the stone steps leading to the shrine. It is time for the summer festival. Black characters are written against the sky as boldly as the clouds, as lightly as kites, as sharply as the big black crows I used to see above the fields in New Hampshire. At festival time there is liquor and food, ritual, discipline, and abandonment. There is music and drunkenness and invocation. There is hope. Another season has come. Another season has gone.

I am racially Japanese. I have a certain claim to this crazy place where the 6 prayers intoned by a neighboring Shinto priest (standing in for my grandmother's nephew who is sick) are drowned out by the rehearsals for the pop singing contest in which most of the villagers will compete later that night. The village elders, the priest, and I stand respectfully upon the immaculate, shining wooden floor of the outer shrine, bowing our heads before the hidden powers. During the patchy intervals when I can hear him, I notice the priest has a stutter. His voice flutters up to my ears only occasionally because two men and a woman are singing gustily into a microphone in the compound, testing the sound system. A pre-recorded tape of guitars, samisens, and drums accompanies them. Rock music and Shinto prayers. That night, to loud applause and cheers, a young man is given the award for the most *netsuretsu*—passionate, burning—rendition of a song. We roar our approval of the reward. Never mind that his voice had wandered and slid, now slightly above, now slightly below the given line of the melody. Netsuretsu. Netsuretsu.

In the morning, my grandmother's sister kneels at the foot of the stone stairs 7 to offer her morning prayers. She is too crippled to climb the stairs, so each morning she kneels here upon the path. She shuts her eyes for a few seconds, her motions as matter of fact as when she washes rice. I linger longer than she does, so reluctant to leave, savoring the connection I feel with my grandmother in America, the past, and the power that lives and shines in the morning sun.

Our family has served this shrine for generations. The family's need to pro- 8 tect this claim to identity and place outweighs any individual claim to any individual hope. I am Japanese.

I AM A JAPANESE-AMERICAN

"Weak." I hear the voice from my childhood years. "Passive," I hear. Our parents 9 and grandparents were the ones who were put into those camps. They went without resistance; they offered cooperation as proof of loyalty to America. "Victim," I hear. And, "Silent."

Our parents are painted as hard workers who were socially uncomfortable 10
and had difficulty expressing even the smallest opinion. Clean, quiet, motivated,
and determined to match the American way; that is us, and that is the story of our
time here.

"Why did you go into those camps?" I raged at my parents, frightened by 11
my own inner silence and timidity. "Why didn't you do anything to resist? Why
didn't you name it the injustice it was?" Couldn't our parents even think?
Couldn't they? Why were we so passive?

I shift my vision and my stance. I am in California. My uncle is in the midst 12
of the sweet potato harvest. He is pressed, trying to get the harvesting crews onto
the field as quickly as possible, worried about the flow of equipment and people.
His big pickup is pulled off to the side, motor running, door ajar. I see two tractors
in the yard in front of an old shed; the flatbed harvesting platform on which the
workers will stand has already been brought over from the other field. It's early
morning. The workers stand loosely grouped and at ease, but my uncle looks as
harried and tense as a police officer trying to unsnarl a New York City traffic jam.
Driving toward the shed, I pull my car off the road to make way for an approaching tractor. The front wheels of the car sink luxuriously into the soft, white sand
by the roadside and the car slides to a dreamy halt, tail still on the road. I try to
move forward. I try to move back. The front bites contentedly into the sand, the
back lifts itself at a jaunty angle. My uncle sees me and storms down the road, running. He is shouting before he is even near me.

"What's the matter with you?" he screams. "What the hell are you doing?" 13
In his frenzy, he grabs his hat off his head and slashes it through the air across his
knee. He is beside himself. "Don't you know how to drive in sand? What's the
matter with you? You've blocked the whole roadway. How am I supposed to get
my tractors out of here? Can't you use your head? You've cut off the whole roadway, and we've got to get out of here."

I stand on the road before him helplessly thinking. "No, I don't know how 14
to drive in sand. I've never driven in sand."

"I'm sorry, uncle," I say, burying a smile beneath a look of sincere apology. 15
I notice my deep amusement and my affection for him with great curiosity. I am
usually devastated by anger. Not this time.

During the several years that follow I learn about the people and the place, 16
and much more about what has happened in this California village where my parents grew up. The issei, our grandparents, made this settlement in the desert. Their
first crops were eaten by rabbits and ravaged by insects. The land was so barren
that men walking from house to house sometimes got lost. Women came here too.
They bore children in 114-degree heat, then carried the babies with them into the
fields to nurse when they reached the end of each row of grapes or other truck-
farm crops.

I had had no idea what it meant to buy this kind of land and make it grow 17
green. Or how, when the war came, there was no space at all for the subtlety of being who we were—Japanese-Americans. Either/or was the way. I hadn't under-

stood that people were literally afraid for their lives then, that their money had been frozen in banks; that there was a five-mile travel limit; that when the early evening curfew came and they were inside their houses, some of them watched helplessly as people they knew went into their barns to steal their belongings. The police were patrolling the road, interested only in violators of curfew. There was no help for them in the face of thievery. I had not been able to imagine before what it must have felt like to be an American—to know absolutely that one is an American—and yet to have almost everyone else deny it. Not only deny it, but challenge that identity with machine guns and troops of white American soldiers. In those circumstances it was difficult to say, "I'm a Japanese-American," "American" had to do.

But now I can say that I am a Japanese-American. It means I have a place 18 here in this country, too. I have a place here on the East Coast, where our neighbor is so much a part of our family that my mother never passes her house at night without glancing at the lights to see if she is home and safe; where my parents have hauled hundreds of pounds of rocks from fields and arduously planted Christmas trees and blueberries, lilacs, asparagus, and crab apples; where my father still dreams of angling a stream to a new bed so that he can dig a pond in the field and fill it with water and fish. "The neighbors already came for their Christmas tree?" he asks in December. "Did they like it? Did they like it?"

I have a place on the West Coast where my relatives still farm, where I heard 19 the stories of feuds and backbiting, and where I saw that people survived and flourished because fundamentally they trusted and relied upon one another. A death in the family is not just a death in a family; it is a death in the community. I saw people help each other with money, materials, labor, attention, and time. I saw men gather once a year, without fail, to clean the grounds of a ninety-year-old woman who had helped the community before, during, and after the war. I saw her remembering them with birthday cards sent to each of their children.

I come from a people with a long memory and a distinctive grace. We live 20 our thanks. And we are Americans. Japanese-Americans.

I AM A JAPANESE-AMERICAN WOMAN

Woman. The last piece of my identity. It has been easier by far for me to know my- 21 self in Japan and to see my place in America than it has been to accept my line of connection with my own mother. She was my dark self, a figure in whom I thought I saw all that I feared most in myself. Growing into womanhood and looking for some model of strength, I turned away from her. Of course, I could not find what I sought. I was looking for a black feminist or a white feminist. My mother is neither white nor black.

My mother is a woman who speaks with her life as much as with her tongue. 22 I think of her with her own mother. Grandmother had Parkinson's disease and it had frozen her gait and set her fingers, tongue, and feet jerking and trembling in a terrible dance. My aunts and uncles wanted her to be able to live in her own home.

They fed her, bathed her, dressed her, awoke at midnight to take her for one last trip to the bathroom. My aunts (her daughters-in-law) did most of the care, but my mother went from New Hampshire to California each summer to spend a month living with Grandmother, because she wanted to and because she wanted to give my aunts at least a small rest. During those hot summer days, mother lay on the couch watching the television or reading, cooking foods that Grandmother liked, and speaking little. Grandmother thrived under her care.

The time finally came when it was too dangerous for Grandmother to 23 live alone. My relatives kept finding her on the floor beside her bed when they went to wake her in the mornings. My mother flew to California to help clean the house and make arrangements for Grandmother to enter a local nursing home. On her last day at home, while Grandmother was sitting in her big, over-stuffed armchair, hair combed and wearing a green summer dress, my mother went to her and knelt at her feet. "Here, Mamma," she said. "I've polished your shoes." She lifted Grandmother's legs and helped her into the shiny black shoes. My Grandmother looked down and smiled slightly. She left her house walking, supported by her children, carrying her pocket book, and wearing her polished black shoes. "Look, Mamma," my mom had said, kneeling. "I've pol-ished your shoes."

Just the other day, my mother came to Boston to visit. She had recently lost 24 a lot of weight and was pleased with her new shape and her feeling of good health. "Look at me, Kes," she exclaimed, turning toward me, front and back, as naked as the day she was born. I saw her small breasts and the wide, brown scar, belly but-ton to pubic hair, that marked her because my brother and I were both born by Cae-sarean section. Her hips were small. I was not a large baby, but there was so little room for me in her that when she was carrying me she could not even begin to bend over toward the floor. She hated it, she said.

"Don't I look good? Don't you think I look good?"   25

I looked at my mother, smiling and as happy as she, thinking of all the times 26 I have seen her naked. I have seen both my parents naked throughout my life, as they have seen me. From childhood through adulthood we've had our naked mo-ments, sharing baths, idle conversations picked up as we moved between show-ers and closets, hurried moments at the beginning of days, quiet moments at the end of days.

I know this to be Japanese, this ease with the physical, and it makes me think 27 of an old Japanese folk song. A young nursemaid, a fifteen-year-old girl, is singing a lullaby to a baby who is strapped to her back. The nursemaid has been sent as a servant to a place far from her own home. "We're the beggars," she says, "and they are the nice people. Nice people wear fine sashes. Nice clothes."

> If I should drop dead,
> bury me by the roadside!
> I'll give a flower
> to everyone who passes.

What kind of flower?
The cam-cam-camellia [tsun-tsun-tsubaki]
watered by Heaven:
alms water.

The nursemaid is the intersection of heaven and earth, the intersection of the 28
human, the natural world, the body, and the soul. In this song, with clear eyes, she
looks steadily at life, which is sometimes so very terrible and sad. I think of her
while looking at my mother, who is standing on the red and purple carpet before
me, laughing, without any clothes.

I am my mother's daughter. And I am myself.   29

I am a Japanese-American woman.   30

EPILOGUE

I recently heard a man from West Africa share some memories of his childhood. He 31
was raised Muslim, but when he was a young man, he found himself deeply drawn
to Christianity. He struggled against his inner impulse for years, trying to avoid the
church yet feeling pushed to return to it again and again. "I would have done anything to avoid the change," he said. At last, he became Christian. Afterwards he was
afraid to go home, fearing that he would not be accepted. The fear was groundless,
he discovered, when at last he returned—he had separated himself, but his family
and friends (all Muslim) had not separated themselves from him.

The man, who is now a professor of religion, said that in the Africa he knew 32
as a child and a young man, pluralism was embraced rather than feared. There was
"a kind of tolerance that did not deny your particularity," he said. He alluded to zest-
ful, spontaneous debates that would sometimes loudly erupt between Muslims and
Christians in the village's public spaces. His memories of an atheist who harangued
the villagers when he came to visit them once a week moved me deeply. Perhaps
the man was an agricultural advisor or inspector. He harassed the women. He would
say: "Don't go to the fields! Don't even bother to go to the fields. Let God take care
of you. He'll send you the food. If you believe in God, why do you need to work?
You don't need to work! Let God put the seeds in the ground. Stay home."

The professor said, "The women laughed, you know? They just laughed. 33
Their attitude was, 'Here is a child of God. When will he come home?' "

The storyteller, the professor of religion, smiled a most fantastic tender smile 34
as he told this story. "In my country, there is a deep affirmation of the oneness of
God," he said. "The atheist and the women were having quite different experiences
in their encounter, though the atheist did not know this. He saw himself as quite
separate from the women. But the women did not see themselves as being separate
from him. 'Here is a child of God,' they said. 'When will he come home?' "

1989

QUESTIONS FOR DISCUSSION

Content

a. What function is served by the questions Noda asks in paragraph 2?
b. What is the distinction Noda draws between Japanese-Americans and other Americans (paragraph 4)?
c. What are the implications of the author's seeing herself "as a person historically defined by law and custom as being forever alien" (paragraph 4)?
d. Discuss this essay as an exercise in self-definition. In what way is classification appropriate to this exercise?
e. Summarize each of the three subsections of this piece by explaining the three ways in which Noda sees herself: as racially Japanese, as a Japanese-American, and as a Japanese-American woman.
f. What was Noda's reaction to learning about the internment of Japanese-Americans during World War II? Why does she describe this reaction?
g. How does the story of the author's getting her car stuck in sand help define her as a Japanese-American? As an individual?
h. Explain what Noda sees when she looks at her mother. What role does the story of the nursemaid play in her defining herself as a Japanese-American woman?

Strategy and Style

i. Is Noda's introduction (paragraph 1) appropriate to this classification essay? Explain.
j. In what ways are paragraphs 5, 12, and 24 alike? What function do they serve? What function do paragraphs 8, 20, 29–30 serve?
k. What light does the story of a West African Muslim in the epilogue shed on Noda's essay?
l. What role does narration play in this classification piece?
m. Noda divides her essay into three major sections and an epilogue. Describe the pattern she uses to organize her three major sections. What is the effect of her organizing all three sections the same way?

SUGGESTIONS FOR SHORT WRITING

a. In paragraph 4, Noda says: "A third-generation German-American is an American. A third-generation Japanese-American is a Japanese-American." What can you infer from this statement about Noda's opinion of the "melting pot" concept? Can you name other ethnic groups who, after three or more generations, are still seen as "hyphenated Americans"?
b. Consider your own family background. Can you identify aspects in your personality, value system, or lifestyle that are directly related to the fact that you are a member of a particular ethnic or religious group? Discuss one or two.

c. Noda defines herself by using ethnic categories. Yet we can define ourselves using categories based on various principles. For example, you might define yourself by grouping your daily activities or responsibilities under various headings: "I am a student," "I am a bank teller," or "I am a parent." Then, again, you might discuss various aspects of your emotional makeup: "I am a romantic," "I am an extrovert," or "I am family-oriented." Using the above as examples, list three or four categories that would help define your emotional makeup, lifestyle, value system, career aspirations, etc. Then, freewrite about each category for about five minutes so as to gather details that show how you fit that category.

SUGGESTIONS FOR SUSTAINED WRITING

a. If you responded to item *c* under the Suggestions for Short Writing, you may have the beginnings of an essay that uses classification to explain your emotional makeup, value system, lifestyle, or other aspect of your character. Use the notes you have made as the raw materials for just such an essay.
b. There is a great deal of talk these days about cultural diversity. Unfortunately, some people are all too happy to define others as members of a particular group rather than as individuals. Yet members of ethnic, religious, economic, gender, or other groups can be very different from one another. Using classification as a method of organization, discuss various types of people you have encountered in a group to which you belong. In the process, explain how you are different from other members of your group. In essence, then, use your essay to define your group and yourself.

The Truth about Lying

Judith Viorst

A contributing editor at Redbook *magazine, Judith Viorst (b. 1931) began her career as a poet in 1965 when she published* The Village Square. *This book of verse was followed by several other volumes of prose and poetry with intriguing titles. Among them are* It's Hard to Be Hip Over Thirty and Other Tragedies of Married Life *(1968),* People and Other Aggravations *(1971),* Yes, Married: A Saga of Love and Complaint *(1972), and* When Did I Stop Being Twenty and Other Injustices *(1987). Viorst has also published several works of children's fiction and nonfiction as well as a musical drama,* Birthday and Other Humiliations. *"The Truth about Lying" first appeared in* Redbook *in 1981.*

I've been wanting to write on a subject that intrigues and challenges me: the sub- 1 ject of lying. I've found it very difficult to do. Everyone I've talked to has a quite intense and personal but often rather intolerant point of view about what we can— and can never *never*—tell lies about. I've finally reached the conclusion that I can't present any ultimate conclusions, for too many people would promptly disagree. Instead, I'd like to present a series of moral puzzles, all concerned with lying. I'll tell you what I think about them. Do you agree?

SOCIAL LIES

Most of the people I've talked with say that they find social lying acceptable and 2 necessary. They think it's the civilized way for folks to behave. Without these little white lies, they say, our relationships would be short and brutish and nasty. It's arrogant, they say, to insist on being so incorruptible and so brave that you cause other people unnecessary embarrassment or pain by compulsively assailing them with your honesty. I basically agree. What about you?

Will you say to people, when it simply isn't true, "I like your new hairdo," 3 "You're looking much better," "It's so nice to see you," "I had a wonderful time"?

Will you praise hideous presents and homely kids? 4

Will you decline invitations with "We're busy that night—so sorry we can't 5 come," when the truth is you'd rather stay home than dine with the So-and-sos?

And even though, as I do, you may prefer the polite evasion of "You really 6 cooked up a storm" instead of "The soup"—which tastes like warmed-over coffee—"is wonderful," will you, if you must, proclaim it wonderful?

There's one man I know who absolutely refuses to tell social lies. "I can't 7 play that game," he says; "I'm simply not made that way." And his answer to the argument that saying nice things to someone doesn't cost anything is, "Yes, it does—it destroys your credibility." Now, he won't, unsolicited, offer his views on the painting you just bought, but you don't ask his frank opinion unless you want *frank*, and his silence at those moments when the rest of us liars are muttering, "Isn't it lovely?" is, for the most part, eloquent enough. My friend does not indulge

212

in what he calls "flattery, false praise and mellifluous comments." When others tell
fibs he will not go along. He says that social lying is lying, that little white lies are
still lies. And he feels that telling lies is morally wrong. What about you?

PEACE-KEEPING LIES

Many people tell peace-keeping lies; lies designed to avoid irritation or argument; 8
lies designed to shelter the liar from possible blame or pain; lies (or so it is rationalized) designed to keep trouble at bay without hurting anyone.

I tell these lies at times, and yet I always feel they're wrong. I understand 9
why we tell them, but still they feel wrong. And whenever I lie so that someone
won't disapprove of me or think less of me or holler at me, I feel I'm a bit of a
coward, I feel I'm dodging responsibility, I feel . . . guilty. What about you?

Do you, when you're late for a date because you overslept, say that you're 10
late because you got caught in a traffic jam?

Do you, when you forget to call a friend, say that you called several times 11
but the line was busy?

Do you, when you didn't remember that it was your father's birthday, say 12
that his present must be delayed in the mail?

And when you're planning a weekend in New York City and you're not in 13
the mood to visit your mother, who lives there, do you conceal—with a lie, if you
must—the fact that you'll be in New York? Or do you have the courage—or is it
the cruelty?—to say, "I'll be in New York, but sorry—I don't plan on seeing you"?

(Dave and his wife Elaine have two quite different points of view on this 14
very subject. He calls her a coward. She says she's being wise. He says she must
assert her right to visit New York sometimes and not see her mother. To which she
always patiently replies: "Why should we have useless fights? My mother's too
old to change. We get along much better when I lie to her.")

Finally, do you keep the peace by telling your husband lies on the subject of 15
money? Do you reduce what you really paid for your shoes? And in general do you
find yourself ready, willing and able to lie to him when you make absurd mistakes
or lose or break things?

"I used to have a romantic idea that part of intimacy was confessing every 16
dumb thing that you did to your husband. But after a couple of years of that," says
Laura, "have I changed my mind!"

And having changed her mind, she finds herself telling peace-keeping lies. 17
And yes, I tell them too. What about you?

PROTECTIVE LIES

Protective lies are lies folks tell—often quite serious lies—because they're con- 18
vinced that the truth would be too damaging. They lie because they feel there are
certain human values that supersede the wrong of having lied. They lie, not for

personal gain, but because they believe it's for the good of the person they're lying to. They lie to those they love, to those who trust them most of all, on the grounds that breaking this trust is justified.

They may lie to their children on money or marital matters.   19

They may lie to the dying about the state of their health.   20

They may lie about adultery, and not—or so they insist—to save their own 21 hide, but to save the heart and the pride of the men they are married to.

They may lie to their closest friend because the truth about her talents or son 22 or psyche would be—or so they insist—utterly devastating.

I sometimes tell such lies, but I'm aware that it's quite presumptuous to 23 claim I know what's best for others to know. That's called playing God. That's called manipulation and control. And we never can be sure, once we start to juggle lies, just where they'll land, exactly where they'll roll.

And furthermore, we may find ourselves lying in order to back up the lies 24 that are backing up the lie we initially told.

And furthermore—let's be honest—if conditions were reversed, we cer- 25 tainly wouldn't want anyone lying to us.

Yet, having said all that, I still believe that there are times when protective 26 lies must nonetheless be told. What about you?

If your Dad had a very bad heart and you had to tell him some bad family 27 news, which would you choose: to tell him the truth or to lie?

If your former husband failed to send his monthly childsupport check and in 28 other ways behaved like a total rat, would you allow your children—who believed he was simply wonderful—to continue to believe that he was wonderful?

If your dearly beloved brother selected a wife whom you deeply disliked, 29 would you reveal your feelings or would you fake it?

And if you were asked, after making love, "And how was that for you?" 30 would you reply, if it wasn't too good, "Not too good"?

Now, some would call a sex lie unimportant, little more than social lying, a 31 simple act of courtesy that makes all human intercourse run smoothly. And some would say all sex lies are bad news and unacceptably protective. Because, says Ruth, "a man with an ego that fragile doesn't need your lies—he needs a psychiatrist." Still others feel that sex lies are indeed protective lies, more serious than simple social lying, and yet at times they tell them on the grounds that when it comes to matters sexual, everybody's ego is somewhat fragile.

"If most of the time things go well in sex," says Sue, "I think you're allowed 32 to dissemble when they don't. I can't believe it's good to say, 'Last night was four stars, darling, but tonight's performance rates only a half.'"

I'm inclined to agree with Sue. What about you?   33

TRUST-KEEPING LIES

Another group of lies are trust-keeping lies, lies that involve triangulation, with *A* 34 (that's you) telling lies to *B* on behalf of *C* (whose trust you'd promised to keep).

Most people concede that once you've agreed not to betray a friend's confidence, you can't betray it, even if you must lie. But I've talked with people who don't want you telling them anything that they might be called on to lie about.

"I don't tell lies for myself," says Fran, "and I don't want to have to tell them 35 for other people." Which means, she agrees, that if her best friend is having an affair, she absolutely doesn't want to know about it.

"Are you saying," her best friend asks, "that if I went off with a lover and I 36 asked you to tell my husband I'd been with you, that you wouldn't lie for me, that you'd betray me?"

Fran is very pained but very adamant. "I wouldn't want to betray you, so . . . 37 don't ask me."

Fran's best friend is shocked. What about you?   38

Do you believe you can have close friends if you're not prepared to receive 39 their deepest secrets?

Do you believe you must always lie for your friends?   40

Do you believe, if your friend tells a secret that turns out to be quite immoral 41 or illegal, that once you've promised to keep it, you must keep it?

And what if your friend were your boss—if you were perhaps one of the 42 President's men—would you betray or lie for him over, say, Watergate?

As you can see, these issues get terribly sticky.   43

It's my belief that once we've promised to keep a trust, we must tell lies to 44 keep it. I also believe that we can't tell Watergate lies. And if these two statements strike you as quite contradictory, you're right—they're quite contradictory. But for now they're the best I can do. What about you?

Some say that truth will out and thus you might as well tell the truth. Some 45 say you can't regain the trust that lies lose. Some say that even though the truth may never be revealed, our lies pervert and damage our relationships. Some say . . . well, here's what some of them have to say.

"I'm a coward," says Grace, "about telling close people important, difficult 46 truths. I find that I'm unable to carry it off. And so if something is bothering me, it keeps building up inside till I end up just not seeing them any more."

"I lie to my husband on sexual things, but I'm furious," says Joyce, "that 47 he's too insensitive to know I'm lying."

"I suffer most from the misconception that children can't take the truth," 48 says Emily. "But I'm starting to see that what's harder and more damaging for them is being told lies, is *not* being told the truth."

"I'm afraid," says Joan, "that we often wind up feeling a bit of contempt for 49 the people we lie to."

And then there are those who have no talent for lying.   50

"Over the years, I tried to lie," a friend of mine explained, "but I always got 51 found out and I always got punished. I guess I gave myself away because I feel guilty about any kind of lying. It looks as if I'm stuck with telling the truth."

For those of us, however, who are good at telling lies, for those of us who 52 lie and don't get caught, the question of whether or not to lie can be a hard and serious moral problem. I liked the remark of a friend of mine who said, "I'm willing to lie. But just as a last resort—the truth's always better."

"Because," he explained, "though others may completely accept the lie I'm   53
telling, I don't."

I tend to feel that way too.   54

What about you?   55

1981

QUESTIONS FOR DISCUSSION

Content

a. Is the essay's thesis explicit? What is it?
b. What arguments does the author offer to defend social lying? What arguments does she offer against social lying?
c. Why does Viorst believe that telling protective lies is a form of manipulation?
d. What else does she find objectionable or dangerous about protective lies?
e. Under what conditions does the author believe that telling protective lies is appropriate?
f. In what way is her position on trust-keeping lies contradictory? How does she respond to that contradiction?

Strategy and Style

g. What is the introduction to this essay designed to do? Does it succeed?
h. To what end does Viorst address the reader directly?
i. What is the effect of her asking "What about you?" at the end of each section?
j. Where and to what end does Viorst use contrast? How does her creating contrast relate to her thesis?
k. Viorst uses examples throughout this essay. What form do these examples take? Are they convincing?
l. Where in the essay does the author engage in definition?
m. Does Viorst's quoting her friends make an effective way to develop this essay? Why or why not?
n. What point does the author make in the conclusion? Does it bring closure to the essay, or is it simply another of the "moral puzzles" she mentions in her introduction?

SUGGESTIONS FOR SHORT WRITING

a. Can you think of another type of lie, one that Viorst does not discuss? Write a short paragraph that explains this category. Like Viorst, include examples and direct quotations from others to develop your point.

b. Respond to Viorst by explaining how you react to what she says about one of the four kinds of lies she discusses. In other words, respond to the question with which she closes each section of this essay: "What about you?"
c. List examples of representative social, peace-keeping, protective, and trust-keeping lies that you tell or are told by others.

SUGGESTIONS FOR SUSTAINED WRITING

a. Write a letter to Viorst explaining why you tell lies like those discussed in her essay or why you refuse to tell such lies.
b. Write a classification essay in which you develop three or four major categories relating to a type of human behavior or activity about which you have mixed feelings. For example, you might discuss "the truth about dieting," "the truth about gambling," "the truth about exercising," "the truth about being assertive," or "the truth about gossiping."

6

Comparison and Contrast

The human tendency to measure one thing against another is so pervasive that it is only natural it to be used as a way to explore and explain complex ideas in writing. Comparison reveals similarities; contrast, differences. Both allow the writer to explain and explore new ideas by making reference to what the reader already knows. One way to begin describing a microwave oven to someone who has never seen one is to liken it to the oven in the conventional kitchen stove with which he or she is familiar. Both use energy to heat and cook food. Both are relatively easy to use, and both are no fun to clean! But there the similarities end. A microwave is quicker and more economical. And whoever heard of making popcorn in a conventional oven? Spend enough time explaining similarities and differences, and you are sure to give your reader at least rudimentary acquaintance with this appliance.

As with all writing, the key to composing effective comparison/contrast papers is to collect important information—and plenty of it—before you begin. Look at your subjects long and hard, take careful notes, and gather the kinds of details that will help you reveal differences and similarities of the most telling kind.

You can use a variety of techniques to develop a comparison or contrast. As suits his purpose, Mark Twain relies heavily on description in "Two Views of the Mississippi" while Lydia Minatoya includes both narrative and descriptive details to create a complex essay about the relationships among cultures. Narration also informs Bruce Catton's brilliant study of Grant and Lee, Mark Mathabane's discussion of superstition in South Africa and in the West, and May Sarton's commentary on loneliness and solitude.

One of the major advantages of using comparison/contrast to explain ideas is that it can lend itself quite naturally to two easy-to-arrange and easy-to-follow patterns of organization. In the point-by-point method, writers address a series of characteristics or features shared by the two subjects; they compare or contrast the two subjects on one point, then move on to the next point.

218

This is how the selection by Deborah Tannen is arranged. In the subject-by-subject method, one subject is thoroughly discussed before the writer moves on to the second. You can see good examples of the subject-by-subject method in the essays by Mark Twain and Suzanne Britt. For example, Twain first describes the beautiful and poetic Mississippi before going on to the dangerous Mississippi

But do not be misled. No writer represented in this chapter is content to follow a predetermined schema. Each author has a specific purpose in mind, and each draws upon other organizational patterns to shape the essay. Indeed, Catton shifts from the point-by-point to the subject-by-subject arrangement so deftly that the reader hardly notices.

The selections in this chapter present a variety of subjects and purposes—from analyzing psychological motivations behind the way men and women communicate to assessing the virtues of solitude. Carefully consider the Questions for Discussion and the Suggestions for Short Writing and for Sustained Writing following each essay. They will lead you to many more insights about using comparison/contrast as a way to explore new ideas and to make your writing more powerful no matter what your topic or purpose.

Grant and Lee: A Study in Contrasts

Bruce Catton

Born in Michigan, Bruce Catton (1899–1978) has come to be regarded as one of the most important historians of the American Civil War. Catton received the Pulitzer Prize and the National Book Award for A Stillness at Appomattox *(1953). Among his other works are* This Hallowed Ground *(1956),* Mr. Lincoln's Army *(1951), and* Gettysburg: The Final Fury *(1974). The piece on Grant and Lee that follows is one of the most frequently anthologized short selections on the subject of the Civil War.*

When Ulysses S. Grant and Robert E. Lee met in the parlor of a modest house at 1 Appomattox Court House, Virginia, on April 9, 1865, to work out the terms for the surrender of Lee's Army of Northern Virginia, a great chapter in American life came to a close, and a great new chapter began.

These men were bringing the Civil War to its virtual finish. To be sure, other 2 armies had yet to surrender, and for a few days the fugitive Confederate government would struggle desperately and vainly, trying to find some way to go on living now that its chief support was gone. But in effect it was all over when Grant and Lee signed the papers. And the little room where they wrote out the terms was the scene of one of the poignant, dramatic contrasts in American history.

They were two strong men, these oddly different generals, and they repre- 3 sented the strengths of two conflicting currents that, through them, had come into final collision.

Back of Robert E. Lee was the notion that the old aristocratic concept might 4 somehow survive and be dominant in American life.

Lee was tidewater Virginia, and in his background were family, culture, and 5 tradition . . . the age of chivalry transplanted to a New World which was making its own legends and its own myths. He embodied a way of life that had come down through the age of knighthood and the English country squire. America was a land that was beginning all over again, dedicated to nothing much more complicated than the rather hazy belief that all men had equal rights, and should have an equal chance in the world. In such a land Lee stood for the feeling that it was somehow of advantage to human society to have a pronounced inequality in the social structure. There should be a leisure class, backed by ownership of land; in turn, society itself should be keyed to the land as the chief source of wealth and influence. It would bring forth (according to this ideal) a class of men with a strong sense of obligation to the community; men who lived not to gain advantage for themselves, but to meet the solemn obligations which had been laid on them by the very fact that they were privileged. From them the country would get its leadership; to them it could look for the higher values—of thought, of conduct, of personal deportment—to give it strength and virtue.

Lee embodied the noblest elements of this aristocratic ideal. Through him, 6 the landed nobility justified itself. For four years, the Southern states had fought a desperate war to uphold the ideals for which Lee stood. In the end, it almost seemed as if the Confederacy fought for Lee; as if he himself was the Confederacy . . . the best thing that the way of life for which the Confederacy stood could ever have to offer. He had passed into legend before Appomattox. Thousands of tired, underfed, poorly clothed Confederate soldiers, long-since past the simple enthusiasm of the early days of the struggle, somehow considered Lee the symbol of everything for which they had been willing to die. But they could not quite put this feeling into words. If the Lost Cause, sanctified by so much heroism and so many deaths, had a living justification, its justification was General Lee.

Grant, the son of a tanner on the Western frontier, was everything Lee was 7 not. He had come up the hard way, and embodied nothing in particular except the eternal toughness and sinewy fiber of the men who grew up beyond the mountains. He was one of a body of men who owed reverence and obeisance to no one, who were self-reliant to a fault, who cared hardly anything for the past but who had a sharp eye for the future.

These frontier men were the precise opposites of the tidewater aristocrats. 8 Back of them, in the great surge that had taken people over the Alleghenies and into the opening Western country, there was a deep, implicit dissatisfaction with a past that had settled into grooves. They stood for democracy, not from any reasoned conclusion about the proper ordering of human society, but simply because they had grown up in the middle of democracy and knew how it worked. Their society might have privileges, but they would be privileges each man had won for himself. Forms and patterns meant nothing. No man was born to anything, except perhaps to a chance to show how far he could rise. Life was competition.

Yet along with this feeling had come a deep sense of belonging to a national 9 community. The Westerner who developed a farm, opened a shop or set up in business as a trader, could hope to prosper only as his own community prospered— and his community ran from the Atlantic to the Pacific and from Canada down to Mexico. If the land was settled, with towns and highways and accessible markets, he could better himself. He saw his fate in terms of the nation's own destiny. As its horizons expanded, so did his. He had, in other words, an acute dollars-and-cents stake in the continued growth and development of his country.

And that, perhaps, is where the contrast between Grant and Lee becomes 10 most striking. The Virginia aristocrat, inevitably, saw himself in relation to his own region. He lived in a static society which could endure almost anything except change. Instinctively, his first loyalty would go to the locality in which that society existed. He would fight to the limit of endurance to defend it, because in defending it he was defending everything that gave his own life its deepest meaning.

The Westerner, on the other hand, would fight with an equal tenacity for the 11 broader concept of society. He fought so because everything he lived by was tied to growth, expansion, and a constantly widening horizon. What he lived by would survive or fall with the nation itself. He could not possibly stand by unmoved in the face of an attempt to destroy the Union. He would combat it with everything he had, because he could only see it as an effort to cut the ground out from under his feet.

So Grant and Lee were in complete contrast, representing two diametrically 12 opposed elements in American life. Grant was the modern man emerging; beyond him, ready to come on the stage, was the great age of steel and machinery, of crowded cities and a restless, burgeoning vitality. Lee might have ridden down from the old age of chivalry, lance in hand, silken banner fluttering over his head. Each man was the perfect champion of his cause, drawing both his strengths and his weaknesses from the people he led.

Yet it was not all contrast, after all. Different as they were—in background, 13 in personality, in underlying aspiration—these two great soldiers had much in common. Under everything else, they were marvelous fighters. Furthermore, their fighting qualities were really very much alike.

Each man had, to begin with, the great virtue of utter tenacity and fidelity. Grant 14 fought his way down the Mississippi Valley in spite of acute personal discouragement and profound military handicaps. Lee hung on in the trenches at Petersburg after hope itself had died. In each man there was an indomitable quality . . . the born fighter's re- fusal to give up as long as he can still remain on his feet and lift his two fists.

Daring and resourcefulness they had, too; the ability to think faster and move 15 faster than the enemy. These were the qualities which gave Lee the dazzling cam- paigns of Second Manassas and Chancellorsville and won Vicksburg for Grant.

Lastly, and perhaps greatest of all, there was the ability, at the end, to turn 16 quickly from war to peace once the fighting was over. Out of the way these two men behaved at Appomattox came the possibility of a peace of reconciliation. It was a possibility not wholly realized, in the years to come, but which did, in the end, help the two sections to become one nation again . . . after a war whose bit- terness might have seemed to make such a reunion wholly impossible. No part of either man's life became him more than the part he played in their brief meeting in the McLean house at Appomattox. Their behavior there put all succeeding gen- erations of Americans in their debt. Two great Americans, Grant and Lee—very different, yet under everything very much alike. Their encounter at Appomattox was one of the great moments of American history.

1958

QUESTIONS FOR DISCUSSION

Content

a. What does Catton mean in paragraph 5 when he says: "[Lee] embodied a way of life that had come down through the age of knighthood and the English coun- try squire"?
b. Catton groups Grant with men who believed: "Forms and patterns meant noth- ing. No man was born to anything, except perhaps to a chance to show how far he could rise" (paragraph 8). Explain what he means by that.
c. Catton's thesis is stated rather early in the essay. What is it? How does it signal the pattern of organization to follow?
d. If this selection is "A Study in Contrasts," why does Catton spend the last four paragraphs discussing the similarities between Grant and Lee?

e. What are some of these similarities?

f. Discuss the other characteristics that Catton attributes to frontier men.

g. How would you explain the Westerner's "deep sense of belonging to a national community," which Catton mentions in paragraph 9? How does this idea differ from what tidewater aristocrats like Lee felt?

Strategy and Style

h. What function do paragraphs 10 and 11 play in the structure of this essay?

i. Catton organizes his prose by alternating the discussion from point to point rather than completing his discussion of one figure before moving on to the next. Is this method effective?

SUGGESTIONS FOR SHORT WRITING

a. Describe what you consider to be the ideal general for today. In your opinion, do generals today share the same qualities as those in Grant and Lee's time?

b. Describe the meeting that might have occurred between Grant and Lee if the Confederacy had won the war.

SUGGESTIONS FOR SUSTAINED WRITING

a. Choose two individuals with whom you have the same kind of relationship: two grandfathers, two aunts, two close friends. How do these individuals differ? List the major differences in their personalities or their outlooks on life. Is one a pessimist, the other an optimist? Is one an introvert, the other an extrovert? Write a well-developed essay that makes the contrast clear.

b. Catton characterized Lee as a "living justification" of the "Lost Cause." Do you see yourself as such an idealist? Do you espouse "lost causes" simply because you think they are right? Or are you more pragmatic and realistic in your approach to life? Whatever your answer, explain it in an essay; cite sufficient examples to be convincing and clear.

c. Select two rival candidates in an upcoming or recent political election (local, state, or national). Isolate and explain the major differences in their ideologies.

d. Catton tells us that both Grant and Lee had "the great virtue of utter tenacity and fidelity." Do you know two individuals who, while otherwise quite different, share one important personality trait or human quality? If so, write an essay comparing them in that regard. Remember, comparison explains similarities, *not* differences. You can choose two people from among your close friends or relatives, or you might write about two figures from the world of politics, art, science, or business about whom you know a great deal.

Talk in the Intimate Relationship: His and Hers

Deborah Tannen

Deborah Tannen (b. 1945) is a professor of linguistics at Georgetown University. Although she has written articles for academic journals, she considers her "mission" to be "the presentation of linguistic research to a general audience." Her many popular nonfiction books do just this: make linguistic issues interesting and important to nonacademic readers. She draws on her experiences teaching English in Greece, studying gender-related language issues, and writing poetry and fiction to create books that are informal and engaging yet soundly researched. These books include Conversational Style: Analyzing Talk Among Friends *(1984) and* Gender and Conversational Interaction *(1993), and* The Argument Culture: Moving from Debate to Dialogue *(1998). The following essay is from* That's Not What I Meant! How Conversational Style Makes or Breaks Your Relations with Others *(1986).*

Male-female conversation is cross-cultural communication. Culture is simply a 1 network of habits and patterns gleaned from past experience, and women and men have different past experiences. From the time they're born, they're treated differently, talked to differently, and talk differently as a result. Boys and girls grow up in different worlds, even if they grow up in the same house. And as adults they travel in different worlds, reinforcing patterns established in childhood. These cultural differences include different expectations about the role of talk in relationships and how it fulfills that role.

Everyone knows that as a relationship becomes long-term, its terms change. 2 But women and men often differ in how they expect them to change. Many women feel, "After all this time, you should know what I want without my telling you." Many men feel, "After all this time, we should be able to tell each other what we want."

These incongruent expectations capture one of the key differences between 3 men and women. Communication is always a matter of balancing conflicting needs for involvement and independence. Though everyone has both these needs, women often have a relatively greater need for involvement, and men a relatively greater need for independence. Being understood without saying what you mean gives a payoff in involvement, and that is why women value it so highly.

If you want to be understood without saying what you mean explicitly in 4 words, you must convey meaning somewhere else—in how words are spoken, or by metamessages. Thus it stands to reason that women are often more attuned than men to the metamessages of talk. When women surmise meaning in this way, it seems mysterious to men, who call it "women's intuition" (if they think it's right) or "reading things in" (if they think it's wrong). Indeed, it could be wrong, since metamessages are not on record. And even if it is right, there is still the question of scale: How significant are the metamessages that are there?

Metamessages are a form of indirectness. Women are more likely to be in- 5 direct, and to try to reach agreement by negotiation. Another way to understand

224

this preference is that negotiation allows a display of solidarity, which women prefer to the display of power (even though the aim may be the same—getting what you want). Unfortunately, power and solidarity are bought with the same currency: Ways of talking intended to create solidarity have the simultaneous effect of framing power differences. When they think they're being nice, women often end up appearing deferential and unsure of themselves or of what they want.

When styles differ, misunderstandings are always rife. As their differing 6 styles create misunderstandings, women and men try to clear them up by talking things out. These pitfalls are compounded in talks between men and women because they have different ways of going about talking things out, and different assumptions about the significance of going about it.

Sylvia and Harry celebrated their fiftieth wedding anniversary at a mountain 7 resort. Some of the guests were at the resort for the whole weekend, others just for the evening of the celebration: A cocktail party followed by a sit-down dinner. The manager of the dining room approached Sylvia during dinner. "Since there's so much food tonight," he said, "and the hotel prepared a fancy dessert and everyone already ate at the cocktail party anyway, how about cutting and serving the anniversary cake at lunch tomorrow?" Sylvia asked the advice of the others at her table. All the men agreed: "Sure, that makes sense. Save the cake for tomorrow." All the women disagreed: "No, the party is tonight. Serve the cake tonight." The men were focusing on the message: The cake as food. The women were thinking of the metamessage: Serving a special cake frames an occasion as a celebration.

Why are women more attuned to metamessages? Because they are more fo- 8 cused on involvement, that is, on relationships among people, and it is through metamessages that relationships among people are established and maintained. If you want to take the temperature and check the vital signs of a relationship, the barometers to check are its metamessages: What is said and how.

Everyone can see these signals, but whether or not we pay attention to them 9 is another matter—a matter of being sensitized. Once you are sensitized, you can't roll your antennae back in; they're stuck in the extended position.

When interpreting meaning, it is possible to pick up signals that weren't in- 10 tentionally sent out, like an innocent flock of birds on a radar screen. The birds are there—and the signals women pick up are there—but they may not mean what the interpreter thinks they mean. For example, Maryellen looks at Larry and asks, "What's wrong?" because his brow is furrowed. Since he was only thinking about lunch, her expression of concern makes him feel under scrutiny.

The difference in focus on messages and metamessages can give men and 11 women different points of view on almost any comment. Harriet complains to Morton, "Why don't you ask me how my day was?" He replies, "If you have something to tell me, tell me. Why do you have to be invited?" The reason is that she wants the metamessage of interest: Evidence that he cares how her day was, regardless of whether or not she has something to tell.

A lot of trouble is caused between women and men by, of all things, pro- 12 nouns. Women often feel hurt when their partners use "I" or "me" in a situation in which they would use "we" or "us." When Morton announces, "I think I'll go for a walk," Harriet feels specifically uninvited, though Morton later claims she would have been welcome to join him. She felt locked out by his use of "I" and his omission of an invitation: "Would you like to come?" Metamessages can be seen in what is not said as well as what is said.

It's difficult to straighten out such misunderstandings because each one feels   13
convinced of the logic of his or her position and the illogic—or irresponsibility—of the other's. Harriet knows that she always asks Morton how his day was, and that she'd never announce, "I'm going for a walk," without inviting him to join her. If he talks differently to her, it must be that he feels differently. But Morton wouldn't feel unloved if Harriet didn't ask about his day, and he would feel free to ask, "Can I come along?" if she announced she was taking a walk. So he can't believe she is justified in feeling responses he knows he wouldn't have.

These processes are dramatized with chilling yet absurdly amusing authen-   14
ticity in Jules Feiffer's play *Grown Ups*. To get a closer look at what happens when men and women focus on different levels of talk in talking things out, let's look at what happens in this play.

Jake criticizes Louise for not responding when their daughter, Edie, called   15
her. His comment leads to a fight even though they're both aware that this one incident is not in itself important.

JAKE: Look, I don't care if it's important or not, when a kid calls its mother the mother should answer.
LOUISE: Now I'm a bad mother.
JAKE: I didn't say that.
LOUISE: It's in your stare.
JAKE: Is that another thing you know? My stare?

Louise ignores Jake's message—the question of whether or not she responded when Edie called—and goes for the metamessage: His implication that she's a bad mother, which Jake insistently disclaims. When Louise explains the signals she's reacting to, Jake not only discounts them but is angered at being held accountable not for what he said but for how he looked—his stare.

As the play goes on, Jake and Louise replay and intensify these patterns: 16

LOUISE: If I'm such a terrible mother, do you want a divorce?
JAKE: I do not think you're a terrible mother and no, thank you, I do not want a divorce. Why is it that whenever I bring up any difference between us you ask me if I want a divorce?

The more he denies any meaning beyond the message, the more she blows it up, the more adamantly he denies it, and so on:

JAKE: I have brought up one thing that you do with Edie that I don't think you notice that I have noticed for some time but which I have deliberately not brought up before because I had hoped you would notice it for yourself and stop doing it and also—frankly, baby, I have to say this—I knew if I brought it up we'd get into exactly the kind of circular argument we're in right now. And I wanted to avoid it. But I haven't and we're in it, so now, with your permission, I'd like to talk about it.

LOUISE: You don't see how that puts me down?

JAKE: What?

LOUISE: If you think I'm so stupid why do you go on living with me?

JAKE: *Dammit! Why can't anything ever be simple around here?*!

It can't be simple because Louise and Jake are responding to different levels of communication. As in Bateson's example of the dual-control electric blanket with crossed wires, each one intensifies the energy going to a different aspect of the problem. Jake tries to clarify his point by over-elaborating it, which gives Louise further evidence that he's condescending to her, making it even less likely that she will address his point rather than his condescension.

What pushes Jake and Louise beyond anger to rage is their different perspec- 17 tives on metamessages. His refusal to admit that his statements have implications and overtones denies her authority over her own feelings. Her attempts to interpret what he didn't say and put the metamessage into the message makes him feel she's putting words into his mouth—denying his authority over his own meaning.

The same thing happens when Louise tells Jake that he is being manipulated 18 by Edie:

LOUISE: Why don't you ever make her come to see you? Why do you always go to her?

JAKE: You want me to play power games with a nine year old? I want her to know I'm interested in her. Someone around here has to show interest in her.

LOUISE: You love her more than I do.

JAKE: I didn't say that.

LOUISE: Yes, you did.

JAKE: You don't know how to listen. You have never learned how to listen. It's as if listening to you is a foreign language.

Again, Louise responds to his implication—this time, that he loves Edie more because he runs when she calls. And yet again, Jake cries literal meaning, denying he meant any more than he said.

Throughout their argument, the point to Louise is her feelings—that Jake 19 makes her feel put down—but to him the point is her actions—that she doesn't always respond when Edie calls:

LOUISE: You talk about what I do to Edie, what do you think you do to me?

JAKE: This is not the time to go into what we do to each other.

Since she will talk only about the metamessage, and he will talk only about 20 the message, neither can get satisfaction from their talk, and they end up where they started—only angrier:

JAKE: That's not the point!
LOUISE: It's my point!
JAKE: It's hopeless!
LOUISE: Then get a divorce.

American conventional wisdom (and many of our parents and English teachers) tell us that meaning is conveyed by words, so men who tend to be literal about words are supported by conventional wisdom. They may not simply deny but actually miss the cues that are sent by how words are spoken. If they sense something about it, they may nonetheless discount what they sense. After all, it wasn't said. Sometimes that's a dodge—a plausible defense rather than a gut feeling. But sometimes it is a sincere conviction. Women are also likely to doubt the reality of what they sense. If they don't doubt it in their guts, they nonetheless may lack the arguments to support their position and thus are reduced to repeating, "You said it. You did so." Knowing that metamessages are a real and fundamental part of communication makes it easier to understand and justify what they feel.

An article in a popular newspaper reports that one of the five most common   21
complaints of wives about their husbands is "He doesn't listen to me anymore." Another is "He doesn't talk to me anymore." Political scientist Andrew Hacker noted that lack of communication, while high on women's lists of reasons for divorce, is much less often mentioned by men. Since couples are parties to the same conversations, why are women more dissatisfied with them than men? Because what they expect is different, as well as what they see as the significance of talk itself.

First, let's consider the complaint "He doesn't talk to me."   22

One of the most common stereotypes of American men is the strong silent   23
type. Jack Kroll, writing about Henry Fonda on the occasion of his death, used the phrases "quiet power," "abashed silences," "combustible catatonia," and "sense of power held in check." He explained that Fonda's goal was not to let anyone see "the wheels go around," not to let the "machinery" show. According to Kroll, the resulting silence was effective on stage but devastating to Fonda's family.

The image of a silent father is common and is often the model for the lover   24
or husband. But what attracts us can become flypaper to which we are unhappily stuck. Many women find the strong silent type to be a lure as a lover but a lug as a husband. Nancy Schoenberger begins a poem with the lines "It was your silence that hooked me, / so like my father's." Adrienne Rich refers in a poem to the "husband who is frustratingly mute." Despite the initial attraction of such quintessentially male silence, it may begin to feel, to a woman in a long-term relationship, like a brick wall against which she is banging her head.

In addition to these images of male and female behavior—both the result   25
and the cause of them—are differences in how women and men view the role of talk in relationships as well as how talk accomplishes its purpose. These differences have their roots in the settings in which men and women learn to have conversations among their peers, growing up.

Children whose parents have foreign accents don't speak with accents. They 26 learn to talk like their peers. Little girls and little boys learn how to have conversations as they learn how to pronounce words from their playmates. Between the ages of five and fifteen, when children are learning to have conversations, they play mostly with friends of their own sex. So it's not surprising that they learn different ways of having and using conversations.

Anthropologists Daniel Maltz and Ruth Borker point out that boys and girls 27 socialize differently. Little girls tend to play in small groups or, even more common, in pairs. Their social life usually centers around a best friend, and friendships are made, maintained, and broken by talk—especially "secrets." If a little girl tells her friend's secret to another little girl, she may find herself with a new best friend. The secrets themselves may or may not be important, but the fact of telling them is all-important. It's hard for newcomers to get into these tight groups, but anyone who is admitted is treated as an equal. Girls like to play cooperatively; if they can't cooperate, the group breaks up.

Little boys tend to play in larger groups, often outdoors, and they spend more 28 time doing things than talking. It's easy for boys to get into the group, but not everyone is accepted as an equal. Once in the group, boys must jockey for their status in it. One of the most important ways they do this is through talk: Verbal display such as telling stories and jokes, challenging and sidetracking the verbal displays of other boys, and withstanding other boys' challenges in order to maintain their own story—and status. Their talk is often competitive talk about who is best at what.

Feiffer's play is ironically named *Grown Ups* because adult men and women 29 struggling to communicate often sound like children: "You said so!" "I did not!" The reason is that when they grow up, women and men keep the divergent attitudes and habits they learned as children—which they don't recognize as attitudes and habits but simply take for granted as ways of talking.

Women want their partners to be a new and improved version of a best 30 friend. This gives them a soft spot for men who tell them secrets. As Jack Nicholson once advised a guy in a movie: "Tell her about your troubled childhood—that always gets 'em." Men expect to do things together and don't feel anything is missing if they don't have heart-to-heart talks all the time.

If they do have heart-to-heart talks, the meaning of those talks may be opposite 31 for men and women. To many women, the relationship is working as long as they can talk things out. To many men, the relationship isn't working out if they have to keep working it over. If she keeps trying to get talks going to save the relationship, and he keeps trying to avoid them because he sees them as weakening it, then each one's efforts to preserve the relationship appear to the other as reckless endangerment.

If talks (of any kind) do get going, men's and women's ideas about how to 32 conduct them may be very different. For example, Dora is feeling comfortable and close to Tom. She settles into a chair after dinner and begins to tell him about a problem at work. She expects him to ask questions to show he's interested; reassure her that he understands and that what she feels is normal; and return the intimacy by telling her a problem of his. Instead, Tom sidetracks her story, cracks jokes about it, questions her interpretation of the problem, and gives her advice about how to solve it and avoid such problems in the future.

All of these responses, natural to men, are unexpected to women, who inter- 33 pret them in terms of their own habits—negatively. When Tom comments on side issues or cracks jokes, Dora thinks he doesn't care about what she's saying and isn't really listening. If he challenges her reading of what went on, she feels he is criticizing her and telling her she's crazy, when what she wants is to be reassured that she's not. If he tells her how to solve the problem, it makes her feel as if she's the patient to his doctor—a metamessage of condescension, echoing male one-upmanship compared to the female etiquette of equality. Because he doesn't volunteer information about his problems, she feels he's implying he doesn't have any.

His way of responding to her bid for intimacy makes her feel distant from him. 34 She tries harder to regain intimacy the only way she knows how—by revealing more and more about herself. He tries harder by giving more insistent advice. The more problems she exposes, the more incompetent she feels, until they both see her as emotionally draining and problem-ridden. When his efforts to help aren't appreciated, he wonders why she asks for his advice if she doesn't want to take it. . . .

When women talk about what seems obviously interesting to them, their 35 conversations often include reports of conversations. Tone of voice, timing, intonation, and wording are all re-created in the telling in order to explain—dramatize, really—the experience that is being reported. If men tell about an incident and give a brief summary instead of recreating what was said and how, the women often feel that the essence of the experience is being omitted. If the woman asks, "What exactly did he say?," and "How did he say it?," the man probably can't remember. If she continues to press him, he may feel as if he's being grilled.

All these different habits have repercussions when the man and the woman 36 are talking about their relationship. He feels out of his element, even one down. She claims to recall exactly what he said, and what she said, and in what sequence, and she wants him to account for what he said. He can hardly account for it since he has forgotten exactly what was said—if not the whole conversation. She secretly suspects he's only pretending not to remember, and he secretly suspects that she's making up the details.

One woman reported such a problem as being a matter of her boyfriend's 37 poor memory. It is unlikely, however, that his problem was poor memory in general. The question is what types of material each person remembers or forgets.

Frances was sitting at her kitchen table talking to Edward, when the toaster 38 did something funny. Edward began to explain why it did it. Frances tried to pay attention, but very early in his explanation, she realized she was completely lost. She felt very stupid. And indications were that he thought so too.

Later that day they were taking a walk. He was telling her about a difficult 39 situation in his office that involved a complex network of interrelationships among a large number of people. Suddenly he stopped and said, "I'm sure you can't keep track of all these people." "Of course I can," she said, and she retraced his story with all the characters in place, all the details right. He was genuinely impressed. She felt very smart.

How could Frances be both smart and stupid? Did she have a good memory 40
or a bad one? Frances's and Edward's abilities to follow, remember, and recount
depended on the subject—and paralleled her parents' abilities to follow and remember. Whenever Frances told her parents about people in her life, her mother
could follow with no problem, but her father got lost as soon as she introduced a
second character. "Now who was that?" he'd ask. "Your boss?" "No, my boss is
Susan. This was my friend." Often he'd still be in the previous story. But whenever she told them about her work, it was her mother who would get lost as soon
as she mentioned a second step: "That was your tech report?" "No, I handed my
tech report in last month. This was a special project."

Frances's mother and father, like many men and women, had honed their lis- 41
tening and remembering skills in different arenas. Their experience talking to other
men and other women gave them practice in following different kinds of talk.

Knowing whether and how we are likely to report events later influences 42
whether and how we pay attention when they happen. As women listen to and take
part in conversations, knowing they may talk about them later makes them more
likely to pay attention to exactly what is said and how. Since most men aren't in
the habit of making such reports, they are less likely to pay much attention at the
time. On the other hand, many women aren't in the habit of paying attention to scientific explanations and facts because they don't expect to have to perform in public by reciting them—just as those who aren't in the habit of entertaining others by
telling jokes "can't" remember jokes they've heard, even though they listened
carefully enough to enjoy them.

So women's conversations with their women friends keep them in training 43
for talking about their relationships with men, but many men come to such conversations with no training at all—and an uncomfortable sense that this really isn't
their event.

Most of us place enormous emphasis on the importance of a primary rela- 44
tionship. We regard the ability to maintain such relationships as a sign of mental
health—our contemporary metaphor for being a good person.

Yet our expectations of such relationships are nearly—maybe in fact— 45
impossible. When primary relationships are between women and men, male-female differences contribute to the impossibility. We expect partners to be both romantic interests and best friends. Though women and men may have fairly similar
expectations for romantic interests, obscuring their differences when relationships
begin, they have very different ideas about how to be friends, and these are the differences that mount over time.

In conversations between friends who are not lovers, small misunderstand- 46
ings can be passed over or diffused by breaks in contact. But in the context of a primary relationship, differences can't be ignored, and the pressure cooker of continued contact keeps both people stewing in the juice of accumulated minor
misunderstandings. And stylistic differences are sure to cause misunderstandings—
not, ironically, in matters such as sharing values and interests or understanding each
other's philosophies of life. These large and significant yet palpable issues can be
talked about and agreed on. It is far harder to achieve congruence—and much more

surprising and troubling that it is hard—in the simple day-to-day matters of the automatic rhythms and nuances of talk. Nothing in our backgrounds or in the media (the present-day counterpart to religion or grandparents' teachings) prepares us for this failure. If two people share so much in terms of point of view and basic values, how can they continually get into fights about insignificant matters?

If you find yourself in such a situation and you don't know about differences 47 in conversational style, you assume something's wrong with your partner, or you for having chosen your partner. At best, if you are forward thinking and generous minded, you may absolve individuals and blame the relationship. But if you know about differences in conversational style, you can accept that there are differences in habits and assumptions about how to have conversation, show interest, be considerate, and so on. You may not always correctly interpret your partner's intentions, but you will know that if you get a negative impression, it may not be what was intended—and neither are your responses unfounded. If he says he really is interested even though he doesn't seem to be, maybe you should believe what he says and not what you sense.

Sometimes explaining assumptions can help. If a man starts to tell a woman 48 what to do to solve her problem, she may say, "Thanks for the advice but I really don't want to be told what to do. I just want you to listen and say you understand." A man might want to explain, "If I challenge you, it's not to prove you wrong; it's just my way of paying attention to what you're telling me." Both may try either or both to modify their ways of talking and to try to accept what the other does. The important thing is to know that what seem like bad intentions may really be good intentions expressed in a different conversational style. We have to give up our conviction that, as Robin Lakoff put it, "Love means never having to say 'What do you mean?'"

1986

QUESTIONS FOR DISCUSSION

Content

a. A key word in this essay is "metamessages" (paragraph 4). How does Tannen define this word? In the few paragraphs that follow, underline or point to phrases that illustrate what metamessages are.

b. Tannen asserts that "[a] lot of trouble is caused . . . by . . . pronouns" (paragraph 12). What kind of trouble is this? Why is it a problem?

c. Does the fact that Tannen is a woman influence how she analyzes men's and women's talk? If your answer is yes, point to several instances in the essay in which a gender bias seems apparent.

d. What are the specific kinds of communication that Tannen compares and contrasts?

e. Tannen occasionally blames stereotypes, such as the "strong silent" stereotype for men (paragraph 23), for causing misunderstandings between men and women. What are some other stereotypes of men and women that she cites? Why do these stereotypes cause misunderstandings?

f. According to Tannen, what do women value or notice as important in a conversation with a man? What do men value or notice as important?

g. Why are women better at remembering stories about people or events and men better at remembering stories about scientific explanations or facts? Do you think that the way men and women remember and tell stories is a factor of biology (i.e., women remember people/events better because they are female) or of cultural training (i.e., women remember people/events better because they have been taught to listen this way)?

Strategy and Style

h. Tannen uses many examples to show how men and women miscommunicate. What is the effect on you as you read all these examples?

i. Does the author use too many examples? If so, what example(s) would you remove and why? How would the removal of the example(s) improve the logic or readability of the essay? If not, how do the examples work together to create a tightly controlled logic and structure?

j. Occasionally, Tannen uses a metaphor or simile to evoke an image. What are the images created and the effects of phrases such as "the barometers to check" (paragraph 8), "you can't roll your antennae back in" (paragraph 9), and "like an innocent flock of birds on a radar screen" (paragraph 10)?

k. Tannen uses simple, direct language, and presents examples as anecdotes. What would happen if she had written this in the academic language of sociologists or linguists?

SUGGESTIONS FOR SHORT WRITING

a. In paragraph 3, Tannen asserts that "women often have a relatively greater need for involvement, and men a relatively greater need for independence. Being understood without saying what you mean gives a payoff in involvement, and that is why women value it so highly." Describe a personal experience that shows how this statement applies or does not apply to you.

b. In your own experiences, what differences have you found in the way men and women talk to each other? Describe a relationship you have with the opposite sex in which there has been miscommunication. (While a romantic relationship may be the first thing you think of, you can also use a friendship, or an acquaintance with a co-worker, student, or teacher.) If you want, write out the conversation as a script like the kind used in a play or television program.

c. Taking item *b* further, compare your scripted dialogue with the examples in Tannen's essay from Jules Feiffer's play *Grown Ups*. Make a list of the metamessages in your conversation.

SUGGESTIONS FOR SUSTAINED WRITING

a. Write an analysis of a male/female conversation in a film, novel, or short story. Base your analysis on the metamessages in the conversation. As a first step in this assignment, reread Tannen's essay and make a list of the metamessages she describes. Use this list both to choose a suitable conversation and to analyze it. Then, explain how these metamessages alter or make more complex the main message(s). You might also extend your analysis to an interpretation of the entire film or literary work.
b. For a less ambitious paper, do the above with the script of one of your own conversations (as described in Short Writing *b*).
c. Find the book by Daniel Maltz and Ruth Borker referred to in paragraph 27. Read the book and write an extended response to it, citing both the book and Tannen's essay. Base your response on your general reaction to the book, on a particular passage that interests you, or on the question, "Do you think the differences in socialization are caused by biological differences or by environmental factors such as home life, school life, culture, etc.?"

Two Views of the Mississippi

Mark Twain

Mark Twain (1835–1910) was, of course, the pen name of Samuel Langhorne Clemens, the Missourian who learned to pilot Mississippi riverboats and who grew to become one of America's leading humorists, social critics, and men of letters. Twain recorded his experiences in numerous newspaper features and columns and in several books, including Life on the Mississippi *(1883),* The Adventures of Tom Sawyer *(1876), and his masterpiece,* The Adventures of Huckleberry Finn *(1885). Indeed, for some literary historians, the true American novel has its beginnings in the work of Twain. In the selection that follows, Twain contrasts his views of the Mississippi first as a novice and then as an experienced river pilot.*

Now when I had mastered the language of this water, and had come to know every 1 trifling feature that bordered the great river as familiarly as I knew the letters of the alphabet, I had made a valuable acquisition. But I had lost something, too. I had lost something which could never be restored to me while I lived. All the grace, the beauty, the poetry, had gone out of the majestic river! I still keep in mind a certain wonderful sunset which I witnessed when steamboating was new to me. A broad expanse of the river was turned to blood; in the middle distance the red hue brightened into gold, through which a solitary log came floating black and conspicuous; in one place a long, slanting mark lay sparkling upon the water; in another the surface was broken by boiling, tumbling rings, that were as many-tinted as an opal; where the ruddy flush was faintest, was a smooth spot that was covered with graceful circles and radiating lines, ever so delicately traced; the shore on our left was densely wooded, and the somber shadow that fell from this forest was broken in one place by a long, ruffled trail that shone like silver; and high above the forest wall a clean-stemmed dead tree waved a single leafy bough that glowed like a flame in the unobstructed splendor that was flowing from the sun. There were graceful curves, reflected images, woody heights, soft distances; and over the whole scene, far and near, the dissolving lights drifted steadily, enriching it every passing moment with new marvels of coloring.

I stood like one bewitched. I drank it in, in a speechless rapture. The world 2 was new to me, and I had never seen anything like this at home. But as I have said, a day came when I began to cease from noting the glories and the charms which the moon and the sun and the twilight wrought upon the river's face; another day came when I ceased altogether to note them. Then, if that sunset scene had been repeated, I should have looked upon it without rapture, and should have commented upon it, inwardly, after this fashion: "This sun means that we are going to have wind tomorrow; that floating log means that the river is rising, small thanks to it; that slanting mark on the water refers to a bluff reef which is going to kill somebody's steamboat one of these nights, if it keeps on stretching out like that; those tumbling 'boils' show a dissolving bar and a changing channel there; the lines and circles in the slick water over yonder are a warning that that troublesome

235

place is shoaling up dangerously; that silver streak in the shadow of the forest is the 'break' from a new snag, and he has located himself in the very best place he could have found to fish for steamboats; that tall dead tree, with a single living branch, is not going to last long, and then how is a body ever going to get through this blind place at night without the friendly old landmark?"

No, the romance and beauty were all gone from the river. All the value any 3 feature of it had for me now was the amount of usefulness it could furnish toward compassing the safe piloting of a steamboat. Since those days, I have pitied doctors from my heart. What does the lovely flush in a beauty's cheek mean to a doctor but a "break" that ripples above some deadly disease? Are not all her visible charms sown thick with what are to him the signs and symbols of hidden decay? Does he ever see her beauty at all, or doesn't he simply view her professionally, and comment upon her unwholesome condition all to himself? And doesn't he sometimes wonder whether he has gained most or lost most by learning his trade?

1883

QUESTIONS FOR DISCUSSION

Content

a. Why does Twain pity doctors?
b. What purpose does paragraph 3 serve? Why does Twain compare the work of a steamboat pilot to that of a doctor? In what way is the conduct of their work similar?
c. Twain fully describes his view of the river as a novice, then goes on to talk about his perception of it as a trained pilot. Does this pattern serve him better than discussing various aspects of the river point by point?
d. What details does Twain offer to prove that at one time in his life the river held grace, beauty, and poetry for him?

Strategy and Style

e. Twain's thesis, which appears in paragraph 1, is presented in an obvious and straightforward manner. How does it help determine the organization of the rest of the piece?
f. The first paragraph is filled with descriptive language that captures a subjective, almost rhapsodic, view of the river. How would you characterize the language found in paragraph 2?
g. What use does paragraph 2 make of the details Twain has already introduced in paragraph 1?

SUGGESTIONS FOR SHORT WRITING

a. Brainstorm a list of metaphors and similes that Twain might have used to describe the Mississippi River. For example, "the Mississippi River is a _____," or "the Mississippi River is like a _____."

b. Write the copy for a travel brochure for a steamboat holiday on the Mississippi.

SUGGESTIONS FOR SUSTAINED WRITING

a. Select a person or place you have known for a long time. Have your views on this individual or place changed significantly over the years? For better or worse? Explain.

b. As children, we become excited, enraptured, and even mystified by the rituals and customs associated with important religious or national holidays: Christmas, Yom Kippur, Thanksgiving, Halloween, the Fourth of July. Think about the holiday you found most exciting as a child. Has your view of it changed? Explain.

c. Twain's training as a pilot seems to have had a negative effect in that it took the romance out of his view of the river. However, learning more about a subject may enhance one's appreciation of it. Can you relate an instance from your own experience to illustrate this notion? For example, mastering the fundamentals of swimming may have given you the confidence you needed to try skin diving. Tuning your first engine may have motivated you to learn more about auto mechanics in general.

d. In a sense, Twain may be hinting at his disillusionment over his life as a pilot. Have you ever become disillusioned with a job? What were the causes of this disillusionment? Explain.

The Rewards of Living a Solitary Life

May Sarton

*May Sarton (1912–1995) was the daughter of a Belgian father and an English mother,
but moved to the United States with her parents when she was four, becoming a U.S.
citizen in 1924. She very early began writing poetry, fiction, and drama. When she was
only twenty-one, she founded the Apprentice Theater at the New School for Social
Research in New York, and acted as its director from 1933 to 1936. During World War II,
she was a scriptwriter of documentary films for the U.S. Office of War Information. She
taught creative and dramatic writing at Harvard University, Wellesley College, and the
Stuart School in Boston, and lectured throughout the country. Sarton was a prolific
writer, having published many volumes of poetry, novels, and memoirs. "Rewards" was
written for the* New York Times *in 1946.*

The other day an acquaintance of mine, a gregarious and charming man, told me   1
he had found himself unexpectedly alone in New York for an hour or two between
appointments. He went to the Whitney and spent the "empty" time looking at
things in solitary bliss. For him it proved to be a shock nearly as great as falling in
love to discover that he could enjoy himself so much alone.

What had he been afraid of, I asked myself? That, suddenly alone, he would   2
discover that he bored himself, or that there was, quite simply, no self there to
meet? But having taken the plunge, he is now on the brink of adventure; he is about
to be launched into his own inner space, space as immense, unexplored and sometimes frightening as outer space to the astronaut. His every perception will come
to him with a new freshness and, for a time, seem startlingly original. For anyone
who can see things for himself with a naked eye becomes, for a moment or two,
something of a genius. With another human being present vision becomes double
vision, inevitably. We are busy wondering, what does my companion see or think
of this, and what do I think of it? The original impact gets lost, or diffused.

"Music I heard with you was more than music." Exactly. And therefore mu-   3
sic *itself* can only be heard alone. Solitude is the salt of personhood. It brings out
the authentic flavor of every experience.

"Alone one is never lonely: The spirit adventures, walking / In a quiet gar-   4
den, in a cool house, abiding single there."

Loneliness is most acutely felt with other people, for with others, even with a   5
lover sometimes, we suffer from our differences of taste, temperament, mood. Human intercourse often demands that we soften the edge of perception, or withdraw
at the very instant of personal truth for fear of hurting, or of being inappropriately
present, which is to say naked, in a social situation. Alone we can afford to be wholly
whatever we are, and to feel whatever we feel absolutely. That is a great luxury!

For me the most interesting thing about a solitary life, and mine has been that   6
for the last twenty years, is that it becomes increasingly rewarding. When I can
wake up and watch the sun rise over the ocean, as I do most days, and know that I
have an entire day ahead, uninterrupted, in which to write a few pages, take a walk

with my dog, lie down in the afternoon for a long think (why does one think better in a horizontal position?), read and listen to music, I am flooded with happiness.

I am lonely only when I am overtired, when I have worked too long without a 7 break, when for the time being I feel empty and need filling up. And I am lonely sometimes when I come back home after a lecture trip, when I have seen a lot of people and talked a lot, and am full to the brim with experience that needs to be sorted out.

Then for a little while the house feels huge and empty, and I wonder where 8 my self is hiding. It has to be recaptured slowly by watering the plants, perhaps, and looking again at each one as though it were a person, by feeding the two cats, by cooking a meal.

It takes a while, as I watch the surf blowing up in fountains at the end of the 9 field, but the moment comes when the world falls away, and the self emerges again from the deep unconscious, bringing back all I have recently experienced to be explored and slowly understood, when I can converse again with my hidden powers, and so grow, and so be renewed, till death do us part.

1946

QUESTIONS FOR DISCUSSION

Content

a. What does Sarton mean by her sentence in paragraph 3, "Solitude is the salt of personhood"? What is the metaphor here?

b. Do you agree or disagree with Sarton's assessment of solitude?

c. To what does Sarton allude with the last phrase of the essay? What is her implication here?

d. What does Sarton use as examples to support her thesis that solitude is better than constant society? How effective are these examples?

e. What might be Sarton's purpose in including a passage of poetry as an entire paragraph (paragraph 4)?

f. Exactly what does Sarton compare and contrast in her essay?

g. Is this an argumentative essay? If so, what is her argument and to whom is she arguing? What does she hope to persuade them to do?

h. How does Sarton define *loneliness*? Do you agree with her definition? How does her definition differ from standard definitions?

i. Have you ever found yourself in the same situation as Sarton's gregarious acquaintance? If so, were your reactions similar to his?

Strategy and Style

j. Sarton begins her essay with an anecdote. What effect does this opening have on you? Does it draw you into the essay? Would the essay be better, or worse, without it?

k. How do you account for the brevity of the essay? Would it be a better essay if it were longer?
l. What allusions or metaphors does Sarton include?

SUGGESTIONS FOR SHORT WRITING

a. Write your definitions of *loneliness* and of *solitude*. How do they compare to what Sarton says of loneliness and solitude?
b. What is your own experience of solitude? Describe a time when you were completely solitary.

SUGGESTIONS FOR SUSTAINED WRITING

a. Write an essay justifying your lifestyle. Decide whether you want to persuade your readers to adopt a similar lifestyle.
b. Write an essay comparing and/or contrasting two or more lifestyles, habits, hobbies, etc.
c. Trying to keep the essay as short as possible, write an essay that captures the essential aspects of a way of life. You may wish to begin with a longer essay, making it more and more compact with each revision.

Neat People vs. Sloppy People

Suzanne Britt

Suzanne Britt teaches English at Meredith College in North Carolina. She writes a regular column for North Carolina Gardens and Homes *and for the* Dickens Dispatch, *a newsletter for fans of Charles Dickens. She has also published articles in the* New York Times, Newsweek, *and the* Boston Globe. *In addition to two composition textbooks, Britt has published two collections of essays,* Skinny People Are Dull and Crunchy Like Carrots *(1982) and* Show and Tell *(1983), from which the following selection is taken.*

I've finally figured out the difference between neat people and sloppy people. The 1 distinction is, as always, moral. Neat people are lazier and meaner than sloppy people.

Sloppy people, you see, are not really sloppy. Their sloppiness is merely the 2 unfortunate consequence of their extreme moral rectitude. Sloppy people carry in their mind's eye a heavenly vision, a precise plan, that is so stupendous, so perfect, it can't be achieved in this world or the next.

Sloppy people live in Never-Never Land. Someday is their métier. Someday 3 they are planning to alphabetize all their books and set up home catalogs. Someday they will go through their wardrobes and mark certain items for tentative mending and certain items for passing on to relatives of similar shape and size. Someday sloppy people will make family scrapbooks into which they will put newspaper clippings, postcards, locks of hair, and the dried corsage from their senior prom. Someday they will file everything on the surface of their desks, including the cash receipts from coffee purchases at the snack shop. Someday they will sit down and read all the back issues of the *New Yorker.*

For all these noble reasons and more, sloppy people never get neat. They 4 aim too high and wide. They save everything, planning someday to file, order, and straighten out the world. But while these ambitious plans take clearer and clearer shape in their heads, the books spill from the shelves onto the floor, the clothes pile up in the hamper and closet, the family mementos accumulate in every drawer, the surface of the desk is buried under mounds of paper and the unread magazines threaten to reach the ceiling.

Sloppy people can't bear to part with anything. They give loving attention 5 to every detail. When sloppy people say they're going to tackle the surface of the desk, they really mean it. Not a paper will go unturned; not a rubber band will go unboxed. Four hours or two weeks into the excavation, the desk looks exactly the same, primarily because the sloppy person is meticulously creating new piles of papers with new headings and scrupulously stopping to read all the old book catalogs before he throws them away. A neat person would just bulldoze the desk.

Neat people are bums and clods at heart. They have cavalier attitudes toward 6 possessions, including family heirlooms. Everything is just another dustcatcher to them. If anything collects dust, it's got to go and that's that. Neat people will toy with the idea of throwing the children out of the house just to cut down on the clutter.

241

Neat people don't care about process. They like results. What they want to 7
do is get the whole thing over with so they can sit down and watch the rasslin' on
TV. Neat people operate on two unvarying principles: Never handle any item
twice, and throw everything away.

The only thing messy in a neat person's house is the trash can. The minute 8
something comes to a neat person's hand, he will look at it, try to decide if it has
immediate use and, finding none, throw it in the trash.

Neat people are especially vicious with mail. They never go through their 9
mail unless they are standing directly over a trash can. If the trash can is beside the
mailbox, even better. All ads, catalogs, pleas for charitable contributions, church
bulletins and money-saving coupons go straight into the trash can without being
opened. All letters from home, postcards from Europe, bills and paychecks are
opened, immediately responded to, then dropped in the trash can. Neat people
keep their receipts only for tax purposes. That's it. No sentimental salvaging of
birthday cards or the last letter a dying relative ever wrote. Into the trash it goes.

Neat people place neatness above everything, even economics. They are in- 10
credibly wasteful. Neat people throw away several toys every time they walk
through the den. I knew a neat person once who threw away a perfectly good dish
drainer because it had mold on it. The drainer was too much trouble to wash. And
neat people sell their furniture when they move. They will sell a La-Z-Boy recliner
while you are reclining in it.

Neat people are no good to borrow from. Neat people buy everything in ex- 11
pensive little single portions. They get their flour and sugar in two-pound bags. They
wouldn't consider clipping a coupon, saving a leftover, reusing plastic nondairy
whipped cream containers or rinsing off tin foil and draping it over the unmoldy dish
drainer. You can never borrow a neat person's newspaper to see what's playing at the
movies. Neat people have the paper all wadded up and in the trash by 7:05 A.M.

Neat people cut a clean swath through the organic as well as the inorganic 12
world. People, animals, and things are all one to them. They are so insensitive. After they've finished with the pantry, the medicine cabinet, and the attic, they will
throw out the red geranium (too many leaves), sell the dog (too many fleas), and send
the children off to boarding school (too many scuffmarks on the hardwood floors).

1983

QUESTIONS FOR DISCUSSION

Content

a. What does Britt mean by the moral distinction between neat and sloppy people? How is this a *moral* distinction? Why, according to Britt's implication, are
   neat people immoral?
b. Do you agree that "sloppiness is merely the unfortunate consequence of . . . extreme moral rectitude" (paragraph 2)? Where is this idea repeated?

c. What kind of neatness and sloppiness is the author actually talking about? She focuses on clutter, but does she imply other kinds of neatness and sloppiness?

d. Is Britt a neat or a sloppy person? How can you tell from the clues she gives in the essay?

e. On the surface, this essay might seem frivolous. Are there serious implications to it?

f. Does the author ever prove that neat people are lazy and mean and that sloppy people are less so?

Strategy and Style

g. Analyze the vocabulary Britt used to discuss sloppy people. How would you describe Britt's tone in this part of the essay? What tone does she use to discuss neat people?

h. Comment upon her use of generalizations. Why does she make statements like "Neat people place neatness above everything, even economics" (paragraph 10)?

i. Britt calls neat people "bums and clods at heart" (paragraph 6). Is she being harsh? If so, does her attitude destroy her credibility, or does it serve another purpose?

j. Where does Britt use irony especially well? How does the irony establish the tone of the piece?

SUGGESTIONS FOR SHORT WRITING

a. Define yourself as neat or sloppy. Write a short description of your bedroom, your closet, or the inside of your car; talk about your grooming habits and your clothing; or discuss the way you go about completing a common task like preparing a meal, painting a bedroom, or packing a suitcase.

b. Britt attributes various character traits to neat and sloppy people. In paragraph 7, for example, she says that "Neat people don't care about process." Challenge one such assertion by using personal experience as a source of information.

SUGGESTIONS FOR SUSTAINED WRITING

a. Turn the tables on Britt, and write an essay in which you argue that sloppy people are immoral, neat people moral. Begin by trying to answer each of Britt's assertions about neat people. Then explain what is immoral about sloppiness. You might find inspiration and information for this assignment in your responses to the second of the Suggestions for Short Writing.

b. Select two other oppositions into which people, animals, or objects can be divided, and write an essay in which you compare and contrast them. Depending upon your topic, consider using the subject-by-subject pattern, seen in Britt's essay, to organize your work.

At the Mercy of the Cure*

Mark Mathabane

Born in Alexandra township, South Africa, Mark Mathabane (b. 1960) came to the United States on a tennis scholarship and attended several American schools, including Dowling College, from which he took his bachelor's degree in 1983. By the age of 26, he had published the first volume of his autobiography, Kaffir Boy: The True Story of a Black Youth's Coming of Age in Apartheid South Africa *(1986). Mathabane describes his birthplace as a land of poverty and violence that can debilitate the strongest spirits.* Kaffir, *a term of extreme disparagement applied to black South Africans, prepares the reader for the physical and psychological degradation visited upon Mathabane's family, friends, and neighbors. Among the author's most vivid memories are the many times policemen raided his shantytown home to arrest his father. Mathabane's parents had emigrated "illegally" from one of the homelands, or tribal reserves, and his father lacked the proper documents to live under the same roof with his family. "At the Mercy of the Cure" is taken from the second volume of his autobiography,* Kaffir Boy in America *(1989). Mathabane is now a freelance lecturer and writer, living in North Carolina. His most recent book is* Out of the Madness: From the Projects to a Life of Hope *(1998), written with and about Jerrold Ladd.*

Upon returning to Dowling in the new year, 1982, I found a letter from home wait- 1 ing for me with the miraculous news: My mother had finally been cured of her insanity. I was overwhelmed with joy. The contents of the letter related how Aunt Queen, the *isangoma,* had spent over a year treating my mother. She was said to have used *muti* (tribal medicine), consisting of special herbs, bark, and roots—and divination, a seeing into the past and future using bones.

Apparently my mother's kindness had done her in. While in South Africa 2 she had, against my protestations and those of the family, taken in as boarders from the Giyani homeland in the Northern Transvaal a tall, raw-boned *nyanga* (medicine man) with bloodshot eyes, named Mathebula, and his family of five. They had nowhere else to go. The shack became home for about fifteen people; some slept under the tables, others curled up in corners and near the stove; there was no privacy. My mother had made it clear that their moving in with us was only a temporary measure, to provide them a roof over their heads while they hunted for their own shack. When months passed without the Mathebulas making any attempts at finding alternative housing, my mother had politely requested them to leave. This angered the wizard, a proud and chauvinistic man. Nonetheless he speedily constructed a shack in one of the rat-infested alleyways. But he never forgave my mother.

From strands of my mother's hair and pieces of her clothing, which he had 3 gathered while he lived in our house, he allegedly concocted his voodoo and drove my mother mad. It took Aunt Queen almost a year to piece together what she

*Editors' title.

deemed a "dastardly plot." Daily, out in the yard, under the hot African sun, with my mother seated cross-legged across from her, my aunt shook bones and tossed them onto the ground. From interpreting their final positions she believed that she was able to name the sorcerer and the method he used to bewitch my mother. To a Western mind this of course sounds incredible and primitive. But witchcraft is a time-honored tradition among many African tribes, where convenient scapegoats are always blamed for events which, through limited knowledge and technology, seem inexplicable. Belief in witchcraft can be compared to a Westerner's belief in astrology holding answers to man's future and fate.

"Now you know the truth," Aunt Queen said to my mother at the end of her 4 confinement, when she was finally cured. The two spoke in Tsonga. "What do you want me to do?"

"Protect my family from further mischief." 5

"Is that all?" 6

"That's all." 7

"Don't you want revenge? Are you simply going to let him go scot-free?" 8

"I'm not a witch. I'm a child of God. I harbor no malice toward him or his 9 family. I seek no revenge." My mother, despite her belief in witchcraft, still considered the Christian God to be all-powerful. This position of course had its contradictions, and since this episode occurred I have pointed them out to her from time to time. She has modified her beliefs and is now more under the sway of Christianity.

"But your ancestors must be satisfied," Aunt Queen said. "And what about 10 the pain he caused you? Do you know that he intended to kill you?"

"But Christ prevented that. He led me to you and gave you the power to 11 cure me."

"You know, Mudjaji [my mother's maiden name], you're so loving that it's 12 impossible for me to understand why anyone would want to harm you. The only thing left for me to do to complete your cure and prevent a relapse is to send the mischief back to its perpetrator." It was believed that no cure of witchcraft was complete until the black magic had reverted to the sorcerer.

"Please don't do anything that would harm him or his family," my mother 13 pleaded.

"The gods will decide," Aunt Queen said. 14

Two weeks after my mother returned to Alexandra, the sorcerer's favorite 15 son was stabbed to death during an argument in a *shebeen.* Hardly had he been buried when another of his sons was stabbed to death by *tsotsis* (gangsters) during a robbery and dumped in a ditch. My mother felt remorse over the deaths and grieved for the sorcerer's family. Aunt Queen told her that there was nothing she could have done to prevent their fate.

Here I was in America, in the heart of Western civilization itself, having to 16 grapple with the reality or unreality of witchcraft. I remember how my mother's incredible story tested my "civilized mentality," my Western education, my dependency on reason, my faith in science and philosophy. But in the end I realized that her insanity, of course, had rational causes, just as did Uncle Piet's gambling, matrimonial problems, my father's alcoholism, and the family's poverty—all of which they tended to blame on witchcraft. Either my mother's undiagnosed and untreated diabetes or the oppressive conditions under which she lived, or a combination of the two, had deranged her. Aunt Queen was the tribal equivalent of a shrink. Her "magical" treatments of diseases owed much to the power of suggestion and her keen knowledge of the medicinal effects of certain herbs, bark, leaves, and roots, from which, it has been discovered, a good deal of Western medicine has gained real remedies. As for the deaths of the Wizard's sons, this was, of course, pure coincidence, since Alexandra, especially the neighborhood in which my family lived, was an extremely violent place: On one weekend over a dozen murders were committed.

I realized all this from the knowledge I had gained since coming to America 17 and discovering that there was a branch of medicine of which I had been completely ignorant while I lived in South Africa: Psychoanalysis and psychiatry. The inhuman suffering experienced by blacks under apartheid had devastating effects on their mental and physical well-being. Given the primitive state of health care in the ghettos, endemic illiteracy, and the sway of tribal beliefs, my mother and most blacks were ignorant of causal relationships. They therefore blamed witchcraft for mental illnesses like schizophrenia and paranoia; diseases like malnutrition and tuberculosis; problems like unemployment, alcoholism, and gambling; and unlucky coincidences, such as being arrested during a pass raid while neighbors escaped, or being fired from a job. Their lack of access to qualified medical doctors, psychotherapists, and social workers forced them to rely on the dubious and often dangerous "cures" of *isangomas,* especially since such "cures" at least offered the victim much-needed psychological relief.

Superstition is present in Western societies as well, astrology being one ex- 18 ample. Some people also blame their misfortunes on the Devil. And many govern their lives through card-reading and palmistry, and rely on charlatans to cure them of cancer, AIDS, blindness, varicose veins, and other diseases. Until education dispelled my ignorance and fortified my reason I was to a degree superstitious and believed in witchcraft.

The psychological problems experienced by blacks in South African ghet- 19 tos are somewhat similar to those experienced by inmates of concentration camps during the Second World War. *From Death-Camp to Existentialism,* by Viktor E. Frankl, explains how psychotic behavior can become a "normal" way of life, a means of survival, for helpless people whose sense of identity and self-worth are under constant attack by an all-powerful oppressor. Jews in concentration camps were at the mercy of their Nazi guards, just as blacks in the ghettos of South Africa are at the mercy of apartheid's Gestapo-like police. Some victims of oppression even come to identify with their oppressors and persecute with relish their own kind. There are cases of Jews, known as Capos, who, in return for special privileges like food and cigarettes doled out by SS guards, treated other Jews sadistically and even herded them into crematoriums and gas chambers. In South Africa black policemen, in return for special privileges such as better housing, residential permits, and passbooks for relatives, shoot and kill unarmed black protesters, torture them in jail, uproot black communities under the homeland policy, and launch brutal raids into the ghettos to enforce Kafkaesque apartheid laws. Such are the evil consequences of unbearable pressures.

1989

QUESTIONS FOR DISCUSSION

Content

a. What is the author's purpose, and how do the comparisons he makes in this essay help him achieve that purpose?
b. Explain how the author's mother reconciled her belief in Christianity and her belief in witchcraft.
c. To what does the author attribute his mother's illness?
d. In what ways are the "cures" of the *isangomas* beneficial?

Strategy and Style

e. How does the frequent use of dialogue help make this complex essay clear?
f. Why does the author bother to tell us that superstition can also be found in the West? Why does he explain that Western medicine owes much to the "herbs, barks, leaves, and roots" Aunt Queen used as medicine (paragraph 16)?
g. Consider Mathabane's definition of terms. Is it important for us to be familiar with these terms? How do they help the author show similarities and differences between cultures?
h. Why did he introduce new ideas in the essay's conclusion? What light do they shed on what he said earlier?
i. This selection is an excerpt from a book. What expectations might the concluding paragraph establish about what will come next in that book?
j. In what ways is this piece typical of other comparison/contrast essays you have read? In what ways is it different? What other methods of development are used in this selection?

SUGGESTIONS FOR SHORT WRITING

a. Africa is not the only place where superstition maintains a strong hold. Mathabane mentions the popularity of astrology, card-reading, and palmistry in the West. List evidence you have observed that superstition has a place in Western society.
b. If you know someone who is suffering from a psychological disorder, drug or alcohol abuse, an addiction to gambling, or any other emotional problem, explain in logical terms the causes of his or her predicament.

SUGGESTIONS FOR SUSTAINED WRITING

a. Write a personal narrative about your mother or other member of the family who has been a powerful figure in the community. Show how that person has helped shape or guide the community. Like Mathabane, include dialogue and, if appropriate, make comparisons/contrasts with other people to reveal your subject's character.

b. Write an extended analytical response to Mathabane's essay. Begin by jotting down your thoughts about, and questions to, each paragraph; then, consider how these thoughts combine to form your overall opinion of, or reaction to, the piece. Finally, tell your readers how you have read and understood the essay, and point out to them what they may not have noticed in a casual reading.

Discordant Fruit

Lydia Minatoya

Lydia Minatoya (b. 1950) was born in Albany, New York. Her parents had emigrated to the United States from Japan, and had moved from the west coast to New York. Growing up so far away from relatives in California and Japan made Minatoya curious about her family and its history, so, after earning a PhD in psychology from the University of Maryland in 1981 and teaching briefly in Boston, she left to teach and travel in Japan, China, and Nepal. This trip prompted her to write Talking to High Monks in the Snow: An Asian-American Odyssey *(1992), which won the 1991 PEN/Jerard Fund Award. In this memoir, Minatoya focuses on her experiences growing up in a predominantly European-ancestry area and on her travels in Asia. "Discordant Fruit" is a chapter from this book; in it, Minatoya describes the awkward cultural tension she experiences during dinner with her upper-class relatives in Japan.*

Once, in a cross-cultural training manual, I came across a riddle. In Japan, a young 1 man and woman meet and fall in love. They decide they would like to marry. The young man goes to his mother and describes the situation. "I will visit the girl's family," says the mother. "I will seek their approval." After some time, a meeting between mothers is arranged. The boy's mother goes to the girl's ancestral house. The girl's mother has prepared tea. The women talk about the fine spring weather: Will this be a good year for cherry blossoms? The girl's mother serves a plate of fruit. Bananas are sliced and displayed in an exquisite design. Marriage never is mentioned. After the tea, the boy's mother goes home. "I am so sorry," she tells her son. "The other family has declined the match."

In the training manual, the following question was posed. How did the boy's 2 mother know the marriage was unacceptable? That is easy, I thought when I read it. To a Japanese, the answer is obvious. Bananas do not go well with tea.

All of my life, I have been fluent in communicating through discordant fruit. 3

"You're not serious about applying to be a foreign exchange student!" ex- 4 claims a high school teacher. "The point is to sponsor an *American* kid." On my application, I deliberately misspell the teacher's name. I cross it out with an unsightly splotch. "Take that you mean narrow man," I gloat in triumph.

"Your mother is so deferential, so *quiet,*" says a boyfriend. "Women like that 5 drive me crazy." *His* mother is an attorney. That morning, I scorch his scrambled eggs. I hide the sports section of the Sunday news. "No insight, loudmouth fool," I mutter. Vengeance, I think, is mine.

The Japanese raise their daughters differently than their sons. *"Gambatte!"* 6 they exhort their sons. "Have courage, be like the carp, swim upstream!" *"Kiotsukete,"* they caution their daughters. "Be careful, be modest, keep safe."

In the old stories, men are warriors: Fierce and bold. But a lady never lunges 7 to slash the throat of an assailant. Instead, she writes a poem about harsh winter; how it can snap a slender stalk. Then she kills *herself* in protest. How the old stories galled me!

My mother was raised in a world such as this, in a house of tradition and   8
myth. And although she has traveled across continents, oceans, and time, although
she considers herself a modern woman—a believer in the sunlight of science—it
is a world that surrounds her still. Feudal Japan floats around my mother. Like an
unwanted pool of ectoplasm, it quivers with supernatural might. It followed her
into our American home and governed my girlhood life.

And so, I was shaped. In that feudal code, all females were silent and yield-   9
ing. Even their possessions were accorded more rights. For, if mistreated, belongings were granted an annual holiday when they could spring into life and complain.

And so, I was haunted. If I left my clothes on the floor, or my bicycle in the
rain; if I yanked on my comb with roughness; if it splintered and lost its teeth (and   10
I did these things often and deliberately, trying to challenge their spell); then my
misdeeds pursued me in dreams.

Emitting a hair-raising keening, my mittens would mourn for their mates.
The floors I had scuffed, the doors I had slammed, herded me into the street. Bro-   11
ken dishes and dulled scissors joined them to form a large, shrill, and reproachful
parade of dutiful ill-treated items. How I envied white children and the simple ab-
solution of a spanking.

While other children were learning that in America you get what you ask for,
I was being henpecked by inanimate objects. While other children were learning   12
to speak their minds, I was locked in a losing struggle for dominance with my
clothing, my toys, and my tools.

The objects meant me no harm; they meant to humble and educate me.
"Ownership," they told me "means obligation, caretaking, reciprocity." And al-   13
though I was a resistant student, in time I was trained. Well-maintained, my possessions live long, useful, and mercifully quiet lives of service.

The consequence, however, is that I cannot view my belongings as mere   14
conveniences. They cannot serve as simple timesavers. For me, acquisitiveness
holds little allure. The indebtedness is much too great.

I am a woman who apologizes to her furniture. "Excuse me," I say when I   15
bump into a chair. My voice resonates with solicitude. In America, such behavior
is viewed as slightly loony.

I am a woman caught between standards of East and West. "I disagree," I say to   16
elders, to the men in my life. My voice rises and cracks with shame. "Razor-tongue,"
relatives say with the pleasure of knowing. "No wonder she still is unmarried."

All these incongruities came flooding back while visiting my Japanese fam-   17
ily. The pull to be deferent. The push to be bold. The tension and richness between.

In the evening, after we left the patriarch's house, Sachikosan prepared a   18
feast. She kneeled before us, cooking a huge skillet of sukiyaki. She plucked
plump morsels of tender beef from the pot and popped them onto my plate. Her
teenaged daughters slipped shyly in and out of the room, bearing flasks of sake
and platters of sushi.

Tadao-san, Yoshi, Mark, and I were seated at the table. Sachiko-san and the 19
girls ate in the kitchen. "Where are the other women?" Mark asked Yoshi. "Yuri-
chan is the guest," he replied. "She is being paid the house's high honor."

Loosened by the sake, chaffing from days of communicating only with me 20
or through me, Mark bombarded Yoshi with questions. Did Yoshi like American
rock and roll? Who were his favorite performers?

Uncomfortable with being the focus of attention, Yoshi attempted to gener- 21
alize every query. "How familiar are Japanese youth with popular American music?" he translated for Tadao-san.

But Tadao-san was not fooled. Excluded in his own house, shunned in favor 22
of his translator, Tadao-san grew increasingly irritable.

"How long has this one been riding autobikes?" he suddenly interjected. 23
"Has he ever had an accident? Would he know how to make repairs should the autobike become disabled?"

At first, the American in me grinned. Clearly Tadao-san had grown weary 24
of his subordinate role. He was asserting his authority. "How are you providing for
Yuri-chan's safety?" his questions implied. "Do not forget you are welcome only
in so far as you provide service to members of my house."

But quickly, the Japanese in me surfaced. The evening was not going 25
smoothly and I was responsible.

"You're putting Yoshi on the spot!" I hissed into Mark's ear. "After all, he is 26
not your host. Address your comments to the household head and try to act with
more deference!"

"No kidding!" exclaimed Mark. He thought everything had been going 27
along just fine.

I smiled apologetically at Yoshi and Tadao-san. My annoyance and bossy in- 28
structiveness had not gone unnoticed. I flushed mightily. I knew my behavior was
most unseemly for a lady.

"So Tadao-san," said Mark heartily, "what do you think about all these 29
protests of American military presence in Japan?"

Yoshi reeled in horror. How could he translate, with delicacy, such an openly 30
confrontational question?

"Don't you think it's a little, uhmmm, *ungrateful?*" continued Mark. "After 31
all, by picking up the bill for your country's defense, America has allowed Japan
to become an economic competitor."

"How can you be so rude!" I croaked in anger. I staggered under the re- 32
sponsibility of having brought a boor into the ancestral house.

"Relax. You're overreacting," snapped Mark. "Besides, this is my conver- 33
sation." Mark was growing tired of my conduct coaching. I could hardly blame
him. Only a few days earlier, as we sat in a coffee shop and I instructed him on the
proper method of ordering, I had overheard a comment. *"Rimokon,"* a woman had
murmured to her companion. She had nodded in Mark's direction. *Rimokon* is a
shortened form of *rimoto-kontororu.* It is the Japanese pronunciation of remote
control: Slang for a henpecked man.

Tadao-san looked questioningly at Yoshi. What was the meaning of all this 34 clamor? Yoshi rushed to translate.

"This is a most difficult question," said Tadao-san after hearing an edited 35 translation.

I cringed. When a Japanese says a question is difficult he is requesting re- 36 lease from an uncomfortable situation.

"I work on a military base," said Mark, "and the sentiment is that Japan is 37 complaining about a free ride."

I wished we never had left the subject of rock and roll. I wished I were not 38 the honored guest. I wished I was with Sachiko-san, in the refuge of the kitchen.

Tadao-san and Yoshi caucused for a while. "Some Japanese believe that 39 America's motives are not fully benevolent," said Yoshi. His voice hesitated with the task of defusing the situation. "They say Americans do not fully view Asians as people. Japan and her people are expendable. Perhaps the point is not to defend Japan but rather to move the site of possible conflict. Asia may be a buffer zone. If war is based from Japan, South Korea, or the Philippines, the soil and civilians of these countries, not America, would be the first at risk."

"I don't know about that," muttered Mark.

"In each country, there are prejudices," said Tadao-san. "We Japanese are 40 prejudiced against the Koreans. I have read your history. Has there not been dis- 41 crimination against Japanese in America? Is there not discrimination today?"

"No," said Mark flatly.   42

"Of course there is!" I cried. We argued hotly for a minute. Then, remem- 43 bering that I was trying to act like a credit to my mother's upbringing, I demurred.

"Mark and I share slight disagreement about this point," I murmured with 44 sudden modesty.

Perhaps Mark was right. Perhaps I was overreacting. Perhaps among men, 45 even in Japan, verbal confrontations and positioning for power are acceptable so- cial forms. Perhaps when two samurai meet, they must engage in hostile sword play and find themselves well matched, before they can be friends.

The exchange of political opinions left me shaken, but Mark, Tadao-san, and 46 Yoshi seemed unscathed. They raised their cups and had a seemingly splendid time.

But then again, perhaps I was right. Before the evening ended, Tadao-san 47 slipped me an envelope. "In case you wish to leave the autobike, to continue, alone, by train," he said. Inside, was a staggering sum of money.

After midnight, Sachiko-san led me to her daughters' room. It was the room 48 of teenagers, a sweet jumble of stuffed animals and pinups of popular singers. Sev- eral pencil sketches were carefully mounted on one wall. Through a window, I saw the crescent moon.

"Come Yuri-chan." Sachiko-san led me to the sketches. "Come and see your 49 past."

The drawings were light, romantic renderings, of princesses all gowned and 50 gloved.

"Your mother lived here briefly, when she was a girl," Sachiko-san ex- 51
plained. "These are her drawings. My daughters found them in storage and thought
them pretty." She paused in reflection. "Your young mother's dreams have been
rescued and honored, mounted here on my little ones' wall."

Through the open window came the sound of a bamboo flute. Sachiko-san 52
looked at me with the warmth of a sister. She touched my hair gently and smiled.
"The hearts of young girls," she whispered to me, "their visions, forever, the same."

1992

QUESTIONS FOR DISCUSSION

Content

a. What does the title mean and why is it appropriate?

b. In paragraph 3 Minatoya says that she has "been fluent in communicating
   through discordant fruit." What are some of the examples she includes of this
   communication?

c. According to Minatoya, how are Japanese sons and daughters raised differently?

d. What are the main attributes of a typical American girl that Minatoya finds appealing? How are these traits seen as negative in traditional Japanese culture?

e. Why does Minatoya feel a sense of obligation to her possessions?

f. What is the "American in me" (paragraph 24) and the "Japanese in me" (paragraph 25)? How are they in conflict?

g. What is the relationship of language—word choice as well as gestures—to behavior? How is some language appropriate and some language inappropriate,
   depending on the culture one is in?

h. Why is it difficult for Minatoya to assess whether the dinner party conversation was hostile or not?

Strategy and Style

i. Why is the comparison and contrast format effective for this essay? What exactly is being compared and contrasted?

j. How does the example about her possessions (paragraphs 9–14) help Minatoya make a point about Japanese women?

k. Where does Minatoya use humor and irony to make a point? Identify specific
   paragraphs. What are the points she makes with humor?

l. What storytelling technique does Minatoya use to make this unlike a "typical"
   essay?

m. What is the purpose of the last section (paragraphs 48–52)? How does it comment on the rest of the essay?

SUGGESTIONS FOR SHORT WRITING

a. Describe your relationship with your possessions. Do you feel responsible toward them? What do your possessions say about you?
b. Write the "script" of a conversation you had or heard in which people misunderstood each other. What were the reasons for the misunderstandings?

SUGGESTIONS FOR SUSTAINED WRITING

a. Compare and contrast two cultures with which you are familiar. If your family recently emigrated to the United States, your choice is easy, but you can also compare and contrast more subtly different cultures, such as comparing home to school, one block in your neighborhood to another block, a rural area to an urban area, or one part of the country to another. Try some of the techniques that Minatoya uses, such as dialogue, personal examples, and humor to make your essay interesting.
b. Compare and contrast acceptable boys'/men's behavior and girls'/women's behavior as you have observed it in your family, neighborhood, and school. Define what you see as the rules for acceptable behavior for each sex. If you see any rules being challenged or changed, discuss these changes.

7

Illustration

Illustration is a natural habit of mind. How often have we offered a "for example" or "for instance" when, as we try to make a point, our listeners respond quizzically or simply shake their heads in disbelief? "What's so unhealthy about my diet?" demands a good friend whose eating habits you have just impugned. "For starters," you respond, "you are a French-fry fanatic, stuffing your face with the greasy, salt-laden sticks at nearly every meal. You eat so much red meat, butter, ice cream, and candy that the *New England Journal of Medicine* ought to report your intake of cholesterol, calories, and fat. And you probably don't even remember what fruits and vegetables look like."

The three examples that explain what you meant by *unhealthy* are products of a powerful and effective technique common to all types of expository or persuasive prose. Good writers are rarely content to tell their readers what they mean; they want to show it. One way to do this is to fill your work with relevant, well-developed illustrations—concrete representations of abstract ideas.

Effective illustrations make possible the explanation of ideas that might otherwise remain vague because they enable the reader to grasp particular realities behind the abstraction, to see specific and pertinent instances of the generality. "My Aunt Tillie is the most unselfish person in town," you may well exclaim. But consider how much more convincing your claim would become if you recalled the times she opened her home to folks who had no place to live, donated her savings to the hospital building fund, and took time off from work to help sick friends and relatives.

The clarity and strength illustration brings to your writing does not depend on the number of examples you include—although sheer volume can be convincing—but on the degree to which each example is clear, well developed, and appropriate to your thesis. William F. Buckley recalls only four or five brief anecdotes to explain why we don't complain more often—and why we should. Each situation is narrated in such detail, however, that readers can picture themselves in his place, and they share both his anger and "mortification."

255

Depending on your purpose, you can choose from several kinds of examples to give your writing variety and power. Annie Dillard ranges widely and freely to gather illustrations from science, philosophy, and her own observations of nature as she considers the mystery that living things must die so that life can go on. Developments in the history of eating, each analyzed thoroughly, provide Peter Farb and George Armelagos with a trove of examples to show how the changes in table manners "reflect fundamental changes in human relationships." Edward T. Hall uses many brief scenarios of intercultural communication to make his point about the necessity of learning about other cultures. And Alice Bloom uses examples from her travels to make a point about American tourists and tourism.

Like most other methods of development, illustration is rarely used to the exclusion of other rhetorical techniques. In the selection by Robertson Davies, for instance, well-chosen examples develop categories (classification) through which the author sheds new and interesting light on the subject. Perhaps the richest variety of materials can be found in Jonathan Kozol's "Distancing the Homeless," where well-researched statistics, first-hand experience, and expert testimony make a compelling argument about the politics of homelessness.

Enjoy the selections in this chapter. They vary significantly in purpose, tone, and subject. Each is effective, however, because it explains an abstract idea in terms that will allow the reader to experience the concrete realities for which that abstraction stands. Each shows us ways to grapple with even the most unwieldy notions in language that is clear, powerful, and convincing.

Why Don't We Complain?

William F. Buckley, Jr.

Perhaps the best-known and wittiest spokesman for political conservatism in the United States, William F. Buckley was born in New York City in 1925 and is the founder of National Review, *a journal for which he once served as editor-in-chief. Since 1966, he has hosted "Firing Line," a weekly television forum for the discussion of important political, social, and moral issues. A prolific writer, he publishes three syndicated newspaper columns each week and contributes regularly to magazines such as* Harper's *and* Esquire, *in which "Why Don't We Complain?" first appeared in 1961. In 1965, he even found time to mount a campaign, albeit unsuccessfully, as a candidate for mayor of New York. He is a graduate of Yale University, which found its way into the title of his first full-length work,* God and Man at Yale, *in 1951. Since then, Buckley has published (among others)* United Nations Journal *(1974);* Stained Glass *(1978);* Atlantic High *(1982), which recounts a transoceanic sailing venture; and ten spy novels. Among his most recent books are* On the Firing Line *(1989),* Tucker's Last Stand *(1990), and* A Very Private Plot *(1994).*

It was the very last coach and the only empty seat on the entire train, so there was 1 no turning back. The problem was to breathe. Outside, the temperature was below freezing. Inside the railroad car the temperature must have been about 85 degrees. I took off my overcoat, and a few minutes later my jacket, and noticed that the car was flecked with the white shirts of the passengers. I soon found my hand moving to loosen my tie. From one end of the car to the other, as we rattled through Westchester County, we sweated; but we did not moan.

I watched the train conductor appear at the head of the car. "Tickets, all tick- 2 ets, please!" In a more virile age, I thought, the passengers would seize the conductor and strap him down on a seat over the radiator to share the fate of his patrons. He shuffled down the aisle, picking up tickets, punching commutation cards. *No one addressed a word to him.* He approached my seat, and I drew a deep breath of resolution. "Conductor," I began with a considerable edge to my voice. . . . Instantly the doleful eyes of my seatmate turned tiredly from his newspaper to fix me with a resentful stare: What question could be so important as to justify my sibilant intrusion into his stupor? I was shaken by those eyes. I am incapable of making a discreet fuss, so I mumbled a question about what time we were due in Stamford (I didn't even ask whether it would be before or after dehydration could be expected to set in), got my reply, and went back to my newspaper and to wiping my brow.

The conductor had nonchalantly walked down the gauntlet of eighty sweat- 3 ing American freemen, and not one of them had asked him to explain why the passengers in that car had been consigned to suffer. There is nothing to be done when the temperature *outdoors* is 85 degrees, and indoors the air conditioner has broken down; obviously when that happens there is nothing to do, except perhaps curse the day that one was born. But when the temperature outdoors is below freezing,

257

it takes a positive act of will on somebody's part to set the temperature *indoors* at 85. Somewhere a valve was turned too far, a furnace overstocked, a thermostat maladjusted: Something that could easily be remedied by turning off the heat and allowing the great outdoors to come indoors. All this is so obvious. What is not obvious is what has happened to the American people.

It isn't just the commuters, whom we have come to visualize as a supine 4 breed who have got on to the trick of suspending their sensory faculties twice a day while they submit to the creeping dissolution of the railroad industry. It isn't just they who have given up trying to rectify irrational vexations. It is the American people everywhere.

A few weeks ago at a large movie theatre I turned to my wife and said, "The 5 picture is out of focus." "Be quiet," she answered. I obeyed. But a few minutes later I raised the point again, with mounting impatience. "It will be all right in a minute," she said apprehensively. (She would rather lose her eyesight than be around when I make one of my infrequent scenes.) I waited. It was *just* out of focus—not glaringly out, but out. My vision is 20-20, and I assume that is the vision, adjusted, of most people in the movie house. So, after hectoring my wife throughout the first reel, I finally prevailed upon her to admit that it was off, and very annoying. We then settled down, coming to rest on the presumption that: a) someone connected with the management of the theatre must soon notice the blur and make the correction; or b) that someone seated near the rear of the house would make the complaint in behalf of those of us up front; or c) that—any minute now—the entire house would explode into catcalls and foot stamping, calling dramatic attention to the irksome distortion.

What happened was nothing. The movie ended, as it had begun *just* out of 6 focus, and as we trooped out, we stretched our faces in a variety of contortions to accustom the eye to the shock of normal focus.

I think it is safe to say that everybody suffered on that occasion. And I think 7 it is safe to assume that everyone was expecting someone else to take the initiative in going back to speak to the manager. And it is probably true even that if we had supposed the movie would run right through the blurred image, someone surely would have summoned up the purposive indignation to get up out of his seat and file his complaint.

But notice that no one did. And the reason no one did is because we are all 8 increasingly anxious in America to be unobtrusive, we are reluctant to make our voices heard, hesitant about claiming our rights; we are afraid that our cause is unjust, or that if it is not unjust, that it is ambiguous; or if not even that, that it is too trivial to justify the horrors of a confrontation with Authority; we will sit in an oven or endure a racking headache before undertaking a head-on, I'm-here-to-tell-you complaint. That tendency to passive compliance, to a heedless endurance, is something to keep one's eyes on—in sharp focus.

I myself can occasionally summon the courage to complain, but I cannot, as 9 I have intimated, complain softly. My own instinct is so strong to let the thing ride, to forget about it—to expect that someone will take the matter up, when the grievance is collective, in my behalf—that it is only when the provocation is at a very special key, whose vibrations touch simultaneously a complexus of nerves, allergies, and passions, that I catch fire and find the reserves of courage and assertiveness to speak up. When that happens, I get quite carried away. My blood gets hot, my brow wet, I become unbearably and unconscionably sarcastic and bellicose; I am girded for a total showdown.

Why should that be? Why could not I (or anyone else) on that railroad coach 10 have said simply to the conductor, "Sir"—I take that back: That sounds sarcastic— "Conductor, would you be good enough to turn down the heat? I am extremely hot. In fact, I tend to get hot every time the temperature reaches 85 degr—" Strike that last sentence. Just end it with the simple statement that you are extremely hot, and let the conductor infer the cause.

Every New Year's Eve I resolve to do something about the Milquetoast in 11 me and vow to speak up, calmly, for my rights, and for the betterment of our society, on every appropriate occasion. Entering last New Year's Eve I was fortified in my resolve because that morning at breakfast I had had to ask the waitress three times for a glass of milk. She finally brought it—after I had finished my eggs, which is when I don't want it any more. I did not have the manliness to order her to take the milk back, but settled instead for a cowardly sulk, and ostentatiously refused to drink the milk—though I later paid for it—rather than state plainly to the hostess, as I should have, why I had not drunk it, and would not pay for it.

So by the time the New Year ushered out the Old, riding in on my morning's 12 indignation and stimulated by the gastric juices of resolution that flow so faithfully on New Year's Eve, I rendered my vow. Henceforward I would conquer my shyness, my despicable disposition to supineness. I would speak out like a man against the unnecessary annoyances of our time.

Forty-eight hours later, I was standing in line at the ski repair store in Pico 13 Peak, Vermont. All I needed, to get on with my skiing, was the loan, for one minute, of a small screwdriver, to tighten a loose binding. Behind the counter in the workshop were two men. One was industriously engaged in servicing the complicated requirements of a young lady at the head of the line, and obviously he would be tied up for quite a while. The other—"Jiggs," his workmate called him—was a middle-aged man, who sat in a chair puffing a pipe, exchanging small talk with his working partner. My pulse began its telltale acceleration. The minutes ticked on. I stared at the idle shopkeeper, hoping to shame him into action, but he was impervious to my telepathic reproof and continued his small talk with his friend, brazenly insensitive to the nervous demands of six good men who were raring to ski.

Suddenly my New Year's Eve resolution struck me. It was now or never. I 14 broke from my place in line and marched to the counter. I was going to control myself. I dug my nails into my palms. My effort was only partially successful.

"If you are not too busy," I said icily, "would you mind handing me a screw- 15 driver?"

Work stopped and everyone turned his eyes on me, and I experienced that 16 mortification I always feel when I am the center of centripetal shafts of curiosity, resentment, perplexity.

But the worst was yet to come. "I am sorry, sir," said Jiggs deferentially, 17
moving the pipe from his mouth. "I am not supposed to move. I have just had a
heart attack." That was the signal for a great whirring noise that descended from
heaven. We looked, stricken, out the window, and it appeared as though a cyclone
had suddenly focused on the snowy courtyard between the shop and the ski lift.
Suddenly a gigantic army helicopter materialized, and hovered down to a landing.
Two men jumped out of the plane carrying a stretcher, tore into the ski shop, and
lifted the shopkeeper onto the stretcher. Jiggs bade his companion goodby, was
whisked out the door, into the plane, up to the heavens, down—we learned—to a
nearby army hospital. I looked up manfully—into a score of maneating eyes. I put
the experience down as a reversal.

As I write this, on an airplane, I have run out of paper and need to reach into 18
my briefcase under my legs for more. I cannot do this until my empty lunch tray
is removed from my lap. I arrested the stewardess as she passed empty-handed
down the aisle on the way to the kitchen to fetch the lunch trays for the passengers
up forward who haven't been served yet. "Would you please take my tray?" "Just
a *moment, sir!*" she said, and marched on sternly. Shall I tell her that since she is
headed for the kitchen *anyway,* it could not delay the feeding of the other passengers by more than two seconds necessary to stash away my empty tray? Or remind
her that not fifteen minutes ago she spoke unctuously into the loudspeaker the
words undoubtedly devised by the airline's highly paid public relations counselor:
"If there is anything I or Miss French can do for you to make your trip more enjoyable, *please* let us—" I have run out of paper.

I think the observable reluctance of the majority of Americans to assert 19
themselves in minor matters is related to our increased sense of helplessness in an
age of technology and centralized political and economic power. For generations,
Americans who were too hot, or too cold, got up and did something about it. Now
we call the plumber, or the electrician, or the furnace man. The habit of looking
after our own needs obviously had something to do with the assertiveness that
characterized the American family familiar to readers of American literature. With
the technification of life goes our direct responsibility for our material environment, and we are conditioned to adopt a position of helplessness not only as regards the broken air conditioner, but as regards the overheated train. It takes an expert to fix the former, but not the latter; yet these distinctions, as we withdraw into
helplessness, tend to fade away.

Our notorious political apathy is a related phenomenon. Every year, whether 20
the Republican or the Democratic Party is in office, more and more power drains
away from the individual to feed vast reservoirs in far-off places; and we have less
and less say about the shape of events which shape our future. From this alienation
of personal power comes the sense of resignation with which we accept the political
dispensations of a powerful government whose hold upon us continues to increase.

An editor of a national weekly news magazine told me a few years ago that 21
as few as a dozen letters of protest against an editorial stance of his magazine was
enough to convene a plenipotentiary meeting of the board of editors to review

policy. "So few people complain, or make their voices heard," he explained to me, "that we assume a dozen letters represent the inarticulated views of thousands of readers." In the past ten years, he said, the volume of mail has noticeably decreased, even though the circulation of his magazine has risen.

When our voices are finally mute, when we have finally suppressed the natural instinct to complain, whether the vexation is trivial or grave, we shall have become automatons, incapable of feeling. When Premier Khrushchev first came to this country late in 1959 he was primed, we are informed, to experience the bitter resentment of the American people against his tyranny, against his persecutions, against the movement which is responsible for the great number of American deaths in Korea, for billions in taxes every year, and for life everlasting on the brink of disaster; but Khrushchev was pleasantly surprised, and reported back to the Russian people that he had been met with overwhelming cordiality (read: apathy), except, to be sure, for "a few fascists who followed me around with their wretched posters, and should be horsewhipped."   22

I may be crazy, but I say there would have been lots more posters in a society where train temperatures in the dead of winter are not allowed to climb to 85 degrees without complaint.   23

1961

QUESTIONS FOR DISCUSSION

Content

a. Relatively speaking, riding in an overheated railroad car and watching a film that is out of focus are minor "vexations." However, what disturbing tendency in the American people does our willingness to endure such discomfort illustrate? Why does Buckley describe that tendency as "something to keep one's eyes on" (paragraph 8)?

b. How would you paraphrase Buckley's thesis? What is his purpose in writing this essay?

c. What are some of the reasons Buckley cites to explain our reluctance to complain? Why, in paragraph 8, does he capitalize "Authority"?

d. What does he mean by "the technification of life" (paragraph 19)? Do you agree that we are being "conditioned to adopt a position of helplessness"? What, according to Buckley, accounts for this "conditioning"?

e. What is the point of paragraph 20? How does it relate to Buckley's discussion of overheated trains and surly airline stewardesses?

f. The author draws upon his own experiences and upon world events for examples. Which of these supports his thesis more effectively?

g. What important events is he alluding to in paragraph 22? What is the function of Buckley's inserting an editorial comment, "read: apathy," when he quotes Khrushchev? In what way does this paragraph serve to emphasize his thesis?

h. Reread paragraphs 9 and 12. How do they help develop the thesis? Why is there so much of Buckley himself in this essay?

i. What does the story of "Jiggs" tell us about Buckley's resolve "to speak out like a man"?

Strategy and Style

j. Is the author's tone at the end of this piece significantly different from what it was at the outset? In what way? Is such a shift important to Buckley's purpose? Why?

k. Can you find examples in this selection of the sarcasm and wit for which the author has become famous? At whom are they aimed? Are they used effectively and, if so, for what purposes?

l. "Why Don't We Complain?" was first published in *Esquire*. Have a look at a recent issue of this periodical. Are Buckley's content, tone, and vocabulary appropriate to the kind of audience that currently reads *Esquire?*

SUGGESTIONS FOR SHORT WRITING

a. Try rewriting paragraph 5 without using any personal narrative (for example, no "I," no dialogue, no storytelling). How does your version compare to Buckley's? What effect does each of the paragraphs create when you read it?

b. Take a paragraph or so of this essay and rewrite it as if it were a speech. How does the tone, structure, and word choice change in order to become spoken rather than written language?

SUGGESTIONS FOR SUSTAINED WRITING

a. Are we becoming a nation of people who are willing to suffer the intolerable rather than to stand up and fight for our rights? If you agree, write an essay in which you support Buckley's thesis with illustrations from your own experience.

b. Do you differ with Buckley on this point? If so, provide illustrations taken from your personal experiences or from events recently in the news that demonstrate our willingness to complain vigorously when conditions call for such action.

c. Is the rail system in this country still deteriorating as Buckley suggests in paragraph 4? What about airlines and bus companies? Are they serving the public as well as they should? Write a letter to the editor of your local newspaper in which you criticize or applaud a specific airline, railroad, or bus company. Look back upon recent trips you have taken on this carrier and recall as many convincing facts as you can to use as illustrations of the service you received.

A Few Kind Words for Superstition

Robertson Davies

*One of Canada's best-known satirists, novelists, and playwrights, Robertson Davies
(1913–1995) was educated at Upper Canada College in Toronto, at Queen's University in
Kingston, and at Oxford University in England. He began his career as a London actor and
then worked as an editor for* Saturday Night *in Toronto and for the* Examiner *in
Petersborough, Ontario. He taught English at the University of Toronto and at Massey
College, and served as Governor of the Stratford Shakespearean Festival in Stratford,
Ontario. He was a fellow of the Royal Society of Canada and was a recipient of the Stephen
Leacock Medal for Humor. He was also the first Canadian to become an honorary member
of the American Academy and Institute of Arts and Letters. Davies published numerous
plays and critical studies on drama and stagecraft and is known throughout Canada for the
delightful satires he wrote under the pseudonym "Samuel Marchbanks." However, his
reputation rests chiefly on his novels.* The Salterton Trilogy, *which includes* Tempest-Tost
(1951), Leaven of Malice *(1954), and* A Mixture of Frailties *(1958), is a study of a fictional
university town in Canada and of its middle-class inhabitants. The* Deptford Trilogy, *which
is made up of* Fifth Business *(1970),* The Manticore *(1972), and* World of Wonders *(1976),
affirms the important part that the irrational plays in an individual's search for spiritual
identity. Other popular books by Davies are* What's Bred in the Bones *(1985),* The Papers
of Samuel Marchbanks *(1986), and* The Lyre of Orpheus *(1989).*

In grave discussions of "the renaissance of the irrational" in our time, superstition 1
does not figure largely as a serious challenge to reason or science. Parapsychol-
ogy, UFO's, miracle cures, transcendental meditation and all the paths to instant
enlightenment are condemned, but superstition is merely deplored. Is it because it
has an unacknowledged hold on so many of us?

Few people will admit to being superstitious; it implies naïveté or ignorance. 2
But I live in the middle of a large university, and I see superstition in its four manifestations, alive and flourishing among people who are indisputably rational and
learned.

You did not know that superstition takes four forms? Theologians assure us 3
that it does. First is what they call Vain Observances, such as not walking under a
ladder, and that kind of thing. Yet I saw a deeply learned professor of anthropology, who had spilled some salt, throwing a pinch of it over his left shoulder; when
I asked him why, he replied, with a wink, that it was "to hit the Devil in the eye."
I did not question him further about his belief in the Devil: but I noticed that he
did not smile until I asked him what he was doing.

The second form is Divination, or consulting oracles. Another learned profes- 4
sor I know, who would scorn to settle a problem by tossing a coin (which is a humble appeal to Fate to declare itself), told me quite seriously that he had resolved a
matter related to university affairs by consulting the I Ching. And why not? There
are thousands of people on this continent who appeal to the I Ching, and their general level of education seems to absolve them of superstition. Almost, but not quite.
The I Ching, to the embarrassment of rationalists, often gives excellent advice.

263

The third form is Idolatry, and universities can show plenty of that. If you 5 have ever supervised a large examination room, you know how many jujus, lucky coins and other bringers of luck are placed on the desks of the candidates. Modest idolatry, but what else can you call it?

The fourth form is Improper Worship of the True God. A while ago, I learned 6 that every day, for several days, a $2 bill (in Canada we have $2 bills, regarded by some people as unlucky) had been tucked under a candlestick on the altar of a college chapel. Investigation revealed that an engineering student, worried about a girl, thought that bribery of the Deity might help. When I talked with him, he did not think he was pricing God cheap, because he could afford no more. A reasonable argument, but perhaps God was proud that week, for the scientific oracle went against him.

Superstition seems to run, a submerged river of crude religion, below the 7 surface of human consciousness. It has done so for as long as we have any chronicle of human behavior, and although I cannot prove it, I doubt if it is more prevalent today than it has always been. Superstition, the theologians tell us, comes from the Latin *supersisto,* meaning to stand in terror of the Deity. Most people keep their terror within bounds, but they cannot root it out, nor do they seem to want to do so.

The more the teaching of formal religion declines, or takes a sociological 8 form, the less God appears to great numbers of people as a God of Love, resuming his older form of a watchful, minatory power, to be placated and cajoled. Superstition makes its appearance, apparently unbidden, very early in life, when children fear that stepping on cracks in the sidewalk will bring ill fortune. It may persist even among the greatly learned and devout, as in the case of Dr. Samuel Johnson, who felt it necessary to touch posts that he passed in the street. The psychoanalysts have their explanation, but calling a superstition a compulsion neurosis does not banish it.

Many superstitions are so widespread and so old that they must have risen 9 from a depth of the human mind that is indifferent to race or creed. Orthodox Jews place a charm on their door-posts; so do (or did) the Chinese. Some peoples of Middle Europe believe that when a man sneezes, his soul, for that moment, is absent from his body, and they hasten to bless him, lest the soul be seized by the Devil. How did the Melanesians come by the same idea? Superstition seems to have a link with some body of belief that far antedates the religions we know—religions which have no place for such comforting little ceremonies and charities.

People who like disagreeable historical comparisons recall that when 10 Rome was in decline, superstition proliferated wildly, and that something of the same sort is happening in our Western world today. They point to the popularity of astrology, and it is true that sober newspapers that would scorn to deal in love philters carry astrology columns and the fashion magazines count them among their most popular features. But when has astrology not been popular? No use saying science discredits it. When has the heart of man given a damn for science?

Superstition in general is linked to man's yearning to know his fate, and to   11
have some hand in deciding it. When my mother was a child, she innocently joined
her Roman Catholic friends in killing spiders on July 11, until she learned that this
was done to ensure heavy rain the day following, the anniversary of the Battle of
Boyne, when the Orangemen would hold their parade. I knew an Italian, a good scientist, who watched every morning before leaving his house, so that the first person he met would not be a priest or a nun, as this would certainly bring bad luck.

I am not one to stand aloof from the rest of humanity in this matter, for when   12
I was a university student, a gypsy woman with a child in her arms used to appear
every year at examination time, and ask a shilling of anyone who touched the
Lucky Baby; that swarthy infant cost me four shillings altogether, and I never
failed an examination. Of course, I did it merely for the joke—or so I thought then.
Now, I am humbler.

1978

QUESTIONS FOR DISCUSSION

Content

a. What is Davies' thesis? Which paragraphs supply examples supporting this
   thesis?
b. Davies asserts in paragraph 11 that "superstition in general is linked to man's
   yearning to know his fate, and to have some hand in deciding it." Do you agree
   with this assertion? Is this a generalization?
c. What examples of superstitions does Davies include? What were his probable
   reasons for including them?
d. Are the examples of superstitions used as persuasive devices? If so, what are
   the readers being persuaded to do?
e. To what does the phrase " 'the renaissance of the irrational' " in the first sentence refer? What examples does Davies use? What examples can you add to
   the list?
f. What is Davies' answer to the last question in the first paragraph? How do you
   know? Why might Davies have used a question rather than a statement?
g. What are the four kinds of superstition? Do you agree with Davies that these
   types of superstition are still prevalent today?
h. Do you believe in any of the superstitions that Davies describes? Do you know
   of people who do? How do you account for belief in superstitions?
i. In the last paragraph Davies admits that what he did jokingly as a college student to ensure passing his examinations was actually done in earnest. Have you
   had any similar experiences?
j. According to Davies, what is the relationship between superstition and religion? Between superstition and science? Between superstition and history?

Strategy and Style

k. Why might Davies have first listed the four forms of superstition and then gone on to a discussion of superstition in general? How do the four forms of superstition establish expectations for the rest of the essay?

l. The author traces the word *superstition* to its Latin origin, "supersisto" (paragraph 7). Look up the origin of the words *divination, idolatry,* or any of the superstitions he lists. How do the origins of these words and superstitions help to illustrate his thesis?

m. What is Davies' attitude toward superstition? How is his attitude revealed through the tone of the piece?

SUGGESTIONS FOR SHORT WRITING

a. Describe the superstitions you or someone you know adhere to. Into which of Davies' categories do they fall?

b. Are the several questions Davies asks merely rhetorical? Try writing an answer to one or more of them.

SUGGESTIONS FOR SUSTAINED WRITING

a. Trace a popular superstition to its origins and write an essay explaining the relationship of the current superstition to its earlier forms. Try to account for the perseverance of the superstition.

b. Interview friends and fellow students, asking them what superstitions they have and how strongly they believe in them. Using these examples as the raw material for your essay, analyze these superstitions, putting forth your theory of why people believe in them.

c. Write a few unkind words for superstition. In what ways does belief in superstition harm society? Why should people try to divest themselves of superstitious beliefs?

Fecundity

Annie Dillard

Born in Pittsburgh in 1945, Annie Dillard made her mark early as a contributing editor to Harper's *magazine from 1973 to 1981. Before she was thirty, she had won a Pulitzer prize for* Pilgrim at Tinker Creek *(1974), a narrative about Virginia's Roanoke Valley, where she once lived. She has served on the U.S. Cultural Delegation to the People's Republic of China and on the National Commission of U.S.–China Relations. From these experiences came* Encounters with Chinese Writers *(1984). She has published two anthologies of narrative essays:* Holy the Firm *(1977) and* Teaching a Stone to Talk *(1982). She has also published poetry, including* Tickets for a Prayer Wheel *(1974). Dillard's most recent books are* An American Childhood *(1988),* The Writing Life *(1992),* The Living: A Novel *(1993), and* Mornings Like This *(1995). "Fecundity" is taken from* Pilgrim at Tinker Creek.

I have to look at the landscape of the blue-green world again. Just think: In all the 1 clean beautiful reaches of the solar system, our planet alone is a blot; our planet alone has death. I have to acknowledge that the sea is a cup of death and the land is a stained altar stone. We the living are survivors huddled on flotsam, living on jetsam. We are escapees. We wake in terror, eat in hunger, sleep with a mouthful of blood.

Death: W. C. Fields called death "the Fellow in the Bright Nightgown." He 2 shuffles around the house in all the corners I've forgotten, all the halls I dare not call to mind or visit for fear I'll glimpse the hem of his shabby, dazzling gown disappearing around a turn. This is the monster evolution loves. How could it be?

The faster death goes, the faster evolution goes. If an aphid lays a million 3 eggs, several might survive. Now, my right hand, in all its human cunning, could not make one aphid in a thousand years. But these aphid eggs—which run less than a dime a dozen, which run absolutely free—can make aphids as effortlessly as the sea makes waves. Wonderful things, wasted. It's a wretched system. Arthur Stanley Eddington, the British physicist and astronomer who died in 1944, suggested that all of "Nature" could conceivably run on the same deranged scheme. "If indeed she has no greater aim than to provide a home for her greatest experiment, Man, it would be just like her methods to scatter a million stars whereof one might haply achieve her purpose." I doubt very much that this is the aim, but it seems clear on all fronts that this is the method.

Say you are the manager of the Southern Railroad. You figure that you need 4 three engines for a stretch of track between Lynchburg and Danville. It's a mighty steep grade. So at fantastic effort and expense you have your shops make nine thousand engines. Each engine must be fashioned just so, every rivet and bolt secure, every wire twisted and wrapped, every needle on every indicator sensitive and accurate.

You send all nine thousand of them out on the runs. Although there are en- 5 gineers at the throttles, no one is manning the switches. The engines crash, collide,

267

derail, jump, jam, burn . . . At the end of the massacre you have three engines, which is what the run could support in the first place. There are few enough of them that they can stay out of each others' paths.

You go to your board of directors and show them what you've done. And what are they going to say? You know what they're going to say. They're going to say: It's a hell of a way to run a railroad.   6

Is it a better way to run a universe?   7

Evolution loves death more than it loves you or me. This is easy to write, easy to read, and hard to believe. The words are simple, the concept clear—but you don't believe it, do you? Nor do I. How could I, when we're both so lovable? Are my values then so diametrically opposed to those that nature preserves? This is the key point.   8

Must I then part ways with the only world I know? I had thought to live by the side of the creek in order to shape my life to its free flow. But I seem to have reached a point where I must draw the line. It looks as though the creek is not buoying me up but dragging me down. Look: Cock Robin may die the most grue-some of slow deaths, and nature is no less pleased; the sun comes up, the creek rolls on, the survivors still sing. I cannot feel that way about your death, nor you about mine, nor either of us about the robin's—nor even the barnacles'. We value the individual supremely, and nature values him not a whit. It looks for the mo-ment as though I might have to reject this creek life unless I want to be utterly bru-talized. Is human culture with its values my only real home after all? Can it pos-sibly be that I should move my anchor-hold to the side of a library? This direction of thought brings me abruptly to a fork in the road where I stand paralyzed, un-willing to go on, for both ways lead to madness.   9

Either this world, my mother, is a monster, or I myself am a freak.   10

Consider the former: The world is a monster. Any three-year-old can see how unsatisfactory and clumsy is this whole business of reproducing and dying by the billions. We have not yet encountered any god who is as merciful as a man who flicks a beetle over on its feet. There is not a people in the world who behaves as badly as praying mantises. But wait, you say, there is no right and wrong in nature; right and wrong is a human concept. Precisely: We are moral creatures, then, in an amoral world. The universe that suckled us is a monster that does not care if we live or die—does not care if it itself grinds to a halt. It is fixed and blind, a robot programmed to kill. We are free and seeing; we can only try to outwit it at every turn to save our skins.   11

This view requires that a monstrous world running on chance and death, ca-reening blindly from nowhere to nowhere, somehow produced wonderful us. I came from the world, I crawled out of a sea of amino acids, and now I must whirl around and shake my fist at that sea and cry Shame! If I value anything at all, then I must blindfold my eyes when I near the Swiss Alps. We must as a culture dis-semble our telescopes and settle down to back-slapping. We little blobs of soft tis-sue crawling around on this one planet's skin are right, and the whole universe is wrong.   12

Or consider the alternative.   13

Julian of Norwich, the great English anchorite and theologian, cited, in the   14
manner of the prophets, these words from God: "See, I am God: See, I am in all
things: See, I never lift my hands off my works, nor ever shall, without end . . .
How should anything be amiss?" But now not even the simplest and best of us sees
things the way Julian did. It seems to us that plenty is amiss. So much is amiss that
I must consider the second fork in the road, that creation itself is blamelessly,
benevolently askew by its very free nature, and that it is only human feeling that
is freakishly amiss. The frog that the giant water bug sucked had, presumably, a
rush of pure feeling for about a second, before its brain turned to broth. I, however,
have been sapped by various strong feelings about the incident almost daily for
several years.

Do the barnacle larvae care? Does the lacewing who eats her eggs care? If   15
they do not care, then why am I making all this fuss? If I am a freak, then why
don't I hush?

Our excessive emotions are so patently painful and harmful to us as a   16
species that I can hardly believe that they evolved. Other creatures manage to have
effective matings and even stable societies without great emotions, and they have
a bonus in that they need not ever mourn. (But some higher animals have emotions
that we think are similar to ours: Dogs, elephants, otters, and the sea mammals
mourn their dead. Why do that to an otter? What creator could be so cruel, not to
kill otters, but to let them care?) It would seem that emotions are the curse, not
death—emotions that appear to have devolved upon a few freaks as a special curse
from Malevolence.

All right then. It is our emotions that are amiss. We are freaks, the world is   17
fine, and let us all go have lobotomies to restore us to a natural state. We can leave
the library then, go back to the creek lobotomized, and live on its banks as un-
troubled as any muskrat or reed. You first.

Of the two ridiculous alternatives, I rather favor the second. Although it is   18
true that we are moral creatures in an amoral world, the world's amorality does not
make it a monster. Rather, I am the freak. Perhaps I don't need a lobotomy, but I
could use some calming down, and the creek is just the place for it. I must go down
to the creek again. It is where I belong, although as I become closer to it, my fellows appear more and more freakish, and my home in the library more and more
limited. Imperceptibly at first, and now consciously, I shy away from the arts, from
the human emotional stew. I read what the men with telescopes and microscopes
have to say about the landscape. I read about the polar ice, and I drive myself
deeper and deeper into exile from my own kind. But, since I cannot avoid the library altogether—the human culture that taught me to speak in its tongue—I bring
human values to the creek, and so save myself from being brutalized.

What I have been after all along is not an explanation but a picture. This is   19
the way the world is, altar and cup, lit by the fire from a star that has only begun
to die. My rage and shock at the pain and death of individuals of my kind is the

old, old mystery, as old as man, but forever fresh, and completely unanswerable. My reservations about the fecundity and waste of life among other creatures is, however, mere squeamishness. After all, I'm the one having the nightmares. It is true that many of the creatures live and die abominably, but I am not called upon to pass judgment. Nor am I called upon to live in that same way, and those creatures who are are mercifully unconscious.

I don't want to cut this too short. Let me pull the camera back and look at that fork in the road from a distance, in the larger context of the speckled and twining world. It could be that the fork will disappear, or that I will see it to be but one of many interstices in a network, so that it is impossible to say which line is the main part and which is the fork. 20

The picture of fecundity and its excesses and of the pressures of growth and its accidents is of course no different from the picture I painted before of the world as an intricate texture of a bizarre variety of forms. Only now the shadows are deeper. Extravagance takes on a sinister, wastrel air, and exuberance blithers. When I added the dimension of time to the landscape of the world, I saw how freedom grew the beauties and horrors from the same live branch. This landscape is the same as that one, with a few more details added, and a different emphasis. I see squashes expanding with pressure and a hunk of wood rapt on the desert floor. The rye plant and the Bronx ailanthus are literally killing themselves to make seeds, and the animals to lay eggs. Instead of one goldfish swimming in its intricate bowl, I see tons and tons of goldfish laying and eating billions and billions of eggs. The point of all the eggs is of course to make goldfish one by one—nature lives the *idea* of the individual, if not the individual himself—and the point of a goldfish is pizzazz. This is familiar ground. I merely failed to mention that it is death that is spinning the globe. 21

It is harder to take, but surely it's been thought about. I cannot really get very exercised over the hideous appearance and habits of some deep-sea jellies and fishes, and I exercise easy. But about the topic of my own death I am decidedly touchy. Nevertheless, the two phenomena are two branches of the same creek, the creek that waters the world. Its source is freedom, and its network of branches is infinite. The graceful mockingbird that falls drinks there and sips in the same drop a beauty that waters its eyes and a death that fledges and flies. The petals of tulips are flaps of the same doomed water that swells and hatches in the ichneumon's gut. 22

That something is everywhere and always amiss is part of the very stuff of creation. It is as though each clay form had baked into it, fired into it, a blue streak of nonbeing, a shaded emptiness like a bubble that not only shapes its very structure but that also causes it to list and ultimately explode. We could have planned things more mercifully, perhaps, but our plan would never get off the drawing board until we agreed to the very compromising terms that are the only ones that being offers. 23

The world has signed a pact with the devil; it had to. It is a covenant to which every thing, even every hydrogen atom, is bound. The terms are clear: If you want to live, you have to die; you cannot have mountains and creeks without space, and 24 space is a beauty married to a blind man. The blind man is Freedom, or Time, and he does not go anywhere without his great dog Death. The world came into being with the signing of the contract. A scientist calls it the Second Law of Thermodynamics. A poet says, "The force that through the green fuse drives the flower/Drives my green age." This is what we know. The rest is gravy.

1974

QUESTIONS FOR DISCUSSION

Content

a. What is Dillard's thesis? What is her purpose?
b. How does nature view the individual? How does this differ from the way human society views the individual?
c. What is Dillard getting at in the railroad analogy in paragraph 5?
d. Who is Cock Robin (paragraph 9), and why does Dillard mention this figure?
e. Explain how Julian of Norwich "sees things" (paragraph 14)? To what end does the author quote this English theologian?
f. In what way, according to Dillard, is fecundity, a sign that there is something "amiss" in the world?
g. What does Dillard mean when she says, "The world has signed a pact with the devil; it had to" (paragraph 24)?
h. Why does the author's quoting W. C. Fields help her develop this essay?
i. In the end, this essay is about a very specific concern: Dillard's own mortality. Trace the development of this essay and explain how the author manages to arrive at that idea.

Strategy and Style

j. What illustrations does Dillard use to develop her essay? Why are they appropriate to her purpose?
k. What other methods of development does she use?
l. Why is Malevolence capitalized in paragraph 16?
m. Find evidence of humor in this selection.
n. What use does the author make of figurative language? Where does she use analogy?
o. Reread the essay's introduction. What about it is so compelling?
p. How would you describe the author's tone? What kind of audience is she writing to?
q. Analyze the style of any one of this essay's longer paragraphs, say 3, 9, 14, or 21. What kind of vocabulary and sentence structure does Dillard use? How does she manage to convey so much energy, excitement, and passion in a piece about so abstract a subject?

SUGGESTIONS FOR SHORT WRITING

a. This essay is filled with a number of provocative statements, such as "Evolution loves death more than it loves you or me" (paragraph 8) and "Either this world, my mother, is a monster, or I myself am a freak" (paragraph 10). Find one such statement that interests you, and interpret or explain it from your own point of view.

b. What do the creek and the library stand for? Write a paragraph or two to explain the analogy Dillard creates by contrasting these two places. Use details from the text to develop your explanation.

c. Write a paragraph in which you agree or disagree with Dillard's notion that nature does not value the individual (paragraph 9). Cite an example or examples to explain your answer.

SUGGESTIONS FOR SUSTAINED WRITING

a. Using Dillard's definition of *fecundity* as a starting point, explain your view of nature by using examples from your reading or experience. Is it a blind force that creates and destroys without plan or concern? Or is it more benevolent and purposeful?

b. Are right and wrong solely human concepts? Or are they present in nature as well? Defend your response by discussing examples of natural occurrences and animal behavior that you have seen or read about.

c. Dillard seems to be trying to come to terms with her own mortality, something human beings have been trying to do for thousands of years. Discuss three or four examples of the ways in which people today deal with or come to terms with death. If you can, discuss at least one way in which we try to achieve immortality.

The Patterns of Eating

Peter Farb and George Armelagos

An anthropologist, naturalist, and acknowledged expert on the American Indian, Peter Farb (1929–1980) wrote numerous studies on the natural history of North America and of its original inhabitants. He also published several introductions to scientific subjects for young readers. Farb was educated at Vanderbilt and Columbia Universities. He worked as feature editor for Argosy *from 1950 to 1952 and as curator for the Riverside Museum in New York City from 1964 to 1971. He also held teaching positions at Yale University and at Calhoun College and served as a consultant to the Smithsonian Institution in Washington, D.C. From 1959 to 1963, Farb wrote a column for* Better Homes and Gardens *and has contributed numerous articles on science and nature to many other popular American magazines. Some of his best-known full-length works include* Living Earth *(1959),* The Forest *(1961),* Face of North America: The Natural History of a Continent *(1963), and* Man's Rise to Civilization as Shown by the Indians of North America from Primeval Times to the Coming of the Industrial State *(1968).*

George Armelagos (b. 1936) received his PhD in anthropology from the University of Colorado and is now professor of anthropology at the University of Massachusetts at Amherst. He has completed extensive research on the relationship between nutrition and human evolution.

Consuming Passions (1980), the book from which this selection was taken, is a fascinating and extremely well documented look at the development of eating habits through the centuries. In it, Farb and Armelagos explain how the rituals we have come to associate with food preparation, table manners, and dietary practices in general have helped both reveal and define our cultural identity. "The interrelation of men and menus," wrote one Time book reviewer, "has filled hundreds of texts. But none of them has digested so many facts so well."

Among the important societal rules that represent one component of cuisine are [1] table manners. As a socially instilled form of conduct, they reveal the attitudes typical of a society. Changes in table manners through time, as they have been documented for western Europe, likewise reflect fundamental changes in human relationships. Medieval courtiers saw their table manners as distinguishing them from crude peasants; but by modern standards, the manners were not exactly refined. Feudal lords used their unwashed hands to scoop food from a common bowl and they passed around a single goblet from which all drank. A finger or two would be extended while eating, so as to be kept free of grease and thus available for the next course, or for dipping into spices and condiments—possibly accounting for today's "polite" custom of extending the finger while holding a spoon or small fork. Soups and sauces were commonly drunk by lifting the bowl to the mouth; several diners frequently ate from the same bread trencher. Even lords and nobles would toss gnawed bones back into the common dish, wolf down their food, spit onto the table (preferred conduct called for spitting under it), and blew their noses into the tablecloth.

273

By about the beginning of the sixteenth century, table manners began to 2
move in the direction of today's standards. The importance attached to them is indicated by the phenomenal success of a treatise, *On Civility in Children,* by the
philosopher Erasmus, which appeared in 1530; reprinted more than thirty times in
the next six years, it also appeared in numerous translations. Erasmus' idea of good
table manners was far from modern, but it did represent an advance. He believed,
for example, that an upper class diner was distinguished by putting only three fingers of one hand into the bowl, instead of the entire hand in the manner of the
lower class. Wait a few moments after being seated before you dip into it, he advises. Do not poke around in your dish, but take the first piece you touch. Do not
put chewed food from the mouth back on your plate; instead, throw it under the
table or behind your chair.

By the time of Erasmus, the changing table manners reveal a fundamental 3
shift in society. People no longer ate from the same dish or drank from the same
goblet, but were divided from one another by a new wall of constraint. Once the
spontaneous, direct, and informal manners of the Middle Ages had been repressed,
people began to feel shame. Defecation and urination were now regarded as private activities; handkerchiefs came into use for blowing the nose; nightclothes
were now worn, and bedrooms were set apart as private areas. Before the sixteenth
century, even nobles ate in their vast kitchens; only then did a special room desig-
nated for eating come into use away from the bloody sides of meat, the animals
about to be slaughtered, and the bustling servants. These new inhibitions became
the essence of "civilized" behavior, distinguishing adults from children, the upper
classes from the lower, and Europeans from the "savages" then being discovered
around the world. Restraint in eating habits became more marked in the centuries
that followed. By about 1800, napkins were in common use, and before long they
were placed on the thighs rather than wrapped around the neck; coffee and tea
were no longer slurped out of the saucer; bread was genteelly broken into small
pieces with the fingers rather than cut into large chunks with a knife.

Numerous paintings that depict meals—with subjects such as the Last Sup- 4
per, the wedding at Cana, or Herod's feast—show what dining tables looked like
before the seventeenth century. Forks were not depicted until about 1600 (when
Jacopo Bassano painted one in a Last Supper), and very few spoons were shown.
At least one knife is always depicted—an especially large one when it is the only
one available for all the guests—but small individual knives were often at each
place. Tin disks or oval pieces of wood had already replaced the bread trenchers.
This change in eating utensils typified the new table manners in Europe. (In many
other parts of the world, no utensils at all were used. In the Near East, for example, it was traditional to bring food to the mouth with the fingers of the right hand,
the left being unacceptable because it was reserved for wiping the buttocks.) Utensils were employed in part because of a change in the attitude toward meat. During the Middle Ages, whole sides of meat, or even an entire dead animal, had been
brought to the table and then carved in view of the diners. Beginning in the seventeenth century, at first in France but later elsewhere, the practice began to go out

of fashion. One reason was that the family was ceasing to be a production unit that did its own slaughtering; as that function was transferred to specialists outside the home, the family became essentially a consumption unit. In addition, the size of the family was decreasing, and consequently whole animals, or even large parts of them, were uneconomical. The cuisines of Europe reflected these social and economic changes. The animal origin of meat dishes was concealed by the arts of preparation. Meat itself became distasteful to look upon, and carving was moved out of sight to the kitchen. Comparable changes had already taken place in Chinese cuisine, with meat being cut up beforehand, unobserved by the diners. England was an exception to the change in Europe, and in its former colonies—the United States, Canada, Australia, and South Africa—the custom has persisted of bringing a joint of meat to the table to be carved.

Once carving was no longer considered a necessary skill among the well- 5
bred, changes inevitably took place in the use of the knife, unquestionably the earliest utensil used for manipulating food. (In fact, the earliest English cookbooks were not so much guides to recipes as guides to carving meat.) The attitude of diners toward the knife, going back to the Middle Ages and the Renaissance, had always been ambivalent. The knife served as a utensil, but it offered a potential threat because it was also a weapon. Thus taboos were increasingly placed upon its use: It was to be held by the point with the blunt handle presented; it was not to be placed anywhere near the face; and most important, the uses to which it was put were sharply restricted. It was not to be used for cutting soft foods such as boiled eggs or fish, or round ones such as potatoes, or to be lifted from the table for courses that did not need it. In short, good table manners in Europe gradually removed the threatening aspect of the knife from social occasions. A similar change had taken place much earlier in China when the warrior was supplanted by the scholar as a cultural model. The knife was banished completely from the table in favor of chopsticks, which is why the Chinese came to regard Europeans as barbarians at their table who "eat with swords."

The fork in particular enabled Europeans to separate themselves from the eat- 6
ing process, even avoiding manual contact with their food. When the fork first appeared in Europe, toward the end of the Middle Ages, it was used solely as an instrument for lifting chunks from the common bowl. Beginning in the sixteenth century, the fork was increasingly used by members of the upper classes—first in Italy, then in France, and finally in Germany and England. By then, social relations in western Europe had so changed that a utensil was needed to spare diners from the "uncivilized" and distasteful necessity of picking up food and putting it into the mouth with the fingers. The addition of the fork to the table was once said to be for reasons of hygiene, but this cannot be true. By the sixteenth century people were no longer eating from a common bowl but from their own plates, and since they also washed their hands before meals, their fingers were now every bit as hygienic as a fork would have been. Nor can the reason for the adoption of the fork be connected with the wish not to soil the long ruff that was worn on the sleeve at the time, since the fork was also adopted in various countries where ruffs were not then in fashion.

Along with the appearance of the fork, all table utensils began to change and 7
proliferate from the sixteenth century onward. Soup was no longer eaten directly
from the dish, but each diner used an individual spoon for that purpose. When a
diner wanted a second helping from the serving dish, a ladle or a fresh spoon was
used. More and more special utensils were developed for each kind of food: Soup
spoons, oyster forks, salad forks, two-tined fondue forks, blunt butter knives, special utensils for various desserts and kinds of fruit, each one differently shaped, of
a different size, with differently numbered prongs and with blunt or serrated edges.
The present European pattern eventually emerged, in which each person is provided with a table setting of as many as a dozen utensils at a full-course meal. With
that, the separation of the human body from the taking of food became virtually
complete. Good table manners dictated that even the cobs of maize were to be held
by prongs inserted in each end, and the bones of lamb chops covered by ruffled
paper pantalettes. Only under special conditions—as when Western people consciously imitate an earlier stage in culture at a picnic, fish fry, cookout, or
campfire—do they still tear food apart with their fingers and their teeth, in a nostalgic reenactment of eating behaviors long vanished.

Today's neighborhood barbecue recreates a world of sharing and hospitality 8
that becomes rarer each year. We regard as a curiosity the behavior of hunters in
exotic regions. But every year millions of North Americans take to the woods and
lakes to kill a wide variety of animals—with a difference, of course: What hunters
do for survival we do for sport (and also for proof of masculinity, for male bonding, and for various psychological rewards). Like hunters, too, we stuff ourselves
almost whenever food is available. Nibbling on a roasted ear of maize gives us, in
addition to nutrients, the satisfaction of participating in culturally simpler ways. A
festive meal, however, is still thought of in Victorian terms, with the dominant
male officiating over the roast, the dominant female apportioning vegetables, the
extended family gathered around the table, with everything in its proper place—a
revered picture, as indeed it was so painted by Norman Rockwell, yet one that becomes less accurate with each year that passes.

1980

QUESTIONS FOR DISCUSSION

Content

a. What were the Last Supper, the wedding at Cana, and Herod's feast? How do
   references to paintings of these events help illustrate important points about the
   history of table manners?
b. Summarize the illustrations Farb and Armelagos use to distinguish manners in
   the Renaissance from those of earlier eras. Does their treatment of the subject
   need to be as graphic as it is?

c. What illustrations do Farb and Armelagos use to explain the European's "ambivalent" attitude toward knives?

d. Who was Erasmus, and how did his ideas help advance table manners?

e. To what are Farb and Armelagos alluding when they tell us that the new table manners adopted by Europeans during the Renaissance distinguished them "from the 'savages' then being discovered around the world" (paragraph 3)? Why is the word *savages* in quotes?

f. This essay attempts to trace various developments that led to "the separation of the human body from the taking of food" (paragraph 7). How would you interpret this statement?

g. The authors claim that, early in the seventeenth century, the family "was ceasing to be a production unit" (paragraph 4). What did this development have to do with the profound changes in the way Europeans prepared and served meat?

h. Explain the Chinese's opinion of European eating habits. Why did the Chinese banish knives from their tables, and how did their doing so affect the development of their cuisine?

i. Why did forks come into use? What other "special utensils" and instruments have since become common in table settings?

j. What accounts for the fact that, in the United States and other English-speaking countries, people still carve large cuts of meat at the table? Why do Farb and Armelagos consider this custom as well as the contemporary American cookout "a nostalgic reenactment of eating behaviors long vanished" (paragraph 7)?

k. How would you describe the work of Norman Rockwell, and why is one of his "revered pictures" mentioned in the conclusion?

Strategy and Style

l. How would you define the terms *Middle Ages* and *Renaissance?* Why does this essay begin with the former? Should the authors have begun with an earlier period of history?

m. What are the "Victorian terms" to which the authors allude in the concluding paragraph?

n. To what extent are Farb and Armelagos making fun of people's eating habits? Point out instances where the tone becomes humorous.

SUGGESTIONS FOR SHORT WRITING

a. Write about what you thought of eating etiquette before you read this essay. In what ways did the essay corroborate or challenge your thinking? Did it change your mind about what is proper etiquette?

b. Describe the eating habits of your family, your roommates, or the students at the campus cafeteria. At which stage of the evolution of eating patterns would you say they belong?

SUGGESTIONS FOR SUSTAINED WRITING

a. Describe and evaluate the table manners people use in your college's dining hall or cafeteria. Like Farb and Armelagos, use as many concrete illustrations as you can to make your writing vivid and convincing. You might want to submit this essay for publication in your college newspaper or literary magazine, so keep your audience in mind!

b. What makes a meal "festive"? Using illustration as your dominant method of development, discuss how this term might apply to your favorite holiday dinner. You need not focus on table manners exclusively. Describing place settings and table decorations or explaining the elaborate rituals that go into preparing traditional family dishes might also help illustrate your idea of "festive."

c. Describe one or more eating or cooking rituals from another culture that you find interesting. You might be able to gather many details about this topic from personal experience, from conversations with the foreign students you meet in your classes, or from chats with people who have immigrated to this country but still follow the traditional culinary practices of their homelands. Address this essay to someone who knows very little about the culture you're discussing, and be sure to include a sufficient number of examples and explanatory detail.

The Anthropology of Manners
Edward T. Hall

Edward T. Hall (b. 1914) is a well-known anthropologist and an expert on cultural differences in communication, manners, and perception of time. He studied at Pomona College; the University of Denver, where he received an AB; the University of Arizona, where he received an MA in 1938; and Columbia University, where he received a PhD in 1942. He did fieldwork from 1933 to 1942 with the Hopi and Navajo, some of which has reemerged in his most recent book, West of the Thirties *(1994). During World War II, Hall taught at the University of Denver and at Bennington College; after the war he worked on the atoll of Truk (Micronesia) helping the Truks and the U. S. Navy personnel understand each other's behavior and cultures. On his return to the United States, Hall became the director of the Point Four program in the Foreign Service Institute, part of the U.S. State Department, from 1950 to 1955. There he designed training programs for workers assigned to posts in Latin America and the Middle East. He has had an active career, bridging both the academic and the commercial worlds. From 1955 to 1960, he was president of Overseas Training and Research, Inc., in Washington, D.C.; founded his own consulting firm in 1960; and he taught anthropology at the Illinois Institute of Technology from 1963 to 1967 and at Northwestern University from 1967 to 1977. Meanwhile, he was writing scholarly and popular books, only a few of which are* The Silent Language *(1959);* The Hidden Dimension *(1966);* Beyond Culture *(1976), from which "The Anthropology of Manners" is drawn; and* Dance of Life *(1983), which discusses time as a cultural concept.*

The Goops they lick their fingers
   and the Goops they lick their knives;
They spill their broth on the table cloth—
   Oh, they lead disgusting lives.
The Goops they talk while eating,
   and loud and fast they chew;
And that is why I'm glad that I
   am not a Goop—are you?

In Gelett Burgess' classic on the Goops we have an example of what anthropologists call "an enculturating device"—a means of conditioning the young to life in our society. Having been taught the lesson of the goops from childhood (with or without the aid of Mr. Burgess) Americans are shocked when they go abroad and discover whole groups of people behaving like goops—eating with their fingers, making noises and talking while eating. When this happens, we may (1) remark on the barbarousness or quaintness of the "natives" (a term cordially disliked all over the world) or (2) try to discover the nature and meaning of the differences in behavior. One rather quickly discovers that what is good manners [1] in one context may be bad in the next. It is to this point that I would like to address myself.

The subject of manners is complex; if it were not, there would not be so 2 many injured feelings and so much misunderstanding in international circles everywhere. In any society the code of manners tends to sum up the culture—to be a frame of reference for all behavior. Emily Post goes so far as to say: "There is not a single thing that we do, or say, or choose, or use, or even think, that does not follow or break one of the exactions of taste, or tact, or ethics of good manners, or etiquette—call it what you will." Unfortunately many of the most important standards of acceptable behavior in different cultures are elusive: They are intangible, undefined and unwritten.

An Arab diplomat who recently arrived in the U.S. from the Middle East at- 3 tended a banquet which lasted several hours. When it was over, he met a fellow countryman outside and suggested they go get something to eat, as he was starving. His friend, who had been in this country for some time, laughed and said: "But, Habib, didn't you know that if you say, 'No, thank you,' they think you really don't want any?" In an Arab country etiquette dictates that the person being served must refuse the proffered dish several times, while his host urges him repeatedly to partake. The other side of the coin is that Americans in the Middle East, until they learn better, stagger away from banquets having eaten more than they want or is good for them.

When a public-health movie of a baby being bathed in a bathinette was 4 shown in India recently, the Indian women who saw it were visibly offended. They wondered how people could be so inhuman as to bathe a child in stagnant (not running) water. Americans in Iran soon learn not to indulge themselves in their penchant for chucking infants under the chin and remarking on the color of their eyes, for the mother has to pay to have the "evil eye" removed. We also learn that in the Middle East you don't hand people things with your left hand, because it is unclean. In India we learn not to touch another person, and in Southeast Asia we learn that the head is sacred.

In the interest of intercultural understanding various U.S. Government agen- 5 cies have hired anthropologists from time to time as technical experts. The State Department especially has pioneered in the attempt to bring science to bear on this difficult and complex problem. It began by offering at the Foreign Service Institute an intensive four-week course for Point 4 technicians. Later these facilities were expanded to include other foreign service personnel.

The anthropologist's job here is not merely to call attention to obvious 6 taboos or to coach people about types of thoughtless behavior that have very little to do with culture. One should not need an anthropologist to point out, for instance, that it is insulting to ask a foreigner: "How much is this in real money?" Where technical advice is most needed is in the interpretation of the unconscious aspects of a culture—the things people do automatically without being aware of the full implications of what they have done. For example, an ambassador who has been kept waiting for more than half an hour by a foreign visitor needs to understand that if his visitor "just mutters an apology" this is not necessarily an insult.

The time system in the foreign country may be composed of different basic units, so that the visitor is not as late as he may appear to us. You must know the time system of the country to know at what point apologies are really due.

Twenty years of experience in working with Americans in foreign lands con- 7 vinces me that the real problem in preparing them to work overseas is not with taboos, which they catch on to rather quickly, but rather with whole congeries of habits and attitudes which anthropologists have only recently begun to describe systematically.

Can you remember tying your shoes this morning? Could you give the rules 8 for when it is proper to call another person by his first name? Could you describe the gestures you make in conversation? These examples illustrate how much of our behavior is "out of awareness," and how easy it is to get into trouble in another culture.

Nobody is continually aware of the quality of his own voice, the subtleties 9 of stress and intonation that color the meaning of his words or the posture and distance he assumes in talking to another person. Yet all these are taken as cues to the real nature of an utterance, regardless of what the words say. A simple illustration is the meaning in the tone of voice. In the U.S. we raise our voices not only when we are angry but also when we want to emphasize a point, when we are more than a certain distance from another person, when we are concluding a meeting and so on. But to the Chinese, for instance, overloudness of the voice is most characteristically associated with anger and loss of self-control. Whenever we become really interested in something, they are apt to have the feeling we are angry, in spite of many years' experience with us. Very likely most of their interviews with us, however cordial, seem to end on a sour note when we exclaim heartily: "WELL, I'M CERTAINLY GLAD YOU DROPPED IN, MR. WONG."

The Latin Americans, who as a rule take business seriously, do not under- 10 stand our mixing business with informality and recreation. We like to put our feet up on the desk. If a stranger enters the office, we take our feet down. If it turns out that the stranger and we have a lot in common, up go the feet again—a cue to the other fellow that we feel at ease. If the office boy enters, the feet stay up; if the boss enters and our relationship with him is a little strained at the moment, they go down. To a Latin American this whole behavior is shocking. All he sees in it is insult or just plain rudeness.

Differences in attitudes toward space—what would be territoriality in lower 11 forms of life—raise a number of other interesting points. U.S. women who go to live in Latin America all complain about the "waste" of space in the houses. On the other hand, U.S. visitors to the Middle East complain about crowding, in the houses and on the streetcars and buses. Everywhere we go space seems to be distorted. When we see a gardener in the mountains of Italy planting a single row on each of six separate terraces, we wonder why he spreads out his crop so that he has to spend half his time climbing up and down. We overlook the complex chain of communication that would be broken if he didn't cultivate alongside his brothers and his cousin and if he didn't pass his neighbors and talk to them as he moves from one terrace to the next.

A colleague of mine was caught in a snowstorm while traveling with com- 12
panions in the mountains of Lebanon. They stopped at the next house and asked
to be put up for the night. The house had only one room. Instead of distributing the
guests around the room, their host placed them next to the pallet where he slept
with his wife—so close that they almost touched the couple. To have done otherwise in that country would have been unnatural and unfriendly. In the U.S. we dis-
tribute ourselves more evenly than many other people. We have strong feelings
about touching and being crowded; in a streetcar, bus or elevator we draw ourselves in. Toward a person who relaxes and lets himself come into full contact with
others in a crowded place we usually feel reactions that could not be printed on
this page. It takes years for us to train our children not to crowd and lean on us.
We tell them to stand up, that it is rude to slouch, not to sit so close or not to
"breathe down our necks." After a while they get the point. By the time we Americans are in our teens we can tell what relationship exists between a man and
woman by how they walk or sit together.

In Latin America, where touching is more common and the basic units of 13
space seem to be smaller, the wide automobiles made in the U.S. pose problems.
People don't know where to sit. North Americans are disturbed by how close the
Latin Americans stand when they converse. "Why do they have to get so close
when they talk to you?" "They're so pushy." "I don't know what it is, but it's
something in the way they stand next to you." And so on. The Latin Americans,
for their part, complain that people in the U.S. are distant and cold—*retraídos*
(withdrawing and uncommunicative).

An analysis of the handling of space during conversations shows the fol- 14
lowing: A U.S. male brought up in the Northeast stands 18 to 20 inches away when
talking face to face to a man he does not know very well; talking to a woman under similar circumstances, he increases the distance about four inches. A distance
of only eight to 13 inches between males is considered either very aggressive or
indicative of a closeness of a type we do not ordinarily want to think about. Yet in
many parts of Latin America and the Middle East distances which are almost sexual in connotation are the only ones at which people can talk comfortably. In Cuba,
for instance, there is nothing suggestive in a man's talking to an educated woman
at a distance of 13 inches. If you are a Latin American, talking to a North American at the distance he insists on maintaining is like trying to talk across a room.

To get a more vivid idea of this problem of the comfortable distance, try 15
starting a conversation with a person eight or 10 feet away or one separated from
you by a wide obstruction in a store or other public place. Any normally encultur-
ated person can't help trying to close up the space, even to the extent of climbing
over benches or walking around tables to arrive within comfortable distance. U.S.
businessmen working in Latin America try to prevent people from getting un-
comfortably close by barricading themselves behind desks, typewriters or the like,
but their Latin American office visitors will often climb up on desks or over chairs
and put up with loss of dignity in order to establish a spatial context in which interaction can take place for them.

The interesting thing is that neither party is specifically aware of what is 16 wrong when the distance is not right. They merely have vague feelings of discomfort or anxiety. As the Latin American approaches and the North American backs away, both parties take offense without knowing why. When a North American, having had the problem pointed out to him, permits the Latin American to get close enough, he will immediately notice that the latter seems much more at ease.

My own studies of space and time have engendered considerable coopera- 17 tion and interest on the part of friends and colleagues. One case recently reported to me had to do with a group of seven-year-olds in a crowded Sunday-school classroom. The children kept fighting. Without knowing quite what was involved, the teacher had them moved to a larger room. The fighting stopped. It is interesting to speculate as to what would have happened had the children been moved to a smaller room.

The embarrassment about intimacy in space applies also to the matter of ad- 18 dressing people by name. Finding the proper distance in the use of names is even more difficult than in space, because the rules for first-naming are unbelievably complex. As a rule we tend to stay on the "mister" level too long with Latins and some others, but very often we swing into first naming too quickly, which amounts to talking down to them. Whereas in the U.S. we use Mr. with the surname, in Latin America the first and last names are used together and señor (Sr.) is a title. Thus when one says, "My name is Sr. So-and-So," it is interpreted to mean, "I am the Honorable, his Excellency So-and-So." It is no wonder that when we stand away, barricade ourselves behind our desks (usually a reflection of status) and call ourselves mister, our friends to the south wonder about our so-called "good neighbor" policy and think of us as either high-hat or unbelievably rude. Fortunately most North Americans learn some of these things after living in Latin America for a while, but the aversion to being touched and to touching sometimes persists after 15 or more years of residence and even under such conditions as intermarriage.

The difference in sense of time is another thing of which we are not aware. 19 An Iranian, for instance, is not taught that it is rude to be late in the same way that we in the U.S. are. In a general way we are conscious of this, but we fail to realize that their time system is structured differently from ours. The different cultures simply place different values on the time units.

Thus let us take as a typical case of the North European time system (which 20 has regional variations) the situation in the urban eastern U.S. A middle-class businessman meeting another of equivalent rank will ordinarily be aware of being two minutes early or late. If he is three minutes late, it will be noted as significant but usually neither will say anything. If four minutes late, he will mutter something by way of apology; at five minutes he will utter a full sentence of apology. In other words, the major unit is a five-minute block. Fifteen minutes is the smallest significant period for all sorts of arrangements and it is used very commonly. A half hour of course is very significant, and if you spend three quarters of an hour or an hour, either the business you transact or the relationship must be important. Normally it is an insult to keep a public figure or a person of significantly higher status than yourself waiting even two or three minutes, though the person of higher position can keep you waiting or even break an appointment.

Now among urban Arabs in the Eastern Mediterranean, to take an illustra- 21 tive case of another time system, the unit that corresponds to our five-minute period is 15 minutes. Thus when an Arab arrives nearly 30 minutes after the set time, by his reckoning he isn't even "10 minutes" late yet (in our time units). Stated differently, the Arab's tardiness will not amount to one significant period (15 minutes in our system). An American normally will wait no longer than 30 minutes (two significant periods) for another person to turn up in the middle of the day. Thereby he often unwittingly insults people in the Middle East who want to be his friends.

How long is one expected to stay when making a duty call at a friend's house 22 in the U.S.? While there are regional variations, I have observed that the minimum is very close to 45 minutes, even in the face of pressing commitments elsewhere, such as a roast in the oven. We may think we can get away in 30 minutes by saying something about only stopping for "a minute," but usually we discover that we don't feel comfortable about leaving until 45 minutes have elapsed. I am referring to afternoon social calls; evening calls last much longer and operate according to a different system. In Arab countries an American paying a duty call at the house of a desert sheik causes consternation if he gets up to leave after half a day. There a duty call lasts three days—the first day to prepare the feast, the second for the feast itself and the third to taper off and say farewell. In the first half day the sheik has barely had time to slaughter the sheep for the feast. The guest's departure would leave the host frustrated.

There is a well-known story of a tribesman who came to Kabul, the capital 23 of Afghanistan, to meet his brother. Failing to find him, he asked the merchants in the market place to tell his brother where he could be found if the brother showed up. A year later the tribesman returned and looked again. It developed that he and his brother had agreed to meet in Kabul but had failed to specify what year! If the Afghan time system were structured similarly to our own, which it apparently is not, the brother would not offer a full sentence of apology until he was five years late.

Informal units of time such as "just a minute," "a while," "later," "a long 24 time," "a spell," "a long, long time," "years" and so on provide us with the culturological equivalent of Evil-Eye Fleegle's "double-whammy" (in *Li'l Abner*). Yet these expressions are not as imprecise as they seem. Any American who has worked in an office with someone else for six months can usually tell within five minutes when that person will be back if he says, "I'll be gone for a while." It is simply a matter of learning from experience the individual's system of time indicators. A reader who is interested in communications theory can fruitfully speculate for a while on the very wonderful way in which culture provides the means whereby the receiver puts back all the redundant material that was stripped from such a message. Spelled out, the message might go somewhat as follows: "I am going downtown to see So-and-So about the Such-and-Such contract, but I don't know what the traffic conditions will be like or how long it will take me to get a place to park nor do I know what shape So-and-So will be in today, but taking all this into account I think I will be out of the office about an hour but don't like to commit myself, so if anyone calls you can say I'm not sure how long I will be; in any event I expect to be back before 4 o'clock."

Few of us realize how much we rely on built-in patterns to interpret mes- 25 sages of this sort. An Iranian friend of mine who came to live in the U.S. was hurt and puzzled for the first few years. The new friends he met and liked would say on parting: "Well, I'll see you later." He mournfully complained: "I kept expecting to see them, but the 'later' never came." Strangely enough we ourselves are exasperated when a Mexican can't tell us precisely what he means when he uses the expression *mañana.*

The role of the anthropologist in preparing people for service overseas is to 26 open their eyes and sensitize them to the subtle qualities of behavior—tone of voice, gestures, space and time relationships—that so often build up feelings of frustration and hostility in other people with a different culture. Whether we are going to live in a particular foreign country or travel in many, we need a frame of reference that will enable us to observe and learn the significance of differences in manners. Progress is being made in this anthropological study, but it is also showing us how little is known about human behavior.

1955

QUESTIONS FOR DISCUSSION

Content

a. What are some of the differences between U.S. and Arab cultures, and between U.S. and Latin American cultures?
b. What is the difference between "taboos" and "habits and attitudes" (paragraph 7)? Why do habits and attitudes cause more problems for outsiders than taboos cause?
c. In paragraph 8 Hall mentions the "rules for when it is proper to call another person by his first name." What are some of the rules that Hall includes in this essay? What other rules can you add to the list?
d. What are some of the ways people of different cultures deal with space, both personal and architectural space?
e. What do anthropologists like Hall do? Why are their skills important?

Strategy and Style

f. Why is the Goop poem at the beginning of the essay so effective?
g. What is an "enculturating device" (paragraph 1)? Give some examples from the essay and from your own experience.
h. Go through the essay and mark or list the examples Hall uses. How many examples does he use for each point he makes?

i. Hall uses multiple examples to make his points, but he uses specific examples to represent a culture as a whole. In your opinion, are there any examples that might misrepresent the culture?

j. Hall writes quite informally. What might the essay sound like if he had written to an audience of scholars and other anthropologists? Why is the informal style more appropriate for general readers? What about Hall's style makes it informal?

SUGGESTIONS FOR SHORT WRITING

a. Reread paragraph 18. Describe the movement from formal to informal address as it occurs in the culture with which you are most familiar.

b. Write a humorous description, in the voice of an anthropologist if you would like, of one of your habits, explaining how that habit reflects your culture.

SUGGESTIONS FOR SUSTAINED WRITING

a. Observe and record behavior in a study area, at a party, at a sports event, at a family gathering, etc. Try to find the rules that people are following but are not conscious of. Write an analytical essay in which you explain the rules, using specific examples from your observations. As a twist to this assignment, you could move from observer to participant, purposely break a rule, and record what happens. For example, in a nearly empty study area, break the rule of personal space by sitting next to a stranger to study.

b. List behaviors or other things from other cultures that puzzle you. Research— in the library but also by interviewing people from that culture—and write an essay explaining the culture to readers unfamiliar with the culture but who are planning to visit that country or countries. Make your goal similar to Hall's: "to open their eyes and sensitize them to the subtle qualities of behavior—tone of voice, gestures, space and time relationships" (paragraph 26).

c. What is "American culture"? Does the United States have a single, unchanging culture? Do you think the United States is a "melting pot" or a "patchwork" of distinctly different cultures? Write an opinion essay about these questions. If you think the United States is a melting pot, describe the American cultural traditions shared by everyone. If you think ethnic groups within the United States will always remain distinct and separate, explain, with examples, why this will be.

Distancing the Homeless

Jonathan Kozol

Teacher, author, and recipient of two National Book Awards, Jonathan Kozol (b. 1936) took his bachelor's degree at Harvard University and did graduate work at Magdalen College, Oxford. He writes extensively on the problems of homelessness, illiteracy, and poverty especially as they affect children. Kozol's best-known works, Death at an Early Age *(1967),* Illiterate America *(1985),* Rachel and Her Children: Homeless Families in America *(1988), and* Savage Inequalities: Children in American Schools *(1991) have helped arouse the conscience of a generation to problems that our presumably affluent society was supposed to have solved. This selection attacks many popular notions about homelessness and the homeless.*

It is commonly believed by many journalists and politicians that the homeless of America are, in large part, former patients of large mental hospitals who were de-institutionalized in the 1970s—the consequence, it is sometimes said, of mis-guided liberal opinion, which favored the treatment of such persons in commu-nity-based centers. It is argued that this policy, and the subsequent failure of society to build such centers or to provide them in sufficient number, is the pri-mary cause of homelessness in the United States. 1

Those who work among the homeless do not find that explanation satisfactory. While conceding that a certain number of the homeless are, or have been, mentally unwell, they believe that, in the case of most unsheltered people, the primary reason is economic rather than clinical. The cause of homelessness, they say with disarming logic, is the lack of homes and of income with which to rent or acquire them. 2

They point to the loss of traditional jobs in industry (2,000,000 every year since 1980) and to the fact that half of those who are laid off end up in work that pays a poverty-level wage. They point to the parallel growth of poverty in fami-lies with children, noting that children, who represent one quarter of our popula-tion, make up 40 percent of the poor; since 1968, the number of children in poverty has grown by 3,000,000, while welfare benefits to families with children have de-clined by 35 percent. 3

And they note, too, that these developments have coincided with a time in which the shortage of low-income housing has intensified as the gentrification of our major cities has accelerated. Half a million units of low-income housing have been lost each year to condominium conversion as well as to arson, demolition, or abandonment. Between 1978 and 1980, median rents climbed 30 percent for peo-ple in the lowest income sector, driving many of these families into the streets. Af-ter 1980, rents rose at even faster rates. In Boston, between 1982 and 1984, over 80 percent of the housing units renting below $300 disappeared, while the num-ber of units renting above $600 nearly tripled. 4

Hard numbers, in this instance, would appear to be of greater help than psy-chiatric labels in telling us why so many people become homeless. Eight million 5

287

American families now pay half or more of their income for rent or a mortgage. Six million more, unable to pay rent at all, live doubled up with others. At the same time, federal support for low-income housing dropped from $30 billion (1980) to $9 billion (1986). Under Presidents Ford and Carter, 500,000 subsidized private housing units were constructed. By President Reagan's second term, the number had dropped to 25,000. "We're getting out of the housing business, period," said a deputy assistant secretary of the Department of Housing and Urban Development in 1985.

One year later, the *Washington Post* reported that the number of homeless 6 families in Washington, D.C., had grown by 500 percent over the previous 12 months. In New York City, the waiting list for public housing now contains 200,000 names. The waiting is 18 years.

Why, in the face of these statistics, are we impelled to find a psychiatric ex- 7 planation for the growth of homelessness in the United States?

A misconception, once it is implanted in the popular imagination, is not easy 8 to uproot, particularly when it serves a useful social role. The notion that the homeless are largely psychotics who belong in institutions, rather than victims of displacement at the hands of enterprising realtors, spares us from the need to offer realistic solutions to the fact of deep and widening extremes of wealth and poverty in the United States. It also enables us to tell ourselves that the despair of homeless people bears no intimate connection to the privileged existence we enjoy—when, for example, we rent or purchase one of those restored town houses that once provided shelter for people now huddled in the street.

But there may be another reason to assign labels to the destitute. Terming 9 economic victims "psychotic" or "disordered" helps to place them at a distance. It says that they aren't quite like us—and, more important, that we could not be like them. The plight of homeless families is a nightmare. It may not seem natural to try to banish human beings from our midst, but it is natural to try to banish nightmares from our minds.

So the rituals of clinical contamination proceed uninterrupted by the eco- 10 nomic facts described above. Research that addresses homelessness as an *injustice* rather than as a medical *misfortune* does not win the funding of foundations. And the research which is funded, defining the narrowed borders of permissible debate, diverts our attention from the antecedent to the secondary cause of homelessness. Thus it is that perfectly ordinary women whom I know in New York City—people whose depression or anxiety is a realistic consequence of months and even years in crowded shelters or the streets—are interrogated by invasive research scholars in an effort to decode their poverty, to find clinical categories for their despair and terror, to identify the secret failing that lies hidden in their psyche.

Many pregnant women without homes are denied prenatal care because they 11 constantly travel from one shelter to another. Many are anemic. Many are denied essential dietary supplements by recent federal cuts. As a consequence, some of their children do not live to see their second year of life. Do these mothers sometimes show signs of stress? Do they appear disorganized, depressed, disordered? Frequently. They are immobilized by pain, traumatized by fear. So it is no surprise that when researchers enter the scene to ask them how they "feel," the resulting reports tell us that the homeless are emotionally unwell. The reports do not tell us we have *made* these people ill. They do not tell us that illness is a natural response to intolerable conditions. Nor do they tell us of the strength and the resilience that so many of these people still retain despite the miseries they must endure. They set these men and women apart in capsules labeled "personality disorder" or "psychotic," where they no longer threaten our complacence.

I visited Haiti not many years ago, when the Duvalier family was still in   12 power. If an American scholar were to have made a psychological study of the homeless families living in the streets of Port-au-Prince—sleeping amidst rotten garbage, bathing in open sewers—and if he were to return to the United States to tell us that the reasons for their destitution were "behavioral problems" or "a lack of mental health," we would be properly suspicious. Knowledgeable Haitians would not merely be suspicious. They would be enraged. Even to initiate such research when economic and political explanations present themselves so starkly would appear grotesque. It is no less so in the United States.

One of the more influential studies of this nature was carried out in 1985 by   13 Ellen Bassuk, a psychiatrist at Harvard University. Drawing upon interviews with eight homeless parents, Dr. Bassuk contends, according to the *Boston Globe,* that "90 percent [of these people] have problems other than housing and poverty that are so acute they would be unable to live successfully on their own." She also precludes the possibility that illness, where it does exist, may be provoked by destitution. "Our data," she writes, "suggest that mental illness tends to precede homelessness." She concedes that living in the streets can make a homeless person's mental illness worse; but she insists upon the fact of prior illness.

The executive director of the Massachusetts Commission on Children and   14 Youth believes that Dr. Bassuk's estimate is far too high. The staff of Massachusetts Human Services Secretary Phillip Johnston believes the appropriate number is closer to 10 percent.

In defending her research, Bassuk challenges such critics by claiming that   15 they do not have data to refute her. This may be true. Advocates for the homeless do not receive funds to defend the sanity of the people they represent. In placing the burden of proof upon them, Dr. Bassuk has created an extraordinary dialectic: How does one prove that people aren't unwell? What homeless mother would consent to enter a procedure that might "prove" her mental health? What overburdened shelter operator would divert scarce funds to such an exercise? It is an unnatural, offensive, and dehumanizing challenge.

Dr. Bassuk's work, however, isn't the issue I want to raise here; the issue is   16 the use or misuse of that work by critics of the poor. For example, in a widely syndicated essay published in 1986, the newspaper columnist Charles Krauthammer argued that the homeless are essentially a deranged segment of the population and that we must find the "political will" to isolate them from society. We must do this, he said, "whether they like it or not." Arguing even against the marginal benefits of homeless shelters, Krauthammer wrote: "There is a better alternative, however, though no one dares speak its name." Krauthammer dares: That better alternative, he said, is "asylum."

One of Mr. Krauthammer's colleagues at the *Washington Post,* the colum- 17
nist George Will, perceives the homeless as a threat to public cleanliness and argues that they ought to be consigned to places where we need not see them. "It is," he says, "simply a matter of public hygiene" to put them out of sight. Another journalist, Charles Murray, writing from the vantage point of a social Darwinist, recommends the restoration of the almshouses of the 1800s. "Granted Dickensian horror stories about almshouses," he begins, there were nonetheless "good almshouses"; he proposes "a good correctional 'halfway house' " as a proper shelter for a mother and child with no means of self-support.

In the face of such declarations, the voices of those who work with and know 18
the poor are harder to hear.

Manhattan Borough President David Dinkins made the following observa- 19
tion on the basis of a study commissioned in 1986: "No facts support the belief that addiction or behavioral problems occur with more frequency in the homeless family population than in a similar socioeconomic population. Homeless families are not demographically different from other public assistance families when they enter the shelter system . . . Family homelessness is typically a housing and income problem: The unavailability of affordable housing and the inadequacy of public assistance income."

In a "hypothetical world," write James Wright and Julie Lam of the Univer- 20
sity of Massachusetts, "where there were no alcoholics, no drug addicts, no mentally ill, no deinstitutionalization, . . . indeed, no personal social pathologies at all, there would still be a formidable homelessness problem, simply because at this stage in American history, there is not enough low-income housing" to accommodate the poor.

New York State's respected commissioner of social services, Cesar Perales, 21
makes the point in fewer words: "Homelessness is less and less a result of personal failure, and more and more is caused by larger forces. There is no longer affordable housing in New York City for people of poor and modest means."

Even the words of medical practitioners who care for homeless people have 22
been curiously ignored. A study published by the Massachusetts Medical Society, for instance, has noted that the most frequent illnesses among a sample of the homeless population, after alcohol and drug use, are trauma (31 percent), upper respiratory disorders (28 percent), limb disorders (19 percent), mental illness (16 percent), skin diseases (15 percent), hypertension (14 percent), and neurological illnesses (12 percent). (Excluded from this tabulation are lead poisoning, malnutrition, acute diarrhea, and other illnesses especially common among homeless infants and small children.) Why, we may ask, of all these calamities, does mental illness command so much political and press attention? The answer may be that

the label of mental illness places the destitute outside the sphere of ordinary life. It personalizes an anguish that is public in its genesis; it individualizes a misery that is both general in cause and general in application.

The rate of tuberculosis among the homeless is believed to be 10 times that 23 of the general population. Asthma, I have learned in countless interviews, is one of the most common causes of discomfort in the shelters. Compulsive smoking, exacerbated by the crowding and the tension, is more common in the shelters than in any place that I have visited except prison. Infected and untreated sores, scabies, diarrhea, poorly set limbs, protruding elbows, awkwardly distorted wrists, bleeding gums, impacted teeth, and other untreated dental problems are so common among children in the shelters that one rapidly forgets their presence. Hunger and emaciation are everywhere. Children as well as adults can bring to mind the photographs of people found in camps for refugees of war in 1945. But these miseries bear no stigma, and mental illness does. It conveys a stigma in the Soviet Union. It conveys a stigma in the United States. In both nations the label is used, whether as a matter of deliberate policy or not, to isolate and treat as special cases those who, by deed or word or sheer presence, represent a threat to national complacence. The two situations are obviously not identical, but they are enough alike to give Americans reason for concern.

Last summer, some 28,000 homeless people were afforded shelter by the city 24 of New York. Of this number, 12,000 were children and 6,000 were parents living together in families. The average child was six years old, the average parent 27. A typical homeless family included a mother with two or three children, but in about one-fifth of these families two parents were present. Roughly 10,000 single persons, then, made up the remainder of the population of the city's shelters.

These proportions vary somewhat from one area of the nation to another. In 25 all areas, however, families are the fastest-growing sector of the homeless population, and in the Northeast they are by far the largest sector already. In Massachusetts, three-fourths of the homeless now are families with children; in certain parts of Massachusetts—Attleboro and Northampton, for example—the proportion reaches 90 percent. Two-thirds of the homeless children studied recently in Boston were less than five years old.

Of an estimated two to three million homeless people nationwide, about 26 500,000 are dependent children, according to Robert Hayes, counsel to the National Coalition for the Homeless. Including their parents, at least 750,000 homeless people in America are family members.

What is to be made, then, of the supposition that the homeless are primarily 27 the former residents of mental hospitals, persons who were carelessly released during the 1970s? Many of them are, to be sure. Among the older men and women in the streets and shelters, as many as one-third (some believe as many as one-half) may be chronically disturbed, and a number of these people were deinstitutionalized during the 1970s. But in a city like New York, where nearly half the homeless are small children with an average age of six, to operate on the basis of such a supposition makes no sense. Their parents, with an average age of 27, are not likely to have been hospitalized in the 1970s, either.

Nor is it easy to assume, as was once the case, that single men—those who come closer to fitting the stereotype of the homeless vagrant, the drifting alcoholic of an earlier age—are the former residents of mental hospitals. The age of homeless men has dropped in recent years; many of them are only 21 to 28 years old. Fifty percent of homeless men in New York City shelters in 1984 were there for the first time. Most had previously had homes and jobs. Many had never before needed public aid.   28

A frequently cited set of figures tells us that in 1955, the average daily census of nonfederal psychiatric institutions was 677,000, and that by 1984, the number had dropped to 151,000. Subtract the second number from the first, conventional logic tells us, and we have an explanation for the homelessness of half a million people. A closer look at the same number offers us a different lesson.   29

The sharpest decline in the average daily census of these institutions occurred prior to 1978, and the largest part of that decline, in fact, appeared at least a decade earlier. From 677,000 in 1955, the census dropped to 378,000 in 1972. The 1974 census was 307,000. In 1976 it was 230,000; in 1977 it was 211,000; and in 1978 it was 190,000. In no year since 1978 has the average daily census dropped by more than 9,000 persons, and in the six-year period from 1978 to 1984, the total decline was 39,000 persons. Compared with a decline of 300,000 from 1955 to 1972, and of nearly 200,000 more from 1972 to 1978, the number is small. But the years since 1980 are the period in which the present homeless crisis surfaced. Only since 1983 have homeless individuals overflowed the shelters.   30

If the large numbers of the homeless lived in hospitals before they reappeared in subway stations and in public shelters, we need to ask where they were and what they had been doing from 1972 to 1980. Were they living under bridges? Were they waiting out the decade in the basements of deserted buildings?   31

No. The bulk of those who had been psychiatric patients and were released from hospitals during the 1960s and early 1970s had been living in the meantime in low-income housing, many in skid-row hotels or boarding houses. Such housing—commonly known as SRO (single-room occupancy) units—was drastically diminished by the gentrification of our cities that began in 1970. Almost 50 percent of SRO housing was replaced by luxury apartments or by office buildings between 1970 and 1980, and the remaining units have been disappearing at even faster rates. As recently as 1986, after New York City had issued a prohibition against conversion of such housing, a well-known developer hired a demolition team to destroy a building in Times Square that had previously been home to indigent people. The demolition took place in the middle of the night. In order to avoid imprisonment, the developer was allowed to make a philanthropic gift to homeless people as a token of atonement. This incident, bizarre as it appears, reminds us that the profit motive for displacement of the poor is very great in every major city. It also indicates a more realistic explanation for the growth of homelessness during the 1980s.   32

Even for those persons who are ill and were deinstitutionalized during the   33
decades before 1980, the precipitating cause of homelessness in 1987 is not illness
but loss of housing. SRO housing, unattractive as it may have been, offered low-
cost sanctuaries for the homeless, providing a degree of safety and mutual support
for those who lived within them. They were a demeaning version of the community health centers that society had promised; they were the de facto "halfway
houses" of the 1970s. For these people too, then—at most half of the homeless
single persons in America—the cause of homelessness is lack of housing.

A writer in the *New York Times* describes a homeless woman standing on a   34
traffic island in Manhattan. "She was evicted from her small room in the hotel just
across the street," and she is determined to get revenge. Until she does, "nothing
will move her from that spot. . . . Her argumentativeness and her angry fixation on
revenge, along with the apparent absence of hallucinations, mark her as a para-
noid." Most physicians, I imagine, would be more reserved in passing judgment
with so little evidence, but this author makes his diagnosis without hesitation.
"The paranoids of the street," he says, "are among the most difficult to help."

Perhaps so. But does it depend on who is offering the help? Is anyone of-   35
fering to help this woman get back her home? Is it crazy to seek vengeance for being thrown into the street? The absence of anger, some psychiatrists believe, might
indicate much greater illness.

The same observer sees additional symptoms of pathology ("negative symp-   36
toms," he calls them) in the fact that many homeless persons demonstrate a "gross
deterioration in their personal hygiene" and grooming, leading to "indifference"
and "apathy." Having just identified one woman as unhealthy because she is so far
from being "indifferent" as to seek revenge, he now sees apathy as evidence of illness; so consistency is not what we are looking for in this account. But how much
less indifferent might the homeless be if those who decide their fate were less indifferent themselves? How might their grooming and hygiene be improved if they
were permitted access to a public toilet?

In New York City, as in many cities, homeless people are denied the right to   37
wash in public bathrooms, to store their few belongings in a public locker, or, in
certain cases, to make use of public toilets altogether. Shaving, cleaning of clothes,
and other forms of hygiene are prohibited in the men's room of Grand Central Station. The terminal's three hundred lockers, used in former times by homeless people to secure their goods, were removed in 1986 as "a threat to public safety," according to a study made by the New York City Council.

At 1:30 every morning, homeless people are ejected from the station. Many   38
once attempted to take refuge on the ramp that leads to Forty-Second Street because it was protected from the street by wooden doors and thus provided some
degree of warmth. But the station management responded to this challenge in two
ways. The ramp was mopped with a strong mixture of ammonia to produce a nox-
ious smell, and when the people sleeping there brought cardboard boxes and newspapers to protect them from the fumes, the entrance doors were chained wide

open. Temperatures dropped some nights to 10 degrees. Having driven these people to the streets, city officials subsequently determined that their willingness to risk exposure to cold weather could be taken as further evidence of mental illness.

At Pennsylvania Station in New York, homeless women are denied the use 39 of toilets. Amtrak police come by and herd them off each hour on the hour. In June 1985, Amtrak officials issued this directive to police: "It is the policy of Amtrak to not allow the homeless and undesirables to remain. . . . Officers are encouraged to eject all undesirables. . . . Now is the time to train and educate them that their presence will not be tolerated as cold weather sets in." In an internal memo, according to CBS, an Amtrak official asked flatly: "Can't we get rid of this trash?"

I have spent many nights in conversation with the women who are huddled 40 in the corridors and near the doorway of the public toilets in Penn Station. Many are young. Most are cogent. Few are dressed in the familiar rags suggested by the term *bag ladies*. Unable to bathe or use the toilets in the station, almost all are in conditions of intolerable physical distress. The sight of clusters of police officers, mostly male, guarding a toilet from use by homeless women speaks volumes about the public conscience of New York.

Where do these women defecate? How do they bathe? What will we do 41 when, in her physical distress, a woman finally disrobes in public and begins to urinate right on the floor? "Gross deterioration," someone will call it, evidence of mental illness. In the course of an impromptu survey in the streets last September, Mayor Koch observed a homeless woman who had soiled her own clothes. Not only was the woman crazy, said the mayor, but those who differed with him on his diagnosis must be crazy, too. "I am the number one social worker in this town—with sanity," said he.

It may be that this woman was psychotic, but the mayor's comment says a 42 great deal more about his sense of revulsion and the moral climate of a decade in which words like these may be applauded than about her mental state.

A young man who had lost his job, then his family, then his home, all in the 43 summer of 1986, spoke with me for several hours in Grand Central Station on the weekend following Thanksgiving. "A year ago," he said, "I never thought that somebody like me would end up in a shelter. Nothing you've ever undergone prepares you. You walk into the place [a shelter on the Bowery]—the smell of sweat and urine hits you like a wall. Unwashed bodies and the look of absolute despair on many, many faces there would make you think you were in Dante's Hell. . . . What you fear is that you will be here forever. You do not know if it is ever going to end. You think to yourself: It is a dream and I will awake. Sometimes I think: It's an experiment. They are watching you to find out how much you can take. . . . I was a pretty stable man. Now I tremble when I meet somebody in the ordinary world. I'm trembling right now. . . . For me, the loss of work and loss of wife had left me rocking. Then the welfare regulations hit me. I began to feel that I would be reduced to trash. . . . Half the people that I know are suffering from chest infections and sleep deprivation. The lack of sleep leaves you debilitated, shaky. You exaggerate your fears. If a psychiatrist came along he'd say that I was crazy. But

I was an ordinary man. There was nothing wrong with me. I lost my kids. I lost my home. Now would you say that I was crazy if I told you I was feeling sad?"

"If the plight of homeless adults is the shame of America," writes Fred 44 Hechinger in the *New York Times,* "the lives of homeless children are the nation's crime."

In November 1984, a fact already known to advocates for the homeless was 45 given brief attention by the press. Homeless families, the *New York Times* reported, "mostly mothers and young children, have been sleeping on chairs, counters, and floors of the city's emergency welfare offices." Reacting to such reports, the mayor declared: "The woman is sitting on a chair or on a floor. It is not because we didn't offer her a bed. We provide a shelter for every single person who knocks on our door." On the same day, however, the city reported that in the previous 11 weeks it had been unable to give shelter to 153 families, and in the subsequent year, 1985, the city later reported that about 2,000 children slept in welfare offices because of lack of shelter space.

Some 800 homeless infants in New York City, reported the National Coali- 46 tion for the Homeless, "routinely go without sufficient food, cribs, health care, and diapers." The lives of these children "are put at risk," while "high-risk pregnant women" are repeatedly forced to sleep in unsafe "barracks shelters" or welfare offices called Emergency Assistance Units (EAUs). "Coalition monitors, making sporadic random checks, found eight women in their *ninth* month of pregnancy sleeping in EAUs. . . . Two women denied shelter began having labor contractions at the EAU." In one instance, the Legal Aid Society was forced to go to court after a woman lost her child by miscarriage while lying on the floor of a communal bathroom in a shelter which the courts had already declared unfit to house pregnant women.

The coalition also reported numerous cases in which homeless mothers were 47 obliged to choose between purchasing food or diapers for their infants. Federal guidelines issued in 1986 deepened the nutrition crisis faced by mothers in the welfare shelters by counting the high rent paid to the owners of the buildings as a part of family income, rendering their residents ineligible for food stamps. Families I interviewed who had received as much as $150 in food stamps monthly in June 1986 were cut back to $33 before Christmas.

"Now you're hearing all kinds of horror stories," said President Reagan, 48 "about the people that are going to be thrown out in the snow to hunger and [to] die of cold and so forth. . . . We haven't cut a single budget." But in the four years leading up to 1985, according to the *New Republic,* Aid to Families with Dependent Children had been cut by $4.8 billion, child nutrition programs by $5.2 billion, food stamps by $6.8 billion. The federal government's authority to help low-income families with housing assistance was cut from $30 billion to $11 billion in Reagan's first term. In his fiscal 1986 budget, the president proposed to cut that by an additional 95 percent.

"If even one American child is forced to go to bed hungry at night," the pres- 49 ident said on another occasion, "that is a national tragedy. We are too generous a people to allow this." But in the years since the president spoke these words, thousands of poor children in New York alone have gone to bed too sick to sleep and far too weak to rise the next morning to attend a public school. Thousands more have been unable to attend school at all because their homeless status compels them to move repeatedly from one temporary shelter to another. Even in the affluent suburbs outside New York City, hundreds of homeless children are obliged to ride as far as 60 miles twice a day in order to obtain an education in the public schools to which they were originally assigned before their families were displaced. Many of these children get to school too late to eat their breakfast; others are denied lunch at school because of federal cuts in feeding programs.

Many homeless children die—and others suffer brain damage—as a direct 50 consequence of federal cutbacks in prenatal programs, maternal nutrition, and other feeding programs. The parents of one such child shared with me the story of the year in which their child was delivered, lived, and died. The child, weighing just over four pounds at birth, grew deaf and blind soon after, and for these reasons had to stay in the hospital for several months. When he was released on Christmas Eve of 1984, his mother and father had no home. He lived with his parents in the shelters, subways, streets, and welfare offices of New York City for four winter months, and was readmitted to the hospital in time to die in May 1985.

When we met and spoke the following year, the father told me that his wife 51 had contemplated and even attempted suicide after the child's death, while he had entertained the thought of blowing up the welfare offices of New York City. I would tell him that to do so would be illegal and unwise. I would never tell him it was crazy.

"No one will be turned away," says the mayor of New York City, as hundreds 52 of young mothers with their infants are turned from the doors of shelters season after season. That may sound to some like denial of reality. "Now you're hearing all these stories," says the president of the United States as he denies that anyone is cold or hungry or unhoused. On another occasion he says that the unsheltered "are homeless, you might say, by choice." That sounds every bit as self-deceiving.

The woman standing on the traffic island screaming for revenge until her 53 room has been restored to her sounds relatively healthy by comparison. If 3,000,000 homeless people did the same, and all at the same time, we might finally be forced to listen.

1988

QUESTIONS FOR DISCUSSION

Content

a. Why did Kozol write this essay? What is his thesis?
b. The author cites several examples of changes in public policy during the 1980s that significantly contributed to increases in homelessness. Identify two or three.

c. In several instances, he challenges our conventional perception of homelessness by picturing homeless people as sane while exposing public policy governing them as quite the opposite. Find and discuss such instances.

d. What is the author's response to those who argue that mental illness precedes and is a major cause of homelessness?

e. How does he answer Dr. Ellen Bassuk's claim that advocates for the homeless have been unable to provide data to prove that these people are not "unwell" (paragraph 15)?

f. Summarize the arguments of those who advocate isolating the homeless from the rest of society. How do you respond to such arguments?

g. What examples does Kozol include to illustrate inconsistency in public policy and attitudes toward the homeless?

h. What examples of public denial does the author cite?

i. Kozol has always been an advocate for children. In what way does this essay reflect that role?

Strategy and Style

j. What use does Kozol make of rhetorical questions? Where can such questions be found?

k. Why does he bother to compare homelessness in America with homelessness in Haiti?

l. What is similar about the way in which mental illness is viewed in the former Soviet Union and in the United States? Why does Kozol make this comparison?

m. Statistics can be powerful tools for illustration; they make abstract ideas clearer and more convincing. Where in this essay does Kozol use statistical or numerical data? Do you find such information convincing?

n. Why does the author bring up the case of the young man he quotes in paragraph 43? Why does he tell us about the woman who stands on a traffic island in Manhattan (paragraph 34)? Would his essay have been more effective had he explained the effects of homelessness on the population as a whole?

SUGGESTIONS FOR SHORT WRITING

a. How do you react when you come upon someone who is homeless? Do some freewriting that captures both your rational and your emotional response to what you see.

b. "A misconception, once it is implanted in the popular imagination, is not easy to uproot, particularly when it serves a useful social role," says Kozol in paragraph 8. Spend a few minutes explaining how this statement might apply to any social problem other than homelessness.

c. Isolate a section of this essay (two or three paragraphs) that argues a specific point about the nature of homelessness, about its causes or effects, or about public policy toward the homeless. Then, write a short statement in which you defend or attack the opinion expressed in those paragraphs.

SUGGESTIONS FOR SUSTAINED WRITING

a. If you responded to the first of the Suggestions for Short Writing above, review what you wrote. Next do some more freewriting about your overall impression of the problem of homelessness, its causes, and its effects. Use all of these notes to begin an essay that explains what, if anything, should be done about the problem.

b. If you live in a city with organizations that help the homeless, volunteer for at least a short time in a soup kitchen or shelter, or get involved in some other way with the organization. Then, write a narrative essay about your experiences, citing Kozol's article when appropriate. Your experiences could also form the basis for an argumentative essay.

c. Using Kozol's organization as a general model, research a critical current issue about which you feel strongly. Begin by becoming familiar with the general background and parameters of the issue, making a list of questions you (and perhaps your readers as well) have about it. Using your list as a guide, try to find facts and statistics that answer the questions. If possible, use the material you have so far to conduct interviews with local people involved in the issue. Then, write your findings as a report with an argumentative bent.

On a Greek Holiday

Alice Bloom

Alice Bloom is a critic and fiction writer, and teaches English at the University of Maine, Farmington. Her articles have appeared in the New England Review, Breadloaf Quarterly, *and* The Hudson Review, *from which the following piece was taken. The selection is an excerpt from a much longer essay with the same title.*

The only interesting question on a trip for me is—what sustains life elsewhere? How deep does it go? Can one see it? This hope, this anticipation, is forcibly blocked. Henry Miller, in 193—, stood in Epidaurus, alone, in a "weird solitude," and felt the "great heart of the world beat." We stand at Epidaurus with several thousand others, some of whom are being called "my chickens" by their tour guide who calls herself "your mother hen," whose counterpart, this time at Delphi, explains several times that what is being looked at is the "belly button of the world, okay? The Greeks thought, this is the belly button of the world, okay?" "These stones all look alike to me," someone grumbles. There is no help for it; we're there with guidebooks ourselves; but this fact—tourism is big business—and others, throw us back, unwilling, into contemplation of our own dull home-soul, our dull bodily comforts, our own dull dwindling purse, our own dull resentments; because the other—in this case, Greece—is either rapidly disappearing or else, self-protective, is retreating so far it has disappeared. You can get there, but you can't get at it. 1

For instance, a study of travel posters and brochures, which in the process of setting dates and buying tickets always precedes a trip, shows us, by projection into these pictured, toothy, tourist bodies, having some gorgeous piece of ingestion: The yellow beach, the mossy blue ruin, a dinner table laden with food and red wine of the region, dancing, skiing, golfing, shopping, waving to roadside natives as our rented car sails by, as though we only go to play, as though all we do here at home is work, as though, for two or four weeks abroad, we seek regression. 2

Also in the posters, but as part of the landscape, there are the natives— whether Spanish, Greek, Irish, etc.—costumed as attractions, performing in bouzouki or bag-pipe bands, or doing some picturesque and nonindustrial piece of work such as fishing, weaving, selling colorful cheap goods in open-air markets, herding sheep or goats. The journey promised by the posters and brochures is a trip into everyone's imaginary past: One's own, drained of the normal childhood content of fear, death, space, hurt, abandonment, perplexity, and so forth, now presented as the salesmen think we think it should have been: One in which we only ate, slept, and played in the eternal sun under the doting care of benevolent elders. 3

And we are shown the benevolent elders, the imaginary natives who also, for a handsome fee, exist now, in the present of the trip we are about to take. ("Take" is probably a more telling verb here than we think.) They exist in a past where they are pictured having grown cheerfully old and wise doing only harmless, enjoyable, 4 preindustrial, clean, self-employed, open-air work, in pink crinkled cheeks, merry eyes, and wonderful quaint clothes, with baskets, nets, toyshaped boats, flower boxes, cottages, sheep crooks, country roads, whitewashed walls, tea shop signs, and other paraphernalia of the pastoral wish. I have never seen a travel poster showing natives of the country enjoying their own food or beaches or ski-jumps or hotel balconies; nor have I ever seen a travel poster showing the natives working the nightshift in the Citroën factory, either.

The natives in the posters (are they Swiss, Mexican, Chilean, Turkish mod-   5 els?) are happy parent figures, or character dolls, and their faces, like the faces of the good parents we are supposed to have dreamed, show them pleased with their own lot, busy but not too busy with a job that they obviously like, content with each other, and warmly indulgent of our need to play, to be fed good, clean food on time, and to be tucked into a nice bed at the end of our little day. They are the childhood people that also existed in early grammar school readers, and nowhere else: Adults in your neighborhood, in the identifiable costumes of their humble tasks, transitional-object people, smiling milkman, friendly aproned store owner in his small friendly store, happy mailman happy to bring your happy mail, happy mommy, icons who make up a six-year-old's school-enforced dream town, who enjoy doing their nonindustrial, unmysterious tasks: Mail, milk, red apple, cooky, just for you, so you can learn to decipher: See, Jip, see.

A travel remark I have always savored came from someone surprised in love   6 for a place, just returned from a month in the Far East (no longer tagged "the mysterious," I've noticed), and who was explaining this trip at a party. She said, "I just loved Japan. It was so authentic and Oriental." Few people would go quite so naked as that, but the charm of her feelings seemed just right. Perhaps she had expected Tokyo to be more or less a larger version of the Japanese Shop in the Tokyo Airport. It is somewhat surprising that she found it to be anything much more.

One of the hushed-tone moral superiority stories, the aren't-we-advanced sto-   7 ries told by those lucky enough to travel in Soviet Russia, has to do with that government's iron management of the trip. There are people who can't be met, buildings that can't be entered, upper story windows that can't be photographed, streets that can't be strolled, districts that can't be crossed, cities in which it is impossible to spend the night, and so on. However, our notions of who we are and what comforts we demand and what conditions we'll endure, plus any country's understandably garbled versions of who we are, what we want, and what we'll pay for, are far more rigid than the strictures of any politburo because such strictures don't say "This is you, this is what you must want," but "This is what you can't, under any circumstances, do." That, though it inhibits movement, and no doubt in some cases prevents a gathering of or understanding of some crucial or desired bit of information, has at least the large virtue of defining the tourist as potentially dangerous. What we meet most of the time, here and abroad, is a definition of ourselves as harmless, spoiled babies, of low endurance and little information, minimal curiosity, frozen in infancy, frozen in longing, terrified for our next square meal and clean bed, and whose only potential danger is that we might refuse to be separated from our money.

Suppose, for a moment, that tourism—the largest "industry" in Greece (it 8 employs, even more than shipping, the most people)—were also the largest industry in America. Not just in Manhattan or Washington, D.C., or Disneyland or Disney World or at the Grand Canyon or Niagara Falls, but in every motel, hotel, restaurant, in every McDonald's and Colonel Sanders and Howard Johnson's and Mom & Pop's, in every bar and neighborhood hangout, truck stop, gas station, pharmacy, department store, museum, church, historical site, battleground, in every taxi, bus, subway, train, plane, in every public building, in post offices and banks and public bathrooms, on every street in every city, town, village and hamlet from West Jonesport, Maine, to Centralia, Illinois, to Parachute, Colorado, and every stop in between and beyond, just as it is in Greece: Tourists.

Suppose that every other business establishment across the country there- 9 fore found it in their best interest to become a souvenir shop, selling cheap, mass-produced "gifts" for the tourists to take back home that, back home, would announce that they had visited America. What images would we mass produce for them? Millions of little bronzed Liberty Bells? Tepees? St. Louis Arches? Streetcars named "Desire"? Statues of Babe Ruth? of Liberty? of Daniel Boone? In Greece we saw miniature bottles of ouzo encased in tiny plastic replicas of the temple of Athena Nike. Could we do something so clever, and immediately recognizable, with miniatures of bourbon? Encase them in tiny plastic Washington Monuments? Lincoln Memorials? Would we feel misrepresented?

Third, suppose that a sizable portion of these tourists wanting gifts, toilets, 10 rooms, baths, meals, dollars, film, drinks, stamps, directions, are Greek; or else, let us suppose that we assumed, that whether actually Greek or not, wherever they come from they speak Greek as a second language. Assume, therefore, that our map and traffic and road signs, postings of instruction and information, advertisements, timetables, directions—"stop," "go," "hot," "cold," "men," "women," "open," "closed," "yes," "no,"—to name a few rudiments of life, plus all the menus in all those sandwich counters, truck stops, fast-food outlets, lunch rooms, and so forth, had to be in Greek as well as in English. We have never been, so far, an occupied country, whether by forces enemy or not. Undoubtedly, if we were, as an ongoing fact of our "in-season" summer months, we Americans, having to offer our multitudinous wares in Greek, would come up with items as hilarious as those we collected from the English side of Greek menus: Baygon and egs. Xamberger steake. Veat. Orange juise. Rost beef. Shrimp carry. Potoes, Spaggeti. Morcoroni. And our favorite, Fried Smooth Hound. (This turned out to be a harmless local fish, much to the disappointment of our children, born surrealists.)

Suppose that we had to post Bar Harbor, Plum Island, Chincoteague, Key 11 West, Bay St. Louis, Galveston, Big Sur and Seattle beaches with "No Nakedness Allowed" signs, but that the Greeks and other tourists, freed from the cocoons of air-conditioned tour buses, armed with sun-oil in every degree of protection, rushed beachwards past the signs and stripped to their altogether, anyway? Would our police sit quietly in the shade and drink with other men and turn, literally, their khaki-clad rumps to the beach, as did the Greek police?

And food. Suppose we had to contrive to feed them, these hungry hordes? 12
They will come here, as we go there, entrenched in their habits and encumbered
with fears of being cheated, fears of indigestion, of recurrent allergies, of breaking their diets, of catching American trots, of being poisoned by our water, fat-
tened by our grease and starch, put off by our feeding schedules, sickened by
something weird or local. Suppose we decided, out of some semiconscious, unor-
ganized, but national canniness, that what these tourists really want is our cobbled
version of their national foods. Whom will we please: The English who want their
teas at four, or the Italians who want supper at nine at night? Or both? And what
will we cook and serve, and how will we spell it?

Or suppose they want to eat "American" food. What tastes like us? What fla- 13
vors contain our typicality, our history, our heroes, our dirt, our speeches, our poets, our battles, our national shames? The hot dog? Corn on the cob? I have eaten,
barring picnics and occasional abstention, probably about 130 meals in Greece.
And Greek food, I feel somewhat qualified to say, contains their history, and tastes
of sorrow and triumph, of olive oil and blood, in about equal amounts. It is the
most astounding and the most boring food that I, an eater, have ever eaten.

Greek food is tragic. Why? Because each bite is a chomp into history, our 14
history. Why? Because this lunch—small fish, cheese, olives, wine, bread—
exactly this lunch, and tomorrow's lunch—fish, cheese, olives, wine, bread—has
been eaten since the time of the glory that will someday be called Greece, the glory
that existed for a moment, the glory that Greece was, and the glory that mankind—
for Greece is that, not Greek, but mankind—might yet be. Each bite is archaeo-
logical, into fine layers of millennia: Fish, oil, cheese, wine, bread—in the par-
taking we join, on the back of the tongue, Amazon forces and single crazy saints,
mythical men who married their mythical mothers, and men, and mothers, who today and tomorrow only dream of it.

One uses a big word like "timeless" with caution, if at all. But there is noth- 15
ing timely about two things in Greece; therefore it is not rhetorical to claim that,
in Greece, the quality of the heat of the sun on the skin and the quality of the food
in the mouth are perhaps as close as we can come to the taste of "timelessness."
Along with the oldest human question—how can we make God happy?—this sun
and this food are among the most ancient sensations recorded.

Under this summer sun every meal, beginning with breakfast, is eaten in 100 16
degrees of heat and hotter—115, 120—by afternoon. The meal, any one of them,
is composed of food that grows best in this climate and yet is entirely unsuited to
it as daily refreshment. No one could possibly, certainly not a tourist, need this oil-
soaked food for fuel in mid-July. It tastes and feels, though, like fuel: Heavy, shiny,
slow-moving food, purple, brown, red—tomatoes, eggplants, fish, lamb, olives,
black wine, blinding white cheese, much bread. We eat this three times a day; three
times a day the tourists eat it and the Greeks eat it. Everyone seems to look forward to the next meal, and all around our table, where we eat again with relish, are
others eating with relish, sometimes even with a look of reprieve and relief. And
there is no escape from it. Who would risk whatever "shrimp carry" might be?

There is no ordering something else—a salad of lettuce for a change, or a thin chicken sandwich. There is nothing but this food with its taste and texture of ancient days, of old crimes, forbidden loves, of something tinny and resigned, something of both gluttony and renunciation.

In addition to being a tragic cuisine, a sacramental cuisine, it is also practical, cheap, crude, and uninventive. The raw materials are without equal: Eggplants hang with the burnish of Dutch interiors; the fish still flap as they are headed oilwards; the lamb chop's mother befouls the yard next to your table; fruit so perfect, so total, that the scent of a single peach in a paper bag perfumes the whole room overnight and brings tears of love of God to the eyes. On a walk into the hills, meadows of thyme and mint and basil are idly crushed under heel. What happens to all this in the pot is a miracle of transformation, of negligence or brutality; or possibly, stubborn evidence of some otherwise lost political knowledge of what draws out the best, most noble, and most beautiful in the masses. 17

For the food is destroyed, each meal, in the process from vine or net or garden to violent table. Its facts are these: It has always been eaten thus, with the exception of the late-coming tomato. It is—lamb, eggplant, olive, fish, white cheese —even now, perfectly indigenous. It is plain cooking. It is cooked for hours, all day; oil is poured on without restraint, discretion, or mercy. Every morsel is the same temperature and consistency by the time it reaches the palate. In a profound way, it is stupid food, overfeeding the flesh while tasting as though one should renounce the flesh forever. 18

We did not, to be fair, eat in a single Greek home. However, we were careful to eat where the Greeks ate, and the Greeks eat out—in family groups, starched, ironed, slicked-down heads, whited summer shoes, strictly disciplined children; or in tense, dark groups of greedy, hasty men; which is how, as families or as men, the Greeks travel through the day. From the second-story, open-air, Greek-family-filled restaurant where we ate most of our meals while on the island, we could, if we had a table near the edge, throw our bread scraps, if we had any left over, straight down into the blue-green sea for the melon and dove-colored fish to mouth; and we could watch the evening sky turn from the day's bleached-out white to a pale English blue, then to lime-green streaked with apricot, and finally, with the fall of night, to a grape-purple that rose, in that instant, up from the sea. 19

1983

QUESTIONS FOR DISCUSSION

Content

a. Although this selection is taken from the middle of a longer essay, the introductory paragraph of this excerpt marks a new direction in the whole essay. As an introduction, what expectations does it set up? In other words, what does it tell you about what follows?

b. After reading the entire selection, go back to the three questions that begin the piece. What do these questions mean? How would Bloom answer them based on her experience in Greece?

c. Who is the "we" that Bloom keeps referring to? Look especially at paragraphs 7, 8, and 9. She is obviously speaking of Americans, but specifically what kinds of Americans?

d. In paragraphs 8 through 13 Bloom presents some hypothetical examples as a way to criticize something. What is it that she is criticizing?

e. At the end of paragraph 9 Bloom asks, "Would we feel misrepresented" if foreign tourists considered mass-produced souvenirs, such as bronzed Liberty Bells, tepees, or St. Louis Arches, as representative of the United States? Would you feel misrepresented by such objects?

f. Bloom asserts that "Greek food is tragic" (paragraph 14) and also that Greek food is "sacramental" (paragraph 17). What does she mean? What adjectives would she, or you, use to describe American food?

g. Why is there so much attention on food? What has food got to do with travel and culture?

Strategy and Style

h. Bloom's tone in the first few paragraphs (2–7) could be described as snide and critical of the travel industry. Underline or point to phrases in these paragraphs that convey this tone.

i. Each of paragraphs 8 through 13 includes "suppose" in the first phrase. Why might Bloom have used so many hypothetical examples?

j. The vocabulary Bloom uses is fairly simple; however, her prose is difficult to read because of sentence structure and length. Find two or three sentences that tripped you up, and paraphrase them.

k. To whom does Bloom seem to be writing? Who are her ideal readers? How do you know? Point to phrases that seem directed to a particular kind of reader.

SUGGESTIONS FOR SHORT WRITING

a. Write a paraphrase or a summary of the opening paragraph of this difficult selection.

b. Notice the logical leap from paragraph 13 to 14, from a brief description of American and Greek food to the statement that "Greek food is tragic." What is the transition here? Write a short transitional paragraph that shows the logical connection between the two paragraphs. Concentrate on making the logic clear; do not worry about matching Bloom's style.

SUGGESTIONS FOR SUSTAINED WRITING

a. In paragraph 3 Bloom shows that the tourist industry sells actual trips by promising another, figurative, trip. She writes, "The journey promised by the posters and brochures is a trip into everyone's imaginary past: One's own, drained of the normal childhood content of fear, death, space, hurt, abandonment, perplexity, and so forth, now presented as the salesmen think we think it should have been: One in which we only ate, slept, and played in the eternal sun under the doting care of benevolent elders."

Find posters or brochures in a local travel office, or ads for exotic travel in a magazine such as *Travel and Leisure* or *National Geographic Traveller.* Write an essay in which you analyze the posters, brochures, or ads, pointing out details of the images and the ad copy that promise something other than the actual, physical trip. Address the questions: What are the figurative journeys promised by these materials? What is the relationship between the figurative journey and the actual trip? In what ways do the images and words implicitly create the promise of another type of journey?

b. In paragraph 9 Bloom lists images that would make good mass-produced souvenirs. Think of the one image or object (from Bloom's list or one of your own) that would say "America" to foreign tourists. Describe the image/object, and explain your choice. What connections are there between the image or object and American culture? What makes this image or object essentially American?

c. Reread Bloom's essay, and write both a paraphrase of it and an extended response to it, pointing out how Bloom structures the essay, how she sequences her examples, and commenting on her choice of examples. Include your opinion of the effectiveness of her structure and content choices.

8

Cause and Effect

If you read Chapter 3, you know that explaining causes and effects is similar to analyzing a process. While the latter explains how something happens, however, the former seeks to reveal why it happens. Causal analysis is often used to explore questions in science, history, economics, and the social sciences. If you have taken courses in these subjects, you may have written papers or essay exams that discuss the major causes of World War I; explain changes in the U.S. banking system brought on by the Great Depression; or predict the environmental consequences of uncontrolled pollution.

Causal analysis is so natural an activity that it appears in the earliest of stages of mental awareness. It is a tool by which we reflect upon and learn from our past: The child who burns her hand knows why she should stay away from the stove. But it is also a common way to anticipate the future. Peering into metaphorical crystal balls, we create elaborate plans, theorize about the consequences of our actions, and make appropriate changes in the way we live. "If I graduate in four years and get a fellowship to law school," dreams the ambitious college freshman, "I might land a job with Biddle and Biddle and even run for city council by the time I'm thirty. But, first, I'd better improve my grades, which will mean studying harder and spending less time socializing."

The student's thinking illustrates an important point about the connection between causes and effects: It is often more complex than we imagine. For example, in "If Hitler Asked You to Electrocute a Stranger Would You? Probably," Philip Meyer cannot theorize about people's willingness to obey authorities until he thoroughly explains Stanley Milgrim's experiment and discusses Milgrim's conclusions.

Keep this example in mind as you begin to use causal analysis as a way to develop ideas. More often than not, each cause and effect you discuss will require a thorough explanation using details that are carefully chosen and appropriate to

306

your purpose. Remember, too, that you can call on a variety of skills and techniques to help you develop your analysis. For example, Ellen Goodman joins illustration with cause and effect, a brilliant combination that reveals the irony behind why planners and nonplanners reap the same rewards.

An important question any time you use cause and effect is where to place your emphasis. Will you discuss what caused a particular phenomenon or will you focus on its effects? Shelby Steele, discusses the relationship between "black power" and "white guilt" and the results these two forces have had on American attitudes and political policy. Marya Mannes, on the other hand, spends most of her time explaining what causes so many people to "deny the existence of any valid criteria" for judging the arts. Of course, you may decide to strike a balance, as does Norman Cousins when he discusses both the reasons for and the effects of our "becoming a nation of pill-grabbers and hypochondriacs."

As with the other kinds of writing in this text, purpose determines content and strategy. You read earlier that causal analysis is used frequently to explain historical or scientific phenomena. For example, take Kathy Svitil's "Nubian Diet Revealed at Last." Such writing is often objective and dispassionate, but causal analysis has many applications. Because it is an especially powerful tool for persuasion, you might even want to use it to express a strong voice over issues to which you are firmly committed. Take your lead from Mannes, for example, who addresses her readers directly and encourages them to adopt aesthetic standards "timeless as the universe itself." Like Cousins, warn your readers about a medical danger. Express concern over the state of the family, as does Barbara Dafoe Whitehead in "Where Have All the Parents Gone?" You might even want to analyze your reactions to social, political, or other types of problems to see what they tell you about yourself.

How Do You Know It's Good?

Marya Mannes

Marya Mannes (1904–1990) was born in New York City into a family of musicians. Her father, David Mannes, conducted the New York Symphony from 1898 to 1912, and was the founder of the Mannes College of Music. Her mother, Clara Mannes, was a professional pianist. Her brother, Leopold, was both a musician and a chemist; along with another musician/chemist, he invented Kodachrome. Marya, however, became a professional writer, editor, and television commentator. She was a feature editor at Vogue; *a columnist for* McCall's, The New York Times, *and United Features Syndicate; and a commentator for Channel 13, a public broadcasting station in New York. She also contributed frequently to several national magazines and was the author of two novels,* Message from a Stranger *(1948) and* They *(1968), and an autobiography,* Out of My Time *(1971). She was best known, however, for her essays, which have been collected in several books, including* But Will It Sell? *(1964), in which "How Do You Know It's Good?" appears.*

Suppose there were no critics to tell us how to react to a picture, a play, or a new 1 composition of music. Suppose we wandered innocent as the dawn into an art exhibition of unsigned paintings. By what standards, by what values would we decide whether they were good or bad, talented or untalented, successes or failures? How can we ever know that what we think is right?

For the last fifteen or twenty years the fashion in criticism or appreciation of 2 the arts has been to deny the existence of any valid criteria and to make the words "good" or "bad" irrelevant, immaterial, and inapplicable. There is no such thing, we are told, as a set of standards, first acquired through experience and knowledge and later imposed on the subject under discussion. This has been a popular approach, for it relieves the critic of the responsibility of judgment and the public of the necessity of knowledge. It pleases those resentful of disciplines, it flatters the empty-minded by calling them open-minded, it comforts the confused. Under the banner of democracy and the kind of equality which our forefathers did *not* mean, it says, in effect, "Who are you to tell us what *is* good or bad?" This is the same cry used so long and so effectively by the producers of mass media who insist that it is the public, not they, who decides what it wants to hear and see, and that for a critic to say that *this* program is bad and *this* program is good is purely a reflection of personal taste. Nobody recently has expressed this philosophy more succinctly than Dr. Frank Stanton, the highly intelligent president of CBS television. At a hearing before the Federal Communications Commission, this phrase escaped him under questioning: "One man's mediocrity is another man's good program."

There is no better way of saying "No values are absolute." There is another 3 important aspect to this philosophy of *laissez faire:* It is the fear, in all observers of all forms of art, of guessing wrong. This fear is well come by, for who has not heard of the contemporary outcries against artists who later were called great? Every age has its arbiters who do not grow with their times, who cannot tell evolution from revolution or the difference between frivolous faddism, amateurish experimentation, and profound and necessary change. Who wants to be caught *flagrante delicto* with an error of judgment as serious as this? It is far safer, and certainly easier, to look at a picture or a play or a poem and to say "This is hard to understand, but it may be good," or simply to welcome it as a new form. The word "new"—in our country especially—has magical connotations. What is new must be good; what is old probably bad. And if a critic can describe the new in language that nobody can understand, he's safer still. If he has mastered the art of saying nothing with exquisite complexity, nobody can quote him later as saying anything.

But all these, I maintain, are forms of abdication from the responsibility of 4 judgment. In creating, the artist commits himself; in appreciating, you have a commitment of your own. For after all, it is the audience which makes the arts. A climate of appreciation is essential to its flowering, and the higher the expectations of the public, the better the performance of the artist. Conversely, only a public ill-served by its critics could have accepted as art and as literature so much in these last years that has been neither. If anything goes, everything goes; and at the bottom of the junkpile lie the discarded standards too.

But what are these standards? How do you get them? How do you know 5 they're the right ones? How can you make a clear pattern out of so many intangibles, including that greatest one, the very private I?

Well for one thing, it's fairly obvious that the more you read and see and 6 hear, the more equipped you'll be to practice that art of association which is at the basis of all understanding and judgment. The more you live and the more you look, the more aware you are of a consistent pattern—as universal as the stars, as the tides, as breathing, as night and day—underlying everything. I would call this pattern and this rhythm an order. Not order—*an* order. Within it exists an incredible diversity of forms. Without it lies chaos—the wild cells of destruction—sickness. It is in the end up to you to distinguish between the diversity that is health and the chaos that is sickness, and you can't do this without a process of association that can link a bar of Mozart with the corner of a Vermeer painting, or a Stravinsky score with a Picasso abstraction; or that can relate an aggressive act with a Franz Kline painting and a fit of coughing with a John Cage composition.

There is no accident in the fact that certain expressions of art live for all time 7 and that others die with the moment, and although you may not always define the reasons, you can ask the questions. What does an artist say that is timeless; how does he say it? How much is fashion, how much is merely reflection? Why is Sir Walter Scott so hard to read now, and Jane Austen not? Why is baroque right for one age and too effulgent for another?

Can a standard of craftsmanship apply to art of all ages, or does each have its 8 own, and different, definitions? You may have been aware, inadvertently, that craftsmanship has become a dirty word these years because, again, it implies standards—something done well or done badly. The result of this convenient avoidance is a plenitude of actors who can't project their voices, singers who can't phrase their songs, poets who can't communicate emotion, and writers who have no vocabulary—not to speak of painters who can't draw. The dogma now is that crafts-manship gets in the way of expression. You can do better if you don't know how you do it, let alone *what* you're doing.

I think it is time you helped reverse this trend by trying to rediscover craft: The command of the chosen instrument, whether it is a brush, a word, or a voice. When you begin to detect the difference between freedom and sloppiness, between serious experimentation and egotherapy, between skill and slickness, between strength and violence, you are on your way to separating the sheep from the goats, a form of segregation denied us for quite a while. All you need to restore it is a small bundle of standards and a Geiger counter that detects fraud, and we might begin our tour of the arts in an area where both are urgently needed: Contemporary painting. 9

I don't know what's worse: To have to look at acres of bad art to find the lit-tle good, or to read what the critics say about it all. In no other field of expression has so much double-talk flourished, so much confusion prevailed, and so much nonsense been circulated: Further evidence of the close interdependence between the arts and the critical climate they inhabit. It will be my pleasure to share with you some of this double-talk so typical of our times. 10

Item one: Preface for a catalogue of an abstract painter: 11

"Time-bound meditation experiencing a life; sincere with plastic piety at the threshold of hallowed arcana; a striving for pure ideation giving shape to inner drive; formalized patterns where neural balances reach a fiction." End of quote. Know what this artist paints like now? 12

Item two: A review in the *Art News:* 13

". . . a weird and disparate assortment of material, but the monstrosity which bloomed into his most recent cancer of aggregations is present in some form everywhere. . . ." Then, later, "A gluttony of things and processes terminated by a glorious constipation." 14

Item three, same magazine, review of an artist who welds automobile frag-ments into abstract shapes: 15

"Each fragment . . . is made an extreme of human exasperation, torn at and fought all the way, and has its rightness of form as if by accident. *Any technique that requires order or discipline would just be the human ego.* No, these must be egoless, uncontrolled, undesigned and different enough to give you a bang—fifty miles an hour around a telephone pole. . . ." 16

"Any technique that requires order or discipline would just be the human ego." What does he mean—"just be"? What are they really talking about? Is this journalism? Is it criticism? Or is it that other convenient abdication from standards of performance and judgment practiced by so many artists and critics that they, like certain writers who deal only in sickness and depravity, "reflect the chaos about them"? Again, whose chaos? Whose depravity? 17

I had always thought that the prime function of art was to create order *out* of chaos—again, not the order of neatness or rigidity or convention or artifice, but 18 the order of clarity by which one will and one vision could draw the essential truth out of apparent confusion. I still do. It is not enough to use parts of a car to convey the brutality of the machine. This is as slavishly representative, and just as easy, as arranging dried flowers under glass to convey nature.

Speaking of which, i.e., the use of real materials (burlap, old gloves, bottle- 19 tops) in lieu of pigment, this is what one critic had to say about an exhibition of Assemblage at the Museum of Modern Art last year:

> Spotted throughout the show are indisputable works of art, accounting
> for a quarter or even a half of the total display. But the remainder are
> works of non-art, anti-art, and art substitutes that are the aesthetic
> counterparts of the social deficiencies that land people in the clink on
> charges of vagrancy. These aesthetic bankrupts . . . have no legitimate
> ideological roof over their heads and not the price of a square
> intellectual meal, much less a spiritual sandwich, in their pockets.

I quote these words of John Canaday of the *New York Times* as an example of 20 the kind of criticism which puts responsibility to an intelligent public above popularity with an intellectual coterie. Canaday has the courage to say what he thinks and the capacity to say it clearly: Two qualities notably absent from his profession.

Next to art, I would say that appreciation and evaluation in the field of mu- 21 sic is the most difficult. For it is rarely possible to judge a new composition at one hearing only. What seems confusing or fragmented at first might well become clear and organic a third time. Or it might not. The only salvation here for the listener is, again, an instinct born of experience and association which allows him to separate intent from accident, design from experimentation, and pretense from conviction. Much of contemporary music is, like its sister art, merely a reflection of the composer's own fragmentation: An absorption in self and symbols at the expense of communication with others. The artist, in short, says to the public: If you don't understand this, it's because you're dumb. I maintain that you are not. You may have to go part way or even halfway to meet the artist, but if you must go the whole way, it's his fault, not yours. Hold fast to that. And remember it too when you read new poetry, that estranged sister of music.

> A multitude of causes, unknown to former times, are now acting with
> a combined force to blunt the discriminating powers of the mind, and,
> unfitting it for all voluntary exertion, to reduce it to a state of almost
> savage torpor. The most effective of these causes are the great
> national events which are daily taking place and the increasing
> accumulation of men in cities, where the uniformity of their
> occupations produces a craving for extraordinary incident, which the
> rapid communication of intelligence hourly gratifies. To this tendency
> of life and manners, the literature and theatrical exhibitions of the
> country have conformed themselves.

This startlingly applicable comment was written in the year 1800 by 22 William Wordsworth in the preface to his "Lyrical Ballads"; and it has been cited by Edwin Muir in his recently published book "The Estate of Poetry." Muir states that poetry's effective range and influence have diminished alarmingly in the modern world. He believes in the inherent and indestructible qualities of the human mind and the great and permanent objects that act upon it, and suggests that the audience will increase when "poetry loses what obscurity is left in it by attempting greater themes, for great themes have to be stated clearly." If you keep that firmly in mind and resist, in Muir's words, "the vast dissemination of secondary objects that isolate us from the natural world," you have gone a long way toward equipping yourself for the examination of any work of art.

When you come to theatre, in this extremely hasty tour of the arts, you can   23
approach it on two different levels. You can bring to it anticipation and innocence, giving yourself up, as it were, to the life on the stage and reacting to it emotionally, if the play is good, or listlessly, if the play is boring; a part of the audience organism that expresses its favor by silence or laughter and its disfavor by coughing and rustling. Or you can bring to it certain critical faculties that may heighten, rather than diminish, your enjoyment.

You can ask yourselves whether the actors are truly in their parts or merely   24
projecting themselves; whether the scenery helps or hurts the mood; whether the playwright is honest with himself, his characters, and you. Somewhere along the line you can learn to distinguish between the true creative act and the false arbitrary gesture; between fresh observation and stale cliché; between the avant-garde play that is pretentious drivel and the avant-garde play that finds new ways to say old truths.

Purpose and craftsmanship—end and means—these are the keys to your   25
judgment in all the arts. What is this painter trying to say when he slashes a broad band of black across a white canvas and lets the edges dribble down? Is it a statement of violence? Is it a self-portrait? If it is *one* of these, has he made you believe it? Or is this a gesture of the ego or a form of therapy? If it shocks you, what does it shock you into?

And what of this tight little painting of bright flowers in a vase? Is the   26
painter saying anything new about flowers? Is it different from a million other canvases of flowers? Has it any life, any meaning, beyond its statement? Is there any pleasure in its forms or texture? The question is not whether a thing is abstract or representational, whether it is "modern" or conventional. The question, inexorably, is whether it is good. And this is a decision which only you, on the basis of instinct, experience, and association, can make for yourself. It takes independence and courage. It involves, moreover, the risk of wrong decision and the humility, after the passage of time, of recognizing it as such. As we grow and change and learn, our attitudes can change too, and what we once thought obscure or "difficult" can later emerge as coherent and illuminating. Entrenched prejudices, obdurate opinions are as sterile as no opinions at all.

Yet standards there are, timeless as the universe itself. And when you have   27
committed yourself to them, you have acquired a passport to that elusive but im-

mutable realm of truth. Keep it with you in the forests of bewilderment. And never be afraid to speak up.

1962

QUESTIONS FOR DISCUSSION

Content

a. What are the responsibilities of the audience? Do you feel qualified (based on Mannes's idea of responsibility) to "make the arts"? Do you think Mannes is asking too much, or not enough, of the audience?

b. Mannes addresses the reader as "you," and her tone is quite authoritative. (See, for example, lines such as this one in paragraph 9: "I think it is time you helped reverse this trend . . .") To whom is she speaking, and why might she want to sound authoritative? What does she want "you" to do?

c. Mannes bemoans what she considers to be a lack of quality, craftsmanship, etc., in the contemporary arts and gives reasons for this lack. But what other causes might explain the state of recent art? What reasons might Mannes have overlooked or conveniently left out of her essay?

d. In paragraph 8 Mannes implies that recent art is in the poor state it is because people no longer care about craftsmanship. Do you agree with Mannes's explanation of this cause-and-effect relationship?

e. Can you infer from the first paragraph what Mannes thinks of critics? Where else in her essay does she reveal her opinion of them?

f. Does she believe that *good* and *bad* can be defined? Does she define those terms? How do you define those terms? Can those terms be defined?

g. In paragraph 2, Mannes uses television programming as an example of the difficulty of defining *good* and *bad*. Which television programs do you consider good, and which, bad? What are your criteria for judgment?

h. In paragraph 4, Mannes states that "it is the audience which makes the arts," an opinion that is implied repeatedly in the essay. Do you agree with this opinion? What effects do you feel an audience has on the arts or on other products?

i. What are the steps Mannes recommends to acquire the standards necessary to determine what is good and what is bad?

j. Mannes focuses her discussion on literature, fine arts, music, and the performing arts. Would her essay apply to other things just as well (for example, architecture, fashion, furniture, even products such as appliances)? If not, do these things require entirely different standards of judgment?

k. Mannes wrote this essay in 1962. Does what she says hold true for today as well?

l. How would you answer the question posed by the title?

Strategy and Style

m. How effective are the examples of critical "double-talk" that Mannes includes in paragraphs 11 through 17? Have you ever come across similar double-talk in magazines, newspapers, or textbooks?

n. Mannes coins a new term in paragraph 9: "egotherapy." What is her implied definition of this word?

SUGGESTIONS FOR SHORT WRITING

a. Go through Mannes's essay and make a list of her suggestions for answering the question posed by the title.

b. Select a work of art in a museum or gallery and write your responses to the questions Mannes suggests in paragraphs 25 and 26. Rephrase her questions to fit the work you have chosen; for example, "What is this artist trying to say when she/he _____?" "Is this a statement of _____?" etc.

SUGGESTIONS FOR SUSTAINED WRITING

a. Using Mannes's suggestions for evaluating the arts, write a review of an art exhibit, play, novel, etc.

b. Write an essay in which you extend Mannes's suggestions for creating one's own standards of bad and good to student essays. Do the same standards fit? Does the "audience" determine the standards?

c. Write a review in which you deliberately try to imitate the critical double-talk that Mannes criticizes. Keep in mind your possible reasons for writing in this style and the effect your words will have on your readers.

d. Find a professional review you believe is especially full of meaningless double-talk and rewrite it in ordinary English. What happens to the authority and to the meaning of the review when it is "translated"?

Pain Is Not the Ultimate Enemy

Norman Cousins

Norman Cousins (1915–1990) served as editor of the prestigious Saturday Review *for more than four decades. From 1978, he was chairman of the editorial board of this journal and senior lecturer at the Medical School of the University of California at Los Angeles. Always interested in international affairs, Cousins was twice president of the World Association of Federalists and of the World Federalist Association. In 1963, he won the Eleanor Roosevelt Peace Award. Shortly thereafter, Cousins was stricken with a disease that left him almost totally paralyzed. His doctors advised him that there was no chance of recovery and that he would remain an invalid the rest of his life. Despite their gloomy predictions, he fought back, often prescribing his own treatment, the foundation of which was an unswerving conviction that he could beat the disease. He wrote two books about his experience,* The Celebration of Life *(1974) and* The Anatomy of an Illness *(1979), in which this selection first appeared. Among Cousins's other well-known works are* Talks with Nehru *(1951),* Who Speaks for Man? *(1953),* Present Tense *(1967),* Albert Schweitzer's Mission *(1985),* The Pathology of Power *(1987), and* Head First *(1990).*

Americans are probably the most pain-conscious people on the face of the earth. 1 For years we have had it drummed into us—in print, on radio, over television, in everyday conversation—that any hint of pain is to be banished as though it were the ultimate evil. As a result, we are becoming a nation of pill-grabbers and hypochondriacs, escalating the slightest ache into a searing ordeal.

We know very little about pain and what we don't know makes it hurt all the 2 more. Indeed, no form of illiteracy in the United States is so widespread or costly as ignorance about pain—what it is, what causes it, how to deal with it without panic. Almost everyone can rattle off the names of at least a dozen drugs that can deaden pain from every conceivable cause—all the way from headaches to hemorrhoids. There is far less knowledge about the fact that about 90 percent of pain is self-limiting, that it is not always an indication of poor health, and that, most frequently, it is the result of tension, stress, worry, idleness, boredom, frustration, suppressed rage, insufficient sleep, overeating, poorly balanced diet, smoking, excessive drinking, inadequate exercise, stale air, or any of the other abuses encountered by the human body in modern society.

The most ignored fact of all about pain is that the best way to eliminate it is 3 to eliminate the abuse. Instead, many people reach almost instinctively for the painkillers—aspirins, barbiturates, codeines, tranquilizers, sleeping pills, and dozens of other analgesics or desensitizing drugs.

Most doctors are profoundly troubled over the extent to which the medical 4 profession today is taking on the trappings of a pain-killing industry. Their offices are overloaded with people who are morbidly but mistakenly convinced that something dreadful is about to happen to them. It is all too evident that the campaign to get people to run to a doctor at the first sign of pain has boomeranged. Physicians find it difficult to give adequate attention to patients genuinely in need of expert

315

diagnosis and treatment because their time is soaked up by people who have nothing wrong with them except a temporary indisposition or a psychogenic ache.

Patients tend to feel indignant and insulted if the physician tells them he can 5 find no organic cause of pain. They tend to interpret the term "psychogenic" to mean that they are complaining of nonexistent symptoms. They need to be educated about the fact that many forms of pain have no underlying physical cause but are the result, as mentioned earlier, of tension, stress, or hostile factors in the general environment. Sometimes a pain may be a manifestation of "conversion hysteria" . . . the name given by Jean Charcot to physical symptoms that have their origins in emotional disturbances.

Obviously, it is folly for an individual to ignore symptoms that could be a 6 warning of a potentially serious illness. Some people are so terrified of getting bad news from a doctor that they allow their malaise to worsen, sometimes past the point of no return. Total neglect is not the answer to hypochondria. The only answer has to be increased education about the way the human body works, so that more people will be able to steer an intelligent course between promiscuous pill-popping and irresponsible disregard of genuine symptoms.

Of all forms of pain, none is more important for the individual to understand 7 than the "threshold" variety. Almost everyone has a telltale ache that is triggered whenever tension or fatigue reaches a certain point. It can take the form of a migraine-type headache or a squeezing pain deep in the abdomen or cramps or a pain in the lower back or even pain in the joints. The individual who has learned how to make the correlation between such threshold pains and their cause doesn't panic when they occur; he or she does something about relieving the stress and tension. Then, if the pain persists despite the absence of apparent cause, the individual will telephone the doctor.

If ignorance about the nature of pain is widespread, ignorance about the way 8 pain-killing drugs work is even more so. What is not generally understood is that many of the vaunted pain-killing drugs conceal the pain without correcting the underlying condition. They deaden the mechanism in the body that alerts the brain to the fact that something may be wrong. The body can pay a high price for suppression of pain without regard to its basic cause.

Professional athletes are sometimes severely disadvantaged by trainers 9 whose job it is to keep them in action. The more famous the athlete, the greater the risk that he or she may be subjected to extreme medical measures when injury strikes. The star baseball pitcher whose arm is sore because of a torn muscle or tissue damage may need sustained rest more than anything else. But his team is battling for a place in the World Series; so the trainer or team doctor, called upon to work his magic, reaches for a strong dose of Butazolidine or other powerful pain suppressants. Presto, the pain disappears! The pitcher takes his place on the mound and does superbly. That could be the last game, however, in which he is able to throw a ball with full strength. The drugs didn't repair the torn muscle or cause the damaged tissue to heal. What they did was to mask the pain, enabling the pitcher to throw hard, further damaging the torn muscle. Little wonder that so many star athletes are cut down in their prime, more the victims of overzealous treatment of their injuries than of the injuries themselves.

The king of all painkillers, of course, is aspirin. The U.S. Food and Drug Ad- 10 ministration permits aspirin to be sold without prescription, but the drug, contrary to popular belief, can be dangerous and, in sustained doses, potentially lethal. Aspirin is self-administered by more people than any other drug in the world. Some people are aspirin-poppers, taking ten or more a day. What they don't know is that the smallest dose can cause internal bleeding. Even more serious perhaps is the fact that aspirin is antagonistic to collagen, which has a key role in the formation of connective tissue. Since many forms of arthritis involve disintegration of the connective tissues, the steady use of aspirin can actually intensify the underlying arthritic condition.

Aspirin is not the only pain-killing drug, of course, that is known to have dan- 11 gerous side effects. Dr. Daphne A. Roe, of Cornell University, at a medical meeting in New York City in 1974, presented startling evidence of a wide range of hazards associated with sedatives and other pain suppressants. Some of these drugs seriously interfere with the ability of the body to metabolize food properly, producing malnutrition. In some instances, there is also the danger of bone-marrow depression, interfering with the ability of the body to replenish its blood supply.

Pain-killing drugs are among the greatest advances in the history of medi- 12 cine. Properly used, they can be a boon in alleviating suffering and in treating disease. But their indiscriminate and promiscuous use is making psychological cripples and chronic ailers out of millions of people. The unremitting barrage of advertising for pain-killing drugs, especially over television, has set the stage for a mass anxiety neurosis. Almost from the moment children are old enough to sit upright in front of a television screen, they are being indoctrinated into the hypochondriac's clamorous and morbid world. Little wonder so many people fear pain more than death itself.

It might be a good idea if concerned physicians and educators could get to- 13 gether to make knowledge about pain an important part of the regular school curriculum. As for the populace at large, perhaps some of the same techniques used by public-service agencies to make people cancer-conscious can be used to counteract the growing terror of pain and illness in general. People ought to know that nothing is more remarkable about the human body than its recuperative drive, given a modicum of respect. If our broadcasting stations cannot provide equal time for responses to the pain-killing advertisements, they might at least set aside a few minutes each day for common-sense remarks on the subject of pain. As for the Food and Drug Administration, it might be interesting to know why an agency that has energetically warned the American people against taking vitamins without prescriptions is doing so little to control over-the-counter sales each year of billions of pain-killing pills, some of which can do more harm than the pain they are supposed to suppress.

1979

QUESTIONS FOR DISCUSSION

Content

a. Why does Cousins believe that aspirin is a dangerous drug? How does his use of aspirin act as an illustration of his thesis?
b. Paragraph 8 may very well be the most important paragraph in this selection. Why?
c. Cousins sometimes refers to medical authorities. What purpose do such references serve? Are they effective?
d. How would you describe the audience Cousins is addressing? Analyze the details, vocabulary, and illustrations he uses as clues.
e. What can you infer about Cousins' opinions of the medical profession, the pharmaceutical industry, and the FDA?
f. Who or what does Cousins imply is mainly at fault for causing or worsening pain?
g. According to Cousins, what are some typical causes of pain? What does he mean when he claims that "90 percent of pain is self-limiting" (paragraph 2)?
h. What are some of the indications that the "medical profession . . . is taking on the trappings of the pain-killing industry" (paragraph 4)?

Strategy and Style

i. What are the solutions Cousins suggests for remedying ignorance about pain and painkillers? Why might he have decided to end rather than to begin his essay with them?
j. How does Cousins define "threshold" (paragraph 7) pain?
k. Describe Cousins's tone in this essay. What is his attitude toward painkillers, and how is that attitude conveyed by his language?

SUGGESTIONS FOR SHORT WRITING

a. Write about a time when you overcame pain of some sort. How did you overcome it?
b. Consider the current state of your health. Write a letter to yourself, proposing some ways in which to improve it.

SUGGESTIONS FOR SUSTAINED WRITING

a. You may know a hypochondriac—someone who has convinced himself/herself that he/she is, has been, or will be afflicted by a variety of serious illnesses. Describe such a person and explain his/her thinking. In doing so, try to demonstrate the fact that hypochondria is itself a dangerous disease. Illustrate some of its more adverse effects, whether physical or emotional, on the "patient." Assume that your reader knows very little about the subject, and provide sufficient explanatory detail to make your point clear.

b. Cousins is obviously warning us about our over reliance on medication to relieve pain. What other methods of trying to cope with pain have you found effective? Illustrate these methods as completely as you can. It would be wise to remember that some readers of your paper might be skeptical of pain-relieving methods that do not require the taking of medication, so be as convincing as you can without exaggerating.

c. Write a counterargument to Cousins's essay in which you try to convince him, or readers who would agree with him, that painkillers are not as dangerous as he says they are.

Watching the Grasshopper Get the Goodies

Ellen Goodman

Ellen Goodman was born in Boston in 1941. She received her bachelor's degree from Radcliffe College and attended Harvard University on a Nieman Fellowship. Goodman began her journalistic career with Newsweek, *then moved to the* Detroit Free Press, *and is now writing for the* Boston Globe. *Her syndicated column, "At Large," appears in more than 200 newspapers across the country. She has won several awards for her commentary, including a Pulitzer Prize in 1980. Many of her columns have been collected in* Close to Home *(1979);* At Large *(1981), in which "Watching the Grasshopper" appears; and* Value Judgments *(1993).*

I don't usually play the great American game called Categories. There are already 1 too many ways to divide us into opposing teams, according to age, race, sex and favorite flavors. Every time we turn around, someone is telling us that the whole country is made up of those who drive pick-up trucks and those who do not, and then analyzing what this means in terms of the Middle East.

Still, it occurs to me that if we want to figure out why people are angry right 2 now, it's not a bad idea to see ourselves as a nation of planners and nonplanners. It's the planners these days who are feeling penalized, right down to their box score at the bank.

The part of us which is most visibly and vocally infuriated by inflation, for 3 example, isn't our liberal or conservative side but, rather, our planning side. Inflation devastates our attempts to control our futures—to budget and predict and expect. It particularly makes fools out of the people who saved then to buy now. To a certain extent, it rewards instant gratification and makes a joke out of our traditional notions of preparation.

It is no news bulletin that the people who dove over their heads into the real- 4 estate market a few years ago are now generally better off than those who dutifully decided to save up for a larger down payment. With that "larger down payment" they can now buy two double-thick rib lambchops and a partridge in a pear tree.

But inflation isn't the only thing that leaves the planners feeling betrayed. 5 There are other issues that find them actively pitched against the nonplanners.

We all know families who saved for a decade to send their kids to college. 6 A college diploma these days costs about the same amount as a Mercedes-Benz. Of course, the Mercedes lasts longer and has a higher trade-in value. But the most devoted parent can be infuriated to discover that a neighboring couple who spent its income instead of saving is now eligible for college financial aid, while they are not. To the profligate go the spoils.

This can happen anywhere on the economic spectrum. There is probably 7 only one mother in the annals of the New York welfare rolls to save up a few thousand dollars in hopes of getting off aid. But she would have been better off spending it. When she was discovered this year, the welfare department took the money back. She, too, was penalized for planning.

320

In these crimped times, the Planned Parents of the Purse are increasingly an-   8
noyed at other parents—whether they are unwed or on welfare or just prolific. For
the first time in my own town, you can hear families with few children complaining out loud at the tax bill for the public schooling of families with many children.

One man I heard even suggesting charging tuition for the third child. He ad-   9
mitted, "It's not a very generous attitude, I know. But I'm not feeling very generous these days." He is suffering from planner's warts.

At the same time I've talked with friends whose parents prepared, often with   10
financial difficulty, for their "old age" and illness. They feel sad when this money
goes down a nursing home drain, but furious when other people who didn't save
get this same care for free.

Now we are all aware that if many people don't plan their economic lives,   11
it may be because they can't. It does no one any good to keep the cashless out of
college, to stash the old and poor into elderly warehouses, to leave the "extra" children illiterate. We do want to help others, but we also want our own efforts to make
a difference.

There is nothing that grates a planner more than seeing a nonplanner profit.   12
It's as if the ant had to watch the grasshopper get the goodies.

Our two notions about what's fair end up on opposite sides. It isn't fair if the   13
poor get treated badly, and it isn't fair if those who work and save, plan and post-
pone aren't given a better shake. We want the winners to be the deserving. Only
there is no divining rod for the deserving.

The hard part is to create policies that are neither unkind nor insane. It is, af-   14
ter all, madness not to reward the kind of behavior we want to encourage. If we
want the ranks of the planners to increase in this massive behavior-modification
program called society, we have to give them the rewards, instead of the outrage.

1981

QUESTIONS FOR DISCUSSION

Content

a. What purpose might Goodman have had in starting her essay with a criticism
   of categorizing and then turning around and categorizing people into "planners
   and nonplanners"? Into which category does she implicitly place herself?
b. According to the author, what happens when you make long-range plans? Is
   she suggesting that people should never plan?
c. What might be her motives for writing this essay?
d. To whom is Goodman probably writing? How would you describe the ideal
   reader of this essay (age, occupation, level of education, opinions, etc.)?
e. What or whom does she specify as the cause of people's anger? Just what are
   people angry about?

f. To what does the title allude? Why is the title appropriate?

g. Do you think that Goodman paints an overly pessimistic picture of what happens as a result of planning?

h. What type of person is Goodman criticizing in the first paragraph? What harmful effects could "the great American game called Categories" have? Would this criticism also apply to those essays in Chapter 5?

Strategy and Style

i. What rhetorical devices does Goodman use to protect herself from counterarguments?

j. What statements in this essay are sarcastic? What does this sarcasm reveal about Goodman? Does it help to place her in one of her two categories?

k. What action is Goodman proposing in the last paragraph? Is the tone of this paragraph different from the rest of the essay?

SUGGESTIONS FOR SHORT WRITING

a. Create another fable that would make the same point that Goodman makes in her essay. Write an outline for the fable or briefly describe the characters.

b. Are you a planner or a nonplanner? Write an anecdote that illustrates that you are one or the other.

SUGGESTIONS FOR SUSTAINED WRITING

a. In this essay, Goodman focuses on money as the cause of unhappiness among planners. Could there be other causes as well? Write an essay in which you show that other things may have caused this unhappiness.

b. Write an essay about a practice, law, or situation that you feel is unfair, not only to you but to a large segment of society. Show the harmful effects this has on people and suggest what might be done to correct the situation.

c. Find another fable with a real-life equivalent. Using this fable as a starting point, describe the real-life situation, explain what is wrong with the situation and what has caused it, and suggest ways to correct the problem.

White Guilt

Shelby Steele

Shelby Steele (b. 1946) is a social critic who teaches literature and writing at San Jose State University. As an undergraduate, he led a student civil rights group called SCOPE, which was philosophically linked to Martin Luther King, Jr.'s, Southern Christian Leadership Conference. Later, however, influenced by Malcolm X, he shifted his energies to the black power movement. While studying for his MA in sociology at Southern Illinois University, he taught African-American literature in an experimental program designed to provide college credit to blacks who could not afford tuition. His experiences as an activist and educator provide a foundation for his sometimes controversial writings. His most well-known book is The Content of Our Character: A New Vision of Race in America *(1990), which won the National Book Critics Circle Award. He also helped to create "Seven Days in Bensonhurst," a film documentary about the racial unrest following the murder of a black teenager in a white New York City neighborhood in 1989. In a 1990* New York Times *profile, Steele said, "Some people say I shine a harsh light on difficult problems. But I never shine a light on anything I haven't experienced or write about fear I don't see in myself first."*

I don't remember hearing the phrase "white guilt" very much before the 1 mid1960s. Growing up black in the 1950s, I never had the impression that whites were much disturbed by guilt when it came to blacks. When I would stray into the wrong restaurant in pursuit of a hamburger, it didn't occur to me that the waitress was unduly troubled by guilt when she asked me to leave. I can see now that possibly she was, but then all I saw was her irritability at having to carry out so unpleasant a task. If there was guilt, it was mine for having made an imposition of myself. I can remember feeling a certain sympathy for such people, as if I was victimizing them by drawing them out of an innocent anonymity into the unasked-for role of racial policemen. Occasionally they came right out and asked me to feel sorry for them. A caddymaster at a country club told my brother and me that he was doing us a favor by not letting us caddy at this white club and that we should try to understand his position, "put yourselves in my shoes." Our color had brought this man anguish and, if a part of that anguish was guilt, it was not as immediate to me as my own guilt. I smiled at the man to let him know he shouldn't feel bad and then began my long walk home. Certainly I also judge him a coward, but in that era his cowardice was something I had to absorb.

In the 1960s, particularly the black-is-beautiful late 1960s, this absorption 2 of another's cowardice was no longer necessary. The lines of moral power, like plates in the earth, had shifted. White guilt became so palpable you could see it on people. At the time what it looked like to my eyes was a remarkable loss of authority. And what whites lost in authority, blacks gained. You cannot feel guilty about anyone without giving away power to them. Suddenly, this huge vulnerability had opened up in whites and, as a black, you had the power to step right into it. In fact, black power all but demanded that you do so. What shocked me in the

323

late 1960s, after the helplessness I had felt in the fifties, was that guilt had changed the nature of the white man's burden from the administration of inferiors to the uplift of equals—from the obligations of dominance to the urgencies of repentance.

I think what made the difference between the fifties and sixties, at least as far as white guilt was concerned, was that whites underwent an archetypal Fall. Because of the immense turmoil of the civil rights movement, and later the black-power movement, whites were confronted for more than a decade with their willingness to participate in, or comply with, the oppression of blacks, their indifference to human suffering and denigration, their capacity to abide evil for their own benefit and in the defiance of their own sacred principles. The 1964 Civil Rights Bill that bestowed equality under the law on blacks was also, in a certain sense, an admission of white guilt. Had white society not been wrong, there would have been no need for such a bill. In this bill the nation acknowledged its fallenness, its lack of racial innocence, and confronted the incriminating self-knowledge that it had rationalized for many years a flagrant injustice. Denial is a common way of handling guilt, but in the 1960s there was little will left for denial except in the most recalcitrant whites. With this defense lost there was really only one road back to innocence—through actions and policies that would bring redemption.

In the 1960s the need for white redemption from racial guilt became the most powerful, yet unspoken, element in America's social-policy-making process, first giving rise to the Great Society and then to a series of programs, policies, and laws that sought to make black equality and restitution a national mission. Once America could no longer deny its guilt, it went after redemption, or at least the look of redemption, and did so with a vengeance. Yet today, some twenty years later, study after study tells us that by many measures the gap between blacks and whites is widening rather than narrowing. A University of Chicago study indicates that segregation is more entrenched in American cities today than ever imagined. A National Research Council study notes the "status of blacks relative to whites (in housing and education) has stagnated or regressed since the early seventies." A follow-up to the famous Kerner Commission Report warns that blacks are as much at risk today of becoming a "nation within a nation" as we were twenty years ago, when the original report was made.

I think the white need for redemption has contributed to this tragic situation by shaping our policies regarding blacks in ways that may deliver the look of innocence to society and its institutions but that do very little actually to uplift blacks. The specific effect of this hidden need has been to bend social policy more toward reparation for black oppression than toward the much harder and more mundane work of black uplift and development. Rather than facilitate the development of blacks to achieve parity with whites, these programs and policies—affirmative action is a good example—have tended to give blacks special entitlements that in many cases are of no use because blacks lack the development that would put us in a position to take advantage of them. I think the reason there has been more entitlement than development is (along with black power) the unacknowledged white need for redemption—not true redemption, which would have concentrated policy on black development, but the appearance of redemption, which requires only that society, in the name of development, seem to be paying back its former victims with preferences. One of the effects of entitlements, I believe, has been to encourage in blacks a dependency both on entitlements and on the white guilt that generates them. Even when it serves ideal justice, bounty from another man's guilt weakens. While this is not the only factor in black "stagnation" and "regression," I believe it is one very potent factor.

It is easy enough to say that white guilt too often has the effect of bending 6 social policies in the wrong direction. But what exactly is this guilt, and how does it work in American life?

I think white guilt, in its broad sense, springs from a knowledge of ill-gotten 7 advantage. More precisely, it comes from the juxtaposition of this knowledge with the inevitable gratitude one feels for being white rather than black in America. Given the moral instincts of human beings, it is all but impossible to enjoy an ill-gotten advantage, much less to feel at least secretly grateful for it, without consciously or unconsciously experiencing guilt. If, as Kierkegaard writes, "innocence is ignorance," then guilt must always involve knowledge. White Americans *know* that their historical advantage comes from the subjugation of an entire people. So, even for whites today for whom racism is anathema, there is no escape from the knowledge that makes for guilt. Racial guilt simply accompanies the condition of being white in America.

I do not believe that this guilt is a crushing anguish for most whites, but I do 8 believe it constitutes a continuing racial vulnerability—an openness to racial culpability—that is a thread in white life, sometimes felt, sometimes not, but ever present as a potential feeling. In the late 1960s almost any black could charge this vulnerability with enough current for a white person to feel it. I had a friend who had developed this activity into a sort of specialty. I don't think he meant to be mean, though certainly he was mean. I think he was, in that hyperbolic era, exhilarated by the discovery that his race, which had long been a liability, now gave him a certain edge—that white guilt was the true force behind black power. To feel this power he would sometimes set up what he called "race experiments." Once I watched him stop a white businessman in the men's room of a large hotel and convince him to increase his tip to the black attendant from one to twenty dollars.

My friend's tactic was very simple, even corny. Out of the attendant's 9 earshot he asked the man simply to look at the attendant, a frail, elderly, and very dark man in a starched white smock that made the skin on his neck and face look as leathery as a turtle's. He sat listlessly, pathetically, on a straight-backed chair next to a small table on which sat a stack of hand towels and a silver plate for tips. Since the attendant offered no service whatever beyond the handing out of towels, one could only conclude the hotel management offered his lowly presence as flattery to their patrons, as an opportunity for that easy noblesse oblige that could reassure even the harried and weary traveling salesman of his superior station. My friend was quick to make this point to the businessman and to say that no white man would do in this job. But when the businessman put the single back in his wallet and took out a five, my friend only sneered. Did he understand the tragedy of a life spent this way, of what it must be like to earn one's paltry living as a symbol of inferiority? And did he realize that his privilege as an affluent white businessman (ironically he had just spent the day trying to sell a printing press to the Black Muslims for their newspaper *Mohammed Speaks*) was connected to the deprivation of this man and others like him?

But then my friend made a mistake that ended the game. In the heat of argument, which until then had only been playfully challenging, he inadvertently mentioned his father. This stopped the victim cold and his eyes turned inward. "What about your father?" the businessman asked. My friend replied, "He had a hard life, that's all." "How did he have a hard life?" the businessman asked. Now my friend was on the defensive. I knew he did not get along with his father, a bitter man who worked nights in a factory and demanded that the house be dark and silent all day. My friend blamed his father's bitterness on racism, but I knew he had not meant to exploit his own pain in this silly "experiment." Things had gotten too close to home, but he didn't know how to get out of the situation without losing face. Now, caught in his own trap, he did what he least wanted to do. He gave forth the rage he truly felt to a white stranger in a public men's room. "My father never had a chance," he said with the kind of anger that could easily turn to tears. "He never had a freakin' chance. Your father had all the goddamn chances, and you know he did. You sell printing presses to black people and make thousands and your father probably lives down in Fat City, Florida, all because you're white." On and on he went in this vein, using—against all that was honorable in him—his own profound racial pain to extract a flash of guilt from a white man he didn't even know.

He got more than a flash. The businessman was touched. His eyes became mournful, and finally he simply said, "You're right. Your people got a raw deal." He took a twenty dollar bill from his wallet and walked over and dropped it in the old man's tip plate. When he was gone my friend and I could not look at the old man, nor could we look at each other.

It is obvious that this was a rather shameful encounter for all concerned— my friend and I, as his silent accomplice, trading on our racial pain, tampering with a stranger for no reason, and the stranger then buying his way out of the situation for twenty dollars, a sum that was generous by one count and cheap by another. It was not an encounter of people but of historical grudges and guilts. Yet, when I think about it now twenty years later, I see that it had all the elements of a paradigm that I believe has been very much at the heart of racial policy-making in America since the 1960s.

My friend did two things that made this businessman vulnerable to his guilt—that brought his guilt into the situation as a force. First he put this man in touch with his own knowledge of his ill-gotten advantage as a white. The effect of this was to disallow the man any pretense of racial innocence, to let him know that, even if he was not the sort of white who used the word *nigger* around the dinner table, he still had reason to feel racial guilt. But, as disarming as this might have been, it was too abstract to do much more than crack open this man's vulnerability, to expose him to the logic of white guilt. This was the five-dollar, intellectual sort of guilt. The twenty dollars required something more visceral. In achieving this, the second thing my friend did was something he had not intended to do, something that ultimately brought him as much shame as he was doling out: He made a display of his own racial pain and anger. (What brought him shame was not the pain and anger, but his trading on them for what turned out to be a mere twenty bucks.) The effect of this display was to reinforce the man's knowledge of ill-gotten advantage, to give credibility and solidity to it by putting a face on it. Here was human testimony, a young black beside himself at the thought of his father's racially constricted life. The pain of one man evidenced the knowledge of the other. When the businessman listened to my friend's pain, his racial guilt—normally only one source of guilt lying dormant among others—was called out like a neglected debt he would finally have to settle. An ill-gotten advantage is not hard to bear—it can be marked up to fate—until it touches the genuine human pain it has brought into the world. This is the pain that hardens guilty knowledge.

Such knowledge is a powerful influence when it becomes conscious. What 14 makes it so powerful is the element of fear that guilt always carries, the fear of what the guilty knowledge says about us. Guilt makes us afraid for ourselves, and thus generates as much self-preoccupation as concern for others. The nature of this preoccupation is always the redemption of innocence, the reestablishment of good feeling about oneself.

In this sense, the fear for the self that is buried in all guilt is a pressure to- 15 ward selfishness. It can lead us to put our own need for innocence above our concern for the problem that made us feel guilt in the first place. But this fear for the self does not only inspire selfishness; it also becomes a pressure to *escape* the guilt-inducing situation. When selfishness and escapism are at work, we are no longer interested in the source of our guilt and, therefore, no longer concerned with an authentic redemption from it. Then we only want the look of redemption, the gesture of concern that will give us the appearance of innocence and escape from the situation. Obviously the businessman did not put twenty dollars in the tip plate because he thought it would uplift black Americans. He did it selfishly for the appearance of concern and for the escape it afforded him.

This is not to say that guilt is never the right motive for doing good works 16 or showing concern, only that it is a very dangerous one because of its tendency to draw us into self-preoccupation and escapism. Guilt is a civilizing emotion when the fear for the self that it carries is contained—a containment that allows guilt to be more selfless and that makes genuine concern possible. I think this was the kind of guilt that, along with the other forces, made the 1964 Civil Rights Bill possible. But since then I believe too many of our social policies related to race have been shaped by the fearful underside of guilt.

Black power evoked white guilt and made it a force in American institutions, 17 very much in the same way as my friend brought it to life in the businessman. Few people volunteer for guilt. Usually others make us feel it. It was the expression of black anger and pain that hardened the guilty knowledge of white ill-gotten advantage. And black power—whether from militant fringe groups, the civil rights establishment, or big city political campaigns—knew exactly the kind of white guilt it was after. It wanted to trigger the kind of white guilt in which whites fear for their own decency and innocence; it wanted the guilt of white self-preoccupation and escapism. Always at the heart of black power, in whatever form, has been a profound anger at what was done to blacks and an equally profound feeling that there should be reparations. But a sober white guilt (in which fear for the self is still contained) seeks a strict fairness—the 1964 Civil Rights Bill that guaranteed equality under the law. It is of little value when one is after more than fairness. So black power made its mission to have whites fear for their innocence, to feel a visceral guilt from which they would have to seek a more profound redemption. In such redemption was the possibility of black reparation. Black power upped the ante on white guilt.

With black power, all of the elements of the hidden paradigm that shape   18
America's race-related social policy were in place. Knowledge of ill-gotten advantage could now be shown and deepened by black power into the sort of guilt from which institutions could only redeem themselves by offering more than fairness—by offering forms of reparation and compensation for past injustice. I believe this bent our policies toward racial entitlements at the expense of racial development. In 1964, one of the assurances Senator Hubert Humphrey and others had to give Congress to get the landmark Civil Rights Bill passed was that the bill would not in any way require employers to use racial preferences to rectify racial imbalances. But this was before the explosion of black power in the late 1960s, before the hidden paradigm was set in motion. After black power, racial preferences became the order of the day.

If this paradigm brought blacks entitlements, it also brought the continuation   19
of the most profound problem in American society, the invisibility of blacks as a people. The white guilt that this paradigm elicits is the kind of guilt that preoccupies whites with their own innocence and pressures them toward escapism—twenty dollars in the plate and out the door. With this guilt, as opposed to the contained guilt of genuine concern, whites tend to see only their own need for quick redemption. Blacks then become a means to this redemption and, as such, they must be seen as generally "less than" others. Their needs are "special," "unique," "different." They are seen exclusively along the dimension of their victimization, so that they become "different" people with whom whites can negotiate entitlements but never fully see as people like themselves. Guilt that preoccupies people with their own innocence blinds them to those who make them feel guilty. This, of course, is not racism, and yet it has the same effect as racism since it makes blacks something of a separate species for whom normal standards and values do not automatically apply.

Nowhere is this more evident today than in American universities. At some   20
of America's most elite universities administrators have granted concessions in response to black student demands (black power) that all but sanction racial separatism on campus—black "theme" dorms, black student unions, black yearbooks, homecoming dances, and so forth. I don't believe administrators sincerely believe

in these separatist concessions. Most of them are liberals who see racial separatism as wrong. But black student demands pull administrators into the paradigm of self-preoccupied white guilt, whereby they seek a quick redemption by offering special entitlements that go beyond fairness. As a result, black students become all but invisible to them. Though blacks have the lowest grade point average of any racial group in American universities, administrators never sit down with them and "demand" in kind that black students bring their grades up to par. The paradigm of white guilt makes the real problems of black students secondary to the need for white redemption. It also cuts administrators off from their own values, which would most certainly discourage racial separatism and encourage higher academic performance for black students. Lastly, it makes for escapist policies. There is no difference between giving black students a separate lounge and leaving twenty dollars in the tip plate on the way out the door.

1990

QUESTIONS FOR DISCUSSION

Content

a. In paragraph 2 Steele writes, "You cannot feel guilty about anyone without giving away power to them." What does he mean by this?

b. According to Steele, what has caused white guilt? Trace the causal links he describes.

c. At the end of paragraph 6, Steele asks, "But what exactly is this guilt, and how does it work in American life?" How does he answer his question?

d. What does he mean when he says that "white guilt was the true force behind black power" (paragraph 8)?

e. What happened in the men's room between Steele's friend and the white businessman (paragraphs 8–13)? What was Steele's friend's "racial experiment"? What went "wrong" and why?

f. Why does the businessman put the twenty dollars in the tip plate?

g. How does Steele define *guilt?* What is the difference between the general term *guilt* and the specific term *white guilt?*

h. According to Steele, what effects does white guilt have on society? What are both its positive and its negative effects?

i. What is the relationship between black power and white guilt?

j. According to Steele, what did the Civil Rights Act of 1964 cause?

Strategy and Style

k. Look up *visceral,* a key word in paragraphs 13 and 17. What does this word mean in the context of these paragraphs? What other words does Steele use in these paragraphs to help define the word? Why was being visceral a problem?

l. What is the effect on you of the example of the "racial experiment"? Is it more of a "visceral" effect or an intellectual effect? What effect might Steele have intended with this example?

m. Look up *paradigm* (paragraph 20). What does the word mean by itself? What does it mean in the phrase "paradigm of white guilt"?

n. How would you characterize the tone of this essay? Does Steele sound calm, angry, impassioned, etc.?

SUGGESTIONS FOR SHORT WRITING

a. Use the statement from the first of the Questions for Discussion and describe an event or two from your own life that illustrates it.

b. Summarize this essay in the form of a letter to your parents telling them about the reading you are doing for this class. Besides your summary, mention the one or two things that strike you as most important about the essay.

SUGGESTIONS FOR SUSTAINED WRITING

a. Do some research into a particular period or event mentioned by Steele—the black power movement of the late 1960s, or the 1964 Civil Rights Act, for examples. Do not merely summarize your research, but use it to come to an understanding of Steele's essay. You may wish to write the paper as a comparison of how you understood the essay on a first reading to how you understand it after your research.

b. By the end of the essay Steele begins to suggest ways to solve the problem of racial separatism; however, he does not elaborate on his suggestions. Write an essay in which you pick up on the points raised in paragraph 20, and present a detailed solution to the problem.

Where Have All the Parents Gone?

Barbara Dafoe Whitehead

Barbara Dafoe Whitehead (b. 1944) is a social historian who heads the Family in American Culture Project for the Institute of American Values. She has written many articles about family issues, including this essay, which originally appeared in New Perspectives Quarterly *in 1990.*

"Invest in kids," George Bush mused during his 1988 presidential campaign, "I 1 like it." Apparently so do others. A growing number of corporate CEOs and educators, elected officials and child-welfare advocates have embraced the same language. "Invest in kids" is the bumper-sticker for an important new cause, aptly tagged the *kids as capital* argument. It runs as follows:

America's human capital comes in two forms: The active work force and the 2 prospective work force. The bulk of tomorrow's workers are today's children, of course. So children make up much of the stockpile of America's potential human capital.

If we look at them as tomorrow's workers, we begin to appreciate our stake 3 in today's children. They will determine when we can retire, how well we can live in retirement, how generous our health insurance will be, how strong our social safety net, how orderly our society. What's more, today's children will determine how successfully we compete in the global economy. They will be going head-to-head against Japanese, Korean, and West German children.

Unfortunately, American children aren't prepared to run the race, let alone 4 win it. Many are illiterate, undernourished, impaired, unskilled, poor. Consider the children who started first grade in 1986: 14 percent were illegitimate; 15 percent were physically or emotionally handicapped; 15 percent spoke another language other than English; 28 percent were poor; and fully 40 percent could be expected to live in a single-parent home before they reached eighteen. Given falling birth rates, this future work force is small—all the more reason to worry about its poor quality. So "invest in kids" is not the cry of the soft-hearted altruist but the call of the hardheaded realist.

Kids as capital has caught on because it responds to a broad set of 5 national concerns. Whether one is worried about the rise of the underclass, the decline of the family, our standing in the global economy, the nation's level of educational performance, or intergenerational conflict, kids as capital seems to offer an answer.

Further, *kids as capital* offers the rationale for a new coalition for child- 6 welfare programs. The argument reaches beyond the community of traditional children's advocates and draws business into the child-saving fold. American corporations clearly have a stake in tomorrow's work force as they don't have in today's children. *Kids as capital* gives the toughminded, fifty-five-year-old CEO a reason to "care" about the eight-year-old, Hispanic school girl.

331

Nevertheless, the argument left unchallenged could easily become yet an- 7 other "feel-good" formula that doesn't work. Worse, it could end up betraying those it seeks to save—the nation's children.

First, *kids as capital* departs from a classic American vision of the future. 8 Most often, our history has been popularly viewed as progressive, with each generation breaking with and improving on the past. As an immigrant nation, we have always measured our progress through the progress of our children; they have been the bearers of the dream.

Kids as capital turns this optimistic view on its head. It conjures up a picture 9 of a dark and disorderly future. Essentially, kids as capital is dystopic—closer to the spirit of *Blade Runner* and *Black Rain* than *Wizard of Oz* or *It's a Wonderful Life.* Children, in this view, do not bear the dream. They carry the seeds of our destruction. In short, *kids as capital* plays on our fears, rather than our hopes. It holds out the vision of a troubled future in order to secure a safer and more orderly present.

There is something troubling, too, in such an instrumental view of children. 10 To define them narrowly as tomorrow's wonders is to strip them of their full status as humans, as children: Kids can't be kids; they can only be embryonic workers. And treating *kids as capital* makes it easier to measure them solely through IQ tests, class standing, SAT scores, drop-out ratios, physical fitness tests. This leaves no place in the society for the slow starter, the handicapped, the quirky, and the nonconforming.

Yet *kids as capital* has an even more serious flaw. It evades the central fact 11 of life for American children: They have parents.

As we all know, virtually every child in America grows up in a family with one 12 or more parents. Parents house children. Parents feed children. Parents clothe children. Parents nurture and protect children. Parents instruct children in everything from using a fork to driving a car. To be sure, there have been vast changes in family life, and, increasingly, parents must depend on teachers, doctors, day-care workers, and technology to help care for and educate their children. Even so, these changes haven't altered one fundamental fact: In American society, parents still bear the primary responsibility for the material and spiritual welfare of children. As our teachers and counselors and politicians keep reminding us, everything begins at home. So, if today's children are in trouble, it's because today's parents are in trouble.

As recently as a dozen years ago, it was the central argument of an ambi- 13 tious report by the Carnegie Council on Children. The Council put it plainly: "The best way to help children tomorrow is to support parents today." Yet, that view has been lost. The *kids as capital* argument suppresses the connection between parents and children. It imagines that we can improve the standing of children without improving the standing of the parents. In the new rhetoric, it is hard even to find the word "parent." Increasingly, kids are portrayed as standing alone out there somewhere, cosmically parent-free.

As a result, *kids as capital* ignores rather than addresses one of the most im- 14 portant changes in American life: The decline in the power and standing of the nation's parents.

Only a generation ago, parents stood at the center of society. First of all, 15 there were so many of them—fully half the nation's households in 1960 were parent households with one or more children under eighteen. Moreover, parents looked alike—Dad worked and Mom stayed at home. And parents marched through the stages of childbearing and child rearing in virtual lockstep: Most couples who married in the 1940s and 1950s finished having their 3.2 children by the time they were in their late twenties.

Their demographic dominance meant two things: First, it made for broad **16** common ground in child rearing. Parents could do a great deal to support each other in raising the new generation. They could, and did, create a culture hospitable to children. Secondly, it made for political clout. When so many adults were parents and so many parents were part of an expanding consumer economy, private and public interests converged. The concerns of parents—housing, health, education—easily found their way into the national agenda. Locally, too, parents were dominant. In some postwar suburbs like Levittown, Pennsylvania, three-quarters of all residents were either parents or children under ten. Not surprisingly, there was little dissent when it came to building a new junior high or establishing a summer recreation program or installing a new playground. What's more, parents and kids drove the consumer economy. Every time they bought a pair of sneakers or a new bike, they were acting in the nation's best interest.

Behind this, of course, lurked a powerful pronatal ideology. Parenthood was **17** the definitive credential of adulthood. More than being married, more than getting a job, it was having a child that baptized you as an adult in postwar America. In survey after survey, postwar parents rated children above marriage itself as the greatest reward of private life. For a generation forced to make personal sacrifices during the Depression and the war, having children and pursuing a private life represented a new kind of freedom.

By the 1970s, parents no longer enjoyed so central a place in the society. To **18** baby boom children, postwar family life seemed suffocating and narrow. Women, in particular, wanted room to breathe. The rights movements of the sixties and seventies overturned the pronatal ideology, replacing it with an ideology of choice. Adults were free to choose among many options: Single, married, or divorced; career-primary or career-secondary; parent, stepparent, or child-free.

Thus, parenthood lost its singular status. It no longer served as the definitive **19** credential of maturity and adult achievement. In fact, as careers and personal fulfillment beckoned, parenthood seemed just the opposite: A serious limitation on personal growth and success. As Gloria Steinem put it, "I either gave birth to someone else or I gave birth to myself."

As the pronatal ideology vanished, so did the close connection between private families and the public interest. Raising children was no longer viewed as a valuable contribution to the society, an activity that boosted the economy, built citizen participation, and increased the nation's confidence in the future. Instead, it became one option among many. No longer a moral imperative, child rearing was just another "lifestyle choice."

Viewed this way, raising children looked like an economic disaster. Starting **21** out, parents had to shell out $3,000 for basic prenatal care and maternity costs; $3,000–$5,000 per child for day care; and $2,500 for the basic baby basket of goods and services. Crib-to-college costs for middle-class Americans could run as high as $135,000 per child. And, increasingly, the period of economic dependency for children stretched well beyond age eighteen. College tuitions and start-up subsidies for the new college graduate became part of the economic burden of parenthood. In an ad campaign, Manufacturers Hanover Trust gave prospective parents fair warning: "If you want a bundle of joy; you'll need a bundle of money."

Hard-pressed younger Americans responded to these new realities in several 22 ways. Some simply chose not to have children. Others decided to have one or two, but only after they had a good job and solid prospects. Gradually, the number of parent households in the nation declined from one-half to one-third, and America faced a birth dearth.

For those who chose the parent option, there was only one way to face up to 23 the new economic pressures of child rearing: Work longer and harder outside the home. For all but the extremely well-off, a second income became essential. But in struggling to pay the bills, parents seemed to be short-changing their children in another way. They weren't taking their moral responsibilities seriously enough. They weren't spending enough time with their kids. They weren't reading to the children or playing with the kids or supervising homework. And, most important, they weren't teaching good values.

This emerging critique marked a dramatic change in the way society viewed 24 parents. In the postwar period, the stereotypical parent was self-sacrificing, responsible, caring, attentive—an impossible standard, to be sure, but one that lent enormous popular support and approval to adults engaged in the messy and difficult work of raising children. Cruel, abusive, self-absorbed parents might exist, but the popular culture failed to acknowledge them. It was not until parents began to lose their central place in the society that this flattering image faded. Then, quite rapidly, the dominant image of The Good Parent gave way to a new and equally powerful image—the image of The Bad Parent.

The shift occurred in two stages. The first-stage critique emerged in the sev- 25 enties and focused on an important new figure: The working mother. Working mothers were destroying their children and the family, conservative critics charged. They weren't feeding kids wholesome meals, they weren't taking the kids to church, they weren't serving as moral exemplars. Liberals sided with working mothers, but conceded that they were struggling with some new and difficult issues: Was day care as good as mother care? Was quality time good enough? Were the rewards of twelve-hour workdays great enough to make up for the loss of sleep and leisure-time? Where did the mother of a feverish child belong—at the crib or at her desk?

On the whole, the first-stage critique was a sympathetic critique. In its view, 26 parents might be affected by stress and guilt, but they weren't yet afflicted by serious pathology. After all, in the seventies, the nation's most suspect drug was laetrile, not crack or ice. Divorce was still viewed as a healthy alternative to an unhappy family life. But as the eighties began, a darker image of parents appeared. In the second-stage critique, . . . parents became toxic.

Day after day, throughout the eighties, Americans confronted an ugly new 27 reality. Parents were hurting and murdering their children. Day after day, the newspapers brought yet another story of a child abandoned or battered. Day after day, the local news told of a child sexually abused by a father or a stepfather or a mother's boyfriend. Week by week, the national media brought us into courtrooms where photographs of battered children were held up to the camera. The sheer volume of stories suggested an epidemic of historic proportion. In even the most staid publications, the news was sensational. The *New York Times* carried bizarre stories usually found only in tabloids: A father who tortured his children for years; a mother who left her baby in a suitcase in a building she then set on fire; parents who abandoned babies dead or alive, in toilets, dumpsters, and alleyways.

Drug use among parents was one clear cause of abuse. And, increasingly   28 child abuse and drug abuse were linked in the most direct way possible. Pregnant women were battering their children in the womb, delivering drugs through their umbilical cords. Nightly images of crack-addicted babies in neonatal units destroyed any lingering public sympathy for mothers of the underclass. And as the highly publicized Joel Steinberg case made clear, middle-class parents, too, took drugs and killed babies. Even those parents who occasionally indulged were causing their children harm. The Partnership for Drug-Free America ran ads asking: "With millions of parents doing drugs, is it any wonder their kids are too?"

More than drugs, it was divorce that lay at the heart of middle-class parental   29 failure. It wasn't the crackhouse but the courthouse that was the scene of their collapse. Parents engaged in bitter custody battles. Parents kidnapped their own children. Parents used children as weapons against each other or simply walked away from their responsibilities. In an important new study on the long-term effects of divorce, Judith Wallerstein challenged the earlier notion that divorce is healthy for kids. She studied middle-class families for fifteen years after divorce and came up with some startling findings: Almost half of the children in the study entered adulthood as worried, underachieving, self-deprecating, and sometimes angry young men and women; one in four experienced a severe and enduring drop in their standard of living; three in five felt rejected by at least one parent. Her study concluded: "Divorce is almost always more devastating for children than for their parents. . . . [W]hile divorce can rescue a parent from an intolerable situation, it can fail to rescue the children."

As a group, today's parents have been portrayed as selfish and uncaring: 30 Yuppie parents abandon the children to the au pair; working parents turn their kids over to the mall and the video arcade; single parents hang a key around their kids' necks and a list of emergency numbers on the refrigerator. Even in the healthiest families, parents fail to put their children first.

The indictment of parents is pervasive. In a survey by the Carnegie Foun-   31 dation, 90 percent of a national sample of public school teachers say a lack of parental support is a problem in their classrooms. Librarians gathered at a national convention to draft a new policy to deal with the problem of parents who send unattended children to the library after school. Daycare workers complain to Ann Landers that all too often parents hand over children with empty stomachs and full diapers. Everywhere, parents are flunking the most basic tests.

Declining demographically, hard-pressed economically, and disarrayed po- 32
litically, parents have become part of the problem. For proponents of the *kids as
capital* argument, the logic is clear: Why try to help parents—an increasingly marginal and unsympathetic bunch—when you can rescue their children?

To blame parents for larger social changes is nothing new. In the past, child- 33
saving movements have depended on building a public consensus that certain parents have failed. Child reformers in the Progressive Era, for example, were able to
expand the scope of public sector responsibility for the welfare of children by exploiting mainstream fears about immigrant parents and their child-rearing practices. But what is new is the sense that the majority of parents—up and down the
social ladder—are failing. Even middle-class parents, once solid, dependable
caretakers of the next generation, don't seem to be up to the job.

By leaving parents out of the picture, *kids as capital* conjures up the image 34
of our little workers struggling against the little workers of Germany and the little
workers of Japan. But this picture is obviously false. For the little workers of Germany and Japan have parents too. The difference is that their parents are strongly
valued and supported by the society for their contributions *as parents.* We won't
be facing up to reality until we are ready to pit our parents against their parents,
and thus our family policy against theirs.

1990

QUESTIONS FOR DISCUSSION

Content

a. What is the "kids as capital" argument (paragraphs 2–6)?
b. What is Dafoe Whitehead's initial response to this argument (paragraphs
   7–14)?
c. Though this essay is in part a cause/effect analysis, it is also an argument. What
   is Dafoe Whitehead arguing?
d. What is the main cause/effect relationship that this argument is based on?
e. Paraphrase and elaborate on paragraph 9. What is Dafoe Whitehead's point in
   this paragraph? Do you agree with her?
f. In paragraph 17, the author refers to a "pronatal ideology." What does she
   mean?
g. What are the stages in the shift from the rosy view of parenthood in the 1950s
   to the dark view of parenthood now? What has happened at each stage to further harm the image of parents?

Strategy and Style

h. Writers who use the cause/effect approach will often use particular words or
   phrases to signal the cause/effect relationships. Some of these words/phrases

that Dafoe Whitehead uses are "as a result," "thus," "behind this," "then," "gave way to," and "lay at the heart of." Find these and other clues in this essay, and explain what the cause/effect relationships are.

i. Dafoe Whitehead begins her essay with several paragraphs (2–6) that present the other side of the argument; she then presents her own argument (paragraphs 7–14). What might have been her reasons for giving the other side so much attention?

j. Paragraph 7 is a transition between the two arguments. How does it link the two arguments? What are the key words that link the "kids as capital" argument with Dafoe Whitehead's argument?

k. Look at the transition words and phrases that frequently begin paragraphs (for example, "unfortunately" in paragraph 4, "further" in paragraph 6, "nevertheless" in paragraph 7, and "as we all know" in paragraph 12). What job do these words/phrases perform?

SUGGESTIONS FOR SHORT WRITING

a. List the points of the "kids as capital" argument (paragraphs 2–6) that Dafoe Whitehead summarizes before she presents her own argument. Then list the points of her own argument (paragraphs 7–14). Write a brief comparison of the two arguments. Which seems stronger?

b. Look up the Joel Steinberg case (mentioned in paragraph 28) in the *New York Times Index* and/or on an electronic database such as InfoTrak. Find and summarize one or two articles about the case.

SUGGESTIONS FOR SUSTAINED WRITING

a. Write a counterargument to Dafoe Whitehead's argument. Before you begin drafting your paper, outline her essay so that you can clearly see its logic and the main points. Then brainstorm a list of points that you could make against her points. Also mark places in your argument where facts and statistics would strengthen it.

b. Conversely, agree with Dafoe Whitehead's argument, and write an essay that expands upon it. Look up in the library the surveys and studies she cites. Use at least one of these studies as the basis for your essay.

c. Dafoe Whitehead does not provide a plan for solving the problem she has described because her intention in this essay is merely to convince us of what the real problem is. She does, however, imply in her conclusion that we must find a way to value parents and to create stability in parenting. Write an essay in which you present a specific plan to achieve this.

If Hitler Asked You to Electrocute a Stranger, Would You? Probably

Philip Meyer

Philip Meyer (b. 1930), earned a BS in 1952 from Kansas State University, an MA in 1963 from the University of North Carolina, and did graduate work at Harvard University during 1966 and 1967. While attending college he worked as the assistant state editor of the Topeka Daily Capital *and as a reporter for the* Miami Herald. *From 1962 to 1978 he was the Washington, D.C. correspondent for Knight-Ridder Newspapers, and from 1978 to 1982 he was Knight-Ridder's director of news and circulation research in Miami. Since then he has taught journalism at the University of North Carolina at Chapel Hill. In 1968 he shared a Pulitzer Prize with the staff of the* Detroit Free Press *for covering the Detroit riots in 1967. He has written several books about journalism, including* Precision Journalism, *which was first published in 1973 and has reappeared in subsequent editions;* To Keep the Republic, *written in collaboration with David Olson in 1975; and* Editors, Publishers, and Newspaper Ethics *(1983); among other books. He also contributes regularly to* Public Opinion Quarterly *and* Esquire. *"If Hitler Asked You . . ." was first published in* Esquire *in 1970.*

In the beginning, Stanley Milgram was worried about the Nazi problem. He doesn't worry much about the Nazis anymore. He worries about you and me, and, perhaps, himself a little bit too. 1

Stanley Milgram is a social psychologist, and when he began his career at Yale 2 University in 1960 he had a plan to prove, scientifically, that Germans are different. The Germans-are-different hypothesis has been used by historians, such as William L. Shirer, to explain the systematic destruction of the Jews by the Third Reich.

The appealing thing about this theory is that it makes those of us who are 3 not Germans feel better about the whole business. Obviously, you and I are not Hitler, and it seems equally obvious that we would never do Hitler's dirty work for him. But now, because of Stanley Milgram, we are compelled to wonder. Milgram developed a laboratory experiment which provided a systematic way to measure obedience. His plan was to try it out in New Haven on Americans and then go to Germany and try it out on Germans. He was strongly motivated by scientific curiosity, but there was also some moral content in his decision to pursue this line of research, which was, in turn, colored by his own Jewish background. If he could show that Germans are more obedient than Americans, he could then vary the conditions of the experiment and try to find out just what it is that makes some people more obedient than others. With this understanding, the world might, conceivably, be just a little bit better.

But he never took his experiment to Germany. He never took it any farther 4 than Bridgeport. The first finding, also the most unexpected and disturbing finding, was that we Americans are an obedient people: Not blindly obedient, and not blissfully obedient, just obedient. "I found so much obedience," says Milgram softly, a little sadly, "I hardly saw the need for taking the experiment to Germany."

There is something of the theatre director in Milgram, and his technique, which 5 he learned from one of the old masters in experimental psychology, Solomon Asch, is to stage a play with every line rehearsed, every prop carefully selected, and everybody an actor except one person. That one person is the subject of the experiment. The subject, of course, does not know he is in a play. He thinks he is in real life.

The experiment worked like this: If you were an innocent subject in Milgram's 6 melodrama, you read an ad in the newspaper or received one in the mail asking for volunteers for an educational experiment. The job would take about an hour and pay $4.50. So you make an appointment and go to an old Romanesque stone structure on High Street with the imposing name of The Yale Interaction Laboratory. It looks something like a broadcasting studio. Inside, you meet a young, crew-cut man in a laboratory coat who says he is Jack Williams, the experimenter. There is another citizen, fiftyish, Irish face, an accountant, a little overweight, and very mild and harmless-looking. This other citizen seems nervous and plays with his hat while the two of you sit in chairs side by side and are told that the $4.50 checks are yours no matter what happens. Then you listen to Jack Williams explain the experiment.

It is about learning, says Jack Williams in a quiet, knowledgeable way. Science does not know much about the conditions under which people learn and this experiment is to find out about negative reinforcement. Negative reinforcement is getting punished when you do something wrong, as opposed to positive reinforcement which is getting rewarded when you do something right. The negative reinforcement in this case is electric shock. 7

Then Jack Williams takes two pieces of paper, puts them in a hat, and shakes 8 them up. One piece of paper is supposed to say, "Teacher" and the other, "Learner." Draw one and you will see which you will be. The mild-looking accountant draws one, holds it close to his vest like a poker player, looks at it, and says, "Learner." You look at yours. It says, "Teacher." You do not know that the drawing is rigged, and both slips say "Teacher." The experimenter beckons to the mild-mannered "learner."

"Want to step right in here and have a seat, please?" he says. "You can leave 9 your coat on the back of that chair . . . roll up your right sleeve, please. Now what I want to do is strap down your arms to avoid excessive movement on your part during the experiment. This electrode is connected to the shock generator in the next room.

"And this electrode paste," he says, squeezing some stuff out of a plastic 10 bottle and putting it on the man's arm, "is to provide a good contact and to avoid a blister or burn. Are there any questions now before we go into the next room?"

You don't have any, but the strapped-in "learner" does. 11

"I do think I should say this," says the learner. "About two years ago, I was 12 at the veterans' hospital . . . they detected a heart condition. Nothing serious, but as long as I'm having these shocks, how strong are they—how dangerous are they?"

Williams, the experimenter, shakes his head casually. "Oh, no," he says.   13
"Although they may be painful, they're not dangerous. Anything else?"

Nothing else. And so you play the game. The game is for you to read a se-   14
ries of word pairs: For example, blue-girl, nice-day, fat-neck. When you finish the
list, you read just the first word in each pair and then a multiple-choice list of four
other words, including the second word of the pair. The learner, from his remote,
strapped-in position, pushes one of four switches to indicate which of the four answers he thinks is the right one. If he gets it right, nothing happens and you go on
to the next one. If he gets it wrong, you push a switch that buzzes and gives him
an electric shock. And then you go to the next word. You start with 15 volts and
increase the number of volts by 15 for each wrong answer. The control board goes
from 15 volts on one end to 450 volts on the other. So that you know what you are
doing, you get a test shock yourself, at 45 volts. It hurts. To further keep you aware
of what you are doing to that man in there, the board has verbal descriptions of the
shock levels, ranging from "Slight Shock" at the left-hand side, through "Intense
Shock" in the middle, to "Danger: Severe Shock" toward the far right. Finally, at
the very end, under 435- and 450-volt switches, there are three ambiguous X's. If,
at any point, you hesitate, Mr. Williams calmly tells you to go on. If you still hesitate, he tells you again.

Except for some terrifying details, which will be explained in a moment, this   15
is the experiment. The object is to find the shock level at which you disobey the
experimenter and refuse to pull the switch.

When Stanley Milgram first wrote this script, he took it to fourteen Yale psy-   16
chology majors and asked them what they thought would happen. He put it this
way: Out of one hundred persons in the teacher's predicament, how would their
breakoff points be distributed along the 15-to-450-volt scale? They thought a few
would break off very early, most would quit someplace in the middle and a few
would go all the way to the end. The highest estimate of the number out of one
hundred who would go all the way to the end was three. Milgram then informally
polled some of his fellow scholars in the psychology department. They agreed that
very few would go to the end. Milgram thought so too.

"I'll tell you quite frankly," he says, "before I began this experiment, before   17
any shock generator was built, I thought that most people would break off at
'Strong Shock' or 'Very Strong Shock.' You would get only a very, very small proportion of people going out to the end of the shock generator, and they would constitute a pathological fringe."

In his pilot experiments, Milgram used Yale students as subjects. Each of   18
them pushed the shock switches, one by one, all the way to the end of the board.

So he rewrote the script to include some protests from the learner. At first,   19
they were mild, gentlemanly, Yalie protests, but, "it didn't seem to have as much
effect as I thought it would or should," Milgram recalls. "So we had more violent
protestation on the part of the person getting the shock. All of the time, of course,
what we were trying to do was not to create a macabre situation, but simply to generate disobedience. And that was one of the first findings. This was not only a tech-

nical deficiency of the experiment, that we didn't get disobedience. It really was the first finding: That obedience would be much greater than we had assumed it would be and disobedience would be much more difficult than we had assumed."

As it turned out, the situation did become rather macabre. The only mean- 20 ingful way to generate disobedience was to have the victim protest with great anguish, noise, and vehemence. The protests were tape-recorded so that all the teachers ordinarily would hear the same sounds and nuances, and they started with a grunt at 75 volts, proceeded through a "Hey, that really hurts," at 125 volts, got desperate with, "I can't stand the pain, don't do that," at 180 volts, reached complaints of heart trouble at 195, an agonized scream at 285, a refusal to answer at 315, and only heart-rending, ominous silence after that.

Still, sixty-five percent of the subjects, twenty- to fifty-year-old American 21 males, everyday, ordinary people, like you and me, obediently kept pushing those levers in the belief that they were shocking the mild-mannered learner, whose name was Mr. Wallace, and who was chosen for the role because of his innocent appearance, all the way up to 450 volts.

Milgram was now getting enough disobedience so that he had something he 22 could measure. The next step was to vary the circumstances to see what would encourage or discourage obedience.

He put the learner in the same room with the teacher. He stopped strapping 23 the learner's hand down. He rewrote the script so that at 150 volts the learner took his hand off the shock plate and declared that he wanted out of the experiment. He rewrote the script some more so that the experimenter then told the teacher to grasp the learner's hand and physically force it down on the plate to give Mr. Wallace his unwanted electric shock.

"I had the feeling that very few people would go on at that point, if any," 24 Milgram says. "I thought that would be the limit of obedience that you would find in the laboratory."

It wasn't. 25

Although seven years have now gone by, Milgram still remembers the first 26 person to walk into the laboratory in the newly rewritten script. He was a construction worker, a very short man. "He was so small," says Milgram, "that when he sat on the chair in front of the shock generator, his feet didn't reach the floor. When the experimenter told him to push the victim's hand down and give the shock, he turned to the experimenter, and he turned to the victim, his elbow went up, he fell down on the hand of the victim, his feet kind of tugged to one side, and he said, 'Like this, boss?' ZZUMPH!"

The experiment was played out to its bitter end. Milgram tried it with forty 27 different subjects. And thirty percent of them obeyed the experimenter and kept on obeying.

"The protests of the victim were strong and vehement, he was screaming his 28 guts out, he refused to participate, and you had to physically struggle with him in order to get his hand down on the shock generator," Milgram remembers. But twelve out of forty did it.

Milgram took his experiment out of New Haven. Not to Germany, just 29 twenty miles down the road to Bridgeport. Maybe, he reasoned, the people obeyed because of the prestigious setting of Yale University.

The new setting was a suite of three rooms in a run-down office building in 30 Bridgeport. The only identification was a sign with a fictitious name: "Research Associates of Bridgeport." Questions about professional connections got only vague answers about "research for industry."

Obedience was less in Bridgeport. Forty-eight percent of the subjects stayed 31 for the maximum shock, compared to sixty-five percent at Yale. But this was enough to prove that far more than Yale's prestige was behind the obedient behavior.

For more than seven years now, Stanley Milgram has been trying to figure out 32 what makes ordinary American citizens so obedient. The most obvious answer—that people are mean, nasty, brutish and sadistic—won't do. The subjects who gave the shocks to Mr. Wallace to the end of the board did not enjoy it. They groaned, protested, fidgeted, argued, and in some cases, were seized by fits of nervous, agitated giggling.

"They even try to get out of it," says Milgram, "but they are somehow engaged 33 in something from which they cannot liberate themselves. They are locked into a structure, and they do not have the skills or inner resources to disengage themselves."

Milgram's theory assumes that people behave in two different operating 34 modes as different as ice and water. He does not rely on Freud or sex or toilet-training hang-ups for this theory. All he says is that ordinarily we operate in a state of autonomy, which means we pretty much have and assert control over what we do. But in certain circumstances, we operate under what Milgram calls a state of agency (after agent, n . . . one who acts for or in the place of another by authority from him; a substitute; a deputy.—*Webster's Collegiate Dictionary*). A state of agency, to Milgram, is nothing more than a frame of mind.

"There's nothing bad about it, there's nothing good about it," he says. "It's 35 a natural circumstance of living with other people. . . . I think of a state of agency as a real transformation of a person; if a person has different properties when he's in that state, just as water can turn to ice under certain conditions of temperature, a person can move to the state of mind that I call agency . . . the critical thing is that you see yourself as the instrument of the execution of another person's wishes. You do not see yourself as acting on your own. And there's a real transformation, a real change of properties of the person."

So, for most subjects in Milgram's laboratory experiments, the act of giving 36 Mr. Wallace his painful shock was necessary, even though unpleasant, and besides they were doing it on behalf of somebody else and it was for science.

Stanley Milgram has his problems, too. He believes that in the laboratory sit- 37 uation, he would not have shocked Mr. Wallace. His professional critics reply that in his real-life situation he has done the equivalent. He has placed innocent and naïve subjects under great emotional strain and pressure in selfish obedience to his quest for knowledge. When you raise this issue with Milgram, he has an answer ready. There is, he explains patiently, a critical difference between his naïve subjects and the man in the electric chair. The man in the electric chair (in the mind of the naïve subject) is helpless, strapped in. But the naïve subject is free to go at any time.

Immediately after he offers this distinction, Milgram anticipates the objection.   38

"It's quite true," he says, "that this is almost a philosophic position, because   39
we have learned that some people are psychologically incapable of disengaging
themselves. But that doesn't relieve them of the moral responsibility."

The parallel is exquisite. "The tension problem was unexpected," says Mil-   40
gram in his defense. But he went on anyway. The naïve subjects didn't expect the
screaming protests from the strapped-in learner. But they went on.

"I had to make a judgment," says Milgram. "I had to ask myself, was this   41
harming the person or not? My judgment is that it was not. Even in the extreme
cases, I wouldn't say that permanent damage results."

Sound familiar? "The shocks may be painful," the experimenter kept say-   42
ing, "but they're not dangerous."

After the series of experiments was completed, Milgram sent a report of the   43
results to his subjects and a questionnaire, asking whether they were glad or sorry
to have been in the experiment. Eighty-three and seven-tenths percent said they
were glad and only 1.3 percent were sorry; 15 percent were neither sorry nor glad.
However, Milgram could not be sure at the time of the experiment that only 1.3
percent would be sorry.

Kurt Vonnegut Jr. put one paragraph in the preface to *Mother Night,* in 1966,   44
which pretty much says it for the people with their fingers on the shock-generator
switches, for you and me, and maybe even for Milgram. "If I'd been born in Germany," Vonnegut said, "I suppose I would have *been* a Nazi, bopping Jews and
gypsies and Poles around, leaving boots sticking out of snowbanks, warming myself with my sweetly virtuous insides. So it goes."

Just so. One thing that happened to Milgram back in New Haven during the   45
days of the experiment was that he kept running into people he'd watched from
behind the one-way glass. It gave him a funny feeling, seeing those people going
about their everyday business in New Haven and knowing what they would do to
Mr. Wallace if ordered to. Now that his research results are in and you've thought
about it, you can get this funny feeling too. You don't need one-way glass. A
glance in your own mirror may serve just as well.

1970

QUESTIONS FOR DISCUSSION

Content

a. Originally, what did Stanley Milgram intend his experiments to test? What unexpected turns did the experiment take?
b. Why did Milgram change the location and the details of the situation after the
   first experiment?
c. What are the probable reasons that the "teachers" in Milgram's experiments
   continued to administer shocks to the "learners"? List reasons Milgram gives
   plus any other reasons you think are likely.

d. What does Milgram conclude about people's willingness to obey?

e. In your opinion, what other changes to the experiment would have made the results different? What might have been these other results?

Strategy and Style

f. The use of "you," starting in paragraph 6, puts you directly into the action, into the role of the "teacher." What effect does this have on you? What is your reaction to the experimenter's requests?

g. What does the startling title and bluntly worded first paragraph make you think the article will be about? Are your expectations met? Are the title and opening effective?

h. What techniques does Meyer use to make this nonfiction article read like a fictional story?

i. Meyer wrote this article for *Esquire,* a magazine aimed primarily for college-educated, fashion-conscious men. How would the effect of the article change if it were written for radically different audiences, such as scholars, psychiatrists, or young children?

j. How does the reference to Kurt Vonnegut's novel, *Mother Night* (paragraph 44), interpret Milgram's experiment? What is Meyer's opinion, as expressed in paragraphs 44 and 45? Do you agree with his take on Milgram's findings?

SUGGESTIONS FOR SHORT WRITING

a. Describe what you would have done as a "teacher" in the experiment. Try to be as truthful as you can.

b. Do you think that Milgram's experiment was ethical? In other words, was it right of him to put his subjects in such a situation? Write a paragraph to explain your opinion about this.

SUGGESTIONS FOR SUSTAINED WRITING

a. Do you agree with Meyer's and Vonnegut's opinion that, if you had been born in Germany, you would have become a Nazi (paragraphs 44 and 45)? Write an argumentative essay in which you expand that basic opinion, explaining why you agree or disagree with their opinion and defending your answer against possible counterarguments.

b. Do you think that continual exposure to violence (on television, on the news, in movies) desensitizes viewers to violence, even makes viewers violent themselves? Write a cause/effect essay in which you argue that, yes, exposure to violence has a direct relationship to increased violent crimes or, no, exposure to violence does not lead to violent behavior. You will need to do some research to support your opinion.

Nubian Diet Revealed at Last

Kathy A. Svitil

An associate editor and writer for Discover *magazine, Kathy A. Svitil took a BS in biology at UCLA and an MA in journalism at New York University. She writes on topics from anthropology, the earth sciences, and biology, and she edits* Discover's *astronomy column. Early in her career, she worked on a science documentary entitled "Innovations" at WNET, a public broadcasting station. Svitil lives in California with her husband and young son. "Nubian Diet Revealed at Last" first appeared in* Discover *in 1994 and has been reprinted in several newspapers.*

The Nubians were kings once: They built pyramids and temples; carved delicate statues and jewelry; controlled trade along the Nile; and for a century or so, beginning in the eighth century BC, even ruled Egypt, their neighbor to the north. 1

Mostly, though, the Nubians have been pawns, invaded by the Persians and Assyrians, dominated by the Egyptians—and finally flooded. 2

When the Aswan High Dam was completed in 1970, the reservoir it created inundated thousands of square miles of land along the banks of the Nile, from Egypt south into the Sudan. 3

Nearly all of what was once the Lower Nubian heartland is now Lake Nasser. 4

Before the flood, however, teams of archaeologists from around the world flocked to the region, hurriedly salvaging what they could of the Nubian past. 5

They recovered tons of ancient artifacts—including the entire Temple of Dendur—and, even more remarkably, hundreds of ancient Nubians. 6

Most of these mummies were ordinary folk, buried in the desert and accidentally preserved by the blistering heat and dry sands. 7

Their bodies dried out so fast that not only the bones but also the skin, hair and muscle were saved from decomposition. 8

And preserved along with the mummies, says Christine White, a physical anthropologist at the University of Western Ontario, is a record of what the ancient Nubians ate—even in the last weeks of their lives. 9

White gleaned that particular bit of information from the mummies' hair. 10

Researchers already knew that the ancient Nubians' diet was inadequate. Besides evidence of arthritis, tumors and parasites, the mummies show clear signs of malnutrition, iron-deficiency anemia and osteoporosis. 11

Yet what that diet consisted of has been something of a mystery. 12

Despite the intensive excavation, no physical evidence—plant or animal remains—was ever recovered. 13

White has now extracted that physical evidence from the mummies themselves by looking at the isotope signatures of their tissue: The distinctive ratios of heavy nitrogen atoms to light ones and of heavy to light carbon that humans acquire from the plants and animals they eat. 14

345

White studied 167 mummies from a site along the west bank of the Nile in   15
the Wadi Halfa region of northern Sudan.

The oldest mummies dated from the period between 350 BC and AD 350,   16
when Lower Nubia was ruled by the Meroitic Empire of Upper Nubia.

White first looked at the mummies' nitrogen signature to find out their   17
source of protein (which is rich in nitrogen).

Grasses and the cows that eat them have a relatively low ratio of heavy ni-   18
trogen 15 to nitrogen 14; scrubs and bushes and the goats and sheep that browse
on them in the Nubian Desert have a higher ratio. Most of the mummies, White
found, had eaten these desert animals rather than cattle.

Some had partaken more than others: Male mummies contained more nitro-   19
gen 15 relative to their body weight than did females. Apparently, the men of ancient Nubia got more than their fair share of the meat.

The ancient Nubians did not just ranch in the desert. They also made it   20
bloom—and with crops that aren't easy to grow in hot, arid conditions.

The ratio of carbon 13 to carbon 12 in the mummies from the Meroitic pe-   21
riod, White says, shows that fully 84 percent of the Nubians' plant intake consisted
of "C3" foods such as wheat, barley and fruit—all of which require more water
than is normally available in the Nubian Desert.

The Nubians, White figures, must therefore have been irrigating their crops,   22
probably using the ox-driven waterwheel—a sort of Ferris wheel with buckets that
dumped water from the Nile into irrigation channels. It was invented in
Mesopotamia and brought to Lower Nubia by Meroitic settlers.

Lower Nubia, White speculates, may have been an agricultural hinterland   23
that produced wheat and barley for Meroe. That might explain why mummies dating from after the fall of the Meroitic Empire around 350 AD ate about 9 percent
fewer C3 plants than their forebears.

"When the Meroitic Empire fell," White says, "the Nubians, who no longer   24
had to grow so much wheat and barley, may have reverted to a more traditional
diet of C4 plants, like sorghum and millet."

Such grains are much easier to grow in the desert than C3 crops, even with   25
irrigation.

Today in the Wadi Halfa, wheat and barley are grown in the fall and winter,   26
with the aid of irrigation and the annual flooding of the Nile, while sorghum and
millet are planted in the spring and harvested beginning in early June.

Could the same crop rotation, White wondered, have been occurring over a   27
thousand years ago?

The mummies' hair said yes.   28

Until White's work, only bone had been used in isotopic analyses, and bone takes   29
between 25 and 30 years to replace its store of isotopes—making its isotope signature
"just a homogenized version of what was consumed over a lifetime," as White puts it.

But isotopes show up in hair two weeks after they're consumed. Thus iso-   30
tope signatures from a hair shaft can reveal any changes in diet that occurred while
the hair was growing.

White cut hair from 14 post-Meroe mummies into 3.25-inch-long segments, 31 each segment representing about two months' growth.

She found that the isotopic signature fluctuated dramatically between seg- 32 ments, indicating that the person had alternated between periods of eating mostly C3 plants and ones of relying on C4 plants.

Furthermore, by looking at the hair closest to the scalp, White could tell 33 what the future mummies had eaten just weeks before they died.

Nearly two-thirds of them had been eating C4 plants. That suggested they 34 died after the sorghum and millet harvest in June, but before the wheat and barley harvest in the winter.

Why would more Nubians have died during summer?   35

Because of heat and malnutrition, White says.   36

C4 plants aren't as nutritious as C3 plants; sorghum is low in vitamin B, for 37 instance, and vitamin B deficiency increases the incidence of pellagra, a disease that causes gastrointestinal and neurological problems.

Moreover, by the end of summer in Nubia, even C4 crops are scarce.   38

Today more residents of the Nubian Desert die in summer than during any 39 other time of year. One thousand years ago, their ancestors may have faced the same hardships.

1995

QUESTIONS FOR DISCUSSION

Content

a. Make sure you are familiar with historical terms such as Nubians, Meroitic Empire, Persians, Assyrians, and Mesopotamia. If not, read more about them in an encyclopedia.
b. What is Svitil's thesis?
c. Why was it possible for archaeologists to recover so much information about the Nubian population and its diet?
d. What evidence did the mummies provide to indicate that the diet of the Nubians was inadequate?
e. What is a "nitrogen signature"? What information did examining the mummies' nitrogen signatures bring to light?
f. What accounts for the theory that the Nubians might have used an ox-driven waterwheel in their farming?
g. How does anthropologist Christine White explain the fact that more of the Nubian mummies she examined had died during summer than during other seasons?

Strategy and Style

h. Where in this essay does Svitil use comparison and to what end?
i. Where does she use description?

j. How does the essay's introduction prepare us for its conclusion?
k. Is Svitil writing to an educated audience? How can we tell?
l. To what extent is this audience grounded in the studies of anthropology, chemistry, and agriculture?

SUGGESTIONS FOR SHORT WRITING

a. Reread "Nubian Diet Revealed at Last." Then list several facts about Nubian society that can be inferred from the essay. For example, it might be fair to say that Nubian women did not fare as well as Nubian men, at least as far as eating is concerned.
b. Complete some brief library research on the diets of another ancient people: the Maya, the Celts, or the Hebrews, for example. Take notes on the kinds of food they ate, the extent and nature of their agriculture, the nutritional aspects of their diets, and the social or religious beliefs associated with raising, gathering, and preparing food.

SUGGESTIONS FOR SUSTAINED WRITING

a. Turn the notes you took for item *b* above (Suggestions for Short Writing) into a full-length essay on the diet of an ancient civilization. Make sure to give sources you researched credit by including internal citations as appropriate and a works-cited or references page.
b. Are you restricted to a special diet because of health, religious, or other reasons? Do you know someone who is? If so, write a cause/effect essay that explains how this regimen affects your subject's life.

9

Analogy

Have you ever taken a test that requires you to evaluate relationships between pairs of items or ideas? A typical question might go something like this:

Truck is to driver as horse is to _____ .

When used to develop ideas in writing, analogies take the form of well-developed comparisons that reveal particular similarities between members of the same or different classes. Like other forms of comparison, analogy introduces new subjects or ideas by referencing and drawing parallels to information with which the reader is already familiar. Writers often use analogy to create unexpected and quite startling comparisons between items from very different classes. Consider Loren Eiseley's discussion of our earthly environment as a kind of cosmic prison and his startling revelation that our perspective on this planet may be as limited as that of a white blood cell traveling through the body of a cat. Nonetheless, the beauty of analogy is that it can be used effectively to shed new light even on items from the same class.

Analogies, then, bring to light important relationships that can help define a term, describe a person, place, or object, or even argue an important point. Scientific writers rely on analogy to make their descriptions of complex mechanisms or obscure phenomena both interesting and accessible to lay readers. Analogy can also be used to emphasize the significance of particular scientific phenomena or issues. The fact that human beings evolved only relatively recently in the history of the planet will not be news to readers of James C. Rettie's "But a Watch in the Night." Nonetheless, charting the history of the Earth on a twelve-month clock helps the author underscore the fact that "We have just arrived. . . ." Of course, analogies sometimes are used falsely, as Alan M. Dershowitz points out in his critique of the well-known analogy of shouting "fire!" in a crowded theater.

Philosophical concepts, by their very nature abstract, also benefit from explanation through analogy. Plato's "The Myth of the Cave" is a cornerstone in the history of ideas; Camus' recounting the Sisyphus myth illuminates his definition of the

349

absurd and explains why fate is a "human matter." Analogy is indeed a versatile tool. Consider the brilliant social commentary of Nichols Fox in "Gawk Shows." Consider too the personal portrait of a writer's anguish in Alice Walker's "Am I Blue?"

The Suggestions for Short Writing and Sustained Writing that follow each selection should help you create and develop interesting analogies of your own. But the essays themselves are so provocative they might even help you come to grips with problems, issues, or concerns that play a significant role in your daily life. Can you compare your current social environment to a prison? Is taking fifteen credits and working twenty hours a week like trying to roll a boulder uphill? Does the way modern college students date resemble courtship rituals among "primitive" peoples (real or fictitious)? If questions like these pop into your mind as you read this chapter, write them down and show them to your instructor; they might make good topics for an essay. At the very least, they will help you begin using analogy as a tool for thinking and for writing.

The Myth of the Cave

Plato

The great Athenian philosopher of the fourth century BC, Plato was the student of Socrates, whom he made the principal speaker in his dialogues. "The Myth of the Cave" appears in book VII of The Republic. *In it, Socrates addresses a series of questions to Glaucon in an attempt to explain that the world in which we live is a world of illusions and shadows—a mere reflection of the "real world" of the intellect. He explains that the "idea of the good" is the "universal author of all things beautiful and right, the parent of light . . . in this visible world, and the immediate source of reason and truth in the intellectual. . . ."*

And now, I said, let me show in a figure how far our nature is enlightened or un- 1
enlightened:—Behold! human beings living in an underground den, which has a mouth open toward the light and reaching all along the den; here they have been from their childhood, and have their legs and necks chained so that they cannot move, and can only see before them, being prevented by the chains from turning round their heads. Above and behind them a fire is blazing at a distance, and between the fire and the prisoners there is a raised way; and you will see, if you look, a low wall built along the way, like the screen which marionette players have in front of them, over which they show the puppets.

I see. 2

And do you see, I said, men passing along the wall carrying all sorts of ves- 3
sels, and statues and figures of animals made of wood and stone and various materials, which appear over the wall? Some of them are talking, others silent.

You have shown me a strange image, and they are strange prisoners. 4

Like ourselves, I replied; and they see only their own shadows, or the shad- 5
ows of one another, which the fire throws on the opposite wall of the cave?

True, he said; how could they see anything but the shadows if they were 6
never allowed to move their heads?

And of the objects which are being carried in like manner they would only 7
see the shadows?

Yes, he said. 8

And if they were able to converse with one another, would they not suppose 9
that they were naming what was actually before them?

Very true. 10

And suppose further that the prison had an echo which came from the other 11
side, would they not be sure to fancy when one of the passers-by spoke that the voice which they heard came from the passing shadow?

No question, he replied. 12

To them, I said, the truth would be literally nothing but the shadows of the 13
images.

That is certain. 14

And now look again, and see what will naturally follow if the prisoners are 15
released and disabused of their error. At first, when any of them is liberated and
compelled suddenly to stand up and turn his neck round and walk and look toward the light, he will suffer sharp pains; the glare will distress him, and he will
be unable to see the realities of which in his former state he had seen the shadows; and then conceive some one saying to him, that what he saw before was an
illusion, but that now, when he is approaching nearer to being and his eye is
turned toward more real existence, he has a clearer vision—what will be his reply? And you may further imagine that his instructor is pointing to the objects as
they pass and requiring him to name them—will he not be perplexed? Will he not
fancy that the shadows which he formerly saw are truer than the objects which
are now shown to him?

Far truer.   16

And if he is compelled to look straight at the light, will he not have a pain 17
in his eyes which will make him turn away to take refuge in the objects of vision
which he can see, and which he will conceive to be in reality clearer than the things
which are now being shown to him?

True, he said.   18

And suppose once more, that he is reluctantly dragged up a steep and rugged 19
ascent, and held fast until he is forced into the presence of the sun himself, is he not
likely to be pained and irritated? When he approaches the light his eyes will be dazzled, and he will not be able to see anything at all of what are now called realities.

Not all in a moment, he said.   20

He will require to grow accustomed to the sight of the upper world. And first 21
he will see the shadows best, next the reflections of men and other objects in the
water, and then the objects themselves; then he will gaze upon the light of the
moon and the stars and the spangled heaven; and he will see the sky and the stars
by night better than the sun or the light of the sun by day?

Certainly.   22

Last of all he will be able to see the sun, and not mere reflections of him in 23
the water, but he will see him in his own proper place, and not in another; and he
will contemplate him as he is.

Certainly.   24

He will then proceed to argue that this is he who gives the season and the 25
years, and is the guardian of all that is in the visible world, and in a certain way
the cause of all things which he and his fellows have been accustomed to behold?

Clearly, he said, he would first see the sun and then reason about him.   26

And when he remembered his old habitation, and the wisdom of the den and 27
his fellow-prisoners, do you not suppose that he would felicitate himself on the
change, and pity them?

Certainly, he would.   28

And if they were in the habit of conferring honors among themselves on 29
those who were quickest to observe the passing shadows and to remark which of
them went before, and which followed after, and which were together; and who

were therefore best able to draw conclusions as to the future, do you think that he would care for such honors and glories, or envy the possessors of them? Would he not say with Homer,

> Better to be the poor servant of a poor master,

and to endure anything, rather than think as they do and live after their manner?

Yes, he said, I think that he would rather suffer anything than entertain these false notions and live in this miserable manner.   30

Imagine once more, I said, such a one coming suddenly out of the sun to be replaced in his old situation; would he not be certain to have his eyes full of darkness?   31

To be sure, he said.   32

And if there were a contest, and he had to compete in measuring the shadows with the prisoners who had never moved out of the den, while his sight was still weak, and before his eyes had become steady (and the time which would be needed to acquire this new habit of sight might be very considerable), would he not be ridiculous? Men would say of him that up he went and down he came without his eyes; and that it was better not even to think of ascending and if any one tried to loose another and lead him up to the light, let them only catch the offender, and they would put him to death.   33

No question, he said.   34

This entire allegory, I said, you may now append, dear Glaucon, to the previous argument; the prison-house is the world of sight, the light of the fire is the sun, and you will not misapprehend me if you interpret the journey upwards to be the ascent of the soul into the intellectual world according to my poor belief, which, at your desire, I have expressed—whether rightly or wrongly God knows. But, whether true or false, my opinion is that in the world of knowledge the idea of good appears last of all, and is seen only with an effort; and, when seen, is also inferred to be the universal author of all things beautiful and right, parent of light and of the lord of light in this visible world, and the immediate source of reason and truth in the intellectual; and that this is the power upon which he who would act rationally either in public or private life must have his eye fixed.   35

I agree, he said, as far as I am able to understand you.   36

Moreover, I said, you must not wonder that those who attain to this beatific vision are unwilling to descend to human affairs; for their souls are ever hastening into the upper world where they desire to dwell; which desire of theirs is very natural, if our allegory may be trusted.   37

Yes, very natural.   38

And is there anything surprising in one who passes from divine contemplations to the evil state of man, misbehaving himself in a ridiculous manner; if, while his eyes are blinking and before he has become accustomed to the surrounding darkness, he is compelled to fight in courts of law, or in other places, about the images or the shadows of images of justice, and is endeavoring to meet the conceptions of those who have never yet seen absolute justice?   39

Anything but surprising, he replied.   40

Anyone who has common sense will remember that the bewilderments of **41**
the eyes are of two kinds, and arise from two causes, either from coming out of the
light or from going into the light, which is true of the mind's eye, quite as much
as of the bodily eye; and he who remembers this when he sees any one whose vision is perplexed and weak, will not be too ready to laugh; he will first ask whether
that soul of man has come out of the brighter life, and is unable to see because un-
accustomed to the dark, or having turned from darkness to the day is dazzled by
excess of light. And he will count the one happy in his condition and state of being, and he will pity the other; or, if he have a mind to laugh at the soul which
comes from below into the light, there will be more reason in this than in the laugh
which greets him who returns from above out of the light into the den.

That, he said, is a very just distinction.   **42**

ca. 373 BC

QUESTIONS FOR DISCUSSION

Content

a. Why does Plato refer to "the world of sight" as a "prison-house"?
b. Does the fact that Plato has cast this extended analogy into a dialogue make it
   more effective than if he had written in conventional essay form?
c. What does the sun represent in Plato's analogy?
d. Consult an unabridged dictionary, encyclopedia, or reference book on ancient
   literature or civilization. Who was Homer? Why does Plato allude to him?
e. What is the "beatific" vision that Socrates describes to Glaucon? Why is it important that one "who would act rationally" experience this vision?
f. How does Plato account for the fact that honorable people, who are able to see
   the truth and to relate it to others, often experience scorn and ridicule?
g. What has Glaucon learned by the end of the dialogue?

Strategy and Style

h. How effective is the dialogue form used in this selection? What is the function
   of Glaucon's brief responses? Of Socrates' questions?
i. How do Socrates' questions help determine the organization?
j. What is Plato's role in this selection? Is he invisible, a mere transcriber of the
   dialogue, or is his voice heard in some way?

SUGGESTIONS FOR SHORT WRITING

a. Write a short dialogue between yourself and Plato or between yourself and one
   of the dwellers in the cave.

b. This is an especially difficult selection. Try to capture the essence of Plato's ideas in a summary of one or two paragraphs.

SUGGESTIONS FOR SUSTAINED WRITING

a. Describe the human condition using another analogy besides the cave.
b. Do you believe that we are prisoners of the material world as Plato suggests? If so, write an essay in which you illustrate how people let their appetites (for food, money, sex, material possessions, for example) determine the course of their lives.
c. Do you believe that whatever is spiritual in a person can prevail? Write an essay in which you illustrate (from your own experiences, from those of people you know well, or from those you have read about) that people will deny themselves physical or material gratification in order to preserve the ethical principles or moral codes they believe in.
d. Create your own analogy by talking about the place where you work, live, or attend school in terms more usually associated with a prison, playground, resort, etc. Or you may want to describe the personality of someone you know well and create an analogy between him/her and an animal, either wild or domesticated, with which your readers might be familiar. You may need to include more than one animal in the analogy.

The Myth of Sisyphus

Albert Camus

Born in what was the French colony of Algeria, Albert Camus (1913–1966) was educated at the University of Algeria. He began his career as an actor and playwright, but he soon gave up the theater for journalism and began writing for Alger Republicain *and for* Paris-Soir *in France. During World War II, Camus was very active in the French resistance and contributed regularly to* Combat, *an important underground newspaper. He is remembered as a leading existentialist, a proponent of the modern philosophical movement (if it can be termed that), which defines the individual as utterly free and totally responsible for his own destiny. For many existentialists, God does not exist, and the world is devoid of meaning except for that which the individual is able to create for him/herself. Unlike the literature of many of his contemporaries, however, the works of Camus expose a view of life that, while hardly optimistic, encourages a belief in the inherent nobility and courage of the human character even in the face of a hostile universe. Though clearly evident in his famous novels,* The Stranger *(1942),* The Plague *(1947), and* The Rebel *(1951), nowhere is this belief expressed more eloquently than in "The Myth of Sisyphus."*

The gods had condemned Sisyphus to ceaselessly rolling a rock to the top of a mountain, whence the stone would fall back of its own weight. They had thought with some reason that there is no more dreadful punishment than futile and hopeless labor. 1

If one believes Homer, Sisyphus was the wisest and most prudent of mortals. According to another tradition, however, he was disposed to practice the profession of highwayman. I see no contradiction in this. Opinions differ as to the reasons why he became the futile laborer of the underworld. To begin with, he is accused of a certain levity in regard to the gods. He stole their secrets. Aegina, the daughter of Aesopus, was carried off by Jupiter. The father was shocked by that disappearance and complained to Sisyphus. He, who knew of the abduction, offered to tell about it on condition that Aesopus would give water to the citadel of Corinth. To the celestial thunderbolts he preferred the benediction of water. He was punished for this in the underworld. Homer tells us also that Sisyphus had put Death in chains. Pluto could not endure the sight of his deserted, silent empire. He dispatched the god of war, who liberated Death from the hands of her conqueror. 2

It is said also that Sisyphus, being near to death, rashly wanted to test his wife's love. He ordered her to cast his unburied body into the middle of the public square. Sisyphus woke up in the underworld. And there, annoyed by an obedience so contrary to human love, he obtained from Pluto permission to return to earth in order to chastise his wife. But when he had seen again the face of this world, enjoyed water and sun, warm stones and the sea, he no longer wanted to go back to the infernal darkness. Recalls, signs of anger, warnings were of no avail. Many years more he lived facing the curve of the gulf, the sparkling sea, and the smiles of earth. A decree of the gods was necessary. Mercury came and seized the 3 impudent man by the collar and, snatching him from his joys, led him forcibly back to the underworld, where his rock was ready for him.

You have already grasped that Sisyphus is the absurd hero. He is, as much   4 through his passions as through his torture. His scorn of the gods, his hatred of death, and his passion for life won him that unspeakable penalty in which the whole being is exerted toward accomplishing nothing. This is the price that must be paid for the passions of this earth. Nothing is told us about Sisyphus in the underworld. Myths are made for the imagination to breathe life into them. As for this myth, one sees merely the whole effort of a body straining to raise the huge stone, to roll it and push it up a slope a hundred times over; one sees the face screwed up, the cheek tight against the stone, the shoulder bracing the clay-covered mass, the foot wedging it, the fresh start with arms outstretched, the wholly human security of two earth-clotted hands. At the very end of his long effort measured by skyless space and time without depth, the purpose is achieved. Then Sisyphus watches the stone rush down in a few moments toward that lower world whence he will have to push it up again toward the summit. He goes back down to the plain.

It is during that return, that pause, that Sisyphus interests me. A face that toils   5 so close to stones is already stone itself! I see that man going back down with a heavy yet measured step toward the torment of which he will never know the end. That hour like a breathing-space which returns as surely as his suffering, that is the hour of consciousness. At each of those moments when he leaves the heights and gradually sinks toward the lairs of the gods, he is superior to his fate. He is stronger than his rock.

If this myth is tragic, that is because its hero is conscious. Where would his   6 torture be, indeed, if at every step the hope of succeeding upheld him? The workman of today works every day in his life at the same tasks, and this fate is no less absurd. But it is tragic only at the rare moments when it becomes conscious. Sisyphus, proletarian of the gods, powerless and rebellious, knows the whole extent of his wretched condition: it is what he thinks of during his descent. The lucidity that was to constitute his torture at the same time crowns his victory. There is no fate that cannot be surmounted by scorn.

If the descent is thus sometimes performed in sorrow, it can also take place   7 in joy. This word is not too much. Again I fancy Sisyphus returning toward his rock, and the sorrow was in the beginning. When the images of earth cling too tightly to memory, when the call of happiness becomes too insistent, it happens that melancholy rises in man's heart: this is the rock's victory, this is the rock itself. The boundless grief is too heavy to bear. These are our nights of Gethsemane. But crushing truths perish from being acknowledged. Thus, Oedipus at the outset obeys fate without knowing it. But from the moment he knows, his tragedy begins. Yet at the same moment, blind and desperate, he realizes that the only bond linking him to the world is the cool hand of a girl. Then a tremendous remark rings out: "Despite so many ordeals, my advanced age and the nobility of my soul make me conclude that all is well." Sophocles' Oedipus, like Dostoevsky's Kirilov, thus gives the recipe for the absurd victory. Ancient wisdom confirms modern heroism.

One does not discover the absurd without being tempted to write a manual of 8
happiness. "What! by such narrow ways—?" There is but one world, however. Happiness and the absurd are two sons of the same earth. They are inseparable. It would
be a mistake to say that happiness necessarily springs from the absurd discovery. It
happens as well that the feeling of the absurd springs from happiness. "I conclude that
all is well," says Oedipus, and that remark is sacred. It echoes in the wild and limited
universe of man. It teaches that all is not, has not been, exhausted. It drives out of this
world a god who had come into it with dissatisfaction and a preference for futile suf-
ferings. It makes of fate a human matter, which must be settled among men.

All Sisyphus' silent joy is contained therein. His fate belongs to him. His 9
rock is his thing. Likewise, the absurd man, when he contemplates his torment, silences all the idols. In the universe suddenly restored to its silence, the myriad
wondering little voices of the earth rise up. Unconscious, secret calls, invitations
from all the faces, they are the necessary reverse and price of victory. There is no
sun without shadow, and it is essential to know the night. The absurd man says yes
and his effort will henceforth be unceasing. If there is a personal fate, there is no
higher destiny, or at least there is but one which he concludes is inevitable and despicable. For the rest, he knows himself to be the master of his days. At that subtle
moment when man glances backward over his life, Sisyphus returning toward his
rock, in that slight pivoting he contemplates that series of unrelated actions which
becomes his fate, created by him, combined under his memory's eye and soon
sealed by his death. Thus, convinced of the wholly human origin of all that is human, a blind man eager to see who knows that the night has no end, he is still on
the go. The rock is still rolling.

I leave Sisyphus at the foot of the mountain! One always finds one's burden 10
again. But Sisyphus teaches the higher fidelity that negates the gods and raises rocks.
He too concludes that all is well. This universe henceforth without a master seems
to him neither sterile nor futile. Each atom of that stone, each mineral flake of that
night-filled mountain, in itself forms a world. The struggle itself toward the heights
is enough to fill a man's heart. One must imagine Sisyphus happy.

1955

QUESTIONS FOR DISCUSSION

Content

a. Who exactly was Sisyphus, and what does Camus mean when he calls him an
   "absurd hero"?
b. How do the various explanations behind his condemnation contribute to his
   portrayal as an "absurd hero"? In what way does the nature of Sisyphus' punishment help define that term?
c. What does Camus mean by the "underworld"? Why are Sisyphus' efforts in this
   place "measured by skyless space and time without depth" (paragraph 4)?

d. What is Camus driving at when he tells us that "There is no fate that cannot be surmounted by scorn" (paragraph 6) and that we "must imagine Sisyphus happy" (paragraph 10)?

e. Does Camus succeed in comparing Sisyphus with a modern human being? Discuss this analogy, and explain in what way a modern human might also be called absurd.

f. In order for Sisyphus to qualify as a "tragic hero," the author tells us, he must know the "whole extent of his wretched condition." In what way does this "lucidity" ennoble Sisyphus?

g. In what works do the famous literary characters Oedipus and Kirilov appear? How do their stories help illustrate "the recipe for the absurd victory"? What is "Gethsemane," which Camus mentions in paragraph 7?

h. What, for Camus, is "sacred" about Oedipus' conclusion that " 'all is well' "? In what way does this remark make "of fate a human matter, which must be settled among men" (paragraph 8)?

i. Discuss the "higher fidelity that negates the gods and raises rocks" (paragraph 10).

Strategy and Style

j. Camus uses the pronouns "you," "I," "one," and "he." To whom does each of these pronouns refer? In what ways do they create a persona for Camus?

k. What does Camus, or at least the persona of the essay, think of Sisyphus?

SUGGESTIONS FOR SHORT WRITING

a. Write a job description for what Sisyphus does.

b. What image does this essay call to mind? Try drawing that image and then writing a short description of it.

SUGGESTIONS FOR SUSTAINED WRITING

a. Through a skillful use of analogy, Camus reveals the relevance of a classical myth to the modern world. Recall an ancient myth, parable from the Bible, folktale, or children's story that has special significance for you. Why is it still meaningful, and what does it tell us about life and people today? In short, what lesson(s) does it offer the modern reader?

b. In paragraph 6, Camus tells us that "The workman of today works every day in his life at the same tasks, and this fate is no less absurd [than that of Sisyphus]." Do you agree? If so, develop your own analogy of the fate of Sisyphus with that of a modern factory worker, storekeeper, or civil servant. In what way is the latter's "fate" similar to that of Camus' mythical hero? Would it be accurate to describe this person as a "tragic hero"? In what way is she or he "tragic"? In what way a "hero"?

"But a Watch in the Night:" A Scientific Fable

James C. Rettie

James C. Rettie was educated at the University of Oregon, Yale University, and the University of London, where he studied economics. Employed by the United States Forest Service for many years, Rettie was able to indulge his love for the outdoors and his interest in conservation. During the Kennedy and Johnson administrations, he served as an advisor to Secretary of the Interior Stuart Udall. Rettie published often in his field, but this is the only essay for which he is widely remembered by the general public. It first appeared in 1948 in a publication of the Department of Agriculture. Rettie wrote it while serving at a Forest Service station in Pennsylvania.

Out beyond our solar system there is a planet called Copernicus. It came into existence some four or five billion years before the birth of our Earth. In due course of time it became inhabited by a race of intelligent men. 1

About 750 million years ago the Copernicans had developed the motion picture machine to a point well in advance of the stage that we have reached. Most of the cameras that we now use in motion picture work are geared to take twenty-four pictures per second on a continuous strip of film. When such film is run through a projector, it throws a series of images on the screen and these change with a rapidity that gives the visual impression of normal movement. If a motion is too swift for the human eye to see it in detail, it can be captured and artificially slowed down by means of the slow-motion camera. This one is geared to take many more shots per second—ninety-six or even more than that. When the slow motion film is projected at the normal speed of twenty-four pictures per second, we can see just how the jumping horse goes over a hurdle. 2

What about motion that is too slow to be seen by the human eye? That problem has been solved by the use of the time-lapse camera. In this one, the shutter is geared to take only one shot per second, or one per minute, or even one per hour—depending upon the kind of movement that is being photographed. When the time-lapse film is projected at the normal speed of twenty-four pictures per second, it is possible to see a bean sprout growing up out of the ground. Time-lapse films are useful in the study of many types of motion too slow to be observed by the unaided, human eye. 3

The Copernicans, it seems, had time-lapse cameras some 757 million years ago and they also had superpowered telescopes that gave them a clear view of what was happening upon this Earth. They decided to make a film record of the life history of Earth and to make it on the scale of one picture per year. The photography has been in progress during the last 757 million years. 4

In the near future, a Copernican interstellar expedition will arrive upon our Earth and bring with it a copy of the time-lapse film. Arrangements will be made for showing the entire film in one continuous run. This will begin at midnight of New Year's Eve and continue day and night without a single stop until midnight of December 31. The rate of projection will be twenty-four pictures per second. 5

360

Time on the screen will thus seem to move at the rate of twenty-four years per second; 1440 years per minute; 86,400 years per hour; approximately two million years per day; and sixty-two million years per month. The normal life-span of individual man will occupy about three seconds. The full period of earth history that will be unfolded on the screen (some 757 million years) will extend from what the geologists call Pre-Cambrian times up to the present. This will, by no means, cover the full time-span of the earth's geological history but it will embrace the period since the advent of living organisms.

During the months of January, February, and March the picture will be desolate and dreary. The shape of the land masses and the oceans will bear little or no resemblance to those that we know. The violence of geological erosion will be much in evidence. Rains will pour down on the land and promptly go booming down to the seas. There will be no clear streams anywhere except where the rains fall upon hard rock. Everywhere on the steeper ground the stream channels will be filled with boulders hurled down by rushing waters. Raging torrents and dry stream beds will keep alternating in quick succession. High mountains will seem to melt like so much butter in the sun. The shifting of land into the seas, later to be thrust up as new mountains, will be going on at a grand scale. 6

Early in April there will be some indication of the presence of single-celled living organisms in some of the warmer and sheltered coastal waters. By the end of the month it will be noticed that some of these organisms have become multicellular. A few of them, including the Trilobites, will be encased in hard shells. 7

Toward the end of May, the first vertebrates will appear, but they will still be aquatic creatures. In June about 60 per cent of the land area that we know as North America will be under water. One broad channel will occupy the space where the Rocky Mountains now stand. Great deposits of limestone will be forming under some of the shallower seas. Oil and gas deposits will be in process of formation— also under shallow seas. On land there will still be no sign of vegetation. Erosion will be rampant, tearing loose particles and chunks of rock and grinding them into sand and silt to be sped out by the streams into bays and estuaries. 8

About the middle of July the first land plants will appear and take up the tremendous job of soil building. Slowly, very slowly, the mat of vegetation will spread, always battling for its life against the power of erosion. Almost foot by foot, the plant life will advance, lacing down with its root structures whatever pulverized rock material it can find. Leaves and stems will be giving added protection against the loss of the soil foothold. The increasing vegetation will pave the way for the land animals that will live upon it. 9

Early in August the seas will be teeming with fish. This will be what geologists call the Devonian period. Some of the races of these fish will be breathing by means of lung tissue instead of through gill tissues. Before the month is over, some of the lung fish will go ashore and take on a crude lizard-like appearance. Here are the first amphibians. 10

In early September the insects will put in their appearance. Some will look like huge dragonflies and will have a wing spread of 24 inches. Large portions of 11 the land masses will now be covered with heavy vegetation that will include the primitive spore-propagating trees. Layer upon layer of this plant growth will build up, later to appear as the coal deposits. About the middle of this month, there will be evidence of the first seed-bearing plants and the first reptiles. Heretofore, the land animals will have been amphibians that could reproduce their kind only by depositing a soft egg mass in quiet waters. The reptiles will be shown to be freed from the aquatic bond because they can reproduce by means of a shelled egg in which the embryo and its nurturing liquids are sealed and thus protected from destructive evaporation. Before September is over, the first dinosaurs will be seen—creatures destined to dominate the animal realm for about 140 million years and then to disappear.

In October there will be series of mountain uplifts along what is now the   12 eastern coast of the United States. A creature with feathered limbs—half bird and half reptile in appearance—will take itself into the air. Some small and rather unpretentious animals will be seen to bring forth their young in a form that is a miniature replica of the parents and to feed these young on milk secreted by mammary glands in the female parent. The emergence of this mammalian form of animal life will be recognized as one of the great events in geologic time. October will also witness the high water mark of the dinosaurs—creatures ranging in size from that of the modern goat to monsters like Brontosaurus that weighed some 40 tons. Most of them will be placid vegetarians, but a few will be hideous-looking carnivores, like Allosaurus and Tyrannosaurus. Some of the herbivorous dinosaurs will be clad in bony armor for protection against their flesh-eating comrades.

November will bring pictures of a sea extending from the Gulf of Mexico to   13 the Arctic in space now occupied by the Rocky Mountains. A few of the reptiles will take to the air on bat-like wings. One of these, called Pteranodon, will have a wingspread of 15 feet. There will be a rapid development of the modern flowering plants, modern trees, and modern insects. The dinosaurs will disappear. Toward the end of the month there will be a tremendous land disturbance in which the Rocky Mountains will rise out of the sea to assume a dominating place in the North American landscape.

As the picture runs on into December it will show the mammals in command   14 of the animal life. Seed-bearing trees and grasses will have covered most of the land with a heavy mantle of vegetation. Only the areas newly thrust up from the sea will be barren. Most of the streams will be crystal clear. The turmoil of geologic erosion will be confined to localized areas. About December 25 will begin the cutting of the Grand Canyon of the Colorado River. Grinding down through layer after layer of sedimentary strata, this stream will finally expose deposits laid down in Pre-Cambrian times. Thus in the walls of that canyon will appear geological formations dating from recent times to the period when the Earth had no living organisms upon it.

The picture will run on through the latter days of December and even up to   15 its final day with still no sign of mankind. The spectators will become alarmed in the fear that man has somehow been left out. But not so; sometimes about noon on December 31 (one million years ago) will appear a stooped, massive creature of man-like proportions. This will be Pithecanthropus, the Java ape man. For tools and weapons he will have nothing but crude stone and wooden clubs. His children will live a precarious existence threatened on the one side by hostile animals and on the other by tremendous climatic changes. Ice sheets—in places 4,000 feet deep—will form in the northern parts of North America and Eurasia. Four times this glacial ice will push southward to cover half the continents. With each advance the plant and animal life will be swept under or pushed southward. With each recession of the ice, life will struggle to reestablish itself in the wake of the retreating glaciers. The woolly mammoth, the musk ox, and the caribou all will fight to maintain themselves near the ice line. Sometimes they will be caught and put into cold storage—skin, flesh, blood, bones and all.

16   The picture will run on through supper time with still very little evidence of man's presence on the earth. It will be about 11 o'clock when Neanderthal man appears. Another half hour will go by before the appearance of Cro-Magnon man living in caves and painting crude animal pictures on the walls of his dwelling. Fifteen minutes more will bring Neolithic man, knowing how to chip stone and thus produce sharp cutting edges for spears and tools. In a few minutes more it will appear that man has domesticated the dog, the sheep and, possibly, other animals. He will then begin the use of milk. He will also learn the arts of basket weaving and the making of pottery and dugout canoes.

17   The dawn of civilization will not come until about five or six minutes before the end of the picture. The story of the Egyptians, the Babylonians, the Greeks, and the Romans will unroll during the fourth, the third, and the second minute before the end. At 58 minutes and 43 seconds past 11:00 PM (just 1 minute and 17 seconds before the end) will come the beginning of the Christian era. Columbus will discover the new world 20 seconds before the end. The Declaration of Independence will be signed just 7 seconds before the final curtain comes down.

18   In those few moments of geologic time will be the story of all that has happened since we became a nation. And what a story it will be! A human swarm will sweep across the face of the continent and take it away from the . . . red men. They will change it far more radically than it has ever been changed before in a comparable time. The great virgin forests will be seen going down before ax and fire. The soil, covered for eons by its protective mantle of trees and grasses, will be laid bare to the ravages of water and wind erosion. Streams that had been flowing clear will, once again, take up a load of silt and push it toward the seas. Humus and mineral salts, both vital elements of productive soil, will be seen to vanish at a terrifying rate. The railroads and highways and cities that will spring up may divert attention, but they cannot cover up the blight of man's recent activities. In great sections of Asia, it will be seen that man must utilize cow dung and every scrap of available straw or grass for fuel to cook his food. The forests that once provided wood for this purpose will be gone without a trace. The use of these agricultural wastes for fuel, in place of returning them to the land, will be leading to increasing soil impoverishment. Here and there will be seen a dust storm darkening the

landscape over an area a thousand miles across. Man-creatures will be shown counting their wealth in terms of bits of printed paper representing other bits of a scarce but comparatively useless yellow metal that is kept buried in strong vaults. Meanwhile, the soil, the only real wealth that can keep mankind alive on the face of this earth is savagely being cut loose from its ancient moorings and washed into the seven seas.

   We have just arrived upon this earth. How long will we stay?   **19**

1950

QUESTIONS FOR DISCUSSION

Content

a. What is the moral of this "scientific fable"?
b. Why does Rettie label this essay a fable? In what ways is it similar to other fables you may have read?
c. Given the fact that this essay was written in the 1940s, is it appropriate for Rettie to spend so much time introducing it with the story of the Copernicans and of their invention of an advanced movie camera? Why does he go to such great lengths to explain time-lapse photography?
d. What is the obvious basis upon which Rettie constructs his analogy?
e. Rettie takes his title from Psalm 90:4 of the King James Version of the Bible. What do you make of this title? Does the last line of the essay shed any light on it? Look up Psalm 90. How does it relate to this selection?

Strategy and Style

f. Does using an analogy aid Rettie in structuring his essay? Explain how Rettie has organized this piece, and describe his use of transitions.
g. Consult an unabridged dictionary or encyclopedia in order to identify the following:

Copernicus	Pre-Cambrian	Devonian
Babylonians	Cro-Magnon man	Neanderthal man
Java ape man	Mammoth	

h. Rettie makes use of scientific language and allusions to develop his essay. Are such terms and references bothersome to a reader without scientific training? Explain. Why does Rettie make it a point to include them?
i. Rettie writes in the future tense. What effect does that have on the narrative? On his argument?
j. Is there a difference in tone between Rettie's treatment of human history and his discussion of geological events? Where does he think we are heading?

SUGGESTIONS FOR SHORT WRITING

a. Write a brief review of Rettie's "film."
b. Continue Rettie's film into the future, writing an extra paragraph that describes, depending on how you foresee it, either the Earth's destruction or its preservation.

SUGGESTIONS FOR SUSTAINED WRITING

a. Rettie's essay is essentially a listing of a number of important events in the history of the Earth and its inhabitants. He singles out several developments as particularly important, including the rise of the mammals, the development of the Rocky Mountains, and the appearance of Java man. Discuss an event or development (within the last fifteen years) that you believe will have an enormous effect on the history of the world. Explain the consequences of that event or development as fully as you can.
b. How would you answer the question Rettie asks at the very end of the essay? What evidence do you see in the world around you that humanity will continue to build, grow, and flourish—that it will prevail over the forces of doom? What evidence points to the very opposite conclusion? Try to be as detailed as you can and to focus on only one or two major developments.
c. Analogy helps us grasp and order difficult concepts by enabling us to compare them to objects, processes, events, or other ideas with which we are more familiar. Compare an experience you are now going through or a problem you are now facing with something that most readers might already be familiar with. Some examples of such analogies are:

- Working at XYZ Company is very much like living in a zoo.
- Driving Route 1 every morning is like playing Russian Roulette.
- By the end of my day, I feel like I've just run a marathon.
- Having dinner at Aunt Tessie's is like eating at an Italian gourmet restaurant.

The Cosmic Prison

Loren Eiseley

An anthropologist, educator, and poet, Loren Eiseley (1907–1977) was one of the most highly respected and prolific scientific writers of this century. Born in Lincoln, Nebraska, Eiseley was educated at the University of Pennsylvania, where he later became professor of anthropology and of the history of science. His other teaching assignments included appointments to the faculties of the University of Kansas and of Oberlin College. The recipient of numerous honors and awards for public service, Eiseley is also known for his work as a conservationist and nature lover. He contributed scores of scientific studies and articles to scholarly journals but has also authored two books of poetry, a genre he found difficult to escape even when writing highly "technical" prose. Eiseley will probably be best remembered for the unique, eloquent, and sometimes verselike style with which he treats subject matter that would otherwise seem cold, abstract, and esoteric. In short, his work represents the best of both the worlds of poetry and of science: perceptiveness, accuracy, insight, and, above all, an ability to make profound contact with the reader. Eiseley's major works include The Immense Journey *(1957),* Darwin's Century *(1959),* The Firmament of Time *(1960),* The Unexpected Universe *(1969), and* The Invisible Pyramid *(1970), from which this selection is taken.*

1   "A name is a prison, God is free," once observed the Greek poet Nikos Kazantzakis. He meant, I think, that valuable though language is to man, it is by very necessity limiting, and creates for man an invisible prison. Language implies boundaries. A word spoken creates a dog, a rabbit, a man. It fixes their nature before our eyes; henceforth their shapes are, in a sense, our own creation. They are no longer part of the unnamed shifting architecture of the universe. They have been transfixed as if by sorcery, frozen into a concept, a word. Powerful though the spell of human language has proven itself to be, it has laid boundaries upon the cosmos.

2   No matter how far-ranging some of the mental probes that man has philosophically devised, by his own created nature he is forced to hold the specious and emerging present and transform it into words. The words are startling in their immediate effectiveness, but at the same time they are always finally imprisoning because man has constituted himself a prison keeper. He does so out of no conscious intention, but because for immediate purposes he has created an unnatural world of his own, which he calls the cultural world, and in which he feels at home. It defines his needs and allows him to lay a small immobilizing spell upon the nearer portions of his universe. Nevertheless, it transforms that universe into a cosmic prison house which is no sooner mapped than man feels its inadequacy and his own.

3   He seeks then to escape, and the theory of escape involves bodily flight. Scarcely had the first moon landing been achieved before one U.S. senator boldly announced: "We are the masters of the universe. We can go anywhere we choose." This statement was widely and editorially acclaimed. It is a striking example of the comfort of words, also of the covert substitutions and mental projections to which they are subject. The cosmic prison is not made less so by a successful journey of some two hundred and forty thousand miles in a cramped and primitive vehicle.

366

To escape the cosmic prison man is poorly equipped. He has to drag portions 4
of his environment with him, and his life span is that of a mayfly in terms of the
distances he seeks to penetrate. There is no possible way to master such a universe
by flight alone. Indeed such a dream is a dangerous illusion. This may seem a
heretical statement, but its truth is self-evident if we try seriously to comprehend
the nature of time and space that I sought to grasp when held up to view the fiery
messenger that flared across the zenith in 1910. "Seventy-five years," my father
had whispered in my ear, "seventy-five years and it will be racing homeward. Perhaps you will live to see it again. Try to remember."

And so I remembered. I had gained a faint glimpse of the size of our prison 5
house. Somewhere out there beyond a billion miles in space, an entity known as a
comet had rounded on its track in the black darkness of the void. It was surging
homeward toward the sun because it was an eccentric satellite of this solar system.
If I lived to see it it would be but barely, and with the dimmed eyes of age. Yet it,
too, in its long traverse, was but a flitting mayfly in terms of the universe the night
sky revealed.

So relative is the cosmos we inhabit that, as we gaze upon the outer galax- 6
ies available to the reach of our telescopes, we are placed in about the position that
a single white blood cell in our bodies would occupy, if it were intelligently capable of seeking to understand the nature of its own universe, the body it inhabits.
The cell would encounter rivers ramifying into miles of distance seemingly leading nowhere. It would pass through gigantic structures whose meaning it could
never grasp—the brain, for example. It could never know there was an outside, a
vast being on a scale it could not conceive of and of which it formed an infinites-
imal part. It would know only the pouring tumult of the creation it inhabited, but
of the nature of that great beast, or even indeed that it was a beast, it could have
no conception whatever. It might examine the liquid in which it floated and decide, as in the case of the fall of Lucretius's atoms, that the pouring of obscure torrents had created its world.

It might discover that creatures other than itself swam in the torrent. But that 7
its universe was alive, had been born and was destined to perish, its own
ephemeral existence would never allow it to perceive. It would never know the
sun; it would explore only through dim tactile sensations and react to chemical
stimuli that were borne to it along the mysterious conduits of the arteries and
veins. Its universe would be centered upon a great arborescent tree of spouting
blood. This, at best, generations of white blood cells by enormous labor and con-
tinuity might succeed, like astronomers, in charting.

They could never, by any conceivable stretch of the imagination, be aware 8
that their so-called universe was, in actuality, the prowling body of a cat or the
more time-enduring body of a philosopher, himself engaged upon the same quest
in a more gigantic world and perhaps deceived proportionately by greater vistas.
What if, for example, the far galaxies man observes make up, across void spaces
of which even we are atomically composed, some kind of enormous creature or
cosmic snowflake whose exterior we will never see? We will know more than the

phagocyte in our bodies, but no more than that limited creature can we climb out of our universe, or successfully enhance our size or longevity sufficiently to thrust our heads through the confines of the universe that terminates our vision.

Some further "outside" will hover elusively in our thought, but upon its na- **9** ture, or even its reality, we can do no more than speculate. The phagocyte might observe the salty turbulence of an eternal river system, Lucretius the fall of atoms creating momentary living shapes. We suspiciously sense, in the concept of the expanding universe derived from the primordial atom—the monobloc—some kind of oscillating universal heart. At the instant of its contraction we will vanish. It is not given us, nor can our science recapture, the state beyond the monobloc, nor whether we exist in the diastole of some inconceivable being. We know only a little more extended reality than the hypothetical creature below us. Above us may lie realms it is beyond our power to grasp.

1970

QUESTIONS FOR DISCUSSION

Content

a. What is Eiseley saying in the last two sentences of this essay, and how do they relate to the analogy he has created? Would it be accurate to say that these ideas comprise his thesis?

b. What is the "fiery messenger" to which Eiseley alludes in paragraph 4? How does it and the analogy of the human life span to that of a mayfly help him convey the immensity of time and space?

c. How would you explain the analogy between humans and the white blood cell that forms the basis of this essay? What makes the analogy logical and consistent?

d. Who was Lucretius, and what was his "atomic theory"? How does mentioning this theory help Eiseley develop the central analogy of his essay?

e. What does Eiseley mean when he says that "some further 'outside' will hover elusively in our thought" (paragraph 9)? Why can we only "speculate" on "its nature, or even its reality"?

f. In paragraph 4, the author tells us that the dream of escaping from the "cosmic prison" is a "dangerous illusion." What does he mean by this curious statement, and why would someone like the U.S. senator quoted in paragraph 3 find it "heretical"?

g. What is "the oscillating universal heart" (paragraph 9) that we can only "suspiciously sense"? How would you define a "monobloc"?

h. How do the quote from Nikos Kazantzakis and the explanation that proceeds from it serve as an appropriate introduction to this selection?

Strategy and Style

i. Define "the cosmic prison" that Eiseley describes in this selection. Why does he call it a prison? How does his use of the term *prison* relate to Plato's use of the word in "prison-house"?

j. How would you characterize Eiseley's tone in this piece? What image of Eiseley himself does the tone project?

SUGGESTIONS FOR SHORT WRITING

a. Find a passage (a sentence or a paragraph) that has meaning for your own life, and write about the connections you see between Eiseley's words and your life.

b. Eiseley writes of humankind's condition from an earthbound position; writing from a position outside the Earth, describe what you see as humankind's relation to the rest of the cosmos. You might try writing from the point of view of Halley's Comet.

SUGGESTIONS FOR SUSTAINED WRITING

a. Write a short essay in which you make clear what Eiseley means by "the cosmic prison." Use analogies of your own making to get your point across.

b. Eiseley has created a startling comparison between the existence of a human being in the universe with the life of a white blood cell in the human body. Create your own analogy by comparing yourself or someone you know well to a fictional character, to a famous historical figure, or even, for that matter, to an animal whose habits would be easily recognized by your audience. Incidentally, the analogy you develop need not be complimentary.

Shouting "Fire!"

Alan Dershowitz

Alan Dershowitz (b. 1938) was educated at Yale and Harvard law schools and has been a professor of law since 1967. He has written many books for the lay reader, some of which are discussions of criminal law, such as Psychoanalysis, Psychiatry and the Law *(coauthored with others, 1967), and* Criminal Law: Theory and Process *(coauthored with others, 1974). Other books are narratives of some of the controversial cases he has taken on, such as* Reversal of Fortune *(1986), about the Claus von Bulow case, and* Reasonable Doubts *(1996), about the O. J. Simpson case.*

When the Reverend Jerry Falwell learned that the Supreme Court had reversed his 1 $200,000 judgment against Hustler magazine for the emotional distress that he had suffered from an outrageous parody, his response was typical of those who seek to censor speech: "Just as no person may scream 'Fire!' in a crowded theater when there is no fire, and find cover under the First Amendment, likewise, no sleazy merchant like Larry Flynt should be able to use the First Amendment as an excuse for maliciously and dishonestly attacking public figures, as he has so often done."

Justice Oliver Wendell Holmes's classic example of unprotected speech— 2 falsely shouting "Fire!" in a crowded theater—has been invoked so often, by so many people, in such diverse contexts, that it has become part of our national folk language. It has even appeared—most appropriately—in the theater: in Tom Stoppard's play *Rosencrantz and Guildenstern Are Dead* a character shouts at the audience, "Fire!" He then quickly explains: "It's all right—I'm demonstrating the misuse of free speech." Shouting "Fire!" in the theater may well be the only jurisprudential analogy that has assumed the status of a folk argument. A prominent historian recently characterized it as "the most brilliantly persuasive expression that ever came from Holmes's pen." But in spite of its hallowed position in both the jurisprudence of the First Amendment and the arsenal of political discourse, it is and was an inapt analogy, even in the context in which it was originally offered. It has lately become—despite, perhaps even because of, the frequency and promiscuousness of its invocation—little more than a caricature of logical argumentation.

The case that gave rise to the "Fire!"-in-a-crowded-theater analogy, *Schenck* 3 *v. United States,* involved the prosecution of Charles Schenck, who was the general secretary of the Socialist party in Philadelphia, and Elizabeth Baer, who was its recording secretary. In 1917 a jury found Schenck and Baer guilty of attempting to cause insubordination among soldiers who had been drafted to fight in the First World War. They and other party members had circulated leaflets urging draftees not to "submit to intimidation" by fighting in a war being conducted on behalf of "Wall Street's chosen few."

Schenck admitted, and the Court found, that the intent of the pamphlets' "im- 4 passioned language" was to "influence" draftees to resist the draft. Interestingly, however, Justice Holmes noted that nothing in the pamphlet suggested that the draftees should use unlawful or violent means to oppose conscription: "In form at least [the

370

pamplet] confined itself to peaceful measures, such as a petition for the repeal of the act" and an exhortation to exercise "your right to assert your opposition to the draft." Many of its most impassioned words were quoted directly from the Constitution.

Justice Holmes acknowledged that "in many places and in ordinary times 5 the defendants, in saying all that was said in the circular, would have been within their constitutional rights." "But," he added, "the character of every act depends upon the circumstances in which it is done." And to illustrate that truism he went on to say:

> The most stringent protection of free speech would not protect a man
> in falsely shouting fire in a theater, and causing a panic. It does not
> even protect a man from an injunction against uttering words that
> may have all the effect of force.

Justice Holmes then upheld the convictions in the context of a wartime draft, 6 holding that the pamphlet created "a clear and present danger" of hindering the war effort while our soldiers were fighting for their lives and our liberty.

The example of shouting "Fire!" obviously bore little relationship to the facts 7 of the Schenck case. The Schenck pamphlet contained a substantive political message. It urged its draftee readers to *think* about the message and then—if they so chose—to act on it in a lawful and nonviolent way. The man who shouts "Fire!" in a crowded theater is neither sending a political message nor inviting his listener to think about what he has said and decide what to do in a rational, calculated manner. On the contrary, the message is designed to force action *without* contemplation. The message "Fire!" is directed not to the mind and the conscience of the listener but, rather, to his adrenaline and his feet. It is a stimulus to immediate *action,* not thoughtful reflection. It is—as Justice Holmes recognized in his follow-up sentence—the functional equivalent of "uttering words that may have all the effect of force."

Indeed, in that respect the shout of "Fire!" is not even speech, in any mean- 8 ingful sense of that term. It is a *clang* sound, the equivalent of setting off a nonverbal alarm. Had Justice Holmes been more honest about his example, he would have said that freedom of speech does not protect a kid who pulls a fire alarm in the absence of a fire. But that obviously would have been irrelevant to the case at hand. The proposition that pulling an alarm is not protected speech certainly leads to the conclusion that shouting the word "fire" is also not protected. But the core analogy is the nonverbal alarm, and the derivative example is the verbal shout. By cleverly substituting the derivative shout for the core alarm, Holmes made it possible to analogize one set of words to another—as he could not have done if he had begun with the self-evident proposition that setting off an alarm bell is not free speech.

The analogy is thus not only inapt but also insulting. Most Americans do not 9 respond to political rhetoric with the same kind of automatic acceptance expected of schoolchildren responding to a fire drill. Not a single recipient of the Schenck pamphlet is known to have changed his mind after reading it. Indeed, one draftee, who appeared as a prosecution witness, was asked whether reading a pamphlet asserting that the draft law was unjust would make him "immediately decide that you must erase that law." Not surprisingly, he replied, "I do my own thinking." A theatergoer would probably not respond similarly if asked how he would react to a shout of "Fire!"

Another important reason why the analogy is inapt is that Holmes empha- 10 sizes the factual falsity of the shout "Fire!" The Schenck pamphlet, however, was not factually false. It contained political opinions and ideas about the causes of the war and about appropriate and lawful responses to the draft. As the Supreme Court recently reaffirmed (in *Falwell v. Hustler*), "The First Amendment recognizes no such thing as a 'false' idea." Nor does it recognize false opinions about the causes of or cures for war.

A closer analogy to the facts of the Schenck case might have been provided 11 by a person's standing outside a theater, offering the patrons a leaflet advising them that in his opinion the theater was structurally unsafe, and urging them not to enter but to complain to the building inspectors. That analogy, however, would not have served Holmes's argument for punishing Schenck. Holmes needed an analogy that would appear relevant to Schenck's political speech but that would invite the conclusion that censorship was appropriate.

Unsurprisingly, a war-weary nation—in the throes of a know-nothing hys- 12 teria over immigrant anarchists and socialists—welcomed the comparison between what was regarded as a seditious political pamphlet and a malicious shout of "Fire!" Ironically, the "Fire!" analogy is nearly all that survives from the Schenck case; the ruling itself is almost certainly not good law. Pamphlets of the kind that resulted in Schenck's imprisonment have been circulated with impunity during subsequent wars.

Over the past several years I have assembled a collection of instances— 13 cases, speeches, arguments—in which proponents of censorship have maintained that the expression at issue is "just like" or "equivalent to" falsely shouting "Fire!" in a crowded theater and ought to be banned, "just as" shouting "Fire!" ought to be banned. The analogy is generally invoked, often with self-satisfaction, as an absolute argument-stopper. It does, after all, claim the high authority of the great Justice Oliver Wendell Holmes. I have rarely heard it invoked in a convincing, or even particularly relevant, way. But that, too, can claim lineage from the great Holmes.

Not unlike Falwell, with his silly comparison between shouting "Fire!" and 14 publishing an offensive parody, courts and commentators have frequently invoked "Fire!" as an analogy to expression that is not an automatic stimulus to panic. A state supreme court held that "Holmes's aphorism . . . applies with equal force to pornography"—in particular to the exhibition of the movie *Carmen Baby* in a drive-in theater in close proximity to highways and homes. Another court analogized "picketing . . . in support of a secondary boycott" to shouting "Fire!" because in both instances "speech and conduct are brigaded." In the famous Skokie case one of the judges argued that allowing Nazis to march through a city where a large number of Holocaust survivors live "just might fall into the same category as one's 'right' to cry fire in a crowded theater."

Outside court the analogies become even more badly stretched. A 15 spokesperson for the New Jersey Sports and Exposition Authority complained that newspaper reports to the effect that a large number of football players had contracted cancer after playing in the Meadowlands—a stadium atop a landfill—were the "journalistic equivalent of shouting fire in a crowded theater." An insect researcher acknowledged that his prediction that a certain amusement park might become roach-infested "may be tantamount to shouting fire in a crowded theater." The philosopher Sidney Hook, in a letter to the New York Times bemoaning a Supreme Court decision that required a plaintiff in a defamation action to prove that the offending statement was actually false, argued that the First Amendment does not give the press carte blanche to accuse innocent persons "any more than the First Amendment protects the right of someone falsely to shout fire in a crowded theater."

Some close analogies to shouting "Fire!" or setting off an alarm are, of 16 course, available: Calling in a false bomb threat; dialing 911 and falsely describing an emergency; making a loud, gun-like sound in the presence of the President; setting off a voice-activated sprinkler system by falsely shouting "Fire!" In one case in which the "Fire!" analogy was directly to the point, a creative defendant tried to get around it. The case involved a man who calmly advised an airline clerk that he was "only here to hijack the plane." He was charged, in effect, with shouting "Fire!" in a crowded theater, and his rejected defense—as quoted by the court—was as follows: "If we built fire-proof theaters and let people know about this, then the shouting of 'Fire!' would not cause panic."

Here are some more-distant but still related examples: The recent incident 17 of the police slaying in which some members of an onlooking crowd urged a mentally ill vagrant who had taken an officer's gun to shoot the officer; the screaming of racial epithets during a tense confrontation; shouting down a speaker and preventing him from continuing his speech.

Analogies are, by their nature, matters of degree. Some are closer to the core 18 example than others. But any attempt to analogize political ideas in a pamphlet, ugly parody in a magazine, offensive movies in a theater, controversial newspaper articles, or any of the other expressions and actions catalogued above to the very different act of shouting "Fire!" in a crowded theater is either self-deceptive or self-serving.

The government does, of course, have some arguably legitimate bases for 19 suppressing speech which bear no relationship to shouting "Fire!" It may ban the publication of nuclear-weapon codes, of information about troop movements, and of the identity of undercover agents. It may criminalize extortion threats and conspiratorial agreements. These expressions may lead directly to serious harm, but the mechanisms of causation are very different from that at work when an alarm is sounded. One may also argue—less persuasively, in my view—against protecting certain forms of public obscenity and defamatory statements. Here, too, the mechanisms of causation are very different. None of these exceptions to the First Amendment's exhortation that the government "shall make no law . . . abridging the freedom of speech, or of the press" is anything like falsely shouting "Fire!" in a crowded theater; they all must be justified on other grounds.

A comedian once told his audience, during a stand-up routine, about the time **20** he was standing around a fire with a crowd of people and got in trouble for yelling "Theater, theater!" That, I think, is about as clever and productive a use as anyone has ever made of Holmes's flawed analogy.

1989

QUESTIONS FOR DISCUSSION

Content

a. Explain the connection between shouting "fire!" and censorship.
b. What is the false connection (analogy) that Dershowitz finds fault with? Why does he find fault with it?
c. What is the valid analogy?
d. Why is it important for us to see the difference between the false analogy and the valid one? What impact does this distinction have on your life?
e. Reread paragraph 8, and paraphrase it. What is the "core analogy" and the "derivative example"? How did Holmes make it "possible to analogize one set of words to another"?
f. Why is it necessary for Dershowitz to explain the concept of shouting "fire!" so thoroughly?

Strategy and Style

g. What is a "folk argument" (paragraph 2)? What is the author's attitude toward folk arguments?
h. Why does he end with the humorous example of shouting "theater!"?
i. Dershowitz relies heavily on quotations from the people and cases he finds fault with. How does he use these quotations?
j. Look also at how Dershowitz writes his sentences so that the quotes sound as if they are part of his own prose. What techniques does he use to do this?

SUGGESTIONS FOR SHORT WRITING

a. Dershowitz uses analogy as a way to define *free speech* and *censorship*. Write definitions of these terms as you understand Dershowitz to define them.
b. Brainstorm a list of other examples of how the "shouting 'fire!'" analogy would apply to real life.

SUGGESTIONS FOR SUSTAINED WRITING

a. Should there be laws limiting free speech? If you believe that speech should be limited, write an essay in which you argue for such laws. What are the limitations you would impose and why? Explain your proposal in detail, and defend it by citing real or hypothetical cases in which your laws would be beneficial. If you believe that speech should not be limited in any way, write an argument in which you show that limitations would have a detrimental effect on society. Again, be detailed and use real or hypothetical cases to illustrate your points.

b. What does Dershowitz's essay have to do with your own life? Write an expository (explanatory) essay in which you first explain Dershowitz's points and then, with examples drawn from your own experience and observation, show the connections between his essay and real life.

Am I Blue?

Alice Walker

Born in Eatontown, Georgia, Alice Walker (b. 1944) attended Spelman College and took her BA at Sarah Lawrence. She has taught and been a writer-in-residence at several prestigious American colleges and universities, but she has also worked for the New York City Department of Welfare, for a Head Start program in Mississippi, and for voter registration drives in Georgia. Among her many literary awards are a Pulitzer Prize and an American Book Award for The Color Purple *(1982), which was turned into a major film. Walker's other fiction includes* In Love and Trouble: Stories of Black Women *(1973) and* The Temple of My Familiar *(1989). She is also a well-known activist, literary critic, biographer, and essayist. She has recently written the memoirs* The Same River Twice *(1996) and* Anything We Love Can Be Saved: A Writer's Activism. *"Am I Blue?" first appeared in* Ms. *magazine in 1986.*

For about three years my companion and I rented a small house in the country that 1
stood on the edge of a large meadow that appeared to run from the end of our deck straight into the mountains. The mountains, however, were quite far away, and between us and them there was, in fact, a town. It was one of the many pleasant aspects of the house that you never really were aware of this.

It was a house of many windows, low, wide, nearly floor to ceiling in the liv- 2
ing room, which faced the meadow, and it was from one of these that I first saw our closest neighbor, a large white horse, cropping grass, flipping its mane, and ambling about—not over the entire meadow, which stretched well out of sight of the house, but over the five or so fenced-in acres that were next to the twenty-odd that we had rented. I soon learned that the horse, whose name was Blue, belonged to a man who lived in another town, but was boarded by our neighbors next door. Occasionally, one of the children, usually a stocky teenager, but sometimes a much younger girl or boy, could be seen riding Blue. They would appear in the meadow, climb up on his back, ride furiously for ten or fifteen minutes, then get off, slap Blue on the flanks, and not be seen again for a month or more.

There were many apple trees in our yard, and one by the fence that Blue 3
could almost reach. We were soon in the habit of feeding him apples, which he relished, especially because by the middle of summer the meadow grasses—so green and succulent since January—had dried out from lack of rain, and Blue stumbled about munching the dried stalks half-heartedly. Sometimes he would stand very still just by the apple tree, and when one of us came out he would whinny, snort loudly, or stamp the ground. This meant, of course: I want an apple.

It was quite wonderful to pick a few apples, or collect those that had fallen 4
to the ground overnight, and patiently hold them, one by one, up to his large, toothy mouth. I remained as thrilled as a child by his flexible dark lips, huge, cube-like teeth that crunched the apples, core and all, with such finality, and his high, broad-breasted *enormity;* beside which, I felt small indeed. When I was a child, I used to ride horses, and was especially friendly with one named Nan until the day

376

I was riding and my brother deliberately spooked her and I was thrown, head first, against the trunk of a tree. When I came to, I was in bed and my mother was bending worriedly over me; we silently agreed that perhaps horseback riding was not the safest sport for me. Since then I have walked, and prefer walking to horseback riding—but I had forgotten the depth of feeling one could see in horses' eyes.

I was therefore unprepared for the expression in Blue's. Blue was lonely. 5 Blue was horribly lonely and bored. I was not shocked that this should be the case; five acres to tramp by yourself, endlessly, even in the most beautiful of meadows—and his was—cannot provide many interesting events, and once rainy season turned to dry that was about it. No, I was shocked that I had forgotten that human animals and nonhuman animals can communicate quite well; if we are brought up around animals as children we take this for granted. By the time we are adults we no longer remember. However, the animals have not changed. They are in fact *completed* creations (at least they seem to be, so much more than we) who are not likely to change; it is their nature to express themselves. What else are they going to express? And they do. And, generally speaking, they are ignored.

After giving Blue the apples, I would wander back to the house, aware that he 6 was observing me. Were more apples not forthcoming then? Was that to be his sole entertainment for the day? My partner's small son had decided he wanted to learn how to piece a quilt; we worked in silence on our respective squares as I thought . . .

Well, about slavery: About white children, who were raised by black peo- 7 ple, who knew their first all-accepting love from black women, and then, when they were twelve or so, were told they must "forget" the deep levels of communication between themselves and "mammy" that they knew. Later they would be able to relate quite calmly, "My old mammy was sold to another good family." "My old mammy was ———— ————." Fill in the blank. Many more years later a white woman would say: "I can't understand these Negroes, these blacks. What do they want? They're so different from us."

And about the Indians, considered to be "like animals" by the "settlers" (a 8 very benign euphemism for what they actually were), who did not understand their description as a compliment.

And about the thousands of American men who marry Japanese, Korean, 9 Filipina, and other non-English-speaking women and of how happy they report they are, *"blissfully,"* until their brides learn to speak English, at which point the marriages tend to fall apart. What then did the men see, when they looked into the eyes of the women they married, before they could speak English? Apparently only their own reflections.

I thought of society's impatience with the young. "Why are they playing the 10 music so loud?" Perhaps the children have listened to much of the music of oppressed people their parents danced to before they were born, with its passionate but soft cries for acceptance and love, and they have wondered why their parents failed to hear.

I do not know how long Blue had inhabited his five beautiful, boring acres 11 before we moved into our house; a year after we had arrived—and had also traveled to other valleys, other cities, other worlds—he was still there.

But then, in our second year at the house, something happened in Blue's life.   **12**
One morning, looking out the window at the fog that lay like a ribbon over the
meadow, I saw another horse, a brown one, at the other end of Blue's field. Blue
appeared to be afraid of it, and for several days made no attempt to go near. We
went away for a week. When we returned, Blue had decided to make friends and
the two horses ambled or galloped along together, and Blue did not come nearly
as often to the fence underneath the apple tree.

When he did, bringing his new friend with him, there was a different look in   **13**
his eyes. A look of independence, of self-possession, of inalienable *horse*ness. His
friend eventually became pregnant. For months and months there was, it seemed
to me, a mutual feeling between me and the horses of justice, of peace. I fed apples to them both. The look in Blue's eyes was one of unabashed "this is *it*ness."

It did not, however, last forever. One day, after a visit to the city, I went out   **14**
to give Blue some apples. He stood waiting, or so I thought, though not beneath
the tree. When I shook the tree and jumped back from the shower of apples, he
made no move. I carried some over to him. He managed to half-crunch one. The
rest he let fall to the ground. I dreaded looking into his eyes—because I had of
course noticed that Brown, his partner, had gone—but I did look. If I had been
born into slavery, and my partner had been sold or killed, my eyes would have
looked like that. The children next door explained that Blue's partner had been
"put with him" (the same expression that old people used, I had noticed, when
speaking of an ancestor during slavery who had been impregnated by her owner)
so that they could mate and she conceive. Since that was accomplished, she had
been taken back by her owner, who lived somewhere else.

Will she be back? I asked.   **15**

They didn't know.   **16**

Blue was like a crazed person. Blue *was*, to me, a crazed person. He galloped   **17**
furiously, as if he were being ridden, around and around his five beautiful acres.
He whinnied until he couldn't. He tore at the ground with his hooves. He butted
himself against his single shade tree. He looked always and always toward the
road down which his partner had gone. And then, occasionally, when he came up
for apples, or I took apples to him, he looked at me. It was a look so piercing, so
full of grief, a look so *human*, I almost laughed (I felt too sad to cry) to think there
are people who do not know that animals suffer. People like me who have forgotten, and daily forget, all that animals try to tell us. "Everything you do to us will
happen to you; we are your teachers, as you are ours. We are one lesson" is essentially it, I think. There are those who never once have even considered animals'
rights: Those who have been taught that animals actually want to be used and
abused by us, as small children "love" to be frightened, or women "love" to be mutilated and raped. . . . They are the great-grandchildren of those who honestly
thought, because someone taught them this: "Women can't think," and "niggers
can't faint." But most disturbing of all, in Blue's large brown eyes was a new look
more painful than the look of despair: The look of disgust with human beings, with
life; the look of hatred. And it was odd what the look of hatred did. It gave him,

for the first time, the look of a beast. And what that meant was that he had put up a barrier within to protect himself from further violence; all the apples in the world wouldn't change that fact.

And so Blue remained, a beautiful part of our landscape, very peaceful to look **18** at from the window, white against the grass. Once a friend came to visit and said, looking out on the soothing view: "And it *would* have to be a *white* horse; the very image of freedom." And I thought, yes, the animals are forced to become for us merely "images" of what they once so beautifully expressed. And we are used to drinking milk from containers showing "contented" cows, whose real lives we want to hear nothing about, eating eggs and drumsticks from "happy" hens, and munching hamburgers advertised by bulls of integrity who seem to command their fate.

As we talked of freedom and justice one day for all, we sat down to steaks. **19** I am eating misery, I thought, as I took the first bite. And spit it out.

1986

QUESTIONS FOR DISCUSSION

Content

a. To what is Blue analogous?
b. In paragraph 5 Walker writes that animals are "completed creations." What does she mean by this? Is she saying that humans are incomplete?
c. According to Walker, what is the usual relationship between animals and humans? What is the relationship that ought to exist?
d. What connections does Walker make between the treatment of animals and slavery?
e. What does Walker assume we will see if we really look into an animal's eyes? What would we see if we really looked into a person's eyes?
f. What is it that animals are trying to tell us?

Strategy and Style

g. Though this essay primarily uses the strategy of analogy, it is also an argument. What is Walker arguing for or against? Is she making more than one argument?
h. The author projects human feelings onto Blue. What mood or tone does this create for the essay? How does it affect the argumentative nature of the essay? Does it make the essay seem less or more convincing?
i. The essay gets increasingly emotional as it progresses. How effective is this strategy?
j. At what point does Walker explicitly mention cruelty to animals? At what point does she mention cruelty to people?
k. Why is the childhood memory described in paragraph 4 necessary? What does it tell us that is essential to understanding the entire essay?

SUGGESTIONS FOR SHORT WRITING

a. What is this essay mainly about? Slavery? Animal rights? Vegetarianism? Another subject? Decide what the main subject of the essay is and write a brief explanation of your choice. Cite examples from the text to illustrate your explanation.

b. Describe the enclosed pasture, from Blue's point of view. What does he think about his life? What does he think of Walker?

SUGGESTIONS FOR SUSTAINED WRITING

a. Use analogy to write an argument. Begin by listing several possible analogies. In Walker's essay, for example, the life of Blue is analogous to the lives of slaves, Native Americans, and women, and to those of other animals. In creating your analogy, think of things that are microcosms, i.e., miniature versions, of a larger world or of an important issue. Consider what you could argue by using such analogies.

   Use Walker's essay as a model for organization and as a guide for generating the kinds of examples to include. Draw on your own experiences and observations for such examples.

b. Write an extended response to Walker's essay. Analyze her use of childhood memories, description, personification, and emotional appeals to create a unified argument. Include your own reactions as you read her essay, both what you felt and what you thought as you read. Finally, explain whether you find her use of memories, description, and so on, effective. In other words, do her strategies help her to persuade you?

Gawk Shows

Nicols Fox

A commentator on the media, culture, and the visual arts, Nicols Fox published "Gawk Shows" in Lear's *magazine in July 1991. She is now a contributing editor at the* New Art Examiner, *is located in Chicago. Fox has also published in the* Economist *and in several other important publications such as the* Christian Science Monitor *and* Newsweek.

I remember the dusty heat of late summer, the yellow and white tent, and the barker strutting on the platform. His voice rose above the sounds of the carnival, hinting of the wonders within the tent, wonders painted in cheap colors on the cracked backdrop: The two-headed baby, the world's fattest man, the bearded woman. I remember the sideshows. I thought they were long behind us.

I turn on the television and see an astonishing sight: A woman. Her soul is beautiful. It penetrates the atmosphere, even across airwaves. Her body is not. It is covered with the lumps and bumps of Elephant Man disease. Sally Jessy Raphael, wearing her trademark red spectacles, cocks her blond head and asks what the woman's life is like. A window is opened into pain. There are more victims of the disease sitting in the audience. We are treated to its various manifestations. We are horrified and amazed: We gawk.

Phil Donahue interviews tiny, wizened children. They have progeria, "the aging disease." With their outsize, hairless heads and huge eyes imparting solemnity and even wisdom, they offer us themselves as a sacrifice to our curiosity. We are compelled into silence, fascinated. We are back in the tent.

While I was living in Europe in the late sixties and early seventies, friends often asked me to tell them what to expect when they visited America. "Think of America as a carnival," I would tell them. "An unending carnival." This was the only way I knew to explain my country. Not just the quality of light and landscape but the excess, the enthusiasm, the love of excitement. We want no limitations on what we can have, on what we can do. We deny ourselves nothing—no objects, no sensations. "The pursuit of happiness": What other nation has made it an absolute right?

The carnival plays on, and we have returned to the sideshows—minus the honesty that made no pretense about what lay behind the curtain, the honesty that divided the world into those who were able to resist satisfying their curiosity at the expense of others and those who were not. Gawking is painted in shades of solicitude now. We justify much in the name of compassion, but we are in fact being entertained in the same ancient tradition. Gawk shows sell.

"I offer no apology," says Donahue. "These children have been unmercifully pressured by their very distinctive appearance." The purpose of the show? "To humanize people who have suffered. It becomes a vehicle for examining our prejudices. Just because it may be true that this kind of show draws a crowd does not condemn it," he says.

381

For Sally Jessy Raphael the rationale is the same: "Teaching the lessons of 7
compassion. Man's triumph over adversity."

These are noble thoughts, and not entirely hypocritical. Compassion and un- 8
derstanding are always in short supply. There is an outside chance that some of each
might be spread around in this exercise. We may also be witnessing exploitation.
"These children are risking their lives to be here," says Sally, introducing children
who will die if exposed to light. What may *she* be risking if they don't appear? As
Donahue says, "If I don't draw a crowd, I could be parking cars for a living."

Donahue is open about the dilemma: "Americans are more interested in 9
Madonna than Managua. The country suffers, in my opinion, from the diminished
interest in serious news. Whichever way you look at it we have a culture of decay." It's tricky playing two sides at once. "It's like walking on eggs. I don't want
to be a dead hero," he says.

We watch our cultural demise in living color.   10

Do you find yourself addicted to sex with prostitutes? Tell Oprah Winfrey and 11
her audience all about it. Did you engage in an affair with your priest? Have your breast
implants started slipping? Geraldo Rivera wants to know. Do you wish you could reverse your sex-change operation? Are you a celebrity subject to diarrhea at odd moments? Does your mother keep stealing your boyfriends? We care, we are interested.
Whatever your problem, there's a television talk show that will accommodate you.

Donahue, Oprah, Sally, Geraldo: They are the virtuosos of voyeurism, lift- 12
ing the skirts of our culture, peering into the closets, airing the national soiled
linen. Sally thinks of her program as a kind of updated town meeting—the modern version of something we no longer have. Electronic gossip, in other words—
the national back fence. Wishful thinking.

As Americans we've been indulging in an orgy of self-analysis and self- 13
revelation—coupled with a natural curiosity now totally unbridled. We've become
a society hooked on the bizarre and the astonishing—living in a perpetual state of
"Can you top this?" Transvestite men marry women on Sally's show, thus proving
an important point, one we all needed to know: Sixty-five percent of all transves-
tites are not homosexual.

Nothing is sacred. There are no memories, no mysteries too precious to re- 14
veal. A woman discusses her husband's sexual addiction. Geraldo asks the husband for details—and gets them. There is nothing we won't share, or watch someone else share, with a million strangers.

We have invented a new social contract on the talk shows: Lay bare your 15
body, your bed, your soul, your emotions, your worst fears, your innermost secrets, and we will give you a moment or two of fame. Every sacrifice can and
should be made to the video god.

Are there topics too hot to talk about?   16

"How to blow up your local post office," says Donahue. He'd draw the line 17
there.

There is no topic Sally wouldn't consider if it "concerns the human condi- 18
tion." She draws the line only at being boring. We have to want to watch it. So we
set the agenda.

Donahue, a man obviously in conflict between his natural honesty and bet-   19
ter instincts and his ambition, admits that his audience calls the shots. Devoting a
recent show to strippers—both male and female—he says, "It must be ratings
week. I don't want to do these shows . . . they make me." Sure they do. But who
is making us watch?

Freedom of expression is not the issue here. Nobody's suggesting censor-   20
ship or even paternalistic decisions based on what someone else thinks is good for
us. The issue is honesty—honesty about why we watch. The talk shows are merely
giving us what we want. The question is, Why do we want it?

In some cultures it was thought that illness or bad luck could be transferred   21
from one person to another by magic. James G. Frazer, in his classic work *The
Golden Bough,* told of one example: "To get rid of warts, take a string and make
as many knots in it as you have warts. Then lay the string under a stone. Whoever
treads upon the stone will get the warts, and you will be rid of them." Something
like that draws us to the tent. We confirm our own normalcy because our worst
fears have been manifested in someone else—the visual equivalent of burying the
string. Or, if we see ourselves in someone who has survived our common plight,
we are reassured; we are not alone.

There is no slouching into the tent today. We walk in shamelessly, casting   22
off inhibitions in the name of openness.

The new openness has, in fact, turned out to be an empty promise. Are things   23
any better than they were two decades ago? Has drug abuse or wife abuse or child
abuse declined as we have learned more? Are we any happier thinking that a friend
who takes a drink is a potential alcoholic, that every stranger is a child-snatcher?

How has this new compassion we are teaching been made evident? Ask the   24
parents who have three HIV-positive sons and found their house burned down because of it. Ask the people who cluster over the grates of subways in our largest
cities. If you were a trapped whale or a little girl down a well, solicitude would
flow your way in great waves. It still helps to be cute or little or white or furry or
totally nonthreatening when you're looking for compassion—or pretty, when you
want a bone marrow transplant.

The potential is there on the TV talk shows for real entertainment—and for   25
service. Oprah scored with a terrific show on female comics. Programs on health
matters or economic questions are valuable. During the first days of the war in the
Persian Gulf, Donahue aired shows that were serious and important contributions
to our understanding of the conflict. "I do have a conscience," he says.

Geraldo, however, ever subject to the temptations of the flesh, spoiled   26
what could have been a serious discussion of breast implants by having Jessica
Hahn as the honored guest and by fondling examples of the implants inter-
minably. Does he have it right? Are we a people who need to watch breast implants being fondled?

What happens when we set aside our last taboo? What happens when we've   27
finally been titillated to a terminal numbness, incapable of shock, on the prowl for
a new high? What manner of stimulation will we need next? Are we addicted? Talk
show codependent?

Which topic affects us more: the discussion of the S & L crisis Donahue did 28
last summer or the interviews with the strippers? Which do you think got the better ratings?

In a free society we get what we want. We shouldn't be surprised when we 29
end up with what we deserve. But we can't transfer blame. It's not the hosts'
fault—it's the viewers'.

1991

QUESTIONS FOR DISCUSSION

Content

a. According to Fox, in what ways are carnival sideshows and television talk
   shows similar?
b. In what important way are carnival sideshows different from television talk
   shows?
c. Reread paragraph 5. In what way does the point Fox is making here relate to
   her thesis? What is her thesis, and where is it most succinctly expressed?
d. Explain the point made in paragraph 4. How does this idea relate to the essay's
   thesis?
e. How do talk-show hosts, such as Sally Jessy Raphael, justify the content of
   their shows?
f. What "dilemma" do talk-show hosts face? How does Fox react to this problem?
g. How does Fox answer those who might say that her essay is an attack on free
   speech? In what way does her response relate to her thesis?
h. What potential for constructive social discourse does the author see in television talk shows? Does her discussion of this potential weaken or strengthen her
   argument?
i. How does Fox respond to hosts who claim their shows teach valuable lessons?
j. In paragraph 15, the author says that "We have invented a new social contract
   on the talk shows." What does she mean? What was the "old" social contract?
k. What theory does Fox offer to explain the reasons that audiences are drawn to
   talk shows?

Strategy and Style

l. The essay begins with a description of a carnival sideshow. Where in the essay
   do we find direct comparisons between the sideshow and the television talk
   show?
m. Is the title of this essay appropriate? Why or why not?
n. What does the fact that Fox chose to create an extended analogy tell you about
   her point of view?
o. How does Fox's citing James G. Fraser affect her argument?

p. Does the author use irony? Where? What is the effect of using this device? How would you describe her tone overall?

q. The last few paragraphs criticize the viewing public. Why didn't Fox begin her essay with these comments?

r. How would you describe the audience for this essay?

SUGGESTIONS FOR SHORT WRITING

a. "Nothing is sacred," Fox claims in paragraph 14. If you were a talk-show producer, would you consider certain topics off-limits? Which ones? Make a list of them and explain your reasons?

b. If, like Sally Jessy Raphael, you believe that only boring topics should be avoided, freewrite for about 10 minutes and explain your point of view.

c. Is Fox criticizing a great majority of American television viewers in paragraphs 12, 13, 14, and 15? If so, do you agree with such an indictment or can such criticism be limited to a relatively small portion of the viewing public?

SUGGESTIONS FOR SUSTAINED WRITING

a. In reference to television talk shows, Fox asks, "Are we addicted?" What's your opinion? Write a well-developed essay in which you argue on one or the other side of this question.

b. Are we addicted to other types of television fare? For example, is the American public hooked on soap operas, sports spectaculars, situation comedies, news magazines, docudramas, game shows, or court TV? Write an essay in which you name and discuss specific examples to prove your point.

c. Write an essay in which you use analogy to discuss common "addiction" other than one to drugs or alcohol. For example, discuss America's addiction to fast foods, sports, exercise, fast cars, television, the movies, or sex.

d. Recently, we have heard a great many arguments about prohibiting minors access to sexually explicit materials on CDs, on television, in the movies, and on the Internet. What's your opinion? Does such a prohibition violate freedom of expression, or should we draw the line somewhere?

10

Argument and Persuasion

Strictly speaking, argument is a rhetorical technique used to support or deny a proposition by offering detailed evidence for or against it in a logically connected fashion. Classical argument relies on deductive and inductive thinking; it appeals to reason and reason alone. Deduction proceeds from a general truth or principle to a more specific instance based on that principle. You would be using deduction if you argued:

All full-time students are permitted to use the college weight room free of charge;
I am a full-time student;
I am permitted to use the weight room free of charge.

Inductive reasoning, on the other hand, proceeds from several specific occurrences to one general truth. Let's say you come down with a bad case of food poisoning—fever, cramps, vomiting, the works! When you feel better, you call up the five people with whom you had dinner; each of them claims to have suffered the same symptoms. It is probably safe to infer that all six of you ate contaminated food.

Sometimes, of course, one's purpose may go beyond simply proving a point. The writer may feel a need to *persuade,* that is, to convert the audience, or even to convey a sense of urgency that will convince readers to act and to act quickly. In such cases, pure logic may not suffice. Thus, while grounding the paper in logic and well-developed evidence, a writer may also wish to appeal to the emotions.

Both methods are legitimate forms studied under the general category of argumentation, and both are represented, to varying degrees, in the essays that follow. Indeed, it is often hard to draw a line. Jonathan Swift's "A Modest Proposal," a model of deductive reasoning expressed in language that is cool, clear, and eminently logical, is couched in a bitter irony that expresses the author's rage over Britain's treatment of the Irish.

Argument lends itself naturally to debate on matters scientific, social, and political. Note the selections by Barbara Ehrenreich, Garrett Hardin, and Stephen

386

Jay Gould. In an essay that recalls a campus incident involving freedom of speech, Nat Hentoff condemns the university's handling of the case. His essay is followed by two letters that attempt to refute his logic. Mike Wallace's "The Press Needs a National Monitor" and its companion piece by Don Hewitt make a strong case that logic and evidence can be used to argue convincingly for and against the same proposal. It is important to note that, as reasoned and clear as these five selections are, each remains unique, varying in tone and urgency according to the proximity from which its author views the subject.

The five persuasive selections illustrate techniques you might use when trying to move your readers or convince them to act. Make sure to read "I Have a Dream" by Martin Luther King, Jr.; it is a classic. However, Rodriguez's "Bilingual Education: Outdated and Unrealistic" and Debra Dickerson's "Who Shot Johnny?" also offer excellent insight into the workings of persuasion, and they are sure to interest and even move you. Finally, the essays by Ann N. Martin and the organization known as The Nature of Wellness will surely get you to consider the issue of animal rights and, perhaps, write a response agreeing with or attacking their points of view.

In fact, that is true of every piece in this chapter. Even though these essays are examples of well-written arguments, you might wish to take issue with the positions they advocate and write a rebuttal to one or two of them. Keep in mind, however, that the essential ingredient in building an effective argument is a thorough knowledge of your subject. Without it, your readers will remain unconvinced despite your ability to stir their emotions. Think of yourself as an attorney. You will have difficulty defending your client unless you know all the facts. Anything less will jeopardize your credibility with the jury. This idea also applies to your role as a writer. Good readers will approach your thesis with a healthy skepticism. They may be open to persuasion—some may even want to be convinced—but most will insist that you provide reasonable, well-developed, and convincing evidence before they give you their trust!

ARGUMENT

Should This Student Have Been Expelled?
Nat Hentoff

Nat Hentoff writes a regular column for The Village Voice, *the New York City weekly, and he contributes frequently to the* Washington Post, *the* New Yorker, *and other major magazines, journals, and newspapers. Born in Boston, he took his BA at Northeastern University and attended Harvard University for postgraduate study. He also studied at the Sorbonne in Paris as a Fulbright fellow. Hentoff describes himself as an "advocacy writer," and his interests range from jazz to educational reform, subjects on which he has written several books and articles. He has also written several novels and biographies. However, Hentoff's reputation rests chiefly on his writings on the First Amendment to the U.S. Constitution. Indeed, he is among America's staunchest defenders of free speech and its most outspoken opponents of censorship. One of his books on this subject is* The First Freedom: The Tumultuous History of Free Speech in America *(1989). "Should This Student Have Been Expelled?," which first appeared in* The Village Voice *in 1991, responds to a letter to the* New York Times *by Vartan Gregorian, president of Brown University, and to a* Times *editorial supporting Brown's expulsion of Douglas Hann. Both the letter and the editorial appear after Hentoff's essay.*

The day that Brown denies any student freedom of speech is the day I give up my presidency of the university.

> —Vartan Gregorian, president of Brown University,
> February 20, 1991

Doug Hann, a varsity football player at Brown, was also concentrating on organi- 1
zational behavior and management and business economics. On the night of October 18, 1990, Hann, a junior, was celebrating his twenty-first birthday, and in the process had imbibed a considerable amount of spirits.

At one point, Hann shouted into the air, "Fuck you, niggers!" It was aimed 2
at no one in particular but apparently at all black students at Brown. Or in the world. A freshman leaned out a dormitory window and asked him to stop being so loud and offensive.

Hann, according to reporters on the *Brown Daily Herald,* looked up and 3
yelled, "What are you, a faggot?" Hann then noticed an Israeli flag in the dorm. "What are you, a Jew?" he shouted. "Fucking Jew!"

Hann had achieved the hat trick of bigotry. (In hockey, the hat trick is scor- 4
ing three goals in a game.) In less than a minute, Hann had engaged in racist, anti-Semitic, and homophobic insults.

He wasn't through. As reported by Smita Nerula in the *Brown Daily Herald,* 5
the freshman who had asked Hann to cool it recruited a few people from his dorm "and followed Hann and his friends."

388

"This resulted in a verbal confrontation outside of Wayland Arch. At this 6 time, [Hann] was said to have turned to one of the freshman's friends, a black woman, and shouted, 'My parents own your people.' "

To the Jewish student, or the student he thought was Jewish, Hann said, 7 "Happy Hanukkah."

There are reports that at this juncture Hann tried to fight some of the students 8 who had been following him. But, the *Brown Daily Herald* reports, he "was held back by one of his friends, while [another] friend stretched his arm across the Wayland Gates to keep the students from following Hann."

John Howard Crouch—a student and Brown chapter secretary of the Amer- 9 ican Civil Liberties Union there—tells me that because Hann had friends restraining him, "nobody seriously expected fighting, regardless of anyone's words."

Anyway, there was no physical combat. Just words. Awful words, but noth- 10 ing more than speech. (Nor were there any threats.)

This was not the first time Hann's disgraceful drunken language had sur- 11 faced at Brown. Two years before, in an argument with a black student at a fraternity bar, Hann had called the student a "nigger." Thereupon he had been ordered to attend a race relations workshop and to get counseling for possible alcohol abuse. Obviously, he has not been rehabilitated.

Months went by after Hann's notorious birthday celebration as Brown's in- 12 ternal disciplinary procedures cranked away. (To steal a phrase from Robert Sherrill, Brown's way of reaching decisions in these matters is to due process as military music is to music. But that's true of any college or university I know anything about.)

At last, the Undergraduate Disciplinary Council (five faculty or administra- 13 tion members and five students) ruled that Doug Hann was to leave the university forevermore. Until two years ago, it was possible for a Brown student to be dismissed, which meant that he or she could reapply after a decent period of penance. But now, Brown has enshrined the sentence of expulsion. You may go on to assist Mother Teresa in caring for the dying or you may teach a course in feminism to 2 Live Crew, but no accomplishments, no matter how noble, will get you back into Brown once you have been expelled.

Doug Hann will wander the earth without a Brown degree for the rest of 14 his days.

The president of Brown, Vartan Gregorian—formerly the genial head of the 15 New York Public Library—had the power to commute or even reverse the sentence. But the speech code under which Hann was thrown out had been proposed by Gregorian himself shortly after he was inaugurated in 1989, so he was hardly a detached magistrate.

On January 25, 1991, Vartan Gregorian affirmed, with vigor, the expulsion 16 decision by the Undergraduate Disciplinary Council.

Hann became a historic figure. Under all the "hate speech" codes enacted 17 around the country in recent years, he is the first student to actually be expelled for violating one of the codes.

The *New York Times* (February 12) reported that "Howard Ehrlich, the re- **18** search director of the National Institute Against Prejudice and Violence, said that he did not know of any other such expulsions, but that he was familiar with cases in which students who had harassed others were moved to other dormitories or ordered to undergo counseling."

But that takes place in *educational* institutions, whose presidents recognize **19** that there are students who need help, not exile.

At first, there didn't seem to be much protest among the student body at **20** Brown on free speech grounds—except for members of the Brown chapter of the ACLU and some free thinkers on the student paper, as well as some unaffiliated objectors to expelling students for what they say, not for what they do. The number of these dissenters is increasing, as we shall see.

At the student paper, however, the official tone has changed from the liber- **21** tarian approach of Vernon Silver, who was editor-in-chief last semester. A February 13 *Brown Daily Herald* editorial was headed: *"Good Riddance."*

It began: "Doug Hann is gone, and the university is well to be rid of him." **22**

But President Gregorian has been getting a certain amount of flack and so, **23** smiting his critics hip and thigh, he wrote a letter to the *New York Times*. Well, that letter (printed on February 21) was actually a press release, distributed by the Brown University News Bureau to all sorts of people, including me, on February 12. There were a few changes—and that *Brown Daily Herald* editorial was attached to it—but Gregorian's declaration was clearly not written exclusively for the *Times*.

Is this a new policy at the *Times*—taking public relations handouts for the **24** letters page?

Next week I shall include a relentlessly accurate analysis of President Gre- **25** gorian's letter by the executive director of the Rhode Island ACLU. But first, an account of what Gregorian said in that letter to the *Times*.

President Gregorian indignantly denies that Brown has ever expelled "any- **26** one for the exercise of free speech, nor will it ever do so." Cross his heart.

He then goes into self-celebration: "My commitment to free speech and **27** condemnation of racism and homophobia are well known. . . .

"The university's code of conduct does not prohibit speech; it prohibits **28** *actions*."

Now watch this pitiable curve ball: **29**

"Offense III [of the Brown code]—which deals with harassment—prohibits **30** inappropriate, abusive, threatening, or demeaning actions based on race, religion, gender, handicap, ethnicity, national origin, or sexual orientation."

In the original press release, Gregorian underlined the word *actions*. There, **31** and in the letter to the *Times*—lest a dozing reader miss the point—Gregorian emphasizes that "The rules do not proscribe words, epithets, or slanders, they proscribe behavior." Behavior that "shows flagrant disrespect for the well-being of others or is unreasonably disruptive of the University community."

Consider the overbreadth and vagueness of these penalty-bearing provi- 32 sions. What are the definitions of "harassment," "inappropriate," "demeaning," "flagrant," "disrespect," "well-being," "unreasonably"?

Furthermore, with regard to Brown's termination of Doug Hann with ex- 33 treme prejudice, Gregorian is engaging in the crudest form of Orwellian newspeak. Hann was kicked out for *speech,* and only speech—not for *actions,* as Gregorian huffily insists. As for behavior, the prickly folks whose burning of the American flag was upheld by the Supreme Court were indeed engaged in behavior, but that behavior was based entirely on symbolic speech. So was Hann's. He didn't punch anybody or vandalize any property. He brayed.

Art Spitzer, legal director of the ACLU's National Capital Area affiliate, 34 wrote a personal letter to Gregorian:

"There is a very simple test for determining whether a person is being pun- 35 ished for his actions or his speech. You just ask whether he would have received the same punishment if he had spoken different words while engaging in the same conduct."

"Thus, would your student have been expelled if he had gotten drunk and 36 stood in the same courtyard at the same hour of the night, shouting at the same decibel level, 'Black is Beautiful!' 'Gay is Good!' or 'Go Brown! Beat Yale!' or even 'Nuke Baghdad! Kill Saddam!'?

"I am confident," Spitzer said, that "he would not have been expelled for 37 such 'actions.' If that is correct, it follows that *he was expelled for the unsavory content of his speech,* and not for his actions. I have no doubt that you can understand this distinction. (Emphasis added.)

"Now, you are certainly entitled to believe that it is appropriate to expel a 38 student for the content of his speech when that content is sufficiently offensive to the 'university community.' . . .

"If that is your position, why can't you deliver it forthrightly? Then the uni- 39 versity community can have an open debate about which opinions it finds offensive, and ban them. Perhaps this can be done once a year, so that the university's rules can keep pace with the tenor of the times—after all, it wouldn't do to have outmoded rules banning procommunist or blasphemous speech still on the books, now that it's 1991. Then students and teachers applying for admission or employment at Brown will know what they are getting into.

"Your recent statements, denying the obvious, are just hypocritical. . . ."   40

And what did the *New York Times*—in a stunningly fatuous February 21 ed- 41 itorial—say of Vartan Gregorian's sending Doug Hann into permanent exile? "A noble attempt both to govern and teach."

The *Times* editorials should really be signed, so that the rest of the editorial 42 board isn't blamed for such embarrassments.

1991

How Much Hate to Tolerate

New York Times editorial, (February 21, 1991)

Free speech and human relations seemed to collide last month at Brown University when it expelled a student for racial and religious harassment. In fact, however, to judge by all that is publicly known, the school walked a fine line with sensitivity toward its complex mission. 1

One mission of a university is to send into the world graduates who are tolerant of many races, faiths and cultures. Another mission is to teach the value of free expression and tolerance even for hateful ideas. But should such tolerance cover racist, sexist or homophobic speech that makes the learning environment intolerable for racial and religious minorities, women and other targets of abuse? Brown found a reasonable basis for saying, clearly, no. 2

Douglas Hann, white, a junior and a varsity football player, had previously been disciplined for alcohol abuse and for racial insults against a black fellow student. Then, one evening last fall, he shouted racial insults in a university courtyard. A Jewish student who opened a dormitory window and called for quiet was answered with a religious insult. Later that evening Mr. Hann directed a racial insult at a black undergraduate. 3

The student-faculty discipline committee found him guilty of three violations of student rules, including another count of alcohol abuse. Vartan Gregorian, the university's president, upheld the student's expulsion last month. He had a sound basis for doing so. If the facts are reported correctly, Mr. Hann crossed the line between merely hateful speech and hateful speech that directly confronted and insulted other undergraduates. 4

Some courts have found that public universities are bound by the First Amendment's ban on state censorship and thus may not punish students for expressing politically incorrect or socially distasteful ideas. Brown, like other private schools, is less directly bound by the Constitution but committed to its precepts. It is trying to avoid censorship but draws a line between strong language and what the courts often call "fighting words." 5

In the adjacent Letters column today, Mr. Gregorian insists that Brown does not punish unruly speech as such but will decide case-by-case whether a student has passed "the point at which speech becomes behavior" that flagrantly disregards the well-being of others or "subjects someone to abusive or demeaning actions." 6

That formula is a noble attempt both to govern and teach. It offers a principled basis for disciplinary action against Mr. Hann for his direct, confrontational conduct. 7

The lines may not be so clearly drawn in other cases. There may also be more of them in the present climate of evidently increasing student intolerance. But when bigots attack other students with ugly invective, universities, whether public or private, need not remain silent. Their presidents, like Mr. Gregorian, may denounce indecency and, in so doing, protect tolerance. 8

Should This Student Have Been Expelled?   Nat Hentoff

393

Brown Expulsion Not About Free Speech

New York Times letter to the editor, (February 21, 1991)

To the Editor:

"Student at Brown Is Expelled Under a Rule Barring 'Hate Speech' " (news arti- 1
cle, Feb. 12) suggests I have instituted "hate-speech" prohibitions at Brown University and that the expulsion of a student who shouted racial and homophobic epithets on campus last October is the first such in the nation based on restrictions
of free speech. Brown University has never expelled anyone for free speech, nor
will it ever do so.

My commitment to free speech and condemnation of racism and homopho- 2
bia are well known. In April 1989, several students were subjected to a cowardly
attack of racial and homophobic graffiti. The words and slogans scrawled anonymously on doors in one of our dormitories were vicious attacks threatening the
well-being and security of Brown students.

I condemned that anonymous poisoning of our community and said I would 3
prosecute vigorously and seek the expulsion of those who incite hatred or perpet-
uate such acts of vandalism. Nothing I said then or have done since should be construed as limiting anyone's freedom of speech, nor have I revised the university's
code of conduct to that effect.

The university's code of conduct does not prohibit speech; it prohibits 4
actions, and these include behavior that "shows flagrant disrespect for
the well-being of others or is unreasonably disruptive of the university community."

Offense III, which deals with harassment, prohibits inappropriate, abusive, 5
threatening or demeaning actions based on race, religion, gender, handicap, ethnicity, national origin or sexual orientation.

"The Tenets of Community Behavior," which outline community standards 6
for acceptable behavior at Brown, have been read for more than 10 years by entering students, who agree in writing to abide by them.

The rules do not proscribe words, epithets or slanders; they proscribe be- 7
havior. The point at which speech becomes behavior and the degree to which that
behavior shows flagrant disrespect for the well-being of others (Offense II), subjects someone to abusive or demeaning actions (Offense III) or is related to drug
or alcohol use (Offense IV) is determined by a hearing to consider the circumstances of each case. The student is entitled to an appeal, which includes review
by a senior officer and a decision by the president.

I cannot and will not comment about any specific case. I regret the release 8
of any student's name in connection with a disciplinary hearing and the exposure
any case may receive in *The Brown Herald.*

Freedom-of-speech questions lie at the heart of any academic community. 9
The very nature of the academic enterprise necessitates that universities remain

partisans of heterodoxy, of a rich and full range of opinions, ideas and expression. Imposed orthodoxies of all sorts, including what is called "politically correct" speech, are anathema to our enterprise.

The university's most compelling challenge is to achieve a balance between 10 the right of its individual members to operate and speak freely, and fostering respect for and adherence to community values and standards of conduct.

VARTAN GREGORIAN
President, Brown University
Providence, R.I., Feb. 21, 1991

QUESTIONS FOR DISCUSSION

Content

a. In a sentence or two, summarize Hentoff's argument against Hann's expulsion.
b. Explain the analogy the author uses in paragraph 12.
c. Why, according to Hentoff, wouldn't Vartan Gregorian "commute or even reverse" Hann's sentence (paragraph 15)?
d. What does Hentoff imply about Brown's president in paragraph 19?
e. What is "Orwellian newspeak" (paragraph 33)? According to Hentoff, in what way is Gregorian engaging in "newspeak"?
f. Explain the test "for determining whether a person is being punished for his actions or his speech" as articulated by Art Spitzer in paragraphs 35–37.
g. Explain the advice Spitzer gave Gregorian as quoted from his letter in paragraph 39.
h. What purpose does Hentoff's conclusion serve? What is his point in the essay's very last paragraph?

Strategy and Style

i. Why does Hentoff include paragraph 10? Is it really necessary?
j. Why does he characterize Gregorian's letter to the *Times* as a "public relations" handout (paragraph 24)? How would you describe Hentoff's attitude toward the newspaper's editorial board?
k. Analyze the structure of the essay. If necessary, write a brief outline that includes its key points and reveals its organization.
l. Where in this selection does Hentoff appeal to authority by quoting expert testimony? Who are those experts? Is their testimony convincing?
m. What advantage does Hentoff achieve by quoting directly from Gregorian's letter to the *Times*? Other than directly attacking the letter's contents, how does he refute Gregorian?

SUGGESTIONS FOR SHORT WRITING

a. Summarize the arguments made by the writer of the *New York Times* editorial "How Much Hate to Tolerate." Then, do the same for Vartan Gregorian's letter to the editor.

b. Are you in favor of unlimited freedom of expression? If so, explain why. In an attempt to anticipate opposing arguments, explain how you would defend the right of others to express themselves in ways you consider immoral, abhorrent, or even dangerous.

c. Do you believe we should limit freedom of expression in certain instances? If so, provide one or two examples.

SUGGESTIONS FOR SUSTAINED WRITING

a. In your own letter to the editor, attack or defend Hentoff's position on the expulsion of Doug Hann and on its implications vis-à-vis the exercise of free speech on college campuses. Whichever position you take, make reference to or quote from Hentoff's essay, the *New York Times* editorial, and/or Gregorian's letter. On the other hand, remember that this is your letter, so rely heavily on your own arguments and insights.

b. The American college is a place where open and free debate should be encouraged. You probably know of several important issues—academic, political, cultural, scientific, theological, economic, and so on—being discussed by students and faculty at your college. Take a clear position on an issue that affects you as a student, that you have studied or read about, or that you have debated with others at your school. You need not choose an issue of universal significance. Interesting and effective arguments can be written on increasing scholarship aid, providing more parking spaces for college commuters, keeping the library open late at night and on Sundays, or giving students access to computer labs free of charge.

A Step Back to the Workhouse?

Barbara Ehrenreich

Barbara Ehrenreich (b. 1941) earned her BA from Reed College in 1963 and her PhD from Rockefeller University in 1968. A noted feminist and socialist, she is a contributing editor for Ms. *but frequently writes for other magazines such as* The Nation, Utne Reader, New Republic, *and* Time. *One of her central concerns is women's status in social institutions such as the health care system, politics, and, as in this article reprinted from* Ms., *the welfare system. The many books she has authored or coauthored deal with these and related concerns; they include* Complaints and Disorders: The Sexual Politics of Sickness *(1973),* Remaking Love: The Feminization of Sex *(1986), and* Fear of Falling: The Inner Life of the Middle Class *(1990). She has been the recipient of several awards, including a National Magazine Award in 1980, a Ford Foundation Award for Humanistic Perspectives on Contemporary Issues in 1981, and a Guggenheim Fellowship in 1987.*

The commentators are calling it a "remarkable consensus." Workfare, as programs 1 to force welfare recipients to work are known, was once abhorred by liberals as a step back toward the 17th-century workhouse or—worse—slavery. But today no political candidate dares step outdoors without some plan for curing "welfare dependency" by putting its hapless victims to work—if necessary, at the nearest Burger King. It is as if the men who run things, or who aspire to run things (and we are, unfortunately, talking mostly about men when we talk about candidates), had gone off and caucused for a while and decided on the one constituency that could be safely sacrificed in the name of political expediency and "new ideas," and that constituency is poor women.

Most of the arguments for workfare are simply the same indestructible 2 stereotypes that have been around, in one form or another, since the first public relief program in England 400 years ago: That the poor are poor because they are lazy and dissolute, and that they are lazy and dissolute because they are suffering from "welfare dependency." Add a touch of modern race and gender stereotypes and you have the image that haunts the workfare advocates: A slovenly, over-weight, black woman who produces a baby a year in order to augment her welfare checks.

But there is a new twist to this season's spurt of welfare-bashing: Workfare 3 is being presented as a kind of *feminist* alternative to welfare. As Senator Daniel Patrick Moynihan (D.–N.Y.) has put it, "A program that was designed to pay mothers to stay at home with their children [i.e., welfare, or Aid to Families with Dependent Children] cannot succeed when we now observe most mothers going out to work." Never mind the startling illogic of this argument, which is on a par with saying that no woman should stay home with her children because other women do not, or that a laid-off male worker should not receive unemployment compensation because most men have been observed holding jobs. We are being asked to believe that pushing destitute mothers into the work force (in some versions of workfare, for no other compensation than the welfare payments they would have received anyway) is consistent with women's strivings toward self-determination.

396

Now I will acknowledge that most women on welfare—like most unem- 4
ployed women in general—would rather have jobs. And I will further acknowledge that many of the proponents of workfare, possibly including Senator Moynihan and the Democratic Presidential candidates, have mounted the bandwagon
with the best of intentions. Welfare surely needs reform. But workfare is not the
solution, because "dependency"—with all its implications of laziness and depravity—is not the problem. The problem is poverty, which most women enter in a
uniquely devastating way—with their children in tow.

Let me introduce a real person, if only because real people, as opposed to 5
imaginative stereotypes, never seem to make an appearance in the current rhetoric on welfare. "Lynn," as I will call her, is a friend and onetime neighbor who has
been on welfare for two years. She is also about as unlike the stereotypical "welfare mother" as one can get—which is to say that she is a fairly typical welfare recipient. She has only one child, which puts her among the 74 percent of welfare
recipients who have only one or two children. She is white (not that that should
matter), as are almost half of welfare recipients. Like most welfare recipients, she
is not herself the daughter of a welfare recipient, and hence not part of anything
that could be called an "intergenerational cycle of dependency." And like every
woman on welfare I have ever talked to, she resents the bureaucratic hassles that
are the psychic price of welfare. But, for now, there are no alternatives.

When I first met Lynn, she seemed withdrawn and disoriented. She had just 6
taken the biggest step of her 25 years; she had left an abusive husband and she was
scared: Scared about whether she could survive on her own and scared of her estranged husband. He owned a small restaurant; she was a high school dropout who
had been a waitress when she met him. During their three years of marriage he had
beaten her repeatedly. Only after he threw her down a flight of stairs had she realized that her life was in danger and moved out. I don't think I fully grasped the terror she had lived in until one summer day when he chased Lynn to the door of my
house with a drawn gun.

Gradually Lynn began to put her life together. She got a divorce and went 7
on welfare; she found a pediatrician who would accept Medicaid and a supermarket that would take food stamps. She fixed up her apartment with second-hand furniture and flea market curtains. She was, by my admittedly low standards, a compulsive housekeeper and an overprotective mother; and when she wasn't waxing
her floors or ironing her two-year-old's playsuits, she was studying the help-
wanted ads. She spent a lot of her time struggling with details that most of us
barely notice—the price of cigarettes, mittens, or of a bus ticket to the welfare office—yet, somehow, she regained her sense of humor. In fact, most of the time we
spent together was probably spent laughing—over the foibles of the neighbors, the
conceits of men, and the snares of welfare and the rest of "the system."

Yet for all its inadequacies, Lynn was grateful for welfare. Maybe if she had 8
been more intellectually inclined she would have found out that she was suffering
from "welfare dependency," a condition that is supposed to sap the will and de-
molish the work ethic. But "dependency" is not an issue when it is a choice

between an abusive husband and an impersonal government. Welfare had given Lynn a brief shelter in a hostile world, and as far as she was concerned, it was her ticket to *independence.*

Suppose there had been no welfare at the time when Lynn finally summoned   9 the courage to leave her husband. Suppose she had gone for help and been told she would have to "work off" her benefits in some menial government job (restocking the toilet paper in rest rooms is one such "job" assigned to New York women in a current workfare program). Or suppose, as in some versions of workfare, she had been told she would have to take the first available private sector job, which (for a non-high school graduate like Lynn) would have paid near the minimum wage, or $3.35 an hour. How would she have been able to afford child care? What would she have done for health insurance (as a welfare recipient she had Medicaid, but most low-paying jobs offer little or no coverage)? Would she have ever made the decision to leave her husband in the first place?

As Ruth Sidel points out in *Women and Children Last* (Viking), most women   10 who are or have been on welfare have stories like Lynn's. They go onto welfare in response to a crisis—divorce, illness, loss of a job, the birth of an additional child to feed—and they remain on welfare for two years or less. They are not victims of any "welfare culture," but of a society that increasingly expects women to both raise and support children—and often on wages that would barely support a woman alone. In fact, even some of the most vociferous advocates of replacing welfare with workfare admit that, in their own estimation, only about 15 percent of welfare recipients fit the stereotype associated with "welfare dependency": Demoralization, long-term welfare use, lack of drive, and so on.

But workfare will not help anyone, not even the presumed 15 percent of "bad   11 apples" for whose sake the majority will be penalized. First, it will not help because it does not solve the problem that drives most women into poverty in the first place: How to hold a job *and* care for children. Child care in a licensed, professionally run center can easily cost as much as $100 a week per child—more than most states now pay in welfare benefits (for two children) and more than most welfare recipients could expect to earn in the work force. Any serious effort to get welfare recipients into the work force would require childcare provisions at a price that would probably end up higher than the current budget for AFDC. But none of the workfare advocates are proposing that sort of massive public commitment to child care.

Then there is the problem of jobs. So far, studies show that existing state work-   12 fare programs have had virtually no success in improving their participants' incomes or employment rates. Small wonder: Nearly half the new jobs generated in recent years pay poverty-level wages; and most welfare recipients will enter jobs that pay near the minimum wage, which is $6,900 a year—26 percent less than the poverty level for a family of three. A menial, low-wage job may be character-building (from a middle-class vantage point), but it will not lift anyone out of poverty.

Some of my feminist activist friends argue that it is too late to stop the work-   13 fare juggernaut. The best we can do, they say, is to try to defeat the more pernicious proposals: those that are over-coercive, that do not offer funds for child care, or that would relegate work clients to a "subemployee" status unprotected by federal labor and civil rights legislation. Our goal, the pragmatists argue, should be to harness the current enthusiasm for workfare to push for services welfare recipients genuinely need, such as child care and job training and counseling.

I wish the pragmatists well, but for me, it would be a betrayal of women like 14 Lynn to encourage the workfare bandwagon in any way. Most women, like Lynn, do not take up welfare as a career, but as an emergency measure in a time of personal trauma and dire need. At such times, the last thing they need is to be hustled into a low-wage job, and left to piece together child care, health insurance, transportation, and all the other ingredients of survival. In fact, the main effect of workfare may be to discourage needy women from seeking any help at all—a disastrous result in a nation already suffering from a child poverty rate of nearly 25 percent. Public policy should be aimed at giving impoverished mothers (and, I would add, fathers) the help they so urgently need—not only in the form of job opportunities, but sufficient income support to live on until a job worth taking comes along.

Besides, there is an ancient feminist principle at stake. The premise of all the 15 workfare proposals—the more humane as well as the nasty—is that single mothers on welfare are not *working*. But, to quote the old feminist bumper sticker, EVERY MOTHER IS A WORKING MOTHER. And those who labor to raise their children in poverty—to feed and clothe them on meager budgets and to nurture them in an uncaring world—are working the hardest. The feminist position has never been that all women must pack off their children and enter the work force, but that all women's work—in the home or on the job—should be valued and respected.

Barbara Ehrenreich's essay stimulated a lively response from Ms. *readers. The following letters were published in the February 1988 issue.*

I was absolutely thrilled when I read Barbara Ehrenreich's article on work- 16 fare ("A Step Back to the Workhouse?" November 1987). As a single mother who received welfare for several years (with no child support) I'm against everything that workfare stands for. I belong to an organization called Women, Work, and Welfare, a group of current and former welfare recipients trying to empower ourselves and become a part of the decisions that affect our lives as poor women. It seems as if everybody but the welfare recipient herself has a hand in the decisions that are made.

CHERI HONKALA
Minneapolis, Minn.

I arrived in Chicago in 1952 with a husband and two children from a camp 17 in Europe. I had another child in 1953, lost a newborn in 1954, had a miscarriage, a hysterectomy, and a divorce in 1955. I never received child support. My ex-husband was remarried within two months.

I *never* received welfare. I worked in another culture, while in very bad 18 health. I found a two-room flat, had no furniture and slept for years on the floor. I even went back to school at night and had to contend with companies like Gulf Oil Corp., which did not believe in promoting women. But I just slugged on.

By the end of the sixties, I had two daughters in college, and I had bought a 19 house. My total earnings for 1970 from three jobs came to a whopping $8,000.

A full-time minimum wage job *can* support one adult and one child. One just 20 has to learn how to do it.

URRSULA SCHRAMM
Hurley, Wis.

I found myself agreeing with the problems that Barbara Ehrenreich outlines 21 in the present workfare program.

Yet deep inside a protesting rumbling exploded when I read that impover- 22 ished mothers should receive sufficient income support to live on "until a job worth taking comes along." *Bullshit!* Sure, we all should have the right to only work a job we love, but how many of us can afford to wait for it? That we are often forced to work at jobs that are not fulfilling says a lot about our society in which more needs to be changed than just the welfare system!

My mother was forced to go to work when I was nine years old. Our family 23 was in dire financial straits and at the age of 50 she took a job in a factory. Was that job "worth taking"? Did it utilize her unique talents? *No!* Did it bring her personal fulfillment? *No!* Did it prevent the bank from foreclosing on our home? *Yes!* Did it give my mother the power to overcome our financial crisis and maintain her autonomy? *Yes!* You tell me if it was "worth taking." That depends on what your self-respect is worth to you.

GAIL FREI
Newtown Square, Pa.

Barbara Ehrenreich omitted a major element in her discussion of the vic- 24 timization of welfare families: The inability or unwillingness of the legal system to award *and enforce* realistic child support. Until it stops being easier to abandon your children than to default on that car loan, women and those who depend on them will be welfare/workfare victims.

SUSAN MARTIN RYNARD
Durham, N.C.

I went on welfare when my daughter was three, when I left my husband. I 25 had a high school education, but had always wanted to go to college. I was 25.

So, with the help of the government, I got my B.S. in nursing. I worked for 26 several years as an R.N. and then returned to school for my master's degree. For graduate school, I lived on savings, loans, and grants. The loans ($19,000 for undergrad and graduate in all) will be paid off in less than a year, in time for my daughter to begin college!

KATHRYN REID
Silverado, Calif.

Although I share Barbara Ehrenreich's concerns about workfare and the 27
plight of her friend Lynn, the conclusions she draws strike me as misguided. We
live in a society where the myths of the work ethic and self-help are deeply em-
bedded in the popular culture; where resort to the dole is frowned upon unless the
need is temporary or arises from disability; where the middle-class majority feels
inequitably taxed, as compared to the wealthy, to support a system that directly
benefits few of its members.

Feminists and other liberals should acknowledge the swelling demand for 28
welfare reform. Our support should be conditional upon the incorporation in any
welfare reform plan of provision for *quality* childcare facilities; upon the mini-
mization of coercion; and upon further efforts to compel ex-spouses to pay their
fair share of support. Nothing in this approach rules out our going ahead simultaneously with other, parallel efforts to question the mystique of work or to expose
the links between welfare and poverty, on the one hand, and capitalism and the
subordination of women, on the other.

DAVID G. BECKER 29
Hanover, N.H.

California is serious about workfare, but we call it GAIN (Greater
Avenues for Independence). It offers welfare recipients vocational counseling,
up to two years of vocational training, and workshops in how to get and hold
a job.

GAIN also pays for child care and transportation. No job need be accepted 30
by the recipient unless she/he will *net* at least as much as their AFDC grant, *including* child care, transportation, and medical insurance. And even then, they will
receive funds to cover these costs for three months after they begin working to
help them make the transition to the work force.

JANE KIRCHMAN
Guerneville, Calif.

QUESTIONS FOR DISCUSSION

Content

a. What does Ehrenreich mean when she writes: "We are being asked to believe
    that pushing destitute mothers into the work force . . . is consistent with
    women's strivings toward self-determination" (paragraph 3)? How is *self-
    determination* used in this context?
b. Where is Ehrenreich's thesis, her argument in a nutshell? What are the two
    main points she uses to support this argument? Evaluate these points. Do you
    agree with the argument?
c. Discuss the stereotype of "welfare dependency" she tries to dispel in this essay.

d. What do the "pragmatists" she mentions in paragraph 13 want? Why won't she oblige them?

e. What, according to the author, are the benefits of the welfare system?

Strategy and Style

f. Why does she begin by attacking opposing arguments? Is her strategy effective? In what other essays in this chapter is this strategy used?

g. In paragraph 5, Ehrenreich tells the story of a woman she knows. Why is narration a particularly effective strategy at this point in the essay?

h. Besides telling Lynn's story, the author uses many statistics. Which is more effective in convincing you? Why?

i. In what parts of this essay does the author use the opinions of authorities on the welfare system to support her arguments?

j. Why does she begin an essay on so serious a subject with sarcasm ("putting its hapless victims to work—if necessary, at the nearest Burger King," paragraph 1)? Does doing so make her argument more effective? If so, in what ways?

k. Point to other uses of irony and sarcasm. How would you characterize the overall tone of this essay?

SUGGESTIONS FOR SHORT WRITING

a. Use freewriting to address Ehrenreich's point in paragraph 3. Do you agree with the author, with Senator Moynihan, or with neither? Explain your position.

b. Reread paragraph 15. Respond negatively or positively to Ehrenreich's premise that "every mother is a working mother."

SUGGESTIONS FOR SUSTAINED WRITING

a. Write an argument for or against workfare in which you take into account the arguments cited in Ehrenreich's essay.

b. Write a letter in response to a recent newspaper or magazine article with which you find yourself strongly agreeing or disagreeing. Submit it as a letter to the editor of that newspaper or magazine.

Lifeboat Ethics: The Case Against Helping the Poor

Garrett Hardin

Garrett Hardin (b. 1915) is a human ecologist who writes, lectures, and teaches about this subject. Though his formal scientific training has been extensive (he was educated at the University of Chicago and at Stanford University, where he received a PhD in biology) and he has written many academic articles, he has always been most interested in making the connections between science and society clear to a wide, nonacademic audience. His desire is to "explain science to the public" and his many books written for lay readers show this. Among his publications are several books on population growth, including Population, Evolution and Birth Control *(1964),* The Limits of Altruism *(1977), and* Living Within Limits: Ecology, Economics, and Population Taboos *(1993). Some of his essays are collected in* Naked Emperors: Essays of a Taboo-Stalker *(1982).*

1 Environmentalists use the metaphor of the earth as a "spaceship" in trying to persuade countries, industries and people to stop wasting and polluting our natural resources. Since we all share life on this planet, they argue, no single person or institution has the right to destroy, waste, or use more than a fair share of its resources.

2 But does everyone on earth have an equal right to an equal share of its resources? The spaceship metaphor can be dangerous when used by misguided idealists to justify suicidal policies for sharing our resources through uncontrolled immigration and foreign aid. In their enthusiastic but unrealistic generosity, they confuse the ethics of a spaceship with those of a lifeboat.

3 A true spaceship would have to be under the control of a captain, since no ship could possibly survive if its course were determined by committee. Spaceship Earth certainly has no captain; the United Nations is merely a toothless tiger, with little power to enforce any policy upon its bickering members.

4 If we divide the world crudely into rich nations and poor nations, two thirds of them are desperately poor, and only one third comparatively rich, with the United States the wealthiest of all. Metaphorically each rich nation can be seen as a lifeboat full of comparatively rich people. In the ocean outside each lifeboat swim the poor of the world, who would like to get in, or at least to share some of the wealth. What should the lifeboat passengers do?

5 First, we must recognize the limited capacity of any lifeboat. For example, a nation's land has a limited capacity to support a population and as the current energy crisis has shown us, in some ways we have already exceeded the carrying capacity of our land. So here we sit, say 50 people in our lifeboat. To be generous, let us assume it has room for 10 more, making a total capacity of 60. Suppose the 50 of us in the lifeboat see 100 others swimming in the water outside, begging for admission to our boat or for handouts. We have several options: We may be tempted to try to live by the Christian ideal of being "our brother's keeper," or by the Marxist ideal of "to each according to his needs." Since the needs of all in the

403

water are the same, and since they can all be seen as our "brothers," we could take them all into our boat, making a total of 150 in a boat designed for 60. The boat swamps; everyone drowns. Complete justice, complete catastrophe.

Since the boat has an unused excess capacity of 10 more passengers, we 6 could admit just 10 more to it. But which 10 do we let in? How do we choose? Do we pick the best 10, the neediest 10, "first come, first served"? And what do we say to the 90 we exclude? If we do let an extra 10 into our lifeboat, we will have lost our "safety factor," an engineering principle of critical importance. For example, if we don't leave room for excess capacity as a safety factor in our country's agriculture, a new plant disease or a bad change in the weather could have disastrous consequences.

Suppose we decide to preserve our small safety factor and admit no more to 7 the lifeboat. Our survival is then possible, although we shall have to be constantly on guard against boarding parties.

While this last solution clearly offers the only means of our survival, it is 8 morally abhorrent to many people. Some say they feel guilty about their good luck. My reply is simple: "Get out and yield your place to others." This may solve the problem of the guilt-ridden person's conscience, but it does not change the ethics of the lifeboat. The needy person to whom the guilt-ridden person yields his place will not himself feel guilty about his good luck. If he did, he would not climb aboard. The net result of conscience-stricken people giving up their unjustly held seats is the elimination of that sort of conscience from the lifeboat.

This is the basic metaphor within which we must work out our solutions. Let 9 us now enrich the image, step by step, with substantive additions from the real world, a world that must solve real and pressing problems of overpopulation and hunger.

The harsh ethics of the lifeboat become even harsher when we consider the 10 reproductive differences between the rich nations and the poor nations. The people inside the lifeboats are doubling in numbers every 87 years; those swimming around outside are doubling, on the average, every 35 years, more than twice as fast as the rich. And since the world's resources are dwindling, the difference in prosperity between the rich and the poor can only increase.

As of 1973, the United States had a population of 210 million people, who 11 were increasing by 0.8 percent per year. Outside our lifeboat, let us imagine another 210 million people (say the combined populations of Colombia, Ecuador, Venezuela, Morocco, Pakistan, Thailand, and the Philippines), increasing at a rate of 3.3 percent per year. Put differently, the doubling time for this aggregate population was 21 years, compared to 87 years for the United States.

Now suppose the United States agreed to pool its resources with those seven 12 countries, with everyone receiving an equal share. Initially the ratio of Americans to non-Americans in this model would be one-to-one. But consider what the ratio would be after 87 years, by which time the Americans would have doubled to a population of 420 million. By then, doubling every 21 years, the other group would have swollen to 3.54 billion. Each American would have to share the available resources with more than eight people.

But, one could argue, this discussion assumes that current population trends 13 will continue, and they may not. Quite so. Most likely the rate of population increase will decline much faster in the United States than it will in the other countries, and there does not seem to be much we can do about it. In sharing with "each according to his needs," we must recognize that needs are determined by population size, which is determined by the rate of reproduction, which at present is regarded as a sovereign right of every nation, poor or not. This being so, the philanthropic load created by the sharing ethic of the spaceship can only increase.

The fundamental error of spaceship ethics, and the sharing it requires, is that 14 it leads to what I call "the tragedy of the commons." Under a system of private property, people who own property recognize their responsibility to care for it, for if they don't they will eventually suffer. A farmer, for instance, will allow no more cattle in a pasture than its carrying capacity justifies. If he overloads it, erosion sets in, weeds take over, and he loses the use of the pasture.

If a pasture becomes a commons open to all, the right of each to use it may 15 not be matched by a corresponding responsibility to protect it. Asking everyone to use it with discretion will hardly do, for the considerate herdsman who refrains from overloading the commons suffers more than a selfish one who says his needs are greater. If everyone would restrain himself, all would be well; but it takes only one less than everyone to ruin a system of voluntary restraint. In a crowded world of less than perfect human beings, mutual ruin is inevitable if there are no controls. This is the tragedy of the commons.

One of the major tasks of education today should be the creation of such an 16 acute awareness of the dangers of the commons that people will recognize its many varieties. For example, the air and water have become polluted because they are treated as commons. Further growth in the population or per-capita conversion of natural resources into pollutants will only make the problem worse. The same holds true for the fish of the oceans. Fishing fleets have nearly disappeared in many parts of the world; technological improvements in the art of fishing are hastening the day of complete ruin. Only the replacement of the system of the commons with a responsible system of control will save the land, air, water and oceanic fisheries.

In recent years there has been a push to create a new commons called a 17 World Food Bank, an international depository of food reserves to which nations would contribute according to their abilities and from which they would draw according to their needs. This humanitarian proposal received support from many liberal international groups, and from such prominent citizens as Margaret Mead, the U.N. Secretary General, and Senator Edward Kennedy.

A world food bank appeals powerfully to our humanitarian impulses. But 18 before we rush ahead with such a plan, let us ask if such a program would actually do more good than harm, not only momentarily but also in the long run. Those who propose a food bank usually refer to a current "emergency" or "crisis" in terms of world food supply. But what is an emergency? Although they may be infrequent and sudden, everyone knows that emergencies will occur from time to time. A well-run family, company, organization or country prepares for the likelihood of accidents and emergencies. It expects them, it budgets for them, it saves for them.

What happens if some organizations or countries budget for accidents and **19** others do not? If each country is solely responsible for its own well-being, poorly managed ones will suffer. But they can learn from experience. They may mend their ways, and learn to budget for infrequent but certain emergencies. For example, the weather varies from year to year, and periodic crop failures are certain. A wise and competent government saves out of the production of the good years in anticipation of bad years to come. Joseph taught this policy to Pharaoh in Egypt more than 2,000 years ago. Yet the great majority of the governments in the world today do not follow such a policy. They lack either the wisdom or the competence, or both. Should those nations that do manage to put something aside be forced to come to the rescue each time an emergency occurs among the poor nations?

"But it isn't their fault!" some kind-hearted liberals argue. "How can we **20** blame the poor people who are caught in an emergency? Why must they suffer for the sins of their governments?" The concept of blame is simply not relevant here. The real question is, what are the operational consequences of establishing a world food bank? If it is open to every country every time a need develops, slovenly rulers will not be motivated to take Joseph's advice. Someone will always come to their aid. Some countries will deposit food in the world food bank, and others will withdraw it. There will be almost no overlap. As a result of such solutions to food shortage emergencies, the poor countries will not learn to mend their ways, and will suffer progressively greater emergencies as their populations grow.

On the average, poor countries undergo a 2.5 percent increase in population **21** each year; rich countries, about 0.6 percent. Only rich countries have anything in the way of food reserves set aside, and even they do not have as much as they should. Poor countries have none. If poor countries received no food from the outside, the rate of their population growth would be periodically checked by crop failures and famines. But if they can always draw on a world food bank in time of need, their population can continue to grow unchecked, and so will their "need" for aid. In the short run, a world food bank may diminish that need, but in the long run it actually increases the need without limit.

Without some system of worldwide food sharing, the proportion of people **22** in the rich and poor nations might eventually stabilize. The overpopulated poor countries would decrease in numbers while the rich countries that had room for more people would increase. But with a well-meaning system of sharing, such as a world food bank, the growth differential between the rich and the poor countries will not only persist, it will increase. Because of the higher rate of population growth in the poor countries of the world, 88 percent of today's children are born poor, and only 12 percent rich. Year by year the ratio becomes worse as the fast-reproducing poor outnumber the slow-reproducing rich.

A world food bank is thus a commons in disguise. People will have more **23** motivation to draw from it than to add to any common store. The less provident and less able will multiply at the expense of the abler and more provident, bringing eventual ruin upon all who share in the commons. Besides, any system of "sharing" that amounts to foreign aid from the rich nations to the poor nations will carry the taint of charity, which will contribute little to the world peace so devoutly desired by those who support the idea of a world food bank.

As past U.S. foreign-aid programs have amply and depressingly demon- 24 strated, international charity frequently inspires mistrust and antagonism rather than gratitude on the part of the recipient nation.

The modern approach to foreign aid stresses the export of technology and 25 advice, rather than money and food. As an ancient Chinese proverb goes: "Give a man a fish and he will eat for a day; teach him how to fish and he will eat for the rest of his days." Acting on this advice, the Rockefeller and Ford Foundations have financed a number of programs for improving agriculture in the hungry nations. Known as the "Green Revolution," these programs have led to the development of "miracle rice" and "miracle wheat," new strains that offer bigger harvests and greater resistance to crop damage.

Whether or not the Green Revolution can increase food production as much 26 as its champions claim is a debatable but possibly irrelevant point. Those who support this well-intended humanitarian effort should first consider some of the fundamentals of human ecology. Ironically, one man who did was the late Alan Gregg, a vice president of the Rockefeller Foundation. Two decades ago he expressed strong doubts about the wisdom of such attempts to increase food production. He likened the growth and spread of humanity over the surface of the earth to the spread of cancer in the human body, remarking that "cancerous growths demand food, but, as far as I know, they have never been cured by getting it."

Every human born constitutes a draft on all aspects of the environment: 27 Food, air, water, forests, beaches, wildlife, scenery and solitude. Food can, perhaps, be significantly increased to meet a growing demand. But what about clean beaches, unspoiled forests, and solitude? If we satisfy a growing population's need for food, we necessarily decrease its per capita supply of the other resources needed by people.

India, for example, now has a population of 600 million, which increases 28 by 15 million each year. This population already puts a huge load on a relatively impoverished environment. The country's forests are now only a small fraction of what they were three centuries ago, and floods and erosion continually destroy the insufficient farmland that remains. Every one of the 15 million new lives added to India's population puts an additional burden on the environment, and increases the economic and social costs of crowding. However humanitarian our intent, every Indian life saved through medical or nutritional assistance from abroad diminishes the quality of life for those who remain, and for subsequent generations. If rich countries make it possible, through foreign aid, for 600 million Indians to swell to 1.2 billion in a mere 28 years, as their current growth rate threatens, will future generations of Indians thank us for hastening the destruction of their environment? Will our good intentions be sufficient excuse for the consequences of our actions?

Without a true world government to control reproduction and the use of   29
available resources, the sharing ethic of the spaceship is impossible. For the foreseeable future, our survival demands that we govern our actions by the ethics of a
lifeboat, harsh though they may be. Posterity will be satisfied with nothing less.

1974

QUESTIONS FOR DISCUSSION

Content

a. What are ethics? How does Hardin use the term in the context of his essay?
b. Summarize Hardin's argument. What is his main point?
c. Hardin uses the lifeboat as the primary metaphor to create a lasting image in
    his readers' minds. Describe this lifeboat as you see it.
d. The other key metaphor is the spaceship. What is the difference between think-
    ing of Earth as a lifeboat and of Earth as a spaceship?
e. What other metaphors does Hardin use?
f. Who are the people Hardin positions himself against? What is the main fault he
    finds with their thinking?

Strategy and Style

g. Hardin asks questions occasionally as a way to guide our thinking (see para-
    graphs 2 and 6 for examples). What other questions could be asked that Hardin
    would not have easy answers to?
h. Does the lifeboat metaphor stand up under close scrutiny? If not, where do you
    think the metaphor is weak?
i. Where and how does Hardin use statistics? What kind of a writer's "voice" do
    these statistics create?
j. Hardin continually refers to "we." Who is "we"? Is Hardin necessarily included
    in this pronoun?
k. In paragraph 19 Hardin backs up his point with an allusion to the Bible:
    "Joseph taught this policy to Pharaoh in Egypt more than 2,000 years ago." In
    the next paragraph, he says that "slovenly rulers will not be motivated to take
    Joseph's advice." What does the biblical reference add to his argument? Who
    might be the slovenly rulers he is referring to?

SUGGESTIONS FOR SHORT WRITING

a. Reread the essay and mark passages that grab your interest because they puz-
    zle, please, or irritate you, or because they connect with things you are learn-
    ing in another class. Choose one such passage and write a brief response to it,

explaining why it puzzles, pleases, or irritates you, or showing the connections between Hardin's essay and ideas discussed in your other classes.
b. Summarize the essay. Since the essay is complex, you may wish to do this summary in a creative way, perhaps in the form of a letter to someone outside the class.

SUGGESTIONS FOR SUSTAINED WRITING

a. Write a counterargument to this selection. Present an alternative solution (or at least a first step in the solution) to the problems of overpopulation and hunger. Do library research to find statistics that will argue with Hardin's statistics. You may want to take a creative approach and write this paper as a letter to Hardin.
b. Find another metaphor that could be used to describe the Earth's current situation. Frame an argument around that metaphor. Some examples of metaphors: race car, leaky barge, tapestry, pond, house.

Sex, Drugs, Disasters, and the Extinction of Dinosaurs

Stephen Jay Gould

Stephen Jay Gould (b. 1941) is a professor of biology, geology, and the history of science at Harvard University, where he has taught since 1967. He was born in New York City, attended Antioch College, and took his PhD at Columbia University. A prolific writer, he publishes a monthly column in Natural History *magazine and has contributed well over a hundred articles to scientific journals across the United States. Among his full-length works are several collections of essays first published in* Natural History. *They include* Ever Since Darwin *(1978),* The Panda's Thumb *(1980),* Hens' Teeth and Horses' Toes *(1983),* The Flamingo's Smile *(1985), and* Bully for Brontosaurus *(1991). He is also the author of* The Mismeasure of Man *(1980) and* Wonderful Life *(1990), which argue against the theory of biological determinism and explain the notion of chance in evolution. Like James Rettie in chapter 9, Gould makes scientific fact and theory appetizing even to the reader with no scientific training. John Noble Wilford, science editor of the* New York Times, *has called him "one of the most spirited essayists of our time." Indeed, his common sense and delightful wit make it seem as if we are reading an article in a popular magazine rather than a reasoned and thoroughly researched scientific study.*

1
Science, in its most fundamental definition, is a fruitful mode of inquiry, not a list of enticing conclusions. The conclusions are the consequence, not the essence.

2
My greatest unhappiness with most popular presentations of science concerns their failure to separate fascinating claims from the methods that scientists use to establish the facts of nature. Journalists, and the public, thrive on controversial and stunning statements. But science is, basically, a way of knowing—in P. B. Medawar's apt words, "the art of the soluble." If the growing corps of popular science writers would focus on *how* scientists develop and defend those fascinating claims, they would make their greatest possible contribution to public understanding.

3
Consider three ideas, proposed in perfect seriousness to explain that greatest of all titillating puzzles—the extinction of dinosaurs. Since these three notions invoke the primally fascinating themes of our culture—sex, drugs, and violence—they surely reside in the category of fascinating claims. I want to show why two of them rank as silly speculation, while the other represents science at its grandest and most useful.

4
Science works with testable proposals. If, after much compilation and scrutiny of data, new information continues to affirm a hypothesis, we may accept it provisionally and gain confidence as further evidence mounts. We can never be completely sure that a hypothesis is right, though we may be able to show with confidence that it is wrong. The best scientific hypotheses are also generous and expansive: They suggest extensions and implications that enlighten related, and even far distant, subjects. Simply consider how the idea of evolution has influenced virtually every intellectual field.

410

Useless speculation, on the other hand, is restrictive. It generates no testable 5
hypothesis, and offers no way to obtain potentially refuting evidence. Please note
that I am not speaking of truth or falsity. The speculation may well be true; still, if
it provides, in principle, no material for affirmation or rejection, we can make
nothing of it. It must simply stand forever as an intriguing idea. Useless speculation turns in on itself and leads nowhere; good science, containing both seeds for
its potential refutation and implications for more and different testable knowledge,
reaches out. But, enough preaching. Let's move on to dinosaurs, and the three proposals for their extinction.

1. *Sex:* Testes function only in a narrow range of temperature (those of mammals
   hang externally in a scrotal sac because internal body temperatures are too high
   for their proper function). A worldwide rise in temperature at the close of the
   Cretaceous period caused the testes of dinosaurs to stop functioning and led to
   their extinction by sterilization of males.
2. *Drugs:* Angiosperms (flowering plants) first evolved toward the end of the dinosaurs' reign. Many of these plants contain psychoactive agents, avoided by
   mammals today as a result of their bitter taste. Dinosaurs had neither means to
   taste the bitterness nor livers effective enough to detoxify the substances. They
   died of massive overdoses.
3. *Disasters:* A large comet or asteroid struck the earth some 65 million years
   ago, lofting a cloud of dust into the sky and blocking sunlight, thereby suppressing photosynthesis and so drastically lowering world temperatures that
   dinosaurs and hosts of other creatures became extinct.

Before analyzing these three tantalizing statements, we must establish a ba- 6
sic ground rule often violated in proposals for the dinosaurs' demise. *There is no
separate problem of the extinction of dinosaurs.* Too often we divorce specific
events from their wider contexts and systems of cause and effect. The fundamental fact of dinosaur extinction is its synchrony with the demise of so many other
groups across a wide range of habitats, from terrestrial to marine.

The history of life has been punctuated by brief episodes of mass ex- 7
tinction. A recent analysis by University of Chicago paleontologists Jack Sep-
koski and Dave Raup, based on the best and most exhaustive tabulation of data
ever assembled, shows clearly that five episodes of mass dying stand well
above the "background" extinctions of normal times (when we consider all
mass extinctions, large and small, they seem to fall in a regular 26-million-
year cycle). The Cretaceous debacle, occurring 65 million years ago and separating the Mesozoic and Cenozoic eras of our geological time scale, ranks
prominently among the five. Nearly all the marine plankton (single-celled
floating creatures) died with geological suddenness; among marine inverte-
brates, nearly 15 percent of all families perished, including many previously
dominant groups, especially the ammonites (relatives of squids in coiled

shells). On land, the dinosaurs disappeared after more than 100 million years of unchallenged domination.

In this context, speculations limited to dinosaurs alone ignore the larger phe- 8 nomenon. We need a coordinated explanation for a system of events that includes the extinction of dinosaurs as one component. Thus it makes little sense, though it may fuel our desire to view mammals as inevitable inheritors of the earth, to guess that dinosaurs died because small mammals ate their eggs (a perennial favorite among untestable speculations). It seems most unlikely that some disaster peculiar to dinosaurs befell these massive beasts—and that the debacle happened to strike just when one of history's five great dyings had enveloped the earth for completely different reasons.

The testicular theory, an old favorite from the 1940s, had its root in an in- 9 teresting and thoroughly respectable study of temperature tolerances in the American alligator, published in the staid *Bulletin of the American Museum of Natural History* in 1946 by three experts on living and fossil reptiles—E. H. Colbert, my own first teacher in paleontology; R. B. Cowles; and C. M. Bogert.

The first sentence of their summary reveals a purpose beyond alligators: 10 "This report describes an attempt to infer the reactions of extinct reptiles, especially the dinosaurs, to high temperatures as based upon reactions observed in the modern alligator." They studied, by rectal thermometry, the body temperatures of alligators under changing conditions of heating and cooling. (Well, let's face it, you wouldn't want to try sticking a thermometer under a 'gator's tongue.) The predictions under test go way back to an old theory first stated by Galileo in the 1630s—the unequal scaling of surfaces and volumes. As an animal, or any object, grows (provided its shape doesn't change), surface areas must increase more slowly than volumes—since surfaces get larger as length squared, while volumes increase much more rapidly, as length cubed. Therefore, small animals have high ratios of surface to volume, while large animals cover themselves with relatively little surface.

Among cold-blooded animals lacking any physiological mechanism for 11 keeping their temperatures constant, small creatures have a hell of a time keeping warm—because they lose so much heat through their relatively large surfaces. On the other hand, large animals, with their relatively small surfaces, may lose heat so slowly that, once warm, they may maintain effectively constant temperatures against ordinary fluctuations of climate. (In fact, the resolution of the "hot-blooded dinosaur" controversy that burned so brightly a few years back may simply be that, while large dinosaurs possessed no physiological mechanism for constant temperature, and were not therefore warm-blooded in the technical sense, their large size and relatively small surface area kept them warm.)

Colbert, Cowles, and Bogert compared the warming rates of small and large 12 alligators. As predicted, the small fellows heated up (and cooled down) more quickly. When exposed to a warm sun, a tiny 50-gram (1.76-ounce) alligator heated up one degree Celsius every minute and a half, while a large alligator, 260 times bigger at 13,000 grams (28.7 pounds), took seven and a half minutes to gain a degree. Extrapolating up to an adult 10-ton dinosaur, they concluded that a one-degree rise in body temperature would take eighty-six hours. If large animals absorb heat so slowly (through their relatively small surfaces), they will also be unable to shed any excess heat gained when temperatures rise above a favorable level.

The authors then guessed that large dinosaurs lived at or near their optimum   13 temperatures; Cowles suggested that a rise in global temperatures just before the Cretaceous extinction caused the dinosaurs to heat up beyond their optimal tolerance—and, being so large, they couldn't shed the unwanted heat. (In a most unusual statement within a scientific paper, Colbert and Bogert then explicitly disavowed this speculative extension of their empirical work on alligators.) Cowles conceded that this excess heat probably wasn't enough to kill or even to enervate the great beasts, but since testes often function only within a narrow range of temperature, he proposed that this global rise might have sterilized all the males, causing extinction by natural contraception.

The overdose theory has recently been supported by UCLA psychiatrist   14 Ronald K. Siegel. Siegel has gathered, he claims, more than 2,000 records of animals who, when given access, administer various drugs to themselves—from a mere swig of alcohol to massive doses of the big H. Elephants will swill the equivalent of twenty beers at a time, but do not like alcohol in concentrations greater than 7 percent. In a silly bit of anthropocentric speculation, Siegel states that "elephants drink, perhaps, to forget . . . the anxiety produced by shrinking rangeland and the competition for food."

Since fertile imaginations can apply almost any hot idea to the extinction of   15 dinosaurs, Siegel found a way. Flowering plants did not evolve until late in the dinosaurs' reign. These plants also produced an array of aromatic, amino-acid-based alkaloids—the major group of psychoactive agents. Most mammals are "smart" enough to avoid these potential poisons. The alkaloids simply don't taste good (they are bitter); in any case, we mammals have livers happily supplied with the capacity to detoxify them. But, Siegel speculates, perhaps dinosaurs could neither taste the bitterness nor detoxify the substances once ingested. He recently told members of the American Psychological Association: "I'm not suggesting that all dinosaurs OD'd on plant drugs, but it certainly was a factor." He also argued that death by overdose may help explain why so many dinosaur fossils are found in contorted positions. (Do not go gentle into that good night.)

Extraterrestrial catastrophes have long pedigrees in the popular literature of   16 extinction, but the subject exploded again in 1979, after a long lull, when the father-son, physicist-geologist team of Luis and Walter Alvarez proposed that an asteroid, some 10 km in diameter, struck the earth 65 million years ago (comets, rather than asteroids, have since gained favor. Good science is self-corrective).

The force of such a collision would be immense, greater by far than the   17 megatonnage of all the world's nuclear weapons. In trying to reconstruct a scenario that would explain the simultaneous dying of dinosaurs on land and so many creatures in the sea, the Alvarezes proposed that a gigantic dust cloud, generated by particles blown aloft in the impact, would so darken the earth that photosynthesis would cease and temperatures drop precipitously. (Rage, rage against the dying of the light.) The single-celled photosynthetic oceanic plankton, with life cycles measured in weeks, would perish outright, but land plants might survive through the dormancy of their seeds (land plants were not much affected by the Cretaceous extinction, and any adequate theory must account for the curious pattern of differential survival). Dinosaurs would die by starvation and freezing; small, warm-blooded mammals, with more modest requirements for food and better regulation of body temperature, would squeak through. "Let the bastards freeze in the dark," as bumper stickers of our chauvinistic neighbors in sunbelt states proclaimed several years ago during the Northeast's winter oil crisis.

All three theories, testicular malfunction, psychoactive overdosing, and asteroidal zapping, grab our attention mightily. As pure phenomenology, they rank about equally high on any hit parade of primal fascination. Yet one represents expansive science, the others restrictive and untestable speculation. The proper criterion lies in evidence and methodology; we must probe behind the superficial fascination of particular claims. **18**

How could we possibly decide whether the hypothesis of testicular frying is right or wrong? We would have to know things that the fossil record cannot provide. What temperatures were optimal for dinosaurs? Could they avoid the absorption of excess heat by staying in the shade, or in caves? At what temperatures did their testicles cease to function? Were late Cretaceous climates ever warm enough to drive the internal temperatures of dinosaurs close to this ceiling? Testicles simply don't fossilize, and how could we infer their temperature tolerances even if they did? In short, Cowles's hypothesis is only an intriguing speculation leading nowhere. The most damning statement against it appeared right in the conclusion of Colbert, Cowles, and Bogert's paper, when they admitted: "It is difficult to advance any definite arguments against the hypothesis." My statement may seem paradoxical—isn't a hypothesis really good if you can't devise any arguments against it? Quite the contrary. It is simply untestable and unusable. **19**

Siegel's overdosing has even less going for it. At least Cowles extrapolated his conclusion from some good data on alligators. And he didn't completely violate the primary guideline of siting dinosaur extinction in the context of a general mass dying—for rise in temperature could be the root cause of a general catastrophe, zapping dinosaurs by testicular malfunction and different groups for other reasons. But Siegel's speculation cannot touch the extinction of ammonites or oceanic plankton (diatoms make their own food with good sweet sunlight; they don't OD on the chemicals of terrestrial plants). It is simply a gratuitous, attention-grabbing guess. It cannot be tested, for how can we know what dinosaurs tasted and what their livers could do? Livers don't fossilize any better than testicles. **20**

The hypothesis doesn't even make any sense in its own context. Angiosperms were in full flower ten million years before dinosaurs went the way of all flesh. Why did it take so long? As for the pains of a chemical death recorded in contortions of fossils, I regret to say (or rather I'm pleased to note for the dinosaurs' sake) **21** that Siegel's knowledge of geology must be a bit deficient: Muscles contract after death and geological strata rise and fall with motions of the earth's crust after burial—more than enough reason to distort a fossil's pristine appearance.

The impact story, on the other hand, has a sound basis in evidence. It can be 22 tested, extended, refined, and, if wrong, disproved. The Alvarezes did not just construct an arresting guess for public consumption. They proposed their hypothesis after laborious geochemical studies with Frank Asaro and Helen Michael had revealed a massive increase of iridium in rocks deposited right at the time of extinction. Iridium, a rare metal of the platinum group, is virtually absent from indigenous rocks of the earth's crust; most of our iridium arrives on extraterrestrial objects that strike the earth.

The Alvarez hypothesis bore immediate fruit. Based originally on evidence 23 from two European localities, it led geochemists throughout the world to examine other sediments of the same age. They found abnormally high amounts of iridium everywhere—from continental rocks of the western United States to deep sea cores from the South Atlantic.

Cowles proposed his testicular hypothesis in the mid-1940s. Where has it 24 gone since then? Absolutely nowhere, because scientists can do nothing with it. The hypothesis must stand as a curious appendage to a solid study of alligators. Siegel's overdose scenario will also win a few press notices and fade into oblivion. The Alvarezes' asteroid falls into a different category altogether, and much of the popular commentary has missed this essential distinction by focusing on the impact and its attendant results, and forgetting what really matters to a scientist—the iridium. If you talk just about asteroids, dust, and darkness, you tell stories no better and no more entertaining than fried testicles or terminal trips. It is the iridium—the source of testable evidence—that counts and forges the crucial distinction between speculation and science.

The proof, to twist a phrase, lies in the doing. Cowles's hypothesis has gen- 25 erated nothing in thirty-five years. Since its proposal in 1979, the Alvarez hypothesis has spawned hundreds of studies, a major conference, and attendant publications. Geologists are fired up. They are looking for iridium at all other extinction boundaries. Every week exposes a new wrinkle in the scientific press. Further evidence that the Cretaceous iridium represents extraterrestrial impact and not indigenous volcanism continues to accumulate. As I revise this essay in November 1984 (this paragraph will be out of date when the book is published), new data include chemical "signatures" of other isotopes indicating unearthly provenance, glass spherules of a size and sort produced by impact and not by volcanic eruptions, and high-pressure varieties of silica formed (so far as we know) only under the tremendous shock of impact.

My point is simply this: Whatever the eventual outcome (I suspect it will be 26 positive), the Alvarez hypothesis is exciting, fruitful science because it generates tests, provides us with things to do, and expands outward. We are having fun, battling back and forth, moving toward a resolution, and extending the hypothesis beyond its original scope.

As just one example of the unexpected, distant cross-fertilization that good   27
science engenders, the Alvarez hypothesis made a major contribution to a theme
that has riveted public attention in the past few months—so-called nuclear winter.
In a speech delivered in April 1982, Luis Alvarez calculated the energy that a ten-
kilometer asteroid would release on impact. He compared such an explosion with
a full nuclear exchange and implied that all-out atomic war might unleash similar
consequences.

This theme of impact leading to massive dust clouds and falling tempera-   28
tures formed an important input to the decision of Carl Sagan and a group of colleagues to model the climatic consequences of nuclear holocaust. Full nuclear exchange would probably generate the same kind of dust cloud and darkening that
may have wiped out the dinosaurs. Temperatures would drop precipitously and
agriculture might become impossible. Avoidance of nuclear war is fundamentally
an ethical and political imperative, but we must know the factual consequences to
make firm judgments. I am heartened by a final link across disciplines and deep
concerns—another criterion, by the way, of science at its best. A recognition of the
very phenomenon that made our evolution possible by exterminating the previously dominant dinosaurs and clearing a way for the evolution of large mammals,
including us, might actually help to save us from joining those magnificent beasts
in contorted poses among the strata of the earth.

1984

QUESTIONS FOR DISCUSSION

Content

a. In paragraph 1, Gould claims that science is a "fruitful mode of inquiry," not a
   set of "conclusions." What does he mean, and how does this assertion help explain his argument? Where is this assertion illustrated in his essay?
b. Why can we "never be completely sure" that a hypothesis is correct (paragraph 4)?
c. Summarize the three hypotheses on the extinction of dinosaurs. What is the
   main element in each that makes it testable or untestable?
d. What distinctions does the author make between scientific hypothesis and
   speculation? Explain his assertion that the "proper criterion lies in evidence
   and methodology" (paragraph 18).
e. Why, according to Gould, is a hypothesis suspect if one cannot mount arguments against it?
f. What does he mean when he implies that science should be fun (paragraph 26)?
   In what way does the Alvarezes' hypothesis meet this criterion? Why are the
   other two theories not fun?

Strategy and Style

g. In paragraph 9, Gould reports that the "testicular theory" had its origins in a respectable scientific study. Why does he say this if he wishes to discredit that theory?

h. What are his views of the various scientists whose studies he cites? Compare his opinions of the team of Colbert, Cowles, and Bogert (paragraphs 9–13); of Siegel (paragraphs 14 and 15); and of the Alvarezes (paragraphs 16 and 17). What words does he use to describe each? How do these words provide foreshadowing?

i. In paragraph 6, Gould writes, "Too often we divorce specific events. . . ." Who is "we"?

j. Is Gould's intended audience limited to scientists or people interested in science? How do you know?

k. What is the effect of quoting poet Dylan Thomas in paragraph 17 ("Rage, rage against the dying of the light")?

SUGGESTIONS FOR SHORT WRITING

a. In paragraphs 15 and 17, Gould quotes from "Do Not Go Gentle into That Good Night" by Dylan Thomas. Find a copy of the poem in your library and read it. Then, briefly explain the significance of the lines that Gould takes from it.

b. Read through the essay once more, writing questions in the margins that you would ask the author if you had the chance to meet with him. For example, you might inquire why he thinks it's "silly" to think that elephants might experience anxiety (paragraph 14).

c. Look around your town or college. Briefly "speculate" about what it or the land it sits on might have looked like 50, 100, or even 1,000 years ago.

SUGGESTIONS FOR SUSTAINED WRITING

a. When he brings in the idea of nuclear war in his concluding paragraphs, Gould suggests that the Alvarezes' theory has implications beyond the scope of paleontology. What other implications might their theory have? Write an essay in which you speculate on these implications.

b. Relying on the basic method of analysis that Gould uses and taking as your subject a current problem of national importance, brainstorm a list of hypotheses to account for the problem's cause. Then, write an essay in which you take three of the hypotheses from your list and discuss how each one could be proved or disproved. Which of the hypotheses is most probable?

The Press Needs a National Monitor
Mike Wallace

Mea Culpa? Not Mea!
Don Hewitt

Mike Wallace (b. 1918) is an internationally known journalist, who is now a coeditor and correspondent for CBS's television news magazine 60 Minutes. *Wallace graduated from the University of Michigan, and he has worked as a radio and television reporter, interviewer, and commentator for more than fifty years. He is the recipient of numerous journalistic honors including eighteen Emmy awards, several George Foster Peabody awards, and two Dupont Columbia Journalism awards. His full-length works include* Mike Wallace Asks *(1958) and* Close Encounters *(1984).*

Don Hewitt (b. 1922) is the executive producer of 60 Minutes, *which he created in 1968. With Douglas Edwards, Hewitt produced the first television network news show, which appeared in 1948. He also collaborated with Edward R. Morrow to create* See it Now, *and he directed the first televised presidential debates between John F. Kennedy and Richard M. Nixon in 1960.*

Both essays appeared in The Wall Street Journal *in December 1996.*

The Press Needs a National Monitor

Mike Wallace

"You arrogant journalists, you spend your lives looking down our throats and 1 holding us up to public obloquy, but you cry foul (or First Amendment) when we want to look down yours!"

 That's the plaint of hundreds of thousands of businessmen, doctors, lawyers, 2 politicians and other public figures who have lost confidence in what we report and in our professed journalistic objectivity.

 And how do we respond? Too often too many of us shrug our shoulders and 3 dismiss the criticism as an occupational hazard, one that comes with the territory, or we suggest a letter to the editor. And if someone really feels his ox has been unfairly gored, his attorney may remind him that he can file a libel suit.

 Is there no better way?   4

 As we reported recently on *60 Minutes*, for the past 26 years an organization 5 called the Minnesota News Council has been taking on these complaints and resolving them with some success.

 Any individual, business or public institution in the state that feels its in- 6 tegrity or reputation has been traduced in a news report may file a complaint with

418

the council. If the council decides the complaint is worth its attention, it'll study the news report, hear from both sides in private and in public, and come to a decision. Either the council's members vote that the complaint is valid, or that the news report in question told its story fairly.

The Minnesota News Council consists of 24 members, half of them jour- 7 nalists and half of them public members—businessmen, lawyers, teachers, other interested citizens. A state Supreme Court justice presides over their public hearings. These 24, chosen over the years by previous council members, study the article or broadcast in question. Then they read written arguments prepared by the news organization and the complainant and sit for a public session, amply covered by all the media, at which each side argues its case. Questions are asked and answered, opinions and rebuttals aired, and finally a vote is taken.

And what happens if the journalists are found wanting? No one goes to jail, 8 no one is put out of business, no money is awarded. Instead, the journalists suffer the same kind of humiliation the objects of our scrutiny are bound to feel when our searching spotlight uncovers their flaws or malfeasances.

Over the past quarter-century, about half the cases filed with the Minnesota 9 News Council have been decided in favor of the journalists. The Minnesota group is not the only such news council currently operating. There is one more, just one, the Honolulu Community Media Council. But there are suggestions that perhaps several regional councils or a national news council should be established.

Back in the 1970s and into the early 1980s, there was just such a national 10 body, spawned by a group of journalists led by Richard Salant, who was president of CBS News. He believed the public should have some means to bring their complaints to someone with the competence and authority to give a public "thumbs up" or "thumbs down" as to the accuracy and the fairness of certain troubling news reports. Something, he felt, more defining than a letter to the editor and less onerous than a libel suit, with its attendant huge legal fees and interminable court procedures.

That early effort to establish a national news council was hampered by a 11 struggle for funding, and by catcalls from inside the hypersensitive journalistic community. It sputtered after a few years and eventually it died, killed off mainly because two heavy hitters, Abe Rosenthal, then the executive editor of the *New York Times,* and Walter Cronkite, then the trusted anchor of "The CBS Evening News," were dead set against it—as was my colleague Don Hewitt, who heads up *60 Minutes.* All three felt they didn't need anyone looking over their editorial shoulders; they were professionals, they said, and if not infallible surely they needed no help from unqualified outsiders.

Today Abe Rosenthal, no longer the man who runs the *Times* but whose 12 columns appear regularly on the paper's op-ed page, hasn't changed his mind one whit. And Walter Cronkite? At a memorial service for Dick Salant a couple of years ago, this was Walter's take: "In the 1970s, I thought it was the worst idea I ever heard in my life, that we should put judgment as to the kind of job we do in the hands of another, somewhere outside our profession, outside our immediate workplace. But I think now, as I look back at it, that Dick was probably right."

At a time when the public trust in us may be even lower than it was in Dick 13 Salant's time, I've come to the reluctant conclusion that Walter's change of mind is right.

1996

Mea Culpa? Not Mea!

Don Hewitt

As I've said to my close friend and esteemed colleague Mike Wallace, bias, like 1 beauty, is in the eye of the beholder. And while I behold bias from time to time in news coverage, I would rather leave it to a good editor to weed it out than to a news council made up of a bunch of guys named Joe (as in Kennedy, who wanted to ride Mike out of town on a rail for giving his son Jack a hard time). Or Henry (as in Kissinger, who wanted to tar and feather Mike because the story he aired about him wasn't as flattering as he thought it should be). Or Alfonse (as in D'Amato, who wanted to take Mike to the woodshed because he didn't like what Mike said about him). Or L. Ron (as in Hubbard, whose Church of Scientology disciples threatened to "get" Mike for what he reported about them). Or Howard (as in Squadron, of the Council of Presidents of Jewish Organizations, who wanted Mike drawn and quartered for reporting that the Jerusalem police were not as innocent as they said they were in the recent temple mount massacre). Or Reed (as in Irvine, of Accuracy in Media, who is convinced to this day that Mike is conspiring with the Clintons to cover up the murder of Vince Foster).

And that doesn't even include what a news council sitting in judgment of my 2 esteemed colleague would have said about him if some old soldiers who refused to die or fade away showed up at a news council to join in the fun after Mike's famous Westmoreland broadcast.

Are journalists as good as they think they are at avoiding bias? No, nobody 3 is. But at least journalists are trained to report fairly—unlike corporate executives, academics, PR types and assorted members of the citizenry who have the time and the inclination to sit on a news council. If anyone thinks certain journalists are unfair, he or she can always complain to, or boycott, the advertisers who pay the reporters' salaries. Or turn them off or tune them out or go buy or watch another news magazine.

It has been my experience that what viewers and readers are most unhappy 4 about is not that journalists slant the news, but that we don't slant it their way. And it's those readers and viewers who would sit on the news councils in Mike's brave new world.

On paper, it may not be a bad idea. But in practice? Whoa there, Mikey, slow ₅ down. Where in the world are you going to find the saints to sit in judgment of us sinners? Mea culpa? Not mea.

1996

QUESTIONS FOR DISCUSSION

Content

a. What are Wallace's reasons for supporting the creation of a "National Monitor"? What are Hewitt's reasons for opposing it?
b. How does Wallace answer the argument of would-be opponents who claim that people who are wronged by journalists can always write letters to the editor or file lawsuits?
c. How might Wallace respond to someone arguing that submitting complaints to a group like the Minnesota News Council would intimidate journalists?
d. Who are each of the following: Joe Kennedy, Henry Kissinger, Alfonse D'Amato, L. Ron Hubbard, Howard Squadron, Irvine Reed, and (William) Westmoreland?
e. Explain the "brave new world" allusion in Hewitt's fourth paragraph.
f. What does Hewitt's title mean? Is it effective?

Strategy and Style

g. Contrast Wallace's tone (his attitude toward his subject) and his style (the kind of vocabulary and sentence structure he uses) with what we see in Hewitt's essay.
h. How does Wallace begin his essay? Is his introduction successful? Why or why not?
i. Comment upon Wallace's conclusion. What can you learn from it about how to close an essay?
j. To what end does Wallace tell us about the positions held by Salant, Rosenthal, Cronkite, and Hewitt?
k. Why does Wallace spend so much time (paragraphs 5–9) discussing the Minnesota News Council?
l. Evaluate Hewitt's introduction. What does he accomplish in the opening lines of his essay?
m. Why does Hewitt cite various incidents from Wallace's career in paragraph 1? How does recalling them help him advance his argument?
n. What use does Wallace make of evocative language? What about Hewitt?
o. What use does Wallace make of rhetorical questions? What about Hewitt?

SUGGESTIONS FOR SHORT WRITING

a. Reread both selections. Then write notes in the margins that question or contradict the ideas and/or opinions the writers put forth.
b. Write a paragraph in which you state several reasons for disagreeing with either Wallace or Hewitt.

SUGGESTIONS FOR SUSTAINED WRITING

a. Write an essay that expands and develops the ideas in the paragraph you wrote when you responded to item *b* of the Suggestions for Short Writing.
b. Write an essay in which you take a position on censoring or controlling the contents of a particular communications or entertainment medium, such as talk radio, the Internet, cable television, adult movies, rap music, or rock videos. Like Wallace and Hewitt, address your essay to the audience of a newspaper, perhaps your own college paper.
c. Read or reread the essays by Alan M. Dershowitz (Chapter 9) and Nat Hentoff (Chapter 10). Then, write an essay in which you explain how each of these men might respond to the arguments put forth by Wallace and Hewitt. This assignment is not as easy as it might seem, for you will have to go beyond explaining whose side Dershowitz and Hentoff would take. You will also have to provide evidence that explains why they would take that side. In fact, you might even want to read other essays by these authors. You can find them in your college library or on the Internet.

A Modest Proposal

Jonathan Swift

Jonathan Swift (1667–1745) was born in Dublin, Ireland; studied at Trinity College, Dublin; and took an MA at Oxford. Ordained an Anglican priest, eventually he was made Dean of St. Patrick's Cathedral in Dublin. He is remembered chiefly for his satires, the most famous of which are A Tale of a Tub *(1704), a vicious satire on government abuses in education and religion, and* Gulliver's Travels *(1726). After the death of Queen Anne in 1714, Swift remained almost the rest of his life in Ireland. There he wrote many essays defending the Irish against English oppression. "A Modest Proposal" is one of a series of satirical essays that exposed English cruelties in Ireland. It demonstrates Swift's keen sensitivity to the problems of the poor in his native country as well as his ability to create satire that is both ironic and incisive.*

It is a melancholy object to those who walk through this great town or travel in the 1 country, when they see the streets, the roads, and cabin doors, crowded with beggars of the female sex, followed by three, four, or six children, all in rags and importuning every passenger for an alms. These mothers, instead of being able to work for their honest livelihood, are forced to employ all their time in strolling to beg sustenance for their helpless infants: Who as they grow up either turn thieves for want of work, or leave their dear native country to fight for the Pretender in Spain, or sell themselves to the Barbadoes.

I think it is agreed by all parties that this prodigious number of children in 2 the arms, or on the backs, or at the heels of their mothers, and frequently of their fathers, is in the present deplorable state of the kingdom a very great additional grievance; and, therefore, whoever could find out a fair, cheap, and easy method of making these children sound, useful members of the commonwealth, would deserve so well of the public as to have his statue set up for a preserver of the nation.

But my intention is very far from being confined to provide only for the chil- 3 dren of professed beggars; it is of a much greater extent, and shall take in the whole number of infants at a certain age who are born of parents in effect as little able to support them as those who demand our charity in the streets.

As to my own part, having turned my thoughts for many years upon this im- 4 portant subject, and maturely weighed the several schemes of our projectors, I have always found them grossly mistaken in their computation. It is true, a child just dropped from its dam may be supported by her milk for a solar year, with little other nourishment; at most not above the value of 2s., which the mother may certainly get, or the value in scraps, by her lawful occupation of begging; and it is exactly at one year old that I propose to provide for them in such a manner as instead of being a charge upon their parents or the parish, or wanting food and raiment for the rest of their lives, they shall on the contrary contribute to the feeding, and partly to the clothing, of many thousands.

There is likewise another great advantage in my scheme, that it will pre- 5 vent those voluntary abortions, and that horrid practice of women murdering their bastard children, alas! too frequent among us! sacrificing the poor innocent babes I doubt more to avoid the expense than the shame, which would move tears and pity in the most savage and inhuman breast.

The number of souls in this kingdom being usually reckoned one million and **6** a half, of these I calculate there may be about 200,000 couples whose wives are breeders; from which number I subtract 30,000 couples who are able to maintain their own children (although I apprehend there cannot be so many, under the present distress of the kingdom); but this being granted, there will remain 170,000 breeders. I again subtract 50,000 for those women who miscarry, or whose children die by accident or disease within the year. There only remain 120,000 children of poor parents annually born. The question therefore is, how this number shall be reared and provided for? which, as I have already said, under the present situation of affairs, is utterly impossible by all the methods hitherto proposed. For we can neither employ them in handicraft or agriculture; we neither build houses (I mean live in the country) nor cultivate land; they can very seldom pick up a livelihood by stealing, till they arrive at six years old, except where they are of towardly parts; although I confess they learn the rudiments much earlier; during which time they can, however, be properly looked upon only as probationers; as I have been informed by a principal gentleman in the county of Cavan, who protested to me that he never knew above one or two instances under the age of six, even in a part of the kingdom so renowned for the quickest proficiency in that art.

I am assured by our merchants, that a boy or a girl before twelve years old **7** is no saleable commodity; and even when they come to this age they will not yield above 3l. or 3l.2s. 6d. at most on the exchange; which cannot turn to account either to the parents or kingdom, the charge of nutriment and rags having been at least four times that value.

I shall now therefore humbly propose my own thoughts, which I hope will **8** not be liable to the least objection.

I have been assured by a very knowing American of my acquaintance in **9** London, that a young healthy child well nursed is at a year old a most delicious, nourishing, and wholesome food, whether stewed, roasted, baked, or broiled; and I make no doubt that it will equally serve in a fricassee or a ragout.

I do therefore humbly offer it to public consideration that of the 120,000 **10** children already computed, 20,000 may be reserved for breed, whereof only one-fourth part to be males; which is more than we allow to sheep, black cattle, or swine; and my reason is, that these children are seldom the fruits of marriage, a circumstance not much regarded by our savages; therefore one male will be sufficient to serve four females. That the remaining 100,000 may, at a year old, be offered in sale to the persons of quality and fortune through the kingdom; always advising the mother to let them suck plentifully in the last month, so as to render them plump and fat for a good table. A child will make two dishes at an entertainment for friends; and when the family dines alone, the fore or hind quarter will make a reasonable dish, and seasoned with a little pepper or salt will be very good boiled on the fourth day, especially in winter.

I have reckoned upon a medium that a child just born will weigh 12 pounds, 11
and in a solar year, if tolerably nursed, will increase to 28 pounds.

I grant this food will be somewhat dear, and therefore very proper for land- 12
lords, who, as they have already devoured most of the parents, seem to have the
best title to the children.

Infant's flesh will be in season throughout the year, but more plentiful in 13
March, and a little before and after; for we are told by a grave author, an eminent
French physician, that fish being a prolific diet, there are more children born in
Roman Catholic countries about nine months after Lent than at any other season;
therefore, reckoning a year after Lent, the markets will be more glutted than usual,
because the number of popish infants is at least three to one in this kingdom; and
therefore it will have one other collateral advantage, by lessening the number of
papists among us.

I have already computed the charge of nursing a beggar's child (in which list 14
I reckon all cottagers, laborers, and four-fifths of the farmers) to be about 2s. per
annum, rags included; and I believe no gentleman would repine to give 10s. for
the carcass of a good fat child, which, as I have said, will make four dishes of excellent nutritive meat, when he has only some particular friend or his own family
to dine with him. Thus the squire will learn to be a good landlord, and grow popular among the tenants; the mother will have 8s. net profit, and be fit for work till
she produces another child.

Those who are more thrifty (as I must confess the times require) may flay 15
the carcass; the skin of which artificially dressed will make admirable gloves for
ladies, and summer boots for fine gentlemen.

As to our city of Dublin, shambles may be appointed for this purpose in the 16
most convenient parts of it, and butchers we may be assured will not be wanting;
although I rather recommend buying the children alive, and dressing them hot
from the knife as we do roasting pigs.

A very worthy person, a true lover of his country, and whose virtues I highly 17
esteem, was lately pleased in discoursing on this matter to offer a refinement upon
my scheme. He said that many gentlemen of this kingdom, having of late destroyed their deer, he conceived that the want of venison might be well supplied
by the bodies of young lads and maidens, not exceeding fourteen years of age nor
under twelve; so great a number of both sexes in every country being now ready
to starve for want of work and service; and these to be disposed of by their parents, if alive, or otherwise by their nearest relations. But with due deference to so
excellent a friend and so deserving a patriot, I cannot be altogether in his senti-
ments; for as to the males, my American acquaintance assured me from frequent
experience that their flesh was generally tough and lean, like that of our school-
boys by continual exercise, and their taste disagreeable; and to fatten them would
not answer the charge. Then as to the females, it would, I think, with humble submission be a loss to the public, because they soon would become breeders themselves; and besides, it is not improbable that some scrupulous people might be apt
to censure such a practice (although indeed very unjustly), as a little bordering

upon cruelty; which, I confess, has always been with me the strongest objection against any project, how well so-ever intended.

But in order to justify my friend, he confessed that this expedient was put **18** into his head by the famous Psalmanazar, a native of the island Formosa, who came from thence to London about twenty years ago: And in conversation told my friend, that in his country when any young person happened to be put to death, the executioner sold the carcass to persons of quality as a prime dainty; and that in his time the body of a plump girl of fifteen, who was crucified for an attempt to poison the emperor, was sold to his imperial majesty's prime minister of state, and other great mandarins of the court, in joints from the gibbet, at 400 crowns. Neither indeed can I deny, that if the same use were made of several plump young girls in this town, who without one single groat to their fortunes cannot stir without a chair, and appear at the playhouse and assemblies in foreign fineries which they never will pay for, the kingdom would not be the worse.

Some persons of a desponding spirit are in great concern about that vast **19** number of poor people, who are aged, diseased, or maimed, and I have been desired to employ my thoughts what course may be taken to ease the nation of so grievous an encumbrance. But I am not in the least pain upon that matter, because it is very well known that they are every day dying and rotting by cold and famine, and filth and vermin, as fast as can be reasonably expected. And as to the young laborers, they are now in as hopeful a condition: they cannot get work, and consequently pine away for want of nourishment, to a degree that if at any time they are accidentally hired to common labor, they have not strength to perform it; and thus the country and themselves are happily delivered from the evils to come.

I have too long digressed, and therefore shall return to my subject. I think **20** the advantages by the proposal which I have made are obvious and many, as well as of the highest importance.

For first, as I have already observed, it would greatly lessen the number of **21** papists, with whom we are yearly overrun, being the principal breeders of the nation as well as our most dangerous enemies; and who stay at home on purpose to deliver the kingdom to the Pretender, hoping to take their advantage by the absence of so many good Protestants, who have chosen rather to leave their country than stay at home and pay tithes against their conscience to an Episcopal curate.

Secondly, the poor tenants will have something valuable of their own, which **22** by law may be made liable to distress and help to pay their landlord's rent, their corn and cattle being already seized, and money a thing unknown.

Thirdly, whereas the maintenance of 100,000 children from two years old **23** and upward, cannot be computed at less than 10s. apiece per annum, the nation's stock will be thereby increased £50,000 per annum, beside the profit of a new dish introduced to the tables of all gentlemen of fortune in the kingdom who have any refinement in taste. And the money will circulate among ourselves, the goods being entirely of our own growth and manufacture.

Fourthly, the constant breeders beside the gain of 8s. sterling per annum by the **24** sale of their children, will be rid of the charge of maintaining them after the first year.

Fifthly, this food would likewise bring great custom to taverns, where the 25
vintners will certainly be so prudent as to procure the best receipts for dressing it
to perfection, and consequently have their houses frequented by all the fine gentlemen, who justly value themselves upon their knowledge in good eating; and a
skilful cook who understands how to oblige his guests, will contrive to make it as
expensive as they please.

Sixthly, this would be a great inducement to marriage, which all wise na- 26
tions have either encouraged by rewards or enforced by laws and penalties. It
would increase the care and tenderness of mothers toward their children, when
they were sure of a settlement for life to the poor babes, provided in some sort by
the public, to their annual profit instead of expense. We should see an honest em-
ulation among the married women, which of them would bring the fattest child to
the market. Men would become as fond of their wives during the time of their
pregnancy as they are now of their mares in foal, their cows in calf, their sows
when they are ready to farrow; nor offer to beat or kick them (as is too frequent a
practice) for fear of a miscarriage.

Many other advantages might be enumerated. For instance, the addition of 27
some thousand carcasses in our exportation of barreled beef, the propagation of
swine's flesh, and improvement in the art of making good bacon, so much wanted
among us by the great destruction of pigs, too frequent at our table; which are no
way comparable in taste or magnificence to a well-grown, fat, yearling child, which
roasted whole will make a considerable figure at a lord mayor's feast or any other
public entertainment. But this and many others I omit, being studious of brevity.

Supposing that 1,000 families in this city would be constant customers for 28
infants' flesh, besides others who might have it at merry-meetings, particularly at
weddings and christenings, I compute that Dublin would take off annually about
20,000 carcasses; and the rest of the kingdom (where probably they will be sold
somewhat cheaper) the remaining 80,000.

I can think of no one objection that will possibly be raised against this pro- 29
posal, unless it should be urged that the number of people will be thereby much
lessened in the kingdom. This I freely own, and it was indeed one principal design
in offering it to the world. I desire the reader will observe, that I calculate my rem-
edy for this one individual kingdom of Ireland and for no other that ever was, is,
or I think ever can be upon earth. Therefore let no man talk to me of other expedients: Of taxing our absentees at 5s. a pound: Of using neither clothes nor household furniture except what is of our own growth and manufacture: Of utterly re-
jecting the materials and instruments that promote foreign luxury: Of curing the
expensiveness of pride, vanity, idleness, and gaming in our women: Of introducing a vein of parsimony, prudence, and temperance: Of learning to love our country, in the want of which we differ even from Laplander and the inhabitants of Top-
inamboo: Of quitting our animosities and factions, nor acting any longer like the
Jews, who were murdering one another at the very moment their city was taken:
Of being a little cautious not to sell our country and conscience for nothing: Of
teaching landlords to have at least one degree of mercy toward their tenants: Lastly,

of putting a spirit of honesty, industry, and skill into our shopkeepers; who, if a resolution could now be taken to buy only our native goods, would immediately unite
to cheat and exact upon us in the price, the measure, and the goodness, nor could
ever yet be brought to make one fair proposal of just dealing, though often and
earnestly invited to it.

Therefore I repeat, let no man talk to me of these and the like expedients, till 30
he has at least some glimpse of hope that there will be ever some hearty and sincere attempt to put them in practice.

But as to myself, having been wearied out for many years with offering vain, 31
idle, visionary thoughts, and at length utterly despairing of success, I fortunately
fell upon this proposal; which, as it is wholly new, so it has something solid and
real, of no expense and little trouble, full in our own power, and whereby we can
incur no danger in disobliging England. For this kind of commodity will not bear
exportation, the flesh being of too tender a consistence to admit a long continu-
ance in salt, although perhaps I could name a country which would be glad to eat
up our whole nation without it.

After all, I am not so violently bent upon my own opinion as to reject any 32
offer proposed by wise men, which shall be found equally innocent, cheap, easy,
and effectual. But before something of that kind shall be advanced in contradiction to my scheme, and offering a better, I desire the author or authors will be
pleased maturely to consider two points. First, as things now stand, how they will
be able to find food and raiment for 100,000 useless mouths and backs. And secondly, there being a round million of creatures in human figure throughout this
kingdom, whose subsistence put into a common stock would leave them in debt
2,000,000*l.* sterling, adding those who are beggars by profession to the bulk of
farmers, cottagers, and laborers, with the wives and children who are beggars in
effect; I desire those politicians who dislike my overture, and may perhaps be so
bold as to attempt an answer, that they will first ask the parents of these mortals,
whether they would not at this day think it a great happiness to have been sold for
food at a year old in the manner I prescribe, and thereby have avoided such a perpetual scene of misfortunes as they have since gone through by the oppression of
landlords, the impossibility of paying rent without money or trade, the want of
common sustenance, with neither house nor clothes to cover them from the in-
clemencies of the weather, and the most inevitable prospect of entailing the like or
greater miseries upon their breed for ever.

I profess, in the sincerity of my heart, that I have not the least personal in- 33
terest in endeavoring to promote this necessary work, having no other motive than
the public good of my country, by advancing our trade, providing for infants, relieving the poor, and giving some pleasure to the rich. I have no children by which
I can propose to get a single penny; the youngest being nine years old, and my wife
past childbearing.

1714

QUESTIONS FOR DISCUSSION

Content

a. Just what is Swift proposing? What is his purpose in making this absurd proposal?

b. At which point in the essay do you begin to suspect that Swift is being satirical?

c. Indirectly, "A Modest Proposal" provides a clear indication of Swift's attitudes toward the poor and the ruling classes. Recalling information from the text, explain his attitude toward each of these segments of society.

d. Swift makes a number of allusions to the politics and history of his time. Consult an encyclopedia or other appropriate reference work in your college library to learn a bit about the history of Ireland during the early 1700s. In particular, make sure you understand the following:

The Pretender	Episcopal curate
Papists	Psalmanazar, a native of the island of Formosa
Roman Catholic countries	Mandarins
Cottagers	

e. Near the end of the essay, we come upon a list of "expedients." Although the speaker claims otherwise, they represent the kinds of solutions to Ireland's problems that Swift actually believes in. What are these solutions? Why does Swift wait until late in his essay to mention them? Why does he mention them at all?

Strategy and Style

f. Swift, the speaker in "A Modest Proposal," is quite different from Swift the author. Describe the speaker. What function does Swift's use of a persona serve?

g. Swift's mention of Psalmanazar serves a particularly ironic purpose. What is it?

h. Swift's solutions to Ireland's problems, though ironic, are explained in a nononsense, businesslike tone. Point to specific passages in which this tone is most apparent.

i. Swift's irony is especially biting when he says: "I grant this food will be somewhat dear, and therefore very proper for landlords, who, as they have already devoured most of the parents, seem to have the best title to the children" (paragraph 12). What other passages reveal his anger toward the ruling class?

SUGGESTIONS FOR SHORT WRITING

a. How did you respond on an emotional level when you read this essay? Write a response in which you describe your "gut reaction" to "A Modest Proposal."

b. Write a paragraph response to this essay from the point of view of one of the poor of Ireland; then write a paragraph from the point of view of a member of the ruling class. Compare the two responses.

SUGGESTIONS FOR SUSTAINED WRITING

a. Like Swift, approach a serious subject in tongue-in-cheek fashion and write your own "modest proposal." For instance, discuss a controversial government policy and, while pretending to defend it, describe those aspects of it that you find most offensive. Or, you might simply try to convince your classmates that there really are "advantages" to becoming a chain smoker, to walking into class unprepared day after day, or to cramming for exams rather than studying for them systematically.

b. One of Swift's real solutions to Ireland's problems is that its inhabitants use "neither clothes nor household furniture except what is of [their] own growth and manufacture." This seems to be the same idea behind the "Buy American" movement. Do you believe that buying only goods manufactured at home will improve our economy? Explain.

c. One aspect of Swift's proposal focuses on the relationship between tenants and landlords. This is still an important issue. Using your own experiences as sources of information, write an essay that argues for the enactment of:

- Laws that keep rents at reasonable levels and protect tenants from unscrupulous landlords.
- Laws that help landlords make a fair profit and protect their properties from irresponsible tenants.

PERSUASION

I Have a Dream
Martin Luther King, Jr.

Martin Luther King, Jr., (1929–1968) had at first planned to become a doctor or a lawyer, but when he graduated from Morehouse College in Atlanta at the age of nineteen, he abandoned these ambitions and went into the seminary. After seminary, he went to Boston University, where he received his PhD in 1955. He was ordained as a Baptist minister in his father's church, the Ebenezer Baptist Church in Atlanta, which he copastored with his father from 1960 to 1968. He was also founder and director of the Southern Christian Leadership Conference from 1957 to 1968, and a member of the Montgomery Improvement Association, an activist group protesting racial segregation. Inspired by Mahatma Gandhi's principles of nonviolent protest, King led this group in several demonstrations. In May of 1963, he was arrested and imprisoned in Birmingham for demonstrating against segregation in hotels and restaurants. It was while in jail that he wrote his famous "Letter from Birmingham Jail," a work that was published in 1963 and expanded and republished in 1968. It was also in 1963 that King made the speech entitled "I Have a Dream" to over 200,000 people at the March on Washington. King received numerous awards for his work for human rights, including the Nobel Prize for Peace in 1964. On April 4, 1968, while talking with other human rights activists on a motel balcony in Memphis, King was assassinated.

Five score years ago, a great American, in whose symbolic shadow we stand, signed the Emancipation Proclamation. This momentous decree came as a great beacon light of hope to millions of Negro slaves who had been seared in the flames of withering injustice. It came as a joyous daybreak to end the long night of captivity.

But one hundred years later, we must face the tragic fact that the Negro is still not free. One hundred years later, the life of the Negro is still sadly crippled by the manacles of segregation and the chains of discrimination. One hundred years later, the Negro lives on a lonely island of poverty in the midst of a vast ocean of material prosperity. One hundred years later, the Negro is still languishing in the corners of American society and finds himself an exile in his own land. So we have come here today to dramatize an appalling condition.

In a sense we have come to our nation's capital to cash a check. When the architects of our republic wrote the magnificent words of the Constitution and the Declaration of Independence, they were signing a promissory note to which every American was to fall heir. This note was a promise that all men would be guaranteed the unalienable rights of life, liberty, and the pursuit of happiness.

It is obvious today that America has defaulted on this promissory note insofar as her citizens of color are concerned. Instead of honoring this sacred obligation, America has given the Negro people a bad check; a check which has come back marked "insufficient funds." But we refuse to believe that the bank of justice is bankrupt. We refuse to believe that there are insufficient funds in the great vaults

431

of opportunity of this nation. So we have come to cash this check—a check that will give us upon demand the riches of freedom and the security of justice. We have also come to this hallowed spot to remind America of the fierce urgency of *now*. This is no time to engage in the luxury of cooling off or to take the tranquilizing drugs of gradualism. *Now* is the time to make real the promises of Democracy. *Now* is the time to rise from the dark and desolate valley of segregation to the sunlit path of racial justice. *Now* is the time to open the doors of opportunity to all of God's children. *Now* is the time to lift our nation from the quicksands of racial injustice to the solid rock of brotherhood.

It would be fatal for the nation to overlook the urgency of the moment and 5 to underestimate the determination of the Negro. This sweltering summer of the Negro's legitimate discontent will not pass until there is an invigorating autumn of freedom and equality. 1963 is not an end, but a beginning. Those who hope that the Negro needed to blow off steam and will now be content will have a rude awakening if the nation returns to business as usual. There will be neither rest nor tranquillity in America until the Negro is granted his citizenship rights. The whirlwinds of revolt will continue to shake the foundations of our nation until the bright day of justice emerges.

But there is something that I must say to my people who stand on the warm 6 threshold which leads into the palace of justice. In the process of gaining our rightful place we must not be guilty of wrongful deeds. Let us not seek to satisfy our thirst for freedom by drinking from the cup of bitterness and hatred. We must forever conduct our struggle on the high plane of dignity and discipline. We must not allow our creative protest to degenerate into physical violence. Again and again we must rise to the majestic heights of meeting physical force with soul force. The marvelous new militancy which has engulfed the Negro community must not lead us to a distrust of all white people, for many of our white brothers, as evidenced by their presence here today, have come to realize that their destiny is tied up with our destiny and their freedom is inextricably bound to our freedom. We cannot walk alone.

And as we walk, we must make the pledge that we shall march ahead. We can- 7 not turn back. There are those who are asking the devotees of civil rights, "When will you be satisfied?" We can never be satisfied as long as the Negro is the victim of the unspeakable horrors of police brutality. We can never be satisfied as long as our bodies, heavy with the fatigue of travel, cannot gain lodging in the motels of the highways and the hotels of the cities. We cannot be satisfied as long as the Negro's basic mobility is from a smaller ghetto to a larger one. We can never be satisfied as long as a Negro in Mississippi cannot vote and a Negro in New York believes he has nothing for which to vote. No, no, we are not satisfied, and we will not be satisfied until justice rolls down like waters and righteousness like a mighty stream.

I am not unmindful that some of you have come here out of great trials and 8 tribulations. Some of you have come fresh from narrow jail cells. Some of you have come from areas where your quest for freedom left you battered by the storms of persecution and staggered by the winds of police brutality. You have been the veterans of creative suffering. Continue to work with the faith that unearned suffering is redemptive.

Go back to Mississippi, go back to Alabama, go back to South Carolina, go 9
back to Georgia, go back to Louisiana, go back to the slums and ghettos of our
northern cities, knowing that somehow this situation can and will be changed. Let
us not wallow in the valley of despair.

I say to you today, my friends, that in spite of the difficulties and frustrations 10
of the moment I still have a dream. It is a dream deeply rooted in the American
dream.

I have a dream that one day this nation will rise up and live out the true 11
meaning of its creed: "We hold these truths to be self-evident; that all men are created equal."

I have a dream that one day on the red hills of Georgia the sons of former 12
slaves and the sons of former slaveowners will be able to sit down together at the
table of brotherhood.

I have a dream that one day even the state of Mississippi, a desert state swel- 13
tering with the heat of injustice and oppression, will be transformed into an oasis
of freedom and justice.

I have a dream that my four little children will one day live in a nation 14
where they will not be judged by the color of their skin but by the content of their
character.

I have a dream today.   15

I have a dream that one day the state of Alabama, whose governor's lips are 16
presently dripping with the words of interposition and nullification, will be transformed into a situation where little black boys and black girls will be able to join
hands with little white boys and white girls and walk together as sisters and brothers.

I have a dream today.   17

I have a dream that one day every valley shall be exalted, every hill and 18
mountain shall be made low, the rough places will be made plain, and the crooked
places will be made straight, and the glory of the Lord shall be revealed, and all
flesh shall see it together.

This is our hope. This is the faith with which I return to the South. With this 19
faith we will be able to hew out of the mountain of despair a stone of hope. With
this faith we will be able to transform the jangling discords of our nation into a
beautiful symphony of brotherhood. With this faith we will be able to work together, to pray together, to struggle together, to go to jail together, to stand up for
freedom together, knowing that we will be free one day.

This will be the day when all of God's children will be able to sing with new 20
meaning

My country, 'tis of thee,
Sweet land of liberty,
    Of thee I sing:
Land where my fathers died,
Land of the pilgrims' pride,
From every mountain-side
    Let freedom ring.

And if America is to be a great nation this must become true. So let freedom 21
ring from the prodigious hilltops of New Hampshire. Let freedom ring from the
mighty mountains of New York. Let freedom ring from the heightening Alleghenies of Pennsylvania!

Let freedom ring from the snowcapped Rockies of Colorado!   22

Let freedom ring from the curvaceous peaks of California!   23

But not only that; let freedom ring from Stone Mountain of Georgia!   24

Let freedom ring from Lookout Mountain of Tennessee!   25

Let freedom ring from every hill and molehill of Mississippi. From every 26
mountainside, let freedom ring.

When we let freedom ring, when we let it ring from every village and every 27
hamlet, from every state and every city, we will be able to speed up that day when
all of God's children, black men and white men, Jews and Gentiles, Protestants
and Catholics, will be able to join hands and sing in the words of the old Negro
spiritual, "Free at last! free at last! thank God almighty, we are free at last!"

1963

QUESTIONS FOR DISCUSSION

Content

a. What does King hope to evoke in his audience by mentioning various historical documents (the Emancipation Proclamation, the Declaration of Independence, the Constitution)?
b. King makes it a point to address issues that are of particular interest to white
   listeners and readers. What might have been his reasons for doing this?
c. Why might King have decided to quote all of the first seven lines of "My Country 'tis of Thee"? Why did he not stop at "Of thee I sing"?
d. What effect does King create when he makes reference to specific places,
   events, and public figures?
e. King makes reference to the Bible and to the faith that has sustained him
   throughout his struggle for civil rights. What effect is created with such references?

Strategy and Style

f. King's speech is especially moving because he succeeds in creating emphasis
   through parallelism. Find a few examples of this technique.
g. What does King mean when he says: "America has given the Negro people a
   bad check" (paragraph 4)? Identify other metaphors that he uses, and explain
   why they are effective.
h. Why does King use the term *marvelous* to describe the "new militancy which
   has engulfed the Negro community"?
i. How would you describe King's tone? Controlled? Angry? Impassioned?

SUGGESTIONS FOR SHORT WRITING

a. In your opinion, has the situation of black Americans changed, or not changed, since King gave this speech?
b. Briefly describe your own dream for a better world.

SUGGESTIONS FOR SUSTAINED WRITING

a. Do some research in your college library by reading several newspaper or magazine articles that chronicle the events leading up to King's address at the Lincoln Memorial. Summarize these events and try to comment on their significance to the civil rights movement of the 1960s. Be certain to footnote or in some way cite the authorship of material you quote or paraphrase.
b. Do you have a "dream" that in the future some social or political injustice will be eliminated, that a cure will be found for a disease, that war and famine will cease? Describe your "dream" and propose ways in which to make it a reality.
c. Has King's dream of equality and opportunity for African-Americans been fulfilled in the decades since he spoke at the Lincoln Memorial? Explain by using as much specific detail as possible.

Who Shot Johnny?

Debra Dickerson

"Who Shot Johnny? "was first published in 1996 in The New Republic.

Given my level of political awareness, it was inevitable that I would come to view 1
the everyday events of my life through the prism of politics and the national discourse. I read *The Washington Post, The New Republic, The New Yorker, Harper's,
The Atlantic Monthly, The Nation, National Review, Black Enterprise,* and
Essence and wrote a weekly column for the Harvard Law School *Record* during
my three years just ended there. I do this because I know that those of us who are
not well-fed white guys in suits must not yield the debate to them, however well-
intentioned or well-informed they may be. Accordingly, I am unrepentant and vo-
cal about having gained admittance to Harvard through affirmative action; I am a
feminist, stoic about my marriage chances as a well-educated, thirty-six-year-old
black woman who won't pretend to need help taking care of herself. My strength
flags, though, in the face of the latest role assigned to my family in the national
drama. On July 27, 1995, my sixteen-year-old nephew was shot and paralyzed.

Talking with friends in front of his house, Johnny saw a car he thought he 2
recognized. He waved boisterously—his trademark—throwing both arms in the
air in a full-bodied, hip-hop Y. When he got no response, he and his friends saun-
tered down the walk to join a group loitering in front of an apartment building. The
car followed. The driver got out, brandished a revolver, and fired into the air.
Everyone scattered. Then he took aim and shot my running nephew in the back.

Johnny never lost consciousness. He lay in the road, trying to understand 3
what had happened to him, why he couldn't get up. Emotionlessly, he told the
story again and again on demand, remaining apologetically firm against all demands to divulge the missing details that would make sense of the shooting but
obviously cast him in a bad light. Being black, male, and shot, he must apparently
be involved with gangs or drugs. Probably both. Witnesses corroborate his version
of events.

Nearly six months have passed since that phone call in the night and my 4
nightmarish headlong drive from Boston to Charlotte. After twenty hours behind
the wheel, I arrived haggard enough to reduce my mother to fresh tears and to find
my nephew reassuring well-wishers with an eerie sang-froid.

I take the day shift in his hospital room; his mother and grandmother, a clerk 5
and cafeteria worker, respectively, alternate nights there on a cot. They don their
uniforms the next day, gaunt after hours spent listening to Johnny moan in his sleep.
How often must his subconscious replay those events and curse its host for saying
hello without permission, for being carefree and young while a would-be murderer
hefted the weight of his uselessness and failure like Jacob Marley's chains? How
often must he watch himself lying stubbornly immobile on the pavement of his
nightmares while the sound of running feet syncopate his attacker's taunts?

436

I spend these days beating him at gin rummy and Scrabble, holding a basin 6
while he coughs up phlegm and crying in the corridor while he catheterizes himself. There are children here much worse off than he. I should be grateful. The doctors can't, or won't, say whether he'll walk again.

I am at once repulsed and fascinated by the bullet, which remains lodged in 7
his spine (having done all the damage it can do, the doctors say). The wound is un-
dramatic—small, neat, and perfectly centered—an impossibly pink pit surrounded
by an otherwise undisturbed expanse of mahogany. Johnny has asked me several
times to describe it but politely declines to look in the mirror I hold for him.

Here on the pediatric rehab ward, Johnny speaks little, never cries, never 8
complains, works diligently to become independent. He does whatever he is told;
if two hours remain until the next pain pill, he waits quietly. Eyes bloodshot, hands
gripping the bed rails. During the week of his intravenous feeding, when he was
tormented by the primal need to masticate, he never asked for food. He just listened while we counted down the days for him and planned his favorite meals.
Now required to dress himself unassisted, he does so without demur, rolling himself back and forth valiantly on the bed and shivering afterward, exhausted. He
"ma'am"s and "sir"s everyone politely. Before his "accident," a simple request to
take out the trash could provoke a firestorm of teenage attitude. We, the women
who have raised him, have changed as well; we've finally come to appreciate
those boxer-baring, oversized pants we used to hate—it would be much more difficult to fit properly sized pants over his diaper.

He spends a lot of time tethered to rap music still loud enough to break my 9
concentration as I read my many magazines. I hear him try to soundlessly mouth
the obligatory "mothafuckers" overlaying the funereal dirge of the music tracks. I
do not normally tolerate disrespectful music in my or my mother's presence, but
if it distracts him now . . .

"Johnny," I ask later, "do you still like gangster rap?" During the long pause 10
I hear him think loudly, I'm paralyzed, Auntie, not stupid. "I mostly just listen to
hip-hop," he says evasively into his *Sports Illustrated.*

Miserable though it is, time passes quickly here. We always seem to be 11
jerking awake in our chairs just in time for the next pill, his every-other-night
bowel program, the doctor's rounds. Harvard feels a galaxy away—the world re-
volves around Family Members Living with Spinal Cord Injury class, Johnny's
urine output, and strategizing with my sister to find affordable, accessible housing. There is always another long-distance uncle in need of an update, another
church member wanting to pray with us, or Johnny's little brother in need of
some attention.

We Dickerson women are so constant a presence the ward nurses and clean- 12
ing staff call us by name and join us for cafeteria meals and cigarette breaks. At
Johnny's birthday pizza party, they crack jokes and make fun of each other's husbands (there are no men here). I pass slices around and try not to think, Seventeen
with a bullet.

Oddly, we feel little curiosity or specific anger toward the man who shot 13
him. We have to remind ourselves to check in with the police. Even so, it feels pro
forma, like sending in those $2 rebate forms that come with new pantyhose: You
know your request will fall into a deep, dark hole somewhere, but still, it's your
duty to try. We push for an arrest because we owe it to Johnny and to ourselves as
citizens. We don't think about it otherwise—our low expectations are too ingrained. A Harvard aunt notwithstanding, for people like Johnny, Marvin Gaye
was right that only three things are sure: Taxes, death, and trouble. At least it was-
n't the second.

We rarely wonder about or discuss the brother who shot him because we al- 14
ready know everything about him. When the call came, my first thought was the
same one I'd had when I'd heard about Rosa Parks's beating: A brother did it. A
non-job-having, middle-of-the-day malt-liquor-drinking, crotch-clutching, loud-
talking brother with many neglected children born of many forgotten women. He
lives in his mother's basement with furniture rented at an astronomical interest
rate, the exact amount of which he does not know. He has a car phone, an $80
monthly cable bill, and every possible phone feature but no savings. He steals Social Security numbers from unsuspecting relatives and assumes their identities to
acquire large TV sets for which he will never pay. On the slim chance that he is
brought to justice, he will have a colorful criminal history and no coherent explanation to offer for his act. His family will raucously defend him and cry cover-up.
Some liberal lawyer just like me will help him plea-bargain his way to yet another
short stay in a prison pesthouse that will serve only to add another layer to the
brother's sociopathology and formless, mindless nihilism. We know him. We've
known and feared him all our lives.

As a teenager, he called, "Hey, baby, gimme somma that boodie!" at us from 15
car windows. Indignant at our lack of response, he followed up with, "Fuck you,
then, 'ho!" He called me a "white-boy-lovin' nigger bitch oreo" for being in the
gifted program and loving it. At twenty-seven, he got my seventeen-year-old sister pregnant with Johnny and lost interest without ever informing her that he was
married. He snatched my widowed mother's purse as she waited in predawn darkness for the bus to work and then broke into our house while she soldered on an
assembly line. He chased all the small entrepreneurs from our neighborhood with
his violent thievery and put bars on our windows. He kept us from sitting on our
own front porch after dark and laid the foundation for our periodic bouts of self-
hating anger and racial embarrassment. He made our neighborhood a ghetto. He
is the poster fool behind the maddening community knowledge that there are still
some black mothers who raise their daughters but merely love their sons. He and
his cancerous carbon copies eclipse the vast majority of us who are not sociopaths
and render us invisible. He is the Siamese twin who has died but cannot be separated from his living, vibrant sibling; which of us must attract more notice? We de-
spise and disown this anomalous loser, but for many he *is* black America. We
know him, we know that he is outside the fold, and we know that he will only get

worse. What we didn't know is that, because of him, my little sister would one day be the latest hysterical black mother wailing over a fallen child on TV.

Alone, lying in the road bleeding and paralyzed but hideously conscious, 16 Johnny had lain helpless as he watched his would-be murderer come to stand over him and offer this prophecy: "Betch'ou won't be doin' nomo' wavin', mothafucker."

Fuck you, asshole. He's fine from the waist up. You just can't do anything 17 right, can you?

1996

QUESTIONS FOR DISCUSSION

Content

a. What is Dickerson's relationship to Johnny? How does she feel about him? What in her words and actions shows us how she feels?

b. How does Dickerson describe herself? How does she differ from Johnny's mother and grandmother?

c. What is Dickerson's attitude toward Johnny's mother and grandmother?

d. What upsets Dickerson most about Johnny's shooting?

e. Who is Jacob Marley, and why does Dickerson compare Johnny to him?

f. At the beginning of paragraph 14 Dickerson writes, "We rarely wonder about or discuss the brother who shot him because we already know everything about him." What does she mean by this?

Strategy and Style

g. What are some of the words Dickerson uses to describe Johnny and the man who shot him? Why are these words effective choices?

h. Dickerson shifts her style from telling a fairly straightforward story in paragraphs 1 to 13 to a hypothetical, generalized, and stereotypical description in paragraphs 14 and 15 of the man who shot Johnny. What might have been her reasons for doing that?

i. Dickerson uses obscenities several times in the essay, and especially at the end when addressing the man who shot Johnny. Why is it important for her to use these words and not words less harsh? How do these words affect you?

j. Where does Dickerson use irony? What might be her purpose for using irony?

k. What persuasive techniques does Dickerson use? In your opinion, how effective are they? What could she have added to the essay to make it even more persuasive?

l. What does this essay teach you about narrative as a strategy for making experiences meaningful?

SUGGESTIONS FOR SHORT WRITING

a. Choose two or three words from this essay whose meaning you do not know. Look them up in a dictionary and write out their dictionary definitions. Then speculate about what they mean in the context of Dickerson's essay.
b. Summarize what happened to Johnny as Dickerson describes it. Then summarize it from Johnny's point of view and/or the point of view of the shooter.

SUGGESTIONS FOR SUSTAINED WRITING

a. In a journal or as a first draft, describe an event in which a family member was wronged and that angered you, including a description of how you dealt with the situation. Then write a persuasive essay in which you try to convey the same sense of anger to your readers.
b. Who shot Johnny? Using Dickerson's essay as a springboard, write a reflective essay in which you discuss Dickerson's answer to this question. Consider Dickerson's comments in paragraphs 14 and 15 about the tragic nature of the attacker, both the real person and the stereotyped image. Questions you might want to address in your essay are: Do you agree with Dickerson's implication that Johnny's attacker represents "black America" for most people? How does your own experience relate to this essay?
c. Research the topic of violent crime in the United States. Is it increasing or decreasing? Have the types of violent crimes changed? Write a report to your classmates about what you find out.

Bilingual Education: Outdated and Unrealistic

Richard Rodriguez

The son of Mexican immigrants, Richard Rodriguez (b. 1944) received a BA and an MA from Stanford University and a PhD in English from the University of California at Los Angeles. In 1982, Rodriguez published Hunger of Memory, *a collection of autobiographical essays in which he describes the challenges of growing up in an immigrant household and of enduring the process of assimilation that eventually led him into the American mainstream. Rodriguez writes regularly for the* American Scholar, Saturday Review, *and other widely read periodicals.*

How shall we teach the dark-eyed child *ingles?* The debate continues much as it 1 did two decades ago.

Bilingual education belongs to the 1960s, the years of the black civil rights 2 movement. Bilingual education became the official Hispanic demand; as a symbol, the English-only classroom was intended to be analogous to the segregated lunch counter; the locked school door. Bilingual education was endorsed by judges and, of course, by politicians well before anyone knew the answer to the question: Does bilingual education work?

Who knows? *Quien sabe?* 3

The official drone over bilingual education is conducted by educationalists 4 with numbers and charts. Because bilingual education was never simply a matter of pedagogy, it is too much to expect educators to resolve the matter. Proclamations concerning bilingual education are weighted at bottom with Hispanic political grievances and, too, with middle-class romanticism.

No one will say it in public; in private, Hispanics argue with me about bilin- 5 gual education and every time it comes down to memory. Everyone remembers going to that grammar school where students were slapped for speaking Spanish. Childhood memory is offered as parable; the memory is meant to compress the gringo's long history of offenses against Spanish, Hispanic culture, Hispanics.

It is no coincidence that, although all of America's ethnic groups are impli- 6 cated in the policy of bilingual education, Hispanics, particularly Mexican-Americans, have been its chief advocates. The English words used by Hispanics in support of bilingual education are words such as "dignity," "heritage," "culture." Bilingualism becomes a way of exacting from gringos a grudging admission of contrition—for the 19th-century theft of the Southwest, the relegation of Spanish to a foreign tongue, the injustice of history. At the extreme, Hispanic bilingual enthusiasts demand that public schools "maintain" a student's sense of separateness.

Hispanics may be among the last groups of Americans who still believe in 7 the 1960's. Bilingual-education proposals still serve the romance of that decade, especially of the late 60s, when the heroic black civil rights movement grew paradoxically wedded to its opposite—the ethnic revival movement. Integration and separatism merged into twin, possible goals.

441

With integration, the black movement inspired middle-class Americans to 8 imitations—the Hispanic movement; the Gray Panthers; feminism; gay rights. Then there was withdrawal, with black glamour leading a romantic retreat from the anonymous crowd.

Americans came to want it both ways. They wanted in and they wanted out. 9 Hispanics took to celebrating their diversity, joined other Americans in dancing rings around the melting pot.

MYTHIC METAPHORS

More intently than most, Hispanics wanted the romance of their dual cultural al- 10 legiance backed up by law. Bilingualism became proof that one could have it both ways, could be a full member of public America and yet also separate, privately Hispanic. "Spanish" and "English" became mythic metaphors like country and city, describing separate islands of private and public life.

Ballots, billboards, and, of course, classrooms in Spanish. For nearly two 11 decades now, middle-class Hispanics have had it their way. They have foisted a neat ideological scheme on working-class children. What they want to believe about themselves, they wait for the child to prove, that it is possible to be two, that one can assume the public language (the public life) of America, even while re- maining what one was, existentially separate.

Adulthood is not so neatly balanced. The tension between public and private 12 life is intrinsic to adulthood—certainly middle-class adulthood. Usually the city wins because the city pays. We are mass people for more of the day than we are with our intimates. No Congressional mandate or Supreme Court decision can di- minish the loss.

I was talking the other day to a carpenter from Riga, in the Soviet Republic 13 of Latvia. He has been here six years. He told me of his having to force himself to relinquish the "luxury" of reading books in Russian or Latvian so he could begin to read books in English. And the books he was able to read in English were not of a complexity to satisfy him. But he was not going back to Riga.

Beyond any question of pedagogy there is the simple fact that a language 14 gets learned as it gets used, fills one's mouth, one's mind, with the new names for things.

The civil rights movement of the 1960s taught Americans to deal with forms 15 of discrimination other than economic—racial, sexual. We forget class. We talk about bilingual education as an ethnic issue; we forget to notice that the program mainly touches the lives of working-class immigrant children. Foreign-language acquisition is one thing for the upper-class child in a convent school learning to curtsy. Language acquisition can only seem a loss for the ghetto child, for the new language is psychologically awesome, being, as it is, the language of the bus driver and Papa's employer. The child's difficulty will turn out to be psychological more than linguistic because what he gives up are symbols of home.

PAIN AND GUILT

I was that child! I faced the stranger's English with pain and guilt and fear. Bap- 16
tized to English in school, at first I felt myself drowning—the ugly sounds forced
down my throat—until slowly, slowly (held in the tender grip of my teachers),
suddenly the conviction took; English was my language to use.

What I yearn for is some candor from those who speak about bilingual edu- 17
cation. Which of its supporters dares speak of the price a child pays—the price of
adulthood—to make the journey from a working-class home into a middle-class
schoolroom? The real story, the silent story of the immigrant child's journey is one
of embarrassments in public; betrayal of all that is private; silence at home; and at
school the hand tentatively raised.

Bilingual enthusiasts bespeak an easier world. They seek a linguistic solu- 18
tion to a social dilemma. They seem to want to believe that there is an easy way
for the child to balance private and public, in order to believe that there is some
easy way for themselves.

Ten years ago, I started writing about the ideological implications of bilin- 19
gual education. Ten years from now some newspaper may well invite me to contribute another Sunday supplement essay on the subject. The debate is going to
continue. The bilingual establishment is now inside the door. Jobs are at stake.
Politicians can only count heads; growing numbers of Hispanics will insure the
compliance of politicians.

Publicly, we will continue the fiction. We will solemnly address this issue as 20
an educational question, a matter of pedagogy. But privately, Hispanics will still
seek from bilingual education an admission from the gringo that Spanish has value
and presence. Hispanics of middle class will continue to seek the romantic assurance of separateness. Experts will argue. Dark-eyed children will sit in the classroom. Mute.

1985

QUESTIONS FOR DISCUSSION

Content

a. Summarize Rodriguez's argument. To what extent do you agree with him?
b. What is bilingual education?
c. What is "middle-class romanticism" (paragraph 4)? What is its relationship to
   bilingual education?
d. Why does Rodriguez say that "every time it comes down to memory" when
   Hispanics argue with him about bilingual education?
e. What are "mythic metaphors" (paragraph 10) and what do they have to do with
   bilingual education?

f. How does Rodriguez describe the groups of people to which he refers in this essay—Hispanics, the middle-class in general (paragraph 4), Mexican-Americans (paragraph 6), and middle-class Hispanics (paragraph 11)? In Rodriguez's mind, how are these groups different from each other?
g. What is Rodriguez's solution to the problems bilingual education creates?

Strategy and Style

h. Rodriguez begins his essay with a question. Does he answer it? If so, where and how? If not, why not?
i. Where does Rodriguez go beyond argument to use persuasive techniques? What persuasive techniques does he use in this essay?
j. What is the purpose of the Spanish terms *ingles* (paragraph 1) and *quien sabe* (paragraph 3)?
k. What effect do the personal examples have on how you read the essay? Why does Rodriguez use so few? Would more personal examples make the essay more persuasive? Why or why not?
l. Rodriguez's tone is one of a professional and an authority. Why might this tone be more effective than an angry, complaining, or pleading tone?
m. What is the effect of the many short sentences in the concluding paragraph?

SUGGESTIONS FOR SHORT WRITING

a. Divide a sheet of paper into two columns. In the left column, list the points that Rodriguez makes to persuade you that bilingual education is outdated and un-realistic. In the right column, list as many counterpoints as you can think of to challenge or refute Rodriguez.
b. Quickly write down your first response to this essay. What did you like or dis-like about it? How did you react to particular paragraphs? Where did you find yourself nodding in agreement and where shaking your head in disagreement?

SUGGESTIONS FOR SUSTAINED WRITING

a. Reply to Rodriguez. If you agree with him, write an extension or follow-up to his essay. If you disagree with him, write an essay in which you challenge him. Or, write an essay in which you point out where you think he is right and where wrong. Whatever option you choose, Suggestion *b* above can help you get started.
b. Find out more about the history or controversies of bilingual education in the United States. Summarize your findings, but also include a discussion of both Rodriguez's essay and your own opinions.
c. Propose a plan that will address the problems of teaching children who don't speak English or whose first language is not English. Back up your plan with details, ex-amples, and statistics or other information from primary or secondary sources.

Food Pets Die For

Ann N. Martin

Ann N. Martin (b. 1944) is an animal rights activist who lives in London, Ontario, Canada. She also researches and reports on pet foods, and her findings can be found in her recently published book Food Pets Die For: Shocking Facts About Pet Food *(1997), from which this essay is exerpted.*

Pets in pet food? No, you say? Be assured that this is happening. Rendered companion animals are just another source of protein used in both pet foods and livestock feeds. 1

Rendering is a cheap, viable means of disposal. Pets are mixed with other material from slaughterhouse facilities that has been condemned for human consumption—rotten meat from supermarket shelves, restaurant grease and garbage, "4-D" (dead, diseased, dying and disabled) animals, roadkill and even zoo animals [Summer '96 *EIJ*]. 2

In 1990, *San Francisco Chronicle,* reporter John Eckhouse wrote a two-part exposé on the rendering of companion animals in California. While the pet food companies vehemently denied that this was happening, a rendering plant employee told Eckhouse that "it was common practice for his company to process dead pets into products sold to pet food manufacturers." 3

Eckhouse's informant, upset that some of the most disturbing information was left out of the *Chronicle* article, subsequently brought his story to *Earth Island Journal.* (After the *Journal* published this insider's extensive report ["The Dark Side of Recycling," Fall 1990], the author placed a frantic call to the *Journal* to say that he was "going underground" because he feared for his safety.) 4

A SEARCH FOR THE TRUTH

I had always assumed that deceased pets were either buried or cremated. I had never heard of rendering. In early 1992, I decided to find out what was happening to the euthanized pets in London, Ontario. 5

Veterinary clinics advised me that dead pets were incinerated by a local disposal company. After hearing U.S. horror stories, I was skeptical. I obtained the name of the company that was picking up the pets, a dead-stock removal operation. Classified as "recollectors," these companies—along with "receiving plants," "brokers," and "rendering plants"—are licensed by Canada's Ministry of Agriculture. 6

I asked the ministry how the recollector disposed of the dogs and cats that it picked up. Two months later, I received a letter along with a document from the dead-stock removal company. This document, addressed to the investigator, was stamped with the warning that the information in the document was "not to be made known to any other agency or person without the written permission of the Chief Investigator." 7

445

Small wonder. The document confirmed that dead pets were, in fact, dis- **8** posed of by rendering (unless cremation was "specially requested" and "paid [for] . . . by their owners or by the veterinary clinic").

The dead animals were shipped to a broker located about 300 miles away **9** who sold the bodies to a rendering plant in Quebec. When I contacted the rendering plant, the owner admitted that cats and dogs were rendered along with livestock and roadkill." Do pet food companies purchase this rendered material?" I asked. Again, his reply was, "Yes."

I was numb. How had this barbaric practice gone undetected all these years? **10**

When I advised the veterinarians in my city about what was happening, most **11** of them immediately ceased using the deadstock company and began using the local humane society where the animals are cremated.

In the United States and Canada, the rendering of companion animals is not **12** illegal. Millions of pets are disposed of by rendering each year. According to the Eckhouse article, an employee and ex-employee of Sacramento Rendering, a plant in California, stated that their company "rendered somewhere between 10,000 and 30,000 pounds of dogs and cats a day out of a total of 250,000 to 500,000 pounds of cattle, poultry, butcher shop scraps and other material." The rendering plant in Quebec was rendering 11 tons of dogs and cats per week—from one province alone.

THE SITUATION IN THE U.S.

If this was the case in Canada, I wondered if the U.S. government was aware of **13** what was happening?

The Food and Drug Administration's Center for Veterinary Medicine **14** (CVM) responded to my query regarding the disposal of pets, stating: "In recognizing the need for disposal of a large number of unwanted pets in this country, CVM has not acted to specifically prohibit the rendering of pets. However, that is not to say that the practice of using this material in pet food is condoned by CVM."

The U.S. Department of Agriculture's (USDA) Food Safety and Inspection **15** Services (FSIS) informed me that dog and cat cadavers are excluded as an ingredient in pet foods under FSIS regulations. But, when I asked the USDA if it could provide me with a list of the companies that were using this inspection service, I was told that only two small facilities were licensed for this service and neither had subscribed to the service for four years.

Pet food companies advertise that only quality meats are being used in their **16** products. As of 1996, however, not one of the major pet food companies was using the USDA's inspection service.

WHAT'S IN THE CAN?

Television commercials and magazine advertisements for pet food would have us **17** believe that the meats, grains, and fats used in these foods could grace our dining tables. Over seven long years, I have been able to unearth information about what actually is contained in most commercial pet food. My initial shock has turned to anger as I've realized how little consumers are told about the actual contents of pet food.

Animal slaughterhouses strip the flesh and send the remains—heads, feet, 18 skin, toenails, hair, feathers, carpal and tarsal joints, and mammary glands—to rendering plants. Also judged suitable for rendering: Animals who have died on their way to slaughter; cancerous tissue or tumors and worm-infested organs; injection sites, blood clots, bone splinters or extraneous matter; contaminated blood; stomach and bowels.

At the rendering plant, slaughterhouse material, restaurant and supermarket 19 refuse (including Styrofoam trays and Shrink-wrap), dead-stock, roadkill, and euthanized companion animals are dumped into huge containers. A grinding machine slowly pulverizes the entire mess. After it is chipped or shredded, it is cooked at temperatures between 220 F and 270 F (104.4 to 132.2 C) for 20 minutes to one hour. The grease or tallow that rises to the top is used as a source of animal fat in pet foods. The remaining material is put into a press where the moisture is squeezed out to produce meat and bone meal.

The Association of American Feed Control Officials describes "meat meal" 20 as the rendered product from mammal tissue exclusive of blood, hair, hoof, hide, trimmings, manure, stomach, and rumen (the first stomach of a cud-chewing animal) contents—except in such amounts as may occur unavoidably in "good processing" practices. In his article, "Animal Disposal: Fact and Fiction," David C. Cooke asks, "Can you imagine trying to remove the hair and stomach contents from 600,000 tons of dogs and cats prior to cooking them?"

DRUGS, METAL, PESTICIDES

Pet food labels only provide half the story. Labels do not indicate the hidden haz- 21 ards that lurk in most pet food. Hormones, pesticides, pathogens, heavy metals, and drugs are just a few of the hidden contaminants.

Sodium pentobarbital and Fatal Plus™ are barbiturates used to euthanize 22 companion animals. When animals eat pet food that has gone through the rendering process, it is likely that they are ingesting one of these euthanizing drugs.

Almost 50 percent of the antibiotics manufactured in the United States are 23 dumped into animal feed, according to the 1996 Consumer Alert brochure, "The Dangers of Factory Farming," Pigs, cows, veal calves, turkeys, and chickens are continually fed antibiotics (primarily penicillin and tetracycline) in an attempt to eradicate the many ills that befall factory-farmed animals—pneumonia, intestinal disease, stress, rhinitis, e-coli infections and mastitis.

While this high-level application of antibiotics means millions of dollars for 24 the pharmaceutical companies, the U.S. Centers for Disease Control, National Resources Defense Council and the U.S. Food and Drug Administration (FDA) all warn that these "levels of antibiotics and other contaminants in commercially raised meat constitute a serious threat to the health of the consumer."

Zinc, copper, and iron are listed on most pet food labels. But the metals in pet foods that do *not* need to be listed on the label include: Silver, beryllium, cadmium, bismuth, cobalt, manganese, barium, molybdenum, nickel, lead, strontium, vanadium, phosphorus, titanium, chromium, aluminum, selenium, and tungsten. 25

The U.S. FDA and Health and Welfare Canada would be very concerned if the level of lead found in pet food were found in the human food chain. For the dog food I had tested, for example, a dog ingesting 15 ounces would receive .43 to 2.4 mg of lead per day. Three mg per day is considered hazardous for a child. But when it comes to pet food, no testing is undertaken by state officials for heavy metals, pathogens, pesticides or drugs. 26

Although the pet food industry is not regulated in the United States and Canada, we as consumers have been lulled into believing that government and voluntary organizations are overseeing every ingredient stuffed into a container of pet food. What is required is government-enforced regulation of the industry. Only state legislatures can turn the tide, but it will be a long and difficult battle to persuade our representatives to take up the fight. 27

In the meantime, let the buyer beware! 28

1997

QUESTIONS FOR DISCUSSION

Content

a. What is Martin's answer to the question she asks to open her essay?
b. What is the process of rendering? Why is it done?
c. According to Martin, why should pet owners be concerned about the ingredients in pet food?
d. Summarize Martin's research. What were her first questions, and how did she go about getting the answers to them? Where did each stage of the research lead her? How long did it take her to find the answers?
e. What obstacles did Martin encounter in her research? Why were they obstacles? How did she deal with them?
f. What questions does Martin still have?
g. What points does Martin make that she supports with statistics or evidence?
h. What points does Martin make that she does *not* support with statistics or evidence?
i. How might a pet food company respond to Martin's claims?

Strategy and Style

j. What images does Martin create to instill in readers a negative image of rendering companies?

k. What is the effect of phrases such as "rendered companion animals" (paragraph 1), "euthanized pets" (paragraph 5), "horror stories" (paragraph 6), and other emotionally laden phrases?
l. What is Martin's tone? How might her background as an animal rights activist influence both her tone and what information she chose to include in the essay?

SUGGESTIONS FOR SHORT WRITING

a. Describe your first, "gut" reactions to this essay. How did it affect you as you read it?
b. Write down the list of ingredients on a can of pet food. Look up ingredients you don't know to find out what they are.

SUGGESTIONS FOR SUSTAINED WRITING

a. Analyze Martin's essay, pointing out the flaws in its argument. For example, where are claims made that are not supported with evidence? Where does she use persuasive techniques unfairly?
b. Using Martin's essay as a starting point and reference, do further research about either the practice of rendering animals or about pet food ingredients. Report on your findings to your classmates.

Next Time You Are Sick, You'd Better Go to the Vet . . .

The Nature of Wellness

The following selection appeared originally as the text of a full-page ad paid for by The Nature of Wellness, a not-for-profit organization based in Glendale, California.

Crazy, isn't it?

If you are reading this, it is because you found the headline totally ridiculous, absurd or both. And you are absolutely right. It is absurd. How can anyone possibly believe that a veterinarian who treats dogs and cats can cure *human* diseases? Ridiculous. [1] [2]

But, unfortunately, millions of Americans have been misled into believing that cures for *human* diseases can be found by conducting experiments on different species of healthy *animals*—animals that are totally different not only from humans *but also from each other.* Equally ridiculous and totally illogical. [3]

If it were true that cures for human diseases could be found by experimenting on animals, your going to the vet when feeling sick wouldn't be such a bad idea. In fact, it would be a darn good idea. And our headline wouldn't be so crazy after all. [4]

But, you see, it has to be one or the other. Either human medicine *cannot* be based on veterinary medicine—in which case animal experimentation is an obvious medical and scientific impossibility—or else, you'd better make an appointment with your local vet next time you need glasses or your appendix taken out. [5]

This madness is costing us plenty. Our health is in a state of collapse because no cures can be found by biomedical research and pharmaceutical testing that base human medicine on veterinary medicine. Little wonder that the "miracle cures" and "medical breakthroughs" that are always "just around the corner" never materialize. Our environment is being systematically destroyed by thousands of pesticides and toxicants that, no matter how destructive, are routinely and conveniently found "safe" based on invalid animal tests. [6]

Consequently, our economic survival is also at stake. In 1995 alone, the United States spent over 1.4 trillion dollars—a figure that is growing exponentially—on what is euphemistically called "health care." [7]

It is time to bury the decaying remains of a medicine based on the medieval ritual of animal experimentation. It is time to stop the latest mind-boggling absurdities such as animal-to-human bone marrow and organ transplantation and genetic manipulation. It's time to usher in the medicine of the 21st century. A medicine based on *prevention, clinical research* and, above all, logic and common sense. [8]

We offer true hope. After all, our way, you won't have to get distemper shots. [9]

450

We invite all Americans to join in a most constructive campaign, aimed at 10
ending animal experimentation—the most horrifying crime ever committed
against both human and nonhuman animals. Your tax-deductible donation is urgently needed. Thank you for caring.

Written by Javier B. Burgos of The Nature of Wellness, copyright 1996, *www.animalresearch.org.*

1997

QUESTIONS FOR DISCUSSION

Content

a. Besides taking a stand against animal experimentation, what else is this selection attempting to persuade you to believe or do?
b. What are The Nature of Wellness's reasons for stopping animal experimentation?
c. If this ad could be said to have thesis, what would it be?
d. What are the counterarguments that The Nature of Wellness addresses in this
   piece?
e. What examples does The Nature of Wellness include to help illustrate its points?

Strategy and Style

f. What is the "madness" of animal experimentation "costing us" (paragraph 6)?
   Why would The Nature of Wellness use the metaphors of madness and cost?
   What other metaphors are used?
g. What words in the piece do you know are meant to bias you against animal experimentation?
h. What words are used to create a positive image of The Nature of Wellness?
i. This selection originally appeared as the text of a full-page advertisement that
   also included a half-page drawing of a family being examined in a pet clinic by
   a veterinarian. What might be the function of this drawing in persuading you
   to be against animal experimentation?

SUGGESTIONS FOR SHORT WRITING

a. Jot down your opinion about animal experimentation, for instance, "I am
   for/against animal experimentation because _____ ."
b. Write an imaginary conversation or debate between a supporter and an opponent of animal experimentation.

SUGGESTIONS FOR SUSTAINED WRITING

a. This piece was originally an advertisement in the magazine *The Animals'*
   Agenda, vol. 16, no. 2, page 37. Find this issue and study the ad. Write an essay analyzing the ad and also discussing the relationship between the text and
   the drawing and between the ad and other pages in the magazine.
b. What would a supporter of animal experimentation write in reply to The Nature of Wellness? Using the writing you did for Suggestion for Short Writing *b*
   as your first draft, revise it into a more formal essay.
c. Call The Nature of Wellness (800-545-5848) to get more information about the
   topic. In addition, research the topic in your school's library to find further supporting evidence as well as evidence that challenges The Nature of Wellness's
   stance. Summarize the opposing viewpoints and add your own opinion, too.

Permissions
Acknowledgments

453

Communications, Inc. *Esquire* is a trademark of Hearst Magazines Property, Inc. All Rights Reserved.

Minatoya, Lydia, From *Talking to High Monks in the Snow* by Lydia Minatoya. Copyright © 1992 by Lydia Minatoya. Reprinted by permission of HarperCollins Publishers, Inc.

Mitford, Jessica, From *The American Way of Death* by Jessica Mitford. Reprinted by permission of Jessica Mitford. Copyright © 1963, 1978 by Jessica Mitford, all rights reserved.

Momaday, N. Scott, "The Way to Rainy Mountain" by N. Scott Momaday, first published in *The Reporter,* 26 January 1967. Reprinted with permission from *The Way to Rainy Mountain* © 1969, The University of New Mexico Press.

Noda, Kesaya E., "Growing Up Asian in America" by Kesaya E. Noda from *Making Waves* by Asian Women United. © 1989 by Asian Women United. Reprinted by permission of the author.

Orwell, George, "A Hanging" from *Shooting an Elephant and Other Essays* by George Orwell. Copyright 1950 by Sonia Brownell Orwell and renewed 1978 by Sonia Pitt-Rivers, reprinted by permission of Harcourt Brace & Company. Copyright © George Orwell 1931. Reprinted with the permission of Mark Hamilton as the Literary Executor of the Estate of the Late Sonia Brownell Orwell and Martin Secker & Warburg Ltd.

Parker, Jo Goodwin, "What is Poverty?" by Joe Goodwin Parker from *America's Other Children: Public Schools Outside Suburbia* edited by George Henderson. © 1971 by the University of Oklahoma Press. Reprinted by permission.

Petrunkevitch, Alexander, "The Spider and the Wasp" by Alexander Petrunkevitch, *Scientific American,* August 1952. Reprinted with permission. Copyright © 1952 by Scientific American, Inc. All rights reserved.

Pickering, Samuel, "Faith of the Father" from *Still Life* by Samuel Pickering. Copyright © 1990 by University Press of New England. Reprinted by permission.

Quammen, David, "Alias Benowitz Shoe Repair" from *Natural Acts* by David Quammen. Reprinted by permission of David Quammen. All rights reserved. Copyright © 1983 by David Quammen.

Rettie, James C., "But a Watch in the Night" By James C. Rettie from *Forever the Land* by Russell and Kate Lord. Copyright 1950 by Harper & Brothers. Copyright renewed 1978 by Russell and Kate Lord. Reprinted by permission of HarperCollins Publishers, Inc.

Rodriguez, Richard, "Bilingual Education: Outdated and Unrealistic," by Richard Rodriguez. Copyright © 1985 by Richard Rodriguez. Reprinted by permission of Georges Borchardt, Inc., for the author. Article originally appeared in *the New York Times.*

Sarton, May, "The Rewards of Living a Solitary Life" by May Sarton. Copyright © 1974 by the New York Times Co. Reprinted by Permission.

Sheehy, Gail, "Predictable Crises of Adulthood" from *Passages* by Gail Sheehy. Copyright © 1974, 1976 by Gail Sheehy. Used by permission of Dutton, a division of Penguin Putnam Inc.

Simeti, Mary Taylor, from *On Persephone's Island* by Mary Taylor Simeti. Copyright © 1986 by Mary Taylor Simeti. Reprinted by permission of Alfred A. Knopf, Inc.

Sontag, Susan, "Beauty" by Susan Sontag. Copyright © 1975 by Susan Sontag. Reprinted by permission of Farrar, Straus & Giroux, Inc.

Steele, Shelby, "White Guilt," by Shelby Steele, first published in *The American Scholar,* Autumn 1990. Copyright © 1990 by Shelby Steele. Reprinted by permission of Carol Mann Agency.

Steinem, Gloria, "Erotica and Pornography" by Gloria Steinem, *Ms.* magazine, November 1978. © 1978 by Gloria Steinem. Reprinted by permission of the author.

Svitil, Kathy A., "Nubian Diet Revealed at Last" by Kathy A. Svitil © 1995. Reprinted with permission of *Discover Magazine.*

Tannen, Deborah, "Talk in the Intimate Relationship, His and Hers" from *That's Not What I Meant* by Deborah Tannen, Ph.D. Copyright © 1986 by Deborah Tannen, Ph.D. Reprinted by permission of William Morrow & Company, Inc.

Toth, Susan Allen, "Cinematypes" by Susan Allen Toth. Reprinted by permission of the author.

Viorst, Judith, "The Truth About Lying" by Judith Viorst originally appeared in *Redbook.* Copyright © 1981 by Judith Viorst. Reprinted by permission of Lescher & Lescher, Ltd.

Walker, Alice, "Am I Blue?" from *Living by the Word: Selected Writings 1973–1987,* copyright © 1986 by Alice Walker, reprinted by permission of Harcourt Brace & Company.

Wallace, Mike, "The Press Needs a National Monitor" by Mike Wallace from *The Wall Street Journal,* December 18, 1996. Reprinted with permission of *The Wall Street Journal* and Mike Wallace, Senior Correspondent, CBS News, 60 Minutes. © 1996 Dow Jones & Company, Inc. All rights reserved.

Whitehead, Barbara Defoe, "Where Have All the Parents Gone" by Barbara Defoe Whitehead from *New Perspectives Quarterly,* Vol. 7, Winter 1990. © by The Center for the Study of Democratic Institutions. Reprinted by permission of The Center and Blackwell Publishers, Inc.

Woolf, Virginia, "The Death of the Moth" from *The Death of the Moth and Other Essays* by Virginia Woolf. Copyright 1942 by Harcourt Brace & Company and renewed 1970 by Marjorie T. Parsons, Executrix, reprinted by permission of the publisher.

Index of Authors and Titles